The Triumph of the Moon

A HISTORY OF MODERN PAGAN
WITCHCRAFT

Ronald Hutton is Professor in History at the University of Bristol. He is the author of *Charles II, King of England, Scotland, and Ireland* (1989), *The Restoration, A Political and Religious History of England and Wales 1658-1667* (1993), *The Rise and Fall of Merry England: The Ritual Year 1400-1700* (1994), and *Stations of the Sun: A History of the Ritual Year in Britain* (1996).

The Triumph of the Moon

A HISTORY OF MODERN PAGAN WITCHCRAFT

Ronald Hutton

OXFORD
UNIVERSITY PRESS

OXFORD
UNIVERSITY PRESS

Great Clarendon Street, Oxford OX2 6DP

Oxford University Press is a department of the University of Oxford.
It furthers the University's objective of excellence in research, scholarship,
and education by publishing worldwide in

Oxford   New York

Athens Auckland Bangkok Bogotá Buenos Aires Calcutta
Cape Town Chennai Dar es Salaam Delhi Florence Hong Kong Istanbul
Karachi Kuala Lumpur Madrid Melbourne Mexico City Mumbai
Nairobi Paris São Paulo Singapore Taipei Tokyo Toronto Warsaw

with associated companies in Berlin Ibadan

Oxford is a registered trade mark of Oxford University Press
in the UK and in certain other countries

Published in the United States
by Oxford University Press Inc., New York

British Library Cataloguing in Publication Data

Data available

Library of Congress Cataloging in Publication Data

Hutton, Ronald.
The triumph of the moon: a history of modern pagan witchcraft/
Ronald Hutton.
Includes bibliographical references and index.
1. Witchcraft—Great Britain—History—19th century. 2. Great
Britain—Religion—19th century. 3. Witchcraft—Great
Britain—History—20th century. 4. Neopaganism—Great
Britain—History. 5. Great Britain—Religion—20th century. I.
Title.
BF1581 .H88 2000
133. 4'3'0941—dc21   99–31586
ISBN 0–19–285449–6

1 3 5 7 9 10 8 6 4 2

Typeset in Minion by
Cambrian Typesetters, Frimley, Surrey

Printed in Great Britain
on acid-free paper by
Cox & Wyman Ltd, Reading

For Palden Jenkins and Lindsay River

⚰ PREFACE ⚰

The subtitle of this book should really be 'a history of modern pagan witchcraft in South Britain (England, Wales, Cornwall, and Man), with some reference to it in the rest of the British Isles, Continental Europe, and North America'. The fact that it claims to be *a* history and not *the* history is in itself significant, for this book represents the first systematic attempt by a professional historian to characterize and account for this aspect of modern Western culture. As such it is an exploratory and tentative work, intended as an initial mapping out of an area which badly needs and deserves serious treatment by more scholars in a number of different disciplines; although—as will be indicated— it is likely to present special difficulties for them.

The geographical emphasis is also important, because the unique significance of pagan witchcraft to history is that it is the only religion which England has ever given the world. The English have always developed their own distinctive versions of other religious systems ever since their state acquired an identity, but this is the first which has ever originated in it, and spread from there to many other parts of the world. That a nation so often associated in stereotype with phlegmatic and restrained qualities should have produced such a spectacularly counter-cultural religion is one of the apparent enigmas which this work is designed to address. As a result, it concentrates upon the homeland of this witchcraft, and only considers other nations or regions where they have made a significant subsequent impact upon its further development in that homeland. Probably the greatest disservice of this concentration is done to Australia, where pagan witchcraft has flourished ever since the 1950s and which is mentioned only in connection with two writers, who both live there but have written on England.

I undertook this research to answer two questions which had arisen naturally from that which I had published before. In *The Pagan Religions of the Ancient British Isles* (1991), I took notice of the fact that pagan religions existed in the modern British Isles which sometimes claimed to represent an unbroken continuity of those which were my principal subject. Virtually all academic scholars of ancient paganism until that time had either ignored them or (in the case of Druids) cursorily dismissed them. My own book came down heavily against the claim of continuity and, indeed, the notion that modern paganisms had very much in common with those of the ancient world. On the other hand, I also formed the opinion that they were perfectly viable modern religions in their own right. My book presented the obvious puzzle of where, when, and why they had in fact arisen, if they had not survived continuously. The present one is intended to suggest answers to those questions, in the case of the first of those religions to appear, and subsequently the most popular and influential of all: pagan witchcraft, most commonly known in its oldest recorded form, of Wicca. In future publications I intend to consider some of the others.

My second point of departure for this book came in the conclusion to my history of the ritual year in Britain, *The Stations of the Sun* (1996). One of the themes of that work was that late Victorian and Edwardian folklorists had been peculiarly determined to regard surviving seasonal customs as relics of ancient pagan religions even when, as later research revealed, this supposition was wildly wrong. My conclusion suggested that instead of belonging to an academic cul-de-sac, such attitudes were part of the high road of British culture in that age, and needed to be thoroughly understood and contextualized as part of its history. I therefore drew attention to what I called an obvious need for a proper study of the treatment of the themes of paganism and witchcraft in the English-speaking world during the nineteenth and twentieth centuries. It was always clear to me that such a study was far beyond the competence of a single scholar, but I soon discovered that pagan witchcraft functioned as a useful microhistory for the analysis of these broader attitudes; indeed, the central argument of the book is that far from being an unusually exotic and bizarre response to specific problems of the late twentieth century, it represented a distillation of certain notions and needs which had been developing in Western Europe, and in England in particular, since the eighteenth. If it is the child of any single phenomenon, then it is the belated offspring of the Romantic Movement.

The title is intended to reflect the way in which this religion honours and embodies certain aspects of the world—most prominently the feminine, the night, the wild nature—which had been subordinated, feared or derided in Western culture since the triumph of Christianity, and in some respects since the dawn of history. It is true, however, that the key decisions which led to the writing of the book were both taken under exceptionally brilliant July full moons. One of those rose over a balcony in Cambridge in 1991, as I sat upon it chatting to a friend who occupied rooms there. It was in the course of the conversation that I decided to carry out some research into the origins of modern paganisms as well as proceeding with the other projects which I had allocated to the decade. The other moon shone upon the Vale of Avalon in 1994, as I drove across it towards the Mendips and home after lecturing at Glastonbury. As I did so I came to the decision that my research into pagan witchcraft alone now necessitated a full-scale book, and that I needed to make this a priority when I had completed my publications concerning the ritual year. At first sight it might seem that the contrast between the two places—the great seat of formal learning and the town of ruins, mists, and myths—neatly represents the two poles between which I found myself operating in the writing of the book, and in a sense this would be correct. It was only so, however, with an irony of a sort which I encountered frequently in the course of the work, for Glastonbury has never yet been a major centre of modern pagan witchcraft, and my lecture there that evening had been on Tudor history. Cambridge however—at least until recently—has certainly been such a centre.

The dominant mode of the book is that of narrative, employing empirical methods. This is the oldest sort of history-writing and the one most clearly connected to the discipline's ancient roots as a bardic art. It depends upon the construction of a story, a genealogy of events with regular components of analysis, which appears in itself to explain why certain things may have happened in the past and why they took a particular form. I have never considered this to be the only way to write history and would indeed think the discipline to be in a parlous state if such an opinion became common. To my mind the healthiest condition of my profession is one in which the largest possible range of methodologies and perspectives are applied to every area of the past, including those which are furthest from narrative. The latter just happens to be the one in which I was trained and have practised hitherto.

Even within this dominant mode, however, *The Triumph of the Moon* in fact embodies, in discrete sections, four distinctively different ways of approaching its material. For the first half, I am X-raying British society between 1800 and 1940 for different features which are subsequently to combine to produce the characteristics of pagan witchcraft. It is a process of selection and combination, whereby I pick on certain individuals, works, or phenomena which seem to me to be particularly significant and revealing, and place them in what I think to be a meaningful pattern. Most of the second half, in which I am writing the recoverable history of pagan witchcraft itself, leaves me much less room to act as a free agent. I am limited to a framework of assertions and narratives already provided by others, and my methodology consists now of checking, amending, refuting, endorsing, or extending, these; only in two chapters (13 and 14) do I return briefly to the first mode of operation. The last chapter departs from both techniques, for it deals, strictly speaking, not with history but with sociology or anthropology, by providing a personal view of contemporary pagan witchcraft. For much of the chapter I operate once again as an empiricist and a free agent, selecting and explaining those features which seem to me to be particularly significant; a piece of higher journalism. In the final section of the chapter I enter completely new territory, by matching my impressions of pagan witchcraft against some models provided by sociologists of religion. This discipline is not my own, and in selecting the models I relied heavily upon those which practitioners to whom I spoke, and works which I read, seemed to identify as especially relevant to my subject. I could no doubt have gone a great deal further, and applied concepts from anthropology, or psychology, or some of the social theories favoured by the new cultural studies, but these disciplines are even further removed from mine, and rather than attempt a crash course in any of them, it seemed sensible for the present to hope that by writing a history of the subject I would tempt skilled and proven practitioners of them to enter the field.

Even that apparently bland statement, however, is fraught with difficulties, because the field concerned is that of a mystery religion, with initiates bound by oaths of secrecy to conceal their identities and activities from the outer world—including the academic world. It is true that some of its leading figures have felt able to publish their key ideas and rituals—to the undying gratitude of professional scholars—but this action has itself been deeply controversial, and aroused powerful conflicting emotions, among other witches. I could not have written this book without the active co-operation and support of many initiates of pagan witchcraft, who trusted me both to honour the demands of objective scholarship and to reserve some mystery to their religion. None of them ever exacted from me any specific promises to ensure the accomplishment of this work; they left me to find my own solution to the dilemma.

I responded to it by observing the following rules. In my statements in this book there are no conscious subterfuges, circumlocutions, half-truths, or significant silences. What I write is what I believe to be correct, based upon evidence which I have gathered by research, and I have not deliberately steered round any issues. I have respected the confidences of pagan witches in just two major ways. First, I have not given any of them their everyday or legal names unless they have already published under these or have specifically asked me to do so; and then I have used the exact version which they have provided to me. Second, I have avoided quoting from any ritual text, save in the briefest and most perfunctory fashion, and have preferred instead to provide an outline of the action and purpose of that particular ceremony. I have done this even where the texts concerned have been published before, in some cases more than once, because (as said) there is still a large number of witches who deeply regret those publications. As an extension of this policy I have tried to avoid referring to unpublished material unless no equivalent published piece exists which will equally well prove the same point. By observing these limitations I have disqualified myself from providing precisely those carefully described, deeply analysed accounts of group behaviour upon which anthropology and sociology commonly depend. I hope at the same time to demonstrate how much history can still be written without them.

It may be helpful now to proceed to some definitions. The meanings of the words 'religion' and 'magic' are explored repeatedly in the body of the book, and especially in the first, fifth, and last chapters. For 'ritual' I adopt Clifford Geertz's lovely definition, of 'consecrated action'; expanded to signify formal, dramatic, and unusually stylized action. In many ways the essence of all modern paganism is consecration; the attempt to make persons, and places, and objects feel more sacred, more invested with inner power and meaning which connects the apparent to a non-apparent world. 'Culture' comprises the body of meaning which a group of people build up in common to make sense of their world. 'Nature' is the world which is apparent to humans but which is not given its obvious and basic form by them. This can in practice lead to a very wide, and sometimes mutually contradictory, set of applications. To Americans and Australians, for example, 'nature' usually signifies the wilderness; to the British, it commonly means the whole non-urban portion of the nation, consisting mainly of pastoral and agricultural landscapes which have been heavily worked and reshaped by humans over thousands of years. Purely because I am writing about Britain, I use the word in this extended form according to the custom of the people whose story I am telling, while remaining deeply uneasy about this usage myself.

In the writing of the book I had to familiarize myself with many aspects of nineteenth- and twentieth-century British culture which had hitherto been but vaguely known to me, and my hope is that my perspective as a scholar of pagan witchcraft provided some views of them which will be of interest to experts. I have probably failed to include some which will later prove to have significance for the subject, and my own suspicion is that the greatest invisble player in the story is spiritualism. This is credited with importance at moments—and the evidence which I uncovered suggested that this treatment was enough—but it may well turn out that an extended examination of it, on the lines of those provided (for example) for cunning craft and woodcraft movements, would have been more appropriate. Such a treatment is only just becoming possible because of the growing quantity of detailed research, and it should be relatively easy to make a study of its relationship with witchcraft and ritual magic in the future.

Two concepts which are missing from this book are reactivity and reflexivity. Reactivity is the effect on a social group created by the scholar studying it; the very process of making such a study can alter, significantly and permanently, the people who are being studied. Reflexivity is the readiness of scholars to be openly aware of the prejudices, preconceptions, instincts, emotions, and personal traits which they bring to their studies and the way in which these can influence the latter. It can also include the impact of the process of study itself upon the personality and attitudes of the scholar. Both have come to be crucially important to social scientists. Reactivity is a more complex matter for historians, whose subjects are usually dead. To change a widespread view of the past is to alter the present, but the effect of these changes is self-evidently not going to be apparent until some time after the scholar has published. None the less, the concept did have some applications to my work. Reflexivity, by contrast, should have an obvious relevance to historians of all kinds, but they have hardly begun to recognize the need for it. Where it is assayed among them, it is still liable to be termed not 'reflexivity' but 'self-indulgence'.

I wrote a section to conclude this book which confronted both issues squarely, and found myself growing more and more uneasy as I did so. In the end, lying awake one night at 3 a.m. I decided to excise the whole passage, and keep it for publication in some separate form, should an appropriate time and context become evident. The pages concerned certainly cast what I think to be fascinating light upon post-Christian British society. Many readers would probably have found them to be the most interesting part of the whole work; but they proved to be too personal, and too painful, for me, and left me feeling too exposed. The problem was that on entering into this project I found myself committed to a dual process which promised a great deal of discomfort. On the one hand I felt honour-bound to represent and defend the ways of academe to

Pagans, and to make more widely known the existence of recent research which challenged beliefs especially dear to some of them. On the other, the same sense of honour compelled me, when asked about my current work by non-Pagans, to dispel prejudice and misunderstanding, and provide what seemed from my research to be more objective information. This seemed to me to be especially important outside the university system. In neither case did I have the inclination to evangelism, always awaiting a specific invitation to address such subjects before I did so; but having been given such requests, I felt that I could not refuse a response without betraying my profession.

The result was a great deal better than I might have feared, upon both sides. Most Pagans, and especially Wiccans and Druids, responded to me with a remarkable warmth, generosity, and fair-mindedness. My university generously paid for my single overseas expedition, my own colleagues treated my work with detachment and myself with continued affability, and I encountered a number of academics who encouraged and inspired me in my research. I won respect as an authority on this subject in all branches of the mass media. On the other hand, there were a number of less pleasant experiences, and whereas on the Pagan side they tended to diminish with time, in the wider society, including the university system, they tended to worsen. To include a section upon reactivity and reflexivity in this book, and not to mention disagreeable aspects of my experience of them, would have represented both cowardice and deception. To retain the whole section carried the risk of perpetuating the very discomforts to which I have referred, and so deprive myself of the chance that, with the publication of this book and a turn to other subjects, I can finally draw a line beneath them.

Why, then, do I even trouble to mention the matter in this introduction? I do so for the sake of young scholars, perhaps undertaking their first research, who might feel inspired by the undoubted fact that more work, of the same and different kinds, is desperately needed to evaluate my own. I tackled this project in a very strong position, holding a tenured post near the summit of my profession and with a proven track record which might confer respect upon subjects which I deemed to be worth tackling; and I still had some problems. Those who lack all those advantages may have a significantly rougher time, and one which they are less well placed to endure.

This said, I have to conclude here by emphasizing that most of the work was tremendous fun, and represented by far the most exciting and challenging research project which I have yet undertaken. If the resulting book does something further to change the climate in which scholars concerned with it can operate, and to make their work yet more pleasurable, then my happiness with it will be complete.

Throughout the text, the following convention has been observed with regard to capitalization: 'pagan' refers to the ancient religions of Europe, while 'Pagan' denotes the modern religions which are partly inspired by their example.

✦ ACKNOWLEDGEMENTS ✦

The single great financial contribution to this research project was made by my own university of Bristol, whose prompt and ample response to an application made possible my journey to read Gerald Gardner's papers in Toronto. Caitlín Matthews, Asherah Brown, and Steve Wilson all provided books for it from their private collections at time when I could not find them elsewhere. I delivered research papers based on work for this book to the day-school on Paganism held at the University College of Bath Spa in May 1993 and to the international conferences on the same or related subjects at the University of Newcastle in September 1994, the University of Lancaster in April 1996, and King Alfred's College, Winchester, in September 1997. Material which was later included in this book was published in *Religion Today* 9 (1994), 29–32; *Paganism Today*, eds Charlotte Hardman and Graham Harvey (HarperCollins, 1996), 3–15; *Antiquity* 71 (1997), 91–9; and *Nature Religion Today*, eds Joanne Pearson, Richard H. Roberts, and Geoffrey Samuel (Edinburgh University Press, 1998), 89–100. A full-scale 'trailer' for the book, containing first drafts of most of its chapters in miniature, is to be published in 1999 as the section on 'Modern Pagan Witchcraft' in *The Athlone History of Witchcraft and Magic in Europe, Volume VI*, ed. Stuart Clark. The book itself, however, contains not only a great deal more material but a large amount of additional research, some of which has substantially changed the opinions which I expressed in the chapter for Athlone.

The whole of this work was read in manuscript, chapter by chapter, by two prominent members of the British Pagan community, of very different viewpoints and experiences: Mike Howard, editor of *The Cauldron*, and Frederick Lamond, author of *Religion Without Beliefs*. Both contributed lavishly in encouragement, criticism, and additional research materials, to an extent which I can hardly ever repay. Separate parts of the book were given the same treatment, by a mixture of pagans of differing traditions and academics, British and American. Steve Wilson and Caroline Wise read chapters 1–5, Owen Davies provided his views on chapter 6, Bill Liddell did the same for chapters 6, 11, and 15, Andrew Chumbley got chapters 6 and 15 (and won the last word on the latter), Chas Clifton gave opinions on chapter 8, Gareth Knight commented on part of chapter 10, Philip Heselton and Brad Verter both worked through chapter 11, Dayonis responded to chapter 12, Maxine Sanders and Vivianne Crowley dealt with chapter 17, and chapter 18 was tackled by Cynthia Eller. Between them all I have gained a rich harvest of information and insights which have greatly augmented the text. This by no means exhausts the number of debts which I have accumulated in the course of this project, and many more are acknowledged in the footnotes. In large part they are a record of new friendships.

❧ CONTENTS ❧

MACROCOSM

1

FINDING A LANGUAGE

✣

Tʜɪs book is to be largely concerned with religion, a phenomenon which itself has never been defined in a manner wholly and universally acceptable to scholars concerned with it; indeed, the many practitioners and commentators who will feature in this present work themselves display a range of approaches to the problem. The term itself derives from the Latin *religio*, signifying those duties and that reverence needed to keep the human world in a good relationship with the divine. People who fulfilled those observances and held that attitude in exemplary fashion would earn the approving adjective *pius*, while the word *superstitio* signified an undesirable extension of them into an excessive fear of the supernatural. These three terms illustrate between them the basic complex of belief regarding human commerce with divinity in ancient Europe. All have only limited relationships with the way in which the English words descended from them have been employed during the last two hundred years. The European cultural world has lost any general sense that the prosperity of humans depends upon the fulfilment of set actions designed to propitiate and please supernatural beings and to retain their goodwill towards the community. Most of the people with whom whom the second half of this book is concerned have lacked any concept of religion as a public duty. This alteration has in turn transformed the status of piety from a social virtue to a personal characteristic. Superstition is a word now usually employed to describe a belief in things which are themselves superfluous or erroneous, not an excessive fear of something real. These shifts sum up a tremendous alteration in mentality between ancient (and medieval) and modern Europe.

The basic modern scholarly definition of religion was provided in 1871 by Sir Edward Tylor, who suggested that its essential component was a belief in the existence of spiritual beings and in the need of humans to form relationships with them. This has been repeatedly questioned since, in a sequence of debates familiar to most students of anthropology and religious studies.[1] In particular, it has been pointed out that some systems generally called religions, such as Theravada Buddhism, do not require belief in supernatural entities. Two things may be said in favour of Tylor's formula for the purposes of the present study. First, that no better one has ever been achieved, all alternatives having run up against equal or worse problems of universal application. Second, that while it certainly has problems when accorded to spiritual systems such as Buddhism, it fits very well the European traditions with which this book is concerned. Within this culturally specific setting, therefore, it will be used as the working basis for the way in which the word 'religion' is used.

Until recently there would have been no equivalent difficulty in defining the original meaning of the term 'pagan'. For over a hundred years writers had commonly asserted that the Latin word *paganus*, from which it was derived, signified 'rustic'; a result of the triumph of Christianity as the dominant, metropolitan, and urban faith, which left the old religions to make a last stand among the more backward populations of the countryside. In 1986, however, the Oxford-based historian Robin Lane Fox reminded colleagues that this usage had never actually been proved and that the term had more probably been employed in a different sense in which it was attested in the Roman world, of a civilian; in this case a person not enrolled in the Christian army of God.[2] A few years later a French academic, Pierre Chuvin, challenged both derivations, arguing that the word *pagani* was applied to followers of the older religious traditions at a time when the latter still made up the majority of town-dwellers and when its earlier sense, of non-military, had died out. He proposed instead that it simply denoted those who preferred the faith of the *pagus*, the local unit of government; that is, the rooted or old, religion.[3] His suggestion has so far met with apparent wide acceptance.

A similar problem attends the equivalent northern European term, 'heathen'. The frequent linkage of 'pagan' to rusticity has produced a similar popular connection of this other word with 'heath', as if it originally indicated people driven to worship the forbidden old divinities in wastelands and wild places. As the *Oxford English Dictionary* makes clear, however, 'heathen' is the English version of the term used throughout the Germanic language group in the early Middle Ages to signify a follower of a non-Christian religion. It was coined originally by the Goths, the first speakers of a Germanic tongue to undergo a mass conversion to Christianity. Unhappily, the similarity to 'heath', so apparent in modern English and German, does not occur in Gothic. Experts have failed to discover any other likely linguistic origin for 'heathen', and the matter will probably remain a mystery.

For the purposes of this book, the actual derivations of 'pagan' and 'heathen' are less important than the fact that both had come by the nineteenth century to have widely accepted associations with the countryside and the natural world; and had done so despite the lack of any clear justification for these. Such linkages are themselves signs of a potent modern cultural tradition at work. This formed, in fact, only one of at least four entirely different languages or (to use the current fashionable academic term) 'discourses', in which paganism was instinctually characterized in British society between 1800 and 1940. One of these was to become that of modern pagan witchcraft; the others were to condition public responses to the appearance of that religious tradition.

*   *   *

In one of these languages, pagans are people who bow down to idols, offer up blood sacrifices, and represent the religious aspect of human savagery and ignorance. It is of course embedded in Christianity, being scattered throughout the Old Testament and echoed by several of the Church Fathers, but it took on a new lease of life in the nineteenth century when it was applied repeatedly to the traditional peoples of Asia, Africa, and the Americas. Such an application had been made, indeed, from the first sustained contacts between these peoples and Europeans in the sixteenth century, but during the eighteenth it had been tempered by other voices. Some of these were represented by the 'philosophes' of the Enlightenment, who found much to admire in the cultures of China and India, others by the proponents of the subsequent fashion for sensibility, who hailed the first reports of the tribal societies of the South Pacific as evidence that humans living closest to nature enjoyed the greatest innocence and happiness of existence. As is well known, these more positive attitudes atrophied as the nineteenth century got under way. The change was due in part to the disillusion inevitably consequent upon closer contact with peoples who had been excessively idealized. It was also one result of the temporary achievement of decisive European technological superiority over the rest of the world, enabling the conquest of most of Africa, Asia, and the Pacific by Europe's major powers and a consequent loss of respect for the indigenous populations. One of the classic themes of British imperial history is the manner in which a long tradition of tolerance and social interaction between the British and the natives in India was terminated in the early nineteenth century. The first consequences were the sensational campaigns in the 1820s and 1830s to end the murderous religious practices of *suti* and *thuggi*, which became part of the epic of the Raj. These catalyzed a more widespread interference with native traditions and institutions, which culminated catastrophically in the great revolt of 1857.

The period's combination of imperialism and evangelism gave rise to a distinctive genre of literature: the memoir of missionary work among tribal societies. Mixing the styles of travelogue, homily, and ripping yarn, it aimed at once to entertain and to edify, to bolster respect for Christianity in the home country, and to inspire the donation of funds for further work. These books supplied European readers with their first information about the religious beliefs and practices of many traditional peoples, and naturally enough gave the most hostile possible impression of them, and the most glowing possible accounts of the consequences of the conversion of the peoples concerned to the Christian faith. These images then soaked into scholarly works and popular fiction alike. A classic example of their impact upon British literature is provided by the books of R. M. Ballantyne, the pioneer of the boy's adventure story.

In his own youth, Ballantyne worked for the Hudson's Bay Company. On returning to London to take up a partnership in a printing and publishing firm, he supplemented his income by writing first factual and then fictional works based on his experiences in the Canadian Arctic. These led him in turn to strike upon the genre which he was to give to the world; tales with boy heroes who fended for themselves through a series of dramatic escapades set against an exotic background. From the 1850s to the 1880s he turned out a steady stream of these, bringing himself considerable wealth and reputation, which soon allowed him to settle comfortably in Middlesex as a professional writer. Indeed, he never stirred from there again, save for a single holiday in South Africa. He certainly never went near the tropical locations in which most of his stories were set, and owed his information upon them wholly to the accounts of others, and especially of missionaries. Here, indeed, was the point. Ballantyne's own mentality was characterized by an ever more fervent Christian religiosity (as a member of the Free Church of Scotland), and his tales were intended partly to infuse the same emotion into his large and impressionable readership.[4] It was crucially important to him that the latter should recognize that in the guise of a romance he was introducing them to real places, peoples, and issues.

This need occasioned regular outbursts of the sort that is found in the twenty-eighth chapter of *The Fugitives, or the Tyrant Queen of Madagascar* (1887). The book consists of an account of the historical persecution of the Christian converts among the Malagasy tribes, by a pagan native government thirty years before, seen through the eyes of the inevitable strapping young British castaways. It includes detailed descriptions of the martyrdom of the converts by burning alive or hurling from cliffs, after one of which appears the exclamation 'We write facts now, reader, no fiction! Men talk of the cruelty of devils! Assuredly there is not a devil in or out of hell who can sink to lower depths of cruelty than fallen man will sink when left to the unrestrained influence of that hateful thing—sin—from which Jesus Christ came to deliver us, blessed be His name!' To Ballantyne, all pagans, by definition, were prey to that 'unrestrained influence'.

The Fugitives was one of the last of his publications, but in this respect the tone had not altered since his first best-seller, *The Coral Island* (1858), which remained his most popular work. In the twenty-sixth chapter of this book comes an almost identical outburst: 'O reader, this is no fiction. I would not, for the sake of thrilling you with horror, invent so terrible a scene. It was witnessed. It is true—true as that accursed sin which has rendered the human heart capable of such diabolical enormities!' The scene concerned, minutely described, consists of the consecration of a new war canoe by Melanesian tribesmen, who launch it over the living bodies of prisoners, crushing them in the process. The first half of *The Coral Island* is devoted to the adventures of three lads who are shipwrecked on an uninhabited Pacific isle, and learn how to survive on it in a manner which represents a cross between *Robinson Crusoe* and *Scouting for Boys*. In the second, however, they encounter successive groups of native islanders, and here Ballantyne's technique is to cull every horror story told about the latter in travellers' accounts, and lay them end to end bracketed by exclamation marks.

The process begins in chapter nineteen, when the reader is informed sweepingly that 'all the natives of the South Sea Islands are fierce cannibals', a point repeatedly illustrated in the rest of the book. Having reached Fiji five chapters later, we are introduced to a giant eel, which is worshipped as a god by the natives and fed live human babies, and to a sacred society which is devoted to the sacrifice of newborn babies: 'the mildest ways they have of murdering them is by sticking them through the body with sharp splinters of bamboo, strangling them with their thumbs, or burying them alive and stamping them to death while under the sod.' The sacrifice of adult humans forms a regular theme of the seven chapters after this; they are buried alive as foundation deposits or because their chiefly powers are failing, strangled to accompany leaders into the next world, or simply offered up in temple forecourts as part of the routine business of native religion.

All of course ends happily, when the protagonists are saved from death in the nick of time by the appearance of a single genteel English missionary, who converts the tribe which is holding them prisoner. The result is amazing; in one instant the natives are bloodthirsty, cruel, treacherous, and debauched, and in the next they have become peaceful, kind, honourable, and modest. The alteration is effected by the burning of the idols of their former deities, as if the latter were literally devils who had possessed them hitherto, and whose hold over them is broken by the cleansing fire. To Ballantyne it was simply impossible to believe that devout Christians could ever torture and slaughter; the white men who sometimes feature in his stories (including this one) as doing evil are always those who have forgotten their religion and so allowed the demons to return. It is easy to smile now at the quintessentially Victorian mixture of piety, sadism, and melodrama in Ballantyne's work, but *The Coral Island*, in particular, has retained its appeal all through the twentieth century. It was last republished in 1994.

The impact of these portraits of tribal religion was given an additional potency by being projected backwards onto the ancient European past. There had always been a tendency to apply Old Testament language instinctually to prehistoric monuments, from the time that these first began to attract the interest of antiquarians in the seventeenth century. In the early part of the nineteenth it was repeated by a popular author such as Sir Walter Scott, who in the nineteenth chapter of *The Pirate* (1821) could make his protagonist contemplate the megalithic structures of Orkney, and comment: 'I knew where the sacrifices were made of yore to Thor and Odin—on what stones the blood of the victims flowed—where stood the dark-browed priest—where the crested chiefs, who consulted the will of the idol—where the more distant crowd of inferior worshippers, who looked on with awe or terror.' It is possible that even at this date such a flight of the imagination was influenced by the stories already trickling back from the frontiers of European exploration. By the mid-century the connection was both explicit and endorsed by apparent objective scholarship. The years between had seen the beginnings of systematic European archaeological research and the achievement of a crude periodization for the prehistoric past. What this work proved conclusively was that the earliest human artefacts were also the most primitive, and that in technological terms Europeans had evolved steadily from a level of culture comparable with the least developed of the tribal groups surviving in the contemporary world. This in turn raised the possibility that the social and ideological structures of prehistoric Europe had likewise been similar to those still existing among these groups. Such a perception cleared the way for a hypothetical reconstruction of the mentalities and customs of the earliest Europeans, by analogy with those of traditional peoples in the contemporary world. It was undertaken in 1865 by the banker John Lubbock, later Lord Avebury, in his book *Prehistoric Times*, which was to remain the basic text upon the subject for a general readership during the rest of the century.[5]

The use of anthropological data to interpret archaeological remains is a good one, although it can rarely suggest more than possibilities. Lubbock's problem was that the data available in 1865 was that provided by the missionaries and by travellers who usually imitated their tone. As a result, when he made a systematic collection of it, the result was a Chamber of Horrors. The native Australians and Americans, the Andamanese and Inuit, all lacked any real concept of religion, and without its comforts they were left terrified of spirits. The Inuit buried old people and orphans alive. Hottentot boys were initiated into manhood with ceremonies 'which are so disgusting that it is difficult to see how they can have originated'. The Fijians were cannibals who inflicted painful tattoos upon themselves, killed their parents, and venerated gods hungry for human sacrifice. So did the Maori, who killed and ate slaves as a sacrament. Human sacrifice was also a habit of the Tahitians, who believed that aristocrats went to heaven and commoners to hell. The tribes of Tierra del Fuego likewise ritually ate human flesh and dreaded 'a great black man in the woods who knows everything'. Lubbock commented that 'savages seem to take a melancholy pleasure in self-inflicted sufferings',[6] and suggested that prehistoric Europeans had existed in the same unhappy spiritual condition.

His readership in the 1860s would have found this notion perfectly logical, for this was the decade in which Darwin's *Origin of Species*, and the theory of evolution, became widely accepted. Victorians who were swallowing the idea that they were descended from apes had no trouble in accepting the concept that savages had been the next stage in human development, especially as the sequence turned the modern Western world into the end product of a triumphal story of increasing technological, cultural, and intellectual progress. This moral was drawn, from the same parallel, in Sir Edward Tylor's *Primitive Culture* (1871), a work which stood in the same parental relationship to the new science of anthropology as *Prehistoric Times* did to archaeology. Tylor commenced the vital work of trying to set tribal beliefs in a broader cultural context which would make sense of them. He was also canny enough to realize that some of the data had to be wrong, pointing out that the assertion that a large number of traditional peoples had no religion was made by people who habitually excluded from the category of religion anything that did not approximate to Christianity.[7] Unhappily, he had no alternative field-work to set beside the sort of sensational story which was repeated by Lubbock, and so accepted both the accuracy of most of the same material and its applicability to prehistoric Europe. 'It is thus plain', he concluded, 'that hideous rites, of which Europe has scarcely kept up more than a dim memory, have held fast their ancient practice and meaning in Africa, Polynesia, and Asia, among races who represent in grade, if not in chronology, earlier stages of civilization'.[8]

It was left to creative writers to reconstruct those 'hideous rites' with unconstrained imagination. Here is the vision provided by late Victorian essayist Grant Allen, of the funeral ceremonies at a neolithic chambered long barrow of what experts now call the Cotswold–Severn group. It was based on the findings of the local antiquarians who excavated a large number of such sites during the period. The objective evidence which they uncovered was of progressive communal disarticulated burial, including, in a very few cases, bones of individuals who had suffered violent injury. From this data, Allen evoked the following picture:

I saw them bear aloft, with beating of breasts and loud gesticulations, the bent corpse of their dead chieftain: I saw the terrified and fainting wives haled along by thongs of raw ox-hide, and the weeping prisoners driven passively like sheep to the slaughter: I saw the fearful orgy of massacre and rapine around the open tumulus, the wild priest shattering with his gleaming tomahawk the skulls of his victims, the fire of gorse and low brushwood prepared to roast them, the heads and feet flung carelessly on the top of the yet uncovered stone chamber, the awful dance of blood-stained cannibals around the mangled remains of men and oxen, and, finally, the long task of heaping up above the stone hut of the dead king the earthen mound that was never again to be opened to the light of day, till ten thousand years later, we modern Britons invaded with our prying, sacrilegious mattock the sacred privacy of the cannibal ghost.[9]

The chief casualty of this gloomy picture of the ancient British was the reputation of the Druid. To be sure, Graeco-Roman authors had left two very different images of Druidry and the Gallo-British cultures in which it has been part, the product of prejudices as strongly marked as those of many nineteenth-century stories concerning traditional peoples. To some, they were philosophers, healers, peacemakers, and benevolent mystics, to others a sinister breed of magus who presided over and encouraged barbaric rites of human sacrifice. The latter sort of text had long been united with the Old Testament imagery to produce a negative view of ancient European paganism, and it was still present in the eighteenth century; yet in that period, on the whole, it was the notion of the Druids as sages which prevailed. John Toland, William Stukeley, James Thomson, and Iolo Morgannwg led a score of lesser authors in crediting them with wisdom, patriotism, serenity, and learning.[10] This benevolent vision of Druidry withered as the nineteenth century came on, along with that of the noble modern savage, both blighted by the chill winds of imperial expansion and the Evangelical Revival. William Wordsworth added to his *Ecclesiastical*

Sketches (1822), a 'Trepidation of the Druids', in which he lamented 'each dreadful rite' with which he believed them to have corrupted their 'patriarchal lore'. 'Guilt and Terror' (1842) includes a panorama of Stonehenge:

> . . . at dead of night, when dreadful fire
> Reveals that powerful circle's reddening stones,
> 'Mid priests and spectres grim and idols dire,
> Far heard the great fane utters human moans.

Down in Cornwall a contemporary poet of very different social stature, the miner and Sunday-school teacher John Harris, experienced the same feelings at the neolithic hill fort of Carn Brea:

> I gained the hill-top, saw in boulders bare
> Some worn by time, some carved by Druid art
> Where oft perhaps the painted Briton prayed
> To Thor and Woden, offering human blood,
> When moral darkness filled our blessed isle.[11]

Where poets led, artists followed. It was still possible to find, until the 1840s, an occasional painting of Druids as wise men gathered in sacred groves. More typical of the period was William Geller's mezzotint *The Druid's Sacrifice* (1832), concentrating upon crowds euphoric with blood-lust, pouring into Stonehenge.[12] In 1843 the commissioners entrusted with the rebuilding of the Houses of Parliament chose six subjects to be painted on the walls of the central corridor: 'in three Britain appears sunk in ignorance, heathen superstition and slavery; in the other three she appears instructing the savage, abolishing barbarous rites and liberating the slave.' The subjects were, respectively, the Phoenicians trading in Cornwall, a Druidical sacrifice, and Anglo-Saxon captives in Rome, and then Captain Cook in Tahiti, the suppression of *suti*, and the emancipation of black slaves.[13] The best-known of all nineteenth-century paintings dealing with Druidry is Holman Hunt's historically impossible *A Converted British Family Sheltering a Christian Priest from the Persecution of the Druids* (1850), now in the Ashmolean Museum.

The same sentiments filtered into private decoration and entertainment. In the garden of his home at Banwell, Somerset, George Henry Law, Bishop of Bath and Wells, had a megalithic folly constructed, with the inscription:

> Here where once Druids trod in times of yore
> And stained their altars with a victim's gore
> Here now the Christian ransomed from above
> Adores a God of mercy and of love.[14]

In Birmingham Central Library is kept a copy of the Victorian ballad 'Barr Beacon', by an unknown author and devoted to a local landmark. The central verses are:

> O Beacon, red with sacrifice,
> High Altar, blood encompassed thrice,

> Lie silent, 'til the doom atone
> With wreckage of the world o'erthrown.
> O Druids, bearded long and white
> With eyes long scant of any sight,
> Beneath old altars lie, where clings
> The blood of vain sun offerings.[15]

This language of paganism, as a religion of gloom and gore, was preserved into the twentieth century, often with more instinctual and less self-conscious expression than in the nineteenth. In 'The Ballad of the White Horse' (1911), G. K. Chesterton could write of the heathen Vikings:

> Their gods were sadder than the sea,
> Gods of a wandering will,
> Who cried for blood like beasts at night,
> Sadly, from hill to hill.

Four years later the traveller Sir Mark Sykes supplied the following description of the Iraqi city of Mosul:

The population is rotted by the foul distemper, corrupted and rendered impotent by drink, stupefied and besotted by vice. The degradation of the city folk is not only physical but mental. Tales are whispered of dark and hideous sorceries and incantations—the noisome stench, as it were, of the charnel house of that dead Paganism which the Cross and Mohammed have slain, but have as yet been unable to annihilate.[16]

Much closer to home, in 1930, the poet W. Force Stead could express his dislike of the atmosphere of the Wychwood district of Oxfordshire in terms of its 'unhallowed emanation', part of 'something sinister that hangs over any heathen or pagan countryside'.[17] Thus the sense lingered into twentieth-century Britain of the old religions as a stain upon the underside of civilization, a nasty and uncomfortable chapter in the communal past; at worst, a force which might rise vampire-like from the past to subvert modern humans, should the power of reason and of education falter.

*   *   *

There was also, however, a second common and well-established language in which paganism was represented during the same century and a half: as a religion which had been associated with magnificent art, literature, and philosophy, and was deficient to Christianity only in its ethics and in its lesser component of divine revelation. This avoided any direct confrontation with the first, in that it referred to a different culture; not to modern or prehistoric tribal societies, nor to the exotic civilizations of the East, but to the familiar, beloved, and respected world of ancient Greece and Rome. It likewise was embedded in Christian culture from the beginning—in the New Testament, where Christ's death is encompassed not by pagans but by his fellow Jews, and the chief pagan character is the confused but well-meaning Roman gentleman, Pontius Pilate. The literature of the classical ancient world remained the basis for European culture, and its deities, now regarded as allegorical or mythical figures, were regular components of written works, painting, and sculpture. Dante's *Divine Comedy*, in the high Middle Ages, enunciated in full development the attitude towards the classical pagan world which was to obtain for the next seven centuries; that it should be admired and loved, and that the triumph of Christianity had only served to perfect it.

This attitude was only compounded in the early modern period, as the ideology developed that the world might be made progressively more perfect by (European) human endeavour, and that Greek and Roman sources could supply important information to assist this task. The increasingly secular tone of political and social language among parts of the international scholarly community, coupled with the persistence of Latin as the language of that community, tended to privilege Roman authors in particular. Likewise, the strengthening admiration for classical forms in art and architecture made the iconography of the Olympian deities even more common and familiar.

The tendencies reached their apogee in the eighteenth century. Dr Johnson could declare in 1781 that 'classical quotation is the *parole* of literary men all over the world'.[18] Conyers Middleton, introducing readers to his *History of the Life of Marcus Tullius Cicero* forty years before, reminded them that it was set 'in a place and age which are familiar to us from our childhood: we learn the names of all the chief actors at school, and choose our several favourites according to our tempers or fancies.'[19] The fashion for landscaped gardens meant that the forms of the old goddesses and gods, long resident in the interior of dwellings on canvas or in marble, overflowed into their grounds. *The Conoisseur* magazine, in March 1756, could remark complacently that 'While infidelity has expunged the Christian theology from our creed, taste has introduced the heathen mythology into our gardens. If a pond is dug, Neptune, at the command of taste, emerges from the basin, and presides in the middle; or if a vista is cut through a grove, it must be terminated by a Flora, or an Apollo.'[20] Peter Gay, in one of the most important modern texts on the culture of the century, concluded of it that 'Classical antiquity was anything but esoteric: it was inescapable.'[21]

This situation endured long into the nineteenth century with some qualitative shifts, the most important being that ancient Greek literature joined and to some extent replaced Latin works as the focus of widespread attention and admiration. A recent historian of mid-century France suggests that 'educated people could probably recite an ode of Horace more easily than verses from the Bible, and Livy and Marcus Aurelius provided them with ideals of virtue as much as the Church.'[22] By then, Germans were self-consciously turning away from Mediterranean to northern models as foci of nationalist culture, but the situation near the beginning of the century is summed up in the title of E. M. Butler's famous study, *The Tyranny of Greece over Germany*.

The infatuation of the Victorian British with the classical pagan world has recently attracted much scholarly attention, of which the work of Richard

Jenkyns is the most significant for present purposes.[23] He has collected a host of quotations which illustrate the intensity of the love affair. Cardinal Newman worried about how, when 'wedded to the Lord', he still yearned for 'scenes of ancient heathen fame'. Henry Alford, Dean of Canterbury, called the Odyssey 'the greatest work of human genius'. John Ruskin informed his contemporaries that 'present education, to all intents and purposes, denies Christ'. At the same time he called 'pagan faith' admirable in itself, for 'all ancient art was religious and all modern art is profane'. Gladstone told a social gathering that, of all places in world history, he would most like to travel back to ancient Athens, and then, realizing that he had forgotten Palestine and Christ, grew ashamed, and substituted a day with the latter. Matthew Arnold thought that Hellenism and Hebraism were the two points between which the human spirit must for ever oscillate. Oscar Wilde went further: 'Whatever . . . is modern . . . we owe to the Greeks. Whatever is anachronism is due to medievalism.' Charles Kingsley expressed a similar sentiment: 'You can hardly find a well-written book which has not in it Greek names, and words, and proverbs; you cannot walk through a great town without passing Greek buildings; you cannot go into a well-furnished room without seeing Greek statues and ornaments.' A glance at the monuments of the age bears him out. Upon the Albert Memorial, Shakespeare sits at the feet of Homer. The politician William Huskisson suffered one of the first truly modern deaths, run down by a railway train, and yet his statue in Pimlico is attired in a toga. The evangelical Christian, Lord Shaftesbury, is commemorated at Picadilly Circus by a statue of the Greek god of love. These may serve as unusually ironic examples of thousands of classical images which still decorate the public places of cities and towns rebuilt during the century.[24]

Richard Jenkyns has also superbly illustrated the struggle of Victorians to preserve amid all this a pre-eminent place for the Christian revelation. Some managed the task by dividing cultures according to function; thus, Frederick Temple suggested that providence had given Judaea, Rome, Greece, and Asia each a different role in the education of humanity, and that of Judaea was in the sphere of religion. The theory of evolution helped the more widespread substitution of a progressive scheme of development. To Newman, 'Pagan literature, philosophy and mythology were but a preparation for the Gospel.' His Protestant counterpart, Bishop Westcott of Durham, praised Greek thought for representing several stages in the unfolding of the divine purpose. Gladstone determined 'to prove the intimate connection between the Hebrew and Olympian revelations', and told the House of Commons that Greek mythology had prepared minds for some of Christ's teachings. Kingsley agreed that it contained essential lessons in the human relationship with the divine, Arnold called the figure of the god Apollo 'the author of every higher moral effort', John Stuart Mill and Benjamin Jowett treated Plato as a form of Scripture, and Lord Macaulay and John Keble hailed works of Aeschylus and Euripides (respectively) as exemplary religious texts.[25]

The task of keeping Jesus at the apex of human religious development was eased by a parallel reappraisal of his own personality and works. Nineteenth-century liberal theologians discounted all the miraculous and magical, and played down the apocalyptic, elements in the Gospels. Christ was remodelled in their hands to become a wise and kindly teacher of an elevated, timeless, and humane ethic, setting the standards for a civilized world. He was now both gentle and reasonable, an appropriate spiritual leader for a progressive and humanitarian society and the clear moral superior of the deities of Mount Olympus.[26]

In this manner, many educated Victorians managed to resolve the competing attractions of the Gospels and the classics, but there is no doubt of the tensions and anxieties involved in the process. They posed a notable problem for practitioners of one characteristic literary form of the period, the historical novel. The first master of the form, Sir Walter Scott, was neither interested in the ancient world nor much impressed by the Greek and Roman classics. He dismissed their pagan deities with the full hauteur of the Age of Reason, as 'personifications of certain evil passions of humanity'.[27] In the mid-century, however, novelists turned to ancient history in significant numbers. To some extent they avoided the religious problem by taking as their subject imperial Rome, when the virtues of classical culture in general could be regarded as badly corroded; but they still had to face it, and adopted a number of solutions.

The closest to that of Scott, and the least typical of his time, was that of Wilkie Collins, in *Antonina* (1850). Uniquely, he turned the full language of evangelical hostility, usually reserved for savages, upon the pagan temples of Rome. To Collins, 'they stand but as the gloomy monuments of the greatest delusion ever organised by the ingenuity of man' (p. 43). This delusion was not merely spiritual, but literal, for the beauties of pagan art and literature were merely snares by which priests would lure victims to 'the wretched impostures, the loathsome orgies, the hideous incantations, the bloody human sacrifices perpetrated in secret, which made the foul real substance of the fair exterior form' (p. 371). Their secrecy, of course, explains why they have left no trace in the historical record. In one temple beside the Tiber, imagined by Collins, girls were persuaded to descend a flight of steps, robed in white and crowned with flowers, to offer a gift at an altar below. Instead they were transfixed by a sword, disguised as the tongue in the head of a bronze dragon, so that their dead bodies could drop into the river and be carried away. The villain of the whole tale is a pagan driven mad by the triumph of Christianity, who murders successive victims as sacrifices until he is burned alive, on a pyre formed of statues of his deities, by a Christian mob.

As the temperature of the writing may indicate, Collins's real talent lay in Gothic fiction. It is significant that he never returned to a historical subject, that he never had much attachment to the classics, and that he was not personally devout. *Antonina* was in some respects a reverence paid to the shade of an obsessively pious father.[28] His approach was not wholly without companions in the world of letters; in the same year a minor poet, Charles Kent, published *Aletheia:*

or the Doom of Mythology, in which the Greek deities are first celebrated and then revealed to be devils, who vanished on the coming of Christ. The other novelists, however, preferred strategies which left some honour to the Olympians and their followers.

One was to declare that the traditional religion of Rome had been dignified and benevolent, but that by the time of the Empire it had been largely forsaken for new, exotic, and pernicious pagan cults which had spread from the East. This argument was deployed very early in the British genre of historical fiction, by Scott's own son-in-law James Lockhart, in his novel *Valerius* (1821). He suggested that, although still noble in outward, especially artistic, form, Roman paganism had become fragmented, confused, and trivialized by the time of the Empire, undermined by the quarrels of opposing Greek philosophers and the appearance of debauched foreign cults such as that of Cybele. Against it, he extolled the firm, simple, faith of the early Christians, as something which conferred serenity, courage, kindness, and dignity upon those who adopted it.

The same line was taken by the most famous work of fiction to deal with ancient Rome in the whole first half of the century: Bulwer-Lytton's *The Last Days of Pompeii*. It appeared in 1834, on the heels of the East India Company's well-publicized campaign against selected Hindu customs and cults, and combined the new invective against oriental religion with the traditional Protestant rhetoric against Roman Catholic priestcraft, drawing at times on the invectives used by ancient Roman writers themselves against what some of them held to be the indolence and corruption of Greek and Syrian culture. The villain of the novel is a priest of the newly arrived cult of Isis, an Egyptian whose swarthy complexion and eastern provenance are repeatedly emphasized. He and his colleagues pretend celibacy while indulging in orgies, and draw wealth from the ignorant multitude with feigned miracles such as speaking statues. The same tactic was employed, this time as part of a Roman Catholic polemic, by Cardinal Newman in 1855. His *Callista* is the tale of a persecution of Christians in third-century North Africa, supported by the cruel, hypocritical, and depraved priesthood of Astarte, Cybele, Moloch, Tyrian Hercules, and other Eastern deities. The clergy of the traditional Roman cults, dignified and genteel, deplore the violence but have lost their popularity. The result is a paganism devoid of coherence or moral purpose, driving the wise to Christianity or to scepticism, and enticing the masses to brutish self-indulgence.

Where novelists had led, scholars followed. In the 1870s Charles Merivale, Dean of Ely, produced a popular history of the Roman world from Julius Caesar to Marcus Aurelius. It informed readers that the old Italian religion was 'comparatively pure and austere', but became corrupted by 'hideous and brutal mysteries of foreign origin'. Likewise, 'it was when the gods of Greece had fallen into utter contempt, that devil-worship first reared itself ostentatiously by the side of their temples.' The latter included the 'curious and sometimes awful rites of initiation, the tricks of the magicians, the pretended virtues of charms and amulets, the riddles of emblematical idolatry, enshrined in the form of brutes or monsters half-brute half-human, with which the superstitions of the East abounded'.[29] In short, the wily oriental had been responsible for the corruption of decent European paganism, which had lacked both the organizational and the moral strength of Christianity, and so easily succumbed.

Charles Kingsley would have none of these evasions, and during a single decade twice confronted the problem of pagan glory and shortcoming in its stronghold, the Hellenistic world. In his novel *Hypatia* (1852) he gave full credit to Neoplatonism as the finest expression of that world, a philosophy that recognized the existence of the one true deity of whom pagan goddesses and gods were merely aspects, and who provided power and unity to all nature. He also recognized that Christianity possessed a potential for demagogy and intolerance from which real evil could result. Still, however, he gave a superior credit to the latter, for having a stronger fundamental sense of morality and compassion. Three years later, addressing a juvenile audience in the preface to his edition of Greek myths, *The Heroes*, he presented a proportionately simpler picture, of natural decay: the Greeks had believed at first in 'the One True God who made all heaven and earth', but then they 'forgot what God had taught them, and though they were God's offspring, worshipped idols of wood and stone, and fell at last into sin and shame, and then, of course, into cowardice and slavery'. In Kingsley's scheme the heroic tales were wholesome because they belonged to the stage at which, although polytheists, the Greeks still had a strong moral sense and worshipped no idols, 'as far as I can find'.

As the century wore out, other novelists returned to the same issue. Walter Pater's *Marius the Epicurean* (1885) made the most sustained consideration of all, and the most sophisticated since *Hypatia*. He portrayed the Roman Empire as admirable in all ways except its spiritual uncertainty, which Christianity had amended with a message of simple hope and benevolence, capable of comforting even the most jaded and overcivilized. He suggested that traditional Roman paganism was lovable and beautiful but suitable only for a primitive and undemanding society. Eight years later, the American general Lew Wallace published *Ben-Hur*, which was a best-seller on both sides of the Atlantic. In its first five chapters he presented a view that the ancient Greek, Egyptian, and Indian religions had, at their prime, all honoured the 'one true God', by the brilliant device of making each of the Three Wise Men of the Nativity story represent one of those faiths. Lest his readership feel that he was taking multiculturalism too far, he added a piece of gratuitous racism by asserting that black Africans had corrupted the pure old Egyptian religion into a false animist polytheism.

In the centre of the book, Wallace judged the quality of classical Greek paganism at the time of Christ, by leading his hero into the sacred grove of Apollo at Daphne and paying full (indeed rhapsodic) tribute to the beauty, sensuality, and assimilation to the natural world of this religion. He then condemned it as a temptation to slide into sloth and amorality, 'the unmixed sensualism to which the East was wholly given'. In that moment Wallace reminded his readers that Daphne was in Syria, and suddenly tarred Greek religion with the common

nineteenth-century charge against Arab and Indian cultures, of idleness, sloven-
liness, and self-indulgence. He coined the aphorism 'Better a law without love
than love without a law.' Ben-Hur is shocked out of temptation, and given a
fresh commitment to puritanical monotheism, by coming across in the grove
what might strike a different observer as an idyllic scene: a pretty young couple
lying asleep in each other's arms on a tiger skin, at the foot of the statue of a
nymph, having just made love. Wallace's point was not merely that the couple
had committed the sin of fornication, but that by lying about in the daytime, in
post-coital torpor, they were wasting time that should have been spent in
productive labour. The Protestant ethic indeed!

In such popular histories and works of fiction, a very large public was inocu-
lated with the instinct that classical paganism had represented some of the lower
rungs on the ascent to the true religion, and that it had left a treasury of images
and ideas which could be enjoyed within limits tightly defined and patrolled by
Christian faith and morality. Should those limits be ignored, the same texts
suggested, then not merely individuals but whole societies would become
vulnerable to spiritual and institutional decay and dissolution of the sort which
had beset the ancient world. The penalty was, in effect, a functional and sociological one; and therein lay the difference in this language from that used to
patrol religious behaviour until the eighteenth century, when the direct wrath of
an offended deity would have been the sanction invoked instead. The European
cultural world of the nineteenth century had grown far too secure, and proof
against natural disasters, to be as nervous of the moods of Jehovah. Instead, the
arguments used to safeguard the established religion were becoming utilitarian;
namely, that its teaching and claim on communal allegiance represented an
important bond within society, any loosening of which might destroy the stability of the whole social order, and imperil the achievements of modernity. In this
language, the legacy of classical paganism wore two aspects. On the one hand it
was so completely built into the fabric of European civilization, and contained
so much of value, that it normally functioned as a source of order, reassurance,
and further edification. On the other, it only retained this supportive role as
long as it was kept clearly subordinate to Christianity in the realm of religion
and ethics. Without this qualification, it possessed the potential to turn into a
profoundly subversive force.

*   *   *

Both of the languages characterized above were traditional and conservative,
although they developed significantly during the nineteenth century. They were
employed to defend the established religion and existing society, had deep roots
in the past, and appealed to widespread instincts and prejudices. In addition,
however, the same century saw the increasing usage of two others, both of which
posed a self-conscious challenge to prevailing religious and cultural norms. The
first of these depended on the notion that there had once existed a single great

world spiritual system, based upon divine revelation, of which the main religions practised by civilized humanity during historical times all contained traces. This automatically denied the claim of Christianity to any special relationship with divinity or any moral pre-eminence, reducing it to a parity with ancient Greek and Egyptian paganism and the principal spiritual traditions of the Orient; indeed, in some respects those other faiths could be compared favourably with that of Christ. Such a language owed its ultimate origin to the project first clearly enunciated by Ficino and succeeding philosophers of the Renaissance, of recovering all that could be known of the wisdom of the European and Near Eastern past in order to create the best possible future. The thinkers of the Enlightenment extended this work in space as well as time, to incorporate the knowledge gained by other major world civilizations.

In 1836 it was given a distinctive twist, with the publication of a two-volume book called *Anacalypsis: An Attempt to Draw Aside the Veil of the Saitic Isis*. This was the posthumous *magnum opus* of a Yorkshire country gentleman, antiquary, occultist, and mystic, called Godfrey Higgins. It asserted that the megalithic remains scattered across the world had been the works of a great nation unknown to history, which had discovered religion and writing. This had given its system of spirituality and philosophy to the ancient Indians, Chaldeans, Hebrews, Egyptians, and Druids alike, based on a veneration of the sun with a threefold personification of deity and a myth of a saviour god who dies and then returns. Higgins identified this nation with the drowned land of Atlantis, hitherto regarded as a myth in itself. This device not only dealt with the question of why no objective evidence of the ancestral civilization remained, but effectively turned the Atlanteans into a blank sheet upon which an ideal religion could be delineated, composed of the writer's favourite aspects of those known to history. In Higgins's scheme, the ancient knowledge had been hopelessly corrupted by the Christian churches, and needed now to be reconstructed.

This idea lay dormant for about forty years, and was then taken up and given a considerable popularity by one of the century's truly international figures, Helena Petrovna Blavatsky. A Russian by origin, she lived for long periods in Italy, Germany, France, Britain, India, and the United States, as well as travelling across much of the rest of the planet. In Paris in 1858 she discovered spiritualism, and with it what she and many others considered to be exceptional personal powers as a medium.[30] In 1875 she brought her interests in spirituality and travel together in New York, by founding the Theosophical Society, dedicated to the fusion of world knowledge of the supernatural and divine. Two years later she published what many came to regard as its manifesto, and the book which established her as a public figure, *Isis Unveiled*.

In more than the title it was a continuation and expansion of Higgins's work. It began by declaring that both modern science and modern theology were too dogmatic, and that a more perfect understanding of the universe would be achieved by joining psychic investigations to those of physical science and the Eastern to the Western mystical traditions. Her main difference of emphasis was that she gave primacy to India in the diffusion of the original religious system. She described the old pagan deities as useful personifications of natural forces, and both honoured and diminished Christ by calling him merely one adept of the ancient 'true' religion. In 1888 she provided a sequel, *The Secret Doctrine*, in which she used Hindu and Buddhist cosmology and symbolism to explain Judaic, Christian, and Egyptian methology. This time she argued more explicitly for the superiority of Eastern over Western spirituality, claiming that the greater materialism of the latter was leading the world towards destruction. She also restated Higgins's argument that Atlantis had been the home of the first, enlightened, civilization, which had produced the original religion.

From the beginning there were two different aspects to Blavatsky's work. On the one hand, it was a scholarly enterprise, dependent upon the study and conflation of many different traditions. On the other, it was presented as a religious revelation. She never credited Higgins with the blueprint from which she had worked; instead, she claimed that the information in *Isis Unveiled* had been taught to her by superior beings, immortals who had given the former universal religion to the Atlanteans and whom she termed the 'Masters of the Hidden Brotherhood' or 'Mahatmas'. She had made contact with these in a permanent physical residence, in the Himalayas (which were both too remote and impenetrable to make verification of her story easy, and harmonized with the widespread old tradition that deities dwell on mountains). She also, however, made the claim that she remained in regular communication with these Masters through psychic channels, the existence of which she demonstrated by use of all her famed powers of mediumship, causing voices to speak or objects to materialize from apparently empty air. The reality of these powers has remained a subject of intense controversy ever since her lifetime.[31]

Was Blavatsky herself a pagan? The answer is provided in a remarkably honest private letter which she sent to her sister Vera:

People call me, and I must admit I call myself, a heathen. I simply can't listen to people taking about the wretched Hindus or Buddhists being converted to Anglican Phariseeism or the Pope's Christianity; it simply gives me the shivers. But when I read about the spread of Russian Orthodoxy in Japan, my heart rejoices. . . . I do not believe in any dogmas. I dislike every ritual, but my feelings towards our own church-service are quite different. . . . Probably it is in my blood. . . . I certainly will always say: a thousand times rather Buddhism, a pure moral teaching, in perfect harmony with the teachings of Christ, than modern Catholicism or Protestantism. But with the faith of the Russian Church I will not even compare Buddhism. I can't help it.[32]

The multi-cultural, supranational Blavatsky remained at heart what she had been as a girl: a Russian Orthodox Christian.

Certainly her movement had a considerable impact upon both East and West. This was probably greater in the former, where it played a major role in reviving cultural self-confidence, and therefore fostering nationalism, in both India and Sri Lanka. In Europe and America, however, its influence was still very important. During the 1880s the writings of her colleague, A. P. Sinnett, introduced the tenets of Buddhism to a mass Western audience for the first time. Anna Kingsford, president of the London Lodge of the Theosophical Society during the same decade, reacted against the oriental emphasis of the parent body by encouraging researchers into Western hermetic traditions which gave a new prominence to the hitherto neglected Gnostic texts.[33] The ideas of theosophy filtered through to large numbers of people who never joined the Society, encouraging them to seek an alternative from the apparent bonds of both traditional Christianity and of the new science in syncretic faiths and heterodox reinterpretations of Christ's teachings, often infusing concepts taken from classical paganism. Indian ideas, however, remained a much greater source of inspiration. The two biggest achievements of Blavatsky's movement were probably to make the notions of a single divine world soul, of which all life is a part, and of reincarnation, both widely known and widely held in the modern European and American worlds.

The language of theosophy to some extent rehabilitated the old religions of Europe and the Near East, and disarmed their traditional enemy, but at the price of diluting them almost beyond recognition, with much larger components taken from other faiths. It was one that paid some genuine respect to paganism, but could only be termed pagan itself by those Christian reductionists who applied this word to all religious traditions other than those of Christ, Mohammed, and Moses.

There was, however, another language in which paganism was characterized between 1800 and 1940. It also offered a challenge to existing norms, and was more directly polemical and confrontational. Like the second language, it lauded the culture of classical Greece and Rome, but it demolished all the constraints placed upon admiration of their religions, characterizing them as joyous, liberationist, and life-affirming traditions, profoundly and valuably connected with both the natural world and with human spirit creativity.

Like the language of syncretic religion, it was a modern phenomenon with long antecedents, in this case the literary tradition of pastoral poetry, itself an ancient form, which visualized an idealized rural landscape in which the human, natural, and supernatural worlds co-existed in a state of tranquillity and bliss. Its appearance in its distinctively modern form is a subject which, as far as the present author is aware, has never been studied hitherto, and the problem has been to some extent obscured by the justly celebrated work of Peter Gay, which was cited above. He entitled the book in question *The Enlightenment: An Interpretation: The Rise of Modern Paganism*. Throughout its pages he termed the eighteenth-century philosophers 'pagan' and hailed them as having given the European cultural world the 'paganism' which has characterized it ever since. The semantic difficulty is that he has used these words in a fifth sense, hardly ever found in the nineteenth century, of a scepticism towards religious belief in general, accompanied by a specific attack upon Christianity. A more appropriate range of expressions for this cast of thought would be deism, Pyrrhonism, or atheism.

As Howard Eilberg-Schwartz has emphasized, building upon Gay's ideas, the Enlightenment *did* contribute themes which would be incorporated into a genuine modern paganism.[34] It set up an antithesis between Christianity and other patriarchal monotheisms and the religions of nature which had preceded them, and regarded the triumph of the former as a disaster. It identified alienation as the central problem facing the human self, and a return to nature as a rediscovery of true humanity. It also blamed that alienation at least partly upon authoritarian and hierarchical social structures, which denied the autonomy of the individual and self-worth. It aimed to abolish or universalize priesthood, it recognized no scripture, and it located the source of truth in the human being. It did so, moreover, by turning to pagan Greek and Roman texts for inspiration and example.

The texts most frequently cited by the *philosophes*, however, were Cicero and Lucretius, who were precisely those ancient writers who questioned most openly the existence of any deities and took a secular view of the human condition. Most of the writers of the Enlightenment linked religious enthusiasm with folly and tyranny; instead they demanded the right to question anything, and viewed the only sensible alternatives to Christianity as being either atheism or belief in some vaguely defined Supreme Being, with whom humans had no personal relationships. They treated mythology of any kind as an opponent to be conquered by reason, and their exemplars were always philosophers and politicians. They classed the pagan religions of the ancient Near East with medieval Christianity, as cultures of error and despotism. The one who made the most sustained consideration of the history of religion, David Hume, postulated a natural evolutionary development from polytheism to monotheism, and while he praised the former for its tolerance, he also considered it to have been vulgar and absurd. In Peter Gay's own words, 'all over Europe and America, for all *philosophes* alike, the ancients were signposts to secularism'.[35]

I would argue instead that the characteristic language of a committed modern paganism has its direct origin in German Romanticism, the result of a fusion in late eighteenth-century Germany of three powerful forces: admiration for ancient Greece, nostalgia for a vanished past, and desire for an organic unity between people, culture, and nature. They were brought together in the 1750s and 1760s by the writings of the person who, more than any other, launched the German craze for classicism: Johann Joachim Winckelmann. These established firmly in the contemporary imagination an association between the ancient Greeks and nature, creativity, and freedom, which could be pitted against a modern world characterized as unnatural, overspecialized, and authoritarian. By 1779 the greatest German writer of that generation, Goethe, was deeply in love with the deities of pagan Greece and Rome; in that year he confided to his diary that 'the beautiful gods continue to visit me'. Goethe had no literal belief in them; rather, he viewed them as symbols for his own deepest experiences, while having a vague faith in a single God who was 'an incomprehensible, inscrutable, being, a highly creative living force with limitless attributes, not to be fashioned by the mind of man; infinite and eternal love manifest in nature'. His personal mythology fused Christian, pagan, and Islamic figures and concepts. For all this, he sometimes wrote like a genuine polytheist, accepting the old deities as metaphor but treating them as real.[36]

It was not Goethe, however, who was to be the exemplar of this attitude, but his contemporary Johann von Schiller, in his poem 'The Gods of Greece', first published in the journal *German Mercury* in March 1788. It was an impassioned lament for a lost classical fairyland, presided over by happy and serene deities, in which the whole of existence and the entire landscape had been invested with divinity:

> O'er the lovely world whilst you were reigning,
> Governing with happiness's soft hand
> Generations blissful neath your training,
> Lovely beings of a fabled land—
> Whilst yet rapturous was the ritual dancing,
> Oh how different then, and better far
> Were those times which crowned your shrines entrancing,
> Venus Amathusia![37]

Schiller's target was not Christianity but a new science, which in his opinion reduced an earth rich in poetry to a compound of chemicals. What impressed many readers, however, was that the pagan ancient world was treated as absolutely good, and the faith of Christ ignored. It made a considerable international impact, and the very next year it was imitated in Germany by Johann Hölderlin, with an ode 'To The Genius of Greece':

> Lovely world, where are you? Gracious seeming,
> Flower of nature's spring-time, oh come back!
> In the fairyland of poet's dreaming
> Lives alone your legendary track.[38]

In 'Bread and Wine' (1801) Hölderlin treated the subject yet more boldly, lamenting the departure of the old religion and identifying Christ with Dionysus, and the Christian communion as a promise that one day the pagan deities would return.

By the first few decades of the nineteenth century this language had reached England and been taken up by virtually all of its first generation of Romantic poets, with varying degrees of enthusiasm. The exception was Coleridge, who admired both nature and Schiller but not Greek mythology. Wordsworth did so briefly and reluctantly, admitting in 'The World Is Too Much With Us' that paganism had enchanted the landscape in a way which Christianity and modernity could not:

> I'd rather be
> A pagan suckled in a creed outworn;
> So might I, standing on this pleasant lea,
> Have glimpses that would make me less forlorn;

Have sight of Proteus rising from the sea;
Or hear old Triton blow his wreathed horn.

Byron made an equally brief accordance with the same sentiments, in
'Aristomenes: Canto First' (1823):

The Gods of old are silent on their shore
Since the great Pan expired, and through the roar
Of the Ionian waters broke a dread
Voice which proclaimed 'The Mighty Pan is dead.'
How much died with him! false or true—the dream
Was beautiful which peopled every stream
With more than finny tenants, and adorned
The woods and water with coy nymphs that scorned
Pursuing Deities, or in the embrace
Of gods brought forth the high heroic race
Whose name are on the hills and o'er the seas.

Just as Wordsworth was at heart too conventional to pursue this theme, so
Byron was too irreverent. The true enthusiasts were Keats and Shelley, especially
in the years 1815–16 when they formed part of a social set gathered around the
London essayist Leigh Hunt. Hunt was deeply interested in the moral effects of
religion, and believed that those of established Christianity had been uniformly
bad. He therefore wished to formulate an alternative, and surrounded himself
with writers and artists who either argued for a reform of the Christian faith or
for its rejection. He never quite adopted the latter position himself, retaining an
admiration for Jesus, a sense of an omnipotent God, and hopes of a happy afterlife. In his search for supplements and alternatives, however, he at times
deployed the language of nostalgia for paganism with an unusually radical edge.

On 15 November 1815 Hunt published in *The Examiner* an article which
contained the following passage:

The Christian mythology personifies Death by an animated skeleton;—the Pagan did it by
the figure of a pale but beautiful female, or with a reconcilement still more agreeable, by
that of a butterfly escaped from its chrysalis. This was death, and the life that followed it, at
once,—the soul freed from the body, and fluttering in the fresh air of Heaven. . . . Even
the absurd parts of the Greek Mythology are less painfully absurd than those of any other;
because, generally speaking, they are on the cheerful side as well as the gloomy. We would
rather have a Deity, who fell in love with the beautiful creatures of his own making, than
one, who would consign nine hundred out of a thousand to destruction for not believing ill
of him.[39]

It is hardly surprising that, almost a year later, his friend Benjamin Haydon
recorded him as saying that 'he prefers infinitely the beauties of Pagan
Mythology to the gloomy repentance of the Christians.'[40]

What is still rather startling is to find the sentiments preserved in a letter of
January 1818, sent to another of his chums, Thomas Jefferson Hogg:

I hope you paid your devotions as usual to the Religion Loci, and hung up an evergreen. If
you all go on so, there will be a hope someday that . . . a voice will be heard along the water

saying 'The great God Pan is alive again—upon which the villagers will leave off starving, and singing profane hymns, and fall to dancing again.'[41]

Nine months after this another of Hogg's own literary circle, Thomas Love Peacock, wrote to say that he had consecrated the valley in which he lived to 'the only true gods, to whom I hope that you continue to pour libations and sing Dithyrambics'. He signed off, 'In the name of Pan, yours most sincerely'.[42] It is impossible now to tell how serious all this was; but even if it was largely in play, that is in itself (as will be made clear later) a hallmark of 'genuine' modern paganism, in which literal belief in deities is not an essential feature of religious practice.

The atmosphere of Hunt's salon made a considerable impact upon the two young poets, both of whom had already lost faith in traditional Christianity. In December 1815 Keats wrote a sonnet in fifteen minutes, entitled 'In Disgust Of Vulgar Superstition'. The 'superstition' concerned was church-going, symbolized by the 'melancholy' and 'gloomy' sound of the bells:

> Still, still, they toll, and I should feel a damp
> A chill as from some tomb, did I not know
> That they are dying like an outburnt lamp;
> That 'tis their sighing, wailing ere they go
> Into oblivion—that fresh flowers will grow,
> And many glories of immortal stamp.

It had generally been assumed by scholars of Keats's work that these 'glories' are poetry and art,[43] but it is worth remembering that for this poet the arts, the natural world, and the classical deities, were all closely interwoven. Nature was the realm of the old religion. The dedication which he wrote for a collection in 1817 captures in concentrated form the spirit of the whole, and also that of the whole language of regret for paganism first articulated by Schiller:

> Glory and loveliness have passed away;
> For if we wander out in early morn,
> No wreathed incense do we see upborne
> Into the east, to meet the smiling day:
> No crowd of nymphs soft voic'd, and young, and gay,
> In woven baskets bringing ears of corn,
> Roses, and pinks, and violets, to adorn
> The shrine of Flora, in her early May.

Keats was generally, however, inclined to mourn rather than to practise or to call for revival. His own religion remained undecided, and from late 1817 he began, like Goethe, to create one for himself around the notion of a single God. His long work 'The Fall of Hyperion' (1819) contains a mixture of imagery culled from medieval Christianity, Judaism, the Greek and Roman classics, the Druids, and ancient Egypt. On his deathbed, two years later, the process was still incomplete; he felt a 'horrible want of faith' and spoke desperately of his need for complete acceptance of the Bible.[44]

Shelley was always more ferociously critical of orthodox religion than Keats, and engaged in the applied paganism of Hogg's social networks. In October 1821 he wrote to Hogg himself: 'I am glad that you do not neglect the rites of the true religion. Your letter awoke my sleeping devotions, and the same evening I ascended alone the high mountain behind my house, and suspended a garland, and raised a small turf altar to the mountain-walking Pan.'[45] As a fervent classicist he translated, rewrote, or imitated hymns to various Greek deities. Behind these divine forms, however, he increasingly sought, and defined, a 'pervading Spirit', a 'soul of the universe', a 'mass of infinite intelligence', superpersonal and lacking any moral sense. Christ became rehabilitated in his thought as a heroic representative of this being. He yearned for a world infused with and interpreted by this 'improved', Neoplatonic, paganism—'a brighter Hellas'—but never lived long enough to decide how it might come about.[46]

This network of friends disintegrated during the 1820s, as its members died or dispersed, and for the next three decades the language of radical paganism is little heard. The silence may be illusory, for the research for this present work has of necessity been confined to major authors. Certainly in 1844 the conventionally devout Elizabeth Barrett Browning felt it necessary to strike a blow against the continuing influence of Schiller's *Gods of Greece*, which she felt to be 'still more dishonouring to poetry than Christianity'. The result was 'The Dead Pan', which claimed that Christians made the best poets, because they were in touch with divine truth, and that the old deities had perished in the moment of the Crucifixion:

> O ye vain false gods of Hellas,
> Ye are silent evermore!
> And I dash down this old chalice
> Whence libations ran of yore.
> See, the wine crawls in the dust
> Wormlike—as your glories must,
> Since Pan is dead . . .

Not everybody agreed. The painter Edward Calvert, who worked from the 1820s to the 1870s and loved Greek subjects, erected an altar to Pan in his back garden. His friends thought that he paid it serious reverence; but then only they knew about it.[47] The outpourings of the early Romantics do seem to have sated the appetite of leading writers for celebrating or mourning the old religions, and it was not until 1866 that another one raised the standard of paganism in the field of revolt, in conscious imitation of Shelley. This was Algernon Charles Swinburne, in his *Poems and Ballads*. Like his hero, Swinburne conceived of liberty as the straightforward destruction of authority, whether in the form of despotic political regimes, Christianity, or prudish conventional morality, and his verses attacked the lot. 'Hymn to Proserpine' portrayed the triumph of Christianity as the suppression of joy, beauty, and a sense of kinship with nature:

Wilt thou take all, Galilean? but these thou shalt not take,
The laurel, the palms and the paean, the breasts of the nymphs in the brake:
Breasts more soft than a dove's, that tremble with tenderer breath;
And all the wings of the Loves, and all the joy before death. . . .
Thou hast conquered, O pale Galilean; the world has grown grey from thy breath. . . .

In 'Laus Veneris', the poet retold the medieval legend of Tannhäuser, while reversing its sympathies; Christianity was again portrayed as a sad and morbid faith, while Venus, in all her powerful beauty, was made the presentative of nature, joy, and vitality. Other poems celebrated the glories of the ancient and natural worlds, and the animal quality within humans, and especially within women. The collection naturally caused a public sensation. Students marched arm in arm round Oxford and Cambridge quadrangles, chanting excerpts, and the book changed publishers in the midst of a fierce literary debate over whether it should be praised or banned.

Swinburne's own reaction, of course, was to bring out a second collection in the following year, *Songs Before Sunrise*. In this, the poet, again like Shelley before him, began to make his peace with Jesus while continuing hostilities against his churches. Even in his first volume, Swinburne had often dramatically, if vaguely, addressed God; now he identified Christ as a heroic radical. 'Hymn to Man' expressed a belief in a single deity dissolved in the natural world, but 'Hertha' turned this deity into a goddess. Although less explicitly directed against Christianity, *Songs Before Sunrise* still subverted it enough to make the future freethinker Havelock Ellis, reading it as a schoolboy, abandon his faith in Christ.[48]

Swinburne's influence upon modern paganism can hardly be overestimated; he was much admired, and quoted by (to name but three figures who will feature prominently in its story) Aleister Crowley, Dion Fortune, and Gerald Gardner.[49] During the controversy generated by *Poems and Ballads*, a fellow radical, William Winwood Reade, wrote to him with the superscription 'To Algernon Swinburne, Pagan, suffering persecution from the Christians'. Swinburne himself, however, never settled the framework of a personal religion. He was attracted to the concepts of reincarnation, an afterlife, and a creative divine intelligence in the universe, but this did not grow into a faith. His interest in attacking social, political, and religious norms waned after those first two major publications. In the end he was buried in a churchyard, but in default of any instruction no service was read over the grave.[50]

Other poets developed some of the same themes with less sensationalism but more stamina. Between the 1850s and the 1900s George Meredith portrayed with increasing confidence a world in which humanity had become tragically separated from nature, aspects of which were represented by various classical goddesses. Over the same period a lesser author, J. B. L. Warren, Baron de Tabley, wrote sets of poems to ancient Greek deities, in imitation of classical hymns. One literary scholar has suggested that the piety in these is so profound that his 'paganism went deeper than neo-pagan affectations'.[51] By 1876, when

John Addington Symonds published his *Studies of the Greek Poets*, he felt obliged to put a health warning on the product. He explicitly denied that he had any 'desire to replant pseudo-paganism on the modern soil' and declared that Christianity had given the world the new virtues of faith, love, purity, obedience, and benevolence, representing a potential for moral progress to combine with the Greek gift for scientific advancement and poetic sense of a living universe, of which humans are an integrated part.[52]

In other words, here Symonds was using the second language characterized in this chapter. This is all the more significant, in that for most of the book he had been using the fourth one, with full force. To him, the ancient Mediterranean had been a world in which

Nature is naked and beautiful beneath the sun-like Aphrodite, whose raiment falls waist-downward to her sandals on the sea, but whose pure breasts and forehead are revealed. . . . What is Apollo but the magic of the sun whose soul is light? What is Aphrodite but the love-charm of the sea? What is Pan but the mystery of nature, the felt and hidden want pervading all?

The Greeks' 'beautiful humanity is so close to the mother ever youthful of all life, to the full-breasted earth, that they seem calling through their art to the woods and waves and rivers'. To Symonds, ancient polytheism represented 'the Many blent and harmonized in the variety that we observe in nature', and he accused Christianity of having driven a false dichotomy between the spirit and the flesh.[53]

By this time, the word 'pagan' had become equipped with connotations of freedom, self-indulgence, and ancient knowledge, which were instantly recognizable to a Victorian reader. In Thomas Hardy's novel *The Return of the Native* (1878), it is used casually three times to create these effects. The heroine has 'Pagan eyes, full of nocturnal mysteries'. Of dancers, Hardy says that 'Paganism was revived in their hearts, the pride of life was in them all, and they adored none other but themselves.' When describing a Dorset village, he asserts that 'the impulses of all such outlandish hamlets are pagan still: in these spots homage to nature, self-adoration, frantic gaieties, fragments of Teutonic rites to divinities whose names are forgotten, have in some way or other survived medieval doctrine'.[54]

As the century drew to a close, the positive language of paganism grew more aggressive. In 1889 the socialist, nature mystic, and pioneer of gay liberation, Edward Carpenter, called for a return of 'cosmic consciousness' to modern 'Man': 'The meaning of the old religions will come back to him. On the high tops once more gathering he will celebrate with naked dances the glory of the human form and the great processions of the stars, or greet the bright horn of the young moon'.[55] This was Hunt's vision of spiritual liberation, restated with an increased power. The following year W. E. Henley founded *The National Observer*, a magazine that ran for half a decade and was designed to oppose 'Puritanism, Labour, and Humbug'. 'Paganism' was now commonly being used in the sense of an antithesis to all three, and especially the first.

Moreover, it looked as if it might be becoming bankable. In 1892 William Sharp founded *The Pagan Review*, with the motto 'Sic Transit Gloria Grundy'. He announced in his first editorial that it would be 'pagan in sentiment, pagan in conviction, pagan in outlook', and herald a new age in which the long hostility between the sexes would end in the resumption of true partnership, and sexual union be recognized as 'the flower of human life'. Unhappily for Sharp, the first issue was also the last. He had written all the contributions (all short works of fiction) himself, under different names, and his talent was not yet sufficient to support one. As the first critic to consider the collection, Peter Green, immediately recognized, two pieces stand out from the others as having an attractive quality, 'The Black Madonna' and 'The Oread'.[56] This is because while the essays in general are risibly bad, these are hilariously so. The former is set in the temple of an Indian mother-goddess, who is served by nude congregations, with large-scale sacrifice of maidens. She materializes because of the fervour of her priest, Bihr, who becomes her lover while vowing that he will die for her; the parallel is explicitly drawn between the couple and the Virgin Mary and Christ. It contains a single memorable piece of dialogue:

THE BLACK MADONNA (trembling and strangely troubled): 'What wouldst thou?'
BIHR: 'Thou!'

In 'The Oread' a young English gentleman, attired in a tweed coat, pursues a naked nymph across a Scottish moor, where he has been stalking a stag. The chase is in vain until he makes the discovery that in order to win her love, he has to take all *his* clothes off as well. After the débâcle of *The Pagan Review*, Sharp fled to the sanctuary of Celtic mythology, from which he emerged to achieve literary success under the pen-name of Fiona Macleod.

The fact that the commercial potential of the P-word had not been damaged by Sharp's efforts was illustrated the next year, when one of the contributors to *The National Observer*, Kenneth Grahame, issued a collection of his own essays under the title *Pagan Papers*. The publisher was John Lane, the shrewdest and most adventurous in England during the decade, who would never have accepted it unless he believed that it would increase sales; indeed, it may have been his proposal. Only three of the pieces have any relevance to the label whatsoever; one on Pan as the spirit of the English countryside, one ('The Centaur') upon the need of humans to reconnect with their animal qualities, and one ('Orion') which looked forward with some excitement to a collapse of civilization and return to hunter-gatherer ways.

If the term 'pagan' had acquired an exciting cachet, conservative critics were now using that of 'neo-pagan' to indicate disapproval of the libertarian attitudes embodied in the latter. In 1891 W. F. Barry made a full-blown attack on 'Neo-Paganism', characterizing it as being concerned with 'the exhuberance of eternal nature, all rhythm and harmonious evolution, a great unceasing festival of flowers and lights and easy sensuous love'. He went on to argue that it was in reality a shallow and corrupting creed, whereas Christianity gave true wisdom and hope.[57] The label 'neo-pagan' was also applied by Punch (then a reactionary journal) to the most celebrated periodical of the *fin de siècle* 'decadents', *The Yellow Book*, published by Lane in 1894.[58]

What Barry and his sympathizers seem to have had chiefly in mind was the tremendous contemporary outpouring of poetry which associated nature, hedonism, and classical paganism in the Keatsian manner, and which will be considered more closely in the next two chapters, as it relates to specific deities. This easily survived the collapse of *The Yellow Book*, the Aesthetic Movement, and the principal coterie of 'decadents' in the wake of the Oscar Wilde trials in the mid-decade, and ran on without slackening into the new century. When E. M. Forster published his first novel, *The Longest Journey*, in 1907, he treated it as natural that his anti-hero, an aspiring author, would write a story about a modern man in love with a dryad. By that time, also, a respected scholar had weighed in upon the side of pagan revival: the classicist G. Lowes Dickinson. In his best-seller *The Greek View of Life*, which went through eleven editions between 1896 and 1917, he took the Symonds line, portraying Greek religion as one that had enchanted the world and inspired humans, while suggesting that such a view was too limited to be suitable for a modern world. In 1905, however, he scrapped the qualification, informing readers of *The Saturday Review* that it had represented 'an ideal of a full and satisfied humanity', as opposed to the arid asceticism of Christianity, and was thus 'more fitted for a new age'.

This article drew a counterblast from the Roman Catholic polemicist G. K. Chesterton, who redeployed the old argument that Christian culture had absorbed all that was good about the pagan world and added a superior ethic. He extended his attack to the 'New Paganism (or neo-Paganism)' of fiction and light literature, complaining that it embodied a largely imaginary view of the ancient Greek and Romans as 'continually crowning themselves with flowers and dancing about in an irresponsible state . . . above all things inebriate and lawless'.[59]

The poems of James Elroy Flecker may stand as a classic example of the sort of Edwardian escapism to which he was referring. In 'The Ballad of Hampstead Heath', Bacchus and his train invade modern London and makes its inhabitants dance, en masse, for a night. 'Oak and Olive' celebrates Flecker's Gloucestershire youth, with verses such as

> Have I not chased the fluting Pan
> Through Cranham's sober trees?
> Have I not sat on Painswick Hill
> With a nymph upon my knees,
> And she as rosy as the dawn
> And naked as the breeze?

The answer, the poem implies, is yes, to both of the above. In reality, of course, he had done so only in imagination, using images from the classical texts dinned into him at Uppingham and Oxford.[60] Fantasies such as these were more rather than less compelling, for both authors and readers, for the fact that they were preposterous.

The First World War put an end to most of them, producing a revulsion of taste in favour of a more sober and gritty modernity. The language of pagan revival diminished accordingly, but also adapted, as the Grecian background was exchanged for a more general association with the powers of nature. Lilian Holmes's poem 'The Pagan' (1917) is actually about a nun who longs to cast off her habit in order to enjoy the 'wild winds' kisses on her neck'.[61] Many of the short stories of Algernon Blackwood, in the 1920s, are about the allure of elemental forces. 'The Glamour of the Snow' contains a typical introductory passage: 'he knew that the spell of Nature was greater for him than all the other spells in the world combined—greater than love, revelry, pleasure, greater even than study. He had always been afraid to let himself go. His pagan soul dreaded her terrific powers of witchery even while he worshipped'.[62]

In 1928 that definitively 'modern' author, D. H. Lawrence, put into the mouth of literature's most famous gamekeeper a paraphrase of the words of his own hero, Carpenter: 'They ought to be naked and handsome, and to sing in a mass and dance the old group dances . . . let the mass be forever pagan'.[63] Four years later the same vision was shared by Harold Massingham, a writer of senti- mental works on the English countryside. He foresaw a time when his compatri- ots would recover their appetite for natural beauty and natural living, the divine spirit of the land would awake, and the 'Lord of Misrule will be proclaimed, and all the blessed sons and daughters of men will gather to the Feast of Fools'.[64] During the inter-war years this language of paganism was still very much alive.

It was, obviously enough, one response to the Evangelical Revival and then to the more sustained phenomena of urbanization, industrialization, and rapid social change. What is particularly significant about it is that it was also very much an English one; and why this should have been so demands some consid- eration. It is fairly easy to suggest an answer in the case of Germany, where the love affair with ancient Greece continued in scholarly circles but waned among radicals during the early nineteenth century, to be replaced by a revivalist nationalism which called for a return to native cultural models.[65] Old German literature, being wholly medieval in composition, was either Christian, or concerned with a semi-secular heroism. The problem is more difficult to solve for the French, who were, as said above, as avid a group of classicists as the English—and indeed sometimes spoke of paganism with the same connota- tions. Baudelaire's 'Pagan's Prayer' is one for sexual release, delivered to the goddess 'Lust'. A visitor to London in 1882 described its prostitutes as having 'pagan smiles'.[66] An art critic in 1896, speaking of a newly exhibited painting of nude sea nymphs, called the latter 'a most certain evocation of the pagan world . . . with their pearly, roseate throats, and the pale azure running in their veins, with their arms that seem to yearn for voluptuous embraces, and their chubby bottoms, whipped by the water's amusing anger.'[67] The distinction is that in France it remained (as these examples suggest) an incidental discourse, of masturbation rather than of revolt or of powerful creative fantasy—apparently because French radicals were at once more anticlerical than their English equivalents and much less enamoured of the countryside. As a result, their assault upon established religion took the form more of outright blasphemy and flirtation, with Satanic imagery.

*   *   *

It must be stressed again that these were languages, not fully formed and mutually exclusive ideological positions. Some individuals moved from one to another, others alternated them, and yet others combined them; in the selection given above, it is obvious that Symonds mixed the second and the fourth, while Sharp (in 'The Black Madonna') blended the first and the fourth. Combinations of first and second were standard, theosophists commonly used first and third, and the third and the fourth appeared together in the thought of the Romantic poets. None of this diminishes the discursive force which each possessed, and they tended to become more, and not less, distinctive with time. It was the fourth, without mixture, that was to become the language of late twentieth-century paganism.

2

FINDING A GODDESS

※ ❦ ※

I N the pagan ancient world goddesses were most commonly patronesses of
cities, justice, war, handicrafts, and home fire, agriculture, love, and learning;
they stood for aspects of civilization and human activity much more often than
for those of the natural world. Furthermore, the overwhelming majority of
ancient pagans genuinely believed that the different goddesses were separate
personalities. In only one text from near the end of the pagan period, the
Metamorphoses of Apuleius, was the writer's favourite female deity declared to
be the embodiment of all other goddesses (or at least of the most important)
and identified with the moon and with the whole of nature. It was, however, that
highly atypical image from Apuleius which became the predominant concept of
a goddess in the modern world. When did it come to do so, and how?

The short answer is, a couple of centuries ago. Throughout the Middle Ages
and early modern period, the emphasis on pagan deities remained just where it
had been in ancient times. A systematic survey of classical themes in English
poetry between 1300 and 1800 reveals that the most popular goddess was Venus,
patroness of love, followed by Diana, representing female chastity and (much
more rarely) hunting, then Minerva, for wisdom, and Juno, symbol of queenli-
ness.[1] A more impressionistic look at intellectual works shows Minerva, not
surprisingly, to be apostrophized most often.[2] As a civic goddess, she also seems
to appear most frequently in urban statuary, from the Renaissance to the nineteenth century.[3]

It is true that in the early modern hermetic tradition there was a concept,
representing a blend of Apuleius and the Neoplatonic notion of a world-soul, of
a female figure identified with the starry heaven, standing between God and the
earth and functioning as a fount of life and inspiration.[4] This tradition was,
however, by definition the preserve of a small minority of specialists.

It is more important that the ancient Greeks spoke of the earth as being feminine in gender and the sky as being masculine (in sharp contrast, say, to the
Egyptians). As most Western science is ultimately based upon Greek thought,
this language became embedded in it. It was reinforced by the mindset of the
patriarchal societies which occupied medieval and early modern Europe, in
which intellectuals in general, and those who dealt with the sciences in particular, were overwhelmingly male. Carolyn Merchant has led a number of writers
in emphasizing the development of a scholarly language which identified the

author and reader as male adventurers occupied in exploring and exploiting a female natural world.[5] A concomitant was that from the high Middle Ages scholastic writers sometimes used a female figure to personify that world, and occasionally this got into creative literature. Its most famous appearance is probably in Chaucer's *Parlement of Foules*, where he felt sufficiently self-conscious about the use of it to cite his source, the twelfth-century cleric Alanus de Insulis.[6]

This was the pattern which prevailed, with remarkable consistency, until the decades around 1800, when it was dramatically altered by that complex of cultural changes known loosely and conventionally as the Romantic Movement. One aspect to this was the exaltation of the natural and irrational, qualities that had conventionally been both feared or disparaged and characterized as feminine. Cultural historians have devoted many works to tracing the course of this revolution in taste, which for the first time gave emphasis to the beauty and sublimity of wild nature and of the night.[7] None has hitherto made a study of its impact upon European images of the divine feminine.

The impact upon English letters is spectacularly clear, and once again the existence of a handy reference work provides an easy means of tracing it in the realm of poetry.[8] Between 1800 and 1940 Venus (or Aphrodite) retains her numerical superiority in appearances, with Diana (or Artemis) coming second. Juno, however, almost vanishes, and so does Minerva after 1830. The third place is now taken by Proserpine, as goddess of the changing seasons or of the dead, and the fourth by Ceres or Demeter, lady of the harvest. A reading of the texts listed discloses a much more striking alternative. Venus now appears not merely as patroness of love but related to the woodland or the sea. Diana is no longer primarily a symbol of chastity or of hunting, but of the moon, the greenwood, and wild animals. Furthermore, when a goddess is made the major figure in a poem, instead of the subject of an incidental reference, the supremacy of Venus is overturned. Diana now leads, or else a generalized female deity of moonlight or the natural world, most commonly called 'Mother Earth' or 'Mother Nature'.

The pattern was clearly established by the 1810s, and shows prominently in the work of Keats and Shelley. From his earliest compositions, Keats felt himself to be enchanted by the moon, and identified it with a goddess, 'Maker of sweet poets, dear delight of this fair world, and all its gentle livers'.[9] His first long and truly ambitious work, *Endymion* (1818) had as its theme the (successful) love of a mortal man for this deity, containing such rhapsodic passages as

> What is there in thee, Moon! that thou shouldst move
> My heart so potently? When yet a child
> I oft have dried my tears when thou hadst smiled.
> Thou seemst my sister: hand in hand we went
> From eve to morn across the firmament.
> . . . And as I grew in years, still didst thou blend
> With all my ardours: thou wast the deep glen;
> Thou wast the mountain top—the sage's pen—

> The poet's harp—the voice of friends—the sun;
> Thou wast the river—thou wast glory won;
> Thou wast my clarion's blast—thou wast my steed—
> My goblet full of wine—my topmost deed:—
> Thou wast the charm of women, lovely Moon![10]

This shimmer of moonlight runs through the work of the Romantics, appearing in some of the least likely places. Traditionally, Druids were regarded as sun-worshippers, but when Vincenzo Bellini wrote the nineteenth century's most famous drama about them, his opera *Norma* (1831), the libretto by Felice Romani made the heroine stand in a sacred grove and invoke the moon, in the most celebrated aria:

> Chaste goddess, who silvers these sacred trees,
> Show your face to us without a veil,
> Bring peace to earth as you have brought it to heaven.

The other favourite way of personifying a goddess at the period was represented by Shelley. When he came to write a wholly original ode to one (as opposed to a translation or imitation), he began:

> Sacred goddess, Mother Earth,
> Thou from whose immortal bosom
> Gods, and men, and beasts, have birth,
> Leaf and blade, and bud and blossom.[11]

By 1820 the dominant image of a goddess in the English poetic imagination was already emerging as the beauty of the green earth and the white moon among the stars. It was thoroughly internalized by the next generation. When the devout Christian Robert Browning tried his hand at a classical subject in 1842, he chose Artemis, and this is how he made her speak:

> Through heaven I roll my lucid moon along;
> I shed in hell o'er my pale people peace;
> On earth I, caring for the creatures, guard,
> Each pregnant yellow wolf and fox-bitch sleek,
> And every feathered mother's callow brood,
> And all that love green haunts and loneliness.[12]

More remarkable is the case of Charlotte Brontë who was the daughter of an Anglican clergyman, chose to return to live in his rectory, and eventually married his curate. She always paid a passionate lip-service to Christianity, and made her heroine, Jane Eyre, contemplate going abroad as a missionary. Emotionally, however, Jane operates within as cosmology where a single supreme God has created nature to be a divine mother for living things, and perhaps in particular for women. It is to this mother (and not to Jesus) that Jane turns for comfort when in serious trouble, and who at one point appears to her out of the moon in a dream-vision, to warn her.[13] It never seems to have occurred to Brontë that this view of divinity was not actually Christianity.

The next stage of the process was to eliminate the creator god, leaving the composite goddess of nature as the single mighty source of all being, and this was taken by Swinburne in 1867, when he gave resounding voice to her under the name of the German earth-goddess Hertha:

> I am that which began;
> Out of me the years roll;
> Out of me, god and man,
> I am equal and whole;
> God changes, and man, and the form of them bodily;
> I am the soul. . . .
>
> First life on my sources
> First drifted and swam;
> Out of me are the forces
> That save it or damn;
> Out of me, man and woman, and wild beast and bird;
> Before God was, I am.[14]

Simultaneously, in 1867 James Thomson was writing a poem entitled 'The Naked Goddess', which he eventually published in 1880. Its heroine is Nature, who comes to a town nude and attended by a train of adults. The adult humans offer her the choice between donning the habit of a nun or the robe of a philosopher. Only the children realize how beautiful she is, and go back with her to the wildwood. During the decades between its production and publication, George Meredith was evolving his own parallel poetic vision in work after work, by which all classical goddesses were different aspects of 'Great Nature' or 'Earth', with whom humans needed to be reconciled in order to be complete once more. By 1880 the composite goddess was both a creatrix and a redeemer.

*   *   *

To understand the hold which she achieved upon the Western imagination during the following thirty years, it is necessary to leave the world of poets for that of scholars, and to make a retreat once more into the eighteenth century. During its last quarter, a debate had developed over the nature of prehistoric religion. Crudely speaking, this was divided between those who suggested that primitive religious belief was a superstitious compound of ignorance and fear, and those who viewed it as an embodiment of sublime truths, which had degenerated and been forgotten among most modern tribal peoples. The first theory was especially popular among thinkers of the French and Scottish Enlightenments, the second among the German Romantics.[15] The Germans assumed that one of these eternal truths consisted of monotheism, and usually linked it to an instinctual understanding of the processes of nature and of human life.

In view of all the above, therefore, it makes sense that it was a German classicist, Eduard Gerhard, who in 1849 advanced the novel suggestion that behind the various goddesses of historic Greece stood a single great one, representing Mother Earth and venerated before history began.[16] As the century wore on, other German, and French, classicists, such as Ernst Kroker, Fr. Lenormant, and M. J. Menant began to adopt this idea, drawing support for it from the assumption that the cultures of Anatolia and Mesopotamia were older than, and in some measure ancestral to, those of Greece.[17] Those cultures did contain some figures of powerful goddesses, identified with motherhood or with the earth (though never with both). The theory meshed with another, which had emerged from a debate between lawyers over the origins of society and of the human family. One of the contesting theories in this exchange, articulated first in 1862 by the Swiss judge J. J. Bachofen, was that the earliest human societies had been woman-centred, altering to a patriarchal form before the beginning of history; what was true in the secular sphere should also, logically, have been so in the religious one.

None the less, by the last decade of the century, the notion was still only tentative, and there was a reluctance to apply it to actual prehistoric data. When the female figurines of the neolithic and Copper Age Cyclades were first described as a group, in the 1880s, there was no attempt to link them to a goddess.[18] The same is true of the Old Stone Age feminine statuettes recognized as a type in the 1890s: they were dubbed 'Venuses' largely in mockery, by comparison with the famous Graeco-Roman statues, rather than because of any religious connection.[19] The director of the British School at Athens in 1901 referred to Greece's neolithic figurines simply as 'idols' and avoided further speculation.[20] When Sir Arthur Evans first discussed the Cretan equivalents, in 1895, he explicitly dismissed the Great Goddess theory, suggesting that they and the similar Balkan figures were symbolic concubines placed in male graves.[21]

The breakthrough in belief occurred with the opening of the new century. In 1901 Evans, now excavating Knossos, underwent a conversion to the idea that prehistoric Crete had venerated a single mighty goddess. He henceforth interpreted all the images of apparent divine females at the site as aspects of this one deity, and male figures as portrayals of an equivalent single god, subordinate to her as her son and consort. This relationship was based on the classical legend of Rhea and Zeus; but his insistence that she had been viewed as both Virgin and Mother, with a divine child, owed an unmistakeable debt to the Christian tradition of the Virgin Mary.[22] By 1921 Evans had firmly associated the neolithic figurines and the historic Near Eastern goddesses with her,[23] and his influence made this the orthodoxy of Minoan archaeology,[24] although there were always a few colleagues who pointed out that it placed a strain upon the evidence.[25]

In 1903 Sir Edmund Chambers, a civil servant who was also a respected scholar of the medieval stage, declared that prehistoric Europe had worshipped a Great Earth Mother in two aspects, creatrix and destroyer, who was later known by a plurality of names.[26] Simultaneously, an influential Cambridge classicist, Jane Ellen Harrison, stated her belief in the same figure, but with a threefold division of aspect. Like Evans, she faced the problem of how to reconcile the apparently incompatible attributes of virginal and material historic goddesses. Instead of solving it with the appropriation of a Christian image, she pointed out that the pagan ancient world had sometimes believed in partnerships of three divine women, such as the Fates or the Graces. She argued that the original single one, representing the earth, had been likewise honoured in three roles. The most important of these were Maiden, ruling the living, and Mother, ruling the underworld; she did not name the third. Extending Evans's ideas, she declared that all male deities had originally been subordinate to the goddess as her lovers and her sons.[27]

One influence upon Harrison's thought in general had been her celebrated Cambridge colleague, Sir James Frazer. He had hitherto avoided the subject of ancient goddesses, but in 1907 he let himself be swept up by the burgeoning enthusiasm for the idea of a prehistoric great one. His acceptance of it was cautious, extending only to the conclusion that in western Asia, at least, the earliest civilizations had believed in a single goddess, 'the personification of all the reproductive energies of nature', with a male son and consort representing the spirit of vegetation, who dies and returns. He got round the problem of how this deity could be both virgin and mother by arguing that primitive peoples had not understood the concept of paternity.[28] Seven years later, Frazer extended the Greek myth of Demeter and Persephone to suggest that all over prehistoric Europe people had venerated a double goddess, mother and daughter, who personified the corn.[29]

This sequence of works was further augmented in 1908, when a distinguished French archaeologist, Joseph Dechelette, proposed that the cult of the Great Goddess had been conceived in the neolithic of Asia Minor and the Balkans and carried thence across the Mediterranean to the whole of New Stone Age Western Europe. Like Chambers and Harrison, he conceived of her as having been visualized both as a giver of life and fertility and as a giver of death and rebirth; a light and a dark goddess.[30] The cumulative effect of this weight of opinion was decisive; by the 1910s it was a staple theme of textbooks upon ancient Greek religion that the worship of the Olympian deities had been preceded by a prehistoric age in which the Great Goddess or Earth Mother had ruled supreme.[31] Whether or not this was actually so is not a question necessary to the purposes of this book; it is sufficient to note that at the dawn of the twentieth century influential scholars had suddenly become very anxious to believe that it was. The problem of why this had happened will be considered, in a much wider context, as part of the seventh chapter of this work. For the present it is only necessary to trace the development of the notion up to the 1940s.

Two important gains were made by it in 1929. The first was proposed by an Englishman, G. D. Hornblower, who linked for the first time the palaeolithic statuettes of women with the neolithic figurines and the notion of the Near Eastern Great Goddess, to project the cult of the latter back to the earliest known human activity in Europe.[32] The second was the work of an American, E. B. Renaud, who made a much more ambitious parallel between apparently female figurines found in the Pueblo cultures of Arizona and those of prehistoric Europe, to suggest that the veneration of the One Goddess, the life-giving mother, had existed all over the world before the coming of civilization. 'The first god was a goddess!' proclaimed Renaud.[33]

Throughout this, however, specialists in the emerging field of north-west European prehistory, and especially of Britain, reserved judgement. This was because their neolithic looked so different from that of the Levant and the Balkans. Its sites had failed to produce any of the female figurines which were such an important prop of the Great Goddess construct in the south-east. Instead the Western European neolithic was characterized by a very widespread monumental tradition, of megalithic tomb-shrines, the structures commonly called dolmens, passage graves, and long barrows. It was true that some of the French tombs contained a carved female figure, which gave some grounds for arguing in favour of a goddess cult; but the decisive evidence was lacking, and archaeologists did not feel able to pronounce upon the matter without it.

As illustrated in the previous chapter, the first scholars of European prehistory applied tribal models to its religions, to produce an impression of savage beliefs and practices. Their successors in the early twentieth century were recoiling from these, as unverifiable given the state of the evidence. Between 1920 and 1940, three leaders of the emerging profession of British archaeology, Gordon Childe, Grahame Clark and O. G. S. Crawford, all published surveys of prehistoric Britain which scrupulously avoided pronouncing upon the nature of its religious cultures. Childe and Crawford suggested that the megalithic tombs had been monuments of a single faith, and Childe even characterized it as spread by missionaries from the East (another comfortable fit with Christianity, and also with Dechelette's theory). Both, however, firmly declined to identify the being or beings upon which it had been focused.[34] No such caution restrained non-academic writers with an interest in archaeology. When Harold Massingham wrote a book about the Cotswolds in 1932 he took his information about their long barrows from Crawford's famous survey, but with the single difference that whereas Crawford had never discussed the religious beliefs of the builders, Massingham repeatedly declared, with perfect confidence, that they had been based on Mother Earth.[35]

For those scholars who wanted to think like Massingham, the barrier was apparently removed at last in 1939, when A. L. Armstrong claimed to have found the unequivocal proof of the worship of an Earth Goddess in the British neolithic. At the bottom of a shaft at Grimes Graves, the big complex of New Stone Age flint mines in Norfolk, he allegedly uncovered a female figurine, seated upon a crude altar, with a vessel for offerings placed before her. From that moment onwards, the statuette appeared in books upon the neolithic in general and Grimes Graves in particular, interpreted as a deity. The Ministry of Works, as custodians of the site, placed a picture of the 'goddess' upon the cover of its official guide-book and reconstructed its 'shrine' for visitors to see.

From the moment of its reported discovery, however, rumours also circulated quietly in some parts of the archaeological community to the effect that it was a fake, planted either by or upon Armstrong. Such was the discretion of that community that not until 1986 did one of its members, Stuart Piggott, raise the matter in print.[36] An investigation into it was carried out by Gillian Varndell, as part of a general reappraisal of the Grimes Graves material, and in 1991 she reported the following points: the excavation was never published; Armstrong's site notebook stopped abruptly on the day of the discovery, without recording it properly; on the day of the find, most unusually, he had directed all other experienced excavators to leave the area; the figurine and vessel look suspiciously freshly carved; and somebody on Armstrong's team was an expert carver, because similar objects made from the same Chalk rock, like an Egyptian sphinx, were among his possessions from the dig.[37]

As no method exists for dating chalk objects, Varndell added, the authenticity of these cannot be objectively tested; but not surprisingly, she concluded that the circumstantial evidence makes their status extremely dubious. This doubt is increased by the fact that since 1939 not a single other figurine has been found in an unequivocally sacred context from the British neolithic. It looks as if the Grimes Graves 'goddess' was a fraud; like the Piltdown skull, it had success because it represented precisely what many were hoping to find at that moment. The way was now open for a general acceptance of the idea that the whole of Stone Age Europe and the Near East had venerated the Great Earth Goddess.

The 'conversion' of Sir Arthur Evans, which had commenced this landslide, had been propelled by a similar piece of apparent objective evidence, this time genuine, but misunderstood. It was the work of the American team which had excavated Nippur in Iraq, then thought to be the world's oldest city, reported in 1898.[38] Evans interpreted the report as saying that the deity found in the earliest levels of its first temple was female, and represented by a clay figurine of the sort now familiar to him from Cretan neolithic sites; he concluded that they all represented the same goddess, to whom the Nippur figure was ancestral.[39] Evans had got the chronology the wrong way round (the Cretan data is older), and the book on the Nippur excavations does not in fact decisively attribute the dedication of that temple to a goddess. What had in fact happened was that he and the scholars who preceded or followed him had projected backwards upon prehistory the goddess who had emerged as pre-eminent in the minds of poets and novelists during the nineteenth century. The actual, known, history of ancient Near Eastern religion had followed a precisely opposite course; the earliest records in each region show a wide plurality of deities, from whom more important figures gradually emerge, until eventually (by the time of Apuleius) some pagans were verging upon monotheism. The orthodoxy which had emerged by the 1940s (correct or not) required a chronological pattern resembling a diamond, whereby an original feminist monotheism had disintegrated into a rampant polytheism, which in turn simplified once more to culminate in a patriarchal monotheism. Or, to put things another way, between 1840 and 1940 historians and archaeologists had turned neolithic spirituality into a mirror of

Christianity, but one which emphasized opposite qualities: female instead of male, earth instead of sky, nature instead of civilization.

Significantly, in this respect amateur historians and prehistorians did not so much follow the emerging group of professionals as lead it. In 1898 a medical doctor, John Arthur Goodchild, published *The Light of the West*, a treatise which suggested that the Great Mother Goddess had been the main divinity of the ancient Celtic peoples, and that Glastonbury had been one of her cult centres; he went on to propose that her worship be restored throughout Western civilization.[40] In his unhappy venture as editor of *The Pagan Review*, William Sharp had already shown interest in the same figure as 'The Black Madonna'; in the 1990s, as Fiona Macleod, he also subscribed to the concept of a Celtic Great Goddess.[41] In 1927 another doctor, Robert Briffault, anticipated Renaud by two years, with the argument that most of the world's peoples had once venerated a Mother Goddess who was believed to have engendered all life, and who was commonly associated with a young god who was her son and consort. He made his own solution to the problem of the virgin mother by asserting that the original meaning of 'virgin' was an essential independence of men.[42] Massingham, in the book in which he had confidently attributed the Cotswold long barrows to her cult, added a portrait of her as remaining the enduring spirit of the English countryside, like a Sleeping Beauty awaiting a recall to life: 'she is so very fast asleep that, if you could win a way through the rose-maze to her, you would think her dead. But the faintest shadow of a smile is upon her divine face, and all these roses are the candid thoughts of her dreams.'[43]

Such a deity remained instinctual to overtly creative writers, who after all had discovered her in the first place. In E. M. Forster's *The Longest Journey*, the main female deity of the ancient people of Wiltshire is suggested as having been 'Erda', the German word for the earth, while human happiness is described as 'Demeter the goddess rejoicing'.[44] In the same (Edwardian) decade, the minor poet Eleanor Farjeon could echo Charlotte Brontë's view of the universe by writing of the stars as the eyes of God watching over nature, 'The Infinite Mother' to whom we all belong.[45] Between the 1890s and the 1910s George Russell (Æ) wrote poems to an earth made sacred by imminent maternal divinity. From the earlier end of the span comes 'Dust': 'Mother, thy rudest sod to me / Is thrilled by fire of hidden day.' At the latter end, with 'The Virgin Mother', rude sods are still numinous, and he chides those who look towards heaven to venerate the Christian Virgin: 'I look, with sudden awe, beneath my feet / As you with erring reverence overhead.'[46]

Algernon Blackwood's story *The Centaur* (1911) concerns the quest of a man for union with 'his great Earth Mother', which culminates in the following ecstasy, in which the goddess meets the Book of Genesis:

And the forms moved down slowly from their mountainous pedastels; the woods breathed out a sigh; the running water sang; the slopes all murmured through their grass and flowers. For a worshipper, strayed from the outer world of the dead stood within the precincts of their ancient temple. He had passed the Angel with the flaming sword those very dead had set there long ago. The Garden now enclosed him. He had found the heart of the Earth, his mother. Self-realization in the perfect union with Nature was fulfilled. He knew the Great Atonement.[47]

It remained a parallel literary cliché to identify the feminine, including the divine feminine, with the moon or with the night sky in general, and, as in the case of the Earth Mother, there were writers vivid enough to keep the image invested with real vigour. One was D. H. Lawrence, who explored it twice, in different moods. In *The Rainbow* (1915) the approach is sensuous and incorporative. At one point the heroine finds herself looking at the full moon and feeling as if she is literally drawing it into herself: 'her body opened wide like a quivering anemone, a soft dilated invitation touched by the moon . . . she wanted more, more communion with the moon, consummation.' At another she lies on her back as her lover enters her, gazing at the sky above and 'it was as if the stars were lying with her and entering the unfathomable darkness of her womb, fathoming her at last'.[48]

Six years later, in *Women in Love*, Lawrence's feelings are much more bitter, and the image is one of alienation from the narrator. He makes his hero cry out against 'the Great Mother of everything, out of whom proceedeth everything and to whom everything must be rendered up. . . . He had a horror of the Magna Mater, she was detestable.' The man expresses this anger against womankind by making futile efforts to shatter the reflection of a full moon, upon a pond, with stones: he calls it the personification of two classical Great Goddesses, 'Cybele' and 'the accursed Syria Dea'. Later still he refers to women as 'the perfect Womb, the bath of birth, to which all men must come', and terms this 'horrible'.[49]

The image of goddess as moon was in fact the only part of this cluster of symbols which underwent any significant development during the first half of the twentieth century, and not until 1948, with the publication of the first edition of Robert Graves's *The White Goddess*. Using his full tremendous talents as a poet, his excellent knowledge of the Greek and Roman classics, and a rather slighter acquaintance with early Irish and Welsh literature, Graves developed the icon of the universal ancient European deity beyond the point at which it had been left in the 1900s. He took Harrison's imagery of three aspects, and related them to the waxing, full, and waning moon, to represent the One Goddess most potently as a bringer of life and death, in her forms as Maiden, Mother, and Crone. He divided her son and consort into two opposed aspects of his own, as God of the Waxing and of the Waning Year, fated to be rivals and combatants for her love. An especially important function of the Goddess, for Graves, was that she gave inspiration to poets; she was the Muse who operated through myths and dreams, in contrast with rational modes of thought which Graves identified with patriarchy, Christianity, and industrial modernity.

A more detailed study of Graves's attitudes to religion will be made later in this work. For the present, two features of *The White Goddess* are especially relevant. The first is that Graves was determined that his readers should not treat it as a personal poetic reverie but as an authentic work of history, an accurate portrait of the Old Religion. The other is that, like most of the other writers discussed above, he treated his Great Goddess as a counter-cultural deity, who stood for values and associations opposed to those dominant in the European cultural world for most of recorded history and especially to those most closely bound up with modernity.

By the time that he wrote, the image of his goddess had been developing for about a hundred and fifty years. No temple had been built to her, and no public worship accorded; yet she had become one of the principal cultural images of the nineteenth and twentieth centuries. She and the modern age had taken shape together, in polar opposition to each other, and truly she needed no tangible monuments as she existed so firmly in the hearts and minds of poets, novelists, polemicists, and scholars alike; the natural world itself had become her shrine.

3

FINDING A GOD

⸙⸙

THE history of modern attitudes to male pagan deities follows exactly the same course as that of images of the divine feminine. The checklist of classical references in English poetry between 1300 and 1800 shows that the god most frequently cited or portrayed was Jupiter, the pattern for rulers and nearest parallel to the Christian Jehovah. He was followed in popularity by Neptune, patron of sailors (suitable for a nautical nation), Mercury, sponsor of commerce, education, and communication, and Vulcan, symbol of industry. This pattern endured until the end of the eighteenth century, when it was altered dramatically by the same culture forces described in the last chapter, which ushered in the modern perceptions of goddesses.[1] The supremacy of Jupiter came to an end, and references to Neptune fell off even more dramatically; indeed, most of the classical male deities became less popular with poets, save for two striking exceptions.

One was Apollo, the favourite god of the early Romantics, who saw him both as the patron of poetry and as the male sovereign of the natural world, in his capacity as a solar deity. After 1830, however, his popularity also atrophied swiftly, to be overtaken by a god who had also been thrust to prominence by the Romantics and who continued to attract more and more favour all through the nineteenth century until he became the most frequently cited male deity in the whole canon of English literature—a phenomenon that has been the subject of a full-length academic study, by Patricia Merivale.[2] He was the one most intimately associated with the wild, disturbing, and exciting aspects of nature: Pan.

Pan's development into a modern icon was a simpler matter than the discovery of the modern goddess, in that the ancient world had bequeathed him in an already substantially complete form. None the less, it must be stressed that his new popularity represented a dramatic alteration. At a few places in the backwoods of classical Greece he may have been 'the great god', but this was far from true of his general reputation. Merivale summed up his ancient reputation as that of 'a comic-grotesque little country god, kept under control by the laughter of the more "civilized" Olympian' deities.[3] The author of the best recent short survey of Greek myths, Ken Dowden, has put it more crisply and cruelly: Pan was 'a Citroen 2CV amongst gods'.[4] It is true that medieval Christian writers

43

occasionally gave him a larger and nobler role. Plutarch's famous story of the rumour of his death at Samothrace was taken by Eusebius as evidence of the destruction of the pagan deities by the crucifixion and resurrection of Christ. Servius and Isidore used the apparent coincidence between his name and the Greek word to signify 'everything', to make him into a universal deity of the natural world. His appearances were, however, still rare, and he makes not a single one in any work written by a major English poet between the mid-seventeenth and the early nineteenth century.[5]

His sudden re-emergence as a major god in the verses of Wordsworth, Keats, and Shelley, and the prose of Leigh Hunt and William Hazlitt, represented a major revolution in taste. These writers established him in the form in which he was to gain popularity for the following hundred years: as the personification and guardian of the English countryside, whose cult burgeoned with that of rural England in general. In most cases, it was the countryside as viewed by the city-dweller (usually a Londoner) on holiday. In Pan's woods and fields it was always summer, and usually a fine summer at that. He was the deity of shady nooks in which humans could lie in the heat of the day, of soft grass in which they could drowse, of lanes nestling in hedgerows, along which they could ramble. It was a landscape in which nobody was ever at work; in which, indeed, the normal agricultural population was invisible. In an emergency, as Matthew Arnold discovered, he could be invoked among the trees of a London park.[6]

This is how the god features in the work of the Romantics named above, and this is how he continued to function later in the century, in the work of Swinburne, Arnold, Roden Noel, Baron de Tabley, Oscar Wilde, James Elroy Flecker, John Cowper Powys, Walter de la Mare, Gordon Bottomley, Geoffrey Sephton, and a host of poetasters whose verses never rose above magazine publication.[7] Between 1895 and 1914 Pan reached the apogee of his popularity, representing, in Patricia Merivale's words, 'the one fashionable subject upon which every minor poet thought that he could turn out a ditty'.[8] The rural English Pan also appeared notably in the prose fiction of Robert Louis Stevenson[9] and the young Kenneth Grahame.[10] By 1907 it was almost inevitable that the unpublished first novel of E. M. Forster's literary antihero, Rickie, would be called 'Pan Pipes'.[11] To cite all this is to ignore the stream of short stories and poems involving Pan in a classical Greek and mythological setting, but with the same character as patron of rural tranquillity, which appeared between 1890 and 1930.

The familiarity of the image, and the ready way in which it could be trivialized, should not be allowed to obscure its power. The nineteenth-century English made the god the expression of all the aspects with which the Romantics had invested the natural world: sublime, mysterious and awe-inspiring, benevolent, comforting, and redemptive. He was pitted directly against the perceived ugliness, brutality, and unhealthiness of the new industrial and urban environment and the perceived aridity and philistinism of the new science. He offered both peace and joy, a return—if only for a few hours—to the lost innocence of a sylvan wonderland. The story of his rumoured death, found in Plutarch, could be made the epitome of the language of nostalgia for a joyous, rural paganism discussed in the first chapter of the present work. It was in exactly this gloss upon the tale that Christina Rossetti scented a real danger to Christianity, calling forth the poem discussed in that chapter.

She was correct to be concerned, although the true subversive potential of the image did not emerge until the very end of her century, when it developed in a number of different ways. One was to turn Pan into the Green Jesus, a wise, protective, powerful, and gentle divine figure, but associated with nature just as Christianity had become firmly linked to civilization. This was first accomplished by Maurice Hewlett in his novel *Pan and the Young Shepherd* (1899), where the horned god is represented as the deity of all creatures except humans, who deny his existence even while secretly fearing him, and so cut themselves off from living in harmony with the world. On page 100 of the novel the deity himself is manifested, with the declaration 'I am Pan, and the Earth is mine', and the hero of the book finds happiness when he accepts that fact. In 1907 Hewlett wrote to an American journalist that he saw the Pan figure as the ideal of 'man as a natural force, differing in no essential way from plants and animals. Then God is reduced to the same expression.'[12] Pantheism had become Pan-theism.

In the next year, 1908, this face of Pan made a much more celebrated appearance in the seventh chapter of Kenneth Grahame's masterpiece *The Wind in the Willows*. The chapter concerned, 'The Piper at the Gates of Dawn', is completely irrelevant to the plot of the book, and its tone is utterly different, suddenly introducing a startling intensity. Pan is never named, but revealed slowly to the reader in heartfelt religious terms, with capital letters for all references to him. He features as the guardian of nature, the protector of the young and the innocent, the finder of the lost. Grahame deals with the problem of how the god can still haunt the English countryside and yet never be seen, by asserting that he confers forgetfulness upon those to whom he (or, rather, He) appears. The central paradox of *The Wind in the Willows*, that its characters are animals who live more or less like humans, rescues the author from any need to clarify the implications of what he is portraying. At times Grahame seems to suggest that the goat-god is the saviour of the natural world just as Christ is of the human one, but he never quite limits himself even to this extent.

The image of Pan as a wise guide and redeemer made its final development in 1923, with Eden Phillpotts's children's story *Pan and the Twins*.[13] Here, the god features as a humane and discerning adviser to youngsters, providing a middle way between pagan debauchery and Christian prudery. He encourages people to love the pleasures of the world but also each other, to enjoy sex but only within marriage, and to behave moderately, responsibly, and morally. There is a remarkable irony in using the least civilized of classical gods as the mouthpiece of social respectability and rational humanism; although unfortunately not one of which Phillpotts seems to be aware. Indeed, at the end Pan almost talks himself out of credibility, by asserting the deities are beings created by human belief, but then undermines this position in turn by pointing out that he himself lingers even though people no longer worship him.

Pan was, however, never entirely tamed by the Victorians and their successors; indeed, some of them found him especially appealing because of his more dangerous and bestial associations, and used his image as a battering-ram against respectability. The earliest deployment of this tactic was to treat him as the patron of poetic inspiration. Traditionally, this role was given to Apollo, and this is how the early Romantics attributed it; Keats could hail England, in 'Sleep and Poetry' as 'great Apollo's land'. It did not remain his for long, because Apollo's classical image, as the deity of moderation, balance, and self-knowledge through reason, was too inimical to the Romantic linkage of the poetic gift to instinct, unreason, and the natural self. In *Endymion* Keats himself came to make Pan the symbol of creative imagination. By 1819 Hazlitt could perceive that 'our poetry has more of Pan than of Apollo' and defend this with the aphorism 'Pan is a God, Apollo is no more!'[14] The same attraction manifested itself later in the century among poets who felt themselves to be in revolt against social norms, and achieved its most self-conscious and oft-quoted expression in 1910, from Richard Le Gallienne. He declared that 'Pan is unmistakeably the father of poets', being both innocent and disreputable, representing truths that transcend convention and respectability.[15]

The half-animal nature of the horned god, after all, gave him a much more obvious parallel in Christian mythology than the figure of Jesus, and one absolutely opposed. There is here, indeed, a fascinating possibility which must be left open, because at present we appear to lack a proper study of images of the Devil in modern culture, to complement a large amount of first-rate scholarship upon those in ancient and medieval times. Between 1100 and 1700, both artistic representation and the confessions extracted from alleged witches certainly portray Satan at times as half-goat, and often with horns. More often, however, the horns are those of a bull, and his more common characteristics are clawed feet, long ears, and wings (of a bat or dragon). He is also featured combined with a wide range of other animals, dog and snake being the most common, or as a black, or black-clothed, man. It does seem as if the standard modern conception of the Devil as a being with cloven hoofs, goat's horns and pointed beard is a nineteenth-century creation, representing a Christian reaction to the growing importance of Pan as an alternative focus for the literary imagination.

What is beyond doubt is that the shocking, menacing, and liberating aspects of the god's image were exciting many writers by the opening of the twentieth century. Forster might have ridiculed poor Rickie for writing about Pan in *The Longest Journey*, but this was because he treated the theme in a trite and naïve way. In the same book, Forster himself suggested that the god was the male deity of the ancient British, and ascribes a sudden eruption of irrational fury among a group of modern schoolboys to the anger of Pan.[16] His very first published work, in 1902, had been the story of a spoiled and unlikeable English boy who gets possessed by the god while on holiday in Italy, and finds a finer self as a result; he eventually escapes into the wild.[17] During the 1890s Aubrey Beardsley had repeatedly drawn Pan as a being at once dangerous and alluring. In 1920 Max Beerbohm recalled how in that decade fauns (the miniature Pans of Greek myth) 'still had an air of novelty about them. We had not yet tired of them and their hoofs and their slanting eyes and their way of coming suddenly out of woods to wean quiet English villages from respectability. We did tire later.'[18]

Beerbohm may have been bored with the theme by 1920, but other writers were only then developing it to its greatest plenitude, at least as far as the greatest faun of all, Pan, was concerned. Nothing in earlier literature could match the sensuous power of Algernon Blackwood's description of the epiphany of the god to a group of modern revellers in the greenwood:

He came with blessing. With the stupendous Presence there was joy, the joy of abundant, natural life, pure as the sunlight and the wind. He passed among them. There was great movement—as of a forest shaking, as of deep water falling, as of harebell shedding its burden of dew that it has held too long because of love. He passed among them, touching every head. The great hand swept with tenderness each face, lingered a moment on each beating heart. There was sweetness, peace, and loveliness; but above all there was—life. He sanctioned every natural joy in them and blessed each passion with his power of creation. . . . Yet each one saw him differently: some as a wife or a maiden desired with fire, some as a youth or stalwart husband, others as a figure veiled with stars or cloaked in luminous mist, hardly attainable; others again—the fewest these, not more than two or three—as that mysterious wonder which tempts the heart away from known familiar sweetness into a wilderness of undecipherable magic without flesh and blood.[19]

In 1915 Lord Dunsany had brought out a collection of short stories, three of which were devoted to the theme that urban civilization was doomed to perish, while Pan would live for ever.[20] A dozen years later he provided the fullest and most remarkable expression of that concept upon which Beerbohm had commented, of the god as saviour of the English from respectability. The vehicle was a novel, *The Blessing of Pan*, in which Pan himself never actually appears.[21] Instead, he leaves his pipes on the edge of a stiflingly quiet, pious, and conventional modern English village, where they are picked up and played by one of its children. At once the pagan past returns 'like something green coming bubbling out of a deep well',[22] and seduces the inhabitants one by one. Near the end the vicar is left alone in a parish church from which he senses all the power has departed, unsupported by ecclesiastical superiors who take a rational view of the world and will not credit what is happening. He prepares for martyrdom (and the reader for tragedy), only to be seized by the magic in turn and to become the high priest of the revived old religion, conducting its rites among the prehistoric standing stones in the wood. The story concludes in gentle happiness, as the village settles down to a new existence of paganism, harmony with nature, and economic self-sufficiency, written off by the surrounding communities as eccentric and by the Church as another congregation lost to religious indifference.

One very obvious area in which Victorian English mores could be challenged was that of sexuality, and the half-goat nature of Pan made him a potential first-class challenger. In particular, he could function as the liberator of those types of sexuality that were either repressed or forbidden by convention, and by the early twentieth century he was doing just that. Into the category of repression fell the female libido. Somerset Maugham later recalled how in the Edwardian period 'God went out (oddly enough with cricket and beer) and Pan came in. In a hundred novels his cloven hoof left its imprint on the sward; poets saw him lurking in the twilight on London commons, and literary ladies in Surrey, nymphs of an industrial age, mysteriously surrendered their virginity to his rough embrace'.[23] Most of the work of these ladies presumably belonged to that ephemeral literature which is hardest for a historian to trace, but enough survives from authors of at least the second rank to lend some credence to Maugham's observation. In 1908 Eleanor Farjeon entitled her first volume of verse *Pan-Worship and Other Poems*, and the title piece includes such lines as

> The Pagan in my blood, the instinct in me
> That yearns back to nature-worship, cries
> Aloud to thee! I would stoop to kiss those feet,
> Sweet white wet feet washed with the earth's first dews.

Teresa Hooley's 'Prayer to Pan' was for rescue from 'the drone from Christian churches' and 'the screech of machines'. It contains an appeal to him to 'Burn! Kindle in me from gold goat-eyes, undying fire, / Red flame-flowers of beauty, white-hot jewels of desire.' To Hooley, Pan and Jesus were both shepherds, who walked the hills together in amity. She wrote some devout poems to the figure of the Christian saviour as well; but never expected him to kindle any fire in her.[24]

The horned god was also the patron of forbidden, which in the Edwardian context meant gay, sexuality. He was invoked in an amazingly brave novel by Forrest Reid, *The Garden God* (1905). The maker of the invocation is a schoolboy falling in love with a male friend, and its recitation marks his departure from conventional restraints and his recognition of his true feelings, and sexual identity. He has memories of a previous life in ancient Greece, when his companion and he were lovers in a legitimate, and supportive, social context, and the two of them call upon the classical pagan deities together on a deserted seashore as they confess their emotions for each other. Six years later another gay author, Hector Munro ('Saki'), published a short story in which Pan punishes a prissy Englishwoman by making a stag gore her to death. Her ostensible offence has been to remove a sacrificial offering left for him by her newly wed husband, his votary, but her real one is to have bullied a contented bachelor into a marriage in which she tries to reform his habits; here the god features as a homosexual icon in a much more subtle, and cruel, fashion.[25]

A third aspect of the gay Pan was as dream-lover, and this was realized by Victor Neuburg in a collection of poetry which appeared in 1910. The title piece, *The Triumph of Pan*, celebrates the poet's rapturous coupling with the god:

> The odour of thy hair
> Thy feet, thy hands shall bring
> Again the Pagan spring,
> And from our bodies' union men shall know
> To cast the veil from the sad face of woe. . . .
> But Pan! Pan! Pan! and all the world shall be
> Mingled in one wild burning ecstasy.

In 'The Lost Shepherd' the goat-god is clearly the one on top, and behaving more like rough trade:

> And he clasped me, slim and light,
> I roared with the pain he gave,
> And he cried, 'I will hold thee here.
> Climax all night,
> My beautiful dark-haired slave.

Neuburg's actual lover at this period was Aleister Crowley, whose response, his 'Hymn to Pan', is much better known, at least among modern pagans and occultists.[26] It differs from Neuburg's verses—indeed may be unique for its time—in using the figure of the god to celebrate bisexuality. The speaker opens with a passionate invocation of the deity, from a classical Greek setting, and then offers his own body to Pan's embrace much as Neuburg had represented himself as doing. The result of the union, however, is different. Whereas the other poet had portrayed himself as arising to become a prophet of the god's message, Crowley actually combines with Pan in the moment of coupling and so takes on his nature, becoming an epitome of ravenous and omnivorous libido:

> I am Pan! Io Pan! Io Pan, Pan! Pan!
> I am thy mate, I am thy man,
> Goat of thy flock, I am gold, I am god,
> Flesh to thy bone, flower to thy rod.
> With hoofs of steel I race to the rocks
> Through solstice stubborn to equinox.
> And I rave; and I rape and I rip and I rend
> Everlasting, world without end,
> Mannikin, maiden, maenad, man,
> In the might of Pan.
> Io Pan! Io Pan Pan! Pan! Io Pan!

It is small wonder that by the 1920s some writers who believed in a syncretic use of ancient pagan and Christian motifs felt that Pan needed reining in. Two in particular, both Anglo-Irishmen, made memorable attempts to do so. One was George Russell ('Æ'), whose 'Farewell of Pan'[27] portrayed the god and his followers as recognizing the limitations of the earthly joy and beauty which they represent. They reveal themselves as being exiles from heaven, and longing to be reunited with its celestial loveliness. More famous is the worsting of the goat-god in James Stephen's *The Crock of Gold* (1928). In this tale Pan actually reaches Ireland, only to be turned back from it by its native god Angus Og, who proves the superiority of the love which he represents himself, spiritualized and tender, over the amoral and physical variety offered by the Greek deity.

By this time, in Patricia Merivale's view, Pan's popularity was in any case on the wane. She has suggested that the 'public' myth of the god was ended by World War One, while a 'private' myth of him continued to be important to some writers.[28] There is much truth in this view, but it requires some important qualifications. The war certainly precipitated a collapse in the taste for the sort of escapist pastoral poetry with classical Greek figures in which Pan had commonly appeared. On the other hand, it must be obvious from the list of works cited above that in the 1920s he was still operating very powerfully as a figure in modern mythology, and as all the items on that list were published, it seems difficult to term that mythology a private one. Furthermore, it represented the same themes which had been developed in the preceding period. The quantity of references had declined, but the quality of the works in which they persisted was comparatively high.

It was really in the 1930s and 1940s that the god made a real departure from works of English literature, and this was because he was undergoing a metamorphosis which had overtaken the modern goddess-figure earlier. It will be traced in detail later in this book; for the time being it is sufficient to state that he was being cut loose from his classical roots and turned into an archetype. Just as Diana, Artemis, Demeter, and Hertha had lost their ancient individual identity and become aspects of a single universal female divinity of the green earth and night sky, so Pan became in the mid-twentieth century the most famous ancient aspect of a being characterized, with increasing frequency, simply as 'the horned god'.

The two deities formed a natural pair; indeed, between 1840 and 1940 writers regularly *had* treated them as a couple, some very different examples being Robert Barrett Browning ('Pan and Luna'), Aleister Crowley ('Pan to Artemis'), and Aldous Huxley (*Cynthia*). Right at the beginning of the nineteenth century, Keats's hero Endymion had invoked Pan and then pursued his own love for the moon-goddess. Throughout that century they had been joint sovereigns and representatives of nature, and by the opening of the twentieth they had become counter-cultural symbols as well. The point can be made neatly from a novel in which neither actually feature, E. M. Forster's *Maurice*, written in 1913–14 but not published until 1971. The reason for the delay was that it was the work in which Forster first expressed his own homosexuality to himself and his friends, but dared not reveal it to the world. He was inspired to write it by a visit to Edward Carpenter, whose rhapsodic vision of a restored paganism was cited earlier.[29] The emotional crisis of the novel comes when the hero decides to acknowledge the truth of his sexual orientation and adopt an active gay lifestyle, with all its attendant social and legal risks. He looks at his fellow Londoners bustling about him and suddenly feels completely cut off from their world; instead, he is now at one with 'the forests and the night'.[30] Those were precisely the domains that civilized humans had traditionally found most alien and frightening; they were those of the two deities to whom the modern imagination, frightened, jaded, and constricted by aspects of civilized living, had turned.

By saying this, I am not necessarily suggesting that the deities themselves are in fact imaginary. Much of the tone of the past two chapters may be taken to imply that they are nothing more than projections—even if passionate projections—of the human heart and mind. This may well be so. It may equally well be true, however, that human belief has actually given them life, or else that they have always existed and have been perceived anew because people now have need of them. These are questions which no historian—indeed no human—can resolve, and the functional nature of my idiom should not be allowed to obscure that fact.

4

FINDING A STRUCTURE

ᴏɴᴇ of the most remarkable aspects of eighteenth-century European culture, and till recently one of the least studied, was a widespread growth of secret societies, into which members were initiated upon an oath to observe confidentiality of proceedings, and which contained a strong ceremonial element. The source, and thereafter the main tradition, of these was Freemasonry. As these bodies were by definition closed to outsiders, and made claims of ancient origins and immemorial transmission of secret wisdom a central component of their appeal, any study of them has, till recently, been extremely difficult. In the late twentieth century, however, those which have survived to the present have generously opened their archives and libraries to the inspection of scholars, and by the 1990s it has at last become possible to piece together an objective history of them.

One of the most important contributions to it has been made by David Stevenson, who has addressed the specific question of the origins of Freemasonry and located them, beyond any reasonable doubt, in Scotland at the end of the sixteenth century.[1] He distinguishes the Freemasons clearly from the medieval 'crafts' or local associations of traders and artisans, although he recognizes that the latter also had a system of local bodies within a wider network, a mythical history, pledges upon joining, and processes of initiation after which trade secrets were taught. He also accepts that medieval stonemasons had an unusually elaborate body of mythology, as they equated their work with the sciences of geometry and mathematics, which were integrally linked (in the medieval mind) to the whole scheme of the universe. In practical terms, Masons were responsible for the construction of the greatest public monuments of the age, churches and cathedrals, into which sacred principles of design were incorporated. By the late Middle Ages, those in England were expounding a pseudo-history to their new members in formal speeches known as 'Charges', which claimed figures such as Solomon and Euclid as founders of their tradition. Masons were also unusual in the mobility which their work demanded, and so evolved, over the same period, a flexible system of organizations based upon building sites in contrast with the normal static craft guilds tied to towns. These were termed 'lodges', after the communal shelters in which their members lived while on site. To solve the problem of recognizing true members of the craft, in such a transitory mode of work, they evolved secret signs which were taught upon admission.

Stevenson has argued, plausibly, that what emerged in Scotland in the 1590s was a development of this tradition, but one so novel as to mark a fresh start: the establishment of a network of lodges permanently based in certain districts, keeping records, admitting members who were not working masons, initiating through a progressive scale of degrees, and concerned far more with the ethical ideas behind masonic lore than with the practice of the work itself. More speculatively, he has attributed this innovation to one man, William Schaw, the royal Master of Works and an architect and diplomat. In 1598–9 Schaw used his powers as warden of all Scottish masons to issue directions for the establishment of these district lodges, with elected officials and a division of members into a higher and lower grade. The same directives reminded masons of the dignity and importance of their inheritance of knowledge, and instructed them to develop the art of exact and retentive memory as well. There can be little doubt that Schaw's orders were directly responsible for the foundation of the first masonic lodges of the modern sort, which were established around Edinburgh and St Andrews in 1600, and have kept continuous records ever since. Some immediately began to admit local gentry to their meetings. In this fashion, masons became Masons.

The context of the development is also plain, for Scotland at the time had a small and cohesive national cultural elite, led by a young king with intellectual ambitions and abilities who was determined to take his nation into the forefront of mainstream European civilization. Schaw had effectively harnessed its masons for this project. The reasons for the success of the venture are also patent, for it furnished local intellectuals with a safe space in which they could discuss any concepts except those relating to religion and politics, with colleagues bonded by an ideology of equality and brotherhood. It also offered some framework of mystical symbolism in a nation whose Church had been more than normally denuded of this by the Reformation.

Stevenson has also traced the development of the new organization through the seventeenth century. It grew in quantity, as more and more lodges were founded, but also qualitatively. By 1630 it had become known as the 'Mason's Word', after the password given on admission. By the middle of the century it had also acquired special marks; that used by one of its most distinguished members at that time, Sir Robert Moray, was the pentagram, which he interpreted personally, by analogy with Greek and Hebrew letters, as representing love and charity. In the 1690s catechisms appear, and it is then that we have our first record of what the password allegedly comprised, being a spoken comment upon the significance of the twin pillars of Solomon's temple, accompanied by a particular handshake.

It is from 1696 that the first information survives of the content of ritual, and there is no way of telling whether this had developed over the century or had been established from the time of Schaw, or before. The record is, at least, comprehensive for that date. It consists wholly of the initiation ceremonies. In the first, the postulant had to ask set questions about the Mason's craft, which were answered by the master initiating him. He was shown the hidden signs and taught the mythical history, and listened to a full description of the decoration and illuminations of an ideal lodge (representing Solomon's Temple), and their symbolic significance, a technique especially associated with the Renaissance 'art of memory', which Schaw had enjoined. He learned how to embrace a brother Mason so that their bodies touched at five points, while they whispered the two halves of a password in each other's ears. He was then given the main 'Masons' Word' on his knees, 'with a great many ceremonies to frighten him', and swore secrecy on the Bible, accepting many terrible penalties for breach of the oath. After that he spoke a set greeting, received a promise, and was accepted. The second-degree initiation ritual involved a different oath, and the learning of new signs and postures, but without any attempt to frighten the candidate. The catechisms suggest that as part of the first-degree rite he was shown a death's head, two pillars, a square, and a compass, and taught the esoteric significance of each.

Stevenson has concluded his survey by showing how Scottish Masons introduced the concepts of their system to English friends in the course of the century; Moray, for example, conveyed some of its symbolism to his friend John Evelyn. By the 1640s ad hoc gatherings were being held in England in imitation, and permanent lodges on the Scottish model were being established there by the 1680s. In Stevenson's scheme of events, the English only added the generic term 'Freemason' and the texts known as the 'Old Charges' (which set forth the pseudo-history of Masonry in a prescribed form) to the Scottish framework. In the early eighteenth century they also incorporated a third degree of initiation, developed a controlling national Grand Lodge, and eclipsed Scotland as the centre for the movement, from which it spread rapidly across Europe.

Since Stevenson wrote, Margaret Jacobs has developed his work further, with a special emphasis on the English contribution to Freemasonry.[2] She has argued convincingly that the English gave 'the Craft' (as the system became commonly known among them) a preoccupation with constitutions, laws, and governance, and a cast of thought very clearly associated with the eighteenth-century Enlightenment; indeed, one which placed the network of lodges firmly within that movement. It pitted Freemasonry against all religious 'enthusiasm' and any identification of the state with a particular denomination, reducing the conventional Protestant piety which appears in the records of the Scottish lodges to references to the 'Supreme Architect of the Universe'. Its lodges, though increasingly dominated by nobles and gentry, admitted all but the very poor, and so attempted to produce an ideal civil polity in microcosm, a group of brethren united to develop wisdom and virtue within a secular constitutional setting.

A number of comments need to be made here concerning the story laid out by these two historians, focusing on themes of especial relevance to the concerns of this book. The first is that in medieval British records the terms 'art', 'craft', and 'mystery' are used interchangeably for any trade or calling which required particular skills. The second is that the same records do not enable us to determine whether or not any actual ceremony was used upon the initiation of new members into the various trade organizations. Those of the masons themselves do suggest that the Charges were a development of the late medieval period—the oldest is the 'Regius Poem', from the end of the fourteenth century—and that they grew more elaborate throughout this period. They instruct the newcomer in rules of conduct, and in masonic tradition, and assume the existence of an assembly of initiates, and (from the 'Regius Poem' onward) have a standard cry of endorsement: 'so mote it be' (the standard Middle English for so *must* it be). None, however, implies any ritual action, of the sort found by the 1690s.[3]

It is also clear that the craft guilds became more and more concerned with secrecy and ceremonial formality during the late medieval and early modern centuries, a tendency which accelerated even as their actual economic power and importance waned. The process can be observed by comparing four different oaths of admission to London livery companies (the metropolitan craft guilds), each fairly typical of its time. That of the Weavers, in 1378–9, is wholly practical, requiring the newcomer merely to observe the regulations of the guild and accept its arbitration in case of disputes. That of 1577 also demands a pledge of allegiance to the reigning monarch and to keep private the content of any discussions at meetings.[4] In 1686 the Cooks used the same form of oath as the last, but added a promise to conceal from non-members 'all the lawful secrets of this Company'.[5] Finally, that employed in 1714 by the Wheelwrights is more or less identical with that of the Cooks, save that it demands the keeping of the secrets of the whole 'Trade, Art or Mystery' as well as those of the company itself.[6] During the Middle Ages English craft guilds in general had developed regular feasts, processions, banners, and ceremonial robes, which became yet more elaborate under the Tudors and Stuarts. Freemasons were thus part of a very broad phenomenon, but distinguished by their greater component of ritual, grander historical claims, and higher moral purpose.

A third consideration is that Masonic ritual (commonly known in Britain as 'Craft working') grew much more elaborate between 1700 and 1740, with a slower growth for the rest of the century, and the lore attached to symbols grew proportionately richer. Soon after its foundation in 1717, the Grand Lodge of England developed feasts and processions 'in proper clothing', the latter including 'coloured ribbands and aprons'; these features were all present when its surviving records begin in 1723.[7] The tract *The Grand Mystery Laid Open* (1726) enumerates the 'five points of fellowship' at which bodies should touch during the ceremonial embrace, as 'foot to foot, knee to knee, breast to breast, hand to back, cheek to cheek', which would accord well with the information given in the initiation ritual of 1696.[8] Another pamphlet in 1754 (likewise consisting of information leaked by disenchanted Masons) gave the full first-degree initiation rite as it had evolved till then. The postulant was put through an exchange of questions and answers, and then brought to a room guarded by a man with a drawn sword. Three more men with swords emerged from it, stripped the postulant naked, and then reclothed him in a loose white robe. He was admitted to the room, knelt, had a sword point held to his throat and took the oath. Then he rose, put his own clothes back on, was given a white leather apron as the main outward symbol of masonry, and taught the main password.[9]

A third tract of this category, *The Mystery of Freemasonry* (1730), shows that the same ritual was associated with various riddles; the postulant was initiated 'neither naked nor clothed' (being covered only in a loose robe), 'neither standing nor lying' (since he was kneeling,) and so forth.[10] As the middle decades of the century passed, other ceremonial elaborations appeared. One was an altar, usually kept in the centre of the lodge, upon which the symbolic ('working') tools were kept and displayed to the new-made initiate with an explanation of their significance; for example, the level stood for solidity, the compass for rectitude, and the plumb-line for directness.[11] By 1775 the whole catalogue of ritual included prayers and responses, anthems, blessings, homages to superiors, salutes, proclamations, invocations of virtue, and the consecration of the lodge with corn, wine, and oil. The standard cry of approbation remained 'so mote it be'.[12]

Between 1775 and 1812 the first-degree initiation took what was to be its enduring form. The candidate had to strip himself of all valuable objects and bare his breast. He was then blindfolded, and a halter put round his neck knotted in a fashion known as the 'cable tow', which left a dangling pair of cords by which he could be led. In this fashion he was taken to the door of the lodge, at which his minder knocked. He was admitted after a challenge with which a sword was held to his bare breast, affirmed his belief in a Supreme Being (to refute charges of atheism commonly levelled at the Craft), and received a first set of instructions. He was then led round the lodge sunwise, and presented to the brethren, after which he knelt to take the oath of secrecy.[13]

By this period, also, the four cardinal points of the compass had been invested with esoteric significance: east stood for wisdom, west for strength, and south for beauty, and leading officers of the lodge took up stations at them for ceremonies. The north was regarded as the place of darkness, and shunned, following a tradition given biblical authority in the Book of Jeremiah and embedded in English folk culture; hence the common reluctance to be buried on the north side of a churchyard or to put a northern door into a church.[14] Ritual closing pronouncements for ceremonies had likewise been adopted by this time, such as this one, which ended the second degree initiation: 'Happy have we met, Happy have we been, / Happy may we part, And happy meet again!' There is a possibility that this was suggested by Joseph Glanvill's very popular book *Saducismus Triumphatus*, which represents a group of Somerset witches as having the parting cry of 'A boy! Merry meet, Merry part'. On the other hand, both the Glanvill expression and that of the Masons may have been rooted in a wider popular tradition of such calls.

Comparatively little seems to have been added or subtracted since to or from Masonic ceremony. During the nineteenth century the fundamental signs of the Craft were settled as the pentagram ('the symbol of the most sacred principles'), the hexagram (known interchangeably with it as the Seal of Solomon), the triangle (symbol of deity and commonly of the first degree), the square (symbol of the second degree), and the compasses (symbol of the third). It had always been the custom that the candidate for the second degree would be spared the blindfolding of the first-degree ritual; now it was expected that he would demonstrate the use and meaning of the various working tools as the major test applied to him. The bound and blindfolded first-degree candidate was described as 'properly prepared' and on admission to the lodge he was presented formally to the quarters of east, south, and west, rather than to the assembled brethren. In this form masonic ritual entered the twentieth century.[15]

It has been a pioneering venture to piece together the sequence of development outlined above, and the results are much in need of expansion; none of the recent historians of Freemasonry has been greatly interested in its symbolism and ritual, although (as shall become obvious) they are of major importance to a study of modern pagan witchcraft. Scarcely more attention has been paid to the development of Masonic historical methology, though here again even a cursory process of research reveals a significant evolution. The medieval pseudo-history expounded in the Old Charges was based firmly upon the only two sources of information about the ancient world available at that period: the Bible and a limited quantity of Greek and Roman literature. Hence they had drawn selectively upon these and medieval legends spun about them to claim a continuous descent for Masonic wisdom from the days of King Solomon, and more specifically from his own Master Mason, Hiram. What happened during the eighteenth and nineteenth centuries was that this basic structure was maintained, but was continuously embellished and extended as more textual and archaeological information came in, and cultural tastes altered. The process was rarely depicted as one of discovery; rather, each new generation of Masons was instructed in the latest version of the package as if it were inherited complete through an oral tradition.

The earlier stages of this development can be seen by comparing the Old Charges with the history given in the most authoritative Masonic writings of the early eighteenth century; the material in the former has been expanded in detail to present a claim of continuous initiation and instruction spanning four thousand years.[16] This was reshaped in turn during the last decades of the century and much of the nineteenth, to introduce a lot of imagery from ancient Egyptian civilization, thought at that time to be the oldest of all, and being progressively revealed by excavation.[17] Other archaeological discovery produced a subsequent infusion during the Victorian period of data from Greek and Roman mystery religions and the cultures of early Mesopotamia, which was blended into the story. Syrian, Babylonian, and Egyptian names for sky-gods joined the familiar Jehovah in prayers to the Supreme Deity.[18] The finishing touches were put in the 1920s, when (in keeping with a new contemporary vogue for anthropology) prehistoric tribal rites from which the Masonic system was claimed to have directly descended were 'reconstructed'.[19]

This process was repeated in parallel all over Europe from the mid-eighteenth century onward, as the original Freemasonry produced scores of successor networks, either by schism or by imitation. A feature of these was that, since they were founded in competition with a tradition which derived a large part of its appeal from a claim of immemorial initiatory descent, they could not be presented as novelties. Instead, either they presented themselves as a reversion to the 'ancient' or 'strict' form of that tradition, or else as the genuine version of it, of which conventional Freemasonry had been a corruption and was now emerging into the open after centuries of secrecy. This phenomenon has been well studied in recent years.[20] The result was not merely a luxuriant proliferation of secret societies, but a multiplication of degrees of initiation and of titles, and of styles of ritual. A typical example of the process of action is furnished by the tract *Krata Repoa*, published in Berlin in 1782 as a revelation of a new branch of Freemasonry launched in the city and initiating members through seven degrees into the secrets of the Old Egyptians; its rituals were clearly based on translations of Graeco-Egyptian texts. Germany was, with its atomized political system, the most fertile breeding-ground for these societies. The most celebrated to appear there in the mid-eighteenth century, the Strict Observance, made an important innovation by claiming, as Blavatsky was to do later, to be directed by secret chiefs (the 'Unknown Superiors') who had preserved the ancient wisdom entire. In the next century the United States became in turn the world centre for the mutation and reproduction of these organizations.[21] Many of them were truly international in character, and many survived into the twentieth century. The last of real consequence to appear, at the opening of that century, was Co-Masonry, which broke with the tradition of its predecessors by admitting women.

*   *   *

There seems as yet to have been no thorough study of the place of Freemasonry in nineteenth-century British culture, to compare (for example) with that by Mark Carnes for the United States in the same period.[22] A superficial impression suggests that it was extremely important; the Craft was patronized by royalty, existed in every part of the nation and its colonies, and in town and countryside alike, and was an accepted part of local life; at the Scottish town of Melrose during the mid-century, the local lodge laid on a public parade on the traditional fire festival of Midsummer Eve. Its officials were elected during the day, and when dusk came the members marched through the streets bearing torches and banners, with a band playing.[23] One very telling sign of the way in which Masonic forms had taken hold of the imagination of British males was the way in which they were reproduced in other sorts of association and confraternity from the late eighteenth century onward. An important example is provided by the early trade unions, the modern successors to the medieval craft guilds. During the 1820s and 1830s many of these organized themselves in local lodges, co-ordinated by a grand one on the Masonic model. Like the Freemasons, also, the unions invested in banners, robes, and ritual regalia, and instituted ceremonies of initiation. At its formation in the 1830s, the Shoemakers' Union at Nantwich, on the salt plain of Cheshire, purchased 'a full set of secret order regalia, surplices, trimmed aprons, etc., and a crown and robes for King Crispin' (the legendary patron of their craft). In the same decade police at Exeter arrested a couple of union members on their way to an initiation, carrying for it 'two wooden axes, two large cutlasses, two masks, and two white garments or robes, a large figure of Death with dart and hour-glass, a Bible and Testament'.[24]

These more formal and elaborate rituals made a national development from the simpler rites of admission which had become common by the opening of the century, and perhaps earlier, for apprentices achieving their formal acceptance into a trade. By the 1820s printers were formed into 'chapels', of which a new member was made a 'deacon' by the following initiatory process:

Holding a wooden sword he headed a processioning of the workplace before kneeling before the father of the chapel. He was exhorted to be observant of his business and not to betray the secrets of the workmen. Beer was poured over his head and he was given a mock title. While he was on his knees the chapellonians worked round him singing an anthem, which is done by adding all the vowels to the consonants in [this] manner: Ba-ba; Be-be; Bi-bi; Bo-bo; Bu-bu; Ba-be-bi-bo-bu- and so through the reset of the consonants. Finally coming out of his time, the apprentice had to endure 'banging out'. He was smeared with printers' ink and led through the workplace, promising beer-money to all the workers.[25]

The equivalent rite among coopers in late nineteenth-century East Anglia was for the lad to be put in a cask holding a brazier, while his elders danced round and doused him with water to keep him from getting burnt. Drovers swore fealty to their craft on a pair of horns. These customs may have been much older, but there is no way of proving the possibility.[26]

Freemasonry had a more spectacular and enduring influence upon the most important of the friendly societies or benefit clubs, private insurance companies to provide working people with care in sickness and old age which appeared in large numbers all across Britain from the end of the eighteenth century; by the 1890s they had at least four million members, compared to one and a half million trade-unionists. Like Masonry, they were found in urban and rural areas alike, so that more than a hundred were founded in the East Riding of Yorkshire alone, in the few years 1838–43.[27] All the societies adopted the lodge system and regalia such as sashes and banners. Some, however, rapidly developed into national associations with colourful titles and trappings, such as the 'Ancient Orders' of Foresters, Druids, or Royal Shepherds, and the Society of Oddfellows. From Freemasonry, also, they borrowed the tradition of claiming an immemorial antiquity; the Oddfellows asserted that they had been founded by Roman soldiers, the Foresters included Alfred the Great and William Rufus among their earlier members, and the Druids named Noah as their founder. None, in reality, sprang from any earlier provenance than the last quarter of the eighteenth century.[28] In the words of one of their foremost historians, Mark Carnes, 'no idea was more commonplace, nor more palpably untrue, than the fraternalists' claims of ancient and venerable origins'.[29]

They also took over from masonry special tokens of recognition—a grip, a word, and a sign—and a system of initiation through successive degrees, with acceptance into the group through a ceremony which involved the taking of an oath of secrecy and some element of ordeal. They wore robes—of scarlet, blue, black, and green—with cords and sashes, carried swords, and invested in other trappings associated with the medieval, Tudor, and Stuart periods to help substantiate their pseudo-histories. Around 1830 a candidate for initiation into the Ancient Order of Shepherds was brought blindfolded into the lodge, to hear 'a rattling of chairs, shaking of sheet iron to imitation of thunder, clashing of swords, stamping of feet, upsetting of furniture and much more. . . . Then in a sudden cessation, the beautiful words of the making would be heard in the otherwise silent gathering'.[30] Every lodge meeting of the Royal Antediluvian Order of Buffaloes began by forming a circle, as a symbol of good fellowship and equality. Initiates had a pipe broken over their heads or shoulders, to test their courage, then had their hair cut or singed, and downed a bumper of wine or spirits.[31] In the early nineteenth century prospective Foresters were prayed over, anointed with oil, and swore an oath to assist their fellows and to keep the order's secrets. They then had to prove themselves by fighting a ritualized sword duel with an existing member.[32] The Druids donned false beards for their ceremonies, the Shepherds carried crooks and rams' heads, and the Foresters wooden axes, bugles, and bows.[33]

The oldest of these affiliated orders was that of the Oddfellows, which developed out of a drinking club which had existed since the early eighteenth century. Between 1810 and 1825 their first-degree initiation began with the blindfolding and binding of the candidate, the baring of his breast, and his passage into the lodge between two guardians, who made challenges. He then heard a rattling of chains, and other strange noises, and was sometimes thrown among brushwood or had his head plunged into a tub of water. When his blindfold was removed he found a sword pointed at his heart by a man who asked the robed and masked company if mercy should be shown. They answered in the affirmative, whereupon the candidate was sworn in, unbounded and then shown a figure of Death and other symbols 'both of holy and profane things'. He was then given the Charge of the Oddfellows by the senior officers.[34] At this period the order initiated through four degrees, of which the symbolic colours were white, blue, scarlet, and gold. The initiation ceremony for the fourth included the following challenge and response:

NOBLE GRAND: 'Whom do you represent?'
SUPPLICANT: 'The son of Onias, the High Priest, who repaired the House of God and fortified the Temple.'
NOBLE GRAND: 'In what light will you appear in the lodge?'
SUPPLICANT: 'As the morning star or the moon at full. I cheer and refresh the minds of my brethren like the Sun on the Temple of the Most High or the rainbow in the heavens.'[35]

Something very apparent about both Freemasonry and the affiliated orders is that the religious language which they used, and the tradition which it implied, was not a Christian one. It implied no necessary hostility towards Christianity, but its determination to produce a spiritual ambience in which all denominations could be at ease, and representing an accumulated wisdom of millennia, passed on through unbroken descent, resulted in a syncretic patriarchal monotheism in which all ancient sky-gods and father-gods were regarded as aspects of the Supreme Being, and Christ was quietly pushed out of the picture. It is hardly surprising that these societies caused disquiet among churchmen, and that some of the latter engaged in outbursts such as that of a minister at Huddersfield in the West Yorkshire wool-weaving area, in 1833, who warned the local Oddfellows that they were 'worse than devils or infidels. . . . if you do not foresake your badges which are emblems of wickedness . . . you will sink down to hell eternal'.[36] In general, however, relations between the secret societies and the churches were much less strained in Britain than in parts of the Continent. The predominance of Old Testament imagery in the former made their practices intelligible and amenable to a Christian culture, and they could be regarded as being supplementary to, and complementary with, Christianity. In any case, the actual religious element in them was always superficial, their rituals being intended as acts of incorporation and sociability rather than of worship; which did not make them any the less powerful.

*   *   *

It was in Scotland, where Freemasonry had begun, that it belatedly evolved into its most colourful and bizarre British form: the Society of the Horseman's Word. Like the Masons themselves, this has only recently been subjected to a process of rigorous research. The result has exactly reversed the chain of historical causation suggested for the society by scholars earlier in the twentieth century. The first was J. M. McPherson, writing in 1929, who suggested that it was the remnant of a pagan cult allied to, or descended from, that which was persecuted in the early modern witch trials.[37] This idea was taken up in 1956 by another folklorist, Thomas Davidson,[38] and then by the pioneer of oral history, George Ewart Evans, who produced a series of books between 1966 and 1979 in which he asserted, with increasing lack of caution, that both Freemasonry and the Horseman's Word derived directly from a pre-Christian fertility religion, which the latter had preserved in a more primitive and 'authentic' form.[39]

Neither Davidson nor Evans carried out any research into Scottish sources themselves, and McPherson confined himself to observations made near the end of the nineteenth century. Had they considered the quite large number of earlier records of the society,[40] then a different conclusion would immediately have become apparent, as it did to another writer on Scottish rural life, Hamish Henderson, in 1962,[41] and then to Ian Carter, who produced the first proper study of the world from which the Horseman's Word had arisen, in 1979.[42]

Carter identified the crucial importance to the process of a different organization, the Miller's Word, which had been formed during the eighteenth century
in imitation of the much earlier and more prestigious Masons' Word, the original Freemasonry. Its purpose was to restrict entry to, and to concert plans
within, what had become the very lucrative and desirable trade, of grain miller.
Like the Masons, it was based upon a system of local groups with initiations,
passwords, and professional secrets; unlike them, it did not pretend to a more
general esoteric knowledge.

Instead, it spiced up its reputation by holding meetings at night and by
spreading the beliefs that its members acquired magical powers over mill
machinery and paid for them by having to read the Bible backwards, three times
over in three years. By the nineteenth century the initiation ceremony had come
to include a strong element of deliberate blasphemy or diabolism. The candidate had to bring a loaf, some jam, and a bottle of whisky, as a mock sacrament,
and had to answer a parody of a catechism before a man impersonating a minister and standing before a bushel of corn representing an altar. At the climax, still
blindfolded, he was told that he had to shake the Devil's hand, and was given a
stick, or heated spade, or a bullock's hoof to hold, while chains were clattered
across the floor.[43] This was a local version of the universal pattern of the secret
societies, that the newcomer faced an ordeal upon initiation; but the diabolism
was novel. It almost certainly derived from traditions of the pacts made by
witches, a notorious feature of the trials which had ended only just over a
century before, and would have been well known in the early nineteenth
century, not merely from memory but from the published work of Sir Walter
Scott and others.

It was at that period that heavy horses became for the first time the main
draught animals in the agrarian districts of northern Scotland, replacing oxen in
the hinterland of Aberdeen and the Moray Firth and ponies in Caithness and
Orkney. The skills required to manage these animals were suddenly much in
demand, representing a new source of reputable and highly paid work. To train
young men for it, regulate competition for jobs, and ensure that both services
and rewards were maintained at a high level, the Horseman's Word was developed in imitation of the Miller's. It rapidly became much more celebrated, being
both numerically stronger (by 1880 three-fifths of farm hands in these arable
areas worked with horses) and much less exclusive. Ian Carter has demonstrated
the direct nature of the borrowing by the Horsemen from the Millers, including
the acquisition of set phrases which made real sense only when spoken in a
mill.[44] From the Millers, likewise, was taken the basis of the initiation ceremony,
including the gifts of bread and whisky, the blindfolding of the postulant, and
the encounter with the Devil.

What the Horsemen did substitute, naturally enough, were their own pieces
of craft knowledge, passwords, oaths, and ordeals. The main Word varied
according to locality,[45] and so did the oaths,[46] although the latter were clearly
modelled on those of Freemasonry (a resemblance which has always been

recognized) and contained the same terrifying range of promised punishments in case of breach. Also thoroughly Masonic was a set exchange of questions and answers. A distinctive trick of the ordeals was to make the candidate swear never to write or otherwise reveal the secret Word, followed by a later command to write it down. If he was foolish enough to forget his oath and start to do so, he was flogged painfully across back or knuckles. Almost needless to say, by the end of the nineteenth century the Horseman's Word declared itself to be the oldest secret society of the lot, founded by Cain, and despised the Freemasons and affiliated orders as newcomers and upstarts.[47]

During the course of that century it spread out of its stronghold in the north-east to other parts of Scotland and to large areas of eastern England, the main arable region of that country; Davidson had noted that it was brought thither by Scots who leased or worked at English farms.[48] As it Anglicized, it became known as the Society of Horsemen, but in all other respects it remained the same.[49] It never achieved the hold on English rural communities that it secured in its homeland; Evans estimated that no more than 1 per cent of Suffolk farms contained men who had the Word.[50] This turned the latter into a small and highly respected elite, but also prevented the society from functioning as a real counter-culture, as it did in its Scottish heartland. There, its satanic initiation rite provided a direct parody of the dominant Presbyterian Christianity of the region, and its meetings were also characterized by hard drinking, and by jokes, songs, and toasts, which deliberately mocked conventional morality. It permitted deliberate misbehaviour in a private and controlled setting, and the whiff of magic and diabolism which hung about its reputation combined with the secrecy of its membership and proceedings, to enable it to function as a very effective means of pressure upon employers.[51]

The story of the society in England is, however, more complex and mysterious than the remarks above would suggest, because on arrival it absorbed and overlapped with much older skills and traditions. A power over farm animals had been one of the immemorial attributions of witches and cunning men, and ever since heavy horses replaced oxen as draught animals on English farms, during the Tudor and Stuart periods, there had been individuals noted as having a special talent for controlling them. The seventeenth-century intellectual Isaac Casaubon cited the case of one John Young, operating in Sussex in 1648, who was famed for making any horse tractable by 'whispering in its ear'. In 1756 the minister at Orwell, on the Cambridgeshire clay plateau, rebuked a servant of his for stopping a team of plough-horses with a wooden rod and a special word.[52] By the nineteenth century men with such skills had become international figures, much sought-after and very highly paid; among those operating in Victorian England were the American James Samuel Rarey and the Australian 'Groovy' Galvayne.[53] Most commentators agreed that the best were Irish, and it was from Ireland that a generic term for them, 'Horse Whisperers', arrived in the early nineteenth century, and subsequently became standard throughout England.[54]

By the second half of the century another fraternity of such experts had appeared there, being especially associated with the East Midlands and East Anglia, but found in places across the rest of England and Wales. It lacked the initiation ceremony of the Horseman's Word or Society of Horsemen and was much more loosely structured, but still disposed of a formidable range of secret techniques for rendering horses (and other farm animals) tractable, immobile, or uncontrollable. The definitive characteristic of its members was the possession of the bone of a toad or frog, often supposedly obtained through an elaborate ritual—an initiation ceremony of sorts—which involved skinning and defleshing the animal and throwing its skeleton into a stream at night. This was popularly supposed to confer the powers of the craft, and because of it the people concerned were given the name of Toadmen. No research has yet been carried out into their history, and all our information consists of memories of them gathered in the mid-twentieth century.[55] It is not clear whether the Toadmen existed before the Horsemen arrived from Scotland, for how long they had been defined by their ownership of the bone, or indeed how far they represented an organization at all, as opposed to a category of individuals working within a common tradition, like the cunning folk.

* * *

Mark Carnes has estimated that by the 1890s up to a fifth of the total population of adult males in the United States belonged to secret societies on the Masonic model.[56] No similar computation seems to have been made for Britain during the same period, but the proportion is unlikely to have been smaller. This means that by the opening of the twentieth century, millions of British men, and hundreds of women, were accustomed to working within closed groups which initiated newcomers through a process that involved blindfolding, a series of challenges and responses, admission to a ritual space, the taking of an oath of secrecy, and the passage of an ordeal. All imparted arcane knowledge to those who were accepted, and all claimed to represent an immemorial body of wisdom and practice—commonly called 'craft'—which had been handed down in private, through initiation and training, from the beginning of recorded time. All had incorporated actual historical figures and events into their own mythological past. All, it is now reasonably certain, had sprung from the original stock of William Schaw's network of Masons; it is most unlikely that any of them were aware of this.

Why did these societies find it so important to believe (or at least to assert) that they descended directly from the ancient past? One answer is a truism, that virtually all humans, at all times, have turned to the past to legitimize and authenticate the present. Another is functional, that a system of initiation in itself begets a sense of continuity and a curiosity about origins, providing an incentive for the development of foundation myths. Two others are more specific to the times and places considered here. One is that a particular value of these bodies is that they provided safe spaces within which members could operate more or less independently of the surrounding public culture; something all the more important, as that culture was suffering the strains of pronounced social, economic, and intellectual change. The sense of safety was much enhanced if the space was believed to have existed from ancient days, surviving all the stresses of the intervening ages. Furthermore, these bodies usually attempted to provide services, skills, and knowledge which would make members more potent in the society which surrounded them. As that society was dominated by institutions which themselves claimed authenticity, at least in part, from the past, and often did so by a system of succession, the ability of these groups to represent independent forces was greatly increased if they could claim a separate and older point of origin, and an even greater continuity.

In the overwhelming majority of cases, the attraction of the safe space depended upon the fact that it excluded not only conflicts of politics and religion, but of gender. It was not simply a model of good citizenship, but specifically of brotherhood, and its ordeals were regarded as tests not merely of a generalized courage and steadiness, but of manliness. The language of these societies, as well as their membership, was remorsely gender-specific. The local religious guilds of the Middle Ages had admitted women on equal terms, and not even the trade guilds had excluded them as absolutely as these later bodies. The recognition of no other deities than a single Supreme Being, who was presumed to be male and identified with the sky, the sun, geometry, and fatherhood, projected the same emphasis into the realm of the divine. These societies were closed systems of patriarchy more absolute that anything that Europeans had produced hitherto.

In an important sense, modern pagan witchcraft was to be the last (or at least the latest) outgrowth from the tradition which had begun with the Mason's Word. In virtually every respect it was to embody and perpetuate the characteristics of the tradition; in one, that of gender, it was to overturn them completely.

FINDING A HIGH MAGIC

⋊⋉

T HE classic definition of magic employed by modern scholars is that formu-
lated by Sir James Frazer at the opening of the twentieth century: practices
designed to bring spiritual or supernatural forces under the control of human
agents. It was this element of coercion and compulsion available to the human
practitioners that was supposed to distinguish magic from religion, in which the
spiritual beings are essentially outside human power and can only be moved by
supplication and praise. Critical to this definition was the human will, for it did
not depend upon the existence of independent supernatural beings, and one
could term magical the effecting of physical changes or the gaining of knowledge by the exertion of the human mind in supersensual and uncanny ways.

This concept of magic has been used throughout the century by historians
and anthropologists,[1] but has always been as problematic, and controversial, as
the definition of religion.[2] In large part, the disputes have concentrated upon its
boundaries, for it has always been obvious that there is a large overlap between
magic, religion, and science, which renders an absolute distinction between the
three, as opposed to a recognition of their core areas of concern, virtually
impossible to achieve. They have also, however, resulted from a growing recognition, itself the result of the ever greater development of the discipline of
anthropology, that all such definitions are themselves culturally specific, and
that different peoples categorize these phenomena according to different strategies of concept and language. It is fortunate for the purposes of the present book
that its concerns lie wholly within the writer's own culture, which is precisely
that which developed the concept of magic articulated by Frazer. There is,
however, one important qualification to be made to this observation: that the
definition concerned was central to the tradition of European and
Mediterranean learned magic which evolved from ancient times to the nineteenth century. From the nineteenth century onwards this tradition has itself
altered some of its key concepts, a development that is one of the concerns of
this chapter.

Despite considerable continuities of information and practice, European
learned magic has passed through a number of distinct phases of development.
It is suggested here that there were five of these. The first was the ancient, which
provided most of the materials for those coming later: the consecrated circle
within which some magicians worked, the importance attached to cardinal

points of the compass, the concepts of elements (fire, water, air, and earth) and of elemental spirits, a belief in the existence of angels and demons, and use of ritual tools, amulets, spells, and invocations, the notion of spiritual correspondences within the natural world, the use of sacred geometry such as pentagrams and triangles, and the drawing of spirits or deities into human bodies, to fuse temporarily with the owners' spirit or to occupy their forms.

The second was the medieval phase, which really began as an aspect of the twelfth-century Renaissance. It placed a new emphasis upon the importance of complex set rituals to gain power over spirits, collected in handbooks ('grimoires') which inspired something of the awe of sacred texts, and usually involving a combination of the circle, the quarters, tools, signs, and invocations. The detail of actions was all-important, with little concern shown for the quality of the practitioner. It was a typical product of a period obsessed with God, geometry, and the angelic and demonic kingdoms, and characterized by an increasing formality and elaboration of religious ritual. The third phase was the early modern one, which retained this medieval magic but drew upon the ancient hermetic texts to put new emphasis upon the figure of the person who worked it, the magus. He was seen as an individual who needed to be both spiritually mature and unusually learned, and thus the mental preparation of the operator of magic was now held to be as important as the operation itself. This was part of the Renaissance stress upon the potential of the human mind, reinforced by a parallel emphasis upon personal spiritual development, visible in the great twin movements of the Reformation and Counter-Reformation. A favourite text of later magicians was to be the *Spiritual Exercises* of Ignatius of Loyola.

The fourth phase was the Enlightenment one, in which the magi and grimoires were eclipsed by the proliferation of secret societies considered above. Many of these, at least on the Continent, employed tools, symbols, concepts, and practices inherited from the tradition of scholarly magic. Finally, there is the modern phase, which is the subject of this chapter.

A good example of how a single symbol could pass through all five stages is provided by the pentagram. Five-pointed stars are found in ancient Egyptian, Greek, and Roman art, and also in that of the Christian early Middle Ages, but there seems to have been no single tradition concerning their meaning and use, and in many contexts they seem simply to have been decorative. The enduring use of the symbol in the Western magical tradition is a product of the twelfth-century Renaissance, which put the pentagram at the centre of its interplay between scripture, divine harmony, and mathematics. In that century both Honorius of Autun and Hildegard of Bingen asserted that the human body is constructed upon the basis of the number five, having five senses, five members, and five figures. This made the five-pointed star the symbol of the microcosmos, the earthly reflection of the divine plan and the divine image.[3] This probably explains the belief against which William of Auvergne wrote in the early part of the next century, that there was an active magical power in its angles. William noted that the figure was now especially associated with Solomon, the most famous magician in Christian legend; a late antique text, *The Testament of Solomon*, had portrayed him as bearing it upon his ring. William also fulminated against a particular text, the *Liber Sacratus*, which taught people how to control demons by using the sacred names of God.[4] This is probably a reference to the book commonly known as the *Liber Sacer*, which was claimed in the preface to have been written by 'Honorius, Master of Thebes' on the basis of Solomon's own teachings. No recensions have survived from the time of William, but there are three in the British Library which between them span the period between the fourteenth and seventeenth centuries.[5] They describe the 'seal of the living God' as consisting of a pentagram and two hexagrams, with the names of God and of angels written around them, and assert that it has power over spirits.

The classic late medieval exposition of the figure is found in the celebrated English poem, *Sir Gawaine and the Green Knight*, which was composed at some time in the second half of the fourteenth century. The author, a devout Christian, placed it upon the shield of his hero, and felt obliged to digress in order to make a defence of his use of it. He restated the ideas that it had been employed by Solomon and that it represented the human, and therefore the divine, form, and added the information that it was commonly known in England as 'the endless knot'. He appropriated it firmly for Christianity by insisted that it also represented the five wounds of Christ himself, an increasingly important religious motif during the period. As such, he argued, it was an especially potent sign for the repulsion of evil. A further stage in its evolving tradition seems to have been supplied by what was perhaps the most famous textbook on magic to be published in sixteenth-century Europe, Cornelius Agrippa's *De Occulta Philosophia*. The various editions of the work contain, reproduced at different points, a diagram of a magic circle which shows a pentagram drawn at each cardinal point, or 'quarter', to protect it.

Thereafter, early modern writers merely elaborated parts of this long-established tradition. The Catholic polemicist Georg Pictorius von Villingen, in his *Subtilissmus Liber Averois* (Strasburg, 1568), condemned the use of the 'Pentagon of Solomon' to rout demons. A writer on hermetic philosophy, Lazarus Meysonnier, devoted an entire book to the symbol, *Pentagonum Philosophico-Medicum* (Lyon, 1659), extending the imagery of it to include representations of the firmament, the planets, and the elements. It is small wonder that the pentagram was taken up enthusiastically by Freemasonry, and that individual Masons made their own interpretations of it, such as that of Sir Robert Moray, mentioned above. Moray communicated an enthusiasm for it, in turn, to his English friend the diarist John Evelyn, to whom it became a potent private image. By such means, and with such a complex of interrelated associations, it reached the modern period.

In approaching the subject of learned magic during that period, the academic historian suffers from a number of disadvantages. The history of ancient, medieval, and early modern magic has recently attracted a relatively large number of scholars, with a proportionate outpouring of publication. By contrast, virtually none has paid attention to the same theme during the nineteenth and twentieth centuries, with the exception of experts in the works of the poet Yeats who have sometimes considered his occult interests.[6] There have, on the other hand, been a number of works of high quality written on the subject by non-academic specialists. Where they differ markedly from those of academics is in their comparative lack of systematic source references; typical in this is one of the finest of these writers, Gerald Suster, who has described footnotes as 'usually tiresome' and felt obliged to offer his readers 'a few words of apology and explanation' when using them.[7] When sources are cited by these authors, they commonly consist of collections in private hands, the location and ownership of which are kept secret. Few university libraries own any of the relevant literature, and even the great national copyright institutions are deficient in it. Some municipal libraries have had surprisingly good holdings, but many of their items have been stolen in recent years. A diligent researcher in the field has no option other than to track down titles through specialist booksellers, which requires time and expense.[8] Further more, ritual magic has its own language, logic, and conceptual structures, demanding a training equivalent to that of music and mathematics and proportionately different for a newcomer to comprehend.[9] It is small wonder that the recent history of it has been left mainly to writers who have amassed private libraries and practical experience.

Having said this, the outline of that history, is now relatively clear. Between 1750 and 1850 the practice of ceremonial magic was more or less in abeyance in Britain's intellectual circles, for reasons which remain speculative. One may have been simply that it had become classed with astrology, alchemy, and a belief in demons and in witchcraft, as part of a mindset of 'enthusiasm' and 'superstition' which eighteenth-century British intellectuals feared and rejected. Another may be that the sort of person associated with such pursuits at earlier and later times was in this one diverted to the still accessible and exciting fields of the new sciences, and into the burgeoning number of secret societies, with their claims to ancient wisdom and immemorial ritual. There were some exceptions, but they were very occasional, the most notable being Francis Barrett, who operated at the junction where applied science, ritual magic, and practical occultisms such as astrology, intersect.[10] His best-known work is *The Magus* (1801), a compendium of earlier English translations of medieval and early modern grimoires, illustrated with a remarkable portrait-gallery of demons. It was not that magi and sorcerers were missing from the imagination of Barrett's generation; indeed, they had an obvious place in it as part of the revival of literary interest in the medieval and the uncanny which produced the genre conventionally known as 'Gothic'. The distinction was that few individuals felt impelled to emulate them.

There remained at this time also a memory, and mythology, of a different sort of admired occultist, the members of the Fraternity of the Rosy Cross, commonly known as Rosicrucians. The origin of the belief in them lies in a sensational series of pamphlets published between 1614 and 1616, which claimed to reveal a hidden society of adepts, equipped with a knowledge of the secrets of the cosmos and dedicated to religion and healing, which had been founded in the fourteenth century. These tracts provoked tremendous excitement, but the existence of the fraternity was never proved, just as the authorship of the works remains controversial. The legend of this group naturally exerted a powerful hold on the minds of an age such as that of Barrett, in which secret societies were proliferating with such speed. Barrett himself claimed to be a Rosicrucian on the title page of *The Magus*. One of the mid-eighteenth-century Continental variants of Freemasonry, the Ancient and Accepted Rite, used imagery from the pamphlets in the ceremonies of its eighteenth degree, which it called 'the Rosy Cross'. When the order reached England near the end of the century, that degree was detached from it to become a new society (the 'Rose-Croix'), in its own right.[11] The occult bookseller used by Barrett, John Denley, was also patronized by the popular writer Bulwer-Lytton,[12] who made Denley's shop the setting for the opening chapter of a novel about ritual magicians, *Zanoni* (1845). The plot of that chapter depended on the idea that the Rosicrucians had not merely existed but survived into the nineteenth century, 'respectable and virtuous', 'severe in the practice of moral precepts', and 'ardent in Christian faith'. He portrayed them as scientists and philosophers working in the mystical traditions of Plato, Plotinus, Pythagorus, and Apollonius of Tyana—all thinkers concerned with the animating spiritual forces within the material universe.

Not even *Zanoni*, however, was sufficient to spark off a revival of the practice of learned magic in Britain. Instead, when such a revival did commence during the next decade, it took place in France, and spilled over from there into other parts of Europe. The deeper social and religious reasons for the emergence of the French as the pioneers of modern ritual magic have not yet been adequately studied, but it is plain that the key figure in the process was Alphonse Louis Constant, who took the pen-name of Eliphas Zahed Levi. Born in 1810 and initially intended for a career in the Catholic Church, Levi dropped out of training after taking deacon's orders, to spend the period between 1839 and 1847 as part of a movement preaching a mystical socialist royalism. The revolution of 1848 and subsequent re-establishment of the Napoleonic dynasty left him disillusioned with politics, and he turned in the 1850s to publishing works on magic. He had already been initiated into some of the secret societies derived from Freemasonry, and thus added to the training in ritual which he had gained during his abortive preparation for the priesthood. He now synthesized a wide range of reading in medieval and early modern magical and alchemical texts, and eighteenth-century philosophers, to provide both a conceptual framework and a set of practical manuals for a new generation of magicians.[13]

There were several aspects to Levi's achievement. One was simply to provide the new magic with a catchy name, 'occultism', signifying the revelation of hidden wisdom. Another was to apply to magical texts the task of recovering all possible sources of human knowledge which had been the guiding principle of European scholarship since the Renaissance, and given a greater range and impetus during the eighteenth century. Levi enunciated the principle that humanity had originally possessed semi-divine powers, which had been allowed to atrophy over the millennia and could be regained by concentrated study and practice. In setting out practical techniques, he boldly developed and reinterpreted the symbols inherited from the past. Once again, the pentagram may stand as an important example. He repeated the idea that it represented the microcosm of the universe, but turned the hexagram into its complement, as the sign of the macrocosm. He restated another old tradition, that the five-pointed star controlled demons, and then extended it to assert that it specifically summoned and directed the demons of the four elements, or elementals, from respective quarters of the consecrated circle. In 1854 he apparently took this to its logical conclusion; hitherto the symbol had been used only to ward off or banish spirits, but in that year Levi seems to have invented the invoking pentagram. He recommended the drawing of the sign in the air according to a particular pattern, above each quarter, to call up the elementals, and the drawing of it in the opposite direction to banish them at the end of the ritual. He also supplied one further development to the mythology of the figure, by informing his readers that with two points down it was the symbol of God, with one point down, it was that of the Devil, and with the two combined, with the satanic pentagram reversed to point inwards, it made the glyph of the holy spirit.[14]

At moments Levi was open about his innovations, describing them in the context of his own magical experiences. It would have been impossible, however, for him to have portrayed his body of work as the exercise in research and imagination which it actually represented, to an audience habituated to the impressive claims to timeless wisdom and continuous tradition made by the secret societies. To be taken seriously, he had both to harmonize with these and to surpass them; and he undertook this task brilliantly. The manner in which he did so was established by Peter Partner in 1981.[15] Back in the eighteenth century, as indicated earlier, the Masonic tradition had posed a real challenge to states which were still identified with a single, intolerant variety of Christianity, and its emphasis upon universal brotherhood was almost as alarming to those still run by closed systems of monarchy and aristocracy. By the end of the century it had become a potent myth among European reactionaries that the French Revolution had been engineered by an international conspiracy of Freemasons, who were still working to destroy the traditional social, political, and religious order.

This theory was given a historical back-projection, by an embittered Jesuit refugee from the Revolution called Augustin de Barruel, and an Austrian civil servant working for the famous reactionary chancellor Metternich, who acquired the name of Joseph von Hammer-Purgstall. Publishing in 1798 and 1818 respectively, they provided between them a pseudo-history to rival any of those claimed by the societies themselves. It revealed a world in which, ever since the time of Christ, evil forces had been working to undermine Christianity, decency, and stability, carrying on the struggle from one secret group to another through the centuries. First had come the Manichaeans and the Gnostic heretics, then the Cathars, Assassins, and Knights Templar, and finally the Freemasons and the Jacobins. This notion, developed by conservatives, fell straight into the hands of their enemies, French and Italian revolutionaries of the early nineteenth century. They preserved it entire, while reversing the sympathies; the chain of wicked conspirators became a secret tradition of revolutionaries who stood for liberal and enlightened values and possessed a hidden knowledge fatal to orthodox Christianity. By the middle of the century both right-wing and left-wing versions of the myth had become commonplace in European society.

It was from a left-wing mystical milieu that Levi had emerged into his career as a magician, and he refashioned the myth as he made the transition. In his version, the succession of secret societies had handed down not just a political commitment but a true knowledge of the nature of the universe, and of how to manipulate the forces of which it was constructed. Thus, he linked ancient Egyptian religion with the Templars and the legend of the Holy Grail, and blended the two greatest early modern European magical systems, the cabbala and the tarot. In the process, he stripped the secret tradition of identification with any one modern political programme; it now supplied a powerful implicit criticism of orthodox Christianity and an alternative history of Western culture which could be taken up by radicals on both the left and the right. He also suggested that instead of descending directly to the modern secret societies, it had been almost wholly lost by the end of the Middle Ages, but could be recovered by the mixture of research and experimentation which his books represented.

This was a heady mixture, and it explains why occultism became the language of radical counter-culture in late nineteenth-century France, just as paganism did in Britain during the same period. Like the theosophy which it was partly to inspire, it offered the thinkers of the age a middle way between a defensive Christian orthodoxy and a science which threatened to despiritualize the universe and question the special status of humanity. Its emphasis upon practical learning and experimentation appealed to the scientific instinct, while its acceptance of supernatural forces and stress upon ancient wisdom appealed to the religious one. Unsurprisingly, it soon began to spread from France to most parts of the European cultural world, including Britain.

*   *   *

The modern British revival of ritual magic began in 1867 (the date is disputed), with the foundation of the Societas Rosicruciana in Anglia, the Rosicrucian Society in England. In an important sense it represented another offshoot from the stem of Freemasonry, for its members were all Masons and membership was restricted to men who held the top Masonic grade. Respectability was (apparently) further safeguarded by a requirement that all also be professed Christians. It represented, therefore, an English Masonic elite, gathered for the purpose of studying the cabbala, the hermetic texts, and other arcane wisdom of the ancient and medieval world. Convention demanded, however, that it claim some initiatory link with an older body devoted to the same aims, and this was supplied by one of the moving spirits, Kenneth H. R. Mackenzie, who claimed to have been initiated into one of the eighteenth-century German mystical societies which had themselves developed (in fact if not in theory) out of the older Freemasonry, the Order of the Gold and Rosy Cross. Mackenzie's story was that he had been received into this by one of its surviving members, a Count Apponyi, while travelling in the Austrian Empire. The Societas was given the structure of the German order, of three lesser orders with three grades in each, all governed by a Most Worthy Supreme Magus. Mackenzie's story may have been true; what is certain is that in 1861 he had visited, and been impressed by, Eliphas Levi.[16]

There were also some links with home-grown occultism. Another formative influence upon Mackenzie, and probably one of the Societas's founding members, was a Freemason and accountant called Frederick Hockley, who had once actually worked in John Denley's bookshop, and admired Barrett's *The Magus*. Hockley had a particular interest in clairvoyance, for which he employed crystals, mirrors, and trances, recording his visions in more than thirty volumes of notes. He also took notes on the cabbala, medieval talismans, and the Enochian system of magic preserved in the papers of the Elizabethan magus Dr Dee.[17] Mackenzie himself defined magic in the short-lived periodical of the society, *The Rosicrucian*, as 'a psychological branch of science, dealing with the sympathetic effects of stones, drugs, herbs and living substances upon the imaginative and reflective faculties'.[18] The professed aims of the group were wholly theoretical, 'to search out the Great Secrets of Nature',[19] and it does not seem to have practised any ritual magic.[20] Instead, it had a body of ceremonies derived from those of Freemasonry, reputedly very old and reputedly discovered by accident in the vaults of Freemasons' Hall, London, by Mackenzie and a friend, the very prominent Mason Robert Wentworth Little, who became the first Supreme Magus of the Societas Rosicruciana.[21] The discovery was amazingly fortuitous; but then this is how things happen in the world of magic. Finally, in 1887, Hargrave Jennings presented the society with a heritage and pseudo-history as grand as anything claimed by Freemasonry, and completely separate. It linked it with the legendary Rosicrucians of the Middle Ages and early modern period, who were declared in turn to have descended directly from the mystery religions of pagan antiquity.[22]

In this manner Levi's project of a quest for the arcane secrets of the cosmos was naturalized in England, and glossed as an experimental science equivalent to the embryonic one of psychology. The quest was given a further, considerable impetus by the advent of theosophy, and most notably by *The Occult World* (1881), a best-seller written by Madame Blavatsky's friend and colleague A. P. Sinnett, which introduced ideas hitherto the preserve of a few enthusiasts to a mass audience.[23] In the next year the Society for Psychical Research was founded in London, by spiritualists, to submit apparently paranormal phenomena to objective study, with the hope of establishing their true causation; members included the Prime Minister, Gladstone, and leaders of the arts and sciences as various as John Ruskin, Lord Tennyson, and Alfred Russel Wallace.[24] Three years later the Theosophical Society itself produced a third body based in the British capital and dedicated to study in this broad area, the Hermetic Society.

The appearance of the latter group indicated a tension within theosophy itself, and between its leaders. On the one hand, Helena Blavatsky herself was another admirer of Levi, and one of the avowed aims of the Theosophical Society was 'to investigate the hidden mysteries of Nature and the physical powers latent in man'. Blavatsky's own spectacular displays of apparent psychic power provided examples of what could be achieved by such work, and could readily be equated with magic. On the other hand, her admiration for the mystical traditions of the East gave her a relative lack of interest in those of Europe and the Mediterranean, and she always forbade her followers to practise ritual magic of the medieval and early modern European kind. To her, paranormal power was better achieved by study and by a psychic link with her semi-divine superiors, the 'Mahatmas', which effectively confined it to her. The blow to her reputation in 1884, when her performances were investigated by a member of the Society for Psychical Research and declared to be impostures, precipitated a schism. It was led by Anna Kingsford, another admirer of Levi and president of the London Lodge of the Theosophical Society. Kingsford's devout Christianity had already caused her to be troubled by Blavatsky's subordination of Western to Eastern traditions, and the allegations against her mistress emboldened her to repudiate the authority of the Mahatmas and to found the Hermetic Society for a concentration upon the European mystical inheritance, and especially the cabbala. In 1888 Blavatsky at last relented and allowed members of the Theosophical Society to form an Esoteric Section for the same purpose. No more than the Societas Rosicruciana, however, did these bodies encourage their members to practise operative magic.[25]

By 1888 most of the first generation of the magical revival—Levi, Little, Hockley, and Kingsford—were dead. A new generation of occult scholars had grown up, trained or inspired by these forerunners, who were anxious to push their researches further; and in that year some of them established a new body for the work. All were Freemasons, and three were leading members of the Societas Rosicruciana. One was Little's successor as Supreme Magus, William Robert Woodman. Another would later succeed him in turn, and was currently secretary of the society, a medical man called William Wynn Westcott. The third was a protégé of Westcott's, Samuel Liddell Mathers. Westcott and Mathers had also been prominent in the Hermetic Society, and formed a powerful complementary pair of talents. The former was a gentle and kindly scholar, with a taste for theoretical structures and an ability to recognize and promote talent in others. He had recognized it most obviously in Mathers, the son of a commercial clerk who was rescued by Westcott from a life of drudgery and supported by him as a full-time student of the occult. The difference in their natures was expressed in their faces, the soft, bearded countenance of the older man contrasting with the bulging eyes and lower lip, and the bristling military moustache, of the younger. Mathers was as capable a researcher as Westcott, but had a far greater interest in the practical application of his studies.

The fourth member of the group was a clergyman, Adolphus F. A. Woodward, and although the least distinguished in arcane researches (he was the only one not a member of the Societas Rosicruciana), he performed one essential service to it. Any new secret society devoted to such pursuits had to possess two features in order to achieve any credibility at this period: a set of distinctive rituals handed down from the past, and an initiatory link with a respected older body. The Societas Rosicruciana had achieved both by a remarkable pair of coincidences; now Woodward came up with another, by discovering a set of initiation rituals into the first five degrees of a quasi-Masonic order, with some elementary teaching to accompany each, in the theory of ritual magic. The grades were those of the eighteenth-century German society into which Mackenzie had claimed to have been initiated, that of the Gold and Rosy Cross, but embellished with concepts drawn from the cabbala, the papers of Dr Dee, and nineteenth-century discoveries of Egyptian archaeology and Graeco-Egyptian papyri, and written in a sixteenth-century cipher. In the more romantic account of the discovery, Woodward made it in a London bookshop. In the more prosaic, he found the papers in a collection left by Hockley, who had, like Mackenzie, been his friend. The documents were translated by Westcott and Mathers, and worked up by them still further to provide the basic hierarchy, ceremonies, and teachings of a new order. Even better was to come, however, for Westcott reported that the manuscripts had contained, hidden in the same cipher, the address of one Anna Sprengel of Nuremberg, an adept of a mysterious society of German Rosicrucians descended from the 'original', medieval fraternity. Once contacted, she formally authorized him to found a new branch of her society, in a charter which Westcott signed and dated on her behalf on 1 March 1888. In this manner there came into being the Hermetic Order of the Golden Dawn. Almost needless to say, the literal truth of these events has been questioned almost since they occurred, and the real story will probably never be known.[26]

The moment for the announcement of the new group, like so much else in this sequence of events, was amazingly fortuitous. Madame Blavatsky herself had recently arrived in London, fuelling interest in the occult, while Anna Kingsford had just died, threatening a crisis in the Hermetic Society. Westcott proceeded to provide it with a lineage and set of teachings capable of rivalling that suggested by Jennings for the Societas Rosicruciana and far more scholarly, which likewise traced its descent back through the German Rosicrucians to the legendary fraternity and through them to ancient philosophies and mysteries.[27] Woodward, the discoverer of the vital papers, had died in 1887, and in 1891

Westcott announced that Frau Sprengel had also died, and that all contact with the presumed parent group in Germany was thus severed, and all enquiries concerning it would be fruitless. In any case, a higher source of authority was now provided. One of the strongest claims of the Theosophical Society had been to the direct link made by its founder with her superhuman leaders in the Himalayas. In 1891 Blavatsky died, and the next year Mathers declared that on a visit to Paris he had been contacted by the same secret chiefs, in her place, and been authorized by them to found an inner order to the Golden Dawn, initiating into three more grades and calling itself the Rosy Cross.

Mathers himself was the sole leader of this, and it had one further significant distinction from the Golden Dawn proper: whereas the latter merely trained its members in mystical and magical systems, and in ceremonies intended to propound and illustrate that training, the higher order allowed them to engage in operative magic, invoking and working with deities and spirits. As the decade wore on, Mathers ran it with an even more absolute and peremptory authority. In parallel to his claims of constant advice from higher planes—the hidden chiefs communicating through various signs when they did not whisper directly in his ears—he embellished his own ancestry, first proclaiming his descent from the Scottish Clan Macgregor and then assuming the titles of a putative Jacobite forebear, Chevalier MacGregor and Comte de Glenstrae. His social insecurity was showing badly, but had it not been for this sense of displacement, it is possible that he would never have dared to break the bounds observed by his middle-class forerunners, and engage in the practice of ritual magic as well as the theory of it. More destructive was his increasing love of military trappings and corresponding tendency to run the Golden Dawn as if it were a regiment under his command. In 1897 Westcott felt obliged to resign because rumours of his occult activities were harming his career; Mathers was now left in total control of the inner and outer orders, with the invisible chiefs as his source of legitimization. A third order of three grades beyond the Rosy Cross was reserved for them.

It needs to be emphasized how remarkable an organization Westcott and Mathers had constructed. In its structure it resembled the Societas Rosicruciana and the Freemasonry upon which the latter had been based, having a graded process of initiation, with accompanying ceremonies, robes, and symbolic tools. Instead of lodges, it had temples, the main one being in London with a scatter of offshoots in Edinburgh and the English provinces. In its attitude to religion and gender, however, it deliberately adopted the open-door policy of the Theosophical Society. Westcott taught neophytes of the new order to regard it as a companion to theosophy, sprung from 'the same stock of Magi—the Scientific Priests of a remote antiquity' and 'allied by mutual understanding and respect'. He emphasized the major role of women in occult researches, paying particular tribute to Blavatsky and Kingsford,[28] and indeed the female members of the order became some of the most celebrated, including the actress Florence Farr, the Irish nationalist Maud Gonne, the patroness of arts Annie Horniman, and others who were best known for their careers as ritual magicians, such as Moina

Bergson who married Mathers.[29] The process of training represented by the five grades of the outer group was remarkably thorough and intense, furnishing a grounding in the main Hebrew, Greek, Graeco-Egyptian, medieval, and early modern esoteric traditions, and the accompanying ceremonies represented a blend of all of these.

They seem to have been almost wholly the work of Mathers, and he performed a parallel service in editing, translating, and publishing some of the main historic texts, a process which defined them for twentieth-century magicians. At times he expounded the meaning of an already famous system, such as the cabbala. At others, he drew attention to an obscure but important work such as the Book of Abramelin, and, at yet others, he collated different recensions of a celebrated one to produce a 'definitive' version; the classic case here is the Key of Solomon.[30] The manuscripts left by the Elizabethan Dr Dee do not, in fact, contain any clear and obvious system of magic, and it was Mathers who integrated them to produce one for the Golden Dawn, which has become known as 'Enochian' after the apocryphal Book of Enoch which was one of Dee's sources of inspiration. Ever since the time of the ancient Greeks, the civilization of Pharaonic Egypt had been regarded as the premier repository of magical lore, being the most stable and enduring of all those that first emerged in Europe and the Near East. Mathers built upon this reputation to incorporate the data unearthed by the many excavations of the nineteenth century; for example, the invocation which he taught to trainees to call upon their Higher Genius or Holy Guardian Angel was taken from a Graeco-Egyptian magical papyrus first published by the Cambridge Antiquarian Society in 1852.[31] The symbolic geometry of Freemasonry was blended with that of the cabbala's Tree of Life, and Egyptian deity-forms with the Enochian magical squares. The admission into the inner order was through a ceremony based on the legend of Christian Rosenkreuz, founder of the original Rosicrucians. Temples were laid out according to the plan of a masonic lodge, with the twin pillars (echoing those of Solomon) and central altar. Masonry also left its mark very clearly on the first-degree initiation rite, which reproduced the structure of blindfolding, binding, challenge, admission, presentation, and oath-taking, followed by the First Instruction. As members studied, so they were also expected to cultivate their psychic abilities, by meditation, visualization, and experimentation with clairvoyance, Tantric techniques, geomancy, numerology, astrology, and the projection of spirit from body.[32]

A more detailed insight into Mather's methods and achievements can be provided by pursuing the same case-study used earlier in this chapter, of the development of the five-pointed star. His most enduring contribution to this was to elaborate Levi's concept of the invoking and banishing pentagram, associated with elemental spirits at each quarter of the circle, into a more elaborate eight-fold system with a different drawing of the figure to call or dismiss the spirits of each element. Air was to east, fire to south, water to west, and earth to north. Mathers strengthened this process of invocation further by adding to it the Tetragrammaton and the Lords of The Watchtowers. The former consisted of the four Hebrew names of God, which had been written at the cardinal points of a magic circle in some medieval and early modern grimoires and were now called, one at each quarter. The latter was a concept taken from John Dee's papers, of good angels who guarded each cardinal point and could be called upon to help the magus; now they were invoked also, as the pentagrams were drawn upon the air with a steel dagger and the Tetragrammaton was recited. This procedure was used for the consecration of a sacred space, together with its purification by the carrying of water and fire around it in a sunwise circle. It was a system which fused a number of different traditions, but was also very powerful and relatively simple.[33]

The first five grades of the order were also related to especial properties of the points of the pentagram, while the ceremonial crown worn by members of the inner order bore a pentagram on each of three sides and a hexagram on the fourth.[34] Mathers also produced two major rituals devoted to the symbol. The Rite of the Pentagram itself was designed to explain its arcane significance further, by relating its points to five of the spheres, or sephiroth, on the cabbalistic Tree of Life. The 'Lesser Ritual of the Pentagram', part of which has become commonly known as the Qabbalistic Cross (Mathers using this spelling for 'cabbala'), was the first ceremony taught to a neophyte, functioning at once as a form of prayer, of magical protection, and of meditation. The celebrant faced each of the cardinal points in turn, starting at the east. At each point she or he had to touch the front of the body in a cruciform pattern, reciting in Hebrew the final few lines of the Christian Lord's Prayer. This was followed by the drawing of Levi's single invoking pentagram in the air with a dagger and the vibrating of one of the four Hebrew divine names. Once the circuit was completed, and the celebrant could imagine the four stars flaming on the air at each quarter, he or she would invoke the four Hebrew archangels, one to guard each cardinal point, and visualize a hexagram shining behind her or him. The cross would then be touched and recited once more at each quarter. The neophyte was expected to carry out this rite every morning, and then repeat it in the evening with the pentagrams reversed to use Levi's single banishing form; the latter version, by itself, could be used as an exorcism.

Mathers also took the Masonic tradition of 'working tools', each carrying a symbolic association, and combined it with the ritual equipment of the medieval and early modern magician, as illustrated in the grimoires. There was no fixed body of such equipment, let alone a standard set of interpretations accorded to it, and so the Golden Dawn assemblage was very much an original creation. It was made by or for a member as part of the transition into the inner order of adepts, and the core consisted of the four 'elemental weapons', the cup or chalice for water, the pentacle (a disc engraved with the five-pointed star) for earth, the dagger for air, and the wand for fire. In addition, she or he required a sword, symbolizing the power of the mind, a wand bearing a lotus emblem for special kinds of working, and the device of a cross bearing a rose, to be worn on the breast of the ceremonial robe. These were all consecrated as part of the initiation rite. Two other symbolic tools or weapons were painted on the temple wall, rather than used: a crook and a scourge, taken from ancient Egyptian iconography and standing for the power to guide and admonish. Two vessels of consecrated foodstuffs were placed upon the altar for ceremonies—a cup or chalice containing wine, and a paten of bread and salt.[35]

Was the Golden Dawn a pagan organization? The question must be answered firmly in the negative, but only in the sense that it was not a religious society at all, but a magical one; and the distinction goes to the heart of the nineteenth-century division between religion and magic. There was a great deal of Christian imagery in the rituals, and devout members of that faith, such as Woodward and the scholar Arthur Edward Waite, were prominent in the order. The latter, after all, drew its ancestry and much of its imagery from the 'original' Rosicrucians portrayed in the seventeenth-century pamphlets, who were pious servants of Christ. The full and correct name of the inner group of adepts was the Rose of Ruby and the Cross of Gold, and the cross was its central symbol. It was traced upon the body of the initiate into that group, from head to foot, as part of the rite of acceptance, and she or he was bound to a wooden cross for a period of meditation. The temple of the inner order, the Vault of the Adepts, was reconsecrated each year at Corpus Christi, the great medieval feast designed to honour the consecrated host. A cross was borne about it, and the Qabbalistic Cross invoked at the quarters, before the Lords of the Watchtowers, the archangels, were called again.[36] The Lesser Ritual of the Pentagram, the basic one taught to every neophyte, was soaked in Christian imagery.

There, however, was the point, for the ceremonies of the order were not acts of worship; their focus was the celebrant. It was far from obvious, in the performance of the Qabbalistic Cross, whether the kingdom, the power, and the glory belonged to God or were being promised to the human carrying out the ritual; this ambiguity no doubt made it acceptable to people with a wide range of beliefs. The founders of the order had, after all, been associated with theosophy, which taught that all the main religious and mystical traditions of the globe reflected the same primal wisdom, and encouraged a syncretization of them to enhance human knowledge and ability. From the seventeenth-century hermetic texts, Westcott and Mathers had taken the image of the 'world soul' mentioned earlier. Upon initiation into the second grade, the former neophyte of the Golden Dawn was taught how to visualize the 'Key of the Universe': 'Within the oval formed of the two circles is a female form, nude save for the scarf that floats around her. She is crowned with the lunar crescent of Isis, and holds in her hands two wands. Her legs form a cross.' Now syncretization set in, for the initiate was informed that this divine figure should be identified not merely with Isis but with the Bride of the Apocalypse, the Cabbalistic Queen of the Canticles, and the 'Great Feminine Kerubic Angel', Sandalphon.[37] She was also identified as the 'Genius of the Order', and its first and main temple was named after her, Isis-Urania. In this aspect she was held to represent the morning star, the herald of the dawn and of the divine sun.[38]

The Golden Dawn thus had a powerful image of female divinity built into its ideological core, even though she could be viewed as the harbinger of a greater male god, and was assimilated to various female figures already existing in Christian and sub-Christian legend. Members of the order could, moreover, draw upon a much wider variety of deity forms. The standard defence of the medieval practitioner of demonic magic, after all, had been that a good Christian, calling upon the power of the One God, was entitled to subdue evil spirits and put them to work for good purposes.[39] It was still easier to conceive of operating with the classical pagan deities in a similar context, once the Renaissance had supercharged the taste for Graeco-Roman art and literature and made the Olympians seem more like morally neutral, rather than satanic, entities. Cornelius Agrippa, in that most celebrated of sixteenth-century magical textbooks, *De Occulta Philosophia* (vol. III, p. 5–7), had asserted that the magician must serve the true God but also be able to work with 'secondary divinities', who were powerful enough to have their value. As a man of his time, he recommended Jupiter above all.

As a man of this time, likewise, Mathers chose differently. Just as the Golden Dawn's presiding goddess was the universal one favoured by the nineteenth-century imagination, so its preferred pagan god was (of course) Pan, who was invoked during the initiation of a new member into the inner order of adepts. In a piece of syncretism typical of the society, he was identified with the Goat of Mendes, the horned figure developed by Levi and itself representing a blend of Pan, an Egyptian god-form and the idol allegedly venerated by the medieval Knights Templar.[40] What was distinctive about the manner in which the Golden Dawn perceived deity forms was the way in which figures from Christian and Hebrew methology were added to the more familiar classical imagery; a further reflection of its roots in the tradition of ritual magic. The result was, more or less, a divine kaleidoscope, which could be adjusted to meet the differing spiritual needs and instincts of the various members. In 1901 Mathers declared that the order 'teaches respect for the truths of all religions, as well as for the religious feelings and ideals of our neighbours'.[41] The crucial point was that deities were not actually worshipped in its rituals; they were either used to represent certain desirable qualities, or invoked to assist the spiritual progress or practical wishes of a person or group, in general terms or at specific moments. Mathers's only prohibitions were that members should not use sexual arousal or intercourse as part of ritual, and should not call upon demons, signifying those spirits whom medieval and early modern Christians had identified specifically as devoted to evil.[42] He himself was well acquainted with such entities, at least in theory, for among the texts which he had edited and translated was the *Goetia*. This is a sixteenth-century grimoire (perhaps older in origin) which purports to give a magician the power to summon and control several million devils, organized into legions commanded by Grand Princes of Hell.[43]

This mixture of tolerance and eclecticism produced a proportionately wide span of attitude and experience within the order. At one extreme were Arthur

Edward Waite and W. A. Ayton, devoted Christians who doubted the wisdom of any operative magic and of invocations to pagan deities. Ayton, himself a clergyman, warned a fellow initiate that 'even the Olympic Planetary Spirits turn against us in the end'.[44] At the other were Alan Bennett and Aleister Crowley, who cheerfully called up demons at their lodgings in Chancery Lane; in one evening (according to Crowley) they identified 316 by name.[45] More mainstream members of the order could be deeply moved by the ancient divine figures which they were invited to contemplate; in 1892 Florence Farr and Elaine Simpson shared a vision of Isis, inspired by ritual, as 'the most powerful of all the world', clothed in green with a jewelled girdle and crown of stars.[46] One of these was Mathers himself, to whom the same goddess appeared in Paris in 1896, ordering him to proclaim her divinity to the modern world. He settled in that city (still the hub of European occultism) with his wife Moina, and they decorated one of their rooms as an ancient Egyptian temple.[47] For the rest of the decade they devoted themselves to writing and performing ceremonies based on Egyptian models and calling upon the deities of that civilization, Isis above all. In 1900 Mathers could inform the Golden Dawn that he recognized no superiors but 'the Eternal Gods'; his language had become imbued with polytheism. Similar work was carried out in sub-groups of the main temple of the Golden Dawn in London, and this began to cause serious concern among members whose first or only loyalty was to Christianity.[48]

Such anxieties combined with personal differences within the order to produce the process by which the Golden Dawn underwent schism after schism between 1900 and 1909, to fragment into four successor bodies:[49] the Isis-Urania Temple continued by Waite, Ayton, and others; the Stella Matutina of R. W. Felkin and (initially) J. W. Brodie-Innes; the Alpha et Omega of Brodie-Innes and the Mathers; and the A∴ A∴ of Crowley.[50] True to the principles of its founders, the first of these confined itself to a Christian mysticism, mediated through ritual, and disavowed the practice of magic. In an equally faithful reflection of the leading spirit, Crowley's organization concentrated upon pagan imagery. The others blended the two, in a more direct reflection of the original order. Most of them either developed into, or gave birth to, other organizations in turn, and thus the basic methods and structures of training developed in the Golden Dawn were continued through the twentieth century, as a distinctive genre of ritual magic.

What, then, was distinctive about that genre, and what magic did the Golden Dawn actually work? The answers take us straight back to the question of definitions, for they illustrate a major conceptual shift, introducing a distinctively modern notion of magic. Hitherto, across all the millennia of European and Near Eastern history, magical operations had been concerned with effecting specific results, or empowering the practitioner for specific ends. For the most part magic was treated as a reactive process, like medicine, employed to deal with particular problems by using means which were believed to manipulate the natural world. The distinctive hallmark of learned ritual magic was that it promised to give the operator control of, or partnership with, forces, which transcended the bounds of that world and placed superhuman powers at the disposal of the magician: demons, angels, or the hidden names of God. Those powers were still, however, expected to be used for practical ends, and to satisfy particular needs. Medieval and early modern occultists clearly had plenty of those; the classic grimoire is designed for somebody who is impoverished, embittered, and (above all) very lonely. This is true of even the most austere and sophisticated of all, the Book of Abramelin the Mage, which although alleged to be late medieval may in fact have been composed in the eighteenth century, the date of the single known manuscript. In sharp contrast to the others, it does away with most of the apparatus of magic circles and geometric forms, and working tools, and places its whole emphasis upon the spiritual development of the magician, the goal of which is the achievement of communication with a Holy Guardian Angel. What the Angel is there to do, however, is to tell the operator how to conjure up demons and reduce them to obedience.[51] Traditional scholarly magic was at basis an elaborate way of ringing for room service.

The alteration brought about by Levi, and continued by Mathers, Westcott, and their successors, was to mix this tradition with a different one, of mystical union with the divine, and infuse the combination with the spirit of optimism and faith in human progress and improvement which was one characteristic of the nineteenth century. It was to this blend that Levi, with his genius for devising handy labels, gave the term haute magie, 'high magic'. The two most important sources of the mysticism with which this magic was imbued were the *Corpus Hermeticum* and the cabbala, which approached the same end from entirely different directions and cultural traditions. The hermetic texts were composed in Greek-speaking Egypt in the second century, and were concerned both with the true place of humans in the universe and with how humans might obtain power over it. The most important for present purposes is the *Pimander*, which suggested that divine powers are latent within human beings, who may recover them by learning their own true natures. The cabbala came out of Hebrew rabbinical culture, and took its enduring form in the thirteenth century. It depended on the notion that the universe is structured around ten names or emanations of the One God, which correspond to the Hebrew alphabet and form together the single great divine name which is also the repository of the informing power of the cosmos. By contemplating and understanding this structure—in effect by ascending it—a human could come to know and understand divinity, and also (perhaps) to share in and employ its power.

What Levi and the occultists of the nineteenth century were trying to do was to develop or release the latent spiritual and mental abilities of humans by using the framework of traditional ritual magic. The object and centre of each operation was now the magician, and its aim was to bring him or her closer to spiritual maturity and potency, by inflaming the imagination, providing access to altered states of consciousness, and strengthening and focusing will-power. It was a therapy designed to enable human beings to evolve further into deities, or to bring forth the divinity already within them; no wonder Mackenzie had likened it to psychology, and the relationship between the two has remained close. The rituals of the Golden Dawn trained initiates to invoke deities and angels, but with the object neither of presenting them with praise and pleas nor of making them do the will of the person invoking; with neither, in short, of the customary aims of religion and magic. They encouraged the practitioners to empower themselves with incantation, within a ceremonial setting, so that they came to feel themselves *combining* with the divine forces concerned and becoming part of them. In the last analysis it did not matter to this work whether or not the entities concerned had any actual existence as long as the magician felt as if they did at the moment of working, and achieved the transforming visions and sensations which were the object of the process. In one sense it represented a revival of the ancient art of theurgy, which had always lain on the hazy boundary between religion and magic and signified an attempt by humans to work with divinities in such a way as to wield divine powers for themselves. In another, it was distinctively modern, being one spiritual reflection of the actual experience of the peoples of the nineteenth-century Western world, as they obtained ever greater political, economic, and environmental control of the globe.

6

FINDING A LOW MAGIC

❧❀❧

THE subject-matter of this chapter differs in one fundamental respect from those treated in the others of this first half of the book. All of the latter are concerned with phenomena which, although often rooted in earlier periods, took their distinctive form in the eighteenth or nineteenth centuries. In this one the emphasis is reversed, for it deals with an area of activity which, although taking on some aspects peculiar to this later period, had not altered in essentials from early modern times. One of the few specifically modern characteristics of it is the label of 'low magic', devised by the 'high' magicians of the occult revival. They used (and use) it to denote all those practices that fell within the broad category of magic and were not part of their self-consciously learned tradition. In particular, such activities belonged to the world of popular belief and custom, concerned not with the mysteries of the universe and the empower-ment of the magus, so much as with practical remedies for specific problems. The focus of the present chapter is upon the practitioners of this operative magic in England and Wales, between 1740 and 1940.

This is, notoriously, an area that has been comparatively neglected by acade-mic scholars. In 1994 Willem de Blécourt declared that the study of it in Europe as a whole 'properly speaking, has yet to start'.[1] The next year, Owen Davies, speaking of British colleagues, suggested that it 'is generally considered that witchcraft and magic is not a relevant or even a valid field of research for the modern historian'.[2] There have been a few useful contributions made to it by scholars using local case-studies,[3] but at the time of writing the only true acade-mic authority is Dr Davies himself, who has pioneered the systematic investiga-tion of the subject.[4] This is not for lack of data; indeed, as I have said elsewhere,[5] it would be easy to write a large book from that surviving for the counties of Somerset and Essex alone, and most other parts of England and Wales are equally rich in relevant source material.

For the purposes of this present study, it is helpful to distinguish between three very different categories of magical operator represented in popular expe-rience and belief. The first consists of witches in the abstract, a group of beings who existed in the same theoretical sphere as fairies, pixies, and gnomes, even though (as in the case of these other entities) belief in their existence could be firm and demonstrably 'real' occurrences were attributed to them. The second comprises actual individuals who were reputed to deal in magic but always firmly denied that they did so. At one end of this category were those who were suspected by one other person or a few other people of having 'ill-wished' or 'overlooked' them and so caused misfortune; a situation which almost always arose out of tensions between neighbours and disappeared if those tensions were resolved. At the other were those who acquired a general and lasting reputation for uncanny dealings. They were invariably people who were in some way out of harmony with the local community. Many were simply isolated and anti-social, others at once aloof and charismatic, and yet others blessed with unusual good fortune which made them prosper while others fared much worse. In no case were any of them proved to have engaged in magical practices, and the belief that they had done so were product of rumour, whether admiring, envi-ous, or hostile.

The third category contains all those who claimed themselves to work in a branch of magic or the occult or to possess arcane powers, and it is a very large one—including, in the two centuries under consideration, many thousands of individuals. It may be subdivided in turn. One distinctive part of it was repre-sented by people who offered no actual services but gloried in a reputation for the ability to work magic if they wished. Some were content to enjoy the enhanced respect and the awe in which they were held as a result, while others went further, to levy a tribute of gifts and payments from neighbours whom they frightened with threats of bewitchment. The rest of the class of self-declared workers of magic was made up of those who were prepared to use their presumed skills on behalf of others, and this may be divided in turn into differ-ent levels. At the lowest were those who specialized in the curing ('charming') of specific ailments in humans or animals, or the provision of specific divinatory services such as astrology or fortune-telling. The charmers were very numerous, especially in rural areas, so that most nineteenth-century villagers would have had access to one in their own parish or another nearby. Astrologers were espe-cially common in London, and in provincial towns, but could build up a widely scattered clientele by use of postal services. Fortune-tellers were also more likely to be urban, though found in many parts of the countryside as well, and often peregrinating, between fairs and parish feasts, and from door to door.

Above the level of these specialists came those practitioners who offered a range of skills linked to the operation of apparent supernatural power: the treat-ment of human and animal illnesses, the finding of lost or stolen goods and the detection of thieves, the removal of destructive magical spells and the punish-ment of the person who had cast them, astrological calculations, and other divinatory techniques. Such an operator was known throughout England as a 'wise-woman' or 'wise-man', with 'wizard' a common alternative for the latter. In southern counties, the Midlands, and Wales, the terms 'cunning-man' or 'cunning woman' were often used instead, while 'conjuror' was sometimes employed for male practitioners in southern England and very frequently in Wales.[6] The native Welsh expression was '*dyn hysbys*', and the Cornish equiva-lent was 'pellar', which folklorists have believed to be a corruption of 'expeller', one who removes evil spirits.[7] Folklore collectors themselves often employed the term 'white witch', but this formulation was very rare in the vocabulary of ordinary people, to whom the word 'witch' almost always signified somebody who worked magic for personal ends of profit or malice.[8]

By whatever name they were known, these practitioners usually carried on their magical work in tandem with another, more conventional, form of employment. They tended to be found most often in towns, local centres where clients would resort to them as for other specialist services, but were plentiful in the countryside as well. Many drew custom only from their own districts, but some, the aristocracy of their craft, had reputations which extended across regions. It needs to be emphasized that such individuals disposed of knowledge which to a degree was the general property of their society. Popular traditions abounded with charms and herbs for the treatment or prevention of disease or the mending of wounds, and spells or rituals for the prediction of future events or the repulsion or removal of hostile magic and the punishment of the person who had operated it. What gave the specialists described above their apparent value was the belief that not only did they possess a broader and deeper knowledge of such techniques and more experience in using them, but that they also either embodied or could work with supernatural power which greatly increased the effectiveness of the operations concerned.

The object of this chapter, is to build upon and to supplement the work of Owen Davies, by examining the world of 'popular' magic in England and Wales during this period, with particular attention to aspects of it which are of relevance to the development of modern pagan witchcraft.

*　　*　　*

The first of these concerns the range of personalities and occupations represented by the category of many-faceted magical practitioner, to which Davies had given the useful blanket term of 'cunning folk'. He himself collected and analysed a sample of forty-one male practitioners for whom relatively detailed information survives, and found that they were overwhelmingly drawn from two closely related economic groups: tradesmen and artisans. The remainder (fourteen individuals) were mainly either herbalists or schoolmasters. Female practitioners formed a large minority of the cunning craft, often being married or widowed. They were every bit as popular and commercially successful as the men, and indeed this was one of the few means by which ordinary women could achieve a respected and independent position.[9] In another essay Owen Davies made a parallel analysis of charmers, and found that they were drawn from the same social groups.[10] The upper ranks (above those of small retailer and farmer) were not represented, as these by definition did not engage in trades or crafts; but agricultural labourers, and the huge mass of the poorest members of society, were likewise almost wholly missing. Davies made two suggestions to account for this last pattern, both reasonable.[11] One was that clients were overwhelmingly drawn from the middle and lower ranks of the social hierarchy and did not like to go for help to their inferiors. The other (which will be considered further below) was that literacy and learning were perceived as integral accomplishments for most types of cunning craft.

What needs to be emphasized here is how large a range of personal style and circumstance could still be comprehended within the categories identified above. Pen-portraits of cunning folk and charmers are relatively scarce, and usually represented only by a single account; thick description is not an option for a scholar of this topic. None the less, enough survive to illustrate the variety of characters involved. The most celebrated cunning man in the whole of nine-teenth-century southern England is probably James Murrell ('Cunning Murrell'), who lived in the market town of Hadleigh, in the clay farmland of south-eastern Essex, overlooking the Thames estuary. His clients were drawn from all over the county, and also from Suffolk and northern Kent, and he regu-larly received post from London to keep him abreast of events there. Born in 1780, he set up first as a surveyor, and then as chemist's assistant in the capital, before returning to his native part of Essex in about 1810, to work as a shoe-maker and to establish his practice as a cunning man which lasted until his death in 1860. Murrell was a small, aloof fellow, who went abroad mostly at night, wearing iron goggles and carrying a basket and a whalebone umbrella; in 'a hard hat and a bobbed tail coat, his hands behind him, he used to walk along humming loudly and lost in thought'. His cottage was hung with drying herbs and lined with books. He cured warts, treated a variety of human and animal complaints with his herbal remedies, and with tough, prayers, and amulets, and offered to restore lost or stolen property. His chief fame, however, was a breaker of evil spells cast by witches, and a discoverer of those who cast the spells; his catch-phrase was 'I am the Devil's master'. The gentry generally disliked him but left him alone, while most ordinary people in his locality deeply admired him.[12]

An almost exact contemporary of Cunning Murrell, and from the same country, was 'Dummy' who lived at Sible Hedingham in similar claylands at the north end of Essex. He was a Frenchman by origin, whose tongue had been cut out at some point in the mysterious past that he had known before appearing in Essex, already at an advanced age. 'He lived alone in a wretched hut full of hoarded walking sticks, umbrellas, and rubbish, and practised fortune-telling.' Among the rubbish were hundreds of scraps of paper upon which his clients had written their questions, for he was deaf as well as dumb. His method of divination is not recorded, nor that of his reply, although he did employ 'ener-getic and somewhat grotesque gestures, which were taken by the rustics gener-ally as cabbalistic and diabolical signs'. His standing was very different from that of Cunning Murrell, for his foreign provenance and his mutilation made him a figure of suspicion and ridicule as well as of arcane reputation. He did not offer to combat witches, and therefore could be taken for one himself. The combina-tion proved lethal; in 1863 he was attacked by a drunken mob led by a woman who claimed that her ill health had been caused by his enchantments. They 'swam' him in a river, according to the traditional test by which water rejects a witch, and the poor old man (by then in his eighties) died as a result.[13]

The equivalent of Murrell in the Northeast was John Wrightson, who died in about 1840 and farmed at Stokesley, where the flood-plain of the Tees runs up to the Cleveland Hills. His catchment area extended all over the adjacent districts of Yorkshire and County Durham. On public occasions he appeared in the dress of a Regency swell, 'a scarlet coat, a long white waistcoat and full-starched shirt frill, crimson knee-breeches and white stockings'.[14] He was 'a man of not unkindly nature, with a pungent flavour of rough humour about him, shrewd and observant'. His consulting room was decorated with a human skull, a globe, and dried herbs, and he received clients clad in a long robe or gown.[15] Officially a veterinary surgeon, he also cured human ailments, traced goods, broke spells, and comforted the depressed.[16] Several pegs below him on the scale of reputation, but still high on it, was his contemporary Nannie Scott, who lived in a 'hovel' up the coast at Sunderland, together with a black dog and cat. She practised astrology, sold a medicinal compound of treacle, laid curses or removed them on request, provided love-charms, and prayed for fair winds at the entreaty of sailors' wives; 'and she did all with an air of solemn strong-mindedness that bore down any approach to discredit'.[17] The bottom of the scale, in the same period, was represented by a 'dirty and ragged' couple who lived along the coast in the other direction, at Scarborough. They bullied food, drink, and money out of servant girls with the threat of the evil eye.[18] Some notion of the profusion of cunning folk in the region during this half of the century may be indicated by the fact that in 1816 Whitby alone had eight resident wise-women or diviners.[19]

The foremost female members of the craft included the healer Bridget Bostock, an old spinster who kept house for a yet more elderly man at Church Coppenhall in the Cheshire salt plain, and became a national celebrity in 1748. Here the refraction of the beholding eye becomes all too obvious. One account stressed her modest simplicity, attired in 'a flannel waistcoat, a green linsey apron, a pair of clogs, and a plain cap, tied with a halfpenny lace'. Another dismissed her 'most dirty attire'.[20] On the rocky coast between Zennor and Treen in west Cornwall, just under a hundred years later, was the solitary hut of 'An Maggey', 'an' signifying 'aunt'. A sailor's widow, like too many women in that harsh land, she kept sheep, goats, dogs, cats, poultry, and tame hares, spun and knitted, prepared cordials and mead, cured skin and eye diseases, and removed bad spells, punishing the perpetrators by using image-magic against them. When entertaining, she was careful to dress up in her best outfit, of a white satin quilted petticoat sewn with blue silk, a blue silk gown, an embroidered muslin apron, and long netted silk gloves. She was more feared than loved in the neighbourhood.[21]

Just as sartorially conscientious was Hannah Henley, whose home was at Membury in the hills at the east end of Devon, in the same period. 'She generally wore short petticoats, with a large white apron, white as the driven snow, a plaid turnover and a satin poke bonnet.' She kept a large number of cats, of all colours, and made superb apple pies and dumplings. She also demanded a tribute from farmers to keep her curses from them, and claimed to be capable of using her magic to kill those who refused. Eventually, one terrified family called in a wise-man from Chard to destroy her with his own spells, and she indeed died suddenly after his arrival.[22] By contrast, another Devonian, old Marianne Vooden, who lived at Bratton in the 1890s, could be called 'indescribably dirty', and yet was a healer of impeccable benevolence and generosity.[23] Sharing Maggey's ambivalent reputation, and Marianne's appearance, was Kilsey Nan, who ran a shop at Skipton, in the Yorkshire Dales, in the early nineteenth century. She sold occult bric-a-brac, and told fortunes by using 'her Guinea pig, and about half a pack of dirty cards'.[24]

Other Victorian cunning folk used John Wrightson's tactic of striking costume or home decorations. Billy Brewer promenaded Taunton in a long Inverness cape and sombrero hat, his hair falling in long dishevelled grey locks. Up at Barmby in the south Yorkshire farmlands, George Wales was equally conspicuous in his long antique coat and tall chimney-pot hat.[25] Jenkyns of Trellech, the famous wizard of the little hills of central Monmouthshire, went out in tails and a box-hat, his dark beard grown long.[26] In Sussex, 'Pigtail' Bridger, 'a very tall, big man, terrible to look at', wore his hair as his nickname suggested, and his dress was likewise described as 'eccentric'.[27] Others cultivated a distinctive demeanour, like a rural wise-man who operated in west Somerset around 1890 and was noted for his 'fish belly white' face and 'diabolical' expression. He succeeded in building up a considerable local reputation both for magical prowess and for evil, which is perhaps why he was eventually found murdered in his cottage.[28] Yet others preferred to be personally less conspicuous but to ensure a suitable ambience for their workspace. In 1857 the fortune-teller and herbalist Clayton Chaffer received clients in a room at Duckinfield, near Manchester, where he prominently displayed his books, his brass instruments, such as horologues, and (pasted on one wall) 'a paper entitled "Raphael's Witch or Oracle of the Future" surrounded by an engraved border representing Warlocks and Witches in a Dance'.[29]

Some pulled out all the stops. Mother Merne of Milborne Down, on the Dorset Chalk hills, was one of the last old-style cunning folk, dying in the 1930s. Even in old age her hair was still 'raven black, her skin was the colour of parchment and her eyes beady, black and penetrating to an alarming degree'. She told the future, healed by touch, and provided herbs, ointments, and charms, from a little four-roomed cottage hung with herbs and equipped with a cauldron in which she brewed her medicinal potions. She kept black hens, a black goat, and a black cat, which sat on her shoulder during consultations. Despite the cat, she also kept guinea pigs, and her home was infested with rats and mice.[30] She must have known that she was a living stereotype, and that doubtless aided her considerable reputation for efficacy.

A hundred years before her, a medical man living in the Mochnant valley of

Montgomeryshire's Berwyn Mountains set himself up as a fortune-teller and magical healer, with the claimed power to call up spirits; he became known as 'bwm-baili'r cythraul', the Devil's bum-bailiff. For his magical operations he donned a unique costume:

a cap of sheepskin, with a high crown, bearing a plume of pigeon's feathers, and a coat of unusual pattern, with broad hams and covered with talismanic characters. In his hand he had a whip the thong of which was made of the skin of an eel and the handle of bone; with this he drew a circle around him, outside of which at a proper distance he kept those persons who came to him, whilst he went through his mystical seances and performances.[31]

The outfit sounds very similar to those of Siberian tribal shamans; this may be coincidental, but this highly literate man may well have taken the idea from accounts of Siberia, just as he may have gained his circle-magic from a grimoire.

This series of images provides some indication of the varied ways in which cunning folk were perceived, and in which they presented themselves to their public, in the period. They certainly represented a distinct, if loose, vocation, and were drawn from a particular band—though a broad one—in the social hierarchy. Within these defining limits, however, they appear as a remarkably heterogeneous collection of individuals, divided by at least as many characteristics as those which they had in common.

*   *   *

One thing they did have in common, as suggested above, is that they were expected to have some learning. Owen Davies has put it crisply: 'The evidence points to the fact that an illiterate cunning person was unlikely to go very far.'[32] The outward sign of their accomplishment was that they possessed books, an immediate distinction in a society in which, even by the mid-nineteenth century, it was exceptional for an ordinary household to own any except the Bible.[33] The presence and importance of these volumes is a recurrent refrain in accounts of the cunning folk, and not merely in those of the elite among them such as Murrell and Wrightson. 'An Maggey', in her hut among the granite outcrops, kept a 'conjuring-book, with large brass clasps and corners . . . full of such queer figures as are put in the almanacs'.[34] Marianne Vooden depended for her healing remedies upon 'an elaborate book of charms and recitations'.[35] In nineteenth-century Wales it was believed that the indispensable basis of a conjuror's skill consisted of occult literature.[36] One of the most famous of these Welsh magicians was Edward Savage (1759–1859), who farmed near Llangurig in the heart of the Cambrian Mountains. His first procedure after hearing a client's request was generally to consult his library; once, upon (more or less) surviving a test designed to discredit him, he exclaimed: 'Well done the old books, they never failed me yet!'[37]

The popular mind did not merely associate cunning people with the printed or written word, but the figures regarded as their natural enemies, and targets, the witches. One of the traits likely to draw upon a person a suspicion of being involved with bad magical dealings was an apparently unnecessary appetite for reading, especially if (rightly or wrongly) the texts were believed to be connected with the occult. In Sussex one informant of a folklore-collector, recalling a long-dead local suspect, stated that 'that kind of wicked old woman always had books—powerful books, which have a great deal of evil written in them'. In about 1920 one reputed witch in that county was removed to the local workhouse because she had become too frail to care for herself. The neighbours insisted that her books were burned as soon as she was carried from her home, rather than taken with her or sold or given away; none dared to see what they actually contained.[38]

This fear of the physical volumes brings home a point that also affected the cunning folk: that books of magical lore were thought not merely to contain information but to possess power of their own, which could affect those who opened them. In a still semi-literate society, the written word was credited as intrinsically potent. A folk tale collected at Abergavenny, the main pass through the Black Mountains of south-east Wales, concerns the misfortunes of the servant of a conjuror, told to carry a volume of invocations as a loan to another, who dared to look into it, and so set loose evil spirits.[39] It was commonly believed that each cunning person was empowered by the possession of one particular volume, from which he or she had learned the essence of the craft and which had an arcane energy of its own; this was told even of those who owned whole libraries. The notion was especially common in Wales, where a language barrier compounded illiteracy, but was found across Britain.[40] In some cases, such as those of 'An Maggey' and Marianne Vooden, there was an element of truth in it.

What *were* the books of the cunning folk? Owen Davies has found complete or partial descriptions of the collections of half a dozen of them, ranging from Henry Harries, the most famous *dyn hysbys* in nineteenth-century Wales, to small fry like Clayton Chaffer.[41] The result is remarkably consistent; they consist of a range of works on astrology, herbalism, medicine, and charms, with a few concerning ritual magic. Some were current astrological tables and charts, published by the London leaders of that art, such as 'Raphael' and 'Zadkiel'. Others were sixteenth- and seventeenth-century classics, such as the works of Cornelius Agrippa, Michel Nostradamus, Reginald Scot, or William Lilley. The same pattern is found in a more impressionistic survey of the works collected by Cunning Murrell.[42] Dr Farrer, who lived at Broomfield in Somerset's Quantock Hills at the end of the eighteenth century, is said to have banished spirits with a rite taken from the famous early modern grimoire, *The Key of Solomon*.[43] Significantly, the finest occult library attributed to any cunning people was amassed by a family which lived in a district as remote as any that nineteenth-century England and Wales could contain. They were the Harries, whose house was Pantcoy, near Cwrt y Cadno in a wooded valley among the southern reaches of the Cambrian Mountains. Their collection was both large and varied, and included works in Greek and Latin, the latter language at least being one in which Henry Harries (1821–49) could perform with some proficiency.[44] Had they resided in a region with easier access to libraries and bookshops, it is possible that they would not have needed to purchase and retain so many volumes.

In addition to collecting published information, cunning folk wrote their own notebooks, of information taken from other printed works, or word of mouth. Murrell compiled several of these, on conjuration, geomancy and astrology. The last of these survived into the 1950s (and may yet), and contained data from books issued in the seventeenth, eighteenth, and nineteenth centuries; it was commenced by an astrologer calling himself 'Neboad', and then passed into the possession of Murrell, who continued it.[45] The volume put together by Timothy Crowther (1694–1761), famed wise-man of Skipton, Yorkshire, contained astrological figures, axioms, incantations, and weather-signs. The antiquarian who read it in the nineteenth century noted down one of the spells, to recover stolen goods. It is a clear example of traditional grimoire magic. The operator had to make a wax plate, and cut the names of 'Sathan' and four other demons into the centre, along with a brief description of the goods and the name of the person who wanted them returned. They had to be ringed with those of the planets. The magician then needed to conjure the spirits in the name of 'God Almighty, Father, Son, and Holy Ghost, and Jesus Christ the son of the Living God' (a theological overkill) to perform the necessary work.[46]

Some of these manuscripts are preserved in national archives. One was put together by a Dr Parkins, who started his practice as astrologer, herbalist, and diviner in Lincolnshire. Dated 1802, it consists mainly of invocations of spirits, with some astrological charts.[47] Henry Harries's own notebooks are now in the National Library of Wales and contain a mixture of incantations, Cabbalistic lore, and astrology.[48] Another Welsh collection includes the miscellany of schoolmaster and *dyn hysbys* Cadwaladr Davies, put together between 1733 and 1745 and consisting of magical recipes, mostly for healing, culled from a range of herbals, astrological treatises and almanacs, and works on medicine.[49]

How did the cunning folk come by this information? For reasons which shall become clear below, most would not have been able to inherit books or receive any formal instruction or apprenticeship. The impression is that they generally bought the former (often by mail order), and picked up their theoretical knowledge from reading and conversation. By the nineteenth century specialist booksellers were serving the market for works on all branches of the occult, publishing advertisements of their stock and receiving requests. In the early part of the century, as in the late part of the twentieth, one of the most famous of these was at Leeds. The greatest source of supply was the capital, represented most prominently until the 1840s by John Denley (whose part in the story of 'high magic' has been mentioned) and thereafter by George Bumstead.[50] Some of Denley's papers survive,[51] and illustrate the wide geographical range of his correspondents within England and Wales. It has been mentioned that Cunning

Murrell kept in regular touch with the metropolis. London also provides the only evidence for anything like occult schools in the period, containing as it did the nation's most famous magicians and astrologers. Dr Parkin may have started out in Lincolnshire, but he moved to Marylebone in order to offer instructions to pupils in branches of magic and divination. In his writings he claimed to have been trained himself by the two most famous metropolitan occultists of his time, Frances Barrett, author of *The Magus*, and Ebenezer Sibley.[52]

The relationship between the capital and the provincial cunning folk is illustrated in a different way, by the reputation of Cunning Murrell. During his own lifetime he had been known throughout the region on either side of the Thames estuary—as large a catchment area as any other of his craft ever seems to have achieved—but not further. What turned him into a national figure was the work of a London writer, Arthur Morrison, who took a holiday at Hadleigh three decades after Murrell's death, met his son, and was told tales of his achievements. Morrison subsequently produced a novel which presented them in a wildly sensational form, and a(n apparently) more objective account of them for *The Strand Magazine*, from which most of our current information about Murrell is derived.[53] These works inflated the name of the old Essex wizard above all others of his craft. Perhaps the most striking insight into the relationship between the capital and the provinces is provided by a letter sent to the London astrologer 'Raphael' in 1840.[54] This individual was famous to the public as the editor of the most popular astrological almanac of the early nineteenth century, *The Prophetic Messenger*, then at its peak of circulation. It had been founded by the brilliant Robert Cross Smith, who had died in 1832 and was succeeded by a sequence of editors who carried on using his pseudonym; the identity of the one operating in 1840 is now disputed by scholars.[55] The letter was from the young Henry Harries, written in his farmhouse at Pantcoy and offering to 'prostrate' himself at the 'venerable feet' of the great man; like virtually all readers of the almanac, Harries did not realize that the original 'Raphael' was long dead. The *dyn hysbys* admitted frankly that he doubted the reality of spirits, and had never succeeded in making any appear, but now begged the Londoner to teach him how to do so, in exchange for payment. Harries envisaged a postal course, through the post office at Llandovery, the nearest town to his remote valley. Whether the editor replied or not is unrecorded, but certainly Harries's local reputation was subsequently enhanced still further by the belief that he had been trained by the great 'Raphael' himself.[56]

All this evidence suggests that before the arrival of the new-style ceremonial magic from Paris, leading to the formation of closed societies dedicated to the spiritual development of the practitioners and the discovery of the inner workings of the universe, any distinction between 'high' and 'low' magic in Britain is meaningless. What we see instead is a common world of knowledge often mediated through common texts, with London firmly at its centre but consisting of a complex network of local hierarchies and business practices, in most cases thoroughly integrated with local society.

There was, however, some distinction between the intellectual universe of the cunning folk and that of the local charmers, with their skill in curing specific ailments. The latter were far more likely to have that skill passed on to them by a personal transmission, and in a few cases (most recorded in the West Country) it was believed firmly that the charm involved could only be spoken, as to write it down would neutralize its power. On the other hand, it was much more common to apply the charm through the written word, by putting a paper on which it was inscribed upon the affected part of the patients, hanging it about them, or having it sewn into their clothing. The real objection was to having a charm printed, which was believed to publish it so widely that its efficacy would be lost—which was, of course, true in a strictly practical sense.[57]

Despite this prohibition, a large number of charms have been collected and printed by scholars, and reveal very clearly that the world of the charmers was not a sealed one.[58] Many were drawn from the general popular repertoire of magico-medicine. Some were religious in nature, and will be considered below. Here it is most relevant to note that some derived from the common stock of traditional occult literature which underpinned cunning craft. A charm sold to a sick man at Rhyader, in the central Welsh mountains, in 1867, consisted of a piece of paper decorated with geometrical designs and the following words:

The fourth is Maynons, one of the powers who hath the ability of superficient administration and protection, that is at one and the same time to be present with many. His presents must be sought by humility and prayer. The fifth good genius is Gaounum, an angel of celestial brightness who hath the peculiar ability of rendering his pupil invisible to any evil spirit whatsoever.[59]

This is an excerpt from an early modern catalogue of good spirits, a parallel to the *Goetia*.

Another was provided to an ailing client by a famous Cornish 'pellar', at Helston in the early nineteenth century. The piece of paper measured one by one and a half inches. On one side was drawn a beast, part angel and part bird, sitting on two eggs. Above it was the word 'Nalgah' and below it 'Tetragrammaton'. On the other side was written 'Jehovah. Jah. Elohim. Shadday. Adonay. Have Mercy On A Poor Woman'.[60] A consumptive girl living near Whitby in the same period received an envelope containing 'one of the signs of the Zodiac, taken from an old almanack, a verse out of Solomon's proverbs and a few dry beech leaves'.[61] A charm given to prevent witchcraft at Fryup Head, in the Cleveland Hills nearby, consisted of an illustration straight from a grimoire: a circle containing a pentagram, with three intersecting triangles forming a hexagram in the centre, and the Tetragrammaton and a passage from the Book of Psalms written round it.[62]

The evidence as its stands therefore tends towards the conclusion that the theoretical and ideological components of the cunning craft and of charming were not closed or self-contained traditions. They formed a continuum both with popular beliefs and remedies in general and with the more specialized genre of learned ritual magic. As such, they are accessible to scholars and recoverable by them, to the same imperfect extent as other aspects of eighteenth- and nineteenth-century British social history.

* * *

What, however, of practical techniques? Here, a vast amount of data survives in the collections of folklorists and in legal records and newspaper archives, and it is necessary to distinguish categories within it. One of those consists of charming, and it is clear enough that charmers concentrated on a few well-defined categories of ailment. They were not concerned with bone-setting, the malfunction of internal organs, cancers, or infectious diseases. Overwhelmingly, they specialized in curing growths or rashes of skin, promoting the healing of wounds, and staunching bleeding, internal or external. What all these afflications have in common is that they are peculiarly responsive to the nervous system and to the patient's morale and mental equilibrium. The essence of the treatment was thus a rapport between the afflicted person and the healer, fostered by the reputation and bedside manner of the latter. Actual methods varied considerably, the most commonly recorded being stroking, rubbing with saliva, and the speaking or writing out of prayers or charms, all of which might be relied upon to produce the necessary effect upon the mind and system of the person under treatment.[63] Theo Brown, who studied charmers still operating in Devon during the mid-twentieth century, noted that their success rate seemed to be total; the one exception known to her being the treatment of a sceptical journalist. She concluded from this that any element of doubt, distraction, or lack of genuine need on the part of the patient was fatal to the process, which is why it could not be subjected to scientific testing.[64]

Thus far, matters comfortably straddle the boundary between the rational and the uncanny. They tip rather more towards the latter in the case of wild animal charmers, like the relatively recent examples of the Cornish rat-catcher who called his victims from their burrows by whistling, or the Devon men who confined adders within a circle drawn on the ground or willed them to death without touching them.[65] The pioneer of spoken history, George Ewart Evans, did rather better with the trick of stilling or starting horses, associated with the Toadmen, Horseman's Word, and Horse Whisperers, as well as with cunning folk. Using some East Anglian testimony, he suggested that the secret lay in manipulating scents which the animals found particularly attractive or terrifying[66]—which might account for most cases of the phenomenon but not (as will be seen in a later chapter) for all. A related problem attends the tales of wise-women and wise-men who could immobilize other people with a look, and keep them so at will, or who caused inanimate objects to dance or fly about. If these are not wholly fictional, then the 'reasonable' explanation is a form of hypnosis, comparable to that used by some modern stage performers; but to suggest this would itself be a statement of faith.[67]

A very widespread device of local magical practitioners was to encourage clients to gaze into a mirror, crystal, vessel of water, or some other reflecting surface, until they saw within it the form of the person who had bewitched them or others, or who had stolen their goods or injured their property. This still reserved credit to the practitioner, because the reflecting object was held to be empowered by magic, but it effectively threw more of the onus of achieving a result onto the client. In practical terms, it could bring to the surface suspicions which already existed, or concentrate the mind of the person concerned more effectively upon the evidence.[68] The psychological screw could be turned in other ways. In the 1930s a farmer near Beaminster in the west Dorset hills consulted a local wise-woman because he wanted to discover the source of some malicious gossip about him. She advised him to drink a glass of beer, silently, in each pub which he passed on his way home from her, and afterwards to explain to people that he was casting a spell to make the word 'liar' form in fiery letters upon the brow of the guilty person. Within a week a woman had come to him to confess the fault and bid him to take the curse off because her forehead was burning.[69] Cunning Murrell filled the mouths of suspected thieves with flour and told them to spit; he reckoned that the guilty would be those who blew dust, for their mouths were dry with fear.[70] None of these devices, however, can account for the reputations of Wrightson, the Lincolnshire cunning man 'Fiddler' Fynes, and a wise-women at Leicester, who were all said at times to exhibit a genuine clairvoyance, detecting thieves, missing persons, and lost or stolen goods by using an unaided visionary power.[71]

To combat bewitchment of humans or cattle, once diagnosed or confirmed, required special methods. The most common one, employed by cunning people throughout England and Wales, was to use a sympathetic magic involving fire. The latter was employed both as a purifying element and as a means of torture, by magical transference, of the witch. Normally, the operation was performed in the house of the bewitched person, or the owner of the afflicted animals. The simplest form was to burn a special powder or incense, provided by the magician. The more elaborate, and frequently recorded, was to take the heart of an animal, stuck with pins, and roast it, or else to put hair, urine, or nail clippings of the sufferer in a pan or bottle, and boil or fry them. The animal concerned could be one of a herd or flock affected by the curse, or sacrificed for the occasion. Sometimes the bottles were buried instead of heated, or bricked up in a building; they occasionally still come to light in such locations. Murrell had his made to order, of iron, by a local blacksmith.[72] It was only a short step from this sort of spell to the use of straightforward image-magic; of fashioning a form (usually of wax) to represent the witch who was harming the client and burning or sticking pins in that. And from that point, of course, it was only a short step more for a cunning person or charmer to accept a fee or reward for laying a curse on somebody against whom a client had a grudge, by the same sorts of device. This was apparently much more rare, but it certainly happened.[73] Occasionally some remarkable reciprocal rackets could develop. A wise-woman with the thoroughly inappropriate name of 'Virtue' lived on the clay plateau north of Norwich in the nineteenth century, and made a good living out of cursing and demanding gifts from her neighbours with the threat of bewitching them if they refused. Cunning folk in nearby villages and towns, meanwhile, constantly profited from removing the spells from people who believed themselves to be her victims.[74]

Such processes could yield obvious positive results. The drama and complexity of the rituals involved in them clearly functioned as an excellent antidote to feelings of depression and persecution, and (as in the case of the charmers) could relieve even physical ailments which had a psychosomatic component. As news of them got about small communities, they could flush out individuals who had harboured bad feelings towards the people who had thought themselves bewitched, forcing them to repentance and amends. The essential problem with them was that they could have no effect upon an illness which sprang in reality from a physical cause. Any lingering and mysterious malady was liable, in the period, to be blamed upon witchcraft, and few of the cunning folk were trained even in the imperfect professional medicine of the time. Their procedures could therefore be tragically ineffective; and even a supremo like Cunning Murrell had his crashing failures, leaving clients resentful and confused.[75]

Otherwise, cunning folk rang the changes on the whole range of quasi-magical remedies. They gave amulets and wrote charms, made healing potions and poultices, cast horoscopes, and read the future in cards and tea-leaves. Some enhanced their reputation by trickery, such as establishing early-warning systems to learn the business of clients before they appeared, practising ventriloquism or 'legerdemain', or (in one case) arranging a crime so that they could then appear to solve it.[76] It is not clear, and never will be, whether the fame of clairvoyants such as Wrightson and Fynes was based upon a particularly adroit practice of such ruses.

Above all, they devised spells and rites according to their own whims and creative talents, and the needs of their customers. One example may help to illustrate the process, the work of a wise-man called Jonathan Westcott who lived at Upleatham, where the North Yorks Moors run down to the sea, in the early nineteenth century. The local suspected witch was a solitary old women called Peggy Flaunders. Westcott was approached by two female clients, one complaining that her butter would not churn and the other that her cow was sick. He suggested that Flaunders was responsible for both problems. To the first, he gave the advice to wash out her churn successively with hot salted water, hot salted water with rowan berries, and with unsalted hot water. With the latter still in it, she then had to drive two rowan-wood pegs into each end and turn it nine times, saying 'This time it's thine, the next time it's mine, and mine for evermore.' He told the other to give a certain cordial to the cow, exercise it, milk it slightly for nine days, and then milk it completely on the tenth, after whispering in its ear 'I'm milking you for Peggy Flaunders.' Rowan (perhaps because of its red berries, which resemble fire and were often used as a ritual substitute for it), was regarded as a tree that had a special power to repel witchcraft; and salted water is a sterilizing agent. All the other details of the procedures, however, seem to have been off the top of Westcott's head; it is not recorded if either of them seemed to work.[77]

*   *   *

Did cunning folk ever work together, or meet in lodges, guilds, or covens? The answer seems to be an almost complete negative, for all the vast body of the eighteenth- and nineteenth-century evidence shows them operating as solitary practitioners, apart from the very occasional husband-and-wife team (like the couple at Scarborough) or pair of brothers (like the Harries, to be considered below). The single real exception was in early nineteenth-century Manchester, where some wisemen gathered round a famed one called Rawlinson. They had, after all, no common system of training or way of functioning, and their fame rested upon individual prowess, rather than group identity or communal solidarity. They were, effectively, competing for custom, even if that custom was ample enough to support some quite dense concentrations (as in Regency Whitby), aided by specialization in the various services provided. Above all, the great majority of cunning people and all charmers regarded their craft as a sideline to their regular employment or source of income, not as a profession in itself.

Some confusion has, however, been caused in this respect by the habit of folklore-collectors in the late nineteenth and early twentieth centuries, of referring to all popular magical practices as 'witchcraft' and to cunning folk as 'white witches'. Owen Davies has, as indicated above, suggested that this was not a terminology often employed by the people who resorted to these practitioners, and the research for the present chapter would bear him out; with a possible exception for west Somerset and Devon.[78] Records for nineteenth-century popular culture certainly abound in references to witches, but these are almost always characterized as the natural opponents of the cunning people: individuals possessed of magical powers who chose to use them maliciously against their neighbours, from motives of revenge or entertainment. Anthropologists have encountered broadly similar beliefs among tribal peoples all over the globe. In England and Wales there was a pronounced gendering of the perception. As said, cunning people tended to be male, by a distinct if narrow margin. The individuals suspected of working malicious magic, by contrast, seem to have been predominantly female, and when abstract notions and stereotypes of such people are considered, that predominance becomes overwhelming.

Another tradition found around the world is that the dedicated workers of bad magic are inspired by an opposition to prevailing social reforms and morality, and gather in secret anti-societies to mock these norms, to celebrate, and to exchange information and concert action. Such ideas certainly existed in Continental Europe, and to a lesser extent in Scotland, and played a prominent part in the witch trials of the early modern period. By contrast, as scholars of the subject have always discerned, English witches were viewed most often as isolated individuals, working alone.[79] This pattern is borne out by the material gathered for the present chapter, with a few exceptions. The outstanding one is the Land's End peninsula of Cornwall, West Penwith. Here, local people believed that witches gathered every Midsummer Eve in the wild granite landscape between Zennor and Nancledra, to feast around a bonfire in imitation of the customary gatherings held that night by the youth of the district.[80] They were also said to gather more irregularly at rocking stones, and the parallel of this tradition to fairy stories is emphasized by the detail that they were supposed to fly there on ragwort stems.[81] A legend was told of a hunter who happened upon a meeting of them in one of the enigmatic local Iron Age tunnels called 'fogous', and was driven mad.[82]

Marie Trevelyan reported many Welsh folk beliefs about such revels, at prehistoric and Roman monuments, on rocky islets, and (above all) on mountain peaks, and it would be tempting to link her evidence to that from Penwith and Scotland, and talk about a Celtic tradition of sociable witches.[83] Unhappily, none of the other rich sources for Welsh folklore contains such information, the closest being an opinion recorded in Monmouthshire that witches flew by night in sets of three, whooping, one on a ladder, one on a grindstone, and one on a hurdle.[84] This matters because Trevelyan's book contains other passages which, like this one, are not attributed to any source, and have no parallels in other collections for Wales but are amazingly similar to some in works of Scottish and Continental folk customs and beliefs. The suspicion must be present, though not proved, that having come late to the field she spiced up an otherwise repetitive body of data with colourful transplants from other nations; or that she was deceived by somebody else.[85]

In the whole of England there is nothing to compare with the well-established and consensual tradition of witch gatherings found at the tip of Cornwall. The latter itself is susceptible to no easy explanation, and may have resulted from close maritime contacts with France and Spain. What English tradition shows instead is a wide scattering of isolated stories and statements. The Lincolnshire tale of 'Fan o'the Fens', a young woman who flew to the witches' Sabbat on her broomstick, leading young men with her to worship Satan, should probably be removed from the ledger.[86] It is not recorded until the twentieth century, and reads like a piece of pure fiction based upon Continental traditions; the very word 'Sabbat', used by French and German demonologists to denote witches' gatherings, is not found in eighteenth- or nineteenth-century English folklore. It is certainly true, however, that some Lincolnshire people believed that witches held conventions at particular locations, Blyborough Top and Dorrington Church being reputed as two of them. A Willoughton man suggested that these gatherings were 'ter discuss their business, an' such like'.[87] Down on the far side of the country, witches were believed to have a traditional meeting-place on Leigh Common, in the Blackmore Vale of Dorset.[88] This is not far away from the Hunter's Lodge Inn, on a main road in east Devon, in front of which lay a large flat stone upon which they were rumoured to have carried out human sacrifices.[89] The only other English tradition of such gatherings is a south Staffordshire one, that each Midsummer Night all the witches of the world met on the moon to determine the fate of ordinary mortals during the next twelve months.[90]

Otherwise, there are a few traces of opinion that witches had informal contacts with each other, concealed from the public. In Sussex one informant said that if two met upon the road, 'they don't speak, and they don't stop, and they don't even nod at each other, however much they may be friends; they just laugh softly, and pass on'.[91] In Essex it was rumoured that those living on opposite sides of the River Crouch would visit each other, individually, sailing across in washtubs or flying upon hurdles.[92] South of the river lay the isolated village of Canewdon, of which much more will be said later. It was notorious in local belief for having a completely unique arrangement, six resident witches who worked separately but could be controlled by a single wizard, the 'Master of the Witches'.[93] Only one person in all the English and Welsh records seems actually to have claimed to have seen a meeting, a millwright in the Cambridgeshire Fens who told how, around 1850, he had hidden in the loft of a derelict cottage near Prickwillow, and watched through the trapdoor as six old witches gathered there. He described how they ate and talked around a fire, and then removed their black cloaks. One was wearing a garter of hair, one garters of viper skin, one breastcups of ferret skin, and one a lambskin chemise.[94] The details sound amazingly closely observed for somebody allegedly spying from above without being detected, and the suspicion must remain that this was a tall story.

It is very likely that a yet more diligent search of the folklore collections and related records would turn up a few more examples of beliefs and opinions like those listed above. What it could hardly alter is their context—that they are infrequent and isolated pieces of information embedded in a huge mass of material testifying to the notion that English and Welsh witches were on the whole, like the cunning people, individuals who worked by themselves, even if they did so within a common tradition. Indeed, to be an anti-social, isolated, figure was itself one of the traits which marked a person out as a probable witch in local opinion. The very word 'coven', generally used in twentieth-century England to indicate a group of witches, is unknown in the earlier material. This because it is not English at all, but Scottish; indeed, as the *Oxford English Dictionary* makes clear, it was not even in popular use in Scotland, but derives from one sensational and very atypical case of alleged witchcraft, the confession of Isobel Gowdie in 1662. Nineteenth-century scholars, from Sir Walter Scott onwards, relied heavily upon this confession for details of how Scottish witches were supposed to have behaved, and so gave the word a wider currency, which it subsequently gained in England also, as writers there drew upon the more dramatic Scottish material.

* * *

Did cunning folk have a separate, secret system of religious belief? Here, again, some confusion has been created by scholarship. In 1976 James Obelkevitch published his famous pioneering monograph upon popular religion in Victorian England, a case-study of the southern part of the Lincolnshire chalk hills. Throughout it, he consistently used the term 'paganism' to describe popular magical practices, on the grounds that some of these almost certainly predated Christianity, and that they embodied a view of the natural world, and of the human place in it, somewhat different from the Christian one. At one point, however, he himself made the comment that although the label was 'convenient', it was also 'misleading', because popular magic represented 'not a distinct and conscious movement or organization but a loose agglomeration of religious phenomena. It was not a counter-religion to Christianity; rather, the two coexisted and complemented each other'.[95] This conclusion was echoed by Willem de Blecourt, surveying what is known of cunning folk in Europe as a whole; their work did not reflect a single cosmology, but was made up of the debris of many.[96] It is endorsed by the whole body of work produced so far by Owen Davies, and cited above.

What this meant in practice is that cunning people varied as much in their religious attitudes as most members of the society around them. Obelkevitch contrasted those of three famous practitioners from his chosen area of Lincolnshire: 'Fiddler' Fynes, who regularly attended church with every sign of piety, John Worsdale of Lincoln, who was a devout Christian but denied the need for professional clergy, and Stainton of Louth, who shunned worship, stating that once a man becomes a wizard, 'the Devil has hold' of him for good. Even Stainton, however, did not regard himself as representing a different religion.[97] An especially tragic extension of his attitude was recorded by a minister in another part of the same county, the Marshland. He was called to the bedside of a dying wise-woman called Mary Atkin, who was in terrible fear that she was damned because she had cursed as well as blessed in the practice of her craft. He did all that he could to console and reassure her, but she died screaming that the Devil had come for her; the horror of the experience was something that he never forgot.[98] Across the rest of England and Wales, the pattern of attitudes found in Lindsey seems to be repeated. Bridget Bostock, Marianne Vooden, John Wrightson, and Jenkins of Trellech were all noted for an unusually intense Christian piety, but the other cunning folk seem to have been wholly unexceptional in this regard.

A different light is shed upon the question by their techniques, which very often contained a large component of Christianity. This was especially true of charming, where prayer was often used as the healing spell in itself. Looking at the recorded charms dispensed by magical practitioners, it is obvious that many—perhaps the majority—are Christian in character. They quote from the Bible,[99] or appeal to the Trinity,[100] or to Jesus,[101] or to saints.[102] In most cases, to be sure, they are using the trappings and symbols of Christianity with little regard to what churchmen would have regarded as its essence; the Bible, for example, is regularly treated as a magical object in itself, with intrinsic benevolent power, rather than as a vehicle for a theological message. This is, however, a large part of what popular Christianity had always been about, and something that had caused learned and devout members of the faith to tear their hair at intervals ever since the time of the Church Fathers. It would have mattered just as much to most clergy of the Church of England that some of the charms were very clearly modelled upon the beliefs and formulae of the medieval Christianity which the Reformation was supposed to have swept away; but these relics of old Catholicism are another feature of popular culture between the sixteenth and nineteenth centuries. At times, the use of religious forms seemed to tip over into blasphemy, such as the recital of the Lord's Prayer or passages of Scripture backwards. On examination, however, the intention seems in each known case to have been pious enough; in one to exorcise the Devil,[103] in another to break the spell of a witch,[104] and in a third to charm out a thorn, as if the reversal of the words reversed the process which had planted it in the flesh.[105] There is apparently no known case of a cunning person or charmer calling upon a pagan deity.

Conversely, there was little doubt about witches in the popular mind; as beings given over to evil and to malice, they had to owe allegiance to the Devil or to demons. All over Wales and its Borders, there was a strong belief that the spell of witches could be broken if they were forced to bless their victims in the name of God.[106] In Shropshire an identical cautionary tale was reported about two different suspected witches in the nineteenth century, Priss Morris and Betty Chidley; that on being made to pronounce the blessing they tried to alter the words to 'my God', but were prevented and so coerced into undoing their magic. The story makes plain that Satan was the alternative being whom they tried to invoke.[107] From Herefordshire and Somerset to Lincolnshire people believed that witches made pacts with him.[108] In East Anglia this tradition took a strongly marked local form, of the familiar or imp, a small demon who was acquired by a witch and imparted the ability to work destructive magic. Most witches were held to own several, multiplying that power. They were usually believed to be visible in animal form. Sometimes this was fantastic, like the cross between frog and rat allegedly owned by a Cambridgeshire woman or the 'creepy-crawly things' which one in Essex was said to feed in a circle, with chopped grass.[109] More often it was that of a recognizable household pet, particularly white mice, which local opinion still held to be somewhat unnatural; and the possession of such pets could be another factor in maturing suspicions of witchcraft against an individual.[110] It is quite possible that pre-Christian mythology lies behind the tradition, but no eighteenth- or nineteenth-century record of popular belief charges witches with worshipping pagan deities.

*   *   *

Did cunning folk and charmers inherit their craft, and were witches presumed to do the same? Here the answer seems to vary sharply between the three groups. The talent required to practise as a cunning person seems to have been as individual and capricious in its appearance as one for music, mathematics, eloquence, or charm, or the possession of physical beauty. The clearest case of a dynasty of such people is the Harries family of Cwrt y Cadno, and here the ability or application effectively lasted for just two generations. It began with Henry (1739–1805), who cannot really be counted as a *dyn hysbys* as he had no reputation for one; he was a yeoman farmer with an interest in medicine and astrology. These interests were developed into a proper practice by his son John (1785–1839), and still further by his elder grandson Henry (1821–49), who was succeeded after his death by the younger one, another John (1827–63). There, however, it ended, for the children of neither Henry nor John showed any inclination to follow their fathers' craft.[111] Owen Davies has uncovered a few more cases in which inheritance played some part. The famous Midland wise-man Richard Morris (1710–93), known as 'Dick Spot' because of a mole on his face, was trained by an aunt. In Yorkshire Hannah Green was succeeded by a daughter and Tim Crowther by one of his sons, while a grandson of 'Old Savage' of Llangurig picked up his ways after a one-generation lapse.[112] In Essex there were the two Pickingills, to be discussed later.

Against these must be set the crashing failures. Both Cunning Murrell and John Wrightson tried desperately to train a son to follow them, with no success; the latter eventually left his books to a nephew, who made a serious attempt to be worthy of them, but ended up completely discredited.[113] A wise-woman at Kettlethorpe, in the Trent valley near Lincoln, died in the 1880s with great hopes that her son had inherited her prowess, but these too were disappointed.[114] It seems that the overwhelming majority of cunning folk were the only people in their families to practise this craft. The largely accidental appearance of the combination of interest and aptitude was to some extent recognized in the popular belief that it manifested with particular strength in seventh children of seventh children; both Murrell and Wrightson claimed this status, and so did a few others.[115]

The situation was different among the more numerous and less prestigious class of charmers. As the skill of each normally consisted of a single technique, for the cure of a specific ailment or group of ailments, it was much more easily passed on through families, or to a close friend. Very often the charm was given by the simple act of writing it down, or embodied in an amulet or other object—in one case a piece of rope. One Devon man claimed that he had received it by being placed in snow just after his birth, and before he was washed. Occasionally the healing power was said to be inherent in a blood-line; a farmer's wife who cured shingles in nineteenth-century Montgomeryshire said that her ability derived from an ancestor who had eaten eagle's flesh, and would continue for nine generations after his time. In the West Country there was a further tradition—not universal even there—that the charm should be passed down between members of the opposite gender: for example father–daughter–grandson. In one Cornish case the charm itself could only work upon members of the opposite sex to the charmer. It seems that this belief is mostly recorded in the twentieth century, and it may have been strengthened by the influence of Sir John Rhys's famous book on folklore, which recorded it as obtaining in the Isle of Man.[116]

The power of witches was also believed at times to descend through kin, but this was largely a side-effect of the simple phenomenon that certain families who had a bad local reputation in general were rumoured to dabble in witchcraft as well as other sorts of anti-social behaviour. The principal recorded examples from the nineteenth century are the Sloleys, at Porlock on the Somerset coast, the Harts, of Latchingdon in eastern Essex, a nameless family at Llanddona on the north coast of Anglesey, another at Denbigh, and a third in the Gwaun valley of Pembrokeshire. The response of the suspects themselves varied greatly. The women of the Llanddona people cashed in on their bad name by demanding charity at nearby farms, with the threat of curses if they refused. Those in the Gwaun, by contrast, regularly attended the Baptist chapel at Caersalem with every sign of devotion; but their neighbours still insisted that they dealt in bad magic.[117]

Far more common was the belief that the power of the witch was a personal one, which was passed on as she approached death and indeed had to be given to a new owner before she could die. Usually this was considered to occur by a transference of spiritual force, such as by breathing into the mouth of the recipient, although it could also do so in the tangible form of custody of the animal familiars or of a book of magic.[118]

The only account of anything resembling an initiation ritual involving witches consists of a cautionary tale from Crosby in the Humberside marshes of Lincolnshire. It describes how an old witch tried to persuade a young apprentice to offer her soul to the Devil by bending over, touching her toes, and saying: 'All that I 'ave a-tween me finger-tips an' me toes I give to thee.' The girl did this, but immediately added the words 'God Almighty', and so escaped damnation.[119]

*   *   *

Did cunning folk and charmers expect payment for their services, and did any make large profits? Here again, there is a difference between the two groups. Charmers usually regarded their healing power as a gift, to be used for the good of humanity, and therefore thought it wrong to demand payment; but there were two qualifications to this rule. One is that it was not observed by all, exceptions including a thrush-charmer at Ilmington in Warwickshire's Red Horse Vale during the 1840s, who charged a fixed fee. The other is that patients usually gave a present to the healer by way of gratitude, and these rewards in kind (such as food and drink) could be a significant supplement to income. Here too, however, there were noble exceptions, such as pious Luke Page (d. 1905), a retired butcher at St Brivael's in the Forest of Dean, who was kept busy curing humans and animals alike, and thought it wrong even to be thanked for what he saw as a duty enjoined by the Christian god. There is some evidence that charmers were more inclined to expect recompense in the nineteenth century, when extra earnings were more crucially needed, than in the twentieth.[120]

With cunning folk, exactly the opposite situation was true; in general, they charged fees for their services as any other craftspeople would do. It is very rare to find one like Mother Herne (mentioned earlier), who did not ask for money but expected a present in kind; she worked, moreover, very late in the tradition, living into the 1930s.[121] The rule was a system of fixed payment, although in an unregulated craft this naturally varied between practitioners. Cunning Murrell charged a halfpenny for curing warts and 2s.6d. for breaking a witch's spell.[122] Henry Harries usually asked £1 for a charm or spell, but moderated this for poorer people.[123] Further north in the Cambrian Mountains, 'Penny Mary' Evans got her nickname because this was her standard rate for telling a fortune—but gentry had to pay 2s.6d. At Birmingham in the 1870s, Ann Archer charged 4d. for the same service.[124] An astrologer operating at Hull in the 1860s levied 2s.6d. for each horoscope, while during the same decade John Rhodes was asking only 1s. for one in the Manchester area; but the clientele of the Hull man was both smaller and socially more select.[125] 'Black Jack', a wizard at Newcastle-upon-Tyne in the early nineteenth century, asked £1 for taking off a curse, while in the 1860s the Staffordshire cunning man James Tunnicliffe had a tariff for the same service: 5s. for human being or horse, 3s.6d. for a cow, and 4s. for a cheese vat. In Lincolnshire Stainton of Louth wanted £2 to remove bewitchment, while 'Fiddler' Fynes, whose catchment area was more localized, required 5s.[126] 'Devil' Dunn, of Dudley in the Midlands' Black Country (d. 1851) asked 1s. for a charm against toothache.[127] Sometimes these rates were proof against alteration in either direction; a farmer in north Dorset during the 1900s offered a local wise-woman £5 for a pot of ointment to cure his eczema, and was informed crisply that the charge was the usual £1.[128]

It was apparently just as common for a system of fees to be ad hoc. Sarah McDonald, a fortune-teller of Bethnal Green, London, gave a woman a series of treatments in 1858, which were intended to cure her of bewitchment and added up eventually to 14s.6d.[129] A 'pellar' at Helston in west Cornwall asked 7s.6d. from an old man for a charm to cure his rheumatism, but exacted a promise of a further £5 if it worked![130] Some preferred payment in kind, such as the Somerset wise-woman who demanded two live hens and a live rabbit for breaking a particular bewitchment.[131] Another, in the Black Country in 1881, received groceries worth 1s.6d. from a female client who wanted the same aid.[132] Bills went up as requests moved into morally dubious areas, so that a Norfolk women charged 2s.6d. to cover her clients' enemies in lice, and a Somerset wise-man required £10 to help a young woman to entrap a man.[133] In the world of magic, as in that of more orthodox crime, the most expensive service was a contract killing. The cunning man who was supposed to have put paid to Hannah Henley received £100 for his work.[134] This was probably considered a good investment in view of the protection racket which she had operated; and she had her counterparts elsewhere. A man at Buxton on the Norfolk clay plateau found himself paying 2s.6d. a week to a self-declared witch in order to keep himself free of her spells. Mother Henley of Burnt Fen in Cambridgeshire went around at night in the 1860s and 1870s putting grave-shaped mounds on the doorsteps of her neighbours. In the morning she would inform them that these were the signs of lethal curses, which she would remove for a fee of 2s.6d.[135]

This panorama suggests that the sums charged by cunning folk were large enough to promise handsome returns if custom were sufficient—and for many it clearly was. The regional fame of Murrell, Wrightson, Harries, and other aristocrats of the craft would have guaranteed them large receipts, and some lesser characters clearly enjoyed considerable success. One was the pale-faced Somerset wizard who was eventually murdered in his cottage; 'on a Sunday afternoon there was a queue of vehicles from carriages and pairs to donkey carts in the lane' outside.[136] One client of the north Staffordshire wise-man Elijah Cotton found six people in his waiting-room, while a pair of women seeking to consult Ann Archer found ten others in the queue ahead of them. 'Devil' Dunn sold his charm against toothache to thousands of customers.[137] Owen Davies has provided some striking examples of the wealth which could result. Hannah Green was said to have left £1,000 upon her death in 1810. It was said of a later Yorkshire wise-woman, who died in the early 1870s, that 'Every drawer in her house was crammed with rich and costly dresses and shawls; and the cupboards contained over three dozen silver or silver-gilt tea and coffee pots, with a vast number of silver cups and silver spoons.' Of cunning men, the Mancunian Richard Morris left a considerable estate in trust, James Baker of Morden, Dorset, was able to buy a house and a few acres of land from his proceeds, and James Tuckett of Exeter was able to lease three properties in 1841.[138]

This needs to be set in perspective. In general, the cunning folk do not seem to have prospered more than other small traders and craftspeople who were good at their work, and those who did best were often precisely the people who combined magic with an equally successful practice of their regular occupation. William Thomas was said to make an average £300 a year at Exeter at the opening of the twentieth century, but that was because he was a noted herbalist as well as a wise-man. Richard Evans, a resident of the mid-Welsh town of Llanidloes in the late eighteenth century, prospered enough to put up buildings; but he was a successful shopkeeper in addition to being a dyn hysbys.[139] Fiddler Fynes ran the school at Kirkstead, played the violin which inspired his nickname, was greatly respected as a cunning man, and styled himself as one of the gentry; yet it was also noted that despite all these sources of income he remained relatively poor, with one decent suit of clothes.[140] It is clear that there were many better roads to riches than through cunning craft, and that the material rewards of the latter merely helped to maintain most of those who practised it in a more comfortable occupation of their existing station in life; or conversely, to prevent them from sliding into poverty in old age. It is fairly obvious also that most of them enjoyed their practice of it, and that the prestige which it gave them was at least as important a motive for their engagement in it as financial benefit.

*   *   *

Did cunning craft, however, make life less comfortable for its practitioners in legal ways? Did they exist in constant fear of prosecution and persecution by Church and State? Here, Owen Davies has, again, made a pioneering study of the evidence. The modern legal history of witchcraft begins with the passage of the so-called Witchcraft Act of 1736, which repealed all the early modern statutes that had prescribed penalties for using witchcraft and made it an offence to call somebody else a witch. It also, however, created a series of punishments for people who *claimed* to work magic, the maximum being a year's imprisonment. It was, in short, a heavy-handed piece of Enlightenment rationalism, based upon the premise that witchcraft and magic were illusory, and that the public needed to be weaned away from a belief in them. Davies has shown that for most of the rest of the eighteenth century the statute remained more or less a dead letter, as educated opinion generally presumed that growing education would eventually take care of the problem in any case, without need of a legal campaign. He has also suggested, with considerable but less secure probability, that there was almost as little attempt to prosecute crowds for direct physical attacks upon suspected witches, to compensate for the formal charges which were no longer possible against them.

In Owen Davies's reconstruction of events, a change in attitudes occurred at the opening of the nineteenth century, as members of the social elite came to perceive that a faith in magic seemed to be as prevalent among the populace as it had been a hundred years before, even while a growing political turbulence among commoners gave their rulers a new interest in the idea of education and civility as stabilizing forces. Ignorance, superstition, criminality, and insurrection seemed increasingly to make up a single package, and one result of this realization was a growing number of prosecutions under the 1736 Act and then considerably more under a new statute which was brought in to reinforce it in 1824. This was commonly known as the Vagrancy Act, and outlawed 'persons pretending or professing to tell fortunes, or using any subtle craft, means and device, by palmistry or otherwise, to deceive and impose'. If enforced wholesale, it would have wiped out cunning folk and charmers, and indeed it did make their existence significantly more difficult. The number of court cases which it generated rose still further after the establishment of professional county police forces in 1851. On the other hand, those same new police forces effectively wiped out the mobbing of suspected witches. That had also been the object of increased prosecution during the early nineteenth century, but the existence of a professional local constabulary meant that people who led crowds to attack suspected witches could be arrested in action, instead of (as hitherto) after the event. Davies has been able to find no case of a witch-mobbing after the death of poor 'Dummy' at Sible Hedingham in 1863,[141] though individual attacks on suspects continued long into the twentieth century. Court appearances by cunning folk were regular though not frequent events throughout the late Victorian and Edwardian periods, and from the 1900s a campaign against astrology and cunning craft was launched in some journals of the new mass-circulation press. On the other hand, an Occultists' Defence League was founded in the 1890s, and from the 1910s prosecutions began to wane, with more sympathy shown for the defendants in newspaper reports. The decline persisted until both the relevant Acts were repealed in 1951.[142]

A closer examination of prosecutions strongly suggests that they represented not a constant menace to cunning people, but an accident which befell a small proportion of them who were either unusually unlucky or behaved with marked folly or mendacity. One part of this category is occupied by those few who simply advertised themselves too wantonly, such as the itinerant wise-man who had twenty thousand handbills printed to proclaim his skills to the people of Radnorshire in 1867.[143] Most of it, however, is comprised of practitioners who were denounced to magistrates or police by dissatisfied customers. Some were simply crooks, masquerading as practitioners of magic, such as Sarah Roxborough, who tried to steal £25 from a Stafford housewife in 1823 under pretence of working a spell for her husband, in which the notes were involved. Another was the female gypsy tried before the Oxford circuit in 1859 for relieving another woman of all her valuables, with the promise that by burying them under a charm she would cause them to multiply.[144] More common were prosecutions brought by clients who were both disappointed and had been charged unusually high fees. James Tunnicliffe, whose fixed tariff for enchantment-busting has been mentioned, pushed his luck over the brink when he took the case of a farmer with a house afflicted by unusually stubborn apparent poltergeist activity. Tunnicliffe deprived the farmer of £37, in instalments, and then the cost of supporting him for almost a year, as the wizard moved in to mount a running battle against the spirits. Eventually his host's patience ran out, and Tunnicliffe ended up on a charge which put him in prison for twelve months. A gypsy woman in Cornwall also went down after repeatedly taking money from a gardener at the little port of St Mawes, to protect him from the evil eye. She carried on this work for twenty-five years, costing him a total of £500, before his credulity suddenly ran out in 1928. Other offenders were cunning folk gone to the bad, like Isaac Rushworth at Leeds, who was put away for eighteen months in 1857 for seducing a girl and defrauding her of her money, threatening to curse her if she reported him; he drove her insane.[145] Occasionally a local protection racket collapsed, such as that of Aquila Hewitt at Great Yarmouth, who was given nine months in 1928 for extorting money from her neighbours with the menace of bewitchment if they refused.[146]

Even well-behaved practitioners could run into trouble with customers. A wise-man living near Whitby in the nineteenth century probably thought that he was doing no more than his duty when he prescribed a charm for a sick girl;

but she had tuberculosis, and when she died her grief-crazed family blamed him and laid a charge. He was given the choice between two months in gaol and refunding the money which he had received for the case, plus the court expenses.[147] A parallel, though less tragic, example is that of the woman at Downside in east Somerset who believed herself bewitched in 1856 and consulted a wise-woman at the local market town of Shepton Mallet. The treatment which she was given made her ill, and she complained to neighbours who had the practitioner put away for six months.[148] Allied to this problem was the less straightforward one that a client who had come to be relieved of a curse, and who did not feel better after successive treatments, might end up convinced that the cunning person was in fact responsible for casting the original spell. In such a case, the client concerned sometimes ran to the law for protection, and that is how Sarah McDonald of Bethnal Green ended up in the dock in 1858, and the Devon wise-man Henry Hillman in 1892.[149] Ann Archer eventually fell foul of the law when she was denounced by two of her hordes of clients, whose fortunes had simply not turned out as she predicted, while a pair of similarly disappointed women were responsible for the apprehension of Clayton Chaffer.[150]

When this whole catalogue is put together, it still gives the impression that it included only a tiny percentage of the people involved in providing magical services, even at the apparent peak of prosecutions in the second half of the nineteenth century. During the eighteenth, as Owen Davies has indicated, cunning folk seem to have been virtually immune from legal harassment, and in the first half of the nineteenth there is no indication that grandees such as Murrell, Wrightson, or Harries ever worried about the law, let alone collided with it. Even in the later, more fraught, period, most accounts of the work of cunning people contain no reference to their legal vulnerability and none to any consequences resulting. The charmers, concentrating upon specific ailments and usually taking payment in kind, were effectively immune from molestation, and so were most magical practitioners in rural areas. A famous magician such as John Rhodes of Salford, operating in an urban area with vigilant authorities in the period of most intense denunciation, should have been particularly at risk. In 1865, indeed, he was reported to the police by a customer and given a seven-day sentence; but the source which records this makes the point that he served hundreds of clients who never betrayed him, and his single week in custody was a small price to pay for such a successful practice.[151] Owen Davies has shown that astrologers (especially in London) advertised openly both with printed cards and in the press, including those very newspapers that were simultaneously inveighing against popular superstition. His own conclusion is that the campaign against cunning craft was ineffective, and admitted to be so even by those who encouraged it.[152] To succeed, it needed the support of local communities, and this was never given; until the early decades of the twentieth century, ordinary people valued magic too much.

* * *

Did cunning craft ever, in fact, decline? The folklorists who collected so much information about it in the period between 1870 and 1940 certainly thought that it was part of a vanishing rural world, and regarded its imminent demise with pleasure or nostalgic regret according to the viewpoint of the writer. It might be more objectively correct to say that it changed character, as some of its traditional functions atrophied and others developed. The availability of better policing and insurance services removed the need to appeal to magic to trace lost or stolen goods. Davies has suggested, to my mind convincingly, that people ceased to fear bewitchment as the almost complete destruction of the old, tightly knit, self-sufficient traditional communities by economic and social changes after the 1860s removed the context which bred such suspicions.[153] It could be added that this transformation allowed the educated disbelief in the literal power of witches to break through to a popular level at last, propelled by the modern mass media. On the other hand, astrology has persisted with considerable vigour and has been incorporated into the very structure of mass-distribution newspapers, and lesser forms of divination, such as card-readings, are still common. The same is true of herbalism and spiritual healing. Jim Tucker of Morchard Bishop in the hills of central Devon was a completely traditional rural charmer, who continued to receive thousands of requests for aid every year until his death—which was in the 1960s.[154] Such demand, and supply, still exists, but the suppliers are no longer likely to be called charmers, but to be identified with one of the techniques within the burgeoning fields of natural healing and therapy, such as naturopathy, homeopathy, hypnotherapy, herbalism, acupuncture, flower remedies, aromatherapy, and colour-healing.

At the time of writing this, in 1997, I have a friend who lives in a medium-sized English city. Her own professional training was in the business world, but, working from home, she also provides a range of services which fall within the categories of healing and divination. She casts horoscopes, reads tarot cards, deals in dietary therapy and homeopathy, and counsels people suffering from anxiety, sometimes merely dispensing advice, and sometimes recommending techniques of mediation and visualization. She also runs classes, or workshops, in the latter. This group of services is united by two themes. The first is that she considers her essential work to be to help her clients to know themselves better and so to operate more effectively. The second is that she believes that the basis of her skill lies in communication with a group of spirits who have been her friends and advisers since childhood. Her religious beliefs are a mixture of Christianity, modern paganism, and native American tradition, but she thinks that the spirit world transcends all formal religious systems. Her skills were acquired by a mixture of reading, contact with other practitioners, and trial and error, all leavening a natural aptitude. She has no family tradition of such work, but it was crucial to her development of it that there was a strong belief in spiritualism, and some practice of exorcism, among her immediate forebears. The income which she earns from it provides a valuable supplement to her main sources, and she is approached by as many clients as she can possibly fit into her available time. All are attracted by a reputation fostered by word of mouth; she does not advertise her occult talents, and does not wish her neighbours to know about them, lest this harm her local reputation. She herself is happy to wear the label of 'wise-woman' when providing such services. It must be fairly obvious that the continuities between her way of operating and that of the old-style cunning folk are more striking than the differences; yet she does not refer to them as the tradition within which she operates, so much as to the contemporary international New Age culture.

It is an irony that, by contrast, many modern pagan witches identify themselves much more closely with traditional cunning craft, and yet, despite some linkages (which will become plain later), in their case the differences are much greater than the similarities. They have much more in common with the stereotypical images of witches in nineteenth-century popular culture; the very beings who were regarded as the natural enemies of the charmers and cunning people, representing the opposite aspect of magic. Even here, however, there are still major distinctions. Each of the chapters of this present book charts the way in which a particular facet of modern pagan witchcraft developed. It is a further paradox that the subject of the present one, which most modern witches have regarded as possessing the greatest obvious relevance, turns out to have had the least.

7

FINDING A FOLKLORE

ⵝⵝ

IN 1996 I published a history of seasonal festivities and rituals in Britain, which opened by questioning the view of the subject most commonly propagated by folklorists for most of the twentieth century.[1] I identified four main components to this. First, it characterized the only interesting calendar customs as rural, different in quality to the observances of towns and cities. Second, it regarded them as essentially timeless and immemorial, relics of a distant, often pagan, past, surviving like living fossils in the static world of English country people. Third, those people were themselves treated as inarticulate, having long lost or distorted any sense of the meaning of their customary behaviour, which could be recovered only by the research of scholarly outsiders. Fourth, this perception was infused with a wider sense of the countryside as a place of charm and of mystery, resistant to the changes of the modern epoch and representing to some extent an antidote to their more troubling aspects.

In the course of the book I repeatedly made the point that this construction of calendar customs has been rejected by folklorists since the 1970s, sometimes with savage criticism. I supported that process of revision, by presenting an alternative view of the ritual year as the object of continual evolution and redevelopment, involving both town and country, which adapted its rituals to the changing needs of the social groups concerned in them. In one part of the conclusion I suggested that further study was needed to answer the obvious question of why it was that so many English scholars between 1870 and 1970 were disposed to view the countryside as a timeless place in which immemorial practices were continued from a blind sense of tradition, and in particular practices that were held to be authentic traces of ancient pagan religion. The present chapter will attempt to provide such an answer.

Two other writers have already considered the problem, in different ways, during the past few years. One is a folklorist, Gillian Bennett, who has faced it head-on, by asking why her late Victorian and Edwardian predecessors were so obsessed with the notion of pagan survivals.[2] She found the answer in the example set by the flagship science of mid-Victorian England, the newly emerged one of geology. Integrated with the equally novel theory of evolution, this provided a view of the Earth's past as recorded in layer after layer of strata, the fossils of which provided evidence of the ascending scale of life-forms. Applied to the development of human culture, the geological model suggested that the minds of all humans worked in essentially the same way, but had developed at different rates, according to culture and class, along the same linear track. Folk customs, therefore, could represent cultural fossils, left over from the earlier stages of civilized societies, and a comparative study of them could provide a general theory of religious development for the human race. They could in fact act as the equivalent of textual evidence for pre-literate peoples.

This approach was pioneered in Britain in the 1870s and 1880s by Sir Edward Tylor, and popularized from 1890 onward by Sir James Frazer. It was especially taken up in the 1890s by the leading figures of the newly founded Folk-Lore Society, to whom it promised a way of rescuing the study of popular belief and observance from mere dilettantism and elevating it to the status of a real science. As Dr Bennett has also shown, this promise failed, as folklorists fell through the gap between the emerging disciplines of archaeology and anthropology, both of which found the comparative method, and the notion of social fossils, deeply flawed by the 1920s.

Gillian Bennett has thus admirably laid out the intellectual framework which supported the concept of folk customs as pagan survivals, and only two additions to her work need to be made for present purposes. The first is to note that the framework concerned was also an outgrowth of German Romanticism, with its quest for a unifying national identity which generated a new interest in rural culture as a promising hunting-ground for a 'definitive' Germanity. This interest inspired the Prussian scholar Wilhelm Mannhardt to make the first systematic collection of contemporary peasant customs, between 1860 and 1880, and to develop from it the first full-blown version of the theory of survivals. As the agricultural customs which he recorded were inevitably concerned overwhelmingly with the produce of humans, livestock, and fields, he tended to overemphasize ancient European religions as concerned with fertility rites, and made a leap beyond the evidence to assert that they had been focused upon the concept of animating spirits of vegetation.[3] Mannhardt functioned as a forerunner to Tylor, and a major influence upon Frazer.

Dr Bennett's work also resoundingly begged the question of why the notion of pagan survivals continued to grow in popularity, and was sustained by folklorists, even after that framework had collapsed inside the academy. Here an important insight is provided by the other author to touch upon the subject in recent years; the classicist Mary Beard. Her subject was the most ambitious and celebrated of all the works that attempted to create a history of religion by using the comparative method, Frazer's *The Golden Bough*, which went through three successive and ever larger editions between 1890 and 1915. She suggested that to Sir James himself, the book had represented a journey through an underworld of belief, in which the familiar rituals of the British countryside were integrally linked with savage and foreign rites in an exciting and unsettling way.[4]

An addition which might be proposed to this picture is that Frazer's own golden bough was the light of human reason, guiding him and his readership through primeval chaos and darkness. The hidden sub-text of both of the greatest

British exponents of the comparative method, Tylor and Frazer, was to discredit religion in general, and Christianity in particular, in order to assist the progress of humanity towards a more perfect rationalism. Both were lapsed Christians from radical Protestant backgrounds, Tylor's parents being Quakers, while Frazer's family were fervent members of the Free Church of Scotland. Both brought out of this inheritance an evangelical Protestant loathing for religious ritual and ornamentation, and for priesthood, to which their loss of faith added a milder contempt for any religious belief.[5]

Of the two, Sir Edward was the more straightforward in this respect. The theory of 'pagan survivals' was a major prop of both his faith in the overall progress of humanity and his determination to break the grip of primitive modes of thought upon modern life, by exposing them for what they were. His Quaker contempt for ritual made the Christian ceremonies of baptism or consecration as absurd to him as those of tribal religion, and he used the comparative technique to ridicule any notion of a spirit world: 'a modern medium is a Red Indian or a Tartan shaman in a dress coat'.[6] He and his fellow rationalist Andrew Lang (like Frazer, a refugee from Scottish Presbyterianism) issued a joint declaration of intent to 'theologians all to expose'.[7] Tylor's evangelical roots were never displayed more clearly than in his adoption of the theory of survivals itself, for although its scholarly application may have taken shape in Germany, in its crude form it had been a tactic developed by sixteenth-century Protestant polemicists to discredit Roman Catholic modes of worship. The device consisted of attempting to demonstrate that most of the ceremonies of the medieval Church had derived from pagan practices. It was extended by the same kind of writer to condemn forms of popular revelry which the reformers wished to suppress as immoral and disorderly, by suggesting that they were relics of heathendom.[8] Tylor was a puritan preacher, reclad as a Victorian liberal humanist.

The case of Frazer is more complex. On the one hand, there is no doubt that during his undergraduate years he became a confirmed atheist or agnostic, and that one of the purposes of *The Golden Bough* was to discredit Christianity.[9] The most important argument of the whole work was that ancient peoples had believed in a dying and reviving god, who represented the animating spirit of vegetation postulated by Mannheim and had been represented in human form by sacred kings, who were killed after a set term or when their power of mind or body failed. Frazer's implication was that the figure of Christ had been an outgrowth from this body of (to him erroneous and unnecessary) belief, and he may well have intended it to be the more effective in that it was never made blatantly. He came closest to stating it plainly in the second edition of *The Golden Bough*, when he suggested that both the Jewish Purim festival and the Christian story of the Crucifixion were derived from the sacrifice of men representing this nature-god.[10] If so, he continued, then this would reduce Jesus to 'the level of a multitude of other victims of a barbarous superstition'. Characteristically, however, he immediately covered himself by adding that a

Christian would see the preceding victims, instead, as part of the preparation for the redemption of humanity by a true Son of God. Frazer was not a Christian, and so the addition was ironic; but most of his readers were not to know that.

A similar sleight of pen is found six years later, in his *Adonis, Attis, Osiris* (1906), a concentrated study of dying and resurrecting gods of the Near East which repeatedly made the implicit parallel with Christ. At one point he broadened the attack to assert that Greek and Roman society had nobly subordinated the interest of individuals to that of the community, making public service the highest ideal of the citizen.[11] He went on to add that this was altered by 'the spread of the Oriental religions' which inculcated the 'selfish and immoral doctrine' that individual communion with the divine and personal salvation should be the main preoccupations of humanity. Frazer blamed this for the 'general disintegration of the body politic' in which the Roman Empire collapsed, and went on to suggest that it obsessed Europe for a thousand years. In his scheme it was the revival of knowledge of the classical ancient world, at the end of the Middle Ages, which restored Europe to 'native ideals of life and conduct' and 'saner, manlier' views of the world. Only then could 'the march of civilization' resume. The passage concludes triumphantly: 'The tide of Oriental invasion had turned at last. It is ebbing still.' What Sir James had done here was very audacious; he had taken the ancient charge that the original Roman culture had been polluted and enfeebled by Eastern cults and manners—used (as said above) by Victorians who wanted to extol Christianity without wholly denigrating classical paganism—and included the Christian faith itself among those cults. He had redesignated it as an alien, morally questionable, Oriental religion, opposed to the 'manly' spirit of Europeans. All that could rescue it, for devout British Christians reading this paragraph, was the assumption that Frazer was referring to the 'corrupt' Church of the Middle Ages, which had been purified by the Reformation. On the other hand, it is possible that some of them, coming across the passage in a discussion of ancient pagan cults, would not have grasped its point at all, as the author so studiously avoided mentioning Christianity by name.

This was, after all, Sir James at his boldest, and other aspects of his life and work suggest that the subtlety of his opposition to the established religion derived from sheer timidity. Throughout his long career as a Cambridge academic, he continued to attend Anglican church services even though he privately rejected their spiritual content—apparently because he thought it good social form to do so.[12] Moreover, the 1900s saw the high point of his covert sniping at Christianity, and in the next decade he drew back from it. In the third edition of the *Bough*, put into sequence between 1911 and 1915, he retracted his speculation that Jesus had been killed as a divine king, and praised his 'beautiful spirit'.[13] The abridged edition of 1922, which was the one most often read by the general public, embodied this softer approach, even though the parallel between the story of Christ and the alleged worship of the dying and returning vegetation spirit remained obvious. The effect was not so much to demolish the claims of

Christianity as to dilute and weaken them by setting them in a more general context of ancient religion.

If the general purpose of both Tylor and Frazer was to debunk spirituality and to elevate reason, they also shared a moral disgust for the practices of the ancient and tribal peoples whom they considered. Tylor's *Primitive Culture* is littered with expressions such as 'hideous', 'atrocious', 'pernicious', 'contemptible', 'savage', and 'barbaric'. Frazer's style was more clinical, but his withering contempt showed through at times. It was never displayed more clearly than in his inaugural lecture as Professor of Social Anthropology at Liverpool University, in 1908. Contemplating the modern folk customs of which he had made such heavy use in his work, he commented loftily that 'superstitions survive because, while they shock the views of enlightened members of the community, they are still in harmony with the thoughts and feelings of others who, though they are drilled by their betters into an appearance of civilization, remain barbarians and savages at heart'.[14] In fairness to both men, it must be pointed out that not only were their attitudes typical of the intellectual culture of their place and time, but that they took care to emphasize that humanity represented a single family, of which barbarism and savagery were the childhood. Tylor in particular urged the need to take seriously, and to study, the ways of tribal peoples, because by this process more advanced nations were learning something about themselves.[15] However patronizing, the language of these scholars was still a liberal and humanitarian one. By contrast, the opposed contemporary discourse which postulated the existence of a golden age of wisdom in the remote past, represented by a single state or people (such as Atlantis), had a more dangerous potential for racism and authoritarianism.

Tylor and Frazer were also linked by the fact that their evangelical aim inspired them to write for the widest possible public, and that they possessed the talent to do so. Tylor's *Primitive Culture* was a model of lucidity and colourful use of example, and enjoyed proportionate fame. Both his care and his ability in this regard were far surpassed by Frazer, who set out to make *The Golden Bough* into a classic work of literature. In a manner extraordinary for most writers, let alone most academic writers, he prescribed the cover picture, the cover engraving, the typeface and size, the quality of the paper, the number of lines per page, and the name of the firm of printers, which he deemed to be essential for the book.[16] All this effort paid off, although the public took more than twenty years to take widespread notice of it and (ironically) it became a bestseller just as respect for it among anthropologists was crumbling. Once its sales had taken off, they became phenomenal; having gone through four editions between 1890 and 1922, the *Bough* hurtled through another fifty-one between 1922 and 1955, and thereafter reappeared as a paperback, which is still in print. Its images became part of the Western popular consciousness, and influenced the work of T. S. Eliot, Ezra Pound, W. B. Yeats, Edith Sitwell, Robert Graves, E. M. Forster, James Joyce, D. H. Lawrence, John Synge, Wyndham Lewis, John Buchan, Joseph Conrad, and a host of lesser creative writers.[17]

It is equally clear, however, that the emotional purpose which had driven Frazer (and Tylor) was not shared by most of this huge readership. The literary impact of *The Golden Bough*, the reviews given to it in popular newspapers,[18] and the use made of it by later folklorists (to be considered below), all testify that it inspired, in varying proportions, a prurient, sensuous, and romantic pleasure. Tylor and Frazer arguably did succeed in doing further damage to the status of Christianity, but fostered not so much an enhanced respect for rationalism and progress as a delight in the primitive and the unreasonable. It is time to commence a systematic analysis of why this was so.

* * *

The first and most obvious component in the phenomenon is the tremendous idealization of rural England which commenced at the end of the eighteenth century and reached an apogee between 1880 and 1930; indeed, it might be called a plateau, as it has not diminished significantly since. It has been well studied in recent years by Raymond Williams, Martin Wiener, Jan Marsh, W. J. Keith, Alun Howkins, and Gillian Bennett.[19] The shift of emotion involved can be attributed to a single and simple process; that in 1810 about 80 per cent of English people lived in the countryside, and by 1910 about 80 per cent lived in towns. The balance tipped neatly around 1850, and to observers in the late nineteenth century the speed and scale of this unprecedented change promised a twentieth-century England consisting of one smoking conurbation from coast to coast.

The new mass urban and industrialized lifestyle was condemned not just because it was frighteningly novel and because its setting was perceived as being ugly, but because it was supposed to be physically and mentally unhealthy. The countryside became credited with all the virtues which were the obverse of those vices. It was not simply regarded as being more beautiful and healthy, but as being stable, dependable, rooted, and timeless. Its working people became credited with a superior wisdom, founded upon generations of living in close contact with nature and inheriting a cumulative hidden knowledge. This organic, immemorial lore was viewed as both a comforting force of resistance to the dramatic and unsettling changes of the nineteenth century and as a potential force for redemption. It was a remarkable revolution in perception, for hitherto rustics had usually been portrayed by leaders of literary taste as the principal reservoir of ignorance, blind superstition, brutal manners, and political reaction, within which towns formed islands of liberalism, education, progress, and refinement. Suddenly the urban centres had turned into monsters, destroying the world about them and spreading ill health, pollution, ugliness, and social instability. The shrinking and depopulating countryside—especially the soft arable and downland landscape of southern England—had become the epitome of continuity, community, and social harmony.

By the second half of the nineteenth century, mere contact with the open country could be represented as an act of grace. Between 1878 and 1880 a

Londoner called Richard Jeffries turned out five popular books on the delights of rusticity. One of them, *The Amateur Poacher*, concluded with the appeal to 'get out of these indoor narrow modern days, where twelve hours have some-how become shortened, into the sunlight and pure wind. A something the ancients called divine can be found and felt there still.' Yes indeed: as illustrated earlier, many writers of the time called that 'something' Pan, while others spoke of Mother Nature or Mother Earth. Most who worked in the genre did not personify it, but still wrote of the rural landscape with the same fervent sense of an animating spirit. As Jan Marsh has put it, 'Love of Nature helped many late Victorians to dispense with God gradually, as it were, without losing their sense of immanent divinity. Others, who continued to believe, found in Nature and Nature poetry an expression of quasi-religious feeling that fed their spiritual needs'.[20]

Jeffries was one of the first authors to serve the full-blown modern cult of rural nostalgia. Others who followed included W. H. Hudson, George Sturt (writing under the name of George Bourne), John Masefield, Edward Thomas, and Harold Massingham. A few creative writers of the first rank took it up and made it their own, most notably Thomas Hardy, Rudyard Kipling, and Kenneth Grahame. The last two in particular drove home the sense of an immemorial accumulation of experience and tradition, changing only in outward forms. Grahame spent his whole professional life in the literal heart of the City of London, the Bank of England, and to him the country represented a haven from a daily work which he loathed. Kipling, as is well known, passed much of his own life in India, and so the eternal and essential England represented a yet more distant fantasy for him than for Grahame; when he eventually retired to Sussex, he described it as 'the most wonderful foreign land I have ever been in'.[21]

This construction of Englishness was not merely produced by native writers, but enjoined upon them by Americans, who saw it as a reassuring emotional tap-root for their own even more dynamic and novel civilization. It was already a central aspect of the work of Washington Irving in the 1810s and 1820s. By the time that Nathaniel Hawthorne addressed an American readership on the subject of *Our Old Home* in 1863, it had long been a commonplace, but no less potent for that. His England was a place in which 'the man who died yesterday or ever so long ago walks the village street today, and chooses the same wife that he married a hundred years ago since, and must be buried again tomorrow under the kindred dust that has already covered him half a score of times'.[22]

This language was meshed from the beginning with another, which was like-wise especially taken up by the newly expanded and enriched urban middle classes. It drew on similar fears of social disorder and breakdown occasioned by the same tremendous economic changes, and was summed up in the two words 'Merrie England'. It has also been the subject of some intense recent study, most notably by Alice Chandler, John Burrow, Fiona MacCarthy, and Roy Judge.[23] This language characterized pre-industrial England as a land of social stability and harmony, operating above all through communal festivity. The same

process of thought (or emotion) led to a conclusion that a revival of such festivities, above all the old May Games, would serve both to stabilize and to revitalize
society. Such ideas were expressed by a succession of literary giants, from Scott,
Wordsworth, and Coleridge near the beginning of the century, through
Tennyson in the middle, to William Morris near the end. In the first half of the
period they tended to be associated most closely with conservatives, above all
the 'Young England' group of the 1840s. In 1858 George Eliot could refer to them
perceptively as 'a little Toryism by the sly, revelling in regret'.[24] By the later
Victorian age, however, they had been taken over wholesale by socialists, and
especially those who felt that working people needed to be redeemed from the
perceived squalor and vulgarity of the new urbanized and commercialized mass
culture.

This was precisely the spirit which inspired some of the most important
figures in the revival of English folk songs and dances which took off from the
1890s. Sir Hubert Parry, inaugurating the Folk Song Society in 1898, said that
such songs embodied 'the quiet reticence of our country folk, courageous and
content', in contrast to 'the boundless regions of sham' represented by the new
commercialized popular music.[25] Similar sentiments moved the other leading
collectors of that decade and the next: Cecil Sharp, Mary Neal, Vaughan
Williams, Sabine Baring-Gould, and Percy Grainger. J. Bruce Glasier, praising
their work in *The Labour Leader* in 1908, declared that 'Not only was "Merrie
England" once a reality, but its reality is full of promise and instruction to us
concerning the Merrier England this is to be.' In the words of their historian, Vic
Gammon, the collectors perceived rural folk singers as 'a sort of musical noble
savage, in a way apart from the modern world'. They helped to foster 'a spurious
myth of "Englishness" divorced from class experience and culture'.[26]

From its foundation in 1878, the Folk-Lore Society was bound up with the
service and propagation of this myth. When its members considered the beliefs
and customs of the modern English, they were almost wholly those of the rural
population, precisely because these were assumed not to be modern. In 1993
Gillian Bennett bemoaned the fact that until the 1960s British folklorists had
been concerned with 'a world of dreams and shadows', 'popularizing an image of
Britain, and particularly England, as a rural haven'. To her, *The Golden Bough*
had completed the legitimization of this work in the eyes of the public, making
folklorists 'the high priests and priestesses of the rural myth'.[27] It is ironic that
exactly a hundred years before, one of the founders of the society had made
more or less the same complaint. This was Joseph Jacobs, who looked, aghast, at
the work of his colleagues and declared that the concept of 'the folk' was 'a fraud,
a delusion, a myth', merely 'a name for our ignorance'. He demanded to know
why modern popular culture such as the music hall was not as fit a subject for
study by the society as the ways of country people.[28] His, however, was an
isolated voice, completely at odds with most of his literary world.

It is important not to overstate the shortcomings of the 'rural myth' or to
underestimate the utility of the work which it helped to inspire. Most of the

individuals who collected folklore in late Victorian and Edwardian Britain were not starry-eyed Londoners but people rooted in the localities about which they wrote, and integrated into them. The vast quantities of information which they gathered represent a major primary source for social history, and although by the standards of later scholarship it is usually badly deficient in context and presentation, it is often remarkably comprehensive; the collectors stockpiled hundreds of pieces of evidence that the 'folk' at the time were often far from being as wise, patient, good-humoured, or perceptive as the myth suggested. Jeffries, Hudson, and the other writers to romanticize the countryside also presented much closely observed and accurate detail about it. The problem is, rather, one of interpretation; that the *meaning* of what these collectors and authors recorded was determined according to a complex of emotions and preconceptions which now appear very questionable. Even those who lived in rural areas were often affected by these, partly because they were responding to a market and to a dominant intellectual metropolitan culture, and partly because they were reacting to the same social and economic processes. The most striking case is probably that of the Edwardian folk-song collector Alfred Williams. He was both rural in origin and working class, being brought up in a village and later making his living in a factory; yet when he published his collections, he romanticized country life as much as any other writer of the time. In the words of his biographer, he 'seemed to possess an ability to ignore anything which was not in keeping with his rose-coloured rural scene'.[29]

*   *   *

At first sight it is still by no means obvious why this sentiment should have attached itself to the notion of *pagan* survivals. After all, medieval and Tudor England (the period most commonly designated 'merrie') was formally a Christian society, and its parish churches remain as enduring and often beloved components of the modern rural landscape. They were certainly more constant, solid, and obvious symbols of communality and stability of the country people of Chaucer's, Shakespeare's, and Victoria's ages alike than maypoles and group dances. The characters of *The Canterbury Tales*, the Robin Hood ballads, and the Arthurian cycle—the most widely-read pieces of medieval English literature in the nineteenth century—are all presented as Christians of varying degrees of education and devotion.

On closer inspection, reasons for the apparent conundrum rapidly appear. The simplest and most obvious is that at no time after 1870 was British intellectual culture prone to a large-scale reaction in favour of established religion. The dominant trends were all in the opposite direction. An equally important, and more subtle, factor in the situation lay in the very nature of a conception of rural England as an organic continuum with ancient roots, preserving timeless wisdom. To foster this, all major upheavals had to be airbrushed out of the picture. The Reformation was one, and the conversion to Christianity another.

The old religious were part of the deep humus of experience out of which the eternal England had grown.

Such a notion was articulated successively by three of the early leaders of the Folk-Lore Society. Sidney Hartland got the ball rolling in the first issue of the society's periodical, in 1890, by interpreting the legend of Lady Godiva as an example of a pagan fertility rite later converted into an occasion for Christian civic pride.[30] The following year Sir Lawrence Gomme endorsed this opinion, pointing out that most folk tales and fairy stories did not have an obvious religious content and arguing from that (more dubiously) that they therefore had to be pre-Christian. In 1892 he repeated this theory, and made a further extrapolation from it, without actual research—that English commoners remained essentially pagan until the seventeenth century, when they were finally converted to Christianity by 'Puritan' evangelism. In his view, therefore, until then the new religion had been understood, and accepted, only by the social elite. To Gomme, the process of conversion was also one of assimilation, the old rites continuing beside the established faith in the form of customary practices. His attitude to the matter was a logical extension of his vision of the English village community, as a unit which 'originated at a stage of development long prior to the political stage' and so was 'of the nature of a survival from prehistoric times'. Thus it incorporated in its beliefs and activities those of 'cave dwellers, hill men, lake dwellers, dolmen builders'.[31]

In 1896 his successor as president of the society, Edward Clodd, produced a complementary view of the same theme by asserting that many medieval churches had been built on or near former pagan shrines, providing 'unbroken evidence of the pagan foundation which, itself resting upon barbaric bedrock, upholds the structures of classical and Christian faiths'. He extended the message of continuity from the physical buildings to the activities within them, by claiming that many Catholic rituals had been developed from those of the older religions; as evidence for this he drew directly upon the invectives of early modern Protestants, cited above, and in particular upon those of Thomas Hobbes.[32] The ideas of both Gomme and Clodd were developed in the next two decades by Walter Johnson, a medical man and keen local antiquary. In a pair of enthusiastically researched and densely illustrated books, published by university presses, he portrayed an English rural landscape of ageless landmarks—yew trees, trackways, and dew ponds—in which virtually every parish church stands upon a former pagan shrine, and both religious rituals and secular customs echo the same pre-Christian past.[33]

Between the 1920s and 1940s the same themes were central to the popular works of Harold Massingham. To him, the ancient religions had inculcated a mystical sense of union with nature, and Christianity had added a superior system of social ethics; so that the two combined, symbolized by the superimposition of churches upon pagan holy places, represented a perfect system of faith. This he evoked, against the 'utter darkness and savagery' which he discerned in modern urbanized culture.[34] He coined the slogan 'Let the Church come back to earth'.[35] Like Gomme and Johnson, he saw the peculiar merit, charm, and power of the English rural landscape as lying in its continuity; in his portrait of the Cotswolds, he traced not merely the region's religion but its social system, economy, and sports, in an unbroken line from the builders of the neolithic long barrows.[36]

During the same period such sentiments continued to be expressed by leading folklorists. In 1933 R. R. Marett informed the English Folk Dance and Song Society that folk customs (at least as interpreted by people like himself) represented 'the higher synthesis that transcends the old, narrow-minded antimony between pagan and Christian modes of hallowing the message of the spring'.[37] Feelings of this sort lay behind much of the literary and popular reception of *The Golden Bough*, discussed above. As said, by placing Christ in a context of dying and resurrecting pagan deities, Frazer had hoped to discredit the whole package of religious ideas. Instead, as some of the literary use of the *Bough* indicates, he actually gave some solace to those disillusioned with traditional religion, by allowing them to conflate the figure of Jesus with the natural world, to produce a kinder, greener variety of Christianity. As shown above, the same exercise was simultaneously being carried out by turning Pan into a Christ-figure, but Frazer's animating vegetation spirit provided an easier and less challenging means of accomplishing it.

It should be stressed that many of these ideas rested upon some truth; the problem is that in every case they went far beyond its bounds. There were certainly gods venerated in the ancient world who were believed to die and return, but they were few and localized. Only under the Roman Empire did one of these (that of Attys) develop into a widespread mystery religion, and this attracted a relatively tiny number of adherents; it may, indeed, have been influenced, or even inspired, by Christianity. It is likewise a fact that some English parish churches are associated with pre-Christian ritual monuments, Knowlton, Rudston, and Taplow being the outstanding examples. At the present day, however, the question of whether most stood upon ancient holy places is still open and likely to remain so; specifically, only a very small minority of churches examined by archaeologists have proved to reveal any sign of pre-Christian activity on the site, but it is not demonstrable that pagan worship would necessarily have left the sort of traces which archaeology can detect. What must be said is that the confident statements of writers such as Clodd and Johnson have not been borne out by investigation.[38] It is also absolutely correct that some British folk customs have descended directly from pagan rituals, such as the fires of Beltane and Midsummer Eve, and the giving of presents and decoration of homes with greenery at midwinter. The majority, however, are either of doubtful ancient provenance or (more often) developed in the Middle Ages or later.[39] The empirical evidence, therefore, is not sufficient explanation for the excitement and dogmatic certainty with which the concepts of pagan origins and of essential continuity were argued.

Nor, however, is the 'rural myth' itself. Even the 'green' Christianity of a writer such as Massingham did not much interest the bulk of folklorists between 1870 and 1970. Their preoccupation was firmly with the old religions which underlay later civilization. Proponents of the theory of continuity were more likely to distinguish paganism and Christian elements than to celebrate the blending of them, and the contrast was rarely to the advantage of the latter. In 1894 Gomme himself told the Folk-Lore Society that it should 'educate' the public 'into understanding that there is sometimes more real humanity in a touch of genuine paganism than in some of the platitudes that at present do duty for higher things'.[40] The society's president was himself using the language of radical neo-paganism so strident in the early 1890s. Moreover, the kind of paganism which the folklorists were seeking was not the familiar kind, of the Greek and Roman classics, of Olympian deities, pillared temples, and Homeric hymns. It was, rather, a world of throbbing drums, fertility rites, ritual dances, painted bodies, and deities who represented primary cosmological forces. What was really going on?

*   *   *

What I think to be the answer was perceived by another modern scholar who made a consideration of *The Golden Bough*, and indeed directly provoked that by Mary Beard, quoted above. This was Edmund Leach, back in 1961, who suggested that the popularity of the *Bough* derived from the fact that, before Freud, Frazer 'was already suggesting the existence of a Dionysian, sex-inspired, primitive undercurrent sapping at the roots of conventional Victorian society'.[41] Such a view is certainly supported by the bulk of the literary use made of Frazer's work, mentioned above, and also by the reviews of it in newspapers and journals; one of the first of the latter, in *The Daily News* on 2 June 1890, commented that until Frazer wrote, 'we never knew how heathenish we are nor how old our heathenism is'.

This does, I believe, get to the heart of the matter, but to concentrate upon *The Golden Bough* while making such a point is at once to flatter and to blame Frazer unduly. One crucially important element in his vision was that he was himself a classicist, in the forefront of what was at his time still the most prestigious of the humanities. As such, his views were only part of a general development in his discipline which took place between 1890 and 1910, running parallel to that within folklore studies and essentially at one with it. It consisted of the adoption of the notion that before the opening of history, and the veneration of the familiar pantheon of deities, the ancient Greeks had worshipped a single female deity. This phenomenon was considered in the second chapter of this present work, but it needs now to be set in a wider context. It was crucial to the Edwardian classicists' view of the ancient world that the difference in deities was also one of quality of religion; the historical world of the Olympians had been that of reason and philosophy, while the older and much more mysterious time of the Goddess had been one of darker, earthier, and more ecstatic rites, concerned with magic and propitiation. It was a mirror image of the vision of the folklorists, except that to the latter the succeeding, familiar, and civilized religion was not classical Greek paganism, but Christianity.

This concept was adopted with considerable speed in the first decade of the twentieth century, although presaged in the 1890s, and Frazer's University of Cambridge was central to its development. In particular, it was the hallmark of a group of scholars gathered around Jane Ellen Harrison, who has been mentioned earlier. Her own attitude to the ancient world was complex. She was careful to declare her disapproval of paganism: 'I am not an archaeologist—still less an anthropologist—the "beastly devices of the heathen" weary and disgust me.' She also described herself as a 'Puritan' and grew to admire Freud only by persevering in the hope that 'below all this sexual mud was something big and real'.[42] A close female friend described her as 'passionate but very pure', and remembered her as saying that she found 'a naked body hideous; a phallus the most degraded of objects'.[43]

Thus far, Harrison's reaction to ancient religion seems to be an extreme version of that already displayed by Tylor and Frazer. Where she differed sharply from both was in the quality of 'passion' noted by the same friend. Savagery and barbarism both frightened and excited her. She admitted that 'ritual seizes me: a ritual dance, a ritual procession with vestments and lights and banners, move me as no sermon, no hymn, no picture, no poem has ever moved me'.[44] Like Tylor and Frazer she had been brought up in evangelical Protestantism—'reared with sin always present, with death and judgement before you, Hell and Heaven to either hand'—and rejected it as she grew up. Unlike them, she came to value ceremony, folklore, and the primitive aspects of religion in their own right, with the shock of a conversion experience.[45] Frazer's work completed it: 'we classical deaf-adders stopped our ears and closed our eyes; but at the mere sound of the magical words "Golden Bough" the scales fell—we heard and understood'.[46] Her acquired love of the theatre of ritual extended to her own teaching methods—in the lecture hall she was 'a tall figure in black drapery, with touches of her favourite green and a string of blue Egyptian beads, like a priestess's rosary. . . . Every lecture was a drama in which the spectators were to share the emotions of "recognition" '.[47]

Her reconstruction of a putative prehistoric religion was shot through with these conflicting impulses. She accepted that the law of evolution made the transition to a more rational religious system inevitable, but at the same time she regretted it, as the loss of the happy childhood of humanity. She yearned for a world in which emotions could be more freely expressed, everyday existence was more imbued with drama and mystery, and humans were more closely linked to the natural world than her own, and she projected this wish into the remote past.[48] It should be emphasized, however, that her perception of that past was merely more positive and vivid than those of other scholars of her generation, who shared the essentials of it and turned them into an orthodoxy. Of her own Cambridge friends and colleagues, Gilbert Murray and Arthur

Bernard Cook both accepted the model of a female-centred religion of magic and unreason preceding that of classical Greece, at once repulsive and fascinating.[49] It was taken up at Oxford by Sir Arthur Evans, who made the Minoans into the exemplars of such a religion, and in France by Joseph Dechelette, both of whom have been discussed earlier. All these had endorsed the idea by 1914; when Lewis Farnell wrote a student textbook on ancient Greek beliefs in 1920, it was represented as established fact.[50] In 1910 another classical scholar, John Cuthbert Lawson, provided a perfect imitation of the work of the folklorists by studying that primal religion in the light of modern Greek peasant customs; in a circular process, the modern customs were used to reconstruct the ancient rituals, and then themselves interpreted according to the significance which those reconstructed rituals were supposed to have possessed.[51]

Parallel work was carried on between 1894 and 1920 by England's leading scholar of the Arthurian legend, Jessie Weston. Directly inspired by the work of the Folk-Lore Society and the Cambridge classicists, she argued that the main motifs of the legend had descended directly from a pagan mystery religion concerned (in Frazerian fashion) with fertility. Unlike the authors cited above, she supplied no source references and at times openly stated that the vital information was provided by nameless friends with occult knowledge who assured her that the same ancient religion had survived in secret up till her own time. She did not belong to any magical groups herself; somebody who knew the world of British occultism well, A. E. Waite, accused her of making use of 'cultist fictions'. Whatever the source of her ideas, they won her a British Academy prize and an honorary doctorate of letters; she seemed to have shown that the greatest literature of medieval England, like its religion, represented a thin Christian screen overlying an essential paganism.[52] Such a vision of the past transcended religious loyalties; Harrison and Murray were romantic agnostics, Cook an evangelical Protestant, and Weston a devout conservative Anglican. It was the common property of a generation.

Once again, it must be asked whence it came. Intellectual lineages do not help here; it is easy to cite the probable influence of Nietzsche or Freud, but thinkers such as these were more part of the same mental world than responsible for it. A possible answer can only be achieved by moving sideways, across area after area of late Victorian and Edwardian intellectual culture. Upon entering that of class relations, we find the obsessive fear of a newly expanded and enriched European social elite, balanced precariously on top of a comparatively impoverished and underprivileged, rapidly growing, and potentially dangerous proletariat. Looking at the enormous contemporary expansion of European tropical empires, we find the same phenomenon, of small colonial elites perched upon large native populations which frequently appeared to the former as savage, contemptible, and frightening. Moving into the realm of religious experience, we find the emotional impact of the theory of evolution, with its revelations that humans are umbilically connected to the beasts. Jumping into that of creative literature, we find these themes treated repeatedly in the best-selling novels and short stories of the age: the fear of the animal or demon within us, of the subversion of respectable society by inward enemies, of the hidden forces of destruction and unreason beneath the veneer of civilization. To name just a few titles in English, such images are central to Robert Louis Stevenson's *Dr Jekyll and Mr Hyde*, Oscar Wilde's *Picture of Dorian Gray*, H. G. Wells's *Island of Doctor Moreau* and *The Time Machine*, Joseph Conrad's *Heart of Darkness*, John Buchan's *Prester John*, and Bram Stoker's *Dracula*.

Freud's construction of the id, ego, and superego was to a great extent a rationalization of them, and the whole developing science of psychology might be regarded as another consequence (rather than a cause) of these anxieties. They represented an interlocking set of visions which were at once terrifying and alluring. The dark, unreasonable forces beneath and inside rational, science-based, progressive modern culture were certainly frightening to the representatives of the latter. The guilt and self-hatred which were often also experienced by the more sensitive of them could make those forces seem potentially redemptive, a means of restoring humanity and truth to a civilization cankered by hypocrisy and injustice. This instinct harmonized with the sense of the redemptive power of the countryside, discussed above.

Such a complex of emotions is quite visible among the scholars who have been considered in the present chapter. Tylor, who was of all of them the most confident and optimistic exponent of the notion of human progress, could still write that 'It is our happiness to live in one of those eventful periods of intellectual and moral history, when the oft-closed gates of discovery and reform stand open at their widest. How long these good days may last, we cannot tell.'[53] Frazer felt that their end could be imminent: 'We appear to be standing on a volcano which may at any moment break out in smoke and fire to spread ruin and devastation among the gardens and palaces of ancient culture wrought so laboriously by the hands of many generations.'[54] Harrison, as said, was far more inclined to recognize defects in modernity and to yearn for aspects of the savage antique world of which she and her colleagues were dreaming. So were Massingham and Gomme, and many of the creative writers, cited earlier, who were inspired by *The Golden Bough*.

All of them were discovering, imagining, and constructing images of a culture which was the antithesis of the civilization to which they belonged, which had preceded it, and upon which it rested; and which, like the bestial nature of humanity, could also be said to be built into it, with a potential to break forth again. This was one aspect of the most pervasive dream—or nightmare—of late Victorian and Edwardian modernity.

*   *   *

If the argument made above is correct, then it explains the compulsive manner in which classicists and folklorists alike sought to uncover traces of this hidden, disturbing, and alluring past, and to reconstruct it. In doing so, the folklorists ensured themselves the widest possible freedom of scope for interpretation. When collecting data upon popular beliefs and customs, none of them attempted more than the most rudimentary investigation of their earlier history, and none made any study of how they might have developed over a span of time; the presumption that rural life was essentially unchanging rendered such an exercise apparently superfluous. Furthermore, it was also assumed that the people who actually held the beliefs and practised the customs would long have forgotten their original, 'real', significance, which could only be reconstructed by scholars. The latter therefore paid very little attention to the social context in which the ideas and actions concerned had actually been carried on during their recent history, when they were best recorded. Many collectors and commentators managed to combine a powerful affection for the countryside and rural life with a crushing condescension towards the ordinary people who carried on that life. Frazer turned this attitude into a general social principle: in his inaugural lecture as professor at Liverpool he informed his audience that most of humanity was 'dull-witted', so that 'disguise it as we may, the government of mankind is always and everywhere aristocratic. No juggling with political machinery can evade this law of nature.'[55] Throughout his compilation of material for *The Golden Bough* he systematically ignored explanations which ancient or tribal peoples or European commoners offered for their own customs. Johnson, the great eulogist of folk memory, could declare that 'the peasant is, in some respects, a child as truly as he is physically a healthy human animal'.[56] Massingham, having convinced himself that the people and traditions of the Cotswolds came down directly from the neolithic, found it irritating that the Cotswold villagers did not share his preoccupations. He warned seekers of ancient monuments that 'you will get no help from the natives, who, when it comes to long barrows, are yawnies indeed'.[57] In 1933 R. R. Marett, himself an academic anthropologist of considerable reputation, informed the English Folk Dance and Song Society that it was a shame that the 'serious purpose' of most folk ritual had been reduced to mere frivolity by its modern practitioners. 'Given merry-making pure and simple as its sole object,' he intoned, 'rustic society is perhaps apt to display that aspect which is covered by the word "boorish".' He called for a restatement of that 'mystic note which haunts these relics of bygone rituals and sacraments', to which those who had apparently preserved them seemed unfortunately deaf. In particular, he wanted people to appreciate how much traditional dances embodied (at least to Marett) 'a straightforward and healthy insistence on marriage and family'.[58]

Such attitudes provided an irresistible temptation to many collectors and commentators to reshape their own source material. Those who specialized in folk song selected from local repertoires those items that seemed to them to be most traditional and archaic, and represented them as a definitive norm.[59] Exactly the same methods were employed by the collectors of folk dances.[60] Once the corpus was put together and standardized, it could be declared inviolable; as late as 1961, another leading figure of the Folk-Lore Society, Violet

Alford, could deplore the continuing development and commercialization of seasonal rituals, and call for them to be frozen in their 'traditional' form. This, in reality, signified the form in which they had been represented by writers such as herself.[61] If the actual performers of customs were not acting sufficiently according to the models of the folklorists, then they could at times be reproved. There was a now celebrated incident at Padstow, Cornwall, in 1931, when another luminary of the society, Mary Macleod Banks, made a second visit to the town's famous Hobby Horse Dance on May Day. Upon her first, two years before, the man dancing before one 'horse' had been dressed as a woman, which perfectly suited her particular theory concerning the pagan origins of the tradition. Now, however, he was attired as a clown, and she accused him of 'spoiling the rite'. On this occasion the instincts of class deference snapped, and he replied angrily that there was no set costume for his part. What she was hearing was valuable folklore, but it made no favourable impression on her because she had already devised an interpretation to which this information was inconvenient.[62] When Violet Alford set about reviving the Marshfield Mummers' Play in 1932, the process represented a series of arguments between elderly villagers, who remembered how it had actually been performed, and herself, who felt that it should have taken a more magical and mystical form. Once they had patched together a set of compromises, that became the 'authentic' version of the drama, in which it has been presented annually ever since.[63] It is not surprising that by the mid-twentieth century the bossy lady scholar, obsessed with pagan survivals, had become a minor stock character in English fiction, notable incarnations being the comic Anna Bünz in Ngaio Marsh's *Off With His Head* (1935) and the tragic Rose Lorimer in Angus Wilson's *Anglo-Saxon Attitudes* (1967).

Unfettered by either history or sociology, the imaginations of folklorists could roam over the material more or less at will. It is known now that the character of Father Christmas was a literary figure who appeared in the 1610s,[64] but to Alice, Lady Gomme, writing in 1929, he was obviously a former pagan god.[65] Research has revealed that the Padstow Hobby Horse Dance represents an amalgam of different traditions put together since the late eighteenth century,[66] but to Mary Macleod Banks in 1938 it was obviously descended from a ritual of sacred marriage between earth and sky.[67] The medieval foliate heads carved in churches and cathedrals are now known to have had nothing to do with the foliage-covered figure which danced in nineteenth-century May Day processions,[68] but to Lady Raglan, in 1939, they were clearly representations of Frazer's ancient spirit of vegetation, which she named 'The Green Man'.[69] The northern English Sword Dance now seems to have been another eighteenth-century development,[70] but to Violet Alford, in 1962, it was a blend of a neolithic rite to waken the sleeping earth of winter, led by matriarchal priestesses, with a patriarchal Bronze Age one to confer manhood.[71] The 1930s seems to have been a particularly febrile decade for such interpretations. In 1937, the annual presidential address to the Folk-Lore Society was delivered by a distinguished academic expert in ancient Near Eastern religion, S. H. Hooke, who suggested that

pancake-tossing had been a magical rite to make crops grow, that Shrove
Tuesday football matches had begun as ritual struggles representing the forces
of dark and light, and that Mother's Day was a relic of the worship of the ancient
Corn Mother.[72]

As said above, the developing scholarly discipline of anthropology rejected
the methods of Tylor and Frazer from the 1920s onward: this development is a
truism of textbooks upon the history of the discipline. It was also noted above
that in the same period *The Golden Bough* began to make its greatest impact
upon the imagination of creative writers. What never seems to have been appreciated, and has certainly not been the subject of any scholarly investigation, is
the influence of Frazer and of the other folklorists of his generation upon other
academic disciplines. In the field of comparative religion, and of the history of
religion, not merely the methodology of Sir James but many of his ideas continued to hold sway; among those who exemplified them in the mid-twentieth
century, and combined high posts in academic departments of religious studies
with a leading role in the Folk-Lore Society, were Hooke (who has just been
cited) and E. O. James. In the first two generations of professional archaeology,
the notions of folklore as pagan survivals of a medieval England which
remained essentially pagan were taken over wholesale and built into the evaluation of data by such giants as Sir Flinders Petrie, Stuart Piggott, and O. G. S.
Crawford.[73] The interpretation of folk customs as remains of archaic religion
was taken into the work of the much-respected and much-read historian of the
medieval and Elizabethan stage, Sir Edmund Chambers.[74] The picture of
medieval English religion as a veneer of elite Christianity brushed over a pagan
populace was absorbed by the greatly esteemed historian of the English Church,
Geoffrey Coulton. His own researches were confined largely to the Church's
actual institutions (above all, to monasteries), employing none of the sources
that later scholars were to use to investigate the actual nature of popular religion. As a result, the few lines which he devoted to the latter consisted of an airy
rhetoric, which was not the less confident for its lack of basis in any primary
sources. Coulton's medieval villagers were 'cheerful semi-pagans'. 'The old idols
remained under the old Christian veneer', and 'in church, the women crowded
around Mary; yet they paid homage to the old deities by their nightly fireside, or
at the time-honoured sacred haunts, grove or stone or spring'.[75] To him, all this
was how things *should* have been.

The greatest success of the early folklorists, however, was with the general
public, whether defined as the masses, or as writers of the popular novels,
screenplays, and radio dramas from which so many people gain, or reinforce,
their notions of history. Padstow may have held out against Mary Macleod
Banks, but it obviously surrendered later to a contemporary of hers among the
leading members of the Folk-Lore Society, Lord Raglan. When I made my own
visit to it on May Day 1985, its leading family confidently explained the Hobby
Horses to me in terms of what were quite recognizably Raglan's theories about
the nature of ancient religion.[76] These were not credited to him, but repeated to

me simply as the accepted facts. Likewise, virtually all the performers of British calendar customs to whom I talked in the 1960s and 1970s firmly believed that they were enacting rites of pagan origin, and explained them to me in the precise terms of the interpretations made by those former scholars. The intention of those scholars, to impose their own framework of thought upon the masses in the name of education, had been all too perfectly realized.

Once installed, that framework became a free-standing entity, to which successive researchers merely added elaborations; a classic intellectual paradigm. To take a particularly distinguished case, the most celebrated figure in the early years of the folk song and dance revival, Cecil Sharp, was careful to base his interpretation of the history of the dances which he recorded on those made by respected scholars, notably Chambers, and altered it as he learned more from them (most obviously to embrace with increasing confidence the idea that they were relics of paganism). At the same time he made what seems to have been distinctive contribution to the 'rural myth' by stressing the communal nature of the pastimes concerned.[77] The Gommes had established the stereotype of 'folk' survivals:

in every society there are people who do not progress either in religion or in polity with the foremost of the nation. They are left stranded amidst the progress. They live in out-of-the-way villages, or in places where the general culture does not penetrate easily; they keep to old ways, practices and ideas, following with religious awe all that their parents had held to be necessary in their lives. These people are living depositories of ancient history—a history that has not been written down, but which has come down by tradition.[78]

Sharp took this a stage further, by suggesting that the practices were the collective inheritance of the communities in which they were recorded; thus, the morris dances which he published were labelled 'The Adderbury Tradition', 'The Ilmington Tradition', and so forth, rather than named after the individuals or teams by whom he was taught them. It is possible that Sharp's own political ideals, which tended strongly towards a mystical socialism based upon collectivism,[79] influenced this process. David Harker has analysed the way in which he both absorbed and reinforced the myth that Edwardian country people were a breed apart from the rest of the English, cut off from both modernity and education.[80] It may be suggested here that he augmented it with the specific notion of the closed village community, within which distinctive customs were passed down unchanging from the remote past, invisible to the outside world until explorers like himself arrived to record and preserve them for the nation.

It is remarkable how little resemblance the view of the ancient pagan past evolved by these late Victorian and Edwardian scholars bears to the world of teeming spirits, and rituals designed to serve complex social and political realities, described by modern anthropologists working among tribal peoples. It has equally little resemblance to the functional pantheons of deities and religious hierarchies revealed by research into the religions of ancient kingdoms and city states. What it reveals instead is a preoccupation with great primal forces—

Earth, Sky, Corn, Vegetation, Nature, Mother, and Father—and with polarity and tension between female and male. It may be suggested that this imagined paganism represented the more important of (to slip into current academic jargon) the Significant Others of modern Western spirituality, the lesser consisting of the Oriental spiritual traditions with which Westerners were now becoming familiar for the first time. As such, the mythology of this archaic religion, and of its enduring presence in the countryside, can be considered both an effect and a contributory cause of the progressive de-Christianization of British culture.

Two aspects of the phenomenon need to be restated in conclusion, as they cannot be sufficiently emphasized. The first is that all parts of it were to some extent anchored in real, proven data, even though it ran beyond this to a very significant extent. The second is that this was no simple matter of an intellectual elite imposing its ideas upon the rest of society. The scholars concerned had those ideas, and made such a favourable impression, because they were so much part of the spirit of their age, and related to so many of its deepest concerns.

8

FINDING A WITCHCRAFT

⊁Ӿ⊰

ONE of the most remarkable shifts of opinion in world history was that which occurred in the seventeenth and eighteenth centuries, when the majority of Europe's social, political, and intellectual elites moved from believing that humans could do damage by uncanny, non-physical means to believing that they could not. The practical result was the repeal, in state after state, of the laws against witchcraft which between 1428 and 1782 resulted in 40–50,000 executions.[1] Statutes against the practice of magic were still enacted, such as those considered in the last chapter; but these were of a radically different nature, treating that practice as fraud or superstition rather than as effective action. This conceptual alteration represents one of the most remarkable processes in the transition of European culture into modernity.

It left scholars with the task of coming to terms with the apparent fact that tens of thousands of people had been officially done to death, and many more tried, for an offence that was wholly illusory. For the *philosophes* of the eighteenth-century Enlightenment, the first to address the matter, there was no difficulty at all; led most obviously by Voltaire, they were only too happy to use the tragedy to condemn those aspects of former European society which they were most anxious to eradicate: obscurantist Churches supported by credulous statesmen and a superstitious and ignorant populace. This discourse—the witch trials as a dreadful mistake—became the dominant one of the nineteenth century.[2] It saturated the work which marked the beginning of systematic study of the trials, Wilhelm Gottlieb Soldan's *Geschichte der Hexenprozesse*, published in 1843. To Soldan, the end of the belief in witchcraft had marked a vital stage in human progress, and responsibility for the prosecution of alleged witches in the early modern period lay squarely with the Roman Catholic Church, which to liberals of his generation had become the most obvious force for reaction and obscurantism in Europe. Soldan's tone was adopted with his research methods by many of the local studies of trials which were made in Germany, France, and Italy during the late nineteenth and early twentieth centuries. It was reproduced and reinforced by Joseph Hansen, a bitterly anti-clerical archivist from Cologne, whose *Zauberwahn, Inquisition und Hexenprozesse im Mittelalter, und die Entstehung der Grossen Hexenverfolgung* (Munich, 1900) was probably the most important work on the subject produced since Soldan. This asserted that the early modern persecution of presumed witches had been consciously fomented by late medieval theologians. It is a measure of how far the notion of the trials as a tragedy produced by ignorance and superstition had sunk into German scholarship by the opening of the twentieth century, that when a Catholic polemicist made a well-researched study of them, he adopted it wholesale and merely attempted to prove that his Church was not peculiarly responsible for the error.[3]

This pattern was to achieve its most notable expression in the United States of America, where it was assimilated into an existing liberal tradition of hostility to religious faith as the root of many human ills. Before Soldan wrote, George Bancroft's *History of the United States* had already used the witch trials to condemn New England Puritanism.[4] This hard rationalist line was further developed in the second half of the century, by intellectuals in the (dominant) Republican party. The most famous of these was probably James Russell Lowell, a Harvard academic and editor of the leading Republican journal *The Atlantic Monthly*, who published in 1868 an essay which described superstition as 'the deformed child of faith' and the early modern persecution of presumed witches as its worst recorded aspect.[5] This theme was married to actual research at the newly founded Cornell College in upstate New York, a non-sectarian institution which came under attack from religious fundamentalists for its secular character. Its president, Andrew Dickson White, struck back in 1896 with a *History of the Warfare of Science with Theology in Christiandom*. As part of his polemic against religious bigotry as the European world's worst force for backwardness, delusion, and oppression, he proclaimed that the witch trials had been the natural result of dogmatic theology and their decline the equally direct consequence of the development of modern science.[6]

White's argument was lent archival support by the energetic researches of his colleague at Cornell, George Lincoln Burr, who co-operated with Hansen upon his visits to German repositories. His stream of publications, which continued all the way through the first half of the twentieth century, encouraged other scholars at liberal East Coast universities to work in the same tradition, such as Wallace Notestein, George Lyman Kittredge, and Henry Charles Lea.[7] The message of these scholars was not wrapped up in academic works alone, for White's *History of the Warfare of Science with Theology* was deliberately populist in tone and he and Burr both wrote for mass-circulation journals such as *The Nation*. By 1940 the American tradition of study of the early modern witch trials was fully established; it represented them as a 'hunt' organized from above by churchmen, and ultimately brought to an end by the benevolent effects of modern scientific thought. Not all the scholars named above supported it with the same fervour and set of emphases, for it represented a spectrum of attitudes ranging from White at one extreme to Kittredge at the other. The latter writer tended to stress the commitment of the populace, as well as of clerics and magistrates, to the process, a result both of his interest in folklore and his concentration upon English records, which revealed a pattern of witch prosecution which was less intense, hysterical, and inquisitorial than that in parts of the Continent (and, in particular, of Germany). In this, however, he was unusual, and he subscribed to the same polarity, of science and reason pitted against superstition and ignorance, as the others.

The situation was different in England, where society was so much more secular in tone than those of either most Continental countries or of the United States, that its writers lacked the sectarian or anti-clerical passions which propelled those abroad. As a result, research into English witch trials began much later; indeed, it was commenced by the American scholars cited above. Not until 1929, with the first of the monographs of L'Estrange Ewen,[8] was anything published on the subject by a home-grown author who had made a systematic study of an archive. When nineteenth-century English writers considered the trials, they usually deployed the international contemporary rhetoric of rationalist disgust. To Charles Mackay, in 1841, the early modern 'Witch Mania' was the result of 'a cruel and absurd delusion'.[9] When Thomas Wright brought out an anthology of tales of witchcraft and sorcery ten years later, he relegated the lot to the category of 'superstition'.[10] Lynn Linton added another, in 1861, 'as landmarks of the excesses to which a blind belief may hurry and impel humanity'.[11] Another four years saw the appearance of W. E. H. Lecky's celebrated eulogy to the triumph of reason and science, in which the execution of presumed witches was declared to have been 'the result of a single superstition, which the spirit of Rationalism had destroyed'.[12]

It would be wrong to conclude that writers like these were engaging in a crude celebration of victory over a dead and defeated foe; rather, the fervour with which they expressed their views derived partly from a real fear that the grip of science and reason might still be a fragile one. If the prosecution of people for witchcraft had resulted from a false belief, ended by a progression of knowledge and a resulting change of viewpoint, then every effort was needed to extirpate that belief completely and to remove any opportunity for it to return. To Edward Tylor, the father of anthropology, a faith in magic was 'one of the most pernicious delusions that ever vexed mankind', and he saw in the contemporary popularity of spiritualism a guise in which it was once again winning a mass following. He invited his readers to hope that:

if the belief in present witchcraft, and the persecution necessarily ensuring upon such belief, once more come into prominence in the civilized world, they may appear in a milder shape than heretofore, and be kept down by stronger humanity and tolerance. But to any one who fancies from their present disappearance that they have necessarily disappeared for ever, must have read history to little purpose.[13]

In this respect, Tylor was to be one of Victorian England's most accurate prophets, both his expectation and his hope coming to pass.

What marked off this English rationalism from its German, and even more from its American, equivalent, was that it did not lay the blame for the delusion upon the elite, and in particular upon churchmen, but upon the whole of a past society. As such, it was as likely to be trained upon popular culture as upon magistrates and demonologists, and indeed formed part of that drive against

cunning folk which was described in the last chapter. At times it could even viti-
ate sympathy for victims of the early modern trials. When *The Times* produced a
leading article commenting upon the mobbing of 'Dummy' in 1863, it came
close to concluding that the poor old fortune-teller had deserved his terrible end
because of the craft in which he had engaged. It went on to consider the early
modern period, and trumpeted that:

We are not disposed to conclude that every witch was unjustly prosecuted. In so far as they
were condemned to a barbarous death for dealing with the Devil, the proceedings were
both shocking and groundless; but if . . . many of these reputed sorcerers did, by their
threats and curses, produce results . . . we cannot really hold them guiltless of crime.[14]

The argument here was still a rationalist one, but of opposite import; that in a
society which believed in magic, presumed witches could blackmail victims
with the threat of using their powers, or even drive them into illness or mental
collapse by making them suppose that they had indeed been cursed. It was
heard again at times during the next seventy years; for example from St John
Seymour, writing about Irish witch lore in 1913. He condemned 'the gross beliefs
of yore' which had resulted in the trials, and yet also noted nervously that the
mind could affect the body and that psychic phenomena were as yet little understood.[15]

Works of popular fiction showed a similar range of attitude. Sir Walter Scott
always spread his colours as a true apostle of the Age of Reason, even though
one attracted to romantic subjects. In *Ivanhoe* (1817) he excoriated medieval
superstition and obscurantism at the highest level, by having the Knights
Templar condemn the beautiful and innocent Jewess Rebecca to death for
sorcery, merely because she is a competent healer and one of the knights has
fallen obsessively in love with her. In *The Pirate* (1821), Scott's fire is directed at
cunning craft, when he introduces readers to a traditional Shetland wise-
woman, of apparently awesome occult powers, only to reveal the artifices by
which she deludes her public into a belief in them. He awards her a fate of
horrific irony, when she proves to be utterly blind to the real nature of developments and her manipulations lead to a tragedy which leaves her broken and
finding consolation in a devout and passive Christian piety. Near the other end
of the century, Thomas Hardy's *Under the Greenwood Tree* (1872) showed early
signs of that romanticization of a rooted and organic rural life which was to be
such a feature of the late Victorian era. His village cunning woman likewise lacks
any actual magical abilities, but is sympathetically presented as a person of
remarkable common sense with a deep understanding of human nature, who
uses these qualities to assist clients.

Alongside these novels of social realism, of course, creative literature continued to evoke witches and sorceresses in imaginary worlds and alternative realities in a wholly traditional manner, from Shelley's gorgeous 'Witch of Atlas'
(1820) to the evil enchantress in William Morris's *The Water of the Wondrous
Isles* (1895). The importation of foreign (mostly German) folk tales in the new

collections such as those of the Brothers Grimm caused the bogey-witches of the kind who try to kill Snow White, and Hansel and Gretel, to reinforce those lingering in native English folk lore. Over the same period the canvases of Victorian painters bloomed with Medeas, Circes, Morgan le Fays, Melusines, Belles Dames Sans Merci, and other famed or nameless enchantresses, as part of the age's ambivalent male engagement with Woman.

By mid-century, therefore, English attitudes to the witch figure were already varied and complex, and that was before a new concept of the witch arrived from the Continent. It originated, like so much else in the story of modern pagan witchcraft, in Germany, and arose from a response to the challenge which the rationalist view of the witch trials had posed to traditional religion. The early nineteenth century was the great age of reaction in Central and Eastern Europe, when clerical and monarchist intellectuals pitted themselves against the ideas which the Enlightenment and the French Revolution had unleashed upon their world. Some of the most determined of them were defenders of the Church of Rome, which had been one of the prime targets of those movements and was now most closely identified (as mentioned above) with reaction. One of these was a young professor of criminal law at the University of Berlin called Karl Ernst Jarcke, who was an enthusiastic journalistic spokesman for the clerical interest. In 1828 he edited the records of a seventeenth-century German witch trial for a legal journal. In his (short) commentary, he suggested that early modern witchcraft had been the degenerate remnant of the former native pagan religion. In his scheme, this had lingered among the common people, had been condemned by Christians as Satanism, and in the course of the Middle Ages had responded by adapting to the Christian stereotype and becoming devil-worship in earnest. As a result, proposed Jarcke, even ordinary people began to turn away from it in disgust, and denounce it to the authorities, who proceeded to extirpate it. In this manner, the young academic brilliantly outflanked the liberals; his explanation of the witch trials equally accepted the non-existence of witchcraft itself, while exonerating the authorities who had persecuted witches as members of an evil and anti-social cult.[16]

Eleven years later another clerical polemicist took up the idea; this time a well-established historian who currently occupied the post of director of the archives of Baden, Franz Josef Mone. Jarcke's theory had the drawback that it besmirched the memory of native German folk culture at a time when Germany was seeking a national identity rooted in its own past. Mone countered this by suggesting that the pernicious secret religion concerned was actually a foreign importation, a degenerate version of the classical mystery cults of Hecate and Dionysos introduced by Greek slaves and kept up by the most debauched members of society. In his scheme, it was loathed both by the practitioners of native paganism and then by the Christians who succeeded them, focused as it was upon the worship of a goat-like god, nocturnal orgies, and the practices of sorcery and poisoning. Conservatives of the time of Jarcke and Mone would easily have recognized the contemporary parallels to their portraits of the witches; in the radical secret societies that were believed (with some truth but much exaggeration) to be the principal agents of revolution and irreligion in early nineteenth-century Europe.[17]

This interpretation of the witch trials was a totally novel one. In 1749 the Italian scholar Girolamo Tartarotti-Serbati had suggested that ancient pagan beliefs and images underlay the later concept of witches' gatherings,[18] and in 1844 the foremost pioneer of German folklore studies, Jakob Grimm, argued effectively that the early modern image of the witch was a conflation of pagan traditions with later medieval stereotypes of heresy.[19] Neither, however, supported the notion that those prosecuted as witches were practitioners of a surviving pagan religion, although both were later misquoted as doing so. That notion seems to have been wholly the work of the two Catholic apologists, and by 1832 it was already widespread enough for Felix Mendelssohn to compose an orchestral piece, *Die Erste Walpurgisnacht*, based on a story of pagan villagers who, attacked by local Christians at a traditional May Eve celebration, pretend to be witches to frighten away their opponents.[20] It was not supported by any actual evidence, Jarcke and Mone having projected their theories without seeking to substantiate them, but in default of any genuine research into the trials it could not easily be challenged.

The anti-clerical liberals therefore had two obvious means of responding. One was to undertake the solid archival work needed to underpin their view of the phenomenon, and after Mone wrote, this was put in hand by Soldan with the results described above. The other and more audacious was to accept the construction made by the two Catholics but to reverse the sympathies, and this was adopted in 1862 by one of the nineteenth century's most famous liberal historians, the Frenchman, Jules Michelet. At that date Michelet had long been an academic martyr, having practised his profession in private life ever since his suspension from his teaching post at the College de France in 1851 because the conservative regime of Louis Napoleon suspected him of sedition—although in fairness to some of the colleagues who voted him out, they were genuinely disturbed by his lack of the objectivity which they felt to be required of a historian.[21] Their disquiet was only partly justified, for when engaged in his heavyweight works of research, most obviously his multi-volume history of France, Michelet could sift through masses of primary source material with an exemplary patience and thoroughness and construct arguments at least as substantial as those of contemporaries working in the same fields. On the other hand, he always saturated them in his own political prejudices and preoccupations, with a passion and colour of prose unusual even for the time, and he would also toss off potboilers which combined the same style with minimal research. He was a zealot and evangelist; in the words of one observer of his college lectures, 'like a priest in his pulpit, Michelet preaches from his chair'. Michelet himself saw the parallel, describing his mission to establish a more just and harmonious society as 'sacerdotal'.[22]

His two principal targets were the Roman Catholic Church and absolute monarchy, and so he developed a bitter detestation of the two epochs in which they had been most dominant: the Middle Ages and the seventeenth- and eighteenth-century *ancien régime*. One of his reflections upon the former may provide a characteristic sample of his rhetoric: 'that bizarre, monstrous, prodigiously artificial condition of life'.[23] Not for nothing did he describe the writing of history as 'a violent moral chemistry, in which my individual passions turn into generalities'.[24] Conversely, his most heartfelt admiration was reserved for the movements which ended both those periods, the Renaissance and the French Revolution; indeed, he has been said to have invented the whole concept of the Renaissance, coining the actual term and representing it as a great renewal of human life, after the hatred of the world and suppression of natural instinct inflicted by medieval Christendom.

That concept was first published by him in 1840. By 1848 he was teaching his students that Christianity itself had now to give way to a new faith suited to a new age. The following year he suggested that such a faith would best be built about the notion of motherhood, and praised the ancient worship of Isis; he was an early example of that drift of French and German intellectuals into the theory of a universal ancient Great Goddess. In 1850 and 1851 he called Woman 'the heart' of society, who could save it from materialism and authoritarianism, and hailed her as the priestess of social reform, 'the living gospel of work', although he also declared that male intellectual discipline was needed to restrain the female tendency to fantasy.[25] After his enforced retirement, Michelet felt himself to be renewed by contact with 'Mother Earth', and wrote two works of natural history in the mid-1850s. He returned to his theme of Woman as redeemer in *L'Amour* (1858) and *La Femme* (1859), declaring at one point 'Don't speak to me of the equality of the sexes; woman is superior.'[26] What he actually meant by this, however, was that women would reform the nation by being model housewives, for he preached the doctrine that menstruation made them unfit for regular work and so confined them to the home under male guidance.

Michelet became interested in the witch trials in the early 1860s, when writing the volumes of his history of France which covered the seventeenth century, and produced his book on the subject, *La Sorcière*, in 1862. It was dashed off in two months[27] and was intended to be a populist and sensationalist work to bring him in the maximum amount of money for the least effort, which would sustain him while he continued the larger, national history; he had started work on a novel to achieve the same end, but abandoned it in favour of the volume on witches.[28] In these circumstances, the research for it had to be minimal, and was. That for the medieval section was more or less non-existent, and it represents an extended poetic reverie, being at times actually composed in blank verse. The seventeenth-century chapters were based upon a small number of pamphlets, which Michelet reinterpreted to suit his own hatred of Catholicism. As the book went on sale, he noted in his journal: 'I have assumed a new position which my best friends have not as yet clearly adopted, that of proclaiming the provisional death of Christianity.'[29]

To Michelet, the witch was an archetypal figure, representing spiritual free-dom, and the rights of women and the working classes. He reversed the picture drawn by Jarcke and Mone to portray witchcraft as a surviving pagan religion which had kept the spirit of liberty alive all through the 'thousand long, dreary, terrible years' of the Middle Ages, and went further than any writer before or since, to proclaim that the Renaissance had been produced when the wisdom preserved by the witches broke surface again to infuse members of the cultural elite. That wisdom was gained from a close knowledge of, and relationship with, the natural world and the life-force, and Michelet believed that women were especially suited to such knowledge and therefore had provided the priestesses of the witch religion. To him, Woman was inherently 'a creature of Enchantment. In virtue of regularly recurring periods of exaltation, she is a Sibyl; in virtue of love, a Magician'.[30] Thus, 'at the Witches' Sabbath woman fulfils every office'. In his imagination of it, it was 'a feast of brothers', without a weapon being present, held on 'a wide heath, often in the neighbourhood of an old Celtic dolmen, or at the edge of a wood'. It was an egalitarian peasant assem-bly, the peasant being 'invariably a leveller at heart', and the witch was a natural rebel, her ceremonies being gatherings at which all prayed for the freedom of the serfs. When not officiating, she communed with animals or the forest trees. 'They awake in her things that her mother told her, her grandmother—old, old things that for century after century have been handed on from woman to woman.'[31]

Michelet cheerfully accepted the suggestion of the two Catholic polemicists, that the deity worshipped by the witches had been a pagan god of fertility, 'Pan or Priapus'. With equal lack of concern he also accepted the notion that this image had been conflated with that of the Christian Devil, which made a posi-tive appeal to Michelet as that of a fellow rebel: 'Is not Satan the outlaw of outlaws? and he gives his followers the joy and wild liberty of all free things of Nature, the rude delight of being a world apart, all-sufficient unto itself.' He could eulogize the witch religion as 'that school of wild nature where Satan lectured a truant band of sorceresses and shepherd lads'[32] (it may be noted in passing that despite his continuous expressions of admiration for nature, Michelet himself lived in Paris whenever it was possible for him to do so). He endorsed also the assertion of Jarcke and Mone that the religion had become increasingly debauched and degenerate with time; the difference being that in his own inimitable fashion, he blamed this upon the infiltration of it by the nobility, whom he regarded as the source of all social evil and vice. His feudal lords were beings of 'savage violence', while their wives were 'bold-faced Jezebels every one, more shameless than the men' (Michelet's respect for women evapo-rated as soon as they ceased to fit his preferred political models). Even in its corrupt form, however, he still thought the witch religion preferable to that of the Church of Rome. Lest his readers believe that its horrors were things of the past, he informed them, without hesitation or supporting evidence, that the same Church still burned people alive in secret, in furnaces or cellars.[33]

Embedded in these torrents of eulogy and abuse were specific flights of imagination which were to take up an enduring place in later popular perceptions of the witch trials: that victims were often selected 'just because they were young and pretty', that the eccentric fifteenth-century text *Malleus Maleficarum* (one of the few medieval sources which he actually read) was 'the guide and beacon-star' of witch-hunters, and that witches had been great healers, upon whose skills much of modern medicine had been based.[34] He adopted the tone of contemporary rationalism when hailing the demise of the trials: 'the great duel of Doctor against Devil, of science and Enlightenment against the spirit of Falsehood and Obscurantism'.[35] His hope for the future was that Woman would foresake her recent preoccupation with 'men's affairs' and rediscover 'her own true role—that of healing, and consoling, that of the fairy that restores to health and happiness. That is her true priesthood—hers by right divine.'[36] In short, the rebel witch was to be reborn as the angel in the house.

La Sorcière was greeted with silence from French literary critics, apparently because they recognized that it was not really history.[37] Nor did it have an impact upon the radical political culture of the nation, probably because French liberals of the time knew all too well that the peasantry, far from being natural revolutionaries, were the greatest reservoir of conservatism and Catholicism. As has been said earlier, the English language of paganism as the religion of a beautiful and sacred countryside did not catch on among writers in a nation where, in sharp contrast to England, the majority of the population remained rural until well into the twentieth century. On the other hand, the book became a popular best-seller, and has, indeed, never yet been out of print; perhaps because of its frequently lurid and sensational content, such as the portrait of an imagined medieval witch-priestess carrying out simulated sexual union with an image of Pan-Satan. In that sense, it served the primary purpose for which the author had intended it—to make cash.

On the whole, the theory that the people persecuted as witches had been pagans made little impression upon late nineteenth-century Continental Europeans. It was the older liberal idea, that the persecution had been the result of a dreadful delusion, which was certainly the accepted one amongst scholars and apparently among the wider literary culture. Only occasionally is an exception found, and then it is partial. The most distinguished example is Freud, who in the early stages of his theorization of psychoanalysis found himself

toying with the idea that in the perversions, of which hysteria is the negative, we may have the remains of a primitive sexual cult, which in the Semitic East may once have been a religion (Moloch, Astarte). I am beginning to dream of an extremely primitive devil religion the rites of which continue to be performed secretly, and now I understand the stern therapy of the witches' judges.[38]

Later, however, Freud changed his mind and subscribed to the theory of delusion; by 1923 he had decided that the confessions of alleged witches were the result of neuroses.[39] *La Sorcière*, therefore, had made no significant impact upon

Michelet's fellow Europeans. It was, however, destined to play a very significant cultural role in a realm in which the patriotic Frenchman had himself displayed very little interest: the English-speaking world.

*   *   *

In the United States, as described, the growing community of scholars of the witch trials endorsed the theory that the victims had been destroyed by a collective insanity propagated by theologians, and had not represented any alternative religion. As indicated above, they had powerful ideological reasons for adopting this position, although to be fair to them it was also one more easily supported by an investigation of the actual trial records than that of Jarcke, Mone, and Michelet. The latter, however, found acceptance by two very unusual Americans, both writing in the 1890s and both subsequently to have considerable impact upon modern popular impressions of witchcraft. One was Matilda Joslyn Gage, a prominent leader of the contemporary campaign for political and social rights for women. In 1893 she published a book entitled *Woman, Church, and State*, which was intended to underpin the claims of that campaigning. It is an early classic of reimagined women's history, written in a tearing hurry and in time snatched from a political activism which left no space for original research. Instead, she took what she needed from existing polemical publications, and one of them was *La Sorcière*. She linked Michelet's witches with another theory going the round of her time, that prehistoric human society had been universally matriarchal. To Gage, they became pagan priestesses who had preserved the secrets of that golden age, especially in the realm of healing, and were persecuted by churchmen not just to wipe out their religion but to complete the breaking of any spirit of female independence.[40]

Some example of the creative boldness with which she used material is provided by the matter of the presumed total number of victims of the witch trials. Previous works upon the subject had either avoided a computation altogether or suggested what seem now to have been serious underestimates. To Grimm, the death-toll was simply 'countless',[41] to Lecky it comprised 'a few thousand',[42] while Mackay talked of 'thousands upon thousands'.[43] It was indeed to be about a hundred years after Gage wrote before research reached anything like a stage at which a proper estimation could possibly be made, so that the field was wide open for anybody's guess. Even so, the scale of her overestimate was breathtaking, especially as it was apparently undertaken on no rational basis whatsoever; she informed her readers, confidently, that nine million European women had died as a result of the early modern persecution of presumed witches.[44] Her influence upon both scholarship and the wider culture was slight until the mid-twentieth century, but in the 1970s it was truly to come into its own.

The other American was Charles Godfrey Leland, a traveller who fell in love with Europe and spent much of his life there, eventually settling in Florence. His principal professional occupation was that of journalist. His political views were radical by European standards, although not by American; as a youth he had taken part in the French Revolution of 1848, which had overthrown the monarchy of Louis-Philippe and established a republic. During those events he may actually have heard Michelet speak, and their later attitudes were practically identical. Leland also nursed a hatred of absolute monarchy and of the Roman Catholic Church, which resulted in a loathing of the Middle Ages and a celebration of the Renaissance.[45] He shared the Frenchman's scientific rationalism, declaring that 'We *know* that there is no truth in anything supernatural',[46] and that 'superstition' arose from primitive fear and illusion, which science would 'put all to shame'. He admitted that he had been impressed by fortune-tellers who had seemed to know things about his own past which could apparently be gained only by uncanny powers, but added that further investigation would certainly reveal a 'rational and natural' explanation.[47]

Like Michelet as well, however, he possessed a strong sense of the beauty, mystery, and sanctity of the natural world, and he felt that folk 'superstitions', although erroneous in scientific terms, often recognized and celebrated those qualities. In 1889 he wrote that 'nature is eternal, and while grass grows and rivers run man is ever likely to fall again into the eternal enchantments. And truly until he does he will have no new poetry, no fresh art.'[48] Three years later he told readers:

Not only is it true that a man who believes—like a Red Indian—that every tree and stone has its indwelling spirit, is always in a kind of fairyland, but what is also worth envying, he is never *alone*. When he sits in woodland wild 'neath green and russet tree, he knows the presence of the Elves, or sees by many a sign where they have passed. Every relic of the olden time, arrow heads, pottery, and hollow flints, have been touched by fairy hands, much more those older relics of an older time, rocks, rivers, and forests.[49]

Here he parted company with the Frenchman, for whereas Michelet eulogized medieval peasants but avoided their modern equivalents, Leland sought out those peoples whom he felt best to preserve this sense of an enchanted Nature— successively, native Americans, gypsies, and cunning folk—and collected and published their stories and beliefs.

His entry into the world of what in England has been termed cunning craft was made in Florence in 1886, when he met a young woman called Maddelena, who came from the Romagna region far to the east of the city. She sounds like an almost classic representative of the type, having inherited a family trove of charms and invocations which were intended to heal, break curses, and invoke spirits, and of tales. He gathered these from her and then hired her as a research assistant, commissioned to bring back more from friends in her native region.[50] For the remainder of the decade, Leland himself was occupied with completing the publication of his collection of gypsy lore, while Maddalena's material came in. He already attached importance to the early modern witch trials, seeing them in classic liberal-rationalist fashion as the obvious disproof of the Roman

Catholic Church's claim to infallibility, which could be used to undermine faith in all its dogmas.[51] From the opening of the 1890s he gave himself over wholly to the arrangement and publication of his Tuscan stories and charms, gained mostly from Maddalena but occasionally from other informants.[52] The results were three successive volumes: *Etruscan Roman Remains* (1892), *Legends of Florence* (1895), and *Aradia* (1899).

The first two make a striking contrast with the last. The former contain absolutely standard European folklore, with local colouring and characteristics recognizable from other contemporary studies of Italian beliefs.[53] There are fireside stories of fairies and spirits, and of witches, who are regarded with fear and hostility as humans motivated by jealousy or malice to work evil magic. In the Romagna it was said that they met in council twice a week to discuss their various projects, and then shifted into animal and other shapes to perform them. One love-spell in the collection suggested that they were a sect who worshipped Cain.[54] Several other stories and charms assumed that two female supernatural beings were the special patronesses of witches and goblins.[55] One was the ancient Italian goddess Diana, who as a deity of night has always possessed such associations, vividly illustrated in Roman literature such as the poetry of Horace. Perhaps reinforced by her high profile as the only goddess mentioned in the New Testament, she retained a place in Italian and other folklore of the medieval and later periods as a night-flying being, often attended by a train of followers.[56] The other was Aradia (pronounced 'Ahradeeah'), the Italianized name of Herodias, the queen who secured the death of John the Baptist and therefore ranks as the principal villainess in the New Testament.

Leland glossed this trove of lore with the preoccupation of many of the leading folklorists of his time, by emphasizing at every possible point that much of it had descended directly from ancient pagan religion. His whole approach was neatly symbolized by his title for the first book based upon it, *Etruscan Roman Remains in Popular Tradition*. On reading the contents it is plain that he was speaking literally; that his material came from the northern, or Tuscan, part of the Romagna. The title, none the less, translated the regional name in such a way as to give an impression of enduring ancient belief. Every time that a story identified a being as an evil spirit, Leland struggled to prove that it had originated as a pagan deity. He conceded that a lot of the stories and spells were soaked in Catholic piety, but dismissed this by declaring (without argument) that the Church's rituals and saints were often themselves of pagan origin and so could be counted themselves as ancient survivals. He also recognized that the popular attitude to witches was usually both hostile and defensive, much of the lore being concerned with breaking or averting the evil magic which they were supposed to work, but asserted (likewise without providing evidence) that this was a prejudice instilled by medieval churchmen. Like his English equivalents, he confused a major issue by referring to cunning folk and bad magical operators alike as 'witches'.[57] The constant tension between data and interpretation in these two books is summed up neatly by Leland's characterization of the Romagna as a remote and backward region of mountains and forests. So might its southern and western parts have been in his time, but at one point he pinpoints Maddalena's own district, from which his collections originated, as lying between Ravenna and Forli.[58] This is on the coastal plain of the Adriatic, a heavily populated and cultivated lowland with good connections to other regions.

For all that, these two works are notable for the fact that whether or not a reader accepts Leland's own glosses upon the material, the latter is set forth in a way which permits independent judgements upon it. He was also careful to point out that although the whole world of popular magic was known to some of his informants as 'the old religion', it did not really add up to a religious system. He argued, with some plausibility, that it did embody a coherent and distinctive cosmology, of a world teeming with spirits with whom humans could work, and that this had descended from ancient times; the more contentious part of his interpretation was that his hatred of Catholicism made him insist that it somehow remained separate from, and inimical to, popular Christianity rather than assimilated into it. For all this, he was careful not to press too far the claim of *stregeria* (cunning craft) to represent a religion in itself; he described it as 'something more than a sorcery, and something less than a faith'[59] which seems to be a fair and a sensitive characterization.

Aradia is strikingly different from these two earlier books. It purports to represent the publication of a single manuscript, the *Vangel* or gospel of a secret religion of witches. In his appendix to it, Leland told how he had heard rumours regarding the existence of such a work since he became interested in Italian witchcraft in 1886; which would certainly conform well with English parallels such as the belief that witches and cunning folk had a Book which was the source of their power. He went on to say that he repeatedly urged Maddalena to obtain a copy of it for him, and that on New Year's Day 1897 she handed over the manuscript which he now printed for the first time. By that date she had long moved out of her native part of the Romagna in her search for material for him, and claimed to have found the necessary information in the Elsa valley, which lies in the Tuscan mountains near Siena. The work which she delivered was in her own handwriting, having either been copied from a written source or sources, or compiled from oral narratives. Leland himself was unsure of this; he was inclined to believe the former but was apparently unable to clarify the matter with Maddalena because she vanished after delivering the work and never reappeared.[60]

The *Vangel* opens with a myth which describes how Diana, goddess of darkness, mated with her brother Lucifer, god of light, after his expulsion from Paradise, and gave birth to Aradia. When this daughter was grown, Diana sent her to earth to teach witchcraft and poisoning to those commoners who had become bandits in the mountains rather than suffer the oppression of feudal lords, that they might strike back against their oppressors. Aradia indeed imparted this wisdom, and then withdrew again, instructing her followers to meet naked in a wild place at each full moon to adore Diana as goddess of witches. They were then to hold a sexual orgy and make a supper of crescent-shaped cakes blessed and baked in the names of Diana and Cain. These meetings would continue until the last of the upper-class oppressors was dead. Aradia then returned to her mother, who granted her the power to gratify those who invoked her with the gift of magical power. A cosmology follows which describes how Diana was the first created being, and divided into two, her other half becoming Lucifer. She went on to create the stars and the rain. The rest of the *Vangel* proper is comprised of invocations and spells which call on the power of Diana, to which Leland added others from different sources, and tales concerning Diana and other female night spirits.

He glossed all this by declaring that this was a (or in some of his passages, *the*) body of 'scriptures' from Michelet's witch religion, which descended in turn from pagan antiquity. He expressed the opinion that this work had come down directly from the Middle Ages, and embodied much older beliefs. He got rid of the apparently unassailable fact that Aradia was a figure from Christian and not pagan mythology by suggesting that she was not the New Testament queen but an ancient Semitic goddess of the same name; no evidence was provided for this derivation, nor for how a Semitic goddess had been transplanted to Italy, nor even for the former existence of this deity. Leland completely forsook any notion that there might be a distinction between *stregeria* and the sort of malevolent witches who were reputed in folklore to hold meetings and cast evil spells, subsuming both within the identity of an Old Religion dedicated to Diana. He went on to assert that it still persisted as 'a fragmentary secret society or sect' and that 'there are in the Romagna entire villages in which the people are entirely heathen and almost entirely governed by *Settimani*' (magicians). His evidence for this was cited as a recent novel, 'several papers published in divers magazines' (he did not explain if these were also works of fiction), and 'my own personal knowledge' (upon which he did not elucidate).[61]

What is one to make of all this? Possible answers may be found within an area bounded by three extreme and polemical positions. The first is that Leland was correct; that this material did indeed represent the sacred book of a secret religion which had survived from antiquity until his own time. It must be admitted that this is not very likely. No other modern Italian folklorist has turned up evidence for anything like the *Vangel*. It is hard to believe that the reactionary Roman Catholic regimes which controlled central Italy until 1859—the Kingdom of Naples, the Empire of Austria (of which Tuscany was a dependency), and the Papal State (which included the Romagna)—would not have noticed the existence of whole villages which rejected Christianity and of a secret sect of pagan witches. This is particularly true because they maintained police systems with the task of detecting secret societies of revolutionaries such as the Carbonari. Leland himself believed that the heyday of the witch society had been in the Middle Ages, and that the *Vangel* came down from that period:

'in this Gospel of the Witches we have a book which is in all probability the translation of some early or late Latin work', i.e. antique or medieval. He continued to say that he 'was not without hope that research may yet reveal in the writings of some long-forgotten heretic or mystic of the dark ages the parallel of many passages in this text, if not the whole of it'.[62] That hope has hitherto been completely vain, despite the fact that medieval Italy possessed ecclesiastical surveillance systems which allowed an inquisitor writing in the 1260s to publish detailed information on almost fifty varieties of heretical sect existing in the peninsula at that time;[63] the 'dark ages' are not as dark as Leland presumed. The list included groups as tiny and obscure as Carpogranites and Atropornofites, but neither this nor any similar work ever mentions followers of Diana or Aradia, save as mythical figures in popular belief.

The source material is still better for the sixteenth and seventeenth centuries. One of the greatest injustices of the view of witchcraft propagated by Michelet and Leland was that their detestation of the Catholic Church led them to hold it primarily responsible for the early modern trials. The truth is that the firmly Catholic states of the Italian peninsula, including that under the direct control of the Popes, remained virtually free of any executions for witchcraft throughout the entire period; the trials were a feature of jurisdictions and societies to the north, which had a less secure religious identity. On the other hand, the inquisitions based in the Italian states relentlessly harried people reported to it for resorting to magical practices or for holding unorthodox beliefs, with penances, fines, and imprisonment. In the process they accumulated a vast number of records detailing the results of their enquiries, which provide a rich source for the historian of popular religion and magic.[64] None of them yet investigated (as most have been) reflects the beliefs laid out in the *Vangel*, let alone reveals a group of people who made them part of a religious cult. When the whole body of data is put together, from Roman times to the present, it proves that some Italians believed in a supernatural being called Diana, who flew by night, and that some also believed that witches prayed to her, and to Herodias, and that they held nocturnal gatherings to plot their evil. It also strongly suggests that the witches concerned had no existence outside mythology.

The second extreme view is that the *Vangel* was partly concocted by Maddalena, to satisfy an employer who ardently wanted to possess the legendary witches' gospel. It is certainly true that she was his main collector of material and that he trusted her absolutely, writing to his niece and later biographer, Elizabeth Robins Pennell, that 'Her memory seems to be inexhaustible and when anything is wanting she consults some other witch and always gets it'. Elizabeth Pennell herself saw 'a huge mass' of letters and manuscripts sent by Maddalena to her uncle, surviving among his papers.[65] She tended to emphasize throughout the biography the way in which Leland acted as a passive and faithful recipient of the information brought to him, and noted that he was very old and ill by the time that he wrote *Aradia*. As he said himself, the manuscript was itself entirely written by Maddalena, from unknown sources. All this information can be used to support the argument that Leland was duped, but none of it comes remotely near proof of the case, and it is balanced by some of the evidence for the third extreme position.

This is, that *Aradia* was to some extent the concoction of Leland himself.[66] There can be no doubt that he had a reputation even in his lifetime for being an unusually unreliable scholar. At the opening of *Etruscan Roman Remains* he noted that he had been accused of inaccuracy in his collection of native American stories, by other experts in the field. Significantly, he made no attempt to deny the charge, just declaring that as he was a pioneer in the area, and dealing with hitherto secretive peoples, he might well have made errors; by saying this, he seemed to be anticipating similar charges concerning his Italian collections.[67] It appears, however, that his critics were prepared to accuse him of more than straightforward mistakes. On his death in 1903, the author of his obituary in the journal of the British Folk-Lore Society, F. York Powell, made the following comment on his methods: 'He could and did make careful and exact notes, but when he put his results before the public he liked to give them the seal of his own personality and to allow his fancy to play about the stories and poems he was publishing.' Coming from a friend and a defender, this is a pretty damning admission, and Powell also admitted that it had given Leland a bad name.[68] It is not, however, a unique pattern for his time. In 1900, the year after the appearance of *Aradia*, Alexander Carmichael published a collection of Hebridean folklore entitled *Carmina Gadelica*, which probably remains the single most popular work of Scottish folklore. Subsequent examination of Carmichael's manuscripts proved that his technique was to collect different versions of a hymn, poem, or charm, and rewrite them as a single 'definitive' one, employing all his own considerable gifts as a poet to invest the verses with a haunting beauty which the originals often lacked; hence the appeal of his work.[69] The same sort of exercise had, of course, been carried out on a grand scale over a hundred years before, when James Macpherson drew on scraps of a genuinely old Gaelic epic to compose a new one, *Ossian*, which he passed off as ancient. Another contemporary of Leland, William Sharp (he of the ill-fated *Pagan Review*), salvaged his literary career by adopting the identity of a Hebridean woman, Fiona Macleod, whose works, steeped in what was presumed to be a peculiarly Celtic sense of enchantment, won a large following. Did Leland do for Tuscany what Macpherson, Carmichael, and Sharp did for the Hebrides?

In considering this question, it needs to be emphasized that Leland may have been old and ill in 1899 but was certainly not a spent force; he went on to complete five more books after *Aradia*. He also invested his edition of the latter with a strong polemical purpose about which he was characteristically candid— to protest against what he saw as the unhealthy benevolence towards the Middle Ages expressed by 'all historians' at that time. To him, this remained a time 'of monstrous abuses and tyranny of Church and State. For then, at every turn in life, the vast majority encountered downright shamelessness, palpable iniquity and injustice, with no law for the weak who were without patrons.' Nothing in the period, for him, mitigated 'the fact that, on the whole mankind was for a long time worse off than before'. To Leland, an age so obviously dominated by his two great *bêtes noires* of the Catholic Church and the feudal nobility could hardly be anything other than horrific.[70] It seemed logical to him that a resistance movement such as that of Aradia's witches *should* have existed, and in the *Vangel* he seemed to possess hard evidence that it had. For wider corroborative data for its existence, he cited Michelet.[71]

He was not, however, a straightforward disciple of the Frenchman. Whereas Michelet had accepted the notion that witches had adored Satan, Leland stated dogmatically that this was an invention of churchmen and that Diana had been their true deity.[72] His position formed a useful soap-box from which to deliver his own views upon contemporary gender relations: that whereas traditional Western society was too disposed to treat women as inferior, and 'the Emancipated, or Woman's Rights woman, when too enthusiastic', was overly disposed to return the same abuse to men, there was hope for a genuine equality between the sexes in the future. The old nineteenth-century radical had lost none of his fire: 'with every new rebellion, every fresh outburst or *débâcle* or wild inundation and bursting over the barriers, humanity and woman gain something, that is to say, their just dues and rights'. To the radical was joined a romantic, equally characteristic of his century: 'there is something uncanny, mysterious, and incomprehensible in woman, which neither she herself nor man can explain. "For every woman is at heart a witch."' The *Vangel* presented Leland with important ammunition for his own beliefs, providing as it did a portrait of a dominant female deity and creatrix to balance the better-known Western patriarchal cosmologies.[73] All this, however, demonstrates that the text suited his political purpose; it does nothing to prove that he created or amended it as a polemical tool.

The three positions explored above are, as repeatedly emphasized, extreme. It is quite possible that the truth lies in a combination of the three; for example, that Maddalena collected local beliefs concerning the principles which witches *ought* to hold, and the activities in which they *should* engage, and put them together as a 'Gospel' for her employer who then believed that he now possessed the text used by an actual secret religion. Such an interpretation would fit all the known facts, but it is only one of a number of possible variations and it is stated here not as a preferred one but merely as an example of one sort of hypothesis which the evidence can sustain; it is itself as unprovable as the others. Will this situation always persist? Perhaps, but it is noteworthy that no modern, scholarly, and properly researched biography of Leland exists, and that a large collection of his papers is preserved by the Historical Society of Pennsylvania. A thorough analysis of the latter should in itself yield interesting results, and eliminate or elucidate some of the possibilities proposed above.[74]

*   *   *

So much space has been devoted to *Aradia* because it was to be one of the most important texts of modern pagan witchcraft, but it needs to be stressed again that it was published by an expatriate American, thoroughly unrepresentative of most of his nation's writers upon witches and witch trials. The theory that the victims of the latter had been pagans was to make most impact upon a country which had neither developed the idea nor been in the forefront of research into the subject. This was England, the only one in which it was to be taken up avidly by mainstream scholars who were part of the current intellectual establishment. It had already appeared there by 1865, in an essay by the antiquarian Thomas Wright 'On the Worship of the Generative Powers during the Middle Ages of Western Europe', which he appended to a privately printed new edition of Richard Payne Knight's eighteenth-century *Discourse on the Worship of Priapus*. The timing of Wright's piece strongly suggests the influence of *La Sorcière*, and his portrait of a medieval witch religion was every bit as supportive as that of Michelet; to him, it represented the ancient pagan veneration of the benevolent power of life and the beauties of nature, driven underground by the life-hating forces of the medieval Church.

Unsurprisingly, this idea really took off in the 1890s, the decade which also saw the full development of the popularity of Pan among English poets, and myth of a timeless, organic, rural Englishness, the language of paganism as a joyous, life-affirming, nature-based religion, and the quest for pagan origins of popular customs. It was expressed most forcefully at the point where most of those concerns intersected, in the newly founded Folk-Lore Society. In 1892 its president, George Lawrence Gomme, informed the world that in his opinion witches had represented a secret society of initiates, through whom elements of prehistoric religion were passed down to the early modern period from the 'conquered pre-Aryan peoples of Europe'. These elements included the traditions of Druidry: 'the witch is the successor of the Druid priestess'. Gomme carried out no research to support this hypothesis; instead he misquoted Grimm as having already proved that witchcraft was basically pagan in character.[75]

Five years later, another distinguished English scholar took a similar leap of imagination. This was Karl Pearson, Professor of Applied Mathematics at University College London and a dabbler in history and anthropology. His view of witchcraft combined that of Michelet with the contemporary speculation about the former existence of universal matriarchy and the worship of a Great Goddess, to provide a parallel to that of Gage (whom he may indeed have read) with the sympathies reversed. To Pearson, likewise, the medieval witch was a young and beautiful priestess, serving the Goddess and sometimes also the latter's consort and junior partner, the god of the natural world, in a religion which celebrated and encouraged the fertility of the land. In the course of the Christian era, he opined, the male deity had become more prominent in the religion and been stigmatized by churchmen as the Devil. It seems to have been Pearson who came up with the idea that Joan of Arc had been one of the last of these traditional pagan holy women and leaders of the common people. The difference between his vision and that of Michelet and Gage was that he declared that the worship of the Goddess had been primitive, cruel, and orgiastic, and that the witch religion had been a yet more degraded version of it. None the less, he continued (like Leland, with one eye on the contemporary New Woman) by suggesting that the recognition that women had once played a leading part in the world—even if they had not played it very well—might abet an improvement in their public position in modern times. To support his theories, Pearson provided a mixture of modern folklore from the German-speaking lands and details culled selectively from early modern trial records.[76]

By the opening of the twentieth century, therefore, the notion that the persecuted witches of Christian Europe had been practitioners of the old religion had earned notable adherents in England. Two years after Pearson wrote, Leland's *Aradia* reinforced the body of literature available to them, and in 1904 *La Sorcière* was at last translated into English and so made available to a wider public in their country; the fact that this work was undertaken in itself indicates that the publisher thought the time propitious for it to attract a large readership. The problem with the theory, at that stage, was that the quantity of scholarly research which underpinned it—especially in comparison with that undertaken by the proponents of the rival notion that witchcraft was a clerical delusion—was lamentably inadequate. What was clearly required by its supporters was a work to defend it, well grounded in the evidence provided by the early modern trials. Such a work was shortly to be forthcoming, from a British writer, and upon its heels would come something which none of the nineteenth-century authors seem to have anticipated; an appearance—or reappearance—of the witch religion itself.

9

MATRIX

HITHERTO, this book has been devoted to identifying certain elements which were to be prominent in modern pagan witchcraft, and tracing their development over a period of one or two hundred years before it appeared. It is time now to examine ways in which some of them were combined in a sample of prominent individuals and organizations operating in the last seventy years before that emergence. The object of this exercise is to illustrate how complex, how personal, and how variable that process of combination could be, and how much it involved negotiation and assimilation with belief systems more conventional in the nineteenth- and early twentieth-century British world. None of the people concerned can be regarded as normative; they were all fairly remarkable by the standards of their day. For all this, their experiences do help to reveal something of the way in which areas of British culture began the transition to a post-Christian society.

The exercise begins with a trio of authors united by the characteristic that all enjoyed exceptional success in serving the market in popular fiction between 1880 and 1910: H. Rider Haggard, Rudyard Kipling, and Kenneth Grahame. Haggard was probably the most widely read writer of colonial adventure stories during the period, dealing continuously with the themes of imperialism, militarism, and race and gender tensions; his all-time best-seller, *She* (1887) is a profoundly hostile portrait of primitive matriarchy. Religion, by contrast, is a subject comparatively understated in his books, and to understand his relationship with it we must look at his life as well as his works of fiction. At first sight it presents a picture of strict Christian piety. The chapter entitled 'A Note on Religion' in his autobiography *The Days of My Life* (1926) declares that he had read the Bible every day for decades. It is known that he led his family and servants in prayers each morning before breakfast. He served as a churchwarden in the Norfolk parish which contained his country seat, and read lessons during services with notable relish. His mother Ella, whom he adored and whose memory he revered, had been conspicuously devout, and one of his biographers, D. S. Higgins, has suggested that it was grief at her death which drove him to this daily regime of worship. In a letter to the *Spectator* in 1887 he equated paganism with agnosticism; the error of looking 'to earth and earth alone, for its comforts and rewards'.[1]

A closer view reveals some remarkable anomalies. Haggard had absorbed from theosophy two doctrines firmly rejected by orthodox Christianity: reincarnation and the law of karma. He married these to an oppressive personal sense of sin, by believing that moral misdeeds in one life led to a loss of future incarnation; an idiosyncratic blend of Hindu, Buddhist, and Christian dogma.[2] This was accompanied by a sense that the Christian Trinity was only the apex of a hierarchy of divinities which included ancient pagan deities: 'I have a respect for Thor and Odin. I venerate Isis and always feel inclined to bow before the moon.' He commissioned an Egyptologist to design him a personal cartouche, reading in hieroglyphs 'H. Rider Haggard, the son of Ella, lady of the house, makes an oblation to Thoth, the Lord of Writing, who dwells in the moon.' He also admitted to at least the possibility of the literal existence of ghosts and spirits and of the effectiveness of magical spells.[3] This rich and idiosyncratic cocktail of beliefs is implicit in the plots of many of his novels, and contributes to their allure.

Kipling professed a much weaker sense of religion but revealed an equally complex set of attitudes towards it. As a young man in 1889 he wrote a confession of faith for a pious young woman with whom he was in love. He rejected the concepts of eternal reward or damnation, of the Trinity, and of sin and redemption, but still believed in

a personal God to whom we are personally responsible for wrongdoing—that it is our duty to follow and our peril to disobey the ten ethical laws laid down for us by Him and His prophets. . . . I believe in God the Father Almighty, maker of Heaven and Earth and in One filled with His spirit who did voluntarily die in the belief that the human race would be spiritually bettered thereby.[4]

Thereafter he remained nominally a member of the Church of England but only attended it for rites of passage, most notably for weddings. He and his wife Carrie were themselves married in church, but they never had their son John baptized as a child.[5]

His books, however, suggest something more than this pallid remnant of formal religion, and the most important for present purposes are the two written for children after his reputation had long been established and he had retired to a country house in Sussex. Having lived in, and identified with, the British Raj in India, this relocation effectively involved the exploration of a new world, as has been noted earlier.[6] This discovery chimed well with a tactical shift in Kipling, provoked by the apparent failure of his former patriotic and imperialist dreams in the Boer War and subsequent settlement of South Africa. He coped with his disillusion by attempting to instil in English youngsters an understanding of, and pride in, their land, to strengthen patriotism in the future.[7] The result was two collections of stories set around his home in east Sussex, *Puck of Pook's Hill* (1906) and *Rewards and Fairies* (1910).

Their essential theme is that the land and the people are one, their association constantly renewed over thousands of years so that the very landscape is a history book. This, of course, harmonized perfectly with the contemporary yearning for a timeless and enduring rural England, and Kipling represented the latter in the character of Hobden, the wily and taciturn old country man who understands the whole story of his district by instinct and tradition. Especially in view of the fact that so many of the stories are set in the Middle Ages, they are notably lacking in Christian piety. It is true that the deities of ancient Near Eastern civilizations and of the Anglo-Saxons are shown as malevolent spirits empowered by the needless belief of their worshippers, cruel orientals, and barbarians respectively, and that Christianity is shown as providing a merciful deliverance from them. Those of ancient Rome, which Kipling saw as a model for imperial Britain, are, by contrast, treated with real sympathy; indeed, Kipling composes a powerful hymn to Mithras, as a god of soldiers dedicated to duty. His main story from the Roman period concerns the fourth-century emperor Magnus Maximus, who was actually a Christian. Kipling, however, makes both him and his followers—who are the heroes of the tale, holding the line on a vulnerable Roman North-West Frontier—pagan. Furthermore, he associates an inherent power with the trees and herbs of the land, especially oak, ash, and thorn, by which the central character of the books, the nature spirit Puck, always swears. His song about them, which closes the very first story, has become a modern pagan classic. One of its verses, in particular, is redolent of that sense of folk customs as enduring representatives of old fertility religions, surviving alongside the established Church, which was becoming dominant in that decade:

> Oh, do not tell the Priest our plight,
>   Or he would call it sin;
> But—we have been out in the woods all night,
>   A-conjuring Summer in!
> And we bring you news by word of mouth—
>   Good news for cattle and corn—
> Now is the Sun come up from the South
>   With Oak, and Ash, and Thorn!

Curiously for a nominal Anglican, Kipling showed no clear approval of the Reformation, portraying it (in the tale 'The Dymchurch Flit') as the time when most of the fairies fled England, disliking the harshness of the new Protestant preachers who had replaced the more magical medieval Catholicism. This fiction might be taken as stressing the more rational, and 'modern', nature of the reformed religion, were it not for the sympathy that Kipling consistently accords to the notion that the land is, and should be, an enchanted place. The contemporary debate over the existence of prehistoric matriarchy also made its impression on him. The tale 'The Knife and the Naked Chalk' presents a curious portrait of ancient Sussex in which a neolithic culture on the Downs co-exists with an Iron Age one in the Weald, but both have a religion run by women: 'Their Priestess was their Ears and their Mouth.' Like many writers of his time, Kipling associated primitive matriarchs with cruelty and superstition, regarding their rule as one feature of the primitive nature of their age, but he still credited them with dignity and wrote about them with respect.

Over this same span of years, however, Kipling's own faith was growing more, rather than less, steady and orthodox. *Reward and Fairies* has less sympathy for paganism than *Puck of Pook's Hill*, and in 1914 Rudyard and Carrie approvingly acted as sponsors for their son, when he chose to have the baptism into the Anglican Church which he had been denied as a baby.[8]

Grahame, who has already featured in the present volume as the author of *Pagan Papers* and of one of the most striking modern literary representations of Pan, exhibits a third personal resolution of the same impulses. He rejected Christianity more completely than either of the others, referring to the brand in which he was brought up as 'Scotch-Calvinist devil-worship'.[9] His replacement for it consisted of a vague (if intense) reverence for the natural world, most immediately represented by the English countryside. The latter, indeed, afforded him a world into which he could take physical and spiritual holidays from his comfortable, lucrative, and detested job in the City of London.[10] His masterpiece, *The Wind in the Willows*, reflects his fears and yearnings in an extreme form. It is famous for its representation of the defeat of working-class revolutionaries (the stoats and weasels) by heroes standing for a paternal society dominated by a propertied bourgeoisie; but Grahame was concerned with more than the conservation of the existing social order. One of the most poignant moments of the book comes in the chapter 'Mr Badger', where it is revealed that the Wild Wood has grown out of the ruins of a city, with the comment that in the end it is the natural world which must always triumph, and that of urban humanity which must pass. In the end Grahame achieved his own triumph over the city, after a fashion, by taking early retirement and moving out to the village of Blewbury in the White Horse Vale of (then) Berkshire, which he characterized in one of the most extreme statements of the English 'rural myth' ever penned:

This is the heart of King Alfred's country, 'Alfred the Great', who beat the Danes close by here; about 860, and nothing had really happened since. True, a tiresome innovator called William the Conqueror came along some years later, and established a thing called the Curfew bell, which still rings here during the winter months, to the annoyance of the more conservative inhabitants, who say that they used to get along very well before these new-fangled notions; but this is all that divides us from Saxon times.[11]

Nobody reading these lines would gain any inkling that the Vale, like most of the English countryside, was undergoing the fastest and most dramatic change in its history, with widespread mechanization, depopulation, and fragmentation of community; Grahame's gaze simply screened all of this off.

Ironically, it was his wife, born Elspeth Thomas, who was initially the more actively 'pagan' of the two and tried to practise the nature-worship that he was preaching. At first she refused a wedding ring, thinking it a hallmark of convention, and it was he who insisted on her acceptance of one. The ceremony took place (in 1899) in the equally conventional setting of the parish church at Fowey, on the south Cornish coast, and Elspeth made one final gesture of rebellion. To demonstrate her communion with nature, she appeared before the altar wearing an old muslin dress which she had soaked in the dew that morning and a chain of daisies around her neck which she had woven herself. The guests certainly, and Kenneth apparently, were embarrassed, and the marriage which ensued was unhappy and unfulfilled.[12]

* * *

It is time now to turn to a different trio of literary men, this time belonging more to the canon of high creative authorship and producing for a more exclusive audience. All, again, were contemporaries, publishing their best-known work between 1890 and 1940: W. B. Yeats, George Russell ('Æ'), and D. H. Lawrence. Much has been printed about Yeats's interest in magic, and he has been mentioned above as a prominent member of the Golden Dawn; considerably less attention has been paid to his religious beliefs, which are of issue here. It can be said that he was possessed of a strong inclination to believe in the existence of a spirit world, and of deities, and to work with them. He once commented that 'I did not think that I could live without religion.'[13] To a great extent he felt that this force was immanent in the world; in 1900 he recalled how 'when we were schoolboys we used to discuss whatever we could find to read of mystical philosophy and to pass crystals over each other's hands and eyes and to fancy that we could feel a breath flowing from them'.[14] During his time in the Theosophical Society, Yeats learned a system which gave him some sense of understanding how this essential power worked and could be worked with: 'every organ of the body has its correspondence in the heavens and the seven principles which made the human soul and body correspond to the seven colours and the seven planets and the notes of the musical scale'.[15]

A good case could be made that he remained a convinced and self-conscious Christian. He was certainly troubled by the more overtly pagan tendencies in the Golden Dawn, and in 1901 he wrote a paper arguing that the order was founded firmly upon Christian principles.[16] The same view had been expressed more succinctly to a worried friend in 1896:

Nor is our order anti-Christian. The very pentagram which I suggested your using is itself, as you would presently have learned, a symbol of Christ. I am convinced however that for you progress lies not in dependence on a Christ outside yourself but upon the Christ in your own breast, in the power of your own divine will and divine imagination and not in some external will or imagination however divine. We certainly do teach this dependence only on the inner divinity but this is Christianity.[17]

At this point, however, some qualifications need to be made. What Yeats was describing was not a Christianity ever preached by established Churches; this notion of an indwelling Jesus had always been, rather, the hallmark of a distinctive strain of radical Christian heresy. On examining the literary works of Yeats it is apparent that Christ is, in fact, rarely mentioned. It is God who features regularly, as 'the Eternal Darkness', 'Supreme Enchanter', 'Ineffable Name', and 'Light of Lights'. Richard Ellman, who studied the poet's view of God, considered that it embodied neither affection or obedience but a sense of a force of nature or of fate. Yeats regarded heaven, hell, and purgatory as states of the human mind; again, a long-established Christian heretical tradition.[18]

Just as in the case of Rider Haggard, Yeats's cosmology allowed for a belief in the existence of lesser deities as well as a supreme one; and for him pagan divinities were bound up with the cause of Irish nationalism to which he devoted much energy in the 1890s. They, and the fairy-folk or Sidhe to whom they were related and allied, were seen by him as spirits of the land which he wanted to free. Maud Gonne, his great love at this period, recalled of it how 'Ireland, we both felt, was powerfully alive and invisibly peopled, and whenever we grew despondent over the weakness of the national movement, we went to it for comfort. If only we could make contact with the hidden forces of the land, it would give us strength for the freeing of Ireland.'[19] In 1888 Yeats made a collection of Irish folklore which he introduced with the assertion that Irish peasants, because of their preservation from the Industrial Revolution, had retained a rapport with the spirit world which had elsewhere disappeared.[20] By 1896 he could write that the time of the old deities had returned:

the Dagda, with his overflowing cauldron, Lu, with his spear dipped in poppy juice, lest it rush forth hot for battle, Angus, with his three birds on his shoulder, Bove and his red swine-herd, and all the heroic children of Dana, set up once more their temples of grey stone. Their reign has never ceased, but only waned in power a little, for the Shee still pass in every wind, and dance and play at hurley, and fight their sudden battles in every hollow and on every hill.[21]

By now his friend George Russell noted that he 'talked much of reviving the Druidic mysteries', and Yeats wrote to 'Fiona Macleod' that 'some sort of new cult is about to be born'.[22]

He wove into his attitude to nature spirits and paganism two other themes commonly heard in the decade. One was (of course) that folk customs represented surviving portions of ancient religion, offering an alternative system of spirituality to set beside the Christian. In 1897 he told readers of *The New Review* that

Nothing shows more how blind educated Ireland . . . is about peasant Ireland, than that it does not understand how the old religion which made of the coming and going of the fields a part of its worship lives side by side with the new religion which would trample nature as a serpent under its feet; nor is that old religion faded to a meaningless repetition of old customs, for the ecstatic who has seen the red light and white light of God smite themselves into the bread and wine at Mass, has seen the exultant hidden multitudes among the winds of May; and if we were philosophical would cry out with the painter, Calvert:—I go inward to God, outward to the gods.[23]

The other familiar theme of the time which he articulated in turn was that 'women come more easily than men to that wisdom which ancient peoples, and all wild peoples even now, think the only wisdom'.[24]

The poet set about bringing such a 'new cult' to birth himself. In the mid-1890s he planned a mystical order to be based in a castle on an island in an Irish lake, 'where we might establish mysteries like those of Eleusis and Samothrace'.[25] During the years 1896–7 he and Maud Gonne extended this plan to one for an Irish nationalist society of mystics based upon a lodge structure taken from Freemasonry and mixing concepts from theosophy and the Golden Dawn with Irish pagan mythology 'to unite the radical truths of Christianity to those of a more ancient world'. He ploughed through contemporary works of scholarship to find correspondences between Irish and Graeco-Roman deities, and in late 1897 he formed a group in London to pursue the work for the new order through guided meditations and other visionary experiences. Most, if not all, were drawn from the Golden Dawn, and they included Florence Farr; in addition he exchanged letters with Moina and Samuel Mathers, George Russell, Maud Gonne, and 'Fiona Macleod', to draw upon their ideas.[26] The result was that

we obtained in vision long lists of symbolic forms that correspond to the cardinal points, and the old gods and heroes took their places gradually in a symbolic fabric that had for its centre the four talismans of the Tuatha de Danaan, the Sword, the Stone, the Spear, and the Cauldron, which related themselves in my mind with the suits of the Tarot.[27]

Throughout this process his tension with those who wanted to discard a Christian component remains obvious; between 1896 and 1902 he wrote, but did not publish, a play called *The Speckled Bird*, in which the hero becomes convinced that the symbols of Christianity must be the central expression of any mystical order. The character who puts the opposite view is clearly modelled upon Mathers.[28] Yeats's own aim was to fuse Christian and pre-Christian traditions as equivalent fulfilments of the some human needs: 'Because the Rose, the flower sacred to the Virgin Mary, and the flower that Apuleius's adventurer ate, when he was changed out of the ass's shape and received into the fellowship of Isis, is the western Flower of Life, I have imagined it growing upon the Tree of Life'.[29] In one sentence there, he had fused Christianity, Graeco-Roman paganism, and the cabbala.

By January 1902 Yeats had completed the initiation rituals for his order, into the grades of the cauldron, stone, sword, and spear successively. At that point, however, the whole supporting framework of his life collapsed, as he suffered disillusion with the Golden Dawn, Maud Gonne, and the Irish nationalist cause.[30] He abandoned his plans for the society, and thereafter his religious ideas reappear only in fragmentary form, embedded in his later poetry and plays. None the less, certain components of them persisted and were augmented, notably his tendency (much influenced by *The Golden Bough*) to relate Christ to Attis, Adonis, Dionysos, and other dying and/or returning gods. In one play he explicitly interpreted the Christian Resurrection as the last episode in a cyclical renewal of spiritual forces through one god after another.[31] Looking back from the 1920s, he could say that 'I had made a new religion, almost an infallible church of poetic tradition, of a fardel of stories'.[32] That comment could fit most of the individuals discussed in this chapter.

It is certainly true of Yeats's friend and collaborator, George Russell. In 1885 the two of them were among the founders of the Dublin Hermetic Society, designed to study the Western mystical traditions, and Russell later became its president and held that post until 1933. He never joined the Golden Dawn (mainly because unlike Yeats he never moved to London) and instead gave his energy in the 1890s to the Theosophical Society and the cause of Irish national-ism. Like Yeats, he blended concepts drawn from theosophy with old Irish mythology, but invested the work with an even greater intensity, seeking to have Druidic Ireland recognized as one of the world's principal ancient civilizations, comparable to Egypt or India.[33] Like Yeats he both foresaw a revival of the veneration of the pagan Irish deities and credited them with genuine existence. In June 1896 he wrote to his friend that

The Gods have returned to Eri and have centred themselves in the sacred mountains and blow the fires through the country. They have been seen by several in vision. They will awaken the magical instinct everywhere and the universal heart of the people will turn to the old Druidic beliefs. I note through the country the increased faith in faery things. The bells are heard from the mounds and sounding in the hollows of the mountains.

Shortly afterwards he told Yeats that he had been granted a vision of the Celtic adept who was to lead the revival; a man with grey-golden hair living in a small Irish cottage. He linked this national resurgence with a global one, the transition from the Age of Pisces to that of Aquarius: 'Pisces is phallic in its influence. The waterman is spiritual so that the inward turning souls will catch the first rays of the new Aeon'.[34] His pen-name, Æ, was an abbreviation of ÆON.

This apocalyptic tone inevitably faded as no gods, adept, or national spiritual renewal appeared, but Russell never shared the bitter disillusion of Yeats. Instead, he developed and consolidated his own spiritual system. It was fully fledged in his treatise *The Candle of Vision*, written in the 1910s, which proclaimed belief in a single original boundless divinity later divided into a Great Father and Great Mother, out of whom all gods and goddesses were formed; but the latter, were also now real and independent entities, communi-cating with humans in vision from a parallel world, the Many Coloured Land. The Father (also called the Lord and King) had created the natural world, and yet the earth itself was a part of the Great Mother, the 'Mighty Mother of Us All', and radiant with her divine power. Christ still had a place in this cosmology as a great and benevolent adept equivalent to Krishna; he was 'the Magician and the Beautiful'.[35] In his poetry between 1890 and 1930 Russell explored these concepts repeatedly, hailing the Father as 'God', or 'The Mighty Master', and the Goddess as 'the Ancient Mother', 'the Virgin Mother', and (following old Irish tradition) 'Dana'. It does seem, however, that the divine feminine moved him to a greater intensity of expression, quotation from which has been provided earlier in this book. Russell's goddess was not merely an immanent divinity, but one who features in poems such as 'Mystery' and 'The House of the Titans' in tangible and human form, materializing in woods and on seashores at twilight to comfort lonely wanderers. He completed his mystical writings in 1933, with *The Avatars*, an account of the birth of religion of Cosmic Consciousness, consisting essentially of a recognition of the divine life in the natural world.

Lawrence stands apart from these two. For one thing he was a much more tormented, embittered, and persecuted individual, with a much more tragic life. For another, he did not emerge from the traditions of theosophy and the Irish literary revival but from the mystical socialism represented by Edward Carpenter. Carpenter was indeed an important direct influence on him[36] as were later Jane Ellen Harrison and Sir James Frazer. These differences make it all the more striking how much he shared with the two Anglo-Irishmen, and with many other writers of their generation: the preoccupations of reconciling humanity with the natural world, man with woman, and Christianity with paganism. In Lawrence's case, a fairly clear linear progress is discernible. It begins properly with *The Rainbow* (1915), which has already been noted as fusing the imagery of woman, moon, and stars in an especially vivid manner. The whole book, however, is intensely religious in tone, being an account of a search for spiritual freedom. It is sprinkled with Christian references, but, through his heroine Ursula, Lawrence seems to be arriving at a religious essentialism, with a syncretism of different traditions, classic of his age: 'The outward form was a matter of indifference to her. Yet she had some fundamental religion. It was as if she worshipped God as a mystery, never seeking to define what He was. And inside her, the subtle sense of the Great Absolute wherein she had her being was very strong.' And again:

Gradually it dawned upon Ursula that all the religion she knew was but a particular clothing to a human aspiration. The aspiration was the real thing—the clothing was a matter almost of natural taste or need. The Greeks had a naked Apollo, the Christians a white-robed Christ, the Buddhists a royal prince, the Egyptians their Osiris. Religions were local and religion was universal. Christianity was a local branch. There was as yet no assimilation of local religions into a universal religion.[37]

There is in all this no special predilection for paganism; indeed, whenever the term 'heathen' is used in the novel, it is dismissive, signifying an absence of religion. By the time that Lawrence wrote *Kangaroo*, in 1923, he was using what was characterized earlier in the present book as the 'first' language of paganism. The twelfth chapter is set in the archaic landscape of western Cornwall, and he repeatedly associates the prehistoric monuments there with blood sacrifice, 'darkness of menhirs', 'savagery', and 'old awful presences'. In the same year he published an essay in *The Adelphi* which declared that all people relate to 'the great God of the End, who is the All-Father of all sources'.[38] Nor, throughout the period between 1915 and 1923, did he have much sympathy for goddesses. It is a simple fact that people in the nineteenth and twentieth centuries who have liked female deities tend to have liked women, and Lawrence at this time was too uncertain in his own sexual orientation and too ambivalent towards human females, to be attracted to the divine feminine. Instead, as has been mentioned earlier, he recognized an inherent power in women, linked to the natural world, and feared it. This anxiety burst out again in his essay 'Pan in America', written in 1924: 'Oh woman, wonderful is the craft of your softness, the distance of your dark depths. Oh open silently the deep that has no end, and do not turn the horns of the night against me.'[39]

All this is true, and yet at the same time other impulses were stirring in Lawrence. In that same chapter of *Kangaroo*, he suggested that the Druids and ancient Celts, although barbaric, understood 'most sensitively the dark flicker of animal life'. He describes how he called out one night to the old Celtic deities, and seemed to feel them approaching from the dark Cornish heathland around his home. Here Lawrence was getting very close to using what I have called the fourth, affirmative, language of paganism; and in 'Pan in America' it becomes dominant, with the horned god employed in his by then traditional modern role, as symbol of 'the live relationship between man and his universe'. To Lawrence in this essay, 'The Pan relationship, which the world of man once had with all the world, was better than anything man has now.'[40] No wonder that in *Lady Chatterley's Lover* (1928), he has Mellors suggest that a pagan revival would be good for ordinary people; although by this time Lawrence was generally hostile to the masses, and made his character add that 'The few can go in for higher cults'. At the same time his fear of women was subsiding, and the novel is in part a celebration of heterosexual union. The association between woman and nature persists, but is far less troubled; thus Constance Chatterley, after sexual satisfaction, is 'like a forest, like the dark interlacing of the oakwood, humming inaudibly with myriad unfolding buds. Meanwhile the birds of desire were asleep in the vast interlaced intricacy of her body.'[41]

In the following year, Lawrence brilliantly resolved all of the tensions traced above, in a short story entitled 'The Man Who Died'. It portrays Christ as surviving his crucifixion and recovering to turn his back upon his old life, followers, and message. He finds sanctuary, and happiness, in a temple of the great goddess, Isis, where he personifies the resurrected Osiris and makes sacred love with the priestess; once again, *The Golden Bough* had proved to be a plank across the chasm separating paganism and Christianity, by implying an equation between Jesus and dying and returning gods. Works published after Lawrence's death in 1930 show other resolutions made in his last years. He had fashioned a bridge of his own between religion traditions by interpreting the Book of Revelation as a representation of the initiation ritual into a pagan mystery religion. Announcing that the true text had been corrupted and disfigured by Hebrew and Christian copyists, and that his had hitherto escaped notice because of the 'terrific prejudice' of scholars, he proceeded to use his instincts to 'restore' it. Thus, the Whore of Babylon was revealed to be 'the great Mother of the cosmos', the Beast or Dragon to represent the divine power within nature, and so forth.[42]

A different posthumous publication provided a full scheme which Lawrence had made of the history of ancient religion. By this, prehistoric people have 'not yet invented gods or goddesses, but live by the mystery of the powers of the Universe, the complex vitalities of what we feebly call Nature'. This spirit survived most admirably into historic times, suggested Lawrence, in the civilization of the Etruscans, which he idealized into a model for humanity.

To the Etruscan all was alive; the whole universe lived; and the business of man was to live amidst it all. He had to draw life into himself, out of the wandering, huge vitalities of the world. . . . The cosmos was one, and its anima was one; but it was made up of creatures. And the greatest creature was earth, with its soul of inner fire.[43]

Lawrence, however, went on to assert that this philosophy was known only to the elite of the time:

The people are not initiated into the cosmic ideas, nor to the awakened throb of more vivid consciousness. Try as you may you can never make the mass of men throb with full awakedness . . . so the actual knowledge must be guarded from them, lest knowing the formulae, without undergoing the experience that corresponds, they may become insolent and impious, thinking they have the all, when they have only an empty monkey chatter.[44]

In this fashion he paid back the common people of Britain, for what he believed to be their consistent failure to understand him or his ideas. He also accounted for the fact that Etruscan art by no means obviously supported the interpretation which he made of it, stating that it was intended to content the populace, while his skilled eye could discern the hidden meaning within it.[45]

To Lawrence, also, the creation of heroes automatically demanded villains, and the loving, carefree, nature-venerating Etruscans had to be pitted against an opposite. He found this in the Greeks and Romans, who had corrupted 'the old religion of the profound attempt of man to harmonize himself with nature' into 'a desire to resist nature, to produce a mental cunning and a mechanical force that would outwit nature and chain her down completely.'[46] In particular, he turned the Romans into a caricature of all that he hated most in modern British culture; a society of philistines devoted to conquest, repression, regimentation, and commercial success.

*　　*　　*

These six individuals were, of course, literary figures and cannot be taken as 'representative' of their society even if three of them wrote deliberately for a mass market; by definition, they were remarkable people. What has been shown here is that a struggle to adapt or reject Christianity, by mixing in or substituting concepts associated with ancient paganism, was one feature of the literary culture of the time. It is necessary now to look at other parts of society to see whether the same forces were at work; and here we are reliant on chance survivals of evidence produced by remarkable circumstances. One of these occurred at the old limestone village of Painswick, on the scarp of Gloucestershire's Cotswold Hills, in 1885. It was then that a new vicar, W. H.

Seddon, took charge of the parish and immediately proved to be a keen classicist and antiquarian. He learned that until the 1830s a procession in honour of Pan had taken place at Painswick each spring, starting at the church and ending in some woods to the north. Seddon decided to revive it. He was especially excited to discover that the rallying cry for the procession was remembered as having been 'Highgates! Highgates!' This was likely in fact to have been 'Hyett's! Hyett's!', meaning the house of Benjamin Hyett, a local worthy who had sponsored the event in the mid- to late eighteenth century and whose mansion in the woods had been its finishing point. Seddon, however, did not know this, and decided firmly that it derived from the Greek *aig aitis*, 'goat-lover', and was the call to Pan used by the original revellers in a pagan ceremony from which the custom had descended. He insisted that it be readopted as part of the restored event, and had a statue of Pan installed near the church tower as a point of commencement. He published a booklet on the village's folklore, *Painswick Feast*, in which he stated that 'Not everything pagan is bad, and our Christian forefathers took a wise view of this matter.' His prime piece of evidence for this last piece of information was the survival of the procession; what he did not realize is that all the actual evidence suggests that the latter was a piece of antiquarian fancy created in the eighteenth century by a group of local gentry with classical enthusiasms, of whom Hyett was a leader. Nobody seems to have criticized Seddon for his revival, nor was he condemned by his superiors. The event long survived him, until 1950, when a more puritanical vicar at last suppressed it and had the statue buried.[47]

It is hard to say how eccentric a figure Seddon was. Late Victorian and Edwardian England was hardly short of clergy with an interest in folklore, the classics, and antiquities; sometimes in all three. In the absence of a local catalyst such as the Pan procession, nobody can reckon how many more of them had arrived at a recognition that the old religions had possessed some merit, of the sort made by members of the laity in this period. What is much clearer, and well documented, is the relationship between paganism and the woodcraft movements. All of the latter were inspired by one man, the American (though Canadian-born) Ernest Thompson Seton, a lover of camping, wildlife, and the natural world, who came during the closing years of the nineteenth century to be heavily influenced by the theories of the popular American psychologist G. Stanley Hill. He drew from the latter the belief that children were best taught by a combination of creative play, self-government, and a reward system based on decorations. In 1900 Seton was propelled into action by the need to reform local juvenile delinquents who were damaging his land. He held a camp for them at which he taught woodcraft with the intention of combining civilized values with the practical skills and knowledge of native Americans. The results were so impressive that from 1902 he advocated his system in *The Ladies' Home Journal*, inspiring the formation of bands of 'Seton Indians' all across the United States. He defined that system as intended to conserve wild animals, foster fellowship, and 'discover, preserve, develop, and diffuse the culture of the Redman'. By 1906 he was holding annual camps and had written a handbook. In that year he lectured in England and asked to meet a public figure noted in that country for his interest in education by outdoor activities, the Boer War hero Robert Baden-Powell. From that meeting, and the ensuing friendship, sprang the Boy Scout movement.

What Baden-Powell did was to apply Seton's methods to his own ends, with amazing success. In 1907 he held his first camp, in 1908 he published *Scouting for Boys*, and by the end of the year his movement already had 100,000 members. Seton was given his due as a godfather by being accorded leadership of the movement across the Atlantic. The two men were, however, pursuing very different ideals. Seton wanted to teach boys to be better humans and to save wildlife; Baden-Powell wanted to teach them to be better subjects and to save the British Empire. The former's model was the tribe, the latter's the army. The contrast is neatly provided by comparing *Scouting for Boys* with Seton's equivalent work *The Book of Woodcraft and Indian Lore* (1912). The former is as much devoted to citizenship, patriotism, and moral instruction as to woodcraft; the latter is not. The alliance between the two men held until the pressures of the First World War blew it apart. The conflict brought out in Baden-Powell's leadership of the Scouts all the jingoism and militarism which had always been latent in it, and Seton resigned in 1915.[48] His departure, however, precipitated a series of secessions by British Scout workers who were likewise dismayed by the tone of the movement and tended more towards Seton's views. In 1916 Ernest Westlake founded the Order of Woodcraft Chivalry, with Seton as honorary Grand Chieftain. John Hargrave followed in 1920 with the Kindred of the Kibbo Kift, from which a further schism in 1924 produced the Woodcraft Folk. Their numbers were tiny in comparison with the Scouts (and the Girl Guides who became a companion movement to the latter)—1,200 in the Woodcraft Chivalry by 1926, 236 in the Kibbo Kift before the secession of 1924—but they have a significant place in the history of British culture and ideas.[49]

In approaching the religious aspect of that history, one common element is obvious; that in absorbing 'lore' and 'craft' from tribal peoples in general and native Americans in particular, the woodcraft movements all to some extent took in the animist view of the world, of a natural universe teeming with spirits, which is inherent in those cultures. This was inevitably going to dilute the Christian element in the movements, as was the different trait that all were open to followers of different monotheist religions. Baden-Powell had laid down from the start that Christians, Jews, and Muslims were to be regarded as divisions of an army serving the same king, and that it was atheists and agnostics who were the enemy. The result was that even in the Scouts, the most conservative and conformist branch, the dominant religion was a very unorthodox Christianity, in which nature was commonly described as Mistress and Mother, God as Creator and All-Father, and Christ as a teacher rather than as God Incarnate. The greatest ceremony of the movement (and of all those derived from it) was the lighting of the campfire, and the adoption of tribal chants introduced a further element of what might broadly be termed paganism. Occasionally this resulted in a flaring of tension; thus, in 1920 Miss Vera Barclay, a devout Roman Catholic and Commissioner for Wolf Cubs, protested when a scout troop used 'the Omaha Tribal Prayer'. She claimed that it taught 'the Great Lies' that it was permissible to 'leave Christ out' of Scout religion, that 'we should go to the heathen for our faith', and that pantheism was tolerable.[50]

What was true of the Scouts was even more so of the smaller and more liberal movements. The Woodcraft Folk much more openly modelled their religion on those of native America, or at least on European perceptions of them, with much talk of a Great Spirit.[51] So did Hargraves's Kibbo Kift, which included such figures as H. G. Wells, Havelock Ellis, and Maurice Hewlett, one of the writers of pastoral fiction in praise of Pan cited earlier.[52] Hargrave set out to 'inoculate' boys with a sense of kinship with nature—vital in his view to redeem them from the evils of urban living—by employing a remarkable range of rites, chants, signs, and songs garnered from native American, African, Polynesian, and Inuit cultures. From Freemasonry he took a system of organization based upon lodges, with a ceremony of blindfolded initiation. He noted good-humouredly in 1919, when still a Scout leader, that 'it has been said "At Hargrave's camp they daren't even light a fire without chanting a heathen incantation over it." '[53] He himself, however, denied that this was 'heathen', for he insisted that tribal peoples worshipped the same deity as Christians, under many names. In *Young Winkle* (1925) he makes the wise teacher of the hero give him the following catechism: 'I believe in the Nameless God who is Time-Space-Matter: And in myself, Winkle, as an actual organic part of the one Great Nameless God.'[54] There were no goddesses in the Kibbo Kift. Hargrave's formal handbook for his Kin, in 1927, denied that it attempted to define or prescribe any religion for its members; instead it included religious *actions*—rituals—and left it to individuals to decide what they meant. To those who objected that this was not Christianity, he replied that it *could* be.[55]

What is particularly interesting—and intriguing—is the manner in which aspects of the woodcraft societies were assimilated by private individuals, in groups which never sought the status of formal organizations. One such, which has gone into history simply because of the memoir published by one of its members, was formed at Middle Wallop in the Hampshire chalk hills by the 1940s. It centred on the music hall actress whose stage name was 'Audrey Ackland', and consisted of middle-class urban people who had moved to the area because of the war. Their practices included vegetarianism, meditation, and the teaching of woodcraft and woodlore to their children. The latter were enrolled as 'Young Soldiers of Pan' or 'Handmaidens of Pan', and at a certain age the boys were initiated as 'Warriors of Pan', swearing an oath to 'take care of the sacred land and the flora, fauna and people upon it'. The circle never considered itself to be pagan, but Ackland herself 'unbaptized' her own nephew as part of the process of admitting him; she considered it necessary to relieve him of a specifically Christian identity.[56]

Most interesting of all the formal societies in this context is the Order of Woodcraft Chivalry, which has recently been the subject of a full-length scholarly study by Derek Edgell.[57] The founder, Ernest Westlake, was born in 1855 of Quaker parents characterized by a 'dogmatic, evangelistic, puritanism'; he became a naturalist, anthropologist, and traveller.[58] Letters written by him to his children from a Tasmanian expedition in 1909 are preserved in Oxford's Pitt Rivers Museum,[59] and provide a remarkable documentation of a middle-aged Edwardian gentleman in the throes of a conversion to heterodoxy. In May he is still very much an exponent of his inherited faith, telling them that 'The religion of Jesus is scientific. It deals with motives and causes which are the real world—and the future belongs to it.' In another letter of this month he invites them to 'surrender yourselves to Jesus'. During July doubts appear. He has become interested in telepathy and fulminates against both Protestants and Catholics for having executed witches, whom he regards as magically gifted people. He cites Matilda Joslyn Gage's figure of nine million executions; and may actually have been reading her. By August the explosion has occurred. He reports having told the local Anglican bishop that women should be 'regarded as an incarnation of God' and 'worshipped in spirit and in truth'. For a failure to recognize this, he faulted even Quakerism and found a converse merit in paganism: 'I trust you will not despise the old gods—all gods even of the lowest savages are true in a measure.'

Westlake's main means of entry to this new world consisted of books, and he now embarked on a learning curve of Himalayan gradient. The works cited in his correspondence and pamphlets are united by a perceived need to liberate the human spirit and to reintegrate people with the natural world. They include Carpenter, Nietzsche, Ellis, Jane Ellen Harrison, Tylor, and Frazer.[60] Of these, the most important proved to be Harrison; a year after founding the Order of Woodcraft Chivalry, Westlake wrote that, 'from the religious side, [it] is an *application* of Miss Harrison's work. . . . Her work might have been written for us.' It was her celebration of the ecstatic and life-affirming in Greek religion which had most seized his imagination, so that he could declare that 'our movement is a Dionysos movement', saving people from 'the cul de sac of intellectualized religion'. In 1921 he added that the vital text for woodcraft was Euripedes' ancient drama about the return of Dionysos to rejuvenate Greece, *The Bacchae*: 'As the Dionysos worship revived old Hellas, so may the same thing, introduced by the Order of Woodcraft Chivalry, revive the greater Hellas of modern civilization.' He decided that the English equivalent to Dionysos was the leaf-clad figure in May Day processions, the Jack-in-the-Green, and thought of taking this as his personal title in the order.[61]

The deity of wine and ecstasy was not, however, the only one favoured by Westlake. In 1921 he decided that the 'Trinity of Woodcraft' consisted of Pan, Artemis, and Dionysos, and also suggested that Aphrodite be revered at times, with the reflection that unless alcohol and sexuality were honoured responsibility and treated as sacred, they would manifest themselves in drunkenness and prostitution.[62] The Westlakes had bought an estate at Sandy Balls on the northern edge of the New Forest, and there the order held its first folkmoot ceremony at the beginning of August 1921, the old feast of Lammas. The sacred fire was lit in the centre of a ritual circle, by four people dressed in colours appropriate to the elemental associations of each quarter, bearing greetings from its powers and proceeding in a succession from east round to north. When it was burning, Westlake delivered the invocation (taken from Socrates): 'Beloved Pan, and all ye other gods who haunt this place, give me beauty in the inward soul and may the outward and inward be at one.'[63] At some point in these years he composed (but apparently did not place) a newspaper advertisement reading: 'An ex-Quaker wishes to unite with some heathen church in England worshipping the other gods, especially Venus and Bacchus.' In 1919 he and his family drew up a plan for a forest park stocked with the surviving fauna of the Old Stone Age, including bison (which would be hunted) and deer. Young women, 'attired like Artemis of old, would follow the deer on foot through the forests, tending and milking them'; this fantastic idea was taken from one of Maurice Hewlett's novels, The Forest Lovers.[64]

All this sounds like hands-on paganism, truly remarkable for its time; but it was not. Even in the eyes of the Westlakes, the order was not a pagan organization, for when Margaret Westlake published a statement as a spiritual teacher she declared that the Woodcraft Chivalry was dedicated to the worship of 'the Great Spirit . . . under whatever manifestation or Name'.[65] It was a formulation almost exactly like that which the Kibbo Kift and Woodcraft Folk were to make, and not very remote even from that of the Scouts. To Ernest himself, the attraction of paganism was not that it would replace Christianity but that it would cope with precisely those areas in which the latter had become deficient, and so (at best) help to revivify it. He coined the aphorism 'one must be a good pagan before one can be a good Christian'.[66] In 1918 he replied to a critic of the order's religious policy by assuring her that 'We proposed to link this movement up with organized Christianity by providing the natural basis of Christianity.' This was no mere politic stance, for in 1922 he wrote to his son Aubrey that Christ had represented the rebirth of God the Father in this world, and that his life was exemplary. He added his belief that after resurrection Jesus had become dissolved into Nature, and so by recognizing inherent divinity in the latter humans were actually becoming better Christians.[67] It is fascinating and frustrating to wonder how Ernest's ideas would have developed had he lived longer; but soon after writing those words he was killed in a road accident. He was laid to rest, not in any conventional burial ground but in a chieftain's tumulus in the woods of Sandy Balls.

His place as British Chief of the Order was taken by Aubrey, but the role of principal representative of paganism in it fell to a much more flamboyant and uncompromising character, a slim, dark-haired and tanned young south Londoner with a strong chin and stubborn mouth called Harry Byngham. Byngham had absorbed to the full Ernest Westlake's belief that the joyous and nature-related aspects of ancient Greek religion could bring benefit to the modern world, but whereas Westlake had been inspired by them, Byngham could be described as intoxicated; he subsequently changed his own first name to Dion, short for Dionysos. Unlike Westlake, he saw nothing in Christianity that deserved saving. Unlike him, also, he espoused another radical cause, that of naturism, being a keen member of the New Gymnosophy Society. Dionysos especially appealed to him as representing the animal part of manhood, and he wrote in the magazine *The Healthy Life* (which promoted naturism and other libertarian ideas) to extol phallic worship as a veneration of the life-force. In 1923 he acquired a parallel platform in the Order of Woodcraft Chivalry, by launching a periodical for it, *Pine Cone*, edited by himself.[68]

In pursuing his ideals within the order, Byngham had to reckon with two aspects of it that were likely to make them profoundly controversial. One was that the appeal of the organization for many members had lain in the fact that it represented the pacifist alternative to the Scouts. As such, it was especially attractive to Quakers, from whom the Westlakes had sprung, and was given recommendation by the Society of Friends. This meant that some—perhaps a large proportion—of its members were not just Christians but personally devout Christians. The second was that it was a movement primarily dedicated to the training of youth, and so anybody who attempted to introduce socially heterodox ideas into it had to reckon with anxious parents, and with co-workers who answered to the latter. Already, in 1919–20, Ernest Westlake's utopian schemes had precipitated many resignations, and he had received heavy criticism from Quaker members to whom Dionysos was an aspect of the Devil.[69] The stage was thus set for a serious clash between Dion Byngham and his friends, and other groups in the order.

It began in July 1923, when the first issue of *Pine Cone* included a call from Byngham for 'the realization of Life. . . . Life is adventure, audacity, revolt. . . . Life springs out of the star-tissued womb of Nature as the virile son of the All-Mother.' Life was, in fact, Dionysos, and Byngham printed an illustration of the thyrsos, the ivy-bound staff of the god, beside the pine cone which was the symbol of the magazine. At the folkmoot in the New Forest that summer, he challenged the singing of Christian hymns and asked instead for readings from Carpenter, Symonds, or William Blake. Complaints poured in from members, but the second edition of *Pine Cone* brazenly carried a cover picture of a nude Dionysos dancing with a pine cone on his thyrsos. The contents were, however, more balanced—the report on the folkmoot was written by a member who spoke of the presence of God in the event—and the third issue contained nothing provocative. The fourth, on the other hand, more than made up for this restraint, containing a photograph of a nude Byngham reclining and playing panpipes while his girlfriend performed 'The Dawn Dance of Spring' above him in a short Grecian tunic which left her legs and one breast bare. It also included a verse play by Victor Neuburg, whose poems to Pan have been quoted earlier and who had contributed verses about union with nature to previous issues; he was now a friend of Byngham and introduced him to the ideas of his own former master, Aleister Crowley.[70]

At the folkmoot of 1924 the inevitable backlash occurred, and Byngham was replaced as editor of *Pine Cone*. Thereafter, the contents were studiously inoffensive, although it is notable that the eighth issue, in June 1925, contained a system of magical correspondences between deities, planets, and colours similar to those of the Golden Dawn and of Crowley. The same moot, moreover, sanctioned the formation of an adult ('Wayfarer') section of the order, in which concepts and practices *might* be tried out without involving adolescents. Byngham suffered another humiliation in 1925, when he was suspended from the Council of Chiefs, but this was not because of his religious beliefs; he and a new girlfriend had posed nude in a Sussex field for press photographs to promote the cause of naturism, and this was felt to have risked the reputation of the order. Unabashed, at the Wayfarers' camp in 1926 he proposed a place for nudity in religious ritual.[71] The following year Aubrey Westlake, as effective head of the Woodcraft Chivalry, intervened in the continuing controversy over religion among members, by publishing writings of his father on the need for the Dionysiac spirit and staying faithful to the family tradition by prefacing them with his own views: that true and good living was based upon a balance between the primitive vigour of Pan and Artemis and the civilized virtues of Christ and Apollo.[72]

During these same years, between 1922 and 1927, the ritual practices and trappings of the order continued to evolve, but in neither a Christian nor a pagan form. The two most potent sources were, rather, Masonic and quasi-Masonic tradition—from which came banners, ensigns, and ritual insignia—and native America, from which the adult section in particular took ceremonial names, the Sunrise Call of the Zuni as one cry for waking up, and the use of tipis.[73] For members, as for so many of their generation, these traditions were regarded as a safe middle ground between religions. None of these measures, however, prevented further polarization over the religious issue (and several others) at the folkmoot of 1928. A compromise was formally accepted, which had been drafted by a sub-committee set up for the purpose; to extol the sanctity of nature and criticize the 'inessential' and repressive aspects of Christianity, but still to hold up Christian ethics as the basis for all morality. The Wayfarers' newsletter in that year recommended Frazer and Harrison as important reading for an understanding of the spiritual dimension of woodcraft. The 1929 folkmoot dealt with the question of divinity by adopting a formula for the order of belief in 'the Great Spirit, wherever found'.[74]

This controversy, and others over issues of personality and principle, placed a severe strain upon the order, and between 1926 and 1930 its membership fell from 1,200 to 400. The nature of compromises, such as that over religion, is to leave extremists on both sides unhappy, and this is what occurred. One furious Christian member in 1928 dubbed the organization 'the Order of Witchcraft Devilry', and in the following year the Society of Friends formally withdrew its recommendation. The year 1928 arguably saw the high point of the pagan faction within the order, whose members stayed on site in the New Forest after the folkmoot to hold a 'dionysian' camp of their own, of which no reports survive, although it is said to have included 'ritual games'. In 1930 further offence was given to conservative opinion when two prominent members married each other in camp, in a ceremony devised for the occasion and termed a 'troth-plighting'. It was based as much on Quaker precedents and English medieval customs as paganism, but represented another breach with convention. On Midsummer morning 1931 some members gathered on Leith Hill, Surrey, to hail the rising sun. Some who died in these years were granted a request to be buried or have memorials placed next to Ernest Westlake's barrow in the woods of Sandy Balls; the marker of one deceased in 1934 displays the Long Man of Wilmington, an old hill figure commonly considered to be pagan.[75]

These gestures, however, were postscripts, for the tensions of the past ten years had created an attrition of radicals as well as of conservatives from the order. Most significant for our purposes was the departure of Dion Byngham, which had occurred by 1931. He moved to the village of Storrington, in the Sussex Weald, just inside the scarp of the South Downs near the prehistoric hill-fort and landmark of Chanctonbury Ring. There he became a part of the community established by a rich Londoner, Vera Pragnell, in 1923 and called 'The Sanctuary'. Pragnell herself was a mystical Christian socialist, inspired by Edward Carpenter, but tolerant enough to permit (though not to encourage) naturism, 'free love', and paganism. Byngham's friend Victor Neuburg had settled nearby at Steyning, and functioned as a semi-detached member of the commune; one of his poems from this period, 'The Druids', was set on Chanctonbury Ring. From this congenial environment Byngham resumed his role as a contributor of articles and letters to *The Healthy Life*, especially in 1934 when he advocated sun-worship, Dionysian rites, and magic (including specific praise of Crowley). In one issue he appeared nude in a photograph, performing 'The Nature Prayer Dance of Pan'. During the mid-1930s, however, his religious enthusiasms waned, as he moved more into a personal, and idiosyncratic, blend of radical politics, which he was to pursue for the next ten years.[76]

Much more serious to the Woodcraft Chivalry was the loss of Aubrey Westlake who, worn out by disputes, resigned as Chieftain in 1933 and withdrew altogether in 1934, depriving the order of its meeting-place at Sandy Balls. After that year, writes its historian Derek Edgell, it was a 'pale shadow' of what it had been in the 1920s.[77] The expression is both accurate and unjust. The order in the late 1930s was a much smaller organization, shorn of various educational and cultural enterprises which it had sprouted in the 1920s and of some of its most colourful leading figures. It was no longer regarded by its members as a potential force for the transformation of society. Dionysos had departed, in more senses than one. On the other hand, it had found peace and stability at last, within a consensual framework which could still be regarded as liberal and progressive according to prevailing cultural norms. Perhaps most impressive of all, it had survived, and still survives to the present as a remarkable association of people characterized by ideals of kindness of humanity and kinship with nature; but it arguably has no more relevance for a historian of modern British attitudes to paganism.

*   *   *

It is time to take stock. What has been shown in this chapter is that a variety of people in early twentieth-century England had come to regard a revival of paganism—in some measure—as a desirable phenomenon. Most wanted such a revival to act as a supplement to Christianity or even to refresh the latter. On the other hand, there were some, like Dion Byngham, who wanted paganism to be restored in its own right. It was out of this second impulse that modern pagan witchcraft was to arise.

GOD (AND GODDESS) PARENTS

꒳ꙮ꒳

THE subject-matter of this chapter is in most respects continuous with the last; an examination of the religious and spiritual ideas of selected individuals who flourished in the first half of the twentieth century. The distinctions are, first, that their best-known work was produced slightly later—between 1900 and 1950—and, second, that they had a direct and obvious influence upon modern pagan witchcraft and have been acknowledged by many modern witches as sources of inspiration.

The first is Aleister Crowley (1875–1947), who has only recently begun to receive the scholarly attention which he deserves. Most of it, naturally enough, has been concerned primarily with his position in the history of modern magic. Of this, the work of Gerald Suster provides far and away the best consideration of the nature and value of Crowley's ideas,[1] although Colin Wilson has perhaps captured the essence of the man's personality more fully than any other writer to date.[2] There remains a great deal of potential to be realized in reintegrating him with other thinkers and writers of his time. For example, he has an important place in the history of modern Western responses to Oriental spiritual traditions, which Suster has highlighted but which is yet to be explored thoroughly. As a literary figure, he shared important preoccupations with others in his generation. Alex Owen has made a beginning by setting him in the context of Edwardian developments of the nature of the self.[3] It would be easy to extend this to compare him with specific individuals who are much more prominent in the literary canon. One would be Nietzsche, with whom Crowley shared, and from whom perhaps he learned, an ecstatic style of writing and a preoccupation with the central importance of the human will. Another is Oscar Wilde, who had in common several devices of poetic ornamentation, a personal and authorial interest in bisexuality, and a preoccupation with the discovery of the true self. The most obvious is probably D. H. Lawrence, who was obsessed with the forces of love and law, fascinated by a reinterpretation of the Book of Revelation, frequently employed phallic imagery, and also possessed a deeply ambivalent, and passionate, attitude towards women related to an ambivalent sexual orientation.

Even in the history of modern magic, there are many connections and relationships yet to be thoroughly worked out, and this is true in that most carefully researched area of all, the story of the Golden Dawn. It may be suggested that the crucial relationship here for Crowley was with Mathers, who acted as his patron and protector in the order until the two men became estranged in 1903. Both were natural scholars, with a genius for studying and synthesizing different magical systems. Both had a yearning for the assumption of more exalted and romantic social identities; the 'Comte de Glenstrae' had his counterparts in the young Crowley's successive assumptions of the identities of a Russian count, a Scottish lord, and a Persian Prince. Both had an unappeasable desire to take charge of any organization with which they were associated and a tendency to quarrel savagely with those who challenged them. In an important sense, Crowley was the true heir of the greatest of Victorian ritual magicians.

Overall, his career represents the spectacle of a double tragedy. One aspect of this was that Crowley formed his identity as a self-indulgent and flamboyant young man empowered by the inheritance of a substantial inherited fortune, which allowed him to pursue his enthusiasms at will and to set about a deliberate flouting and provocation of social and religious norms. His wealth insulated him against any consequences of an outraged public opinion, until by his middle age he had squandered it all. At that point he acquired a need to please a wider public in order to support himself, and his sulphurous reputation now weighed in against him, wrecking one promising project after another and condemning him to an impecunious old age dependent on the charity of a few admirers. The second tragic aspect of his story is that he always believed himself to be one of the outstanding individuals of his time, and due a proportionate acclaim. In reality he possessed a genuine but limited talent as a poet, novelist, and journalist. His only truly remarkable distinction lay in the field of magic, and that was not one which earned much interest or respect in his society.

In this field, however, the laurels are unmistakably his own. Like Mathers, he explored every major Western magical tradition; but he did so in much greater depth, and added to them a proportionately profound study (and experience) of Eastern mystical practices. The preoccupation of the present book is not with this, central, work of his life but with an issue at once integrally associated with it, and oblique to it: his attitude to religion. An analysis of that presents certain difficulties. The largest is that Crowley was not very interested in religion itself, and as shall be illustrated, his attitudes to it were complex. His lack of any systematic attention to it is reflected in his lack of reference to sources of information and inspiration in it. His list of heroes and recommended authors in the fields of literature and magic was long and well acknowledged by him, Swinburne and Blake being pre-eminent.[4] By contrast, the single authority cited by him in the field of religion is Frazer, who is called 'the only man worthy of our notice' in it, while *The Golden Bough* is 'invaluable'.[5] Jane Harrison clearly also had some influence on Crowley's thinking, as will be seen, but was not mentioned.

Another cluster of problems results from his literary personality, and style of expression. When writing seriously about abstract matters, he did not always express himself clearly, his sentences becoming at times laboured, tortuous, and obscure. Furthermore, he did not always write seriously, for one of the most remarkable and attractive things about Crowley as a spiritual leader is his capacity for irreverence. He frequently paid homage to the vital role of the trickster, riddler, and clown in the gaining of wisdom, and personified it, delighting in this sort of sentence: 'Holy, Holy, Holy are these truths that I utter, knowing them to be falsehoods, broken mirrors, troubled waters.' That particular example concludes an apparently serious exposition of cosmology.[6] More of Crowley's pronouncements on the divine are wrapped up in an ecstatic and enraptured poesy than a reasoned argument. It is also true that at times a reader is left wondering whether Crowley himself was aware of some of the ironies embodied in his work: for example, his novel *Moonchild* (1929) makes a passionate appeal for love as the greatest force in the universe, and for the essential unity of being, while indulging in a series of vicious caricatures of former colleagues in the Golden Dawn, the most savage and unjust being reserved for his old patron Mathers.

On proceeding to an examination of his religious beliefs, it may be helpful to deal first with some of the more lurid aspects of his popular reputation. Gerald Suster, who has refuted many of the specific stories and assertions associated with the latter, has also provided the most commonly repeated recent comment upon it: 'Perhaps the best known and least interesting facts about Crowley are that he enjoyed sex and took drugs. So what?'[7] In one sense this is spot on. In another it misses a major point: if Crowley advocated or practised the incorporation of sex or drugs in a system of spiritual practice, then this was sufficiently at odds with the prevailing mores of his time to become interesting. In the case of drugs there is no evidence that he advocated any such thing, although some of the ecstatic and visionary experiences which he underwent in some of his magical workings may not be unrelated to his consumption of them. Here is one example, taken from a diary of such workings:

5.20 am . . . Her teeth was moonlight and her tongue ambrosia; to her throat nectar, in Her Body the one God of whose Pure Body she could fresh Her Blood. So, with my body shuddering, retching, fainting and convulsed; with my mind tempest, my heart crater, my will earthquake, I obeyed Her lash. Not then did I gain grace, God came not to his Host. Not even when she had added her mouth's sweetness to His strength; but I passed ordeal, I took oath; I am indeed High Priest. . . . 9.30 am. end of cocaine.

Sexuality was far more important to both his theory and practice of magic. It is hard to examine his art, poetry, or prose for very long without running into a phallic symbol. This was not unusual for his generation, such imagery having cropped up already in the present book, quite incidentally, in discussions of George Russell, Dion Byngham, and D. H. Lawrence; and their time was also, of course, that of Freud. In Crowley's case, however, sexual symbolism was propelled by a libido of more than usual vigour. As a Cambridge undergraduate, he wished that physical love could be delivered to his door along with other necessities of life,[8] and even in his sixties, when he was worn out by constant ill health, his diaries reveal him regularly trekking round London on 'shikar' in search of it.[9] It is a preoccupation of much of his poetry, and his 'magical record' for the 1910s is largely one of sex magic, undertaken with a succession of professionals and close friends, and carefully noted up.[10] As mentioned above, his tastes were bisexual, but they had a pronounced bias towards heterosexuality; his homosexual relationships seem to have been much fewer, and all concentrated in his youth,[11] and it is notable that all the erotic dreams recorded in his later diaries involved women. Even here, however, his attitudes remained deeply ambivalent; in one book he could write that 'Life is as ugly and necessary as the female body'.[12] His declared opinion upon sexual preference was that nobody should have a right to interfere with any type of manifestation of sexual impulse in others, that all should follow their own inclinations, and that neither homosexuality nor heterosexuality was more noble than the other.[13] In a more liberal age, these sentiments may seem as admirable as they were shocking to the majority of his contemporaries. With Crowley, however, there is almost always a qualification, for he could be as viciously petty and unscrupulous in some moods as he could be courageous and high-minded in others; and he did not hesitate to sneer at some opponents for being homosexual.[14]

So what did he think of religion, and of the divine? It would be possible to make a good case that he was an atheist, or sceptic. In 1911 he proclaimed that all religions were more or less bankrupt, and that it was time to start again by doubting the lot, and so take charge of one's own mind. In 1929 he defined 'True Will' as the setting of oneself in harmony with a universe in which all things were probably connected, although humans did not actually know how they were. Elsewhere in that same year he asked 'what is religion? The consummation of the soul by itself in divine ecstasy. What is life but love, and what is love but laughter? In other words, religion is a joke.'[15] *Liber V vel Reguli* has the magician say: 'I am identical with All and None. I am in All and all in me; I am apart from all, and lord of all, and one with all. I am a God, I very God of very God'.[16] *Liber O vel Manus et Sagittae* (1909), section 2, announces that 'In this book it is spoken of the Sephiroth, and the Paths; of Spirits and Conjurations; of Gods, Spheres, Planes and many other things which may or may not exist. It is immaterial whether they exist or not.' *Liber Oz* (1941) states the matter more crisply in its preface: 'There is no god, but man.'

Crowley repeatedly stressed the relationship of 'magick', as he termed his system of occult practice, to science rather than religion. He provided at least three definitions of it. The famous one, in 1929, is 'the art or science of causing change in conformity with will'. In the same work he also called it 'the Science of understanding oneself and one's condition . . . the Art of applying that understanding in action'. He emphasized that magick and science progress together, and elsewhere described magick as a branch of physics.[17] In the 1940s he termed it 'the study and use of those forms of energy which are (a) subtler than the ordinary physical–mechanical types, (b) accessible to those who are (in one sense or another) "Initiates" '. The latter would certainly be true of modern physics. In this same, late, series of letters, he insisted that magick is 'the exact opposite of religion; it is, even more than Physical Science, its irreconcilable enemy. . . . Magick investigates the laws of Nature with the idea of making use of them.' Faced with the suggestion that his own belief system could be taken as a religion, he conceded that it could be only 'just in so far as a religion means an enthusiastic putting-together of a series of doctrines, no one of which must in any way clash with Science or Magick.'[18]

This streak of rationalism was blended with a celebrated contempt for and detestation of conventional Christianity, based on a reaction against the especially narrow and fanatical variety professed by his parents, who were Plymouth Brethren. It took a form which bore a close resemblance to deliberate and sustained blasphemy; it is well known, and true, that Crowley identified himself with the Beast 666 of the Book of Revelation and the satanic idol, Baphomet, allegedly worshipped by the medieval Knights Templar, and transposed another section of Revelation to make the Whore of Babylon a symbol of victory and life. It is equally true, and less famous, that to the end of his life he sent 'Antichristmas cards' every December (the list of recipients made out conscientiously in his diaries), and that he wished his living female Muses, his Scarlet Women, to be 'principally, an anti-Christian social force'.[19] The text of his which he came closest to regarding as holy writ, the *Liber AL vel Legis* ('Book of the Law') (1904) preaches an almost precise reversal of the morality of the New Testament. He extolled Set, the ancient Egyptian deity commonly associated with evil—or at least with destruction—and dated one of his works, *The High History of Good Sir Palomedes* 'Anno Pseudo Christi MCMXII'. Notoriously, in his main book upon magick, in 1929, he recommended blood sacrifice as a particularly efficacious means of magical working, and especially that of a young male child; he claimed that 'Frater Perdurabo' (his own magical name) had performed this act an average 150 times per year between 1912 and 1928.[21] It is easy to see how he acquired a public reputation as a Satanist of a particularly wicked type.

It is equally easy for anybody who makes even a cursory study of Crowley to refute this reputation. In order to be a Satanist, it is necessary to believe—literally or symbolically—in Satan, and Crowley did not. He rejected the whole cosmic structure of good pitted against evil upon which traditional Christianity was built, and the figure of the Devil with it.[22] His appropriation of those of the Beast, Baphomet, and the Whore did not involve an acceptance of the Christian attributes accorded to them, but a reworking to invest them with positive values, such as that also attempted by Lawrence. Thus, to Crowley the Beast 666 symbolized a divine, human, and animal self, conjoined in harmony.[23] His claim of having sacrificed hundreds of male children was (of course) a joke, referring to the theory of Aristotle, adopted by medieval Catholicism, that sperms were tiny male humans; Crowley was counting his orgasms. In the same book in which he did so, he wrote that 'Whatever I do to another, I do also to myself. If I kill a man, I destroy my life at the same time', and in another work of the same year he condemned abortions as 'dastardly crimes'.[24] It is certainly true that despite his taste for fancy dress he never (unlike Mathers) made a cult of uniforms, and he always avoided military service of any kind. He did commit blood sacrifice on at least one occasion—slitting the throats of a pair of pigeons as part of a major ritual in Algeria in 1909[25]—but did not make it a regular, let alone an intrinsic, part of his system.

His attitude to Christians was likewise more complex than at first appears. In 1910 he wrote: 'I am coming round to the belief that the best test of a religion is the manhood of its adherents rather than its truth.' He went on to say that he hated Christianity 'as Socialists hate soap', but would rather be saved with Christian heroes such as Livingstone and Gordon than damned with the sort of mediocrities who attacked their faith in his own time.[26] Three years before he had written a series of hymns to the Virgin Mary, in the manner of a devout Catholic, as an exercise to develop his own personality by taking on an alien world picture, and in the community which he led in Sicily during the 1920s he invoked Jesus along with other god-forms, thinking it 'pedantic and priggish' to leave him out.[27] At the end of that decade, in his novel *Moonchild*, he quotes 'the gospel' as saying 'If Satan be divided against Satan, how shall his kingdom stand?', and speaks of 'the sign of the cross, the symbol of Him who gives life through his own death, or of the instrument of that life and of that death, of the Holy One appointed from the foundation of the world as its redeemer'.[28] There is more than a faint whiff of whitewash about *Moonchild*, however, and it is also unclear whether this 'Holy One' is Jesus or Frazer's divine sacrificial pagan king. In the same work Crowley reaffirms his specific rejection of modern Christianity as the religion of 'the Bourgeois, whose character is based on fear and falsehood';[29] once again one suspects that his middle-class parents are in the target. In one of his last writings he provided a condemnation of all philosophical systems which consider the physical world to be a curse and its phenomena to be sorrows. In these he included Buddhism and some Hinduism but asserted that Christianity introduced 'the poison in its foulest and most virulent form'.[30]

It would be possible to make a case, by use of the same selective quotation which can represent Crowley as a sceptic, that he was a mystical monotheist. His poetry not infrequently contains references to 'God' and 'the Lord'. He addressed the Statue of Liberty in 1915 with an appeal to 'the one true God of whom the Sun himself is but a shadow'. The daily rite of his community in Sicily was a prayer to the sun, made four times under different Egyptian god-names.[31] One of the instructions which he wrote for his Ordo Templi Orientis runs 'In the macrocosm is one sole God, the Sun.' Another informs the trainee that the aim of the order is to find 'the One True God', and yet another declares that 'God in Spirit and Truth is one'.[32] In 1913 he wrote an anthem later included in his Gnostic Mass, in which he declares himself to be a part of a single entity, 'centre and secret of the Sun' and 'hidden spring of all things known'.[33]

The same theme is sounded in the two great public works of 1929, *Magick in*

Theory and Practice and *Moonchild*. The former informs readers that the point of all magickal ritual should be union with God, a being above gender and so representable in no human form. Ideally,

the Magician becomes filled with God, fed upon God, intoxicated with God. Little by little his body will become purified by the internal lustration of God; day by day his mortal frame, shedding its earthly elements, will become in very truth the Temple of the Holy Ghost. Day by day matter is replaced by Spirit, the human by the divine; ultimately the change will be complete; God manifest in flesh will be his name.[34]

Moonchild sums up its view of the cosmos in a poem which hails a single 'Sire and Lord of All', 'the spring of Life, the axle of the Wheel, All-mover, yet the One Thing immobile', 'the Central Spirit', abiding 'in silence of all deed, or word, or thought, So that we name It not, or name It Naught. This is the truth behind the lie called God'.[35]

It is not surprising, therefore, that he could work well with ritual systems derived from monotheist traditions. He thought his association with Freemasonry 'more fertile than almost any other study'.[36] The Golden Dawn's 'Lesser Ritual of the Pentagram', with its four Hebrew names of God, was performed daily in his Sicilian community.[37] Above all, he found the cabbala 'so handy and congenial' that he used it more than any other spiritual tradition 'for daily use and work'.[38] And yet—in the same, very late, sequence of letters in which he declared that, he also totally rejected monism, a belief in the essential unity of the universe, saying that 'I hate this doctrine so rabidly that I can hardly trust myself to represent it fairly!'[39] So will the real Mr Crowley stand up?

An examination of his attitude to paganism enhances a suspicion that in religious matters the 'real' man may not in fact have existed. At times he spoke all four of the 'languages' characterized at the beginning of the present book. The 'third', or unifying and theosophical one, is implicit in some of his monotheist statements above. The 'first' appears in *Moonchild*, when he speaks of 'the fearful deities of man's dawn, when nature was supposed to be a personal power of cruelty, delighting in murder, rape, and pillage' and 'children were cast into the fire, or thrown to bears, or offered up in sacrifice on bloody altars'.[39] The 'second', of a noble Graeco-Roman polytheism inferior only to monotheist revelations, is embedded in many of his rituals, especially the 'Paris Working' with Neuburg of 1913–14, in which the two magicians invoked most of the major Graeco-Roman deities, treating them essentially like spirits to be summoned and worked with according to a system of corresponding colours. On 20 January 1914, however, the 'fourth' language suddenly burst out in the ceremonies, when the classical deities informed Crowley (through Neuburg) that they 'wished to regain their dominion on earth, and that the two brethren . . . were as fiery arrows' shot by the Olympians in their war with 'slave gods' such as Christ, Buddha, and Allah. The eclecticism of the rites may, however, be indicated by the fact that the deities chose to speak not in Greek or Latin but in Enochian, the magical language devised by the Christian Elizabethan, John Dee.[40]

The Olympians were not in fact, Crowley's favourite pagan pantheon, for he followed long-established Western tradition in regarding Egypt as the home of magic, and accorded his deities a special place of honour. Near the end of his life he declared that the 'Egyptian Theogony is the noblest, the most truly magical, the most bound to me (or rather I to it) by some inmost instinct' and that he used it 'for all work of supreme import'.[41] The Book of the Law itself was written (or dictated by a spirit) in Cairo, as a revelation from three deities in ancient Egyptian form: the star-goddess Nuit, the earth god Hadit and the war god Ra-Hoor-Khuit. In 1928 he asserted that all 'true' deities were 'derived' from this Trinity; but while saying it he depersonalized them into cosmological forces, so that Nuit represented infinite space, Hadit the atom, and Ra-Hoor-Khuit the unity of all things.[42] It would be possible to suggest that these are the 'Three in One' and 'One in Three' who feature in the poem in *Moonchild* published that same year, and that their combination represents the central entity of which that work speaks. 'The Creed' in *Liber XV O.T.O. Ecclesiae Gnosticae Catholicae Canon Missae* (1915) (the Gnostic Mass) had, however, defined a different Trinity: of Chaos, the 'Father of Life', 'one secret and ineffable Lord', 'of whose fire we are created', plus Babalon, the 'one Earth, the Mother of us all', 'one Womb wherein all men are begotten, and wherein they shall rest', plus Baphomet, 'the Serpent and the Lion'.[43] The instruction on the nature of the gods given at the seventh degree of the Ordo Templi Orientis, as said, emphasized the single nature of true godhead, and it also declared local and tribal deities to be unimportant; but it did add that the universal, and more admirable, forces with which the divine had been associated were fire, Moon, Mountain, Ancestor, Yoni (female genitalia), Snake, Lion, Egg, Eagle, Tree, Stars, and (above all) Phallus.[44] Crowley appears here as religious chameleon, teaching different systems according to the tradition within which he was trying to work: Egyptian, Gnostic, or Templar. In 1913 he seemed to produce a rationalization of the three systems in which Nuit, Hadit, and Ra-Hoor-Khuit ruled supreme, with the 'seeming duality' of Chaos and Babalon below them and 'the reflection of All is Pan; the Night of Pan is the Annihilation of the All'; but the work concerned was the *Book of Lies*.[45]

In his autohagiography, Crowley defined his task as 'to bring oriental wisdom to Europe and to restore paganism in a purer form'.[46] He never, however, defined what he meant either by paganism or by a purer form of it. In *Moonchild* the usage of the former term is of a kind of personality rather than a religion, and not unequivocally admiring: 'a type perfectly pagan, whatever the creed', 'robust and subtle, spiritual and sensual, adroit in its manipulation of inferiors and superiors alike'.[47] In a different mood again, when writing to a friend in about 1914, he declared that

the time is just ripe for a natural religion. People like rites and ceremonies, and they are tired of hypothetical gods. Insist on the real benefits of the sun, the Mother-Force, the Father-Force and so on; and show that by celebrating these benefits worthily the worshippers unite themselves more fully with the current of life. Let the religion be Joy, but with a worthy and dignified sorrow in death itself; and treat death as an ordeal, an initiation.... In short be the founder of a new and greater Pagan cult.[48]

These lines perfectly capture the spirit which was driving people like Lawrence, Westlake, and Byngham, and was a fairly good prediction of what modern pagan witchcraft was actually to be; but it is notable that Crowley was not interested in establishing such a religion himself, as opposed to the fervent creativity which he invested in his magical orders. Instead, he was suggesting to the friend, George Jones, that he undertake the work; and Jones did not.

The question of the specific and personal contribution which Crowley made to modern witchcraft will be discussed in subsequent chapters of this book, and for the present it is sufficient to note certain innovations which he made in the practice and theory of magic which were to be of relevance. One was in the concept of female divinity. Like so many writers since the Romantics, Crowley instinctually conceived of it as taking the form of a single major goddess, Nuit or Babalon, identified with the night sky or the earth; but to him she featured most often as a giver of passion and ecstasy, a redemption through the saturation and intoxication of the senses. He also provided a vital link in the evolving modern conception of the triple goddess, between Jane Harrison and Robert Graves. It came in 1929, in *Moonchild* where he explained that the nature of the moon was threefold:

For she is Artemis or Diana, sister of the sun, a shining Virgin Goddess; then Isis-initiatrix, who brings to man all light and purity, and is the link of his animal soul with his eternal self; and she is Persephone or Proserpine, a soul of double nature, living half upon the earth and half in Hades ... and thirdly she is Hecate, a thing altogether of Hell, barren, hideous and malicious, the queen of death and evil witchcraft.

To Crowley all these natures represented those of womanhood: 'Artemis is unassailable, a being fine and radiant; Hecate is the crone, the woman past all hope of motherhood, her soul black with envy and hatred of happier mortals; the woman in the fulness of life is the sublime Persephone'.[49]

Another significant development lay in his use of the working tools which Mathers had adapted for ritual magic from their Masonic predecessors. He retained the wand, cup, pentacle, dagger, and sword, and added others, of which the most important in this context were as follows. first, the scourge, which was taken from its place in a wall-painting and turned into a solid object, to represent one aspect of the will of the magus. Second, a container of consecrated oil, to be used for anointing those who took part in a rite. Third, a bell, for summoning them—and sometimes supernatural entities as well. Fourth, a censer, to hold sacred fire and perfume the working space, and, fifth, a book of charms and spells, compiled by the magician and also acting as a record of workings.[50] He also redeemed the inverted (one point down) pentagram, which Levi had declared to be the sign of Satan and which the Golden Dawn had therefore vehemently avoided, by using it simply to signify the descent of spirit into matter.[51]

It is time to sum up. What must be clear by now is that Crowley invested in the subject of religion nothing like the interest, energy, or clarity of thought which he brought to the subjects of magic, morality, or will-power. To him the greatest aim of the magician was to merge with a higher power connected to the wellsprings of the universe, but he did not trouble himself too much to define that power consistently; sometimes it was God, sometimes the One, sometimes a goddess, and sometimes one's own Holy Guardian Angel or higher self. In the last analysis he was content for the nature of divinity to remain a mystery. As a result he wrote at times like an atheist, at times like a monotheist, and at others like a polytheist. Near the end of his life he instructed a pupil simply to 'choose the religious system most convenient to you and to your work'. He went on later in the same course of instruction to say that 'My observation of the Universe convinces me that there are beings of intelligence and power of a far higher quality than anything we can conceive of a human . . . and that the only chance for mankind to advance as a whole is for individuals to make contact with such Beings.' He added yet later that he felt gods to be real personalities, and 'not mere collocations of the elements, planets and signs as are most of the angels, intelligences and spirits'.[52] He did not, however, make any more attempt now than before to declare a firm belief in what they were, from where they came, and how they functioned. It was enough that they seemed to communicate.

Crowley's greatest, and least tangible, bequest to later paganism and magic(k) was to be his reputation. When he died in 1947 it was, as said, at a relatively low point. His most potent single action in preparing the way for its revival—although in the event not quite as he bargained—was to make a young man called John Symonds his literary executor. Symonds's first public use of his role was to write a biography of the dead magician called *The Great Beast*, which appeared in 1951. It was both hostile and sensational, but these very qualities gave it a commercial success which established Crowley in the public mind as the most notorious, and most interesting, figure in the world of early twentieth-century Western ritual magic. It also opened the way for Symonds to publish an increasing number of the master's manuscripts during the next two decades, which consolidated that reputation during the great burgeoning of interest in the occult which occurred in those years. As a result, Crowley became a dominant figure in later pagan culture, a name to be conjured with by those seeking to enhance their own reputations or those of their traditions. This in itself produces major problems for a historian, which will be considered later.

*　　*　　*

The second figure who must be included here is Violet Firth (1890–1946), who came to use the pen-name of Dion Fortune. Like Crowley, she emerged from the milieu of Edwardian magical societies to found her own, and to become a leader in the world of early twentieth-century British occultism. Indeed, because of her writings she is now its foremost female figure, and the subject of pioneering biographical studies by Alan Richardson and Janine Chapman.[53]

A distinction between the two great magicians lay in their education. Crowley had a full traditional one, including public school and Cambridge, and supplemented this with very extensive travels, especially in Asia. Fortune (like most women of her time) never went to university, and seems to have had no interest in travelling other than that of the mind. As a result, Crowley's experience of magic and mysticism was brushed onto his large knowledge of conventional history, geography, and literature, while Fortune's grasp of these subjects was absorbed largely through her occult studies. One striking result of this is that he never had any time for the myth of Atlantis, while a belief in its literal truth became a central prop of her world picture.

Her training in meditation and ritual magic was an extensive one. Her mother was a keen Christian Scientist, and so was she during her adolescence. By 1914 she had become a theosophist, and within ten years she was a prominent member of its Christian Mystical Lodge. In 1919 she was also initiated into the London temple of one of the successor orders of the Golden Dawn, the Alpha et Omega, and during the 1920s she was a pupil of an occultist called Theodore Moriarty. He taught that 'the Bible is a compilation of the Universal Theosophy which was first taught in Atlantis' and which had descended through history in the dicta of Horus, Mithras, Quetzalcóatl, Buddha, and other figures in whom 'the Christ Principle' had manifested. During 1922 she founded a Fraternity of the Inner Light as an 'outer court' of the Alpha et Omega, and from 1926 onward she began to publish books steadily, under her own name upon ethical issues, and as Dion Fortune when dealing with occultism. By 1928 she had left both the Theosophical Society and the Alpha et Omega, and established the Inner Light as a fully independent body, initiating its members through three degrees on the Masonic model.[54]

Given this background and training, it is hardly surprising that the Dion Fortune of the period 1914–30 was a devout mystical Christian. She was certainly a very unorthodox one. Neither then nor later did she have a good word to say for clergymen, always portraying them as sanctimonious fools. She never expressed allegiance to any formal church, and she found serious fault with modern Christianity, for its loss of mystical content, while rejecting traditional doctrines such as that of heaven and hell.[55] Her own faith, however, is unmistakable. In the 1910s she took 'The Master Jesus' as her personal spirit guide.[56] At the end of her collection of short stories, *The Secrets of Doctor Taverner* (1926), the narrator of the tales finally achieves enlightenment, at the foot of a giant cross— although admittedly it is a Celtic cross. The next year, in *The Demon Lover*, she pitted a Christian heroine against the forces of darkness, at one point getting her to rout that great icon of Edwardian paganism, Pan, by reciting the child's prayer 'Gentle Jesus, meek and mild'. At another, she actually defended the Inquisition, asserting that although it might have killed a few innocent people, it 'safeguarded mankind from evils little suspected by modern men'.[57] In *The*

Esoteric Orders and their Work (1928), she declared that 'the Master Jesus is the Master of Masters for the West',[58] and in *The Training and Work of an Initiate* (1930), that 'in any school of Western mysticism the author and finisher of our faith must be Christ Jesus, the Great Initiator of the West'.[59]

Her morality was of a piece with this devotion. In her writings of the 1920s she called abortion an abomination, and masturbation an activity which undermined health; she condemned homosexuality, sadism, and masochism as perversions, and warned that homosexuality was an infectious mental disease; such assertions were given some spurious professional status by the fact that she had set herself up as a psychologist operating out of a London clinic. She cautioned her readers that promiscuity arouses 'the antagonism of the group mind of the race'. She stated firmly that the only good sex occurs within marriage and urged those tempted to it outside that institution to think of God and (hilariously) to engage in a sort of psychic masturbation. They were advised to imagine putting a psychic hand on a psychic swelling at the base of the psychic spine, and giving it a good psychic squeeze. At the same time a different theme runs through these writings from the beginning, which was to remain of significance in her work; of the sacramental nature of sex, and of the extraordinary effects achieved by sublimating the current of erotic attraction between a woman and a man, and channelling it into magical operations.[60]

The reference to 'the race' quoted above is also characteristic of her work, and one aspect of a general fear of contamination by other nations, races, or classes which runs through her books at this time and, although hardly rare in the inter-war years, is still strong enough in her to count as a personality quirk. In the Dr Taverner story 'The Return of the Ritual', the narrator remarks on a middle-class girl in a courtroom as 'seeming to belong to another race from the irregular Cockney features about her'. Another, 'The Soul That Would Not Be Born', takes a distinctly elitist view of reincarnation, distinguishing those souls who have 'ancient lineages and great opportunities' from the common sort. Other tales in the collection comment on the 'wily Teuton' and the 'savage races' of the Balkans. By contrast, 'Recalled' shows a real sympathy for Indians, and their treatment at the hands of the snobbish British of the Raj; like the belief in reincarnation, an inheritance of her training in theosophy. This, however, wore thinner in subsequent years, so that a theme of her writings became the assertion that traditions of wisdom are racial, and so those of the East were unsuitable for those of the West. She added that Indian doctrines might have done Britain some good in the 1880s, but that the new hostility of Indians towards British rule invited a corresponding British repudiation of their ideas. Such a stance, of course, provided part of the reason for her breach with the Theosophical Society.[61] Throughout her work, her vision of Atlantis (for her as for many theosophists, the birthplace of the world's wisdom) was to remain that of a rigidly hierarchical society, ruled by a theocratic elite segregated from the common people, which maintained its talents by selective breeding.

It is true that by the late 1920s she was starting to recognize some merit in ancient Egyptian religion, but only as a preparation for the higher truth of Christianity. Her book *The Esoteric Orders and their Work* put it on a scale of evolution above tribal practices and equal with Eastern religions, but below that of Christ.[62] One of her Taverner stories is entitled 'A Daughter of Pan', and talks wistfully about the freedom and wildness of a nature-loving paganism. None the less, it still concludes that such attitudes bar people from 'higher things' and a true 'spiritual self'. Two years, later, in *Sane Occultism*, she was still harsher, condemning a 'pagan' celebration of free love as an animal way of behaviour.[63]

Things began to change for her during the 1930s, at least in part because of the influence of three different men. One was D. H. Lawrence, whose book *The Rainbow* she admired so much that her own novels *The Winged Bull* and *The Goat-Foot God* contain clear tributes to it. As the tale of a woman's quest for spiritual fulfilment, transcending all established religions and intensely invoking the sexual magnetism possible between woman and man, its appeal to her is easy to understand. A second probable influence upon her was that of her own husband, Thomas Penry Evans, whom she married in 1927. By 1933 he was delivering a course of four lectures to her Fraternity of the Inner Light, on 'The Four Elements', 'The Celtic Gnosis', 'The Christ Within', and (finally) 'The Pan Within'. This was a balance of traditions characteristic of groups as different as the Golden Dawn and the Woodcraft Chivalry, but not one found hitherto in Fortune's own work. Evans's interest in the premier modern pagan god seems to have been strong and enduring, for two decades later he named his retirement home in Buckinghamshire 'Pan'.[64]

A third figure who may have been the most important in this context is Charles Seymour, a recruit to the Inner Light from Freemasonry who became Fortune's main magical partner between 1934 and 1937. In a set of lectures beginning in December 1934 he taught members of the Inner Light that modern Christianity had become largely an empty faith, but that its deficiencies could be made up by a revival of the ancient pagan mystery religions. In Seymour's view, these religions were not merely a stage in the ascent towards Christianity but contained timeless truths which the latter lacked—above all an experience of the divine as manifest in nature, and through beauty and joy. He was using, in fact, a powerful form of what was earlier called the 'fourth' modern language of paganism. To him the old deities were timeless and perfect forces with whom people could still work, and the most important of all was the Great Mother.[65] At Midsummer 1938 he entered in his personal record of meditations 'the idea of linking the old symbolism of indigenous women's mysteries with the pagan mysteries of England down to the present day, and through the witchcraft period'. A week later his principal working partner by that time, Christine Campbell Thomson, entered in her own diary a vision of 'little pictures of Ishtar worship through the ages, the most common being one of silhouetted witches in pointed hats and ragged skirts dancing round a fire. Then it seemed to focus a little more steadily and I was aware of the goddess standing before us mistily veiled. . . . she stressed again the necessity for Joy in worship and that she was the goddess of Love of Life'.[66] These were exactly the sort of images from which Wicca was to arise, but it does not seem as if either writer did anything to take them out of dreamland. In the end, the greatest public impact of Seymour's ideas was made by their precipitation or encouragement of the change in those of Dion Fortune herself.

This came about slowly. During the period between 1930 and 1934 she published very little, and this time of comparative withdrawal seems also to have been one of hard rethinking. As part of this, she shunted the purely Christian work of the Inner Light into a sub-division of the order run by Charles Loveday. It seems to have been at this time, also, that the rooms of her home in London's Bayswater district were redecorated so that each represented an ancient mystery tradition, of which Christianity was only one.[67] In an essay in 1932 she defined magic as 'a highly developed, highly stylized, form of mystical religion, with an elaborate philosophical basis'. She went on to suggest that the old gods had represented 'glyphs of the racial unconscious' and 'true psychological formulae', and that the old ceremonies for 'abreacting' them could be used to awaken areas of the human mind. In this somewhat agnostic and functionalist manner, she was starting to accord them some positive value.[68]

It was during 1934 that her period of withdrawal came to an end, to be succeeded by five years of frantic writing in which she produced all her best-known work. Her articles in the magazine of the Inner Light remained Christian in tone throughout this period, and her book on the cabbala in 1935 was firmly rooted in Judaeo-Christian tradition.[69] During 1934, in a book on Glastonbury, she had at last declared that both pagan and Christian mysteries had their place, and complemented each other, but still identified herself with the latter. She told readers that her own two most powerful experiences had been in the ruins of Glastonbury Abbey and at communion in Westminster Abbey, and the list of recommended reading appended to the book is all of mystical Christian texts. She recognized the allure of 'the fiery pagan forces that make the heart leap and burn' but did not identify with them; instead, her three British centres of spiritual power were the three most famous early medieval monasteries: Iona, Lindisfarne, and Glastonbury.[70]

It was in 1935 that her allegiance started to wobble. She wrote an essay in which she praised, in Seymour's fashion, the value of a classical education in conditioning people to understand the ancient mysteries, and asserted that while all true religion was essentially one, there were many outward forms of it.[71] During that year she published a novel, *The Winged Bull*, which preached the same message, with the more radical assertion that the pagan deities were equally good and valid faces of a one God of whom the Christian deity was merely one aspect. To her now it was humanity itself which perceived, and thus created, the faces. Furthermore, she was starting to attack the faith of Christ itself, as something that had once been 'mighty potent' in its original, lost form, but which had been hopelessly distorted by 'those two crusty old bachelors, Paul and Augustine'. As such, it had become a religion of the mean-minded and repressed, 'so darned lop-sided' that it could not stretch 'round the circle of experience'. Thus, 'peppery old Jehovah with his long beard and golden crown could go into the discard without anybody being damned'. And again: 'Man can't get on without a dash of paganism; and for the most part, he doesn't try to.' The figure of the wise pagan magician in the story bears a distinct resemblance to Seymour; and Fortune used the tale to provide a second definition of magic: 'the practical application of a knowledge of the little-understood powers of the human mind'.[72]

It was in 1936 that she changed sides, with another novel, *The Goat Foot God*, which did honour to Pan as the prime symbol of a paganism needed to heal the modern world, in the way traditional among English writers for over a hundred years. She charmingly referred to this resurgent force as 'Vitamin P'. Christianity was still allotted its place as one of the 'Paths to the Light', but one which had become overemphasized, to the serious detriment of humans, so that a revived paganism was needed to restore a healthy balance; this was precisely the language of Seymour (and, before him, of Westlake and several others). Fortune added two further concepts to justify it, both of them also well rehearsed by this time. One was that medieval churches overlay pagan temples and medieval saints were 'really the Old Gods with a coat of whitewash'; so a pagan revival involved abandoning neither familiar holy places nor familiar heavenly figures. The other was of the essential unity of divinity; in Fortune's formulation, 'All the gods are one god, and all the goddesses are one goddess, and there is one initiator. The All-Father was celestial Zeus—and woodland Pan—and Helios the Life-giver. He was all those things, and having known Pan, a man might pass on to the heavenly gate where Helios waits beside the Dawn.' By such a route theosophy could flower into modern paganism.[73]

From Pan she was now free to turn to the Great Goddess, whom she personified above all, in the central theosophical tradition, as Isis. During the years 1937–9 she repeatedly performed a ceremony in which she took the part of the goddess herself, often with Seymour as her magical partner.[74] The literary results were her most famous novel, *The Sea Priestess*, which meant so much to her that she published it herself in 1938 after several rejections from firms which doubted its commercial potential, and its unfinished sequel, *Moon Magic*. In the former she still hedged her theological bets a little, suggesting that the Virgin Mary was also an aspect of the Goddess, repeating the creed that the Goddess herself was only the female aspect of the single original initiator, and talking (rather confusingly) of Nature as the self-expression of God.[75] Christ, however, was now conspicuously absent, and even Pan features only occasionally, as a complementary male divinity in invocations of the Great Goddess. The latter dominates the whole story, and is described as presiding over the living world as Isis, associated with the moon, stars, and sea, and with the world of death and rebirth as Persephone; the light and dark goddesses already perceived by Edwardian writers. Fortune also incorporated the nineteenth-century vision of ancient matriarchy, by declaring that religion was once the preserve of priestesses, and built this in turn into her vision of Atlantis. In *Moon Magic* the balance has tilted still further; the text declares that the One God is the source of all nature, but that Isis *is* Nature, and then proceeds to treat her effectively as the only deity. Once again it is stated that Christianity has left humanity out of balance, but now it is specifically the divine feminine, 'the moon-forces', which are required to set things right.[76]

This pair of novels is also remarkable for the reinforced emphasis which Fortune places in them upon the essential magical power of polarity, and the manner in which the whole world is constructed on binary opposites: moon/sun, dark/light, passive/active, negative/positive. The greatest of these remained for her that of female/male, and it is notable that the power of this increases in her books even while her heroines grow ever more powerful—until her last one is hardly human at all—and her heroes get steadily weaker. These last two novels are extended poems to the intensity of effect which is created when a woman and man sublimate a mounting sexual attraction in acts of magic; in *Moon Magic* the couple at the centre of the story barely touch each other, but the air between them virtually burns. This especially vivid sense of magical polarity, and a body of poetry to support it, was to be Fortune's single greatest legacy to modern pagan witchcraft.

It was in 1939 that her tremendous flow of literary output came to an end, in what looks like a sudden crash in her creative life. The reasons for this remain mysterious, and to some extent disputed, but three developments of that year are likely to be relevant. One was that Seymour, having become increasingly dissatisfied with her and with constant repetition of the Isis ritual, abandoned their magical partnership. A second was that her husband left her for a younger and prettier woman. Both the people who may have stimulated her change in religious thought were therefore removed, just in time for the third event, the outbreak of the Second World War, which provided an incentive to concentrate upon more patriotic and conventional themes.[77] The precise impact of each development will probably never be known,[78] but the results are very clear. *Moon Magic* was left unfinished,[79] and she never published another book. Instead, her messages in the magazine of the Inner Light took on a more pronounced Christian tone once more, and in the most elaborate visualization which she prescribed to help the defeat of Germany, the Master Jesus was firmly back at the top, supported by Arthur, Merlin, and the Virgin Mary. An alternative one required Inner Light members to concentrate upon the image of the Rosy Cross, and another involved 'angelic images'. Her new principal working partner was W. K. Creasy, a mystical Christian of narrow-minded piety. Fortune became involved in spiritualism, a movement rooted in Christianity, and was reputed to be working on another book on the cabbala. This new set of emphases remained constant until her death in 1946, and the Inner Light has remained an explicitly Christian organization ever since.[80]

There remain, however, some tantalizing hints that she may have been considering a fresh change of direction, and they derive from her relationship with Crowley. Amazingly, in view of their different natures and interests, her opinion of him was a warm one. It has been rumoured among British occultists that she visited him in the 1930s to ask how to invoke Mercury,[81] and in an undated survey of 'the occult field' written after 1936, she called his services to its literature 'immense' and the man himself 'a genuine adept', even if some of his practices, such as first invoking the north (place of darkness) rather than the east (place of light) seemed dangerous to her.[82] In 1942 she exchanged chatty letters with him, playfully calling him 'Dear 666', and in early 1945 the exchange suddenly accelerated, the pace being forced by her. Kenneth Grant, Crowley's secretary at the time, has remembered that she visited him twice at that time and discussed 'the possibility of reviving the pagan attitudes to cosmic and elemental forces'. There is some confusion in the surviving evidence here, because Crowley's diary apparently does not mention actual visits in that period, and the two letters preserved by Grant from the correspondence do not discuss paganism, although Fortune does hint that she might make a public acceptance of Crowley's ideas regarding 'the law of New Aeon' in the future.[83] The diary does, however, record these letters, and bear out Grant's general point of a sudden intense interest in the magician's views taken by Fortune at that time; in one letter (received on 1 February) she enclosed money enabling the impecunious Crowley to make three replies to her.[84] Further progress on it, and any consequences, were prevented by the illness which eventually led to Fortune's death. Crowley preserved both the letters to him and copies of his replies, but the latter were later lost in America, apparently destroyed.[85]

There are thus some puzzles in the story, and indeed the whole sequence of events which I have proposed above is heavily dependent upon my own perspective and the sources available to me. To a cabbalist, for example, her spate of publication in the 1930s could be quite reasonably characterized as engendered by her first really considerable work, *The Mystical Qabalah* (1935) and devoted to working out a set of ideas dependent upon the latter. Another perspective would emphasize the continual interplay in her life of three different traditions, hermetic and ritual magic, paganism, and mystical Christianity, and suggest that all that altered was the current balance of interest which she maintained between them. Her apparent gaps in publication were spanned by her regular expression of views in the magazine of her order, the Inner Light, which was not available to me; although (according to those who have had access to it) they broadly reflected the shifts of interest found in her books. Throughout the Second World War she issued letters to her members, weekly until 1942 and monthly thereafter, and these showed a preoccupation with hermetic philosophy, astrology, and similar esoteric matters, as well as with national defence. It seems certain that had she not died so soon after the end of the war, then this material would have been developed into more books; and indeed she left a number of unpublished manuscripts containing material from the war years, upon such matters as esoteric medicine and cabbalistic symbolism, which have remained in the custody of the (now) Society of the Inner Light.[86] Although the course of events which I have suggested above still seems to stand up, with a more Christian period in the 1920s, a more pagan one at the time of her greatest flowering of work in the late 1930s, and a more Christian and abstractly esoteric one after 1939, she was clearly a complex thinker, whose career defies any simple formulations.

*   *   *

The third individual to be considered here is Robert Graves (1895–1985), who unlike the first two is a celebrated member of the pantheon of mainstream modern literature, being honoured by critics as one of the finest English poets of the twentieth century and among the general public as one of its most popular authors of historical novels. His impact upon modern pagan witchcraft, however, derives mostly from a single work of prose non-fiction, *The White Goddess* (1948). Its importance to the evolution of the favourite modern image of pagan goddess and god has been emphasized above; here it needs to be placed in the context of Graves's own life and creative development. It falls into a sequence of prose in which he gradually reinterpreted some of the fundamental texts of his civilization according to his own, very personal, views. This was presaged by a novel in 1925, *My Head! My Head!*, which provided his rereadings of the Old Testament stories of Moses and Elisha. It truly began, however, while Graves was living in a village in South Devon during World War Two, cut off by the hostilities from his beloved expatriate home in Majorca and needing to write novels instead of poems to bring in more money. Between 1942 and 1943 he produced his own version of one of the most famous Greek myths, the tale of the Golden fleece and the Argonauts, and this work filled him with a sense of a personal relationship with the great Triple Goddess and the matriarchal society over which she was imagined to have presided in prehistoric Greece, as revealed long before in the work of Jane Harrison. In August 1943, a month after finishing *The Golden fleece*, he felt himself bursting with a sense of revelation, which found expression in January 1944, when in three weeks of feverish writing he produced a survey of myth and history built around the figure of the Goddess, called *The Roebuck in the Thicket*. Having completed it, he laid it aside, partly because he felt frightened of it himself, partly because he needed to write another commercially viable work to maintain a steady income, and partly because he wanted to settle accounts with Jesus Christ before proceeding further.

During those five months between *The Golden Fleece* and *The Roebuck*, he had drafted a novel which provided his personal version of the life of Christ, and he returned to this in early 1944, completing the book in the following year; it was published in 1946 as *King Jesus*. Having finished the writing of it, he felt able to devote the rest of 1945 to the reworking and expansion of *The Roebuck*, into a book which he now called *The Three-Fold Muse*. He completed it and dispatched it to the press in January 1946, under its final name of *The White Goddess*. A few amendments were made to the manuscript during the remainder of the year, in which he returned to Majorca, and it was published in England in May 1948 and in the United States three months later. Graves rounded out his goddess-related writings in the rest of the decade with a translation of the ancient Roman text which best supported them, the *Golden Ass* of Apuleius (1950), and a novel which imagined a future in which matriarchal religion and society had been restored, *Seven Days in New Crete* (1949). Apart from the isolated early work of *My Head! My Head!*, therefore, *The White Goddess* stands in a run of prose which otherwise consisted of three novels and a translation.[87]

Throughout this body of work, certain themes remain constant. One is a resolutely sceptical and rationalist attitude to miracles and marvels. Graves allows very little credit to the human imagination; instead he is determined to interpret apparently fantastic episodes in terms of real events, and to him virtually all myth which concerns human action is distorted history. In *My Head! My Head!* all the plagues visited upon Egypt are shown to have had natural causes; the death of the first-born children, traditionally the hardest for scientists to explain away, is shown to have resulted from the activities of an Israelite hit-squad! Moses is portrayed as a man equipped with a superb knowledge of the workings of nature, which he manipulates with constant fraud and trickery in order to deceive, coerce, impress, and destroy the simpler human beings around him. In his view of the voyage of the Argo, the stress is again upon reconstructing the 'reality' of the event: the Harpies are not monsters but carrion birds, the golden apples of the Hesperides are oranges, the dragon which guards the Golden Fleece is only a large python, Icarus does not fall from the sky but from a ship's prow, the Centaurs are merely a tribe with a horse totem, and so forth. The priestesses who dominate religion are just as adept as Moses at lying, deceiving, and engineering miracles to retain power over their followers, while oracles shape their answers in response to force, bribery, and self-interest. It is a very cynical view of organized religious behaviour. Nor is Christ allowed any miraculous power. In *King Jesus* he can heal only those nervous conditions which are amenable to a placebo effect; the 'leprosy' which he is alleged to have cured is revealed to be a skin complaint produced by stress and mistaken for a true leprous condition. Achievements such as the feeding of the five thousand and the turning of water into wine are declared to be misunderstandings caused by a literal reading of statements and actions of Jesus which were in fact allegorical.

The picture is complicated, however, by the fact that Graves still wishes to believe in the supernatural. In *Seven Days in New Crete* he has the narrator recount two apparent personal encounters with ghosts, which were in fact autobiographical. Part of the plots of both *My Head! My Head!* and *King Jesus* rests upon a curious concept that it is possible to restore to life a person who has just died by offering to substitute one's own life instead, within a short span; so the Crucifixion is Jesus's payment for the raising of Lazarus. Graves in fact both endorses a view of Jesus as an admirable figure, of exceptional spirituality, integrity, and nobility, and leaves open the possibility that his resurrection in a heavenly form might have been a genuine event.

This is linked to the poet's view of divinity; that deities are real beings, but they are only empowered by the faith of believers. In *My Head! My Head!* it is asserted that the strength of Jah (Jehovah) is no greater than the strength of his people; without the Hebrews he is nothing. The Triple Goddess of *The Golden Fleece* admits to a devotee that she has been so enfeebled by the accession of power given to her son Zeus by the comparative growth in the number of his adherents, that she can no longer exert her will directly upon earth. One of the central arguments of *The White Goddess* is that once people start to believe in her in large numbers again, her reign will recommence in earnest. *Seven Days in New Crete* portrays a world in which just that has occurred, and the Goddess takes visible forms and intervenes directly in the affairs of humans for their own collective good. The Christ of *King Jesus*, on the other hand, is immune to her because he has never called upon her or had sex with a woman, and so he can vanquish the magic of her adherents; yet fortune or destiny causes him to fail in his mission and to die in the traditional way of a sacrifice to her.

It was important to Graves that readers should realize that his reconstructions of the 'real stories' behind these bodies of sacred literature, even in the form of novels, represented not merely one possibility of what had occurred, but *the* truth, reached by a superior process of scholarly deduction. In *The Golden Fleece* this is described as a process of comparing the very different versions which exist of the legend, and then 'choosing for my own account whatever version of any incident makes the best sense, and even occasionally in improvising where a gap cannot be bridged by existent materials'.[88] This in fact greatly understates the extent to which Graves reworks the story. In *King Jesus* he is more specific as to texts; his interpretation is based on material taken from the Gnostic Gospels, which is read in turn in the light of 'secret lore' taken from medieval Irish and Welsh works, 'and they yield their full sense only in the light of Babylonian astrology, Talmudic speculation, the liturgy of the Ethiopian Church, the homilies of Clement of Alexandria, the religious essays of Plutarch, and recent studies of Bronze Age archaeology'.[89] He never, however, cites the material taken from each source, and explains how it all fits together; this parade of erudition appears to be simply intended to impress the uninformed reader. *The White Goddess* adopts identical tactics; a personal interpretation of texts taken from a very wide range of cultures, bridged by unsupported personal assertions of faith. Graves specifically aims it at the general public, declaring from the start that critics and scholars are not going to take it seriously and making this expectation into a point of pride, on the grounds that academics are too corrupted by professional timidity and myopia to recognize the truth of unorthodox opinion.[90]

Another constant theme is Graves's complete acceptance of the reality of ancient matriarchy, in both society and religion, of the sort suggested by writers since the mid-nineteenth century. This already features in *My Head! My Head!*, where it is assumed to have been an excellent system, and its replacement with patriarchy to have introduced a period of misery lasting until the present. Two decades later, in *King Jesus*, he was more equivocal, declaring that the question whether one 'is a better solution to the eternal problems of the relations of men and women' than the other must remain open.[91] What is really remarkable to a liberal humanist reader is how unattractive a picture of matriarchy Graves actually seems to present. In *The Golden Fleece* the priestesses who dominate the old religion sacrifice or cripple male children, tear animals to pieces in frenzy, and put (male) strangers to death on whims. In *King Jesus* the rituals at the Goddess's great temple at Hieropolis include 'sacrifices of sheep, goats, and children' and 'holocausts of live beasts hung from terebinth-trees'. This is the classic, hostile, Old Testament vision of ancient paganism, but applied to a religion of which Graves seems to approve.

In the same novel he goes on to make a significant adaptation to Frazer's image of the divine king, sacrificed as representative of the dying and returning god all over ancient Europe and the Mediterranean basin, by assuming that he must have been sacrificed to the Goddess, 'decked with the green branches, crowned with whitethorn, flogged and ill-treated in a manner shameful to record, and finally roasted alive; while his companions dressed in bull-hides dance around the pyre. But his soul escapes upward in the form of an eagle . . . and becomes immortal, while the bull-men feast eucharistically on his remains'.[92] This theme—that a man can gain immortality by being first tortured and then killed in the service of the Goddess—is a recurrent one of Graves's work. In *Seven Days in New Crete* a young boy is ritually butchered in a public performance as part of a twice-yearly sacrifice, by priestesses who then feast upon his flesh. The Goddess herself materializes to reassure the narrator, who is at first appalled, that he was a willing victim and that his family are greatly honoured. The last words of *The Golden Fleece* concern the death of Orpheus, the character with whom, as a poet and personal devotee of the Goddess, Graves most clearly identifies. He is torn to pieces by priestesses, winning the author's comment that 'the Goddess has always rewarded with dismemberment those who love her best, scattering their bloody pieces over the earth to fructify it, but gently taking their astonished souls into her own keeping.'[93] Why do such intensely masochistic images keep appearing in Graves's work?

The short answer is that he was an intense masochist, who depended for his own creative inspiration upon being dedicated to the service of a specific woman, dominated by her, and made unhappy by her. This is an issue upon which his two biographers, Martin Seymour-Smith and Richard Perceval Graves, who disagree upon much else, are wholly at one. It is plain from the story put together independently by each that three successive women fulfilled this role between his birth in 1895 and the opening of his Goddess-centred period in 1940. The first was his mother, a powerful figure of profound Christian piety who used affection and punishment as instruments to encourage her offspring to succeed in the world. Under her influence, Robert spent his childhood and adolescence as a devout and somewhat priggish Christian. Her influence was broken in 1918 by his marriage to his first wife Nancy Nicholson, who immediately became the new dominant force in his life. She was a pronounced feminist, and pushed him into a decisive loss of faith in Christianity by declaring that any religion with a male deity must be 'rot'. It can be no coincidence that he acquired his lasting belief in ancient matriarchy during this period. The marriage became a time of acute unhappiness for him, from which he was rescued by falling under the spell of his third and greatest guiding figure, the writer Laura Riding, with whom he lived from 1926 to 1940. Riding proved to be more domineering than either of her predecessors, and actually believed herself to be something more than human, and to deserve the reverence accorded to a goddess. She inspired Graves to some of his best work, and eventually to his greatest pitch of frustration and misery, before abandoning him. He was rescued by Beryl Hodge, who became his second wife and gave him a supportive love and understanding which he had never received before. He thus achieved a lasting domestic happiness, and yet lost that insecurity and emotional pain which he was gradually coming to recognize as essential to his ability to write poetry. His solution, from 1950 onward, was to fall in love with a series of young women whom he termed his Muses (more strictly, successive faces of *the* Muse, the lovely and cruel Goddess) and whom he pursued through doomed romances which afforded him the necessary excitement and torment. The main sequence of Goddess-centred writings, therefore, occurred in the gap, when he was bereft of such a figure in his own life and coming to terms with his need for one. To somebody of Graves's personality, what was true for him had to be true for everybody else; this absolute moral certainty was one of the enduring bequests made to him by his mother.[94]

This emotional pattern led to some fascinating consequences for his interpretation of deity. Harrison had conceived the notion of the threefold Great Goddess, but only shown any interest in her aspects as Maiden and Mother. Crowley had recognized and defined the third, of the old woman, but reacted to it with fear and loathing. Graves, by contrast, found that third, waning-moon personification the most fascinating and alluring of all, as it represented the divine feminine who gives pain and death in order to give reward and new life. Repeatedly he saw her as the sow who eats her own farrow, and this image of the destructive sow-goddess was one which he imposed on the historical evidence, most tellingly upon the Welsh figure of Ceridwen. The latter features in Welsh legend as a witch and in later Welsh bardic poetry as a muse. Nobody associated her with a sow form until Graves twisted an interpretation of her name by Canon MacCulloch (itself now rejected by philologists) to give her one and so assimilate her to his notion of the dark, or destructive, aspect of goddess.[95]

The same effect of propulsion of personal need is found in his redevelopment of male deity, by splitting Frazer's vegetation spirit into two forms, the gods of the waxing and waning year who duel with each other. Such an image may well have come to him from the legend of the annual combat between Gwyn ap Nudd and Gwythyr in *The Mabinogion*[96] or from an eighteenth-century local Welsh custom of an annual mock fight between Kings of Winter and Summer, reported in popular collections of folklore such as that of Marie Trevelyan.[97] The idea was given a particular power for Graves, however, by his belief that one of the humiliations which the Goddess must inflict upon her favoured devotee as part of his ritual destruction is to foresake him for a rival; something which did indeed occur to Graves spectacularly in the cases of Nicholson, Riding, and most of his later 'Muses'.[98]

As has been said earlier, a central role of the Goddess for Graves was to give the gift of poetry; but his definition of the latter was, again, deeply personal and very narrow. *The White Goddess* is not merely a diatribe against the modern world but against modern poets, who are not named in the text but from Graves's other writings clearly included T. S. Eliot, Ezra Pound, W. H. Auden, Dylan Thomas, and the other leading figures in his generation. It is a great irony, therefore, that the book only gained acceptance by a publisher because of the heroically generous intervention of Eliot, who persuaded Faber to take it on with an assurance that it possessed literary merit. Not that Graves thought any better of earlier verse, dismissing all that of classical Greece and Rome and 'nine-tenths of what passes as English poetry', including most of its most famous practitioners. The work which he considered to pass the test, in fact, consisted of his own, that of Laura Riding (until their separation), that of the relatively obscure Tudor writer John Skelton, that of a very few other equally marginal figures, and that of archaic Greece and early medieval Wales and Ireland (at least as he 'restored' it).[99]

His biographers also supply many insights into the process by which Graves 'restored' texts to their 'true' meaning, which proves to be one of instinctual imposition of personal vision exactly comparable to that which Lawrence applied to Etruscan art; except that Graves articulated it more openly in theoretical terms. He termed it 'associative' or 'analeptic' thought, the application of poetic insight and appropriation of ideas and images taken from many different contexts to 'solve' problems which were intractable to reason alone. He fully understood that what he was propounding might not actually be true; but in poetic terms that did not matter, for he could declare that 'literal truth is comparatively unimportant, as an artist can tell the truth by a condensation and dramatization of the facts'. His reading public, however, would be given the impression that what he was telling *was* literal truth; hence the way in which he rewrote the facts of his own life in his famous autobiography *Goodbye To All That* (1929).[100] He dismissed any criticisms of his theory of the career of Christ in *King Jesus* as those of 'prose men' who did not understand poetic thinking. To Graves, 'philosophical truth' was higher than factual truth. In one example of his logic given by his friend Martin Seymour-Smith, 'while Dylan Thomas might not actually have syphilis ("at present"), *philosophically* he was riddled with it'. He apparently applied this tactic to those around him as well; another friend once burst out 'that Graves did not perceive people, but rather invented them—and afterwards came to believe in his own inventions'.[101]

All this may sound like a more personal analysis than has hitherto been found necessary in this book; a study *ad hominem* rather than simply of literary work. With Graves, however, the latter really is even more closely based upon an idiomatic individual view of the world than most. The point can be made very neatly by considering the description which he provided of the entity who was to be his great gift to modern pagan witchcraft, the fully formed image of the Triple Moon Goddess, Maiden, Mother, and Crone. On page 24 of *The White Goddess* he portrays her in her Mother and Bride aspect, with a particularity of detail which has often surprised readers; she is pale-faced, hook-nosed, fair-haired, blue-eyed, red-lipped, lovely, and slender. The reason for the precision of the portrait is simply that it is one of a real woman, a friend of his family called Irene Gay, who was staying with them while he was writing that part of the book, and with whom the poet was a little in love.[102] It is also, however, a picture of his lost love and greatest Muse, Laura Riding, as she had been at the beginning of their affair.

*　　*　　*

The fourth and last person to be considered here is Margaret Murray (1862–1963). Her life story shows certain striking similarities to those of Jane Harrison and Jessie Weston, two other members of the first generation of women to make a serious impact upon the world of professional scholarship. Like them, she never married, dedicating her life to her work. Like them, she owed many of her earlier ideas to a mentor, who had helped to launch her career and whom she revered and followed uncritically; in her case this was Sir Flinders Petrie, in that of Harrison, Dugald MacColl, and in that of Weston, Alfred Nutt.[103] All three produced work which aroused great controversy, and defended it virtually as an article of faith. Like Weston, Murray came to the life of scholarship relatively late, both being in their forties when they entered it. The distinction of Margaret Murray, however, lies both in the wide range of fields in which she worked and the huge volume of her publications, and in her ardent feminism, which caused her to campaign actively for female suffrage, and to speak bitterly about the prejudices against women within academe. Linked to a combative and self-assertive nature, it gave her a great pride in herself and her achievements—in her autobiography she constantly provides examples of her physical toughness and belligerent courage—and a tendency to deny any good motives or virtues to those who criticized her theories.[104]

The core of her academic career lay in Egyptology, but she came to write on a wide variety of topics linked to the theme of ancient religion. Her significance here, and the one which has provided her widest public reputation, is that she appeared to become the first person to provide apparent supporting evidence, based upon systematic research, for the long-rehearsed theory that the victims of the early modern witch trials had been practitioners of a surviving pagan religion. In her autobiography, she described how she had come across the idea in London during World War One, when the fighting had stopped her getting back to her work in Egypt and left her at a loose end. She forgot who had suggested it to her; obvious channels for it are the Folk-Lore Society, of which she was an enthusiastic member and which had been led by one notable proponent of the theory, Sir Lawrence Gomme, and the University of London, where she taught and where another one, Karl Pearson, had been a colleague. She cited the latter in the introduction to her own first book on the subject, *The Witch Cult in Western Europe* (1921). Her ideas were first aired, however, to the Folk-Lore Society, and published in its journal in 1917 and 1920, encouraged by the immediate praise and worthies of the society such as Charlotte Gomme, who commented that they made perfect sense in the context apparently established by *The Golden Bough*.[105] This was a perfectly accurate perception, for Murray was a lifelong admirer of Frazer. In 1919 she tested her research again in another respected scholarly body, the Royal Anthropological Institute, which published two more of her papers. Another was brought out by the *Scottish Historical Review*.[106] The groundwork was therefore well laid for the presentation of her book to Oxford University Press, which accepted it easily after receiving a supportive report from the respected scholar Henry Balfour.[107]

The Witch Cult in Western Europe rested upon a small amount of archival research, with extensive use of printed trial records in nineteenth-century editions, plus early modern pamphlets and works of demonology. Most of the material was Scottish, with some from England and a little from the Continent, and Murray combined it all to give an impression of a fairly uniform pagan religion, surviving all across Western Europe until the seventeenth century. In her portrait it was a fertility cult focused upon a horned god who represented the generative powers of nature and was personified at the rites by a human being, usually male. It was organized in covens of thirteen, run by men or women (the latter being called 'Queens of the Sabbat') who owed allegiance to a 'Grand Master' controlling several such covens. People entered these either by being dedicated as children or initiated as adults. Covens held meetings known as 'esbats', to transact business, and held 'sabbats' four times a year, at the old quarter days which opened the seasons (Candlemas, May Day, Lammas, and All-Hallows) to provide religious ceremonies for all local believers in the old religion. The rites included feasting, ring and processional dances (to promote fertility), acts of magic, sacrifice of animals and children, ritualized sexual intercourse to encourage fertility in humans, and (most important) the paying of homage to the person representing the god. She took up Pearson's suggestion that Joan of Arc had been a member of the religion, and added one of Joan's contemporaries, Gilles de Rais, as another prominent member of 'the ancient religion'.

The tone of the book was generally dry and clinical, and every assertion was meticulously footnoted to a source, with lavish quotation. When advancing theories which she sensed to be potentially controversial, Murray usually became hectoring, characterizing scholars who had made different interpretations of the evidence as possessed of 'bias', 'prejudice', and 'unscientific attitudes'. In reality, her portrait of the religion was constructed by choosing vivid details of alleged witch practices provided in sources scattered across a great extent of space and time, and declaring them to be normative: the full plan of the four sabbats was taken from a single deposition at Forfar in 1661. Her copious use of quotation masked the fact that she ruthlessly ignored in her sources anything which did not support her case, and, by removing it from the extracts which she printed, she was effectively altering the tone and import of documents. This tactic was later to be heavily, and understandably, criticized,[108] but in fairness to her it was simply an extension of that long employed by respected anthropologists and folklorists: to assume that the people under study would not themselves understand the genuine meaning of their actions, which could only be detected by trained modern experts.

A decade passed, in which Murray returned to Egyptology, and then in 1933 she brought out a sequel to *The Witch Cult*, entitled *The God of the Witches*. It represented a restatement and reinforcement of the thesis of the earlier book, with two major aspects to it. The first was a change in tone, for the second book was put out by a popular press, Sampson Low, and aimed far more obviously at a mass market. The approach was no longer analytical, but celebratory, the 'Old Religion' (Murray having picked up Leland's phrase) being characterized as a joyous and life-affirming one, contrasted with the gloom of Christianity; the picture of it was now being soaked in the characteristic language of neo-paganism. She still accepted that it included blood sacrifice, but insisted that this was in a degenerate form produced by Christian persecution.

The second new aspect was, as the title suggests, a much heavier emphasis upon the nature of its deity. The book represented the culmination of the cult of Pan in modern England, for it asserted the doctrine that the horned god of the greenwood had been the oldest male deity known to humans, and traced his worship across Europe and the Near East, from the Old Stone Age to the seventeenth century. This was achieved by seizing every prominent representation of a horned god in European or Near Eastern art and literature (ignoring all others) and identifying it with him while reasserting the idea that he had been the focus of worship for the witches, and the origins of the figure of the Christian Devil. At the same time, paradoxically, she helped to eclipse Pan himself, by asserting that the Greek god had been only one aspect of the deity, and not necessarily the most important. Amongst alternatives which she cited, two were to be of special significance for the future: the Arabic Dhu'l Karnain, or 'horned one', applied to the ram-horned images of Alexander the Great, and the Gallic deity Cernunnos. The latter, although strictly speaking attested by name (and that doubtfully) from one site in Paris, was declared by her to have been 'one of the greatest gods, perhaps even the supreme deity, of Gaul' (modern France); by implication, the main form of the god in north-western

Europe.[109] This process satisfied two impulses of the time: the first, a weakening hold of the classics upon British literary culture, which made Greek and Roman deities less automatically familiar to the modern mind, and the second, a new sense of the importance of universal images in the human imagination, hardened by Carl Jung into the theory of archetypes.

The book was significant in other ways. It embedded the putative medieval witch religion in a much richer context of associations, linking it with fairy stories, the Robin Hood legend, surviving folk customs, and historical figures such as William Rufus and Thomas à Becket, who were declared to have died as human sacrifices according to Frazer's theory of divine kingship, and Edward III, who was revealed as having founded the Order of the Garter in imitation of it. Items were added to the institutions and iconography of the 'cult'; garters were found to be a distinctive part of its costume, and covens were now described as having been run by a supreme Chief (usually male), who deputed power to an Officer (also normally a man) and a Maiden (always female), the latter being the more important of the two. The role of Officer could double with that of Summoner, the person who carried information around coven members and their local supporters.

A case-study of the way in which Murray could appropriate and redevelop an image in the book is provided by her treatment of a rock-painting at Cogul in north-eastern Spain. This she characterized as the only scene in palaeolithic art 'which can be identified as a religious ceremony performed by several persons'. To her, it was unmistakably a 'dance of nine women around a standing male figure' who 'wears a garter on each leg'. An illustration of the painting was provided which shows well the features to which she wished to draw attention.[110] Leaving aside the point that the painting is not palaeolithic (Old Stone Age) but from the more recent mesolithic, a look at fuller illustrations of it—let alone at the original—reveals certain discrepancies. The actual group of figures consists of three bulls, two ibex, nine deer, one pig, nine female humans, and three males. Two of the men are hunting stags. The women appear not to be dancing in a ring but standing in a row, five facing towards the onlooker and four facing away. The third man is placed in the centre of their line and is very stylized, his only features being the phallus which indicates his sex and the leggings which Murray interpreted as garters. The whole composition, however, is not a straightforward group of figures but a sequence in which layers of them were superimposed upon each other, possibly at widely differing times. The row of women was painted over an unidentifiable animal, one of the deer was painted over them, and the man with the leggings was superimposed on one of the women; it might be argued that the men belong to a hunting scene which was added to the rock after the line of women and has nothing to do with them.[111] Almost needless to say, Murray's illustration of the paintings is reduced simply to those aspects which she thought significant and shows none of these problems; her treatment of visual sources matched that of written texts.

In 1934 she made another significant contribution to medieval scholarship, by contributing an essay on 'Female Fertility figures' to the *Journal of the Royal Anthropological Institute*. It suggested that the enigmatic carvings of naked women which appeared in some medieval churches were representations of pagan goddesses of fertility, and further proof of the enduring hold of the old religion upon the bulk of people throughout the medieval period. This idea was the direct inspiration for the theory propounded five years later by her colleague in the Folk-Lore Society, Lady Raglan, that the foliate heads found in fourteenth- and fifteenth-century churches were images of Frazer's vegetation god, 'The Green Man'. This linkage of church carvings with paganism was arguably to be the most influential idea which Murray produced outside Egyptology, and it persisted among folklorists, historians, and archaeologists alike until the 1980s.[112]

It needs to be stressed that all this work was generated by Margaret Murray during what were effectively holiday periods from her own discipline, the study of ancient Egypt—and the reckless abandon with which she treated material may well attest to this spirit. Her much more voluminous contributions to Egyptology itself, although idiosyncratic at moments, were sober and well researched, and are still worthy of respect.[113] None the less, she herself took her theories concerning the witch trials very seriously, and was proud of them, and they probably came to provide the most prominent element in her public reputation. They represented, indeed, a considerable achievement. Between 1917 and 1921 she had appeared to provide sound documentary support for the theory that medieval and early modern witchcraft had been a pagan religion. In the period 1931–34 she had extended this work to furnish some evidence for the belief that this religion had represented an enduring component in ancient European paganism—perhaps the most important—which could be traced from the palaeolithic to the early modern period, and retained the allegiance of most of the population until the end of the Middle Ages. How, then, were her theories received?

Among that small number of scholars who were familiar with the trial records, they never had a chance. The use of source material which underpinned them was too blatantly flawed, and this was made immediately apparent by expert reviewers of *The Witch Cult*. One was W. R. Halliday, to whom the book was sent by the journal of Murray's own Folk-Lore Society and who relentlessly laid bare the way in which she had ripped quotations free from their historical context.[114] From 1929 onwards L'Estrange Ewen brought out his succession of books on the English trials based upon close and comprehensive use of the archival material, which left no room for doubt that those tried were not pagans. Murray herself reacted to this informed criticism with the same lack of scruple which had characterized her attitude to sources. Her own reviews of Ewen's work in the Folk-Lore Society's periodical were amazingly ungracious, avoiding any engagement with his actual arguments or evidence and dismissing him completely in general terms as 'unscientific', 'uncritical', 'dull', and so valueless and worthy only to be ignored.[115] In her autobiography she declared that she had long given up reading reviews of her own books, and that opponents of her theories about the witch trials had been motivated primarily by Christian prejudice. She added airily that critics of them were always ignorant of the original sources, of which she possessed an unsurpassed knowledge.[116]

She could afford to brazen things out in this way, because her work in the field found an immediate and lasting favourable reception among readers— sometimes major scholars—who were not expert in it. It appealed to so many of the emotional impulses of the age; to the notion of the English countryside as a timeless place full of ancient secrets, to the literary cult of Pan as its deity, to the belief that until comparatively recently Christianity had represented only a veneer of elite religion covering a persistence of paganism among the masses, and to the characterization of modern folk customs as survivals from that paganism. Furthermore, it appealed not just to the emotions but to common sense. The notion that the witch trials had resulted from some kind of collective madness, propounded by most experts in the subject, seemed much more far-fetched than the suggestion that they represented the persecution of an actual rival religion; especially as in Murray's formulation, like those of Michelet, Gage, and Leland and unlike those of Jarcke and Mone, it was possible to sympathize more with the oppressed faith than with Christianity.

For these reasons, it is not surprising that the reviewer of *The Witch Cult* for *The Times*, in the delighted phrase of her editor at the press, 'swallowed it whole', and with notices such as that on her side she could afford to ignore criticisms made later in learned journals.[117] The same remark could be applied to the respected historian of medieval monasteries, G. C. Coulton, who built it into his major work on them in 1923,[118] and of the best-selling writer of popular fiction, John Buchan, who based a novel upon it, *Witch Wood*, in 1927. Its most obvious early impact, however, was upon British occultists, who took it up rapidly and with enthusiasm; among those who endorsed it in the years between 1917 and 1940 were Dion Fortune and her partner Charles Seymour, the mystical Celticist Lewis Spence, the prominent publisher of esoteric works Ralph Shirley, and J. W. Brodie Innes, leader of one of the successor orders to the Golden Dawn.[119] It was also taken up by a related genre, of sensationalist popular histories of witchcraft; one in 1929, by the American Theda Kenyon, linked Murray's 'witch cult' with Leland's *Aradia* and both traditional and ritual magic, and suggested that it had survived to the present, in a way that was to presage the appearance of pagan witches and may possibly have acted as one blueprint for them.[120] Murray herself acquired a further, potent hold over the public imagination when she was invited to write the entry on 'Witchcraft' in the most prestigious British encyclopaedia, the *Britannica*. She stated her own ideas there as if they were proven and accepted fact, and they remained in its successive reprintings until the 1960s.

None the less, what was to become known as 'the Murray thesis' was a relatively slow-burning fuse. In its first thirty years in print, *The Witch Cult in Western Europe* sold only 2,020 copies. *The God of the Witches*, designed as a populist work, was remaindered after two years. The turning-point for both came in the 1940s, when interest in *The God* picked up again. It was republished after the war, and became a best-seller in the last years of the decade. At the opening of the 1950s, Oxford University Press and Faber bought the rights to it for a paperback imprint, and in this same period the sales of the more academic *Witch Cult* began to pick up at last.[121] The reputation of the thesis in scholarly circles followed the same trajectory. Halliday's withering review may well explain the silence concerning it in the Folk-Lore Society for the rest of the 1920s. In 1935, however, two essays appeared in the society's journal which supported and extended it,[122] and between 1946 and 1955 contributors to the same periodical regularly praised it, usually in the context of an attack upon somebody else with different ideas.[123] In 1945 another prominent member of the society, Christina Hole, brought out a popular book on witchcraft which accepted the thesis with a few reservations about details.[124] In the same year, one of the most reputable of academic historians, Sir George Clark, issued a second edition of a widely used textbook which he had first published in 1929. The first version had taken the tradition, rationalist line on the witch trials as an exemplar of bigotry and superstition, to be vanquished by science. The revised one replaced this with the Murray thesis.[125] In 1947 the latter was incorporated into no less than three history books of different kinds: a survey of witchcraft beliefs by another reputable academic, Trevor Davies, a study of folklore by a professional scholar, Arne Runeberg, and a sensational work on the Middle Ages by the amateur historian Hugh Ross Williamson.[126] It was in the late 1940s that the Murray thesis truly seized the imagination of the British; and the public emergence of pagan witchcraft followed directly upon this development.

What did Margaret Murray herself believe about religion and magic? Like Graves, she had been brought up by an unusually devout Christian mother, and initially took up her faith with proportionate zeal, becoming a Sunday School teacher.[127] By the time that she entered academic life she had rejected it, and in the Folk-Lore Society she acquired an enduring reputation as 'a whole-hearted sceptic and rationalist'.[128] This was not wholly accurate. In her autobiography she declared an awareness of 'an unseen over-ruling Power', 'the 'Infinite', which rules the universe, and 'which science calls Nature and religion calls God'. She did add that most traditional religions had been 'childish legends' about that Power, but this did not diminish its reality, and she looked forward to being brought to a higher knowledge of it upon death.[129] Nor was her attitude to magic consistently dismissive. It is true that in an interview given to a Sunday newspaper she dismissed witchcraft as 'superstition and superstitious fear', empowered only by credulity, yet in her autobiography she professed a belief in clairvoyance.[130] Moreover, private sources reveal her parallel enthusiasm for both the theory and practice of sending out curses. Once she carried out a ritual to blast a fellow academic whose promotion she believed to have been undeserved, by mixing up ingredients in a frying pan in the presence of two colleagues. The victim actually did become ill, and had to change jobs. This was only one among a number of such acts of malevolent magic which she perpe-trated, and which the friend who recorded them assumed (rather nervously) to have been pranks, with coincidental effects.[131] So they may have been, but there is a letter extant in which another friend of hers, with even more disquiet, quoted a conversation in which she discussed her technique of putting curses on victims with every sign of conviction.[132]

A different aspect of her belief system is revealed in a book by a popular writer on crime and related issues, Donald McCormick. It concerns the interest which Murray took in one of the most spectacular unsolved murders of the twentieth century, the beating and hacking to death of a farm labourer called Charles Walton on Meon Hill, Warwickshire, in 1945. Five years after the event, when the police investigation had been closed, Murray launched her own, by taking a holiday in the district disguised as an artist. According to McCormick, she then gave an interview to *The Birmingham Post*, in which she claimed that Walton had been sacrificed by 'people who still believe in a religion practised in Britain before Christianity, whom we call devil worshippers'.[133] McCormick recorded how he then went to visit her himself, and that she told him that the local villagers (who had expressed indignation at her opinion) were colluding to conceal their knowledge of the cult—if true, it is an extreme example of the tradition that scholars understood country people better than they did them-selves. She then allegedly told him that several other unsolved murders in the recent past—especially of children who had been sexually molested before death—were likewise the work of 'black' witches.[134]

If this is true (and the only reason for caution in accepting it is the lack of corroborative evidence), then she had softened her line in the following year, when she told the *Sunday Dispatch* that although a few witches survived to the present day, 'most' of them were 'white'.[135] It was still softer three years later, when she became an almost literal godmother to modern pagan witchcraft by writing a supportive foreword to the first book devoted to it, Gerald Gardner's *Witchcraft Today*. This declared that ancient and tribal rituals were all 'acts of worship according to the Almighty Giver of Life', inspired by a common feeling of 'grati-tude to the Creator and hope for the constance of His goodness'. She accepted that much of the witchcraft portrayed in the book was at least 'descended' from ancient rites and was a 'sincere expression' of a 'feeling towards God' represented 'perhaps more decorously, although not more sincerely' by Christianity.[136] This was generous, and also embodies a heartfelt manifestation of that instinctual monotheistic piety which balanced much of her public rational scepticism. It was also a somewhat peculiar comment upon a book which portrayed a religion based on a stark duotheism, in which a goddess was the senior partner; but here, just as before when dealing with witchcraft, she was ignoring those aspects of the source material which did not suit what she wished to believe.

This consideration of Margaret Murray has brought us to the appearance of modern pagan witchcraft itself. It is time to confront that phenomenon directly at last, and to see what can be done to tell its story.

MICROCOSM

GERALD GARDNER

✄ ✄

THE foundation story of modern pagan witchcraft was first published in 1960, in the biography of the person most prominently associated with its appearance, Gerald Brosseau Gardner (1884–1964). The book was formally credited to Jack Bracelin, and written, in reality, by the well-known author on Sufiism, Idries Shah; but as Gardner himself was the source of virtually all its information, it is effectively autobiographical.[1] It told the story of a long and relatively uneventful working life, spent first as the owner or manager of tea and rubber plantations in Ceylon, North Borneo, and Malaya, and then as an inspector in the Malay customs service. The setting is the one on which Joseph Conrad's novels were fashioned, and in the single photograph printed from those days, Gardner appears very much a Conradian hero, a tall, muscular, moustachioed man with a resolute smile, standing upon a riverboat with a revolver at his side. His memoirs, however, are resolutely unheroic, and the one episode which begins to approximate to drama, an anticipated attack on his plantation by headhunters, is rapidly deflated as the report turns out to be a false alarm, and Gardner's posturing with a rifle is turned into a joke against himself. The impression is given of a self-contained individual, whose lonely existence came to an end when he married a nurse, Dorothea (usually called Donna), in a whirlwind romance when he was forty-three; the partnership lasted until her death four years before his own.

In two respects, however, the book emphasizes Gardner's distinction from the norm of colonial society. One was in his keen interest in the supernatural, which led him to read widely about religion and the occult, to discuss them repeatedly with like-minded people, and to gain first-hand experience of Freemasonry, spiritualism, Buddhism, and tribal magical practices. The other was an equally active antiquarianism, which propelled him to become a pioneer of Malay archaeology, numismatics, maritime history and folklore, and an author of respected monographs in these fields.

In 1936, aged fifty-two, he retired to London, and two years later moved to the New Forest, where his collections of Far Eastern artefacts would be safer if war broke out. On a cycle ride he discovered the Rosicrucian Theatre at Christchurch, Hampshire, and joined its company in order to find companions while Donna was distracted by nursing duties. Some of its members introduced him in turn to a wealthy local lady called 'Old Dorothy', who turned out to be the leader of a surviving witch coven of the ancient religion. He was initiated into it at her home in September 1939, and he worked with it until the late 1940s. In 1946, related Gardner, he visited Crowley and was initiated into the latter's Ordo Templi Orientis. Gardner, however, thought Crowley 'a charming charlatan'. He died while Gardner was in America, and many people there regarded Gerald himself as the obvious new leader for the order; but he did not want the job. Instead, he was increasingly dedicated to the task of informing the world of the survival of pagan witchcraft.

This process commenced in 1946, when the witches gave him permission to represent some of their rituals and beliefs in the disguise of a novel, *High Magic's Aid*, which was published in 1949. In 1951 the repeal of the Witchcraft and Vagrancy Acts allowed witches to advertise their existence without fear of prosecution, and Gardner at once began to give press interviews to do so. Three years later he brought out a book, *Witchcraft Today*, in which he posed as a disinterested anthropologist who had been lucky enough to discover its survival as a secret and initiatory system of pagan religion.

The rites of that religion were now revealed to consist mainly of dances intended to promote fertility, and of feasting upon consecrated food and drink. The performers were naked, in the belief that this more easily released magical power from the body. They venerated a goddess and a god, whose names were secret, the former predominant in summer and the latter in winter. They worked within a circle, formed with a consecrated sword or knife and carefully purified, to contain the energy which they raised. They held the north to be the most sacred of the four cardinal points, believed in reincarnation, and trained themselves to develop latent psychic powers. The religion was organized in covens, led by a high priestess supported by a high priest, which subdivided into couples for training purposes. Training, like initiation, was always between the sexes. As part of this polarity they revered the life-force within the world and regarded acts of worldly love and pleasure as sacred. They had eight ritual tools, of which the most important were the knife, the censer, and the cord. Their seasonal festivals were the four quarter days which opened the seasons. Trance and ecstasy were important components within their rites, and they aimed not merely to address their deities, but to feel as though they had become them.

No academic historian has ever taken seriously Gardner's claim to have discovered a genuine survival of ancient religion, and it was dismissed in the review given to it by the journal of the Folk-Lore Society. Members of the latter generally found the religion described by him so totally unlike the traditional English witchcraft beliefs which they had recorded themselves and found recorded by earlier collectors, that they rejected his assertions out of hand.[2] These considerations would at least make Gardner's witchcraft worthy of study as a part of modern history, but until now the only significant research into its origins has been carried out within the modern pagan community. In particular, four writers have produced work for which any subsequent scholar must be profoundly grateful. Janet and Stewart Farrar collaborated with Doreen Valiente between 1981 and 1984 to make the first analysis of the key ritual texts associated with the religion. In addition, Valiente has conducted research of her own, and is an important source of evidence in herself, as a major personality in the development of modern witchcraft. The fourth individual is Aidan Kelly, who continued their work in a series of investigations into Gardner's own papers, culminating in 1991. In addition, two other key witnesses survive from the 1950s and have furnished information for this chapter: Frederic Lamond, and the Pagan harper known as 'Bran'.

It should be said that there is nothing inherently implausible in Gardner's claim to have been initiated into an existing religion. The account which he provides of his earlier life in the biography is sober and understated, where he might at several points have taken advantage of its exotic setting to romanticize it. It is striking also that he describes a coven composed partly of Rosicrucians and led by a wealthy lady, instead of announcing that he had discovered a group of witches hidden in a rural working-class community, presided over by a more conventional cunning woman. In view of the cultural patterns outlined above, it is precisely from this more educated esoteric milieu that one would expect a modern pagan revival to commence.

Nor did Gardner include in the biography some of the more dubious claims which he made for himself in daily life, such as his possession of two university degrees, including a PhD which entitled him always to style himself 'Dr'. Doreen Valiente has exposed these as bogus,[3] and it is noteworthy that by assuming them Gardner stood in a long tradition of leading figures in English occultism, who seem frequently to have felt the need to claim titles of honour to reflect a status in the world at large which they considered to be truly due to them. As said, Mathers and Crowley postured as aristocrats. A more precise parallel is with Kenneth Mackenzie and Dion Fortune's mentor Theodore Moriarty, both of whom claimed university degrees which they did not possess; Alan Richardson has made the comment that among magicians 'doctorates appear like invoked spirits'.[4] In the biography, however, Gardner never gives an account of a university career and does not even leave any room for one; so he implicitly withdraws his own deception. How then, does the life story in the book stand up to closer inspection?

*   *   *

The obvious starting point for any search for further information regarding the coven into which he was allegedly initiated is the figure of 'Old Dorothy', the leader and one member whose name is given. The biography, as said, describes her as a rich lady with a big house near Christchurch, and adds the detail that she always wore a fine pearl necklace. In conversation with his own initiates, Gardner gave this person a last name, Clutterbuck, and claimed that the ritual sword which he used in ceremonies had once been hers. Dorothy Clutterbuck is thus a key figure, functioning with regard to Gardner's witchcraft as Count

Apponyi did to the Societas Rosicruciana in Anglia or Anna Sprengel to the Golden Dawn—as the legitimating figure connecting the new body of people to the old initiatory descent. Unlike the other two, however, she has been proved beyond doubt to have had an actual existence; by Doreen Valiente, who has revealed her to have been born in India in 1880, to Thomas and Ellen Clutterbuck, her father being an officer in the Indian imperial army. She lived at Highcliffe during the 1930s and 1940s, the overgrown village just to the east of Christchurch where the Gardners also settled in 1938, and died in January 1951 leaving an estate worth £60,000, including some valuable pearls.[5] So all this fits.

Gardner added one more detail to his portrait of her; that when France fell in 1940 and the invasion of Britain seemed imminent, 'Old Dorothy called up covens right and left; although by witch law they should not be known to each other'. The result was 'Operation Cone of Power', in which a Great Circle was cast at night in the New Forest and a cone of magical energy raised and directed against Hitler, as one had according to tradition been sent against the Spanish Armada and Napoleon. This was repeated four times until the coven elders called a halt; the strain of the work upon those present was severe, and many died a few days later.[6] This dramatic episode became Gardner's favourite story about the coven. He provided many extra details to Doreen Valiente, including the vital one that the power was raised by frenetic dancing and chanting, and that it was these exertions which had proved fatal to many of the older people.[7]

At this point it is necessary to digress, to consider a claim made by Amado Crowley, a writer who has presented himself as one of Aleister's illegitimate sons, that the whole story was stolen by Gardner from an actual ritual held by Aleister himself in Ashdown Forest, Sussex. It features in two out of three collections of anecdotes concerning Amado Crowley's boyhood life with his father which have been published so far,[8] under the code-name of 'Operation Mistletoe'. This was requested of Aleister Crowley by MI5 itself, to add an occult dimension to moves against Hitler, and involved a flaming dummy in Nazi dress launched along a cable from a church tower, within two circles of soldiers wearing robes over their uniforms. 'Old Mother Clutterbuck' was Crowley's own code-name for the occasion, and the result was the remarkable mission of Rudolph Hess to Britain, resulting in his capture, in 1941. Amado himself was present for the whole ceremony. This story was confirmed a year after its appearance, by Cecil Williamson, an owner of museums of witchcraft who will feature later in the present book. He claimed that as a member of MI6, he had helped to organize the ritual and chosen the site for it. He supported every detail supplied by Amado Crowley and added some of his own.[9] We therefore appear to have here two independent, first-hand witnesses. Is there any objective source against which their testimony can be checked? Yes indeed: the diaries and letters of Aleister Crowley.

Crowley kept diaries of one sort or another for most of his life, and many of these have survived. For our purposes the most important are those covering the last eleven years of his life, from 1936 to 1947. For the first nine of that span, they are very detailed, itemizing even apparently trivial incidents during each day, and his correspondence. Only in the last two, as he grew increasingly ill, do they dwindle into a bare record of visitors, appointments, and work undertaken, with few comments. They are now in the archive of the Ordo Templi Orientis in the United States, but complete copies were made by Crowley's friend Gerald Yorke, and are now in his deposit in the Warburg Institute, London.[10] I have been able to check these against extracts from the originals and found them to be completely accurate;[11] and the information within them conforms with all else that is certainly known of Crowley's life during this period, including the data obtainable from his published work and surviving correspondence and working papers.

There is absolutely no trace in the diaries of 'Operation Mistletoe' or the relationship with MI5 which led up to it. On 14 February 1941 Crowley did have the idea for a union of magicians to beat the Nazis, but he did nothing subsequently to form one. The diaries also tell the story of his attempts to gain employment with the government intelligence and propaganda services, from the outbreak of war until 1941 when he received a final curt letter of rejection; the correspondence itself is preserved in a file in the same archive.[12] More disturbing, there is no trace in these diaries of *any* of the events remembered by Amado Crowley in his memoirs; indeed, no trace of Amado Crowley himself. On the date upon which Aleister is supposed to have been introduced to this son, of whose existence he hitherto had not known, in a scene of great emotional intensity, the relevant diary entry records a routine day, of which the highlights were that Crowley finished a lecture and that a friend of his was swindled out of 15s. 8d. by a confidence trickster.[13] Nor, for that matter, do the diaries record the personal relationship which Cecil Williamson claims to have enjoyed with the old magus; the 'Cecil' who features often in them as a friend was Robert Cecil. Until these discrepancies are resolved, it seems more likely that the story of the event in Ashdown Forest was inspired by that in the New Forest, and not vice versa.

It is time to return to Dorothy Clutterbuck. The family graves in Highcliffe churchyard and wills in Somerset House tell the story of how she came to the district; her parents settled there when Thomas retired from the army, renting a pretty house by a stream. To describe the setting as 'the New Forest' is in fact slightly misleading, as Highcliffe is a few miles south of the forest proper and its true socio-cultural context is as a part of that genteel conurbation which stretches along the coast between Poole and Lymington, with a healthy climate and picturesque hinterland which has made it especially attractive to people in retirement, including many ex-colonials such as the Clutterbucks and the Gardners. Her father died in 1910 and her mother in 1920, leaving Dorothy a comfortable private income. Now a middle-aged spinster with no immediate family, she continued to live in the house by the brook.

At this point the local newspaper, the *Christchurch Times*, takes up her chronicle. Its successive issues show that by the late 1930s she had become a major society figure, the wife of Rupert Fordham who resided at a local mansion called

Latimers, at which the two held court together; this was apparently the big house at which Gardner claimed to have been initiated into witchcraft. Fordham was in his seventies, a landed gentleman of considerable estate and a former Justice of the Peace. The couple held a succession of garden parties each summer, of which the greatest was the annual one for the local Conservative Association, attended by various politicians and titled figures. Both were exceptionally committed Tories, Dorothy being even more dedicated to the party than her husband; each year she presented awards to the members who had enrolled the greatest number of newcomers. Highcliffe lay in one of the safest Conservative seats in the country, so that such efforts were hardly necessary; but it must have added a triumphalist air to the occasion. This existence terminated in May 1939, when Rupert was fatally injured in a road accident. Dorothy cancelled the whole summer season of parties, and seems to have withdrawn into a shell from which she only gradually emerged during the 1940s, to return to her role as a leading local hostess and patroness. Her favoured organizations were still those built into local social respectability: the Conservatives again, the Horticultural and Bee-Keepers' Associations, the British Legion, the Girl Guides and Boy Scouts, the Silver Band, and the Seamen's Mission. She died in January 1951.[14]

All this means that Dorothy Clutterbuck must have lived one of the most incredible double lives in human history; a pillar of conservatism and respectability who was also the leader of one witch coven and capable of summoning up others. And what of Rupert? He was either one of the least observant husbands on record or her partner in the whole remarkable charade. There is absolutely no incompatibility between pagan witchcraft and Conservative politics—as will be shown—but it is unusual to find modern pagan witches who are quite so prominent—and ostentatious—in supporting conventional social and political values. The impression of hypocrisy is increased by the fact that, according to Gardner, in September 1939, when she was still in her period of mourning and seclusion following the shock of Rupert's death, she was initiating him into her witch religion at her home, and then holding a celebration at which everybody danced and made merry till dawn. Could she had lived such a double life?

There is certainly a puzzle concerning her marital life. Local gossips whispered that she and Rupert were not legally married because he had an existing wife who was incurably insane.[15] It is certainly true that Dorothy is described as a spinster and by her maiden name in her own will, and that when Rupert died intestate an initial judgement in favour of her as his natural heiress was subsequently overturned by his relatives; final judgement was given against her in 1941.[16] She herself continued to use the name of Mrs Fordham in everyday life, and to receive it from others, until the day of her death. She declared herself to be Rupert's wife on his tombstone. This raises another oddity in Gardner's testimony: why did he use her maiden name, instead of the one which she herself would have chosen? To help conceal her identity? In that case, why did he leave such clear pointers to it in every other respect?

Other doubts hang over the question of Dorothy's religion. To all outward appearance she was a church-going Anglican, on better than usual terms with the local vicars. One collaborated with her in fund-raising for charities in the 1930s, while a later incumbent received one of the largest bequests in her will (the main beneficiary of which was an Arthur Stuart Beazley who died in 1984 and has no known connection with witchcraft).[17] This all may have been an insurance policy to safeguard her hidden identity; but what then do we make of the family graves? In her own will, Dorothy's mother asked to be cremated and her ashes deposited wherever her daughter wished. It must have been Dorothy, therefore, who decided to put them into her father's grave in the churchyard, covered with a stone bearing a fervently Christian declaration. Still more remarkable is the large memorial cross which she raised to Rupert over his grave in the same yard, into which her own ashes were put in turn. It bears one of the longest and most impassioned affirmations of faith in salvation through Jesus Christ that I have ever read upon any funerary monument, made by Dorothy herself as his wife. If she was initiating Gardner into pagan witchcraft at almost exactly the same time, then this goes beyond duplicity and achieves the status of schizophrenia. What is needed to resolve the puzzle is some kind of personal record left by her and equivalent to Crowley's diaries. It would be a miracle if such a document had survived; but the miracle has occurred.

In 1986 three of Dorothy's diaries, covering the years 1942–3 (when she was allegedly functioning as a witch priestess) were discovered in a cupboard of what had been her firm of solicitors. They were dense volumes, carefully illustrated with paintings, and placed upon exhibition at Bournemouth Reference Library and in London.[18] After this they were left in the custody of their discoverer, and there they remain, and I have been able to read them.[19] They are not diaries in the conventional sense, but daily poems with accompanying illustrations, reflecting an incident or idea which had occurred during each date. The woman they reveal is a simple, kindly, conventional, and pious one. Absolutely none of them—including those at the time of the four major witch festivals— have any relevance to paganism or the occult.

Ian Stevenson, the resident historian of Highcliffe, grew up there when Dorothy and Gerald Gardner were inhabitants, and confirms what the *Christchurch Times* strongly suggests: that their social worlds never overlapped. She was a well-known and well-loved figure at the centre of the community's life, while his friends visited from outside it and he was regarded in Highcliffe as an exotic, mysterious, and rather sinister figure. There were no known connections between her and the Rosicrucians at Christchurch; both were keen on dramatic productions, but she had her own separate troupe, the Mill House Players. The Rosicrucian Theatre staged Shakespeare and their own mystical compositions, while she preferred Gilbert and Sullivan.[20]

While engaged upon this research, I was furnished with two vivid illustrations of how perception can be affected by belief. One came when another of the district's local historians passed me the information that she had discovered a newspaper report of a car accident in which Dorothy had been involved while on her way to attend a Rosicrucian meeting at Christchurch. This greatly excited me, being the first solid evidence of contact between them of which I had learned. When I was on my way to see it, she corrected herself, with commendable thoroughness and probity, by sending another message; that, on second reading, Dorothy's destination had turned out to be communion at Christchurch Priory, with a clergyman as her passenger. So it proved to be. My second such experience occurred when I was being entertained, with great kindness, by the present owners of Dorothy's house by the brook—the survivor of her two homes, as Latimers has been demolished. One of my hosts remarked that in an adjoining room there was a relic from her time, a carving of a goddess between two goats' heads. On being shown eagerly through to it, I found a splendid wooden fireplace, probably Victorian, with a Regency-style cameo of a woman's head in the centre and a ram's head at either end, plus other decorations. What had produced the initial misreading of the material, in both cases, was the 'knowledge' that Dorothy Clutterbuck had been a famous witch, recently spread about the village by such books as the Farrars' *The Witches' Way*. Had either the newspaper report or the fireplace perished after that first interpretation, then the latter would have become a historical 'fact'. By such means can personal testimony be created.

None of this proves that Dorothy Clutterbuck was not a witch; indeed, it would be impossible to do so, for every piece of evidence to the contrary could be interpreted as yet another ploy upon her part to conceal her identity as one. It must be suggested here, however, that for the first time there is serious reason to doubt the assertion. There are at least two motives, quite mutually compatible, which might be imputed to Gardner for misrepresenting her as one. The less honourable is that a man of his undoubted mischievous sense of humour could have gained private delight from the thought that people would imagine this pillar of conventional Anglican Tory society summoning up covens and leading frantic naked dances in the New Forest. The more honourable is that he used her to divert attention from somebody else in the district who can actually be proved to have worked with him as a witch priestess; for such a person certainly existed.

*   *   *

This person is the only individual who can be securely identified as working witchcraft with Gerald Gardner before he announced the religion to the public: a private teacher of music and elocution whom he called 'Dafo'. She lived near Christchurch, and Doreen Valiente, who met her in 1952, found her 'an elegant, graceful lady with dark hair'. Dafo had hitherto been Gardner's main partner in ritual.[21] Once she is substituted for Dorothy Clutterbuck, all the problems found in the latter's case disappear. Her close friendship with Gardner can be documented through most of the 1940s, and she was not merely a member of the

Rosicrucian Theatre; she was its leading lady and stage director. Her husband took minor roles.[22] The theatre itself was the creation of an actor called G. A. Sullivan who used the stage name of Alexander Matthews. He was partnered in the venture with Mabel Besant-Scott, daughter of the famous theosophist and socialist Annie Besant. Having left the Theosophical Society after her failure to succeed her mother as leader, she had continued to work in Co-Masonry, the tradition of Freemasonry which accepted women and which had been founded by Annie Besant. Within this, she and Sullivan established a mystical order working quasi-Masonic rituals (much as the Societas Rosicruciana did), called the Rosicrucian Fellowship of Crotona (this being the name of the ancient city where Pythagoras had lived). They opened the theatre to fulfil Sullivan's dream of educating the public in mysticism through drama, but the public was not sufficiently interested and the plays lasted for only one season, from June to September 1938, when Gardner claimed to have discovered and joined the group. In 1939 the theatre building was hired out as a Methodist meeting-hall and a cinema, until war came. Then the Fellowship tried again, by organizing a series of talks and classes devoted to religious and philosophical subjects. These petered out in turn in April 1940, and Sullivan and his colleagues tried staging vaudeville and musical comedy in a last desperate attempt to attract audiences, before resigning themselves to providing nothing more than an annual lecture. Sullivan himself died in 1942, and by then it seems that Dafo's husband had gone also.[23]

Between 1939 and 1944 Gardner is largely invisible in the recorded public life of the area, although shown as resident at Highcliffe in Kelly's Directory. His duties as an air-raid patrol warden, described in his biography, would amply account for this.[24] Then in 1944 he reappears in the Christchurch Times, with Dafo as his constant companion. In June he was elected co-president of the Bournemouth Historical Association, and she gave the first lecture of his term, on the need for accuracy in plays with historical themes. For the rest of the summer they campaigned together to establish a museum of local history in Christchurch, addressing various local bodies.[25] Donna Gardner, though much loved by Gerald, had never showed any interest in sharing his intellectual and spiritual enthusiasms;[26] now he had a companion who did. The project for the Christchurch Museum came to nothing, and Gardner's leadership of the Historical Association expired in 1945. From that time onward, with the war over and London once again safe to live in, his energies began to turn back towards the capital, and further afield. The year 1946, in which he claimed to have met Crowley and decided to publicize the witch religion, seems to have represented a turning-point for him; and as in the case of the Rosicrucian Theatre, he seems to be telling us something which has a symbolic—if not a literal—truth. By 1947 he was certainly embarked upon a course which he was to follow for the rest of his life.

In that year he and Dafo became partnered in another enterprise, which was to have far more momentous consequences than those which they had shared before. This was a company called Ancient Crafts Ltd, whose single purpose was to pool the shareholders' capital to buy and own a plot of land adjacent to a naturist club near St Albans in Hertfordshire, just north of London.[27] Gardner was a member of this club, having become convinced of the therapeutic effects of sunbathing, and thus of naturism, during his colonial career. Upon this land the company erected a remarkable building, a complete 'reconstruction' of a sixteenth-century witch's cottage, made of half-timber and having cabbalistic designs upon the inner walls, which had been built as one exhibit in the open-air Abbey Folklore Museum at nearby New Barnet. The museum had been owned and designed by a friend of Gardner, J. S. M. Ward, another former colonial in Far Eastern service and a noted writer on the history of Freemasonry and its putative pagan origins. It had closed in 1945 and Ward had moved to Cyprus during the following year, leaving Ancient Crafts Ltd to acquire and transplant the building.[28] It provided a very atmospheric setting for a working group of magicians, on a secluded site next to a club from which some at least of its membership would be drawn and which could provide a further cover for its activities. This is exactly what happened, and a coven flourished there under the leadership of Dafo and Gardner by the opening of the 1950s. By late 1952 she had withdrawn from it, partly because of ill health but mainly because she feared for her reputation and livelihood as Gerald became more determined to publicize the existence of their practices.[29] Until the reality of the New Forest coven or of any earlier group is securely established, this spot in Hertfordshire is the best-documented place on earth to bear the name of the birthplace of modern pagan witchcraft.

By 1958 Dafo was living with a staunchly Christian niece, and very anxious that her past involvement in witchcraft should not become known.[30] I took a difficult decision to respect those wishes and not to trace her heirs in the hope that she left any personal effects or papers of relevance to my research. In doing so, I was comforted by the thought that she would probably not have allowed such evidence to survive, in view of her desire to bury that aspect of her life. During 1958 she was approached by three different factions of witches, each asking her to verify Gardner's story about the origins of his rituals. She avoided both confirmation and denial when responding to two of them; to the third, she protested that she possessed only a theoretical interest in the occult and had not sought any personal experience of it.[31] In this manner the first clearly recorded modern witch priestess passes out of history.

*   *   *

What other evidence exists for the presence of a coven in the New Forest during the 1940s? The most famous piece appeared in 1970, in a history of modern ritual magic in England written by Francis King. King recalled how in 1953 he had met Louis Wilkinson, a novelist who had been one of Aleister Crowley's friends. The latter had told him that during the late 1930s or early 1940s he had been friendly with a group of witches operating as a coven in the New Forest. It was a peculiar mixture of middle-class intellectuals with 'the local peasantry' and in Wilkinson's opinion it had fused 'an authentic surviving folk tradition with a more intellectual middle-class occultism'. It had worked nude, using a heavy grease based on bear's fat to protect the bodies of its members from cold, and took small doses of the toxic mushroom fly agaric to achieve hallucinations. In May 1940 it had held a ritual to ward off Hitler, which offered up a voluntary human sacrifice when the oldest and frailest member left off his protective grease and so died of exposure. The night was so cold, however, that two others also perished as a result of the rite.[32] As an apparent record of first-hand acquaintance, this has to be taken seriously, but there are three aspects of it which provoke caution. The first is the airy imprecision of Wilkinson's memory; he was talking in 1953 about events which had occurred only just over a decade before, and yet spoke vaguely of the 'late 1930s or early 1940s'. The second is that his account looks like a somewhat garbled and sensationalized version of Gardner's—bear's fat has never been a commodity readily obtainable in England since customs records begin in the late Middle Ages. The third is that, as has already been apparent in the case of 'Operation Mistletoe', even first-hand or eye-witness testimony is not always reliable, and there is a real risk that Wilkinson had picked up Gardner's story about the coven and retold it as his own, with some distortions produced in transmission to him or by his own imagination.[33] This is therefore an important piece of evidence that should be treated with respect, but is unfortunately not conclusive.

With that, the data runs out. Folklore collections made in and around the area in the hundred years before 1950 provide no clues; indeed, although reasonably well supplied with fairy stories, the New Forest had actually fewer associations with witches than the rest of Hampshire.[34] Nor can traditions within the modern Pagan community, if unsupported by documents, get a historian any further. In the course of my enquiries I have met a woman who had made something of a name for herself in one district as a traditional witch. One device which she had used to nurture this was to describe herself as the granddaughter of Dorothy Clutterbuck, with some reminiscences of her grandmother's personality. In another region I was shown 'the original book of rituals of the New Forest coven', by a set of witches who had inherited the manuscript. The woman was a perfectly pleasant and effective person, with every sign of complete conviction, and the people with the book firmly believed what they had been told of it when it was passed to them. The only reason that I had for doubting their stories was the simple fact that they were impossible; the real Dorothy never had any children and the book concerned was a fairly standard set of modern witch rituals of a sort which did not take that form until the end of the 1950s. There is a real danger that as modern witches acquire more knowledge of their history without all of them also acquiring a greater sense of historical relativism, then the misinformation is only going to become more sophisticated.

There is a last question to be considered before leaving the New Forest; could

Gardner's coven there have actually been the Order of Woodcraft Chivalry? This suggestion has been put forward in the Druid magazine *Aisling*, and has much to commend it.[35] The order, after all, worked in the same forest, within a sacred circle which had quarters cast in the same pattern, and a pagan section amongst its members who honoured a horned god and moon goddess (plus Dionysos) and believed in ceremonial nudity. I contributed information to the argument made in the journal, and can now add another piece; that by the 1950s if not before, Gardner was apparently friendly with members of the Woodcraft Chivalry. One of the latter, who came to know him well, claims to have seen him beside the sacred fire in the centre of the folkmoot circle at Sandy Balls one evening, chatting to the people there.[36] There are, however, a number of difficulties in making an identification of the order with the coven. Two are incidental: that the pagan element in the Woodcraft Chivalry never showed any recorded interest in witchcraft, and that Sandy Balls and Highcliffe are a long way apart, at opposite ends of the forest. One is major: that the chronology is wrong. By the time that Gardner retired to England, as described earlier, the pagan element in the order had departed. Because of the resignation of Aubrey Westlake, it did not meet at Sandy Balls between 1934 and 1945. From 1939 to 1944, the vital years for Gardner's relationship with the coven in his own life-story, there were no summer camps or moots at all, communication between different sections of the Woodcraft Chivalry—none of which seems to have remained in the New Forest area—being maintained only by newsletters. From 1945 onward the order returned to Sandy Balls and met there regularly thereafter; but the date seems too late for it to have played the role of the witches in Gardner's account.[37] With this reflection, the forest seems to have given up its known store of evidence.

*   *   *

It is time to consider Gardner's relationship with Crowley, an issue in itself greatly complicated by subsequent claims and assertions. Some of these cluster around the question of when they first met. Gardner, as said, claimed that the relationship consisted of a visit which he had made to the magician in 1946, at the guest house to which he had retired at Hastings, Sussex. Valiente heard more details of the encounter from Gardner's friend Arnold Crowther, a stage magician who sought out Crowley himself and decided to introduce the two men. Crowther added that Gardner repeated the visit by himself on a number of occasions.[38] In 1988, however, a writer in a publication of the modern Ordo Templi Orientis has suggested that Gardner and Crowley knew each other for more than ten years before the latter's death; the evidence consisted of a cigarette case now owned by a Colonel Lawrence whose family run a witchcraft museum in the United States. It is said to contain a note, allegedly in Crowley's hand, reading 'Gift of GBG, 1936. A. Crowley'.[39] In the 1990s Amado Crowley has asserted that the two men first met in his own presence in 1940, while E. W. Liddell has stated that both Francis King and Gerald Suster argue that they knew each other for 'several years' before Crowley died; he provides no references for their views, but adds that there is 'no tangible evidence' for such a belief.[40]

Indeed there is not, but there is some very good evidence against it: Crowley's diary, which makes it clear beyond all reasonable doubt that he first met Gerald Gardner, with Arnold Crowther, upon May Day 1947, and that Gardner returned alone to spend the 7th, 14th, and 27th of May with him.[41] Gardner and Crowther were telling the truth; but the former's memory was a year out of place. It is much harder to provide such a definite resolution to the other controversies surrounding the relationship. One was started by Francis King, who stated that he had heard that Gardner paid Crowley to write the rituals which the former then passed off as those of the New Forest Coven. King apparently told the American academic James Baker that he had received this information from Gerald Yorke.[42] If so, then it was something that Yorke came to surmise after several years rather than learned at first hand, for Crowley's diary shows that Yorke himself was not in Hastings at the time of Gardner's visits, and in 1953 or 1954 he was still unsure of the origins of the witch religion revealed by Gardner. In a note which Yorke himself wrote on his copy of Gardner's book, *High Magic's Aid*, he recorded that all the rituals in the novel which had not been taken from *The Key of Solomon* had been given to Gardner by 'the witch society'; an exactly opposite story to what which he allegedly reported to King.[43]

Wherever it came from, the story has taken root. It was confidently repeated by Gerald Suster, in his study of Crowley which was praised earlier in this book. Amado Crowley has specified the exact price paid by Gardner for the work; three guineas per page. E. W. Liddell has provided a more sophisticated version of the tale; that Louis Wilkinson confided in Francis King that Crowley's papers included drafts of many of the rituals which were later to be key texts of the witch religion, including the greatest of all, 'the Charge of the Goddess' (of which more below).[44] As Aidan Kelly has pointed out, the complete and standard body of modern witch rituals was still in the process of composition during the 1950s, and so Crowley cannot be called their author;[45] but this does not do away with the possibility that he provided some first versions which formed the basis of them.

All that can be said of this possibility is that the existing evidence is all negative. There is no mention of any such work in Crowley's diary or in a subsequent important letter to him from Gardner (which will be considered below). There is certainly a lot of Crowley's work in the earliest known versions of the witch rituals, which may well be the source of the whole rumour that he wrote them; but it appears in chunks, copied or slightly adapted from his earlier publications, and interspersed with other material which is not in Crowley's style at all. Such a pattern is far more consistent with composition by another person who borrowed from works of the magus. Nor have any of the drafts mentioned by Liddell turned up in the various surviving collections of Crowley's papers. A rumour swept the American Pagan community in 1993 that the collection held by the University of Texas contains a draft of one major text from Gardner's witch rituals, 'The Legend of the Goddess', sent by Gardner to Crowley for his correction. A copy of this, allegedly 'bootlegged' from that archive, was passed around some Pagans in the United States.[46] I have, however, been assured by the Research Librarian of that university that there is no record of such a document, or any others connected with Gardner, existing in the collection either now or in the past.[47] Crowley's diary makes fairly plain that Gardner was much more interested in him than he was in Gardner. The old man was very ill and weak in May 1947—indeed he was not to survive the year—and his main preoccupation in that month was with visits from the only son of whom he knew, the little boy whom he had called Ataturk.

A different sort of story first appears in the biography of Gardner, where the only account given of what was said between him and Crowley at their meeting was that the latter declared that he would not himself enter the witch religion because 'he refused to be bossed around by any damn woman' and could not understand the lack of financial profit in it.[48] Ten years later one of Gardner's initiates into witchcraft, Patricia Crowther, claimed that she had met Crowley in 1945 or 1946 and that although he knew a lot about witches he personally rejected their tradition, as 'he wasn't the type to be bossed about as by a woman' and 'preferred to leave witchcraft to females as it was intended to be'. In the same year, 1970, Francis King reported that Louis Wilkinson, and 'two other, independent, sources' had informed him that as a young man Crowley had been offered initiation into the witch religion, but had refused because he 'didn't want to be bossed around by women'.[49]

Then in 1974 E. W. Liddell gave the story a quantum leap by telling the world, from inside information, that Crowley had actually been initiated into the witch religion in 1899 or 1900, having been introduced to it by his friend in the Golden Dawn, Allan Bennett, who had been a pupil of the witches. Liddell had heard about a photograph clearly showing Bennett with the famous cunning man George Pickingill, who was stated in the same revelations to have been the most famous witch of the time. Another figure in the same photograph may have been Crowley. According to the same account, Crowley himself was expelled from the coven because its high priestess thought him 'a dirty minded, evilly disposed, vicious little monster'. In recent years both Cecil Williamson and Colonel Lawrence have supported this story. The former has attested from personal knowledge of both men that Crowley 'heard about Pickingill from Gerald's chatter about his New Forest witches' and sent him down to Pickingill's village to learn more about the old cunning man. The latter has claimed that his own great-grandmother studied under Pickingill and was introduced to Crowley while doing so.[50]

It is necessary to look at some details of this body of testimony and then at the broader implications of it. First, it is notable that the subject of witchcraft is not mentioned in either Crowley's diary entries on Gardner's visits, nor in the surviving items of the correspondence which resulted. Instead, Crowley noted that Gardner was a Doctor of Philosophy of the University of Singapore and a

Royal Arch Freemason. The former claim, as said above, was bogus, and as the Royal Arch is the highest, most exclusive and most prestigious of all Masonic degrees, there is a possibility that the latter was also. What is clear is that Gardner was presenting himself as an establishment figure, a man of repute both in the academic and the Masonic worlds. The earliest mention of a discussion of witchcraft between them comes in an account of their meeting which Gardner gave to John Symonds in 1950, when he was starting to spread the news of his witch religion. He said that Crowley 'was very interested in the witch cult, and had some idea of combining it with the order, but nothing came of it. He was fascinated with some snaps of the witch's cottage.'[51] The 'order' here was plainly the Ordo Templi Orientis, and the cottage the one in Hertfordshire. It is a notably different version of the story than that in the biography, and raises the possibility that Gardner invented the latter at some point in the 1950s and spread it about the world of English occultists until it reached Francis King, elaborated, from three different sources.

What, however, of Patricia Crowther's independent and first-hand endorsement of it? It is true that she is not mentioned in Crowley's diaries, which would be under her maiden name of Dawson; but as a young woman coming to visit a man of dubious reputation, she might well have used an alias. An 'Eva Collins' called on Crowley on May Day 1947 as well as Gardner and Arnold Crowther (later Patricia's husband), and might have been her, accompanying them under that assumed name. The real problem with her testimony, however, is a much bigger one; that in her book *Lid Off The Cauldron* (1981) she says that she only met Arnold in 1956, and then became acquainted with Gerald Gardner through him;[52] and this is the version of her life which she has repeated ever since. Clearly, both versions cannot be correct, and she seems by implication to have scrapped her claim to have known Crowley by telling the second one.

There is no better evidence to support the grander version of the story told by E. W. Liddell. He has reported that the photograph which is the objective proof of his assertions was 'purloined' on the death of the owner.[53] Cecil Williamson's testimony with regard to Aleister Crowley has already been shown to be problematic, in the matter of 'Operation Mistletoe'. He does not actually endorse the whole of Liddell's assertions, but does provide support for a connection between Crowley, Gardner, and Pickingill. Unhappily, this evidence is not only itself unsupported, but is coupled with other assertions, based on the same claimed personal knowledge, that Gardner and Crowley were introduced by Gerald Yorke (which is wrong) and that the former paid the latter £25 a time for a course of instruction, from which Gardner was ejected acrimoniously for being a bad pupil (which seems to be contradicted by their subsequent letters). As for Colonel Lawrence, he also claims that his same great-grandmother studied under Leland before moving to Pickingill, which Michael Howard, the most open-minded of Pagan editors, has declared to be 'certainly too good to be true'. On the other hand, it must be emphasized that there is no *disproof* of all these statements apparent either. Furthermore, E. W. Liddell was not the originator of the statement that Crowley was initiated into a coven; it was told to Gerald Yorke as early as December 1953, in an interview with a member of Gardner's own witch group who seems, from the magical name which she used, to have been Doreen Valiente. She provided the story to explain why it was that obvious quotations from Crowley's work appeared in the witch rituals, and added the detail that the famous magician had left witchcraft because he 'would not be ruled by women'. Valiente herself never repeated this assertion in her later books, and the latter make clear that her sole source of information regarding the earlier history of Gardner's coven and related groups was Gardner himself.[54]

There seem to be three different stories here: that Crowley heard of the witch religion from Gardner and said that it was not for him; that Crowley was offered initiation into it as a young man; and that he actually was initiated into it. It may be that one, two, all, or none of them is true. Further progress in the matter can only be made by looking at Aleister Crowley's relationship with witchcraft. He certainly wrote about it in the abstract, twice, and his views upon it will be considered in more detail later, but there is nothing in his published works which indicates any acquaintance with the actual religion revealed by Gardner. Aidan Kelly has noted this and used it to challenge the information relayed by Bill Liddell, who has responded by pointing out that none of Crowley's works mention his humiliation by the famous mystic Georgei Gurdjieff, who berated him and threw him out of Gurdjieff's community at Fontainbleu in 1925, as related in a well-known book by James Webb.[55] This particular example backfires, however, because Webb never provided a reference for the anecdote and it seems to have been a piece of gossip. Suspicion that it was a false one, inspired by Crowley's generally bad reputation, is strengthened by the statement of Gerald Yorke to his namesake Gerald Suster, that he was the sole witness of Crowley's only actual meeting with Gurdjieff and that the latter was a total non-event; the two men just 'sniffed around one another'.[56]

What disturbs me is not that there is no apparent reference to the witch religion in Crowley's published works, but none in his *unpublished* works—which are numerous—either. He did not himself publish any direct reference to his bisexuality, which actually brought him within risk of criminal prosecution, but it is plain enough from his poetry, his close friendships, and his records of rituals. He was careful to conceal from the public his savage anti-Semitism, but it breaks out repeatedly in his private writings, especially his diaries.[57] So do his personal grudges and resentments, against those who had foreswoken, criticized, or thwarted him; the manner in which these spilled over into *Moonchild* has been noted, and his personal papers contain items such as an appallingly petty and undignified denunciation of his talented former secretary Israel Regardie.[58] It does seem hard to believe that he was initiated into a coven and then ejected from it without harking back to the incident in the most bitter terms; instead his pronouncements on witchcraft are few and clinical. It is more directly to our purpose that he was not the pupil of the witches in the tradition reported by E. W. Liddell; this distinction went to his close friend

Allan Bennett. Now, notebooks complied by Bennett himself survive, from that very period in the late 1890s when he was living with Crowley and supposed to have been working with the witches as well.[59] They are an apparently full reflection of his magical studies at that time, including information from Hebrew, Egyptian, and Buddhist traditions; and there is not a single mention in them of either witchcraft or George Pickingill. This is the problem with E. W. Liddell's information—not that the evidence refutes it so much as that the very kinds of source which ought to support it never do.

It is harder to make any evaluation of the 'softer' versions of the story—that Crowley commented on Gardner's sort of witchcraft or had heard of it as a young man—other than with the comments offered above. In his autohagiography he noted his acquaintance with 'a sort of secret cult' at Pembroke College, Cambridge, when he was at the university in the 1890s, run by one of the fellows, 'a clergyman called Heriz Smith'. It was said to have seven degrees of initiation, in the highest of which the candidate was flogged, and 'was disrespectfully called by outsiders the Belly-banders'. Crowley took the first degree, but it made so little impression upon him that by the time of writing he had 'altogether forgotten what took place. I remember that I was alone in the man's room with him. He blindfolded me. I waited for something to happen; it did not. I was utterly unable to divine what purpose might lie behind the scheme.' He therefore did not persevere with the other degrees, though he later wondered whether 'a method of psycho-analysis' might have lain behind Smith's system.[60] Whatever the latter was, it had nothing apparent in common with Gardner's witch religion except the blindfold (which was found in all post-Masonic traditions) and flagellation (but only rumoured, and only in the final degree). This matters, because, of all the actual magical or religious groups referred to by Crowley in any of his writings, it is the only one which bears even that much similarity to modern pagan witchcraft.

Having necessarily devoted a great deal of space to undocumented claims made after the event, it is heartening to report that there actually is good contemporary material for an evaluation of the relationship between Gardner and Crowley which has never been noticed or discussed. As said earlier, after the initial meeting they spent three whole days together in the course of May 1947. Crowley's diary makes no comment on what was discussed, but some of the content is indicated by letters written by the two men after the meetings. Following the second one, on 9 May, Crowley wrote to Gerald Yorke, introducing Gardner and asking Yorke to send him an extra copy of Crowley's book *The Equinox of the Gods*, which contained many of his most important texts. He added that Gardner had bought his own stock, of four copies, already. This is clearly an excessive number for personal consumption, so that the purpose seems to have been to distribute them, and a letter from Gardner to Crowley, on 14 June, reveals the reason. It calls Crowley by his name as chief of the Ordo Templi Orientis (OTO), 'Baphomet', thanks him for a letter dated the 10th which enclosed a list of people whom Gardner needed to contact, and promised to write to them. It asked Crowley how much individuals should be charged for initiating them into the Minerval [first] degree of the OTO and revealed that Gardner himself had received all the degrees up to the seventh. It is signed 'Scire', the Latin for 'to know', the magical name and motto which Gardner must have adopted upon initiation.[61]

What this seems to prove is that Gerald Gardner was attempting to revive the OTO in England. The order itself first appeared in Germany in 1904, as an offspring of mystical Freemasonry, influenced by the writings of Eliphas Levi, Indian traditions of tantra and yoga, and the eighteenth-century myth of the medieval Knights Templar, as bearers of arcane wisdom taught to initiates. In 1912 it contacted Crowley, as a celebrated magician with ideas apparently similar to its own, and made him its leader in England, whereupon he had heavily rewritten its rituals.[62] By 1947 he was more or less regarded as the head of the whole organization, but although it was flourishing in the United States and still active in Continental Europe, it was moribund in England. This was the situation which Gardner was trying to remedy, an interpretation reinforced by the survival of another letter, from Crowley to the London occultist W. B. Crow, informing him that 'Dr Gardner' could now put all of Crow's 'following in the London district . . . properly through the Minerval degree'.[63] Gardner claimed in his biography that Crowley had chartered him to found a 'camp' of the order, and although the charter itself seems to have disappeared, these letters prove that it must have existed. The situation thus revealed seems to admit of three explanations: either Gardner had temporarily lost interest in witchcraft and was striving to make the OTO his vehicle instead; or he was involved in both alongside each other; or he had not yet conceived the idea of 'reviving' the ancient witch religion and, looking for a magical group to install in the 'witch's cottage', he had turned to the famous Crowley for inspiration and taken up the latter's order.

Whichever is the true story, his enthusiasm for the OTO soon cooled. Writing to John Symonds in 1950, by which time he was fully committed to witchcraft, Gardner said that his attempts to 'start an order' had been foiled first by illness, which had caused him to leave the country on a convalescent holiday, and then by a discovery that the people whom he had expected to join (probably the names furnished by Crowley) were either serving abroad with the armed forces or lived too far away to work with him.[64] He certainly did go abroad in late 1947, to Memphis, Tennessee, where he was living when Crowley died near the end of the year. The latter's friend Frieda Harris then wrote to Karl Germer, leader of the OTO in America, that it was supposed in England that Gardner would now be the head of the order in Europe. Germer received a letter from Gardner in January 1948, saying that he was sailing for England from New York on 19 March and could meet Germer there before he departed.[65] In his letter to Symonds, Gardner claimed that the meeting had taken place, and Germer had indeed recognized him as European leader of the OTO. His failure to revive the order, and abandonment of the plan to do so, must therefore have followed in 1948.

During that year he must have sent to press a novel published in 1949 and entitled *High Magic's Aid*. That stands at a sort of crossroads, for its sympathies are divided equally between the witch religion and the 'high magic' of learned magicians; it portrayed some of the rituals of both. At the time of completing it, Gardner still regarded himself primarily as an OTO grandee, for he published it under his initiatory name (misspelled 'Scrire') and printed the order's initials and his degree (again given somewhat inaccurately, in Golden Dawn not OTO form) underneath it.

*　　*　　*

The only remaining clues to the origins of Gardner's witchcraft lie in his own writings. Those from the 1930s conform very closely to the story given in the biography. Between 1933 and 1939 he published a number of monographs on Malay culture and archaeology and ancient Cypriot metalwork, which testify to the range and energy of his mind and his particular preoccupation with swords and daggers (especially the latter) and their magical associations. They also refer to his personal collection of such weapons, almost all Malay and exceeding a hundred items.[66] His first novel, *A Goddess Arrives* (1940), bears out the assertion in the biography that it was written before his discovery of the witch religion. It is, in fact, a rationalist and sceptical work. The whole plot is based upon the premise that the cult of the goddess Aphrodite owes its origin to the appearance of a human woman who deludes the Cypriots into taking her for a divinity. She is herself a witch, possessed of genuine powers of divination and versed in old and arcane knowledge, working her rituals nude and employing for them a wand and sword, the sacrifice of black cats, goats, sheep, and the occasional human to Hecate, the marking of magic circles in blood, chanting in a strange tongue, and the raising of smoke from a brazier full of roots and herbs, in which the pattern of the future may be seen. She is not, however, the protagonist of the story, and functions very much like a heroine in contemporary (and later) sword-and-sorcery comics; she is young, beautiful, fights in battle, and wears very little—indeed for much of the time nothing at all. She also knows how to lean upon the hero when weary and to faint into his arms when lightly wounded. The protagonist, with whom Gardner clearly identifies, is a male member of a society of swordsmen with special signs and gestures like those of Freemasons. He derives his strength from Higher Powers who abominate sacrifice, doubts the value of the conventional pagan religion carried on by his compatriots in Cyprus, and derides the 'Old Ones' venerated by the witch as creations of human minds, onto whom are projected powers which actually occur within human beings. There is no doubt allowed that he represents a finer sort of spirituality than hers and she comes to accept this. The book ends with a plea for the theory of group reincarnation articulated by the famous German theosophist Rudolph Steiner.

Parallel records reveal his membership of two bodies which are played down in the biography. One was the Folk-Lore Society, which he joined in 1939, presenting as a debut paper an account of a box of apparent relics of witchcraft, some allegedly associated with the famous Essex witch-finder Matthew Hopkins, which he had recently acquired. One notable feature of the paper was its citation of Margaret Murray as one of the two scholars (the other being J. S. M. Ward) whom he had approached for verification of the objects; it is the first record of the association between them which was to culminate in her preface to *Witchcraft Today*.[67] The war, and his removal to Hampshire, suspended his activities within the society, but they resumed at a higher level in March 1946, after his return to London, when he took a seat on its council. From that year, also, comes the first apparent record of his membership of the Circle of the Universal Bond, commonly called the Ancient Druid Order, the most active and prominent group of practitioners of mystical Druidry in the country, best known for their public ceremony at Stonehenge each midsummer. By December 1946 he sat on the governing council of that as well.[68]

His next publication after *A Goddess Arrives* was in 1949, being the novel *High Magic's Aid*, which has been mentioned several times; and with this we are in a different stage of his life, for (as said) it represents his first, fictionalized, announcement of the rituals of the witch religion. The book was brought out by Michael Houghton, owner of the Atlantis Bookshop in London and as such one of the grandees of the British occult book trade. Another famous London magician, Madeline Montalban, later claimed to have typed out the manuscript for him; and Gardner's own typing was so bad that it is credible that someone would have performed this service. He later used the novel as a test for prospective initiates, giving it to them to read and seeing how they reacted to the portrait of the witch rituals.[69]

Its basic structure bears marked similarities to that of *A Goddess Arrives*: a tale of adventure set in times of political and military turmoil, in which a hero joins forces with a witch to achieve his ends. Once again, he is the more powerful figure, setting the pace and directing the events of the action, and she defers to him. Once again, she is repeatedly shedding her clothes to work ritual, and indeed on public occasions (the witches' sabbats) her nudity becomes the emblem of her religious office: 'I am Priestess, and so must appear as their Priestess, or I lose my power, so clothes are forbidden me.' There are, however, important shifts between the two novels. The single male protagonist of the first is now divided into three main male characters, one representing wisdom, leadership, and proficiency in magic, one being the virile and martial figure with whom the witch forms a romantic partnership, and one being boyish, innocent, and mercurial. The heroine has grown in dignity, so that although she follows the will of the first of the male trio (as all do), she achieves a dominance over the younger two, and initiates them into her religion. The latter is shown as possessing an equal status to the 'high' ritual magic worked by the dominant male, being more closely linked to the forces of nature and to the common people, while the other is better suited to an intellectual elite.

The witch religion portrayed is that of Margaret Murray's *God of the Witches*, in virtually every detail, including its dedication to a single male deity of fertility, whose name is given here (again taken from Murray) as Janicot. The setting of the story is the central Middle Ages, at which time, according to the Murray thesis, that religion was most highly developed. There is, however, much added to Margaret Murray's picture. The initiation rituals credited to the religion, and described in detail, are found nowhere else. Gardner adds a distorted reference to the cult portrayed in Leland's *Aradia*, describing a divinatory rite used by 'Greek' witches and dedicated to the goddess 'Artemis' (the Greek name for Diana, of course) and her daughter 'Ardrea'. He also ascribes to the witches a ritual based upon the seventeenth-century myth of the Black Mass (in which a naked woman is used as the altar), as reinterpreted by Crowley: 'At the Great Sabbat the living body of a priestess does form the altar. We worship the divine spirit of Creation, which is the life-spring of the world, and without which the world would perish.'

The powerful dynamism of sexual polarity which features in Dion Fortune's novels is given a new twist: the magus works robed but in partnership with a nude woman, in order to perfect his ability to operate magic without temptations of the flesh. 'For a Magus must never work with a naked woman till nudity is naught to him, lest an evil or mischievous spirit should appear thus, and distract his mind at the critical moment, and so ruin an operation.' Furthermore, her nudity means that 'the natural magnetism in the human body could flow unhindered to the support of the Magus'. Murray's emphasis upon the joyous and life-affirming character of the witch religion is powerfully expressed, and developed into a mystical sense of unity with the natural world. In one episode, the witch, having bathed, walks naked to a silver birch which is moving in the breeze:

The tree was not only living and dancing, but it sang as it danced, as an act of worship, obeying a law and performing a ritual that was ancient even when the world saw its first dawn. Drawn to the silver birch, Morven paced a wide circle in which she began to dance, full of the wild exhilaration of being alone and the mistress of herself for the first time in months. Yet there was nothing Bacchic in her revel, rather was it a pattern of postures, in which her young body bent and swayed in rhythm with that of the tree; a slow wreathing of arms as though they were branches, and an intricate pattern of her feet as if she wove a spell about the Dryad of the Birch.[70]

This preoccupation with the magical and religious power of nude female beauty was by no means peculiar to Gardner; indeed, it was a minor theme of early twentieth-century English literature. In J. W. Brodie Innes's novel *The Devil's Mistress*, the witch Isobel Gowdie draws on the power of the moon for a spell, by invoking it naked, three times and in three aspects. Robert Graves returned repeatedly to such imagery. In *The Golden fleece*, the women of Lemnos madden themselves to do the Goddess's murderous work, 'by chewing ivy leaves and dancing naked in the moonlight'. The principal witch in *Seven Days in New Crete* casts spells by removing her clothes and prowling in a circle about the object of her magic. Even more dramatic and significant is the moment in which the narrator of the tale makes his personal surrender and commitment to the Goddess; it comes when her earthly representative, the land's sacred queen, appears before her people clad only in her 'moon-mirror crown'.

The 'high magic' in the novel comes plainly from one source, Mathers's edition of the *Key of Solomon*. This he borrowed from Crowley's friend Gerald Yorke, according to a private note scribbled by Yorke upon the title page of his own copy of *High Magic's Aid* (now in the Warburg Institute). It seems a reliable source as it was not meant for public consumption, and, as stated above, Gardner and Yorke were introduced by Crowley in May 1947. This would place the composition of the bulk of the work in late 1947 or 1948, which is rather as one would expect for a book published in 1949. This does produce a puzzle over Gardner's claim in the biography that it was in 1946 that he was given permission by the coven to publicize their beliefs, and wrote the novel. He may well have drafted it earlier, but the delay in completion seems odd; as in the case of his meeting with Crowley, he may just have forgotten the true year. A different conundrum hangs over his claim made later in a private letter, that he 'wanted to write about a witch, and what she'd told me', and she only gave him permission to do so if he did not include any actual 'witch magic'; hence he put in the rites from the *Key* instead. Why then did 'she' allow him to publish the actual first- and second-degree initiation rites, in full? Gardner confronted this problem obliquely in 1950, when writing to John Symonds, saying that the witches read the novel in manuscript and 'went up in steam' that he had included the ritual for the third degree as well, and forced him to delete it. He did not, however, explain why they allowed the first two to appear in such detail.[71]

It is clear that the puzzles surrounding Gardner's relationship with witchcraft cannot be solved by an analysis of his publications alone. The most important and enduring literary work towards which he contributed was, however, one that was intended never to be published: the collection of instructions and rituals which represented the sacred text of his witch religion and to which he gave the evocative name of the Book of Shadows. An analysis of this must apply, at the least, a great deal of additional information.

*   *   *

Gardner himself published several extracts from the Book, and pirated versions of the whole work were available in print from 1964 onward, as will be seen. Between 1981 and 1984 Janet and Stewart Farrar, aided by Doreen Valiente, produced a critical edition of it which attempted to establish a standard text, identifying the differences between the successive early recensions and the sources for those of its contents which had been copied from or modelled on earlier pieces of literature or composed by known persons in the 1950s. Between them, they therefore managed to reconstruct an 'original' text of 1953 and highlight a number of rituals with no known provenance.[72] In 1991 Aidan Kelly took the process further by publishing researches commenced many years before, into the archive of papers which Gardner had left at his death, and which had since been transferred to private hands in Toronto; it will henceforth be known here as 'the Toronto collection'. His greatest service to scholarship was his recognition of the peculiar importance of one manuscript, entitled by Gardner 'Ye Bok of ye Art Magical', which he identified beyond reasonable doubt as the precursor of the 1953 Book of Shadows, and therefore the earliest known version of the witch liturgy.[73] Owing to the constraints of time upon him in studying it, he tended, naturally enough, to concentrate upon those of its contents that were to feature later in pagan witchcraft; and his critics in recent Pagan magazines have done the same. It may be profitable to attempt a different approach, of treating the manuscript as a complete work.

It is, as Aidan Kelly recognized, an elaborate and complex work, created by binding large sheets of paper into a handsome leather cover, taken from a book whose contents had been removed. Onto these pages were copied selected passages from a range of sources concerned with ritual magic, consisting of biblical verses, the Mathers editions of the *Key of Solomon* and of another early modern grimoire, the *Goetia*, a work on the cabbala, three different books by Crowley, the Waite-Smith tarot pack, and one or two unidentified grimoires. Between and after these were added rituals with no known provenance, which have a particularly close association with the witch religion. Another of Kelly's major insights was that the entries were made over a significant period of time, with two to four pages initially left blank between each so that they could be filled later with further material; and such a filling occurred through most of the book. To assist the process and to prevent confusion, contents pages were created at the front and entered up at different periods as material came in; although this practice was abandoned long before the additions were complete. To this extent, the volume functioned as a notebook within which items could be collected around a certain theme.

It was, however, much more than that, at least for a significant period; it was intended to be a grimoire in its own right, designed to resemble a medieval or early modern one. This was the point of the leather cover, and also probably of the fact that much of the material copied was misspelled. Gardner was not dyslexic, as his letters prove (although he was a terrible typist), and the aberrant spelling seems to have been part of the attempt to give the contents an archaic appearance. The latter were written in a number of different ornate scripts, with careful colouring and decoration of the letters; most of the volume is a work of art. The lettering is usually large enough to be easily read from a short distance, and those parts intended to be repeated by initiates (such as the initiation oath) are particularly plain and striking. It is impossible to say whether or not the intent was deliberately to deceive those who saw it into thinking it an old manuscript, but it seems a reasonable speculation that it was designed to function as the ritual book used by the group which Gardner and Dafo were forming at the 'witch's cottage'. This is because of the likely dating of the work. It was certainly commenced at some time before the writing of *High Magic's Aid*, because the initiation rituals portrayed there are those in 'Ye Bok', as amended and completed in that text. One of the major sources from which extracts are taken, and one used relatively early in the career of the volume, was the *Key of Solomon*. If Gerald Yorke's private note is correct, then Gardner did not obtain this until May 1947 at the earliest. It may therefore be suggested that the bulk of the manuscript was written between mid-1947 and late 1948.

The work forms a loose but clear thematic whole, the contents being concerned with a set number of interrelated subjects—the power and importance of magic, the preparation of tools, clothing, and spaces for ritual work, the invocation of spirits, the sanctity of the whole human body, and the potency, for magical operations, of nudity and of binding and scourging. The scriptural quotations, for example, relate to those issues rather than to witchcraft as such, and most are deftly removed from context to give them a connotation not obvious in the original verses; which lends an ironic humour to their designation in the contents pages as 'Holy Writ'. In general, the theme of ceremonial ritual magic is dominant in the earlier entries, and that of witchcraft only enters in what seems to be the mid-life of the volume and becomes central in the later passages. Likewise, the element of theory in the contents is strongest at first, and the sequences of ritual gradually take over as the main preoccupation of the book. When the first original material is included, consisting mainly of the witch initiation ceremonies, deliberate effort seems to have been made to disguise its nature; unlike the quotations, it is entered in a shorthand (much of it based on Masonic convention) and sometimes in portions divided between the pages left blank among earlier entries; a procedure which was not necessary as there was still plenty of space at the back of the manuscript. Such devices would have made it very difficult for a stranger to understand its meaning.

My personal opinion is that the text does not provide any conclusive evidence for the question of whether Gardner composed those entries which have no known provenance or copied them from a pre-existing source; in other words, whether he was initiated into an existing religion or created one himself. In favour of the former hypothesis are the following points. first, at times he corrected details of the rituals in 'Ye Bok' and wrote comments upon them, both actions compatible with a copyist. Second, some texts have apparent slashes in them which may be a calligrapher's convention to indicate breaks in an original document. Third, the rituals associated with witchcraft are written with stylized abbreviations not found in the others. All these arguments, however, are vulnerable to criticism. The corrections and comments may have been those of an author amending his own work; the slashes may be stylistic flourishes rather than indications of line breaks; and, as said above, the shorthand in the rites seems to have been part of a deliberate camouflaging of their nature from strangers. It is not even certain that the manuscript was the work of a single hand, as it contains different scripts, but there is enough basic similarity to make lone authorship perfectly possible.

What, then, are the contents of the rituals? The most substantial consist of those for initiation into the three degrees of the religion. All are designed to be given by a man ('the Magus') to a woman ('the Witch'); the same partnership as that at the centre of both Gardner's novels, save that in the actual ceremonies portrayed in *High Magic's Aid* the woman performs the initiations. Each initiation ends with the option of proceeding immediately to the next one, so that it would have been possible in theory for a complete newcomer to be transformed in one evening first into a priestess and witch, and then into a twice-consecrated high priestess and witch queen. The only ability which she would have to acquire in the interval between first and second degrees, and to demonstrate for the second, would be the knowledge of how the various working tools operated; and indeed, in *High Magic's Aid*, the two initiations are given just forty-eight hours apart. The third degree is only referred to obliquely in the novel, being (like the higher grades of Crowley's OTO) an actual or symbolic act of sex magic. The outlines of the first two rituals are very clearly Masonic; but that is true (as should be plain by now) of most initiation rituals in English secret societies since the eighteenth century. The structure of the first is absolutely in that tradition. First comes the challenging of a bound and blindfolded postulant upon the edge of a consecrated space, followed by a password, entry, and presentation to the cardinal points. Next there is an ordeal, an oath of secrecy, and a presentation and explanation of the working tools. The second degree initiation follows the same process, save that (again as in Freemasonry) the postulant is bound but not blindfolded and it is necessary to demonstrate competence in the symbolism of the Craft. The working tools are essentially those of Crowley—sword, dagger, wand, censer, pentacle, and scourge. The major differences are that the cup or chalice, though present and used for other rituals, is no longer counted among them. Instead, two daggers are used, with black and white handles, as in the *Key of Solomon*, and cords are added, as symbols of the enforcement of the witch's will. There is also much more prominence given to the scourge, as 'the sign of power and dominance', and as the ritual agent of 'suffering and purification', used to administer the ordeals.

The principal working tool, however, is made the black-handled knife, and this is another major innovation as the supremacy of this instrument is found neither in the Golden Dawn and Crowley traditions nor in the *Key of Solomon*. In 'Ye Bok of ye Art Magical' (and later Books of Shadows) it is termed 'the true Witch's weapon', having in concentrated form all the powers of the more traditional dominant consecrated sword, to form magical circles and control spirits. 'Ye Bok' also gives the name by which it was to become central to modern pagan witchcraft, of 'athame' (conventionally pronounced 'athaymee'). This is derived from the *Key of Solomon*, but only in a few recensions of the work. The markings to be placed upon the handle when the knife is consecrated are taken from the

Mathers edition of the work along with so much other material in 'Ye Bok', but the name 'athame' does not appear in that edition.

The problem with the *Key*, as Mathers discovered, is that it is not a standard text, but a framework for ritual within which various copyists in the sixteenth to eighteenth centuries added or mutated details. Mathers compiled his 'standard' text by conflating seven different versions in the British Museum. The number and functions of the ritual weapons varies significantly between these, and only one of them gives the black-handled knife a name (which Mathers ignored), of *arclavo* or *arclavum*.[74] There is, however, an eighth manuscript in the same collection, which Mathers did not notice, and this provides the terms *arthanus* or *artamus* for the instrument; the white-handled equivalent is the *arthany*. In the Bibliothèque de l'Arsenal, Paris, is yet another, and here the word for the black-handled knife is *arthame*, which is closest to Gardner's version.[75] There is no evidence that Gardner consulted any of these manuscripts, but he was an avid reader of modern works on the occult, and two in the early twentieth century published details of the last pair cited above: C. J. S. Thompson's *The Mysteries and Secrets of Magic* (1927) used the terms from the London manuscript, and Grillot de Givry's *Witchcraft, Magic and Alchemy* (1931) prominently cited the Paris text, including a fine photograph of a page of it describing the *arthame*. The American fantasy writer Clark Ashton Smith copied de Givry's information to make the *arthame* feature prominently in a short story, 'The Master of the Crabs', published by the magazine *Weird Tales* in 1947, when Gardner was in America. The origins of the term are not known; perhaps the simplest and most likely source is that proposed by James Baker: the Old French verb *attame*, meaning 'to cut'.[76] There is no evidence to explain Gardner's omission of the 'r' in the word; perhaps he first heard it orally and guessed at the spelling, perhaps he decided to simplify it, or perhaps the error was in a source which he was copying.

None of this, however, accounts for why this knife becomes 'the true Witch's weapon'. Two explanations may be proposed, which are entirely compatible. One is that a black-handled knife is a powerful magical weapon in Irish folk tradition, employed to banish malevolent fairies and other unwelcome spirits.[77] As a prominent member of the Folk-Lore Society, Gardner may well have come across these stories. The second is that he himself had a preoccupation with ritual knives, of which he had collected scores, and in particular with the Malay *kris*, upon which he was one of the world's experts. It may have been he who decided to make such a knife, with a distinctive name parallel to that of the *kris*, the indispensable ceremonial tool of the witch religion which he was to publicize.

One very striking way in which the witch rituals in 'Ye Bok' redeveloped Masonic tradition was provided by their version of the old Masons' ceremonial embrace, the five Points of Fellowship. It became an adoration and celebration of the whole human body as a sacred vessel, made by woman to man and man to woman: the five-Fold Kiss. Likewise, at about the time that the initiation rites were entered into the volume, a blessing for the consecration of wine was provided, which symbolized the sexual union of female and male; a union which was, as said, the central feature of the third-degree initiation.[78] The parallel was drawn there with the OTO and, appropriately, much of the actual text of the third-degree initiatory rite is drawn from Crowley's own passionate poetry in his 'Gnostic Mass'. The consecration of the wine was probably modelled upon the sixth-degree initiation of the OTO itself, in which a man dipped the point of a holy lance in a cup of wine held by a woman; save that Gardner's rite reversed the poles, and had the man hold the cup for the woman's *athame*.[79]

Crowley had drawn in turn upon oriental traditions of tantra, and it is possible that Gardner made direct borrowings from these himself, either from his own experience of the East or through English works such as *Shakti and Shakta* by 'Arthur Avalon' (Sir John Woodroffe) who described an Indian rite called the panchamakara. In this, women and men sat alternately in a circle at midnight, presided over by a leader and by a beautiful naked priestess representing a goddess. A ritual meal was followed by sexual intercourse as an act of worship. The seating plan of the participants is exactly that of Gardner's witches, who also had a presiding couple in which a woman represented a goddess—although the purpose of the witch coven meetings was not sexual congress.[80] In its symbolism, the witch religion publicized by Gerald Gardner carried forward that resacralization of sexuality and the human body which had been a feature of the magic(k) of Crowley and of the writings of D. H. Lawrence and Havelock Ellis (among others). The eroticism encoded in the rites was intensified by the tradition that all participants worked naked, something that was a feature of the witches' sabbats imagined by early modern writers (as part of the general transgression of moral codes imputed to them) and has a long and worldwide association with ritual magic; but hitherto was probably unknown in the history of religion.[81] Dion Fortune had directed that magicians should be nude under their robes, 'as nothing mundane is worn in magic', and in her writings portrayed powerfully how this custom could increase greatly the creative sexual tension between her female and male protagonists.[82] Gardner's rituals got rid of the robes.

One other entry in 'Ye Bok' can be suggested as belonging to this middle-term phase of its compilation; a ritual for preparing and casting the magic circle within which the initiations were to take place. It directs that the circle be drawn with sword or athame and sprinkled with 'exorcised water', meaning the mixed salt and water blessed according to the formula entered up in 'Ye Bok' from the *Key of Solomon*. Then candles are lit with an 'Exorcism Prayer', the circle sealed with the drawing of pentagrams at the 'doors', the Banishing Ritual of the Pentagram performed (as in Crowley's texts), and the elemental powers called with a single pentagram (of earth) according to the mode of Eliphas Levi. In *High Magic's Aid*, however, a different version of the preparation is given; in place of the rite of the pentagram, the witch uses an eleven-line chant commencing:

Eko; Eko; Azarak
Eko; Eko; Zomelak.
Bagabi Lacha Bachabe
Lamac cahi achababe
Karrellyos[83]

This incantation is a good example of how the composer of these rituals worked, for it was constructed by cobbling together two equally mysterious (or meaningless) chants found in different twentieth-century sources. The first two lines are taken from an article published in 1926 by Crowley's erstwhile friend J. F. C. Fuller, who used them to preface a four-line incantation which he claimed to be 'a sorcerer's cry in the Middle Ages';[84] he did not cite any source for it and none has since been discovered. The rest had appeared in two popular works on the history of magic, Grillot de Givry's *Witchcraft, Magic and Alchemy* (1931), which has been cited as a probable source of the term 'athame', and Kurt Seligmann's *History of Magic* (1948).[85] This time the source is very clear; a thirteenth-century play called *Le Miracle de Théophile*, composed by one Ruteboeuf. The invocation was used by one character, an evil sorcerer called Salatin, to conjure up the Devil. Neither piece is in any known language, and both seem to have been pieces of gibberish intended to produce a suitably mystifying effect. To Gardner, reasonably enough, all that mattered was that they were apparently medieval incantations, suitable for inclusion in that context in a novel set in the period; but both were to reappear—as shall be seen—in the Book of Shadows.

Between mid-1947 and late 1948, therefore, Gardner had put together a book of rituals which a group based at the 'witch's cottage' could work. They consisted, thus far, of a sequence of initiatory rites based on Masonic practice and Crowley, with some novel features, plus a blessing for wine, and a set of ceremonies and declarations of theory drawn from existing published sources. There is an obvious puzzle in this conclusion; if he was trying at this time to revive the Ordo Templi Orientis—as seems proven—why did he not simply use Crowley's rituals for that order? All that can be suggested without better evidence is that either the latter were not to his taste, or the time-scale involved is even more truncated and 'Ye Bok' was composed in 1948 after he had given up on the idea of resurrecting the OTO and decided to propagate the witch religion instead. Whatever the truth, by the end of 1948 at the very latest, the basic framework for that religion was going into place.

*   *   *

Between 1949 and 1952 Gardner either acquired or created the remaining components of that framework. One inspired decision, almost certainly his own, was to give the set of rituals which was being collected the romantic name of 'Book of Shadows', to replace the traditional and functional 'grimoire'. Doreen Valiente has discovered that the term was borrowed from an article published in *The Occult Observer* in 1949, about an ancient Sanskrit manual of that name which taught how to tell a person's destiny from the length of their shadow. James Baker has noted in turn that the same article probably gave Gardner or his collaborators the idea of adding to the first-degree initiation a rite whereby the initiator 'takes the measure' of the postulant by tying knots in a cord which indicate the various dimensions of her or his body. This is regarded as to some extent capturing them, so that the initiator can then either keep the cord in order to ensure that the initiate holds to the oath of secrecy (on pain of having destructive magic worked with the measure) or return it to the initiate as a sign of trust. Baker's suggestion is borne out by the fact that this gesture does not feature in the initiation procedure in *High Magic's Aid*, nor in the first form of it in 'Ye Bok of ye Art Magical', but was added to the latter while it was still intended for use in ritual; which would argue well for its adoption in 1949 or soon after.[86] Another publication of that period yielded a second charismatic term; Hugh Ross Williamson's novel *The Silver Bowl* (1948) portrayed a seventeenth-century witch cult based on the theories of Margaret Murray and described by members as 'the Craft of the Wise', an expression which Gardner subsequently used for his religion.

The development of that religion during this period can best be traced in the additions to 'Ye Bok of ye Art Magical', which went through two further phases after 1948 and before 1952. In the first, Gardner had ceased to enter new material in the contents lists—perhaps because he now knew it so well—but still intended to use it as a working grimoire because the additional material was still entered in large and ornate script. In the second, he stopped employing the volume in ritual and used it instead as a scrapbook in which further rites and expositions of principle were drafted in a rapid and untidy hand before being entered up properly in a new ceremonial text. That text, as Aidan Kelly has realized, was the earliest known recension of the Book of Shadows, as identified by the Farrars and Doreen Valiente.

The ceremonies in the former category consist of seasonal rituals, for the four festivals identified by Murray as the main witches' sabbats, and a speech for a priestess personifying a goddess. The appearance of such rituals is logical at this point because hitherto the witch religion had acquired distinctive initiation rites, and one for the blessing of wine, but no other set practices to perform in circle which were not taken from identifiable texts, themselves not associated with witchcraft. The relative haste with which the festival ceremonies were composed is indicated by the fact that each incorporates material transposed from an existing source. Thus, that for Hallowe'en opens with the whole of Salatin's invocation from *Le Miracle de Théophile*, mentioned above, and those for May Eve and August Eve both contain a verse from Kipling's 'Puck's Song'. Quotations from Crowley's Gnostic Mass are interpolated directly or in paraphrase in the invocations prescribed for each one. Some of the motifs, such as the entry of the coven riding brooms or staves or carrying torches, and the bearing of a phallic wand by the high priest, are taken from

Murray's portrait of the medieval witch cult. On the other hand, there is also some that is original, such as other parts of the invocations, and the very heavy emphasis on the use of ritual flagellation; what appeared in the initiation ceremonies as an ordeal features here as an essential purificatory operation. There is also a constant prescription of dances and games, to balance the solemnity of invocation with joy, in the manner which Margaret Murray had visualized for the sabbats in her *God of the Witches*.

These later additions to 'Ye Bok' show other significant developments. One is in the nature of the presumed practitioners. The earlier entries, copied from standard texts of ritual magic, naturally assumed that the person working them is a (male) magician. The initiation rites are written with the presumption that a 'magus' will be initiating a 'witch', with the possibility but not guarantee that others will be present. As Aidan Kelly noticed, in the seasonal ceremonies, for the first time, appears the assumption that those working them will be a coven led by a high priestess and high priest. A similar process can be observed in attitudes to deities. The earlier, provenanced texts, like those from the *Key of Solomon*, speak of God, demons, and spirits, in the traditional fashion of medieval and early modern ceremonial magic. The initiation rites are mainly concerned with the elemental powers of the quarters, and only at the very end of the third-degree one, and apparently as a later addition to it, are deities mentioned. The names given are 'Airdia' (Gardner's garbled form of Aradia) and 'Cernunnos') the witch-goddess of Leland's text and the witch-god of Margaret Murray.

In the seasonal ceremonies, by contrast, the two divine figures are highly developed and essential to the action. At Hallowe'en the god is addressed as giver of death and keeper of its realm (seen as a resting-place before reincarnation). He presides in the same guise at February Eve, and on both occasions it is the high priest who represents him, his spirit being invoked into the man by the high priestess. On May and August Eves the goddess presides, as the bringer of fruitfulness, invoked into the high priestess by the high priest. The sabbat rituals are proceeded by a passage entitled 'Leviter Veslis' (the lifting of the veil), in which the goddess herself speaks—presumably through the high priestess—as the Great Mother so dear to nineteenth- and early twentieth-century writers, representing in one all of the great female divinities of the historic ancient world. Her words consist of a linking together, with some paraphrasing, of some of those delivered in the two most notable manifestations of the divine feminine to appear in English letters since 1890: Leland's *Aradia* and Crowley's Nuit in his 'Book of the Law'. The single strikingly original addition is a line referring to ancient Spartan practices of ritual flagellation, used here to justify the prominence of the scourge in the rituals.[87]

It is hardly possible to postpone further a consideration of the heavy emphasis of this element in the 'original' ceremonies in 'Ye Bok' and in the witch religion which Gardner later propagated. It is obvious to any researcher, and a central theme of Aidan Kelly's book is that it represents the essential component of the rituals once all the borrowings from known sources are deducted. He has suggested that the rites can be boiled down to a set of practices designed to induce sexual excitement by scourging, and that this was Gardner's distinctive personal contribution to, and main emotional investment in, what was otherwise a pastiche of borrowings from other texts. The process at work seems to have been rather more complex than that. Kelly is absolutely correct to emphasize the prominence of the binding and flogging, which is the principal practical link between all the initiatory and seasonal rituals. Gardner's novels, however, are not works of flagellant fiction. Among his papers preserved in Toronto are scrapbooks of pictures and stories which he found interesting or attractive, including some of erotic character (within the very formal and restrained limits available to legally published material, which is all that Gardner drew upon, in the 1940s and 1950s). What they show is that he was fond of images of pretty, nude young women; not an uncommon taste among heterosexual males, and one which itself hardly amounted to an obsession, as these pictures make up only a small fraction of the whole collection. None of the pictorial or literary items in the books is concerned with binding or flogging. This is not the profile of a straightforward flagellant.

Nor are the operations involved in the rituals standard acts of sadomasochism. What they define instead is a highly idiosyncratic and thoroughly unusual way of attaining an ecstatic trance, which is explained in detail in two of the sections added to the later Book of Shadows.[88] The cords are used to apply a gentle restriction of the blood circulation to produce dizziness, and the scourge is applied very lightly and steadily to induce a rhythmical tingling sensation. The infliction of pain and the breaking of skin are explicitly discouraged. This is one of eight methods for the achievement of trance defined in another passage added to the Book of Shadows,[89] and there is no doubt that it was the one which Gardner himself preferred; the same document expresses his distrust of drugs, and a personal communication from Fred Lamond, who worked with him, informs me that his asthma prevented the old man from engaging in other techniques open to younger members of the coven, such as running in a linking circle or dancing. A very personal set of circumstances therefore lies behind this major motif in the rites.

Had it been the only important aspect of the latter, then the religion which had begun to be defined in them would never have appealed to more than a small number of asthmatic mystics. What they outlined as well, even at this early stage, was a very radical system of religious belief and practice which distilled the import of the cultural developments discussed in the first ten chapters of this book. By uniting paganism with the figure of the witch, in the Leland and Murray tradition, it automatically pre-empted any easy reconciliation of the result with Christianity or with conventional social mores; it was full-blown counter-cultural religion of the sort after which people such as Dion Byngham had hankered. This was supercharged by the fact that it paid no reverence to any Great Spirit, Prime Mover, or World Soul, who might be equated with Jehovah, but to the nature-goddess and the horned god who had arisen in the nineteenth century as the favourite deities of the positive, life-affirming, language of paganism. Although both were invoked at different times in the various rituals, with equal honours, it was only the goddess who had been given a set speech to her worshippers; the divine feminine had been accorded a distinct edge over the masculine in a manner which was, again, startlingly radical.

Like Freemasonry and Co-Masonry, the ceremonies taught knowledge and skills through three progressive degrees of initiation, and included 'working tools'. Like Co-Masonry and the Golden Dawn, they involved women members on an equal basis, and like the Golden Dawn they operated practical magic; the seasonal rites always left space for ad hoc magical workings. Like the Golden Dawn, also, they attempted to draw divinity into, or from, human beings. Unlike all of these, they were conducted by groups led by a high priestess and a high priest, whose relationship mirrored that of the two deities. Freemasonry, following long-established Christian tradition, shunned the north as the place of darkness; Gardner's ceremonies not only recognized the north as a place of divinity and elemental power, as Mathers and Crowley had done, but treated it as the quarter of greatest sanctity. By forcing its members to recognize the merit in the dark, as in its feminism, its unqualified paganism, its counter-cultural deities, and its insistence upon complete nudity during rites, it was challenging a whole series of norms in the most dramatic way. It challenged another in its resacralization of the human body and sexuality, the devices noted earlier being enhanced by the attribution to sexual intercourse of the name 'the Great Rite' and the direction that it should be performed at the end of each seasonal festival, preferably in actuality or in symbolic form (such as the dipping of the athame in the cup) if this was not desirable; though Doreen Valiente has recorded that among Gardner's witches sexual acts never took place in the consecrated circle, but afterwards and in private between members.[90]

The self-image of the witch formed a crucial function in nerving people up to crash the barriers of convention in these ways. Like all the magical or quasi-magical societies which had flourished since the seventeenth century, this one concealed innovation under a language of continuity or restitution; except that it went one better than the lot, by claiming to descend from the palaeolithic in the manner suggested by Margaret Murray. Beneath this label of 'the Old Religion' an extraordinarily novel one was taking shape. In its own way, it was seeking to drive a battering ram against the boundaries of the present, and of the possible.

*   *   *

The final set of additions to 'Ye Bok' were made, as said, after it had been retired from use as a working grimoire designed for reading in ceremony and become a scrapbook within which passages intended for the new grimoire—the Book of

Shadows—could be drafted before being written up in fair hand in that successor volume. The latter would contain virtually none of the selections from existing works of ritual magic, which had comprised the earlier entries in 'Ye Bok', but would include the initiation ceremonies and other rites specifically associated with the witch religion, with the new material. The purpose of the latter was to set the ceremonies in a historical background, by adding explanations and enlargements intended to substantiate the claim that they derived from an old and secret religion, now surfacing after centuries of persecution.

One was intended to preface the whole of the new book and to give the impression that it was the first item to be written in the whole collection— instead of, as the truth was, one of the last, hastily jotted on the back of a page. It purported to derive from the period of the witch trials and directed the newly initiated witch to copy the book in her or his own hand and to claim if arrested that it represented a private fantasy world, thereby protecting other members of the religion. The dubious nature of the history represented in it was obvious to Doreen Valiente; it assumes that witches were systematically tortured and then burned in early modern England, as in Germany, and neither was true. Indeed, it proves that 'Ye Bok' was used after its retirement from ceremony as a drafting volume not just for one but for two successive Books of Shadows written between 1949 and 1953. The earlier, seen by Valiente in Gardner's possession, did not contain this preface; the later, used for her own initiation in 1953, did.[91]

The other late additions include an invocation to the goddess, based upon Crowley's poem 'La Fortuna', to be used in times of bad luck, followed by a passage on the discipline to be kept in the coven by the high priest or priestess; the punishment in every case was to be by scourging, and the standard number of strokes for ritual occasions, in a set sequence, was prescribed. Appended to this was a recipe for an aromatic perfume in a grease base, to be applied to parts of bodies before entering the circle; this may possibly have been the origin of Wilkinson's story (as reported by Francis King) that members of the New Forest coven had greased themselves against the cold. Later in 'Ye Bok' were jotted chants, and directions for a hypnotic technique designed to soothe and thus to help heal the sick, both allegedly used 'of old'. Another jotting dealt with the cat as a symbol of the moon and of witchcraft, and one inserted at the end of the Hallowe'en ritual further exalted the role of the high priestess, by stating that if no man existed in a coven of suitable rank to take the part of the god, then the priestess could do so, wearing a sword.[92]

This, then, was the corpus of rituals which existed by the time that Gardner's witch religion emerged into public view in the early 1950s. By 1950 he was circulating news of its existence within the London occult community,[93] and it was announced to the national press in the summer of 1951, as shall be described. What can be suggested here about its origins? first it may be helpful to compare my own opinions with those of Aidan Kelly, whose pioneering work into the key documents has often been cited in this chapter. At virtually every point, they seem to be more negative and less conclusive than his. On the one hand, he took for granted the existence of the New Forest coven and proposed a list of members for it; I regard its existence as unconfirmed, and if it did exist then the only member whose presence in it I would take as certain is Dafo. On the other, he suggested that it was virtually certain that Gardner composed the witch rituals in 'Ye Bok of Art Magical' to suit his own tastes, and that also I regard as unproven. Where I do accord with Aidan Kelly completely is in his central insight that the rituals concerned do not seem to have been given to Gardner en bloc by an existing tradition, but were amended and augmented by him fairly steadily over a period of some years. Indeed, my view of this is stronger than Kelly's, because he had no knowledge of the Warburg documents, and so no indication of when 'Ye Bok' commenced. As far as he was concerned, it might have been started in the 1930s, before he ever met or helped to form the New Forest coven, and the witch rituals added at any point between 1938 and 1948. If 'Ye Bok' was not commenced until mid-1947, at the earliest, then the question of why Gardner did not simply enter up the witch rituals in it at the beginning, without wasting time on so much ritual magic which was to prove of no utility to him, is posed much more sharply.

There seem to me to be at least three different readings of the evidence possible at this point. One is that Gardner's story is true, with the correction of 1946 to 1947 for his meeting with Crowley. It must be stressed that this is still possible, although for reasons which must be plain from the discussions provided above, it now does not seem to me to be very likely. The second is that Gardner's account is correct, but with Dafo substituted for Dorothy Clutterbuck as leader and moving spirit in the New Forest coven. This amendment would eliminate most of the problems in the first version, and indeed the only major one remaining would be the development of the rituals, as analysed above. Gardner initially passed off the whole body to Doreen Valiente as those of the old witch religion. When she spotted that many passages in them derived from other sources, such as Crowley, he answered that the ceremonies of the New Forest coven had been 'fragmentary' by the time that he discovered it, and so he was obliged to flesh them out with borrowings from other texts in order to make them viable for revival.[94] It seems strange that a person like Dafo, so well trained in theatre and ritual, as leading lady, Rosicrucian, and Co-Mason, and with a group allegedly composed in part of friends with the same background, should not have developed more than 'fragmentary' ceremonies. This interpretation would also fail to explain Gardner's brief but intense involvement with Crowley and the OTO.

There is also a third reading of the evidence, which has never been proposed before, but seems to me now to be worth suggesting. According to this, Gerald Gardner retired to England in 1936 bursting with energy and determined to find a new, fulfilling, and prominent role for himself in his new, leisured circumstances. First, he tried the route of scholarship, publishing more of his Malaysian material, joining the Folk-Lore Society, and visiting archeological digs. Then, when the approach of war drove him out of the capital to Highcliffe, he joined the Rosicrucian Theatre and then threw himself into air raid patrol duties. When these were less urgent he turned to local history, leading the appropriate society and campaigning to found a museum. The failure of this project and the end of the war encouraged his return to London and attainment of high administrative office in the Folk-Lore Society and the Druid Order. From 1946 onward he determinedly sought a leading role in ritual magic, acquiring the perfect setting for a working group near London and then approaching England's leading ritual magician for advice and authorization. Having obtained both, he attempted to revive the OTO in England as a vehicle for his plans, and having failed to do so, turned at once to reviving the ancient religion of pagan witchcraft, as described by Margaret Murray but in a form suited to his own tastes and experience, instead. This time he succeeded, spectacularly, and so won his place in history. Such a version of events fits the known evidence relatively well, but it falls foul of Louis Wilkinson's claim to have known the New Forest coven, even if this is not decisive in itself. Furthermore, it is not proven, any more than the others.

What seems to be established beyond doubt is the central role of Gerald Gardner in developing and propagating the religion, if not in conceiving it (with or without the contributions of Dafo and others). He was, beyond doubt, a remarkable man, a pioneer of Malaysian archaeology and numismatics even while he was still in full-time employment in the colonial administration, and then one of modern history's exemplars of how retirement can provide a more productive outlet for frenetic energy than formal work. As a founder of a modern pagan religion (if he was such), his qualifications were probably unrivalled, given his experience of tribal animism, spiritualism, Freemasonry, Co-Masonry, the Fellowship of Crotona, the OTO, the Folk-Lore Society, the Ancient Druid Order, and the Order of Woodcraft Chivalry, not to mention his wide reading and field work in history and archaeology. He was a published author of learned monographs and of novels, as well as his later books on pagan witchcraft. He was perfectly capable of the trickery, dissimulation, and plagiarism needed to pass off as an ancient survival a religion which he had developed out of various older materials; anecdotes from very different sources testify to his capacity to be at times (depending on one's viewpoint) either a liar or a prankster.[95] The rituals possess certain idiosyncracies which seem particularly suited to his own tastes and views.

Even if he had compiled the rituals himself and founded the first modern pagan coven, however, it would still not be wholly just to describe him as having 'invented' or 'made up' modern pagan witchcraft. In religious terms, it might be said that he was contacted by a divine force which had been manifesting with increasing strength during the previous two hundred years, and that it worked through him to remarkable effect. A secular way of saying the same thing, more commonly found among historians, is that cultural forces which had been developing for a couple of centuries combined in his emotions and ideas to produce a powerful, and extreme, response to the needs which they represented. It is the capacity, or destiny, to function in this sort of way that makes certain human beings especially significant in the historical record. I would emphasize again, however, that it has not been proven here that he did in fact fulfil such a role. In the last analysis, the old rascal is still in charge of the early history of his movement.

GERALD'S PEOPLE

Ж Ж

THE 1950s were the decade in which Gerald Gardner announced the existence of his witch religion to the world, and succeeded in establishing it as a lasting component of modern spirituality. In 1954 his book *Witchcraft Today* gave that religion a generic name, of 'Wica', adapted by the 1960s to its enduring form of 'Wicca', by which it will be known hereafter in this book. The word in Gardner's spelling occurs only in *Chambers's Dictionary of Scots-English*, where it means 'wise', and this volume may well have been his source for it.[1] The later adaptation resulted from the older and more precise connotation of the Anglo-Saxon *wicca*, signifying a male witch (female version *wicce*). The double 'c' in these words was pronounced 'ch', to produce a sound very close to the modern word 'witch', but custom and convenience has made Wiccans prefer a hard, 'k' pronunciation.

The derivation, and thus fundamental significance, of the words *wicca* and *wicce* is lost in an etymological swamp studded with the arcane terms prefixed by asterisks which philologists coin to indicate putative archaic root-words. Gardner himself blended the Scots word and Hugh Ross Williamson's designation of pagan witchcraft as 'the Craft of the Wise', to declare that 'Wica' meant 'wise people'. A more recent theory is that the Anglo-Saxon words derive from a Proto-Indo-European root meaning 'to bend' or 'to shape'. This, however, apparently confuses a root with a homonym. It seems only possible now to say that the Anglo-Saxon terms seem to be cognate with other words in old Germanic languages signifying 'awakener', 'sacrificer', 'adviser' or 'diviner'.[2] For the purposes of this book, the modern connotations of the word 'witch', like those of 'pagan', are more important than the origins; it is significant that between the 1950s and 1970s it was most commonly taken to indicate a possessor of hidden knowledge, and that in the 1980s it became more associated with a person who shapes or transforms things.

Various descriptions survive of Gardner himself during this last, and most public, period of his life. Doreen Valiente remembers him near the opening of the 1950s as tall, white-haired, clean-shaven, kind, and intelligent, wearing fine tweed clothes and a silver ring bearing his OTO name in Theban script. Her first sight of him as a high priest was equally impressive: 'tall, stark naked, with wild white hair, a sun-tanned body, and arms which bore tattoos and a heavy bronze bracelet. In one hand he brandished "Old Dorothy's" sword while in the other he held the handwritten "Book of Shadows" as he read the ritual.'[3] Later in the decade he grew a beard and moustache, and became more frail. Somebody who had turned into a bitter enemy wrote a recollection of him on a sickbed in the mid-1950s: 'Rheumy grey eyes blinked at me out of a waxy emaciated face. His hair stood on end in long tufts of grey thistle-down, and above an uncombed goatee beard his lips twitched in a strange, nervous smacking sound.'[4]

Although left by a vindictive pen, there is still something endearing about this picture, and most recollections of him in old age emphasize his vivacity, humanity, and charm. Sir James Laver, a high official at the Victoria and Albert Museum, thought that 'he radiated friendliness and understanding. . . . he was quite plainly and obviously a *good* man'. The French newspaper *Le Matin* observed with Gallic dash that 'he has a triangular face, a beard fierce as if in battle; eyes blue, astonishingly young and sparkling'.[5] His initiate Patricia Crowther found him tall and gentle, with long arms and legs, a soft voice, and bright eyes. He would laugh heartily at jokes, banging the table and saying 'Damned good!'[6]

She also noted that in the late 1950s he was regularly ill, and indeed it would have been astonishing had he not been so. In 1951, when he first came to public attention as a witch, he was already sixty-seven years old, and was to spend the remaining decade of his life under considerable pressure. He must have thought it possible that he would die at any moment, and this alone would account for the urgency which he brought to the task of ensuring that his religion would survive. In the apt phrase of Frederic Lamond, who joined his principal coven in 1957, he was 'an old man in a hurry'.[7] The pace of his activities, which had taken off with such verve in 1947 and had resulted in his drafting three successive books of rituals during the next six years, was scarcely to falter until the day of his death. He announced his religion to the press when only the basic format of its ceremonies and beliefs had been established; Wicca was a tradition that hit the ground running.

The publicity campaign began with a convergence of interests between himself and Cecil Williamson, a former film producer who was aged forty-six in 1951. The latter had decided to move from films into the museum business after the war and (doubtless also influenced by personal interest) decided to fill a gap in the market by devoting one to witchcraft. His first attempt, at Stratford-upon-Avon, failed because of local opposition, and so he tried again at Castletown on the Isle of Man, which had a rich lore of witches and fairies, an adequate tourist season, congenial local laws for the establishment of museums, and more tolerant neighbours. The repeal of the Witchcraft and Vagrancy Acts in June 1951 provided a suitable occasion for the launch, and from April onwards a popular weekly, *The Sunday Pictorial*, was primed with stories to publicize it. Williamson claimed to be on friendly terms with at least a dozen witches, and to intend to invite a coven from the south of England to practise at his museum when it opened. He told reporters that its members included respectable middle-class people, called upon spirits to work good, carried out seasonal fertility rites, and danced in the nude. This was fairly clearly a reference to Gardner's coven in Hertfordshire, and indeed he was duly advertised in the *Pictorial*'s issue on 29 June as 'the resident witch' of Williamson's institution. In July he performed for Williamson the opening ceremony of 'the Folklore Centre of Superstition and Witchcraft'.[8] For Williamson, these reports represented a means of promoting his museum (and the attached restaurant), while for Gardner, they furnished an opportunity to promote his religion, at a safe distance from its current centre or centres.

Their interests, moreover, overlapped. Williamson had his own enthusiasm for the occult, and in 1952 he presented himself to a popular magazine, *Illustrated*, as a full-time consultant on witchcraft, specializing in removing spells from people who felt themselves to be cursed, in exactly the fashion of an old-style cunning man. Clients were invited to write to him at his Centre. He stated candidly that he found the counter-spells in books, so that he would have been using some of the actual material from the traditional cunning craft.[9] At the same time he was intending to establish his own set of magicians at the Centre. A month before his interview for the magazine, he wrote to Gerald Yorke to say that he had set the museum up in the hope of using it to attract like-minded people with whom he could form a small group to work non-cabbalist magic. He had not succeeded as yet, and felt that the dead Aleister Crowley 'wanted to help'. Crowley's reputation had just been greatly increased by the appearance of Symonds's sensational biography, and Williamson now wrote to Yorke, as the friend of the late magus, to admit that he 'knew nothing' of Crowley's work and wondered if Yorke could send some of his rituals.[10] Gardner had apparently concealed from Williamson the extent of his own knowledge of the great magician and of his writings. At the same time Williamson took care to publicize Gardner's own witch religion, providing *Illustrated* with a comprehensive outline of its festivals and deities, and providing the first account in print of the alleged ritual in the New Forest to hold back Hitler.[11]

From the start, such publicity was to prove a two-edged weapon. The interviews with Williamson and Gardner reported in the *Pictorial* and *Illustrated* had been written by a journalist called Allen Andrews, who was consistently respectful and objective. Others, lacking such direct comment and reliant on gossip circulating in the capital, resorted to the opposite tactic, of raising the hue and cry after 'secret societies', practising 'black magic', and the *Pictorial* took to printing this sort of material from the autumn of 1951. A sensational piece at Hallowe'en that year included mention of 'a nudist camp where midnight rites were performed with nude devotees of both sexes'. The Hallowe'en issue in 1952 ran a story entitled 'Witches Devil-Worship in London', warning that covens led by priestesses were engaging in sacrificial and sexual rites in temples around the capital.[12] The information about Wicca which Gardner had been circulating among London magicians since 1950 was starting to rebound, and the comment about the 'nudist camp' was altogether too close to home. It is small wonder that Dafo was frightened into withdrawing from her place as high priestess, as described earlier.

What journalists took away, however, they also gave, for among the readers of the piece in *Illustrated* was Doreen Valiente, then thirty years old and possessed of a keen interest in witchcraft and magic. The information about Wicca fired her imagination, and she wrote to Williamson, who passed her letter to Gardner. He arranged a meeting with her near the end of 1952, at Dafo's house, which was conveniently near to Valiente's home in Bournemouth. The interview went well for all concerned, and she was initiated into Wicca there at Midsummer of the next year, when Gardner came down to stay with Dafo to attend the annual Druid ceremony at Stonehenge; he had by now given up the house at Highcliffe in order to divide his movements between one in the Isle of Man and a flat in North London, conveniently close to the covenstead in Hertfordshire. It was at that flat that she subsequently met the coven, now numbering eight to ten people, mostly members of the naturist club to which the 'witch's cottage' was attached. She never learned anything of its previous history; the others clearly preserved the absolute discretion about its origins maintained by Dafo. In time she became its high priestess.[13] Gardner thus acquired the second great creative partnership of his life, replacing that now ended by Dafo.

*   *   *

The years 1953–4 brought about other significant developments in Gardener's career. Williamson lost interest in the museum at Castletown and sold it to Gardner, who thus acquired the perfect home for his own collection of weapons and other artefacts. It was to remain his main residence for the remainder of his life. Williamson himself returned to England and started a new museum of witchcraft, which (with successive changes of location) he was able to maintain until his final retirement in 1997. The two men clearly parted upon bad terms, Gardner subsequently writing Williamson out of his account of his own life, while the latter has lost little opportunity to disparage his former partner and diminish his reputation after his death.[14] The end of their collaboration, however, left Gardner with a secure and congenial base, and he followed this achievement by publishing the book which built on the newspaper reports by announcing the existence of Wicca to the public, *Witchcraft Today*. Just as in the technical production of *High Magic's Aid* he apparently had skilled help (from Madeline Montalban), so in the writing of this he had more, from his friend Ross Nichols, one of the leaders of the Ancient Druid Order and subsequently the founder of the Order of Bards, Ovates, and Druids.[15]

The book set out to establish Wicca as a viable religion in its own right, with a lineage reaching back deep into the past and a set of characteristics that were entirely its own and not an imitation or derivation of any other. He claimed that he had first encountered its members through 'spiritualist and other societies', and was determined to record its characteristics, as an anthropologist, before it died out. He regarded its historical context, and validity, as established, by the work of Margaret Murray and the scholars who had endorsed it from the late 1940s, as described earlier. The problem of its concealed transmission to the present was confronted by representing it as largely a family-based tradition, inculcated into members from a very early age together with oaths of absolute secrecy. While concealing the names of the deities and the details of most rituals, Gardner then provided a great deal of information upon beliefs and practices, which fill out that provided by 'Ye Bok of ye Art Magical' and the subsequent Books of Shadows, and give a good idea of the continuing development of the religion.

For example, there is a full description of a midwinter ceremony, not found in 'Ye Bok' which had only provided rites for the main sabbats to be held on the quarter days which opened the seasons. It opened with the usual casting of the circle and 'purification' (by scourging) of celebrants, and then the goddess was invoked into the high priestess (thus contrasting with the dominance of the god at Hallowe'en and February Eve). This process was called here for the first time by the evocative and lovely name of 'Drawing Down The Moon', a term taken from ancient Greece. In actual fact, as so often, Gardner's Wicca was putting its own creative spin upon an idea which had formerly had a quite different significance: the ancient tradition that the malign power of Thessalian witches was so great that the mightiest of them could pluck the moon from the sky and force it to the earth. The main texts here are Lucan's *Pharsalia*, Philostratus' *Life of Apollonius of Tyana*, and Lucian's *Lovers of Lies*. In Wicca it had been blended with the modern association of goddess, woman, and moon, to signify the union of human and divine feminine. In the Yule ritual, the high priestess representing the goddess stood by a burning cauldron in the centre of the circle, and the high priest led a circle of witches, bearing torches lit at the cauldron, dancing in a circle about them. This was the rite of 'the Cauldron of Regeneration and the Dance of the Wheel'. The former motif is an old one from Welsh and Irish mythology, well known in nineteenth- and early twentieth-century editions, while the latter was a ritual suggested by Murray as performed at the witches's sabbat of February Eve, or Candlemas.[16]

A different and much more important rite also made its first datable appearance in the book, as 'The Myth of the Goddess', later also called 'The Legend of the Goddess' or 'The Descent of the Goddess'. It was printed as 'The Central Myth of Witchcraft', and was subsequently incorporated into the second-degree initiation ritual. It told how the goddess of the witches descended into the realm of death, ruled by its god, to understand why the latter caused all things to fade and perish. The god of death fell in love with her and won her heart, teaching her (and all who hear the story) that he provided rest and peace for humans before they returned to new lives, if they had made themselves worthy of this by love. Those who love most truly will be reborn at the same time and place as those to whom they are devoted, so that they may know each other again. The latter comforting concept was very dear to Gardner, having represented the closing message of his first novel *A Goddess Arrives*. This myth was, as he said, based upon the Babylonian one of Ishtar and the Indian one of Shiva, but different from both; it was in fact an elaboration of the doctrine of reincarnation, as popularized in the modern West by theosophy.

The book took great pains to emphasize the importance of actual mystical experience to the religion. Its fundamental premise—that of Levi and the other nineteenth-century 'high magicians'—was that apparently supernatural abilities such as clairvoyance and prophesy are latent within human beings and can be brought out by training and practice. It was essential 'to quicken and stir the blood, in which life resides'. By acting the part of deities, witches entered into communion with them, 'and once you have known the goddess, does anything else really matter?' And again: 'To do magic you must work yourself into a frenzy; the more intense you feel, the more chance of success.'[17]

Witchcraft Today therefore both embodied and justified the continuing eclectic evolution of the ceremonies of Wicca, to which the presence of Doreen Valiente now contributed a powerful creative infusion. She was a handsome woman of striking, dark-haired, aquiline looks, possessed of a strong, enquiring, candid, and independent personality, and a gift for poetry and for ritual. Gardner utilized her talents both to promote his religion and to augment it. He played up especially to the belief that the public would respond best to Wicca if it were represented by young, attractive, and charming women. In October 1952 he and Williamson tried to win further interest in the Castletown museum by presenting a pretty witch for a televised interview, but the British Broadcasting Corporation 'got cold feet' and Gardner was confined to going on alone, explaining the working tools of the craft to the public. As soon as Valiente was initiated, he employed her in similar fashion, representing her to Gerald Yorke as a daughter of one of the traditional pagan witch families about whom he had told the world. To some extent she played along with this, feeding Yorke information by letter and then meeting him (in December 1953) to provide more and to reinforce the impression of an ancient and hereditary religion.[18]

Her greatest contributions, however, were to the Book of Shadows. From the start, Gardner not merely encouraged but propelled her to improve rituals; at her first midwinter as an initiated witch, that of 1953, he informed her after lunch that she had to write an invocation for use in the Yule ceremony to be held that evening. She rose to the challenge and, inspired partly by a Hebridean song in Carmichael's *Carmina Gadelica*, produced the poem 'Queen of the Moon, Queen of the Stars', which immediately became (and remains) a permanent part of the midwinter liturgy. It was printed, as a traditional part of that rite, in *Witchcraft Today*. Needing a standard chant to perform while raising power by dancing in a circle, she and Gardner together wrote 'The Witches Rune' (the latter word being an Anglicization of the Gaelic *rann* or rhyme, as popularized in *Carmina Gadelica*). Celebrating the elements, working tools, and deities, it culminated in the enigmatic lines attributed by Fuller to a medieval sorcerer, 'Eko; Eko; Azarak', which had featured in *High Magic's Aid* and was now given a lasting setting. Other poetry by Valiente augmented seasonal ceremonies for midsummer and the equinoxes, which began to take their place alongside the quarter days which Murray had designated as the main witch festivals.[19]

Her greatest single contribution to Wicca, however, lay in her revision of 'Leviter veslis', the words spoken by the invoked goddess which had first been recorded in 'Ye Bok of ye Art Magical'. In the mid-1950s she remonstrated with Gardner about the quantity of material obviously attributable to Crowley in it, as the latter's reputation (thanks largely to Symonds) was both so great and so bad that it would help bring Wicca into disrepute. He invited her to rewrite it, and this she did, keeping the material taken from Leland as more 'traditional', and replacing most of the Crowley with words of her own, first in verse and then (following the wishes of her coven) in prose. The result has been published many times now, but is given in summary here because of copyright issues and other qualms. It begins with the summons of Leland's Aradia, to humans to assemble and adore her with secret and joyful rites, receiving freedom, ecstatic joy, and the secrets of magic in return: 'for behold I am the Mother of all living, and my love is poured out upon the earth'. In the second part of the speech, the priestess representing the goddess identifies herself as the soul of Nature in all its beauty, from whom all things proceed and must return. She commands a religion of love and pleasure, with a balancing of qualities such as reverence and mirth, and tells worshippers that the true knowledge of her lies within themselves. As an expression of the union between human and divine, individual and absolute, it is superb, and carries the listener on an outpouring of passionate poetry. Known by the Masonic expression of 'the Charge', it has remained ever since the principal expression of Wiccan spirituality.[20]

These alterations also marked something of a break in Gardner's own relationship with Crowley's memory. As has been shown, the dead magician had been very significant both in the inception of Gardner's career as leader of a magical group and in the creation of its first rituals, although it may as fairly be claimed that his work was used in a very different context from that which he would have chosen himself. In the mid-1950s, as one initiate later recalled, Gardener still spoke 'reverently' of Crowley,[21] but by 1960 the need to distance himself in public had sunk in and he did so in the biography of him published that year. His description of the dead man as a charming charlatan, quoted earlier, at least avoided the tone of pious horror in which Crowley was normally described in print, but still counts as one of the few ungracious acts which Gardner ever committed. It is hardly surprising that friends and followers of Crowley have treated him with dislike ever since—Gerald Yorke himself turning against him—and that this has reflected upon his reputation in turn, such as in the rumour that he paid Crowley to write the Book of Shadows. The ghost of the old man still hovered over Wicca, even Valiente's 'Charge' knowing its touch in places; her words 'for my law is love unto all beings', for example, surely echoes Crowley's famous phrase 'love is the law, love under will', and there are other such moments.[22] His yet more famous dictum, the Law of Thelema—'do what you will shall be the whole of the law'—was (with a significant qualification) the basis of the Wiccan Rede, the witch religion's great statement of ethics: 'Do what ye will an ye harm none.'

The self-conscious archaism of the language in this phrase is typical of several additions to the Gardnerian Book of Shadows in the later 1950s, as material continued to enter it in harmony with the notion that an old religion was vouchsafing its secrets. Much of this emanated from Gardner, but to his credit he was equally insistent that all Wiccan initiates should not merely copy the existing rituals and statements of belief but alter and add to them according to their own tastes and abilities, just as Valiente had done.[23] A major occasion of this occurred in 1958, when the Hertfordshire coven objected to the fact that whereas the main sabbats, at the quarter days, were celebrated on the actual dates, the festivals at the solstices and equinoxes were held at the nearest monthly meeting, which was pegged by the full moon, as a sign of their lesser status. They asked Gardner if they could accord them equal importance, and hold them on the calendar dates. He agreed at once, and this created the standard, eightfold, pattern of Wiccan seasonal festivals.[24] It was adopted by Ross Nichols when he founded his own Order of Bards, Ovates, and Druids in 1964, and has become ubiquitous in modern paganism. Other additions were made to the Book of Shadows during the rest of the 1950s and early 1960s, and older ceremonies (such as circle-casting) were revised.[25] As the process was continuous, this means that copies of the book made by initiates at any one point of the period are likely to vary significantly in detail from those made at any others, and, as new covens were founded, their recensions were going to diverge still further. Gardner's own last Book of Shadows, kept in the Isle of Man after his death and recently added to the Toronto Collection, contains invocations and a wedding ceremony found, in my knowledge, nowhere else.

* * *

Throughout the mid-1950s Gardner continued to promote Wicca with press, radio, and television interviews, and once again this public profile brought liabilities as well as rewards. In May 1955, the original platform from which the religion had been announced, *The Sunday Pictorial*, decided to attract readers by reviving a campaign against modern witchcraft as devil-worship. Its star witness was a Birmingham woman claiming to have been a former high priestess who seems (to judge both from her tales and from police reactions) to have been deranged. When Gardner protested, the paper turned upon him as a 'whitewasher', using the journalist Peter Hawkins, who had written its original attacks upon witchcraft in 1951.

In 1956 other journals began to cash in on the interest aroused by the stories, aided by the reappearance of the woman who had been the star witness in the previous year,[26] and under this pressure the Hertfordshire coven began to divide. Valiente and the older members believed that Wicca should make itself as invisible to the mass media as possible, and argue its case through books, over the content of which it had complete control. They were opposed by some newcomers to the group, led by Jack Bracelin, a tall, spare, and moustachioed young man with a passion for naturism and the diffusion of libertarian ethics in society. He was supported by his girlfriend, a young woman of elfin beauty who became well known in the world of modern witchcraft under the name of Dayonis. Bracelin had been attracted to Wicca by the very press attacks which had appeared in 1955, and which seemed to him (accurately) to be a defamation of an exciting and socially radical religion; he was being entirely consistent, therefore, in expecting that further reportage would bring in other like-minded people. The tactic advocated by him and Dayonis was to find sympathetic journalists working for mass-circulation newspapers and put their own case through them.[27]

Gardner's policy was to combine both approaches: to work on a book and to talk to the press, and the latter policy drove Valiente's faction to desperation in 1957. They drew up thirteen 'proposed rules for the Craft' to regulate the behaviour of Wiccans, most intended to ensure mutual consultation and secrecy. Gardner, taking this as mutiny, replied from Castletown with a set of 'traditional' 'Laws of the Craft' which he held to bind Wiccans instead. They were written in archaisms which seemed to Valiente to be very clearly artificial, and she suspected them of having been invented for the occasion. Furthermore, although much of the content dealt with relationships within and between covens in a sensible and practical fashion, she was especially enraged by clauses which limited the authority of high priestesses and seemed to be a clear riposte to her opposition to Gardner's policies. The heated exchange of letters which followed led to the secession of her group from the Hertfordshire coven, leaving Dayonis and Bracelin to take over as high priestess and priest.[28]

The latter were now free to pursue their policy of setting up newspaper stories, and contacted a journalist called Neville Stack, who seemed to be sincerely open-minded and agreed to write a fair account of Wicca for *The People* newspaper in exchange for admission to part of a ritual and photographs of members engaged in it. The interview took place at a house in North London, which had become an alternative meeting-place for the coven, and included a profile of Dayonis, who made the now customary claim that she had been brought up by one of the surviving pagan witch families. Stack's story was indeed taken up by *The People*, being split between the two editions on either side of Hallowe'en and making headline news for the first. It broke, spectacularly, the promise of a fair hearing, for his objective account of the ritual and the interview with Dayonis was larded (probably as an editorial decision) with the now conventional condemnations of all witchcraft as 'repulsive' and 'barbaric'. Stack kept faith with the Wiccans to the extent of refusing to print their names, and by tipping them off at the following Hallowe'en when *The Sunday Pictorial* planned a raid (with cameras) on the coven at the 'witch's cottage'. This raid was itself, however, an indication that the press was closing in, and *The People* administered what it expected to be the death blow in January 1959, when it printed names, occupations, and photographs of all the witches interviewed by Stack. The women went into hiding for a time, and the coven spread the story amongst journalists that exposure had forced the disbanding of the group and abandonment of the cottage. In reality, it survived, and still does to the present day, at a different location in North London. Bracelin's hope of attracting new recruits through the press received an ironic reward when a young man, reading the first coverage in *The People*, felt attracted to the religion attacked there and wrote to the paper to protest. The editor forwarded his letter to the coven, which initiated him; he later became its high priest, and has remained so for more than thirty years.[29]

To the present writer, the most striking aspect of the newspaper reports is the degree of dedication and sincerity shown by the Wiccans concerned. The enthusiasm of Dayonis for her religion, 'eyes blazing', shines out from the interview. All of the people who talked to Stack clearly believed in the reality of the divine powers with whom they were working, and were utterly committed to them. Upon exposure in January 1959, they were all entirely unrepentant, and prepared for what was, effectively, martyrdom. Valiente, remembering her own early days as a witch in 1953–5, has paid tribute to the real sense of freedom and of spiritual fulfilment which the rituals gave her. Dayonis expressed the same feelings, with a characteristic addition of wildness, in a letter to Gardner about a ceremony held by her coven at the ancient megalithic circle of the Rollright Stones on Midsummer Eve 1959. All night the witches, fifteen strong, had leaped a bonfire and danced about the circle: 'I wanted to roll over and over like a young animal'.[30] In its simple way, this phrase expresses perfectly the feelings of release and blissful communion with nature and the past which the witch religion gave. Frederic Lamond, who was one of the coven at the time, remembers that he found Gardner himself a kind, friendly, and unassuming old gentleman, and an excellent raconteur with an eye for the absurdities of humanity and a childlike enjoyment of life. He inspired love, but entirely lacked the charisma normally associated with religious leaders. Instead, Lamond felt a power reaching out from the experience of the rituals and magical workings themselves, and from the deities to whom they were dedicated; especially the goddess.[31]

This was very much the sensation with which Gardner wanted to put people in touch if they wished it. After the secession of Valiente, he passed Dayonis all the letters which he had received from interested individuals, with a request to initiate as many of them as possible; when the coven was overburdened or thought people to be unsuitable, he often gave the initiation himself, after minimal preparation. By this hit-and-miss process, there emerged between 1957 and 1963 a set of remarkable high priestesses independent of both successors to the former Hertfordshire coven. In the North of England was Patricia Crowther, who founded covens in Yorkshire and Lancashire, while Eleanor ('Ray') Bone established one in South London. Monique Wilson had set up two in Scotland by 1961, and an initiate of hers founded the first securely recorded Wiccan group in the United States during 1963. All their lines were to prove fruitful. They are named here because of the prominence which they were to achieve as media personalities, but there were others who remain much more obscure, and even Gardner's main friends and supporters in Wicca completely lost track of the number and names of his initiates. The successor of Dayonis as high priestess of the Hertfordshire coven wrote to him reproachfully in 1962 that he scattered new Wiccan groups across the landscape in the hope that they would turn out well, without real monitoring or support of the results. Half of those of whom she had heard had either disbanded or lost contact with her, and there were bound to be others of whose existence she was completely ignorant. She finished by saying that she had given up remonstrating with him on the issue: 'I have decided that you must be allowed to do exactly what you want as you are determined to do anyway.'[32]

The one disaster which resulted from this behaviour has provided a windfall for the historian. It centred upon a young woman using the name of Olive Greene, to whom Gardner gave all three degrees at his flat in North London, after the Hertfordshire coven had refused her. She was both pretty and well educated; members of the coven had found her variously either too superior or too ingratiating in her attitudes.[33] Their suspicion was justified, for either she had from the start been employed as a spy by a rival of Gardner, or else turned to this man when she became disillusioned with Gerald. What is clear is that her initial apparent enthusiasm for Gardner became first disappointment, and then bitter hatred. He eventually found it necessary to secure a solicitor's injunction to restrain her from bombarding him with furious letters; he believed that the latter had hastened the death of his wife Donna. The rival witch mentioned above persuaded her to publish an attack on Gardner after the latter's own death, using the story that she had been acting as an undercover agent for the other man all the time.[34]

The result is a mine of information for a study of Gardner in the late 1950s. The worst that Greene could find to say about him was that he was a silly old man; she never claimed that he had tried to seduce her or to bring her under his control. What emerges very powerfully is his anxiety that she should use her initiations to found a coven, as soon as possible, and to use it to work good for others. He taught her that magic occurred if you held an image in the mind and worked up the will-power to achieve it, by 'getting the blood to course' through scourging, kissing, or some other personally preferred means. He thought it permissible to use witchcraft to get oneself a new house, but only if a fair price was paid for it. He evaded all questions about the origins and antiquity of his tradition. A strong impression that he was a Conservative in politics, suggested by his colonial career and choice of Highcliffe as a retreat, is supported by the title of a book noted by Greene as prominent among those which he used to help form a magic circle: *The Left is Never Right*. His physical frailty, making him so different a figure from the commanding one who had initiated Valiente only just over half a decade before, is also very apparent. None of these details was germane to Greene's attack on him, and their very irrelevance induces some—though not complete—belief in their truth.

Another aspect of Greene's memoir which also rings true is her recollection of Gardner's bitterness over his breach with Valiente and his sorrow that his various high priestesses did not like each other better. This last regret is amply borne out by the body of letters to him preserved in the Toronto Collection. It admittedly gives the worst possible impression of the people concerned because it is confined wholly to missives which brought news of conflict and so were retained in order to work through the problems—a trouble-shooting file. None the less, they make it clear that by the early 1960s the Wiccan community existed in a condition of chronic low-level civil war. The qualities required to make a good high priestess—strength, dedication, and independence—did not easily lead to co-operation and compromise. What these letters also convey, however, is the determination of all the women concerned to carry on their work, and their love and respect for the old man at Castletown.

His last years were dedicated to more than training, initiating, visiting, and dealing with a large and difficult correspondence. He published a last book, *The Meaning of Witchcraft*, in 1959, which amplified the historical background to Wicca provided by Margaret Murray and defended the religion systematically against the press attacks. He continued to take holidays abroad, visiting Robert Graves in Majorca on one occasion in 1961.[35] He was taking another in February 1964, when he was well into his eightieth year, on a cruise ship off the North African coast. On the morning of the 12th he had finished his breakfast in the restaurant and was reading a book on magic, when a heart attack suddenly carried him off; he was dead before he could be taken to his cabin.[36] It was a merciful end. The English gentleman who had lived most of his days abroad, and returned home for a time to shape the history of his country, was buried at Tunis. In his will, preserved at Somerset House, he remembered Jack Bracelin and Dora's sister, but divided the bulk of his estate between Dayonis's successor in Hertfordshire, Patricia Crowther, Monique Wilson, and Doreen Valiente. He offered his museum to his assistant there, but specified that if that man did not wish to undertake it, it should pass to Wilson; and this is what occurred. At the end of his life the old man, childless himself, knew that his true heiresses were his daughters in the Craft.

13

THE WIDER CONTEXT: HOSTILITY

I⊤ has been noted in the previous chapter that the announcement of Wicca to the public was greeted in some newspapers by automatic condemnation, and that witchcraft was equated in some with Satanism. To a certain extent this reaction hardly requires explanation, for such a blatantly counter-cultural religion was hardly likely to meet with approval from all journalists. Furthermore, the old connotations of menace associated with the witch figure in folk tales were inevitably going to colour responses to those who now identified with it. None the less, the specific form which condemnation took does demand comment, for it was articulated within a structure which was as much a product of the nineteenth and twentieth centuries as Wicca itself.

There were a number of different components to that structure. The most recognizably traditional consisted of the continuing struggle between eighteenth-century rationalism and the human love of marvels and mysteries which manifested in its most enduring modern form in the genre of Gothic fiction. Caught directly in the tension between the two were novelists such as the Victorian William Harrison Ainsworth. His best-regarded work, *The Lancashire Witches* (1849) was in part a plea for tolerance of the sort presented by the Enlightenment *philosophes* and Sir Walter Scott, so that the heroes are liberals opposing the persecution of the suspected witches. At the same time, Ainsworth's romantic love of the magical and supernatural caused him to represent the witches as having genuine arcane powers; the result is a total moral confusion. A later novelist of equal fame, John Buchan, was rescued from this predicament by Margaret Murray, whom he followed in *Witch Wood* (1927) by representing the witches of seventeenth-century Scotland as practitioners of a surviving pagan religion. Buchan, however, made its rites depraved and disgusting, and hinted that genuine superhuman powers of evil and good were involved in the contest between it and the Christian hero.

Two other writers of the early twentieth century, representing opposite approaches to the same dilemma, are particularly relevant to the issue raised in this chapter. One is the American H. P. Lovecraft, who published works of pure fantasy fiction in the 1920s and 1930s. They took to an extreme degree that theme so common in Victorian and Edwardian high culture; that civilization is a veneer over a morass of primeval horror and excitement. In Lovecraft's cosmology, the latter was represented by 'the Old Ones', monstrous extra-terrestrial entities which had ruled the world before and desired to do so again if they could attain entry points to it. Megalithic monuments and ancient pagan rites of human sacrifice were treated as aspects of the veneration of these beings, and witches were portrayed as their votaries, seeking to restore their rule. Lovecraft wove images of witches' sabbats, taken from Murray and from early modern demonologies, into his tales, to give an impression of a religion of utter evil.[1] What underpinned this vision was Lovecraft's own fear of racial pollution, revealed in letters in which he railed against the threat to the wholesome English values and genes of the United States represented by Jews, Mexicans, blacks, and every variety of Southern and Eastern European immigrant.[2] Beneath these attitudes in turn lay a more general sense of human existence as a dream encircled by a nightmare. All his works could be summed up by one sentence from *Arthur Jermyn* (1920): 'Life is a hideous business, and from the background behind what we know of it peer daemoniacal hints of truth which make it sometimes a thousandfold more hideous.'[3]

The other author is Montague Summers, who reversed the equation presented by Lovecraft: his best-known works were of non-fiction and it was his life which partook of the quality of romance. He had launched his career as an exceptionally flamboyant Oxford undergraduate, idolizing and imitating Oscar Wilde. His choice of a role model was no doubt aided by his sexuality, which was gay. In 1908 he was ordained into the Church of England, but his career there was ruined the next year because of a charge of pederasty. At once he turned to the Church of Rome, only to be barred from priesthood in it, presumably because of his record. It is possible that at some point thereafter he received illicit orders within it, but he never appeared upon any official list of its clergy. Only two things are certain in the matter: that he became an incurable spinner of fictions about himself, and that from the 1910s he acted as though he were a Roman Catholic priest, dressing as one and defending the interests of this Church, especially against the presumed forces of evil. His actual career was that of a schoolmaster until 1926 and a professional writer thereafter. It is also clear that in his youth he had an intense interest in Satanism and the occult, and one writer has suggested that the unrelenting hostility towards magic which he displayed in his later writings was produced by a desire to expiate what he had come to regard as sinful youthful inclinations upon his own part.[4]

He was certainly no mean scholar. His work on Restoration literature, in particular, inspires respect, and when dealing with demonology he tracked down early modern authors who had been wholly neglected until his researches. When writing of witchcraft, however, he took his pose as a Catholic churchman to an extreme and an excess. In three works published between 1926 and 1928 he reacted to Margaret Murray by embracing her idea that early modern witches had been adherents of a rival religion to Christianity. Like her, also, he conformed to modern tenets of rationalism by agreeing that witches had no supernatural powers, although he regarded the existence of the Devil and of demons as a possibility. To him, however, the witch religion was not paganism but Satanism, a parody and perversion of Christianity dedicated to evil as Christians were to good. Thus the early modern accounts of witches' sabbats were accurate in most details, and the witch trials had represented the praise-worthy suppression of a real danger: the witch was

a social pest and parasite; the devotee of a loathly and obscene creed; an adept at poisoning, blackmail, and other creeping crimes; a member of a powerful sect or organization inimical to Church and State; a blasphemer in word and deed; swaying the villages by terror and superstition; a charlatan and a quack sometimes; a bawd; an abortionist; the dark counsel-lor of lewd court ladies and adulterous gallants; a minister to vice and inconceivable corruption; battening upon the filth and foulest corruptions of the age.

Nor had the early modern executions completely eradicated the threat, for to Summers witchcraft was both an ancient and a perennial evil, and the scholarly establishment which insisted that it had been an imaginary one was 'reprehensi-ble and dishonest', blinding society to a serious menace.[5] His views made no impact upon academic experts (to whom their faults were and are obvious), but they had greater success with the general public; in 1946, two years before his death, he restated them in an omnibus edition which roped in voodoo and 'high' ritual magic to his picture of Satanism to declare: 'The cult of the Devil is the most terrible power at work in the world today.'[6] Like that of Murray and Lovecraft, his work reached its greatest popularity in the mid-twentieth century; his main History of Witchcraft was reprinted three times between 1965 and 1973.

A different strand of the negative stereotyping of witches was fashioned out of that thoroughly modern phenomenon, the nineteenth-century revival of interest in ceremonial magic. This presented its practitioners with an apparent difficulty which many of them never worked through; that if, on some level, the techniques characterized as 'magic' had some genuine efficacy, then would not malevolent or destructive magic be equally effective in reality, and should not then its operators be punished? To admit the existence of destructive spirits and the literal utility of curses was virtually incumbent upon any modern magician who was not sufficiently wary of the implications and equipped with an alterna-tive definition of, and explanation for, evil. At the beginning of the revival in England, Madame Blavatsky herself warned theosophists to avoid ceremonial magic because 'geometrical designs and figures especially have a power in them of reacting on the awakening of . . . the half blind and brainless creatures of the elements'.[7]

To those who ignored her advice and yet retained a commitment to Christianity, the temptation to place their work in the context of a supernatural battle between good and evil was often irresistible. One was Arthur Machen, an initiate of the Golden Dawn who later became a friend of Summers; in 1894 he reacted to the contemporary eulogization of Pan by identifying the god as an ancient spirit of corruption, madness, and destruction equivalent to the Christian Devil. Its sequel made out the ancient pagan peoples of Britain to be practitioners of human sacrifice whose descendants still dwell underground in remote rural areas and creep forth in search of victims.[8] If Machen made pagan-ism his target, then J. W. Brodie-Innes, leader of one of the successor groups of the Golden Dawn, turned on witches. He wrote articles for *The Occult Review* taking note of the undoubted propensity of some cunning folk to accept money for laying curses, and declaring that 'this must be done in the Devil's name'. He anticipated Summers by suggesting that the witches accused in the early modern trials had been Satanists, and added a theory that they had accom-plished their evil deeds by projecting their bodies onto the astral plane. To accompany and illustrate these ideas he produced two novels about witches in early modern Scotland, which articulated a theory that Druidry had been the ancient faith of the British Isles, a wise and benevolent religion anticipating that of Christ, and that witches had perverted its power to the service of the Evil One, to harm and dominate fellow humans. In both books they are defeated by the power of Jesus.[9]

Further cautions were provided by the three most famous Christian initiates of the Golden Dawn's successor orders. Two came to the decision that magic was bad in itself. One was the poet and mystical writer Evelyn Underhill, whose novel *A Column of Dust* (1909) warned that those who raised elemental spirits could be possessed by such entities. In that case the only release was in death and ascent to Christ's mercy in heaven. The other was Charles Williams, who achieved national distinction between 1930 and 1945 as a writer of 'theological thrillers'. A common feature of these was the appearance of ceremonial magi-cians as figures of evil, and the last in the sequence, *All Hallows' Eve*, was also the most explicit in its condemnation of magic as a pursuit essentially selfish, wicked, and destructive.[10] By then the publishing firm Faber had persuaded him to write a non-fictional work, *Witchcraft* (1941), which it hoped would cash in on the success of the novels. It proved to be a milder version of Summers, based upon minimal research and dedicated to providing 'a brief account of the history in Christian times of that perverted way of the soul which we call magic or (at a lower level) witchcraft'. The mildness lay in his insistence that by tortur-ing and executing alleged witches instead of trying to redeem them, the early modern authorities had been almost as guilty of flouting Christ's teachings as their victims.

The third writer was Dion Fortune, in her earlier and more fervently Christian days, and she differed from the other two in her sustained belief that magical forces could be legitimately employed to defeat the powers of evil. In her novel *The Demon Lover* (1927), this is exactly what the Christian heroine does. Her occultist hero Doctor Taverner frequently engaged in combat against 'Black Lodges' of wicked magicians, the worst of whom have long hair, consume odd brands of coffee and cigarettes, and live in Chelsea.[11] Members of the world of early twentieth-century British occultism who rejected Christianity could be just as concerned with the dangers from malevolent magical forces. One of the most original, Austin Osman Spare, had a low-level obsession with the power and menace of witches. He regarded their sabbats as having been real events in history, and claimed in old age to have once ridden upon a London bus with a ghostly assemblage of them, all bound for one.[12]

The greatest member of that world fitted the same pattern. Given that his reputation represented the biggest glass house in contemporary ceremonial magic, Aleister Crowley was in no position to throw stones himself; but this is what he did. His most overtly populist work, *Moonchild* (1929) pitted a hero clearly identified with himself against Black Lodges of evil rivals in just the manner of Doctor Taverner, save that his 'black' magicians were recognizable caricatures of former colleagues with whom he had fallen out. This was no doubt deeply satisfying, and it also provided Crowley with an apparent easy answer to the attacks upon his own name; that there were indeed wicked magicians about, but that he was one of the good guys. In his more serious writings he addressed the nature of bad magic more delicately. *Magick in Theory and Practice*, also in 1929, defined 'the Brothers of the Left Hand Path' as those who worked for pure self-aggrandisement, ignoring any higher or more general good. In a series of letters written to a trainee near the end of his life, he repeatedly warned against the 'Black Brothers', who sought only their own ends.[13] This was a long way from talking about Satanists, but the villains of *Moonchild* raise 'vile things' from the Underworld, and the notion of a world divided into the right and the wrong sort of magician, both capable of working with superhuman entities, presented a strong parallel to Christian cosmologies.

Nor did Crowley neglect to condemn witchcraft, although only in two brief passages. In doing so he treated it as an abstraction, based upon traditional imagery and used as a contrast with 'magick' of the sort which he expounded. In 1909 he identified it as the shadow of true cabbalistic work, dedicated to animal pleasures and communication with the lower sort of demon, undertaken by old and jealous hags for selfish ends. Twenty years later, he repeated these views, with the same instinctual suspicion and detestation of post-menopausal women. Deprived by age of the power of motherhood and the joys of the flesh, Crowley's witches venerate the moon, as 'the burnt-out, dead, airless satellite of earth'. He explicitly states that a young witch is a contradiction in terms, and that the works of witchcraft are illusory, dependent upon altering things to give the impression of change, without the deep transformative power of magick.[14] In such ways Crowley provides a perfect illustration of how even a modern magician who rejected the whole notion of Satan could at the same time play his part in reviving old stereotypes of supernatural menace.

* * *

By the 1920s, therefore, fictional images of secret societies of evil magicians, produced by occultists themselves, were circulating among the British reading public. It was but a short step from them to the notion that such groups actually existed in contemporary Britain. Such a step had been taken long before in France, where the modern revival of ceremonial magic had begun, and where occultism had been a language of the radical intelligentsia in general. During the 1890s the country was swept by assertions, given very prominent publicity, that Satanists were at work there, and growing rapidly in power and numbers. The stories centred upon the ritual of the Black Mass, a blasphemous and erotic parody of the Roman Catholic service, and were spread principally by an intelligent and articulate individual who claimed to have been a member of the network and witness to its ceremonies. Upon investigation, the tales turned out to be baseless, and the key witness a self-promoting prankster; but their exposure was not made apparent to all of those who had read the original allegations; and the concept of the Black Mass entered the modern consciousness—both in France and far outside it—as the most striking single image of Satanism at work.[15]

Similar scaremongering was slower to commence in Britain, but during the inter-war years it grew into a distinct, if minor, literary genre there. The catalyst to it was probably a book by the American Theda Kenyon, which has been mentioned before: *Witches Still Live* (1929). It linked Margaret Murray's witch religion, cunning craft, Satanism, and tribal animist beliefs under the labels of 'witchcraft' and 'the Black Art', to declare that 'more than half of the people on earth today' were dominated by the evil 'Power' which lay behind these phenomena. This was the language of the nineteenth-century missionaries, but whereas they portrayed the forces of devildom as contracting inexorably before the Word, Kenyon, writing in the more defensive and anxious world of the new century, warned her readers that they were permeating the civilized nations themselves. The same theme was taken up, and localized in England, by Elliott O'Donnell, a writer of ghost stories who was also possessed by a passionate enmity towards spiritualism, which he regarded as false religion and a trafficking with dangerous entities. Having published repeatedly against that, he widened his target in 1934 to include the whole world of metropolitan occultism.

The result was a modern parallel to those catalogues of heresies issued by medieval and early modern churchmen to warn the faithful against error. It is impossible to say how accurate O'Donnell's sources of information were, as he always wrote in the style of a sensational novelist. Most of what he reported was clearly hearsay, although he included—honestly or not—a few declared first-hand experiences. A major motif of the book was racism—readers were warned against the contamination of Britain by the foul practices of Africans, Orientals, and Southern Europeans. Another, in the style set by Victorian novelists, was to treat the young and idle rich as peculiarly corruptible by exotic and bizarre pleasures. As a result, credulity or disbelief in the scores of cults which he describes is a matter for arbitrary decision. It seems hard to take seriously his insistence that the long-extirpated cult of *thuggi* had been revived and brought from India to London, where its practitioners were regularly murdering sacrificial victims without the police ever noticing; nor that 'the Black Magic Cult' was engaging in vampirism. The Rosicrucians, on the other hand, certainly did exist (and do), and could be accused in the book of nothing worse than being 'silly and presumptuous'. It is hard to tell whether one category or the other should include O'Donnell's feminist neo-pagan sect, 'the Gorgons', who were allegedly based in a big house on the Thames above the capital, and 'love open-air life and cocktails but have no liking for men'.[16]

In 1941 William Seabrook produced a book modelled upon Kenyon and updating her, entitled *Witchcraft: Its Power in the World Today*.[17] Once again, tribal religion, ritual magic, and Satanism were all lumped together under that label, and for his sections on London, Seabrook copied O'Donnell's material wholesale. He added a few extra colourful cults, called the Rosicrucians 'horrible' (without enlargement), and claimed to have met Satanists in person; although they did nothing more spectacular than to try to invoke spirits with chalked pentagrams, and fail. Between these two works an additional, and independent, contribution was made to the genre from within the world of ritual magic. It came in 1936 when a young initiate of one of the successor orders of the Golden Dawn, Rollo Ahmed, brought out *The Black Art*.[18] This provided a history of magic in the world, which swallowed whole the views of Summers on early modern witchcraft and the reports of Satanism in nineteenth-century France. It went on to assert that secret societies of 'black magicians' existed all over Europe, comprising mostly wealthy people hoping to obtain yet greater power, and recruiting through spiritualist churches.

Ahmed described one of these in detail, as wearing black cloaks with animal-head hoods, and worshipping in a temple hung with black and scarlet cloths and focused upon an altar dedicated 'to the Prince of Darkness, Isis, or any other male or female deity of sorcery'. They feasted, danced naked, sacrificed animals, and indulged in 'all the vices . . . avarice, gluttony, drunkenness, homosexuality, and the like'. The imprecision of the details here make them sound like the products of gossip, or else of Ahmed's own imagination; as will be explained below, he was trying to produce a work sensational enough to become a best-seller. It is strange that contemporaries of his with much longer and broader experience of international occultism, such as Crowley, Fortune, Gardner, or Brodie-Innes, should never have noticed anything as lurid as this going on. It is certainly true that there were individuals around in London during the late 1930s who were potential Satanists; two of them wrote to Crowley, excited by his sulphurous public reputation, to profess themselves willing to be recruited into 'black magic'. These, however, were no debauched plutocrats or ambitious politicians, but lonely middle-aged spinsters, and he did not recruit them into anything.[19] It is also interesting to note in passing that in none of these alleged catalogues of cults and societies was there anything resembling Wicca.

Belief in the existence of a Satanist Underground in modern Britain was given an apparent infusion of expert testimony in the 1950s, in the memoirs of a retired policeman, Robert Fabian. Prominent in both criminal investigations and the Vice Squad in previous decades, 'Fabian of the Yard' (as he styled himself) augmented both his pension and his reputation by publishing two volumes of his most interesting cases, and in doing so became perhaps the nation's best-known member of his profession. The first, in 1950, had the pick of the bunch. Among them was the unsolved murder of Charles Walton, referred to before in the present book as a crime thought by some to have been an example of human sacrifice. Fabian stated this theory in his treatment of the case, as one put forward by some of the local police, but did not press it himself with any especial zeal.[20]

The tone of the second book, published in 1954, was different. In the first, Fabian had written as a scientist, operating the forensic skill of detection. Now he was starting to scrape the barrel of entertaining experiences, and dealing more with his work in the Vice Squad, and he wrote as a guardian of social ethics: 'if vice is allowed to go unchecked it will destroy the moral stability of the whole nation.' He was especially hostile to gay men, informing readers with all the spurious authority of his former rank that homosexuality represented a serious danger to society, a vile perversion which often led to worse crimes in those who gave way to it. Lest these views be taken as merely typical of his time, it must be pointed out that they represented an intervention in a major contemporary debate over the decriminalization of homosexuality in Britain—which eventually occurred. Fabian was deploying his professional reputation most unscrupulously—for his actual examples did not suffice to support his sweeping assertions—to ensure the continued persecution of a sexuality against which he had a vehement personal animosity. To other policemen, law-enforcement was a job; to Fabian, at least in this set of memoirs, it was a crusade.

The chapter upon 'black magic' took this tone to an extreme. It commenced by informing readers that 'There is more active Satan-worship today than ever since the Dark Ages, when witches were publicly burned on Tower Hill.' The latter was a completely nonsensical piece of pseudo-history, for no executions for witchcraft are known from the 'Dark Ages' (the nineteenth-century nickname for the early Middle Ages), English witches were hanged and not burned, and none was ever executed on Tower Hill, a place reserved for noble traitors. The rest of the chapter was strikingly at variance with the rest of the two books, for it contained not a single actual case. Instead, it consisted of assertions, made confidently (even hysterically), to the effect that Black Masses were celebrated in the plusher districts of London and that people congregated in secret temples there for rites involving nudity and blood sacrifice.

The only actual evidence which Fabian furnished for any of this was a single Scotland Yard file concerning a woman of twenty-one years, who was recovered by the police for her parents and found to be 'almost insane from exposure to occult obscenities'. He noted that no evidence had been found upon which any prosecution could be based, and attributed this to the fact that the woman had been 'willed' to forget everything that had been done to her. At another point, he claimed that it was impossible for the police to infiltrate these groups because their spies would probably be hypnotized, or compromised by involvement in the 'orgies'. This being so, one is left wondering how Fabian obtained the information which he was providing with such lack of hesitation; he only said that if readers had doubts then they should read the allegations concerning Satanic practices being published in newspapers. As these allegations themselves lacked firm supporting evidence, this was an astonishing declaration for a supposed expert to make. One particularly baffling part of Fabian's chapter concerned the 'Rite of Abramelin', which he characterized as the raising of devils by the binding of a naked girl to an altar. As anybody even slightly expert in the history of ritual magic knows, the actual Rite of Abramelin is one of the most austerely Christian of the whole genre, a process prescribed to enable a magician to gain the conversation of his guardian angel, carried on alone, and involving celibacy as one of the requirements for performance.[21] It remains an open question whether Fabian's amazing distortion of it was produced by an actual group of London Satanists, by the prurient imagination of an unknown informant, or by his own. His targets in this chapter, at least, were both obvious and broad; occult bookshops, spiritualists, and anthropologists who lectured upon 'tribal rites'. All, in his view, were recruiting-grounds for Satan. He was, in fact, as narrow-minded a bigot in matters of spirituality as he was in those of sexuality, and glossed both with the prestige of his former professional standing.[22]

With members of the new orders of magicians writing about fictional societies practising bad magic and others warning against them in real life, it is not surprising that more mainstream authors of fiction picked up the same themes in the same period. First off the mark was Somerset Maugham, who met Aleister Crowley and proceeded to caricature him and his practices in a novel, *The Magician*, published in 1908. The villain is a devious and vicious sorcerer, who has uncanny powers of hypnosis and astral projection, and ritually sacrifices his own wife in a bid to achieve the power to create life. He is eventually killed by the strait-laced and pugnacious hero, who employs counter-magic. A point made in the story, which was to be repeated constantly in the genre, is that the greatest defences of evil magicians in the modern world are its scepticism and rationalism, which prevent belief in their prowess and so allows them to operate unchecked. During that decade and the next Algernon Blackwood included among his short stories one which expressed a literal belief in the existence of Satanic witchcraft and several starring his equivalent to Doctor Taverner, the psychic detective John Silence. In tale after tale, the latter defeated servants of 'the Dark Powers', including a sect of German devil-worshippers.[23] In 1929 A. E. W. Mason drew on the French scare of the 1890s to create a detective novel, set in France, in which the hero exposes a group of modern Satanists, who are linked both with early modern witchcraft and with ancient paganism.[24]

All this must have made some impact upon the popular imagination; but that was nothing as to what followed, and again the decisive step in the process was taken by a ritual magician—indeed, by Crowley himself. In 1934, desperate to gain public recognition as an author, he sent a complimentary copy of his *Magick in Theory and Practice* to a young novelist who had made a sensational success with his own first book. The man concerned thanked Crowley warmly,[25] and proceeded to draw heavily upon his material for a second novel, entitled *The Devil Rides Out*. The newcomer was called Dennis Wheatley, and Crowley had, unwittingly, committed the greatest single disservice to himself and to his life's work that he was to produce in his whole career.

*   *   *

There were, in fact, a number of similarities between Wheatley and Crowley. Both had inherited fortunes based upon the drink trade—the former in wine, the latter in beer—and then lost them, although, whereas Crowley simply spent his, Wheatley was ruined by the Great Depression. Both combined a strong political conservatism with an ethic of sexual libertinism. Both had an instinctual liking and respect for Germany and a hatred of Russians, although in both cases also this seems to have post-dated the October Revolution, and derived from the fact that Russia had become the first superpower to succumb to Communism, which both men detested and feared. They seem, in fact, to have met each other and to have got on well enough, although Wheatley, characteristically, later put a tale into one of his novels to the effect that Crowley had driven himself mad by invoking Pan at one point in the 1920s, and lost all his magical powers; the falsehood of this has been exposed by Gerald Suster. On the other hand, Wheatley also apparently met Montague Summers, and repaid him for the acquaintance in worse coin by later providing a hostile account of their meeting and caricaturing him (in a very obvious portrait) as the villain of a novel; as in the case of his canard about Crowley, Wheatley waited until his victim was dead before abusing his memory.[26] At the same time he did not scruple to use material from Summers's books for his own. This was, in fact, the principal distinction between Crowley and Wheatley; that whereas the former made magic(k) his life's work and had only reasonable talent as a writer, the latter saw the world primarily as a source of ideas for his novels, and was a brilliant author of popular fiction. He wrote, in all, seventy-four books, which were translated into thirty other languages and sold an aggregate of fifty million copies.[27]

Virtually all of these works were 'thrillers', set either in previous historical times or else in the present, and dealing with political and military events. Only seven, written over thirty-eight years,[28] made magic a central part of the plot, but it is for those that he seems to be best known in popular repute. There is a central paradox in this reputation. On the one hand, the novels always carried a disclaimer to the effect that Wheatley himself had never taken part in any acts of magic himself, so that he was innocent of any implication in the lurid scenes which he was describing. On the other hand, the confidence with which he wrote of these matters somehow vested him with the authority of an expert in them, not merely as a genre of fiction but in 'real' life. One admirer, the actor Christopher Lee, declared that whereas other romancers, such as Rider Haggard and Conan Doyle, invented most of their material, Wheatley did not. He was telling people about real dangers, and so had probably saved many from them.[29]

How much access, then, did the novelist have to 'actual' data? On the whole, his own disclaimer was perfectly accurate. The single exception was home-made, when a friend's wife Joan, a psychic, allowed herself to have 'the Powers of Light' invoked upon her by a friend in Wheatley's presence, involving 'a lot of palaver with a sword and roses'. Joan then lay on a couch and talked, apparently in a trance, about a previous life in ancient Egypt. An interesting aspect of the rite is that she chose to strip herself naked for it, illustrating again the instinctual connection between magic and ritual nudity (especially female nudity) made by some in the early and mid-twentieth century.[30] For the material in his novels, however, Wheatley remained wholly dependent upon second-hand material, gained mostly from reading and to a lesser extent from conversations with British occultists. It seems very likely that Crowley's gift, mentioned above, first propelled him towards an interest in ritual magic, but once he had begun research for a novel which treated the subject, his most valuable informant was Rollo Ahmed, who fed him the sort of sensational material which was to appear in Ahmed's own work. The partnership between the two men was of great mutual benefit, for Ahmed gave Wheatley information, and Wheatley got Ahmed his publishing contract for *The Black Art*, the 'non-fictional' accompaniment to *The Devil Rides Out*.[31] There, however, it ended; Ahmed sank back into obscurity, and Wheatley became a household name.

Only in 1971, almost forty years later, did the novelist produce a book on witchcraft and magic himself, and then his reluctance was patent. He explained to readers that he was pressed into the project by his publisher and his wife, the latter persuading him that by 'nearly sixty years of serious reading, I had acquired more knowledge than I could have by a few years spent at any University'. The 'serious reading' listed in his bibliography turned out to be a catalogue of populist works upon the subject, which he fastened together with hooks of his own logic. For example, his view of medieval witchcraft neatly combined those of Margaret Murray and Summers. It declared that the former's joyous Old Religion had been abandoned by 'decent' people during the sixteenth century as Europe became more thoroughly Christianized, and left to society's baser elements, which perverted it into Satanism and so justified its suppression.[32] He repeated these ideas in the same year, in a foreword to a reprinting of Summers's edition of that eccentric and semi-demented text *Malleus Maleficarum*. Summers had termed the latter 'the most solid and important work in the whole vast library of witchcraft', and so Wheatley now completed the process which Michelet had begun, of making it the most celebrated product of early modern demonology in the modern period.[33]

His book on witchcraft is as revealing of Wheatley's opinions of the universe as of his notions of history, and he furnished more evidence for both a few years later, in his memoirs. Together they reveal that he was certainly not himself a Christian; he despised the ancient Hebrews as bigots, doubted the miracles of their prophets, denied the divinity of Christ, and firmly believed in reincarnation, which is a theme of his novels. His theology was, instead, a perfect modern representation of one of the great traditional challenges to Christianity, feared and condemned by it since the third century: Manichaeism. Wheatley certainly did not reach this point by studying it in the past; rather, it embodied his instinctual view of the universe, as a battleground for two mighty, independent, and opposed forces of good and evil. In his contemporary cosmology, the former were represented by capitalism, Christianity, and some of the major Eastern spiritual traditions, and the latter by Communism and Satanism, which to Wheatley were hand in glove. Thus Wheatley could utilize Christian language and symbolism without accepting its belief-system, for it did not matter to him that its claims were literally false, because its intentions were good and it acted in practice as a force for stability and order in the modern world, especially in the great fight against Communism.[34]

In writing most of his novels, he expressed the viewpoint of a traditional British political conservative, and often took care to articulate other viewpoints, if only to refute them more thoroughly in the course of his plots. Only a careful inspection of them, and the final confessions of his memoirs, reveal quite how extreme his opinions were. He never accepted any responsibility on the part of the rich to assist the poor, and bitterly resented having to pay income tax, complaints against which are scattered through his fictional works. His memoirs make clear his resentment that he was not allowed to keep the whole of his earnings, as an early Victorian entrepreneur would have done. Wheatley did not believe that society should be organized into a rigid hierarchy, for it was part of his creed that every person had the ability to achieve riches if possessed of enough ability and enterprise; his two great examples to substantiate this were that of his grandfather, who rose from a penniless labourer to a wealthy merchant, and his own, by writing his way out of financial trouble after the family trade failed.[35] He regarded socialism as a means of destroying the capacity of the working class for self-improvement, and condemned the British Labour Party as a stalking-horse for Communists. His commitment to democracy was limited, his belief being that each person should have one vote, but that those of wealth and social standing should have extra, to deprive the masses of decisive power. He openly admired the fascist regimes of the Continent, and to the end of his days praised not merely Franco but Mussolini, as having done 'a splendid job' of 'cleaning up' their countries. His attitude to the Nazis, by contrast, became one of hostility, as the great national enemy, but there is every sign that it was very different before the outbreak of the Second World War. Indeed, he was later amused to discover that Hitler's regime had considered installing him as gauleiter of north-west London, in the event of a conquest of Britain.[36]

The single reservation which that regime had expressed about him, however, was a significant one; that he had Jewish friends. He never forgot that those friends had kept him afloat financially when his business crashed,[37] and a Jew was one of the team of five friends who were the leading characters of his first two novels, and of a succession of others later on. He was, admittedly, the weakest of the team, and closest to a physical caricature, but to feature him as a hero at all makes a contrast with the views of other fascist sympathizers of Wheatley's generation. This did not, however, rescue the novelist from being a racist in general. He approved of the British, Germans, Americans, and French, as a natural family of peoples, although he thought that nobody should be allowed to become a member of the British Parliament whose family had not been settled in Britain for at least a century.[38] His detestation of Russians, however, only increased with time, until by the late 1940s (with the fall of Eastern Europe to Communism) he regarded all Slavs as inherently treacherous and debased human beings.[39] Asians were treated in his books as cultured but alien, and best segregated from Europeans,[40] while he consistently portrayed black Africans (at home and abroad) with fear and loathing; to Wheatley, black magic and black people went naturally together.

In another respect, he was a radical rather than a traditional right-winger; the sexual libertarianism mentioned earlier. Through all his books Wheatley preached that sexual intercourse, both inside and outside marriage, was a healthy and desirable activity for both sexes. There seems little doubt that the ebullient eroticism of passages in most of his novels contributed greatly to their popularity. What this amounted to in practice, however, was to make the maximum number of female characters sexually available to the male heroes with whom he identified. Indeed, Dennis Wheatley's books are a striking demonstration of how much a writer could portray of erotic activity in mid-twentieth-century English fiction, without fear of censure, as long as the scenes concerned were properly packaged. In the historical novel *The Shadow of Tyburn Tree* (1943), the hero, a dashing and clean-cut young Englishman called Roger Brook, invades the bedroom of a woman after she has undressed, hits her in the face and stomach, throws her naked onto the bed, flogs her with a parasol and then prepares to rape her. The sympathies of the reader are never expected to waver from Roger, however, for the woman is a Russian and is so excited by this treatment that she immediately falls in love with him; this being (Wheatley assures his readers) the way in which Russian men show true affection.[41] The same hero actually does commit rape twice in subsequent novels of the series, and in both cases his victims are virgins.[42] His behaviour is justified by the fact that he believes that both are experienced, and have led him on; and of course, once possessed by him, they come to love him and to be his willing mistresses. Reading such scenes, it is worth emphasizing not merely that Wheatley was a wildly popular author but that he was a respectable one, his devotees including King George VI.[43] His attitude to sexuality was an exact parallel to his attitude to economics: that the world should be a free market with no barriers to a talented, ruthless, and enterprising male.

Wheatley's portrait of Satanism was of a highly organized international conspiracy to subvert the 'Western' world, in alliance with Communism, modern music and art, and 'progressive' education. Its rites, as portrayed in his books, consisted of the Black Masses and sexual orgies associated with devil-worship in the works of Summers and Ahmed. Wheatley also, however, incorporated into it the degree system of the Golden Dawn, as laid out for him in

Crowley's book, and associated Satanism with witches in general, tribal animist religions, cunning craft, and ancient paganism, as if they were all parts of the same spiritual system, dedicated to the Devil. As Wicca became publicized in the 1950s, he simply added features of it to his portrait of that system, and his 1971 history of witchcraft warned people away from modern covens on the grounds that members would become 'pawns of the Power of Darkness'. Conversely, it would be very hard for any reader of his works before that history to conclude that he was not a Christian, for he so cheerfully appropriated Christian texts and trappings—holy water, crucifixes, the Lord's Prayer—into his fictional struggles with Satan and his followers; and always with efficacy. In Wheatley's novels, magic actually works, and must be fought with supernatural power in turn. Although this was wholly in the modern tradition of romantic fiction, it also reflected his personal beliefs, for he fully credited the potency of premonition, hypnotism, faith-healing, and telepathy, believing them to be scientific techniques as yet imperfectly understood.[44] Above all, he had a literal belief in the existence of supernatural powers, warring for the possession of the world. As in the contest between capitalism and Communism, he could see no compromise possible, and all humanity had to be ranged upon one side or the other.

Montague Summers, Robert Fabian, and Dennis Wheatley: these were the three defenders of British decency whose names were invoked to condemn modern pagan witchcraft when it appeared. None of them had any direct knowledge of the subject, nor indeed of any branch of the occult, with the possible exception of Summers, who hinted darkly in later life at a youthful experience of demonic magic. All were, however, accepted as authorities upon it.

*   *   *

Media attacks upon ritual magicians, as practitioners of Satanism and menaces to the moral and social order, had commenced almost with the twentieth century itself—specifically directed against Aleister Crowley, who courted both positive and negative publicity in his flamboyant and courageous manner. Between 1910 and 1933 he was made the object of clusters of defamatory articles. The onslaught which developed in the 1950s, however, was novel in its intensity, and in the broadness of its targets. It was launched, as said earlier, by Peter Hawkins in *The Sunday Pictorial*. He specifically cited Summers as a source of inspiration. As other journals took up the hue and cry in 1956, *The Sunday Graphic* enlisted both Fabian and Wheatley to write against the presumed menace from devil-worshippers; Wheatley was given a whole series, and continued to contribute pieces on the same theme to Sunday newspapers well into the 1960s. Journalists working for those newspapers went to considerable lengths to gain condemnations of witchcraft and magic from the established Church, but it is noteworthy that the response was very muted; one bishop (of Exeter) obliged, but otherwise the only fulminations were provided by a few scattered parish clergy—repeatedly quoted—who had an existing animosity against spiritualism. It is interesting also to note that a parallel theme of the same journals consisted of horror stories about alleged rituals involving animal sacrifice and demonic possession among black peoples, either in Africa or in the New World; bubbling away in this brew of journalistic anxiety were powerful issues of racism and decolonization, as imperial Britain made its uneasy transition to the late twentieth century.[45]

Where newspapers led, novels and films were happy to follow, with an augmented cargo of sensational images. Robert Neill's novel *Mist Over Pendle* (1951), which enjoyed considerable success, took the Summers view of early modern witchcraft. It portrayed the Lancashire witches tried in 1612 as a network of criminals, preying upon respectable society and justly trapped and condemned by the forces of law. In 1957 Columbia Productions turned an old M. R. James story about an evil magician into a film, *Night of the Demon*, which became a classic of Gothic cinema. In Charles Bennett's screenplay, the original magus, who wields powers gained from a medieval grimoire, was given a coven of rural disciples and associated with witchcraft and pre-Christian British religions.

Three years later, the historical novelist Nora Lofts, using a pseudonym, made a foray into the subject of modern witchcraft with a tale set in a contemporary Essex village, where the 'old ways' have been carried on without interruption from the remote past. These turn out to focus upon a cult of the Devil, conducted by witches led by a high priestess, who celebrate the four main seasonal festivals of Wicca with sexual orgies, naked dancing, and gluttonous feasts. Lofts credited them with genuine magical powers, bestowed by the spirit of evil whom they venerate. The cult is kept secret by careful removal of all traces of the rites, and drugging or blackmailing of villagers who are not part of it. The most chilling aspect of the tale is that the witches are detected and defeated by an obsessive, celibate spinster with a history of mental instability, who is a newcomer to the community and knows about Satanism from books. The moral seems to be that such a person, by spying upon and exposing her neighbours, can be a heroine and defender of society.[46] The novel found a wide readership, and was turned into a film after a few years. By the mid-1960s, therefore, the notion that modern England was menaced by secret societies of witches and Satanists (usually conflated) had become a familiar literary theme.

It is equally clear that many took it as fact. An early, and spectacularly silly, example of the sort of panic which could result occurred at Chigwell, where the Essex countryside runs into the London suburbs, in 1956. The caretaker of an empty mansion found a curious collection of leaves and feathers upon the table of a summer house in the grounds. Primed by the newspaper articles, he immediately interpreted it as a temple set up by a group of Satanists. The police prepared to mount a surveillance operation, the local vicar stood by to exorcise the place, and the national and local press both took up the story with cries of horror. The latter turned to laughter within two days, when a group of embarrassed schoolboys confessed that the caretaker had happened upon a store of materials which they had been collecting for their nature study class.[47] In this case the boys were brave and honest enough to come forward, but at regular intervals throughout the late 1950s and early 1960s local people would interpret unfamiliar sights and sounds in just the same way, and without any further corrective to them.

There were, however, more sinister aspects to the media campaign. These were discerned by one of England's most prominent occultists, Madeline Montalban, who suggested in the November 1956 issue of *Prediction* magazine that by focusing upon images of devil-worship, journalists would instruct the public in them and so produce the very phenomenon against which they claimed to be warning. This seems, to a limited extent, to be what actually occurred. One feature of Satanism which the scare-stories emphasized was the desecration of Christian images and monuments, and the series of articles by Hawkins in the summer of 1955 was followed directly by a series of attacks upon graveyard memorials, the most vulnerable kind of such monument. The *Sunday Pictorial* immediately fastened upon these as further evidence of 'Black Masses', never stopping to wonder for a moment whether it might have precipitated the desecrations by its own stories. During the years 1962–4 another wave of attacks followed, with churches in Sussex now being ceremonially desecrated as well, and sporadic incidents in cemeteries continued for the rest of the decade.[48]

None of those responsible for these acts was ever apprehended or confessed to them, and so it remains entirely unclear as to whether they were the work of groups of magicians working Satanic rituals (as the press commonly suggested), or of people having destructive nights of fun within a symbolic framework suggested by the press itself; the fact that such occurrences were either unknown or very rare before the media stories about devil-worship appeared suggests a strong element, at the least, of the latter. My own late childhood and adolescence was spent in the Chigwell area of Essex, referred to above, and I can state categorically that by the mid-1960s it had become a tradition for the roughest of the local lads to amuse themselves by counterfeiting devil-worship in order to shock and frighten respectable neighbours; they held bonfire parties on wastelands with dancing and chanting, left upside-down crosses, and hung up dead animals, and let off terrifying screams and animal noises at night around the fringes of housing estates. These activities were always certain to produce the desired effect, of horrified gossip and local newspaper articles speculating about Satanism. The symbolism employed by the youths was itself gained by reading press reports, and their japes were totally devoid of any spiritual content; rather, they represented occasional alternative forms of entertainment to gang warfare, conventional vandalism, and petty crime. Likewise, among the more law-abiding local adolescents, Dennis Wheatley's novels were eagerly read and despoiled of ideas and images to liven up parties with risqué imagery. For my generation of Essex teenagers, they represented the essential primer in diabolism; though the latter was never treated in anything other than a spirit of fun. Meanwhile, not a scrap of decisive evidence has emerged since to confirm the presence of actual working groups of Satanists in Britain during the first six decades of the twentieth century.

*　　*　　*

There was, however, another side to the picture, and one provided by Wicca itself. In interview after interview, Gerald Gardner drove home the point that his sort of witchcraft was not merely a symbolic system of honouring the natural world and venerating certain deities; it was an effective system of magical operation. His aim was at once to persuade the public that witchcraft actually worked, and that it was in the hands of people who could be trusted to work it for good, especially for healing. That was why his story of the ritual in the New Forest to turn back Hitler was so important to him, for it helped establish the image of Wiccans as patriotic and public-spirited individuals intent upon safeguarding the whole community.[49] The problem with such a strategy, of course, lay in readers and listeners who believed him when he stated that witchcraft worked but not when he added that witches would invariably use it benevolently; it was an extreme manifestation of the basic problem which dogs modern magicians. It attends them, indeed, right up to the present; in a book published in 1987, a prolific and long-established writer upon occult subjects, Colin Wilson, reasserted both the efficacy of magic and the reality of the spirit world, with the suggestion that modern society might be improved by an acknowledgement of both. He took as a particular example of the reality of magic at work, that allegedly operated by a set of people put to death in a famous series of trials, for attempting to kill James VI of Scotland by witchcraft. The glaring question which he then ignored was whether, in that case, they had deserved their fate.[50]

This problem shades into a yet greater one, which will be introduced here by a pair of personal experiences. A few years ago I was lunching in a hotel restaurant with a classic English county lady, from an old family, who was well educated and daintily mannered as most of her kind. For a minute I let my attention wander from her conversation in an attempt to catch a waiter's eye. Discerning this, and misunderstanding it, she asked me if I had seen a 'fetch' behind her. When I questioned her as to the significance of this statement, she explained that she had inherited through blood an ability to see apparitions of different kinds, at fairly regular intervals. Instinct had suggested to her that I possessed the same trait, and was therefore sympathetic to others who did; she was wrong in the first point, though correct about the sympathy. Knowing that she was a loyal Anglican, I asked her about the relationship between these visions and her Christian faith, and she replied that the latter had been the one in which she had been brought up, and to which she still trusted in the great matters of religious allegiance and of salvation. She had also, however, long realized that there were aspects of life in this world which the modern Church of England did not seem to understand, and therefore were not its concern. Her propensity to see spectral beings was one of those, and since it was a family gift she regarded it as something entirely positive and interesting, to be lived with comfortably and privately in the manner of her forebears.

Three months later I was lunching in a pub with a somewhat younger woman friend, who belongs to one of Britain's historical re-enactment societies. She is craggily beautiful, with the slightly bloodshot eyes and rapid and abrasive wit which are almost inseparable from the social life of the society concerned; her background is in the provincial working class. I told her about my research for the present book, and she immediately mistook this for an interest in 'psychic' matters in general. Being thus emboldened, she told me that she some-times saw, or felt the presence of, ghostly figures, and that she had observed one at a gathering in the camp on the previous night; it had also been watched by another woman in the group, who had the same ability. Both had felt perfectly comfortable with this experience. She also sensed that certain places exuded spiritual power, and she enjoyed the feeling of being in them and taking it into herself. I asked her if she had any religious beliefs. She looked embarrassed and replied that she kept clear of that kind of thing. I asked her if she had inherited her gifts, and she answered that she had not; on the contrary, her family had always been troubled by them and preferred to ignore them, but the fact that she did share them with a few other friends put her at ease with her situation.

These encounters are absolutely typical of many that I have had over the years, and especially during the last few, when my research into paganism and witchcraft has encouraged people to speak to me more openly about them. They have convinced me that there is a significant minority of people within British society (and doubtless in many—perhaps all—others) who regularly see, hear, or feel phenomena which most others do not perceive to be present, but which are very real to them. These phenomena can, indeed, be experienced in the same way by other individuals with the same characteristic. The latter seems to be most common among women, though by no means exclusive to them, and is often passed down through families. Let no readers of these paragraphs feel that their personal belief systems are being challenged; the experiences concerned may be the product of chemicals in the brain, or of communications from God Almighty, the Goddess, angels, the spirits of the dear departed, or a range of other entities. The only limitation that I myself would place upon interpretation of them is that the empirical evidence causes me to reject the notions that they are caused by mere overactive imaginations, or by general mental imbalance. I also find it highly significant that modern Western society is apparently unique in the human record in that it provides no generally accepted frame of reference for them and no system of explanation within which they may be sustained or discussed.

This was not expected to be the final situation by the Enlightenment authors who did their utmost to demolish the previous system of interpretation, in terms of good or evil spirits. Sir Walter Scott, in his *Letters on Demonology and Witchcraft,* argued vehemently against a literal belief in such entities; but he did not deny that humans often appeared to see or hear them. He suggested instead that an improved understanding of the natural world would eventually yield a scientifically viable explanation for such phenomena. Almost two hundred years have passed since his time, and yet that explanation has not been achieved; instead, the tendency has been to ignore or deride such experiences, leaving those who undergo them to come to terms with them within private frames of reference, and greater or lesser degrees of ease and comfort according to their circumstances. The principal consequence is that large numbers of people in this society have to live with phenomena of which their dominant models of physical and metaphysical explanation do not take account—indeed, which they do not recognize at all. Such a situation has some obvious implications for the ways in which individuals have either been attracted to modern pagan witchcraft, or have reacted to news of its existence with instinctual hate and fear.

Since the mid-twentieth century, two different models of hostility to pagan witchcraft have operated within British culture, blending with each other at the edges. In one, there are no supernatural or uncanny forces involved at all, and what is at stake is the presumed existence of Satanist groups which indulge in practices which threaten the moral or physical safety of the wider society about them and so should be exposed and suppressed upon purely rational and objective grounds. To be sustainable, this position depends simply on the need to prove that such groups do indeed exist, and that pagan witches can be identified with them; although neither proof has in fact hitherto been furnished.

The other model adopts all the physical structure of the first but accepts in addition the notion that the devil-worshippers concerned are in reality working in contact with effective supernatural powers. Such a thought structure should in theory be rare among the modern British, and is certainly not articulated in mainstream public discourse. It may, however, be more common and deep-rooted than at first appears, and operate quite independently of any formal religious beliefs. The most disturbing recurrent experience which I have personally undergone since I began research for this book has been encountered in social situations shared with middle-class people of high education and professional ability: fellow academics, lawyers, schoolteachers, civil servants, and occupants of leading posts in commercial and industrial organizations. The overwhelming majority of these have been agnostics, atheists, or individuals who answer to the name of Christian but do not attend church except for rites of passage. When I have informed such people of my research, far and away the most frequent question which they ask of modern witches is not 'From what social and economic groups are they drawn?' or 'What motivates them to take up such a spirituality?' or 'How does their religion compare and contrast with others?' or even 'What do they believe?' It is, again and again, '*Do their spells really work?*'

14

THE WIDER CONTEXT:
REINFORCEMENT

᙭ ᙭

THE previous chapter emphasized those factors in mid-twentieth century British society which would tend to encourage a hostile response to modern pagan witchcraft. The most important single argument of this book, however, is that this witchcraft was the result of a particular combination of major cultural trends which had developed in that society since 1800; and that during the twentieth century most of these trends were still in force. It is necessary, therefore, to look now at aspects of mid-twentieth-century Britain which tended to reinforce the self-image of pagan witchcraft, and to encourage an acceptance of it among non-initiates.

The simplest and most easily documented was the continued activity of figures who had contributed towards that self-image. One was Robert Graves, who communicated his idea that the entire ancient world had worshipped the Triple Moon Goddess to a much wider public with his two-volume retelling of *The Greek Myths*, published in 1955. It has been mentioned that Gardner visited him in 1961. Graves may already have published by that time a short story entitled 'An Appointment for Candlemas', which was a good-humoured and sympathetic portrait of a Wiccan coven in contemporary North London, based either upon Gardner's writings, or the press reports, or both; if it dates from after the visit, then it was a direct literary product. He subsequently produced an essay on Wicca, which swallowed whole Gardner's account of his discovery and revival of it. The piece incorporated further information upon contemporary witches, probably furnished by another of them, a character known as 'Taliesin' who will be discussed later.[1]

Margaret Murray also remained active throughout the 1950s. In 1954 she produced her third book on her putative medieval witch religion, *The Divine King in England*, which suggested that every violent royal death and almost every execution of a failed politician in England between 1066 and 1600 had in fact been a human sacrifice, representing Frazer's dying and returning god, under the laws of the Old Religion. It was her most imaginative and least plausible work, and won no acceptance in the world of professional scholarship; but it was presumably believed by at least some of the general public. In 1963 she brought out *The Genesis of Religion*, a personal view of ancient spirituality in which she whole-heartedly endorsed the idea that the prehistoric European and Mediterranean world had worshipped a single supreme female deity.

At the same time, her original thesis about the nature of medieval and early modern witchcraft was continuing to gain adherents. This was due in part to her own promotion of it in the popular press, especially Sunday newspapers and magazines, where she was treated throughout the 1950s as the leading expert on the subject. In 1963 the American-based academic expert, Russell Hope Robbins, gave a series of lectures in Britain in which he restated the traditional view that witchcraft as such had never existed, and that the victims of the early modern trials had been victims of delusion, malice, and superstition. This had been the nineteenth-century orthodoxy, and was still dominant among the handful of specialists in the subject (mostly American). By the time of his visit, however, journalists had become so habituated to the Murray thesis that they treated Robbins's views as a sensational, and dubious, piece of revisionism.[2] Throughout the 1960s and early 1970s popular books on witchcraft (which multiplied dramatically during these years) accepted Margaret Murray's ideas on the subject as the established truth.[3]

A few of these texts deserve consideration in their own right. One was published under a pseudonym by Idries Shah, the friend of Gerald Gardner and Robert Graves who was to become famous as a popularizer of Sufiism in the West, although other experts in the field have questioned the authenticity of his teachings. Shah claimed that Murray's witch religion, and the Wicca derived from it, had originated not in native paganism but as a secret society which had spread from Moorish Spain in the early Middle Ages and was itself rooted in the Berber culture of North Africa. His evidence consisted of apparent similarities in symbolism and the names for ritual tools (such as *athame* for the Wiccan ritual knife, which Shah compared to the Arabic *al-dhamme*, 'blood-letter'.[4] Another was encouraged by Murray herself, being a book by a fervent admirer of hers, an author of historical potboilers called Michael Harrison who was best known for his works on the fictional character Sherlock Holmes. Taking the Murray thesis as 'conclusive' and accusing its critics of mere prejudice against a female scholar, he developed it further by identifying witchcraft with Druidism as a wise and gentle religion wholly compatible with early Christianity. He held up this faith as an example to 'these desperate times', in which Western humanity was cut off from the natural world, preyed upon by 'the Income Tax vampires', and 'inevitably and obviously slipping' into 'anarchy'. He approved of the Catholic Legion of Mary as a revival of the veneration of the Great Goddess, and disliked the 'noisier contemporary "Liberators"' who led the modern women's movement.

Two aspects of Harrison's work call for particular comment. One was that he had obtained some Wiccan texts, and concluded that the apparently nonsensical lines of the 'Bagabi Rune' and 'Eko; Eko; Azarak' actually derived from Basque, then thought to be an exceptionally ancient language. This, to Harrison, was further proof of the antiquity of the witch religion. He was clearly unaware of the literary providence of both items, and no linguist has endorsed his idea; but it is still sometimes repeated among Wiccans. The second is that he provided apparent dramatic supporting evidence of the links between paganism and medieval Christianity by quoting the distinguished architectural historian, Geoffrey Webb, who allegedly told Harrison himself, in the late 1940s, that 90 per cent of altars found in English churches built before the Black Death proved on examination to have a stone phallus, representing the pagan god of fertility, concealed inside.[5] There are two very odd things about this anecdote. One is that Webb, a confident and self-assertive scholar, does not record this startling piece of information in any of his own writings, including his magnum opus, *Architecture in Britain: The Middle Ages* (1956). The other, and more fundamental, is that as any historian of the Reformation knows, all medieval altars standing in English churches were, without exception, smashed up and removed in the reign of the Protestant Edward VI.[6] There simply are no survivors upon which Webb's alleged remark could have been based; and yet it is also still heard in places at the present day.

Murray also gave encouragement to another writer who repaid her with absolute devotion to her ideas: the archaeologist T. C. Lethbridge. Always distinguished by a keen interest in paranormal phenomena and a dedication to dowsing, he also did good service as curator of the Cambridge University Museum of Archaeology and Ethnology, but his status as a scholar never really rose above that of an unusually lively local antiquary. In large part this was his choice; he prided himself upon his character of an upper-class dilettante, with a private income and a contempt for professionalism in all fields. When the university became more the preserve of salaried career scholars after World War Two, he was increasingly bored and irritable there, referring to 'academic trade-unionism'. The breach came in 1957, when other archaeologists refused to accept his claim to have rediscovered a set of prehistoric hill figures at Wandlebury Camp, near Cambridge. He resigned his post and devoted the rest of his life to writing about ancient religion and psychic phenomena, producing nine books on these topics before his death in 1971.[7]

In 1957 and 1962 he published two books which were wholly or partly concerned with pagan witchcraft, and consisted of working the ideas of Frazer and Murray into specific features of the English landscape.[8] He also contacted Wiccans, accepting them as the direct descendants of medieval witches and incorporating some of their beliefs into his picture of the Old Religion. To him, that was essentially a worship of the original Great Mother Goddess, with two male consorts, one horned and one solar. He suggested that the latter was later Christianized as SS Michael and Andrew, enabling him to identify all medieval churches with those dedications as former pagan shrines to the sun. A case-study of the way in which Lethbridge could both draw upon and reinforce modern witchcraft is provided by the figure of Black Annis. Her story begins with a real woman, a late medieval anchoress called Agnes Scott, who lived a life of prayer in a cave in the Dane Hills near Leicester. She was born nearby, at Little

Antrum, and buried in Swithland Church, beneath a gravestone with a fine portrait of her which still survives. To receive such an honour suggests that she was popular, as one would expect of a holy woman living in such a manner at this period. By the eighteenth and nineteenth centuries, however, the memory of her had been distorted into the image of Black Annis, an ogress who lived upon human flesh in the Dane Hills, and who was used in stories as a bogey to frighten and subdue children. It is possible that the distortion was the result of the Protestant Reformation, bitterly hostile to anchorites and anchoresses, as it was to monks and friars.

As such, she had become the most colourful figure in the folklore of Victorian Leicestershire, and as scholars of popular beliefs and customs became enchanted by the notion of pagan survivals, as described earlier, it seemed natural to some (who did not know the story of Agnes) to suggest that she might represent a memory of a pagan deity. This possibility was given some spurious support by the apparent similarity between the name Annis and that of Anu, a genuine ancient Irish goddess.[9] Lethbridge took up this identification, as if it were proven fact, and gave considerable prominence to Black Annis as one of the most striking English personifications of the Great Goddess in her crone aspect. As such, she was taken into the liturgy of some Wiccan groups, and is still represented there. The gentle and pious Agnes seems therefore to have been turned first into a local saint, then into a local demon, next into a Celtic goddess, and finally into a witch goddess; and all the while her bones have rested in apparent peace at Swithland.

All these writers were either working outside academe or—in Lethbridge's case—in self-imposed exile from it. Within its walls, however, the Murray thesis found almost as many supporters during this period. In 1962 a Canadian scholar, Elliott Rose, complained that 'the Murrayites seem to hold ... an almost undisputed sway at the higher intellectual levels. There is, among educated people, a very widespread impression that Professor Murray has discovered the true answer to the problem of the history of European witchcraft and has proved her theory.' Ironically, while Rose himself challenged many aspects of the latter, and suggested that Wicca was an independent, modern development, he substituted a medieval witch religion of his own for that suggested by Murray, a secret society of herbalists and troubadours which reached Britain in the early modern period.[10] In 1965 an Italian scholar pronounced that despite serious defects, the Murray thesis had 'ended by prevailing', while the first great work of one of the most celebrated of modern French historians, Emmanuel Le Roy Ladurie, built a picture of a genuine religion of rebel witches into its portrait of early modern France.[11]

In England there was no significant scholarly publication upon the early modern witch trials between the last of L'Estrange Ewen's works in 1941 and Hugh Trevor-Roper's essay in 1967; and in the gap Margaret Murray's ideas found several powerful supporters. The endorsement of them by Sir George Clark and Trevor Davies has been mentioned earlier, and the former's textbook was one of the most heavily used by schools and universities during the 1950s and 1960s. In 1962 Oxford University Press reissued *The Witch Cult in Western Europe* as a paperback, with a commendatory preface by another of Murray's friends, the leading medievalist Sir Stephen Runciman. Its argument was also absorbed into the work of Christopher Hill, one of Britain's foremost Marxist historians and probably the most prolific and respected author on Stuart England at that time. He endorsed it repeatedly in the years 1964–7, not least in his own textbook *Reformation to Industrial Revolution*, which became the standard alternative to older and more conventional histories for socialist schoolteachers.[12]

The main redoubt of the traditional belief that the witch trials had been products of delusion remained the United States, and that country (by no coincidence) contained most of the academics who were still actually conducting research into the trials, Russell Hope Robbins, Erik Midelfort, and William Monter being prominent among them. It was from there that Robbins launched his mission to Britain to question the Murray thesis in 1963, referred to above. Even in America, however, absolute scepticism regarding that thesis was rocked at the end of the 1960s as word spread of the work of a young Italian historian, Carlo Ginzburg. In 1966 the latter had published a first book, *I Benandanti*, concerning a tradition found in sixteenth-century Friuli (the north-eastern province of Italy), that people born with a caul grew up to possess the gift to leave their sleeping bodies at night and do battle in spirit form with witches, for the good of the crops. Such individuals, known as *benandanti*, sometimes did go into deep sleep or trance, and dreamed vividly that they were engaged in such a struggle. Part of Ginzburg's concern was to show the cultural context from which such beliefs derived, and part was to trace the way in which the *benandanti* gradually became confused with demonic witches, at all social levels, in the course of the seventeenth century. The result was a masterpiece, a wonderful fusion of insights drawn from history and folklore studies, which launched a glorious international career and helped to establish the modern genre of 'microhistory'. It also, however, caused some confusion in the study of early modern witchcraft.

The book was not translated into English until 1983, and most American experts in the subject do not read Italian. Hence, its impact in the United States was initially filtered through William Monter, who in the process created a widespread impression that Ginzburg had revealed the existence of a 'genuine' surviving pagan witch religion in early modern Italy. Jeffrey Burton Russell declared that 'no firmer bit of evidence has ever been presented that witchcraft existed', and included this statement in a book which broke ranks with the sceptical tradition to argue that Murray's witch cult had been a sect of lapsed Christians who had combined heresy with memories of ancient fertility rites. Erik Midelfort stated more cautiously that the *benandanti* 'remain to date the only authentic witch cult in early modern Europe'.[13] In his preface to the long-awaited translation, Carlo Ginzburg himself indignantly disowned these views, with the categorical statement that his work left the existence of 'real' early modern witch organizations an open question. On the whole, this is what it did, but as a result of self-contradiction rather than a clear conclusion. For most of the book, the activities of the *benandanti* are treated as belonging to a dream-world. Then, towards the end, it is accepted that they represented the common imagery of a real, sectarian association of people, while qualifying this with the statement that the evidence does not suffice to prove that either they or witches ever held meetings. On the very next page, however, it is suggested that real social events lay behind the stories of the witches' sabbats—using, amongst other material, the *Malleus Maleficarum*—and that this 'lends plausibility to the hypothesis' that the benandanti met in reality as well.[14] It is easy to see why some readers got confused.

In his preface of 1983, Ginzburg asserted unequivocally that there had been a 'kernel of truth' in the Murray thesis. He identified two different elements in that thesis; that witchcraft had its roots in an ancient fertility cult, and that witches' meetings and rituals actually took place. He felt that he had demonstrated the first point, and that this constituted the 'kernel';[15] these views were restated on a grander scale in his later survey of the beliefs which came together to produce the model of the sabbat.[16] It may, however, be suggested that he had not even proved the first point, because dreams do not self-evidently constitute rituals, and shared dream-imagery does not add up to a 'cult'. Ginzburg's assumption was that what was being dreamed about in the sixteenth century had in fact been acted out in religious ceremonies, themselves descended from pagan times, at an earlier date. That this had ever occurred was an inference of his own, representing a striking late application of what anthropologists had come to characterize, and abandon, as 'the ritual theory of myth', one associated especially with Jane Ellen Harrison's 'Cambridge group' half a century before, and with Sir James Frazer.[17] The whole of Ginzburg's interpretation, indeed, was heavily Frazerian, Sir James himself being credited as an authority in footnotes along with Arne Runeberg, who had himself been influenced by both Frazer and Murray, and the nineteenth-century scholar Wilhelm Mannhardt, who had first pushed Frazer towards the notion that modern folk customs descended from ancient fertility rites. It was wholly in harmony with the methods of *The Golden Bough* that Ginzburg found a belief recorded in early modern Friuli, and a similar one in Livonia at about the same time, and concluded it to be 'obvious' that both were the sole survivors of a 'single agrarian cult' which was once found across the whole expanse of Europe between. At another point he asserted confidently that the Christian feasts of the Ember Days (when the *benandanti* were supposed to be most active) were descended from ancient agricultural festivities. The source reference which underpins this statement, however, is to a single scholar whose work, the footnote goes on to admit, has long been challenged. Another passage refers as fact to groups of young people gathering to celebrate 'fertility rites' in early modern Italy under the patronage of a saint; the source reference states merely that no satisfactory study of youth associations in the period exists.[18] It must be restated that Carlo Ginzburg's early work represented an important and enduring contribution to the study of history; but this single aspect of it—his claim to have vindicated part of the Murray thesis—rests upon imperfect material and conceptual foundations.

In the short term it had the effect of shaking scepticism regarding the thesis among some of those who had formerly rejected it. Among most members of the British public who were aware of, or interested in, that field, no such scepticism existed by the 1960s. Whether they took their learning from newspapers, the *Encyclopaedia Britannica*, or textbooks, they would have absorbed the idea that early modern witches had been practitioners of a surviving pagan religion.

* * *

The 1950s and early 1960s also witnessed the apogee among academic scholars of the idea that neolithic Europe had worshipped a single great goddess, associated with the earth. The development of this notion was the subject of the second chapter of the present work, which noted that the apparent discovery of a figurine of a goddess in 1939 at Grimes Graves, Norfolk, provided the objective evidence—previously lacking—for the veneration of such a deity in Britain. Under the impact of this discovery, the previous restraint of British archaeologists in the matter soon crumbled. Its impact can be seen immediately upon a wife-and-husband team very prominent among them, Christopher and Jacquetta Hawkes. In 1940 and 1945, respectively, they published textbooks in which they suggested that the megalith builders of Western Europe had been converted to the religion of the Great Goddess of fertility, by missionaries moving through the Mediterranean from the old centre of her cult in the Balkans and Levant. This religion was replaced in turn, so both argued, by new cults introduced by the Beaker People, conquering westward from Central Europe.[19]

During the early 1950s they parted, first professionally and then personally. Christopher Hawkes did not return to the subject of the Great Goddess, concentrating instead upon later prehistory. Jacquetta, by contrast, developed it with passionate enthusiasm, as part of a change of lifestyle in which she remarried, to the writer J. B. Priestley, and became herself a professional author, of novels, plays, poetry, and (above all) popular works of history and archaeology. The latter earned her an enormous readership, even while she continued to command respect and affection among archaeologists of her generation. She was awarded the Order of the British Empire and an honorary doctorate, and became one of the two British members of the United Nations's cultural organization, UNESCO. By 1951 she had developed a view of the neolithic which she was to elaborate far into the 1960s—essentially that of Jane Harrison and Harold Massingham, with some input (explicitly acknowledged) from Robert Graves. Like theirs, her New Stone Agers were woman-centred, peaceful, creative, and living in harmony with Nature, worshipped as a single goddess. This happy religion had united the whole of Europe from one end of the continent to the other until destroyed by patriarchal invaders worshipping sky gods. Hawkes's personal contribution to this vision was to identify the invaders with the Indo-Europeans, and to make the Beaker People their Western manifestation.[20]

This imagery was shot through with powerful personal emotions. One of these was the one which had most clearly united and propelled previous exponents of the notion of a universal prehistoric goddess; a hatred and fear of modern industrial and urban civilization. Hawkes's own favourite period was the eighteenth century, when in her opinion the English had managed to develop the comforts of a sophisticated civilization while maintaining the beauties of the rural world; like most of her compatriots, she managed to regard an intensively managed and long-developed set of agricultural landscapes as 'nature'. With the Industrial Revolution, as she saw it, England grew 'hard, dirty and hideous', and 'the Great Goddess was seen in her aspect as Cinderella, with soot in her hair and dust upon her skirt'.[21] To her, modern science was 'a Frankenstein's monster', leaving the present world 'in helpless expectation of a searing death', and the computer was 'a parasite of the Apollonian mind'.[22] Her hatred of technology was joined to a suspicion of socialism, as a means of computerizing and standardizing humanity; to her, the neat identical buildings of the American nuclear weapons research station at Los Alamos were an exemplar of 'what socialism would achieve if it had its head'. Her reason for believing that an ancient society ruled by women had to have been preferable was because of the 'conservative power' displayed—to Hawkes innately—by human females. The word 'conservative' is used here in both its customary senses, but she was no straightforward Tory of the time; her detestation of destructive machinery led her to make a prominent contribution to the Campaign for Nuclear Disarmament.[23]

For Hawkes, as to so many writers before, the salvation of modern humanity lay in a renewed sense of kinship and unity with Nature; indeed, she personified the latter as the Great Goddess.[24] In several respects, her work enhanced the geological and archaeological dimension of the English 'rural myth' beyond the point at which authors such as Massingham had left it. A return to the countryside for Hawkes was a cleansing of the soul; notwithstanding which, she herself lived in London's plushest suburb—Hampstead—throughout her most productive literary period.[25] One of the most—perhaps the most—popular of all her works was her *Guide to the Prehistoric and Roman Monuments of England and Wales* (1954). It was really a guide to those in rural settings, dismissing in a sentence all which survived in modern towns or cities. A large part of its appeal lay in the poetic passion with which it related the sites to the surrounding ecology and geology, all filtered through her own states of mind. One entirely typical example is furnished by her treatment of Chanctonbury Ring, in Sussex:

The rampart and ditch of this little circular fort standing on the scarp above the village of Washington are quite inconspicuous, but some eighteenth-century landscape gardener planted the interior with beech-trees and now the clump, sleek and smoothly rounded as a sleeping cat, is a landmark showing for miles alike from the Weald and from distant points on the Downs. When as a child I first stepped across the Iron Age rampart among the slender beech-trunks, I felt that I had left the sun for a strange shadowy cage, a world entirely of its own. Although I did not know that the foundations of a Romano-Celtic temple (dedicated probably to some local Celtic divinity) were buried beneath my feet, I was possessed by a most potent sense of natural sanctity; the tree-trunks through which I could see the bright world of the Downs on one side and the swooning distances of the Weald on the other were themselves the pillars of a temple. In this tense and fragile atmosphere a chaffinch burst abruptly into song, that spate of notes which is so full of vitality yet not of light-hearted joy. It seemed to me that here was the guardian spirit of the place and the moment of its spell sank into the depths of my consciousness. As these words themselves testify, I have never lost the memory and it still seems to me that Chanctonbury Ring is one of those places where the past still lives with some peculiar power.[26]

The quantity of actual archaeological and historical information conveyed here is minimal; what this passage is mostly about is Jacquetta Hawkes herself. On the other hand, the very self-indulgence of the writing, the vividly personal nature of the perceptions, succeed in conveying a powerful sense of the site concerned as a numinous place, inviting a visit, and it is easy to see why Hawkes's work was so admired by a large public in the 1950s and 1960s. It provided the prehistoric counterpart to the sentimental conservatism represented in the same period by the histories written by Sir Arthur Bryant and the guides to English counties produced by Arthur Mee.

Within the British scholarly community, Hawkes was only the most impassioned and overtly ideological representative of a broader trend. Whether or not there ever was an Age of the Goddess in neolithic Europe, there certainly was one among European intellectuals between 1951 and 1963. During the mid-1950s three giants of British archaeology, Gordon Childe, O. G. S. Crawford, and Glyn Daniel, declared their belief in the veneration of a single female deity by New Stone Age cultures from the Atlantic littoral to the Near East.[27] Childe was the most tentative, and Crawford the most enthusiastic, being converted to the notion in 1953 and subsequently devoting a large and euphoric book to it.[28] Both projected the image into later ages; Childe asserted that it lay behind the medieval Christian veneration of female saints, while Crawford simply absorbed the whole pagan-survival theory of folklore, to find traces of his goddess in a variety of popular customs, such as the making of corn dollies.

With such a volume of endorsement from leading prehistorians, the existence of a neolithic Great Goddess was taken as proven fact by contemporary writers on the history and theory of religion,[29] and these made an impact in turn upon archaeological theory. One of the obvious needs of the theory of a universal goddess was for a stepping-stone in the western Mediterranean, to connect the megalithic monuments of the western coasts, which were now credited to her cult, to the figurines of the Levant. This was now provided by the neolithic and Copper Age remains of the island of Malta. It is worth noting that the scholars who had pioneered the study of its remarkable prehistoric temples, such as Sir Themistocles Zammit and John Evans, had failed to find any self-evident interpretation of the nature of the religions which had been practised there. It seems to have been Gertrude Levy, a theorist concerning the development of religion, who first cautiously suggested that a (selective) argument from statuary and shapes of temples might be used to support the suggestion that the Great Goddess was worshipped there.[30] By the 1950s, the general surveys of prehistory took this argument as orthodoxy. Popular works on the history of art also picked up the concept of the universal goddess as proven fact, and in turn it governed the interpretation of new sites by some excavators. The most spectacular example of this was the partial exploration of the world's largest known neolithic site, Çatal Höyük in Turkey, by James Mellaart in the early 1960s. Mellaart's gift for publicity, much of it through popular journals such as *The Illustrated London News*, rapidly established Çatal Höyük in the public imagination as a former cult centre of 'the Mother Goddess', served by priestesses.[31]

The most remarkable illustration of a wider impact of the image on intellectual culture is provided by the field of psychology. Freud seems to have said nothing directly about the matter, although his work did emphasize the universal importance of mother figures. Jung, in view of his famous theory of archetypes, was surprisingly offhand when dealing with that of the goddess. Declaring that the essential archetype was that of the mother, he saw the deity as merely one derivation from it, and not of immediate concern to psychologists because the modern world rarely worshipped goddesses; indeed, he seemed to imply that he only considered her at all because historians of religion made such a fuss about her.[32] It was left to his devoted disciple Erich Neumann to argue in 1963 that the evidence for the universal goddess indicated that the archetype of the Great Mother had been a constant 'inward image at work in the human psyche'. Neumann developed this argument into an elaborate theory of human spiritual development, in which the goddess stood for 'the archetypal unity and multiplicity of the feminine nature' and even now 'determines the psychic history of modern man and of modern woman'.[33] A process of perfect circularity was now created; Neumann had based much of his argument upon the data assembled by archaeologists who had developed the notion of the Great Goddess, and his work in turn inspired Jacquetta Hawkes to declare that in-depth psychology had proved that such an image was natural to human beings, and so provided the final evidence of its importance in prehistory.[34]

As in the case of the Murray thesis, that of the goddess had achieved the kind of apogee that comes before a fall; and its decline occurred more swiftly. In 1962 a young archaeologist, Peter Ucko, published an essay questioning the interpretation of the Near Eastern figurines as images of a single female deity, and so rocked the foundations of the whole structure of theory.[35] His arguments inspired a leading figure in the profession, Stuart Piggott, who more than a decade before had apparently been the only one in Britain to view the neolithic as patriarchal with the same instinctual leap of faith which carried others towards a matristic interpretation. Even Piggott had briefly been carried away by the rush in the 1950s to accept that it venerated a goddess, but after Ucko's work he felt able to attack the whole idea.[36] Ucko himself pressed forward his critique at the end of the decade, and was joined then by another rising scholar, Andrew Fleming, who uncoupled the chain of reasoning which had supported the notion of the goddess at the other end, by challenging the idea that the Western European megaliths could definitely be associated with such a cult.[37]

The effect upon professional prehistorians was to make most return, quietly and without controversy, to that careful agnosticism as to the nature of ancient religion which most had preserved until the 1940s. There had been no disproof of the veneration of a Great Goddess, only a demonstration that the evidence concerned admitted of alternative explanations. Nobody at the time put up a determined fight against this shift of opinion. Margaret Murray sent Ucko a furious letter, informing him that he had no right to speak about the goddess, because he was, first, far too young, and, second, a man;[38] but she had never established a reputation as a prehistorian, and she died soon after sending the missive. Jacquetta Hawkes referred to his work irritably in a condemnation of the whole of the so-called 'New Archaeology' of the 1960s, but was later content to declare that as the worship of the goddess had not actually been disproved, she continued to believe in it as a personal opinion.[39]

What must be emphasized is that the change of view occurred within an increasingly professional world of academic prehistory; it had still not reached many members of the general public even by the 1990s. Ucko and Fleming had only expressed their ideas in learned journals and a monograph; at the same time Hawkes's popular works, and the textbooks issued in the 1950s, continued to be reprinted and to spread the idea that the neolithic veneration of the goddess was proven fact to a yet larger audience. In the late 1970s that audience was swollen further by the books of Michael Dames, who interpreted the Avebury ritual monuments in terms of the cult of that deity, relying heavily on the ideas of Hawkes, Briffault, Graves, and other writers in that tradition. He did not reject the arguments against it; rather, he was completely unaware of any reinterpretations and assumed that he was stating the scholarly orthodoxy.[40] In the process he made mistakes which no trained archaeologist would ever have committed, such as assuming that long barrows and henges were in use during the same period. These errors, however, themselves enhanced the appeal of his works to the uninformed, and especially to the growing number of people who were seeking a feminist alternative to conventional spirituality, by claiming all the megalithic monuments of the British Isles for the goddess's worship. Such people were especially numerous in the United States, where the notion of an 'Age of the Goddess' was to acquire an emotional power even greater than that which it had possessed hitherto. The change in academic opinion had served mainly to widen a gap which was opening between professional archaeologists and the public.

* * *

In the same years most popular works on folklore continued to treat traditional customs as pagan survivals, and new publishing served only to reinforce this belief. Marian McNeill's comprehensive and populist survey of Scottish folk beliefs and rituals published in three volumes between 1957 and 1968, *The Silver Bough*, was not only the homage to Frazer that the title suggests but incorporated the Murray thesis. Nor did anything change for most of the 1970s. The very popular series of books edited by Venetia Newall for the Batford County Folklore series treated popular customs as the products of an almost wholly amorphous past, without a chronological perspective. So did coffee-table volumes on the subject, such as those by Homer Sykes and Brian Shuel, and the *Reader's Digest Book of British Folklore*. Ralph Whitlock's *In Search of Lost Gods* (1979) was a classic example of a potboiler written by a respected local folklorist, which played up the theme of pagan origins without any attempt to investigate or substantiate it; the 'search' consisted of no more than a portrayal of existing customs. During the 1980s, a powerful critique did at last develop of this approach to the subject, from within the Folk-Lore Society,[41] but like that of the Great Goddess it was long confined to learned journals and monographs, while the older ideas were still offered to the public at large. Even in the early 1990s members of the older generation of writers on the subject were still offering to a general readership a mixture of Frazer and Murray.[42] This all mattered the more in that the 1960s and 1970s witnessed the second great wave of interest in folklore and folk culture of the modern period; the local folk club was perhaps the most significant formal gathering-place of the youth counter-culture of those years.

One of the most significant and influential examples of these ideas at work is provided by the books of the pioneer of the collection of spoken history in England, George Ewart Evans. Born to a working-class family in a Welsh mining valley, he worked as a schoolteacher in Cambridgeshire and London before taking early retirement and settling in the isolated Suffolk coastal village of Blaxhall, where his wife had secured the post of headmistress of its school. Having time on his hands, he took an interest in its traditional life, and then began to publish on it in order to supplement the family income.[43] With his first book of this material, in 1956, he became nationally famous, and produced ten more before his death in 1988, while a posthumous collection followed five years after that. In all his works, he recorded interviews with ordinary people who had grown up in the late nineteenth or early twentieth centuries, and who described their domestic and working lives during that period. In the process he made a significant, and novel, contribution to the writing of modern social history.

Evans's research was propelled not merely by curiosity or poverty but by an emotion already noted in many of the protagonists of the present book, a suspicion and fear of modern urban and industrialized life. His zeal in recording traditional skills arose from a feeling that they would be needed again when twentieth-century mechanized processes collapsed; thus, his volume on horse-management was explicitly a text for a future generation which had to abandon the internal combustion engine.[44] Most of his works harped upon the dehumanizing and polluting character of contemporary civilization, and his opposition to chemical fertilizers was based on a traumatic personal experience, when nitrates poisoned the well from which his household drew its water at Blaxhall.[45] Such opinions did nothing to affect the quality of his research, and some of his books are exemplars of reportage, allowing the individuals interviewed to speak for themselves without any authorial interference.[46] Most, however, did not, and these included his most popular works. Like many of the scholars of folk culture who had preceded him, Evans believed that ordinary people were essentially wise and good, but that their wisdom did not extend to interpreting their own beliefs and actions without expert, and external, assistance. His own interpretations conformed to a few, deeply entrenched, prejudices.

One was a rationalism which caused him to reject any magical explanations of phenomena and to manipulate his data determinedly to find a 'real', 'scientific' motivation for popular actions and beliefs. To him, the countryside was a place of practical values and common sense, and anything which did not fit this image had to be ignored or explained away.[47] Another prejudice was atheism, to which he had turned when rejecting his Welsh Baptist upbringing, and which caused him to mete out the same treatment of suppression or reinterpretation when he encountered Christian elements in popular culture.[48] He had to admit to the prominence of the Devil in folk tales, but dealt with this by declaring that he was not a Christian figure at all, but 'the old chthonic god of the pre-Christian religion'.[49] Ancient paganism, in fact, had a number of attractions for Evans. He had a lifelong love of classical Greek and Roman mythology. As a 'practical' religion, venerating the earth, paganism suited his notion of rural common sense. The idea that every medieval parish church covered a pre-Christian shrine enabled him to treat them as timeless religious monuments belonging to no particular faith. Above all, paganism seemed to be long and safely dead, a religious system belonging to the youth of the human race, and so to pose no threat to a secular and rational culture. When he learned about Wiccans (through mass media reports), his anger and indignation were immediate; he informed his readers that they were impostors who took their ideas from books, were inspired by Aleister Crowley, a 'pretender to magic', and performed 'rituals like the Black Mass'.[50]

This hasty condemnation is ironic, because at the same time Evans was reinforcing the stock of ideas and images upon which Wicca drew. He stressed the perennial and unchanging nature of English rural life until the opening of the twentieth century, so that what was true of it under Victoria could be taken as 'basically unaltered from earliest times'.[51] Repeatedly, he referred to this timeless body of knowledge as 'the Old Beliefs', 'the oral tradition', or 'the authentic tradition'. Such an attitude freed him from a task to which he was not temperamentally suited in any case; of carrying out research into local records to discover the actual history of what he was recording from living memory. He did write a great deal about the past, but relied for this upon an application to his material of the ideas of Margaret Murray, Tom Lethbridge, Sir James Frazer, and Robert Graves; for Graves, indeed, he acquired an admiration close to hero-worship, and corresponded with him for many years.[52] The knowledge that some of these writers were not favoured by mainstream scholars only increased their attraction for Evans, because his own research had initially been rejected by the Agricultural History Society and this sharpened an animosity towards academe inherent in his own status as an autodidact. In 1966 he published an attack on academics as narrow-minded and unimaginative individuals as bitter as those of Lethbridge and Graves themselves. Ten years later he acknowledged that university departments had adopted his own methods of recording spoken history, but in 1987, at the very end of his life, his hostility welled up again. He informed his readers that academics resisted anybody 'who does not accept unquestioningly the *received* way of interpreting the distant past'. His evidence for this was their continued obstinate refusal to acknowledge the (to him self-evident) truth of Graves's *The White Goddess*.[53]

If a mass readership of non-fiction was absorbing the ideas and arguments of the books surveyed above, the same imagery was being conveyed to a still larger public in novels, and above all by three English authors of the 1950s and 1960s. One was Mary Renault, who took Frazer's and Graves's concepts of the divine sacrificial king and of ancient goddess-worshipping matriarchy, and built them into her best-selling stories of archaic Greece.[54] Another was Henry Treece, who embodied the same themes in his novels about the ancient and medieval worlds which took to an extreme degree the Victorian notion of pre-Christian religion as a brutal, savage, and thrilling business.[55] The most important for present purposes was Rosemary Sutcliffe, who made her name as a writer in the mid-1950s and continued for almost thirty years to produce novels which represented the most complete, sustained, and compelling fusion in popular fiction of the ideas of Frazer, Graves, and Murray. Millions of people—above all children and adolescents—who had never heard of those authors, internalized their images of the Old Religion through her work.[56] During the last three decades of the twentieth century, many individuals who adopted a self-consciously Pagan identity said that to do so felt like coming home. Perhaps this was due to memories of past lives, or acknowledgement of long-established contacts with the divine, or simply the discovery of a spirituality which perfectly corresponded to their own instincts and needs. It is also, however, possible that much of this feeling was due to the fact that such people had spent their youth reading books of the sort described above.

Such literary works, then, provided constant reinforcement of the body of ideas which had shaped Wicca. It must be plain enough that those works, in turn, fed off powerful emotional currents within modern British culture—a yearning for a reunion with the natural world and one's own imagination, for a spirituality of liberal self-expression and self-actualization, and for a greater parity and partnership between the sexes, especially in religion—which only strengthened as the twentieth century passed its meridian. The 1960s, in particular, witnessed an explosion of articulations of those needs and attempts to realize them. Out of hundreds of possible texts which might furnish illustration of that phenomenon, I choose one produced by a historian of cinema, Sean French, who describes how films of the decade turned an elitist artistic hedonism 'into a mass-market industry. It was the democratizing of Eden that the 1960s would promise: if we let our hair grow, lie in the sun and cast off our inhibitions imposed by clerics, old people and other tyrants, the result will be a Utopia of the senses'. French described this process as a revival of 'a pagan, classical tradition of sensual pleasure',[57] and indeed the whole passage, like many others from or concerning the time, is soaked in the 'fourth', libertarian, modern English language of paganism. In the definitive era of the counter-culture, counter-cultural religion came into its own.

Linked to these fairly obvious forces were others, perhaps more subtle but not the less profound. One was the continuing erosion of traditional communities by the atomizing effect of modern living. As the church and chapel lost their places as communal foci, so privatized spirituality came to seem more and more natural, and pagan witchcraft was a private spirituality *par excellence*. Furthermore, as the natural world became tamer and tamer, and the recesses of the globe more familiar, so Westerners began, more than ever before, to treat their own minds and souls as wild places, worthy of exploration. The new witchcraft, which united religion and magic, provided for some a particularly exciting way of entering those inner landscapes.

OLD CRAFT, NEW CRAFT

THE reality of Gardner's claim to have discovered an existing religion is only one of two large problems which confront a historian concerned with the origins of modern pagan witchcraft. The other, closely related, is whether any other groups of pagan witches existed at the time when he was forming his own. It was central to his portrayal of this process that he was believed to be reviving an old and secret faith that had almost died out; built into that portrayal, therefore, was the suggestion that other adherents of that faith might have survived in the manner of the New Forest coven, and could surface now that Gardner had initiated the process of emergence. In order to do so credibly, however, such groups would either have to approximate to the Gardnerian model of what pagan witches ought to be like, or else to challenge that model as fraudulent or inadequate. For anybody who wanted to follow the former course, an outline of Wiccan belief and practice was provided in Allen Andrews's article in *Illustrated*, in September 1952, much augmented from 1954 by the information in *Witchcraft Today*, to which could be joined that available in *High Magic's Aid*, five years before. Between them, these publications supplied any attentive reader with the data for a rough simulacrum of Gardnerian Wicca. By the early 1960s an unknown number of copies of the Book of Shadows (in different recensions) had vanished into society at large with individuals initiated through the Gardnerian network, and the whole Book was published in 1964, in a pirated edition issued by Charles Cardell.

In previous chapters of the present book, some indication has been provided of the richness and diversity of the different concepts and images which came together to form Wicca, and the widespread power of the emotional currents which vivified them. There is nothing inherently improbable in the notion that pagan witch groups could have evolved independently of Gardnerian Wicca, drawing upon the same pool of ideas and impulses. Such groups could have possessed genuine roots of inheritance or training in the earlier world of popular magic. Charmers and cunning folk were so numerous before the twentieth century that tens of thousands of people in contemporary Britain (at the least) must be descended from them. A knowledge of charms and spells was found far more broadly in society than among these specialists, and seems to have been especially common amongst women; so that there may well have been millions of individuals in mid-twentieth-century Britain who had possessed at least one grandmother or great-aunt who had manifested it. It remains an open question, moreover, how many of the consumers of the 'neo-pagan' literature which burgeoned from the 1890s internalized or even acted out its ideas; how many admirers of the classics and of Romantic verse followed Shelley and Calvert in building altars to Pan.

The simple problem is that Gardner's pagan witchcraft was not merely the first to surface but remains the first to be securely documented. It is entirely possible that members of other witch groups which pre-dated 1950 deliberately avoided the creation of any written record of their activities, and avoided detection by any except the more discreet of their relatives, friends, and neighbours. It is also true, however, that the terms in which Gardner announced the existence of Wicca (following a grand cultural tradition which by then included Freemasonry, the Oddfellows and similar orders, the Rosicrucians and the magical societies) made it impossible for about thirty years for anybody to gain credibility for a coven unless it likewise claimed to be part of an ancient and enduring line. There is also a logical bind upon historians confronted with this impasse. From the late 1980s onwards, academics in Britain and America have confronted claims of ritual abuse and sacrifice of children by networks of Satanists, and after careful investigation have concluded that there is no evidence that such networks exist, nor that such rites have taken place. Modern witches who may be grateful for this work cannot then expect scholars to suspend the same absolute demand for evidence when evaluating their own claims to the antiquity of their traditions.

The documentary record from before 1950, therefore, yields nothing except the Gardnerian material. It has been noted that none of the magical or pagan groups listed and denounced by O'Donnell and Seabrook as active in the 1930s included anything like Wicca; but then those surveys were confined to London and its immediate hinterland, and covens may have existed elsewhere. *The Illustrated Police News* on 28 April 1939 printed the 'confession' of a female artist aged twenty-two, who claimed to have attended the revels of a devil-worshipping coven in a Sussex wood, led by a prominent Londoner and an older woman and including feasting, nude dancing, and copulation. The article asserted that hundreds of people would celebrate in like manner upon the next May Eve. All this may well be an account of an actual group; but it does sound rather like one of the most famous episodes in Dennis Wheatley's novel, *The Devil Rides Out*, which had been published four years before. On the night of the May full moon of 1949, a passer-by allegedly saw five cloaked figures dance widdershins about the famous prehistoric monolith in the Cotswolds known as the King Stone. They then prostrated themselves before it, and pressed their bodies against it (climbing the surrounding railings to do so); it may have happened, and the dancers may have been pagan witches.

The same article which publicized this incident, written in 1952, stated that covens were operating by then at various points upon the south coast, in Liverpool, and in Cumbria. It commented that a Sussex group, inspired by books, had developed a pretty Candlemas ritual which they worked upon the South Downs. The Cumbrian set numbered eleven, and held ceremonies in the celebrated prehistoric stone circle at Castlerigg; one commented that 'you get so close to God'.[1] Most of the piece consisted of an interview with Cecil Williamson, and it is not certain whether the information concerned was obtained from him, rather than directly from group members; the last two items of it, however, seem remarkably circumstantial. The comment from the Cumbrian one is a rather odd one to hear from an alleged pagan witch, and does raise the question of whether sets of people experimenting with rather different kinds of alternative spirituality were being gathered under the label of 'witch-craft'. Some indication of the sort of alternative variety of witch at work in the 1950s is provided by an experience of Gardner's Hertfordshire coven. At the end of the decade it was joined by a wealthy woman who claimed to be a member of a hereditary coven in East Anglia. She had been in touch with Gardner himself to discover what other witches did, drawn by the publicity given to his coven, and worked with the latter for a time. All that she told it of her own group's practices was that they were very different, often consisting of sitting in a circle, clad in robes, holding hands and concentrating upon what was to be done. One of the Hertfordshire coven's high priestesses, Lois Bourne, has told how she eventually joined the East Anglian group and discovered that this description was more or less accurate. It was led by a Lord and Lady, although the regular affairs were conducted by deputies, the Magister and Magistra. The members were generally affluent individuals, numbering about thirty-six; all were expected to attend four 'great sabbats', but not necessarily the meetings between. It was organized on various different levels, and honoured a god and goddess, with the former as the senior partner. There was a heavy emphasis on silent meditation.[2]

Most of the evidence relating to non-Gardnerian pagan witchcraft before 1960, however, derives wholly from retrospective testimony, and this must form most of the subject-matter of the present chapter. Two such claims became the foundation stones of important traditions, and will be given the space due to them in the chapters immediately following this one. The remainder can be treated here.

*   *   *

By far the most celebrated of these was first articulated in 1974, when a writer calling himself Lugh began to contribute articles to what was then the principal magazine of British witchcraft, *The Wiccan*. He later revealed himself to be an Englishman called E. W. Liddell, who had emigrated to New Zealand in the early 1960s and subsequently moved to Australia. His pieces in *The Wiccan* made sensational claims concerning the history of pagan witchcraft, which he restated and amplified from 1977 onward as he switched his allegiance to a new journal, *The Cauldron*, edited by Michael Howard; his contributions to that have continued to the time of writing. They have won and then lost a number of supporters. The original editor of *The Wiccan* became markedly less sympathetic to them. A subsequent editor, Leonora James, was inspired by them to conduct some research of her own into areas with which they dealt; but in the course of the 1980s she totally lost faith in Liddell's veracity. Doreen Valiente was also initially receptive to his material, but grew more sceptical of it. It has generated an actual living tradition (or set of traditions) of pagan witchcraft in Australia and the United States, but its only sustained champion in the United Kingdom has been Michael Howard himself. His defence has been limited and measured; he has declared many of Liddell's claims to 'seem too fantastic to be true', while insisting that most remain without disproof and should be treated with respect until or unless such refutation is provided. The two men have greatly facilitated debate by editing the material in book form, under the title *The Pickingill Papers*, in 1994. As yet, however, the only academic scholar to have considered it seems to be the American James W. Baker, who has dismissed it as a hoax.[3]

This brief history provides some impression of the controversy and doubt which has settled over this information. If anything, it prejudices me in favour of Bill Liddell and his assertions, for the simple reason that one of the quickest ways to create a major impact in academe is to prove the truth of something that has hitherto been derided or dismissed. Furthermore, he himself has contributed most generously to my researches, corresponding with me at length and in detail. On the other hand, it must be admitted that his way of answering questions, both in print and in private, is often slow and oblique, and that his material is not always presented with the greatest clarity. It is claimed to derive from three different sources: a hereditary tradition of pagan witchcraft, a separate tradition which was given its distinctive qualities by George Pickingill of Canewdon, Essex, in the late nineteenth century, and Liddell's own experiences as a child of a witch family, an initiate of both these traditions, and a member of a 'cunning lodge', with all of which he worked in the 1950s before his emigration. Most of his information is said to derive from the Elders of these two different traditions, using him as a mouthpiece, although as a working member of the groups concerned he apparently has some first-hand experience of their ways. This has permitted him to disclaim personal responsibility for the provenance, and truth, of much of the material, but it is generally presented as a seamless whole and as given fact, without any distinction as to the origins of each piece of data. Furthermore, the whole collection of assertions has been assembled over a period of twenty years, article by article. The actual communications from Liddell's Elders are said to have ceased in the early 1980s, so that what has been published since either consists of material delivered then and brought out in measured stages, or of comments upon it made later by Liddell himself. The result is that an original simple claim has grown into a complex and not entirely coherent body of alternative history.

Aspects of that history which refer to the relationship between Aleister

Crowley, Gerald Gardner, and traditional witchcraft have already been considered in Chapter 11 of the present work, with disappointingly negative results. The remainder, which may be regarded as the core of his information, may be summarized (with difficulty) as follows. The medieval European religion of pagan witchcraft became divided into distinctive national variants. There was the English, which was male-led, and had two degrees of initiation, although in another place it is said that it had no degrees but three 'rites'. There was the French, which had three 'rites', which apparently were the same as degrees, was led by priestesses, and had adopted from Saracens the customs of the fivefold kiss of adoration and the ritual use of cords. There was the Scottish, distinguished by the use of a ritual black-handled knife and the prominence of a 'Black Book' in which rites were recorded. finally, there was the Scandinavian, which was also led by women, and had the custom of initiating people across genders, so that women initiated men, and vice versa.[4]

In a personal communication Liddell has added the important information that none of these derived from a surviving ancient paganism, but represented a new religion which first emerged in fifteenth-century France and resulted from popular disenchantment with late medieval Catholicism. This account of witchcraft breaks decisively and explicitly with the Murray thesis and aligns itself more with Jeffrey Burton Russell's view of the witch religion as a Christian heresy—or even represents a softer form of that propounded by Montague Summers. In the same century, according to the same communication, Moorish initiates into Muslim magic formed secret lodges in Western Europe to undermine Christianity and introduce the adoration of Lucifer, as the indwelling divinity in the human mechanism. These allied with landowners seeking to record the secrets of traditional European cunning craft, to produce a network of 'cunning lodges' dedicated to Lucifer which persists to the present day.[5] This history has never, it seems, been revealed to the world before. It seems at first sight to sit uneasily with the assertion made at the opening of the 'Lugh' communications, that the Pickingills were hereditary priests of the pagan Old Religion from the eleventh century.[6]

At one point the material insists that hereditary covens, although divided into factions, have certain 'infallible criteria' for recognition as authentic: mandatory sexual induction into the group by the Magister or the Lady, a proscription of the use of metal at meetings, and the lack of any common book of ritual copied by each member, the Magister or his male lieutenant sometimes keeping a single coven book of rules. In another place, however, it states that sexual induction 'all but disappeared' during the eighteenth century, leaving the Magister to pass the power to candidates of both sexes. In another, it is stated as 'axiomatic' that 'English covens have always been led by men', producing the presumption that 'the Lady', who is mentioned again elsewhere as being in a leading triad with the Magister and his male deputy, is somehow of inferior status to them. In the next decade, Liddell informed readers that 'the true Hereditary tradition' consisted of rural witches passing down knowledge through families and never joining covens.[7] Such a pattern would be consistent with a single individual changing his mind about the nature of what traditional witchcraft should have been, in response to changing contemporary circumstances and growing knowledge. It is also, however, one which fits Liddell's own insistence that his data has come from different, and sometimes opposed, sources; through he always provides it in a single, dogmatic, authorial voice.

The same difficulties are found in the accounts of George Pickingill. The first, in 1974, announced that he was not merely 'England's most notorious witch', but 'acknowledged as the world's greatest living authority on witchcraft, Satanism and black magic. He was consulted by occultists of every hue and tradition who came from all over Europe, England and even America.' He himself came from a famous family of witches, practising a distinctive form of craft which amalgamated native practices with others brought by Danish and French immigrants who represented their own national traditions. The result was that in Pickingill covens 'all of our rites are conducted in toto by a woman'. George himself went on to develop the rituals further, and imparted them to nine covens which he founded, over a period of sixty years, in Norfolk, Essex, Hertfordshire, Sussex, and Hampshire. In 1980 it was added that one of his innovations had been to introduce a manual for each coven which was used by every member, the ancestor of the Book of Shadows.

In 1984 the data took a leap, when Liddell told readers that Pickingill had drawn heavily upon the rites developed by a coven of Cambridge academics in the 1810s and founded by the occultist Francis Barrett. These in turn had drawn on ancient texts, such as Apuleius. They included most of the apparatus of later Wicca, including ritual nudity, nature worship, female leadership, priority to a goddess, the fivefold kiss, Drawing Down The Moon, a Charge of the Goddess, the Legend of the Goddess, initiation through three degrees and between opposite sexes, and the use of magical cords. Pickingill was said to have found these ceremonies in the archives of the cunning lodges, to several of which he belonged. He was also, it was claimed, a famed gypsy sorcerer and learned in Saracen magic and in medieval grimoires, upon all of which he drew as well. The three officers of his covens were Priestess, Maiden, and Priest, reversing the male predominance in the Traditional English Craft; likewise, they always honoured a goddess, whereas most English covens had only recognized the horned god. A few years later, however, Liddell declared that 'the Old Craft' (apparently the same as the Traditional) 'maintains that two goddesses have always ruled over these islands'.[8]

The attitude of *The Pickingill Papers* towards Gerald Gardner shows some significant shifts. In 1974 (when Liddell was writing for a Gardnerian editor), Gardner was 'the spiritual heir of Pickingill', continuing the public revival of 'the Old Religion' commenced by the latter. Ten years later (when Liddell was more concerned to identify himself with non-Gardnerian witches), his system was a 'travesty', the result of 'perfidy' to the Hereditary Craft. By 1994 the views had become more balanced, in response to the challenge to both Gardnerians and

Liddell mounted by Aidan Kelly; Gardner was 'quite a magus in his own right', but also 'an arch-dissembler, as well as an inveterate liar'.[9]

So from where did Gardner gain his Wiccan rituals? In 1974 Liddell told readers that he developed them in collaboration with Aleister Crowley, who had been initiated into one of Pickingill's nine covens even as Gardner had much later been admitted into another. Six years later his informants had remembered that a former Magister of his own parent coven in Essex had been present when Gardner was accepted into the Hertfordshire coven which had been founded by Pickingill, and that Gerald had advanced to its third grade, becoming a Magister himself. In the New Forest coven, by contrast, 'he did not advance far'. During the 1980s it was announced that the New Forest coven used rites altered by the Fellowship of Crotona, that Gardner had only received the second 'rite' from the Hertfordshire one, and that he had received the third from another East Anglian coven, led by a Magister known to Liddell. Later the same year, the latter added that this coven had been his own one, in Essex; confusion was increased by his habit of referring to these groups as hereditary, while making clear that Pickingill's tradition was considered a heresy by hereditary witches, while he had earlier stated that these two covens were themselves in the Pickingill tradition. A year later his readers learned that Crowley and Gardner had deliberately introduced metal working tools, formerly forbidden, to render 'the ancient guardians' powerless. In the 1990s it was added that they had borrowed the use of the black-handled knife and of a common book of rules and rites from the Scottish Craft. The position of the New Forest coven was also clarified, in that it had been the Hampshire one founded by Pickingill, which had changed many of its procedures because of an influx of new members.[10]

This by no means exhausts the contributions alleged by Liddell as having been made by George Pickingill to modern magic and witchcraft. He is said to have been contacted in the 1850s by the Freemasons who subsequently founded the Societas Rosicruciana in Anglia, and heavily influenced the rituals and teachings of that body. 'Many leading Masons' got in touch with him, and two, Hargrave Jennings and W. J. Hughan, became his pupils. Jennings then collaborated with him to develop the ceremonies which became those of the Societas, and in turn influenced those of the Golden Dawn. It has been noted earlier that, according to Liddell, Pickingill was still taking pupils from the community of London ceremonial magicians in the late 1890s, and that a prominent one was Allan Bennett. Liddell has recently added the information that he gave talks at country houses, which were attended by (among others) Moina Mathers, wife of the dominant figure in the Golden Dawn, and also in Masonic temples; he 'astonished the middle-class intelligentsia for decades'. 'Eventually he outlived his usefulness as stories of "black magic" and "Satanism" tarnished his reputation.'[11]

Even this summary of Bill Liddell's assertions involves a measure of contraction and simplification, and leaves out information that he supplies on other topics, such as the news that the ancient British Druids worked with quartz crystals and the energy-bearing earth currents which became a focus of belief in the 1970s under the name of ley-lines. What is to be made of it? There are two classic means of vindicating a body of evidence. One is by independent witnesses, and the other is by supporting documentation. None of the former has emerged; indeed, at no point in the many years since Liddell first published his claims have any of the 'Elders' and 'Brethren' whose views he is supposed to articulate been discovered by anybody else. He is the sole source of testimony for their very existence. If they formed a single, tightly knit group, then this would not be a matter for comment, but by his own testimony they represent 'at least four affiliated covens' plus or including 'Elders from such disparate factions as a cunning lodge, Pickingill covens and Hereditary "companies" '.[12] Somehow all of these very different and sometimes mutually antagonistic groups have remained outside every other network of modern pagan witches, and the gaze of all other observers or researchers, and for some reason they have all persisted in using Liddell as their sole mouthpiece in an effort to preserve the secrecy of their identities. If their motivation for behaving like this is obscure, then its consequence is not; it ought to have made Bill Liddell himself into the foremost authority upon the history of Western European witchcraft and magic, able to inform modern witches, ritual magicians, and ley-hunters alike of the true origins of their traditions. That he has not in fact achieved that position, at least in Europe and America, has been because of the doubts which many people in all those groupings have expressed concerning the truth of his claims.

The situation regarding documentary evidence is no better. It was remarked in Chapter 11 that Liddell did claim to have heard of a photograph which proved the link between Pickingill and the London ritual magicians, but that this was subsequently reported to have disappeared. He cited a fifteenth-century French miniature showing a group of people worshipping a goat, as proof that the essential features of Wicca were already in place by the late Middle Ages, in the rites of the French Craft. A hostile critic might reply instantly that the reverse is true; that Liddell or his informants have invented the whole notion of a French Craft from this picture, which he or they know from its reproduction in Pennethorne Hughes's popular history of witchcraft. In fact, the original, in Oxford's Bodleian Library, does not seem to be a scene of witchcraft at all; the context is that of a libel upon the Christian heretics known as the Waldensians.[13] At times Liddell does cite tantalizing scraps of written evidence—his own 'documented family tree' in the Hereditary Craft from the eleventh century onward, the rituals of Pickingill's Nine Covens which are 'still extant' and which any 'impartial observer' should recognize as the origins of Wicca[14]—but they have never been produced.

Liddell's account of history does in fact give an immense scope for documentation. Many 'intellectuals' are said to have entered the Hereditary Craft during the seventeenth and eighteenth centuries, and intellectuals leave more papers than most people. Pickingill is said to have taught ritual magicians from both Europe and America for fifty years, and these are individuals, again, who create records. In this context, it is amazing that not a scrap of corroborative evidence survives. Satanism (which is the most extreme activity which Liddell imputes to the cunning lodges) was not actually illegal in seventeenth- and eighteenth-century England. Homosexuality was, and yet we have copious evidence of that. Prostitution and ritual magic were socially marginal and dubious activities, and both are well represented in the records. During the breakdown of censorship and ecclesiastical surveillance in the 1640s, writers compiled enormous catalogues of all the unorthodox varieties of religious and spiritual belief existing— or even rumoured to exist—in England; the most famous of these are Daniel Featley's *The Dippers Dipt*, Ephraim Pagitt's *Heresiography* and Thomas Edwards's *Gangraena*, all published in 1645–6. Secret societies such as the Freemasons rapidly attracted attention and comment. In none of these sources is there even a whisper of the widespread systems of 'cunning lodges' or covens described by Liddell. Nor, of all the educated and literate people who are supposed to have visited or entertained Pickingill, did a single one, anywhere in the world, leave any known reference to him, either in praise or condemnation. There is not even a rumour recorded anywhere of an association between metropolitan ritual magicians and an Essex cunning man. The published works of Hargrave Jennings are barren of such information; but so too are the private notebooks of Frederick Hockley, one of the founder members of the Societas Rosicruciana, which were compiled during just the period in which Pickingill is supposed to have been training his friends.[15] The world of these magicians was not a close-knit and self-protective one; rather, it was riven with feuds, from the quarrels between Mackenzie and Hockley to those which destroyed the Golden Dawn. In none of these did any participant allege an association with an increasingly disreputable village magician against another.

Some specific issues of source material now need to be addressed. Liddell's identification of an early nineteenth-century Cambridge coven as the major source of Wiccan rituals is buttressed by a citation of Montague Summers's last book, *Witchcraft and Black Magic* (1946). Here, Summers asserted that Francis Barrett had founded a sodality of academic magicians in Cambridge which had continued into recent years; this last part represented one of those dark hints of which he was so fond. Against this piece of information must be placed the view of Barrett's biographer Francis King, that there is absolutely no evidence for such an organization, and that Summers seems to have invented the whole story for reasons of his own.[16]

Much more complex is the matter of George Pickingill himself. He was virtually unknown to folklorists until the 1950s, when an author called Eric Maple made the first systematic collection of nineteenth-century witch traditions in the south-eastern quarter of Essex. His findings were published in the journal of the Folk-Lore Society between 1960 and 1965.[17] Much of his material was drawn from the village of Canewdon, standing isolated on a ridge of land between the rivers Roach and Crouch. It had a sinister local reputation, being supposed always to be the home of six evil witches, old women from both rich and poor families who rode hurdles through the air and crossed rivers in tubs rowed by feathers. Although they worked 'individually and without organisation', they were all subject to a male wizard, the 'Master of the Witches'. Resident in the village during the late nineteenth century was George Pickingill, a farm labourer whose wife was dead and who occupied a cottage with his two sons. He was 'a tall unkempt man, solitary and uncommunicative', with long fingernails and intense eyes. He practised cunning craft as a sideline to his regular work, curing warts and other ailments with chants and passes, and finding lost property; for these services he never charged money, although he expected favours such as having water fetched for him. He was reputed to be able to draw game birds from the hedgerows and to immobilize farm animals and machinery, and levied money from farmers with the threat of deploying this last skill. Village gossip had it that he flew through the air, made ornaments do the same, and could force the witches to come to their doorways or dance for him in the churchyard. He died at an advanced age in 1909, and although one of his sons inherited some of his powers, he hardly bothered to practise them. Eric Maple called Pickingill 'the last and perhaps the greatest of the wizards' of Canewdon; but as the latter is a small as well as a remote village, this was not saying much. Maple commented that Pickingill had a large catchment area of clients, but that again was to speak in very local terms, the most striking example which he provided being that the wizard was once consulted by two labourers from Dengie Hundred, which is on the opposite side of the Crouch.

Matters took a further turn when Maple combined his own field work with reading into early modern records and other folklore collections, to produce a sensational popular history of witchcraft, *The Dark World of Witches*, published by Hale in 1962. In this, he inflated the south-eastern corner of Essex into the 'witch country' of England *par excellence*, a claim which can hardly be seriously sustained. The sources used for the second chapter of this present book indicate that, whether judged by the number of cunning folk or that of reputed witches, west Cornwall, the Cleveland area of Yorkshire, and the borderland where Somerset, Dorset, and Devon meet, can all be considered to have been 'witch country' in Victoria's reign as much as any part of Essex. Maple went further, moreover, in suggesting that the Rochford Hundred (which contains Canewdon) functioned as the last reservoir of English witch traditions; of beliefs and powers which had died out elsewhere. Pickingill took his place in this picture as one of the last bearers of these. Eric Maple had effectively taken his own favourite nook of England, the scene of his own research, and given it a spurious national status. The process certainly served him well, as however much his colleagues in the Folk-Lore Society rued his abandonment of scholarly standards, the enormous public success of his book enabled him to retire to the life of a full-time writer of potboilers on witches, devils, and ghosts; he died in 1994.[18]

Maple had also, however, made Pickingill himself into a star, and this reputation continued to grow throughout the 1960s. When the American Charles

Lefebvre toured England collecting material for his own sensationalist book on witchcraft, published in 1970, he found that most of the pagan witches whom he met had heard of the old wise-man. Gossip among them now had it that Pickingill possessed an ageless body, was the last survivor of an old witch family, held Black Masses and orgies in the churchyard, made people ill by touching them with his stick, had Romany relatives, was visited by 'black magicians' from all over Europe, and was eventually killed by the sign of the cross. It is not clear whether these were the fantasies of his informants or of Lefebvre himself; but they certainly suited the latter's polemical purpose, in declaring that witchcraft was an evil which should be made illegal once more.[19] Liddell's opinion of Pickingill, which appeared only four years later, is essentially a more benign view of the same image.

Is there any independent material against which it can be checked? Such data certainly existed in the 1960s, when people still survived who had lived in Canewdon at the opening of the century and known Pickingill. One was 'Granny' Lillian Garner, who had been one of Maple's chief informants. Another was Jack Taylor, then in a retirement home at Rayleigh. In April 1967 I spent some time in the district myself, inspired by Maple's book to collect further information. What I found exactly supported his original body of material, which is hardly surprising as it was gained from the same sources, but none of the more lurid tales reported by Lefebvre. It confirmed the impression given by Maple, that Pickingill's clients, though numerous, were drawn mainly from rural south-east Essex. My only significantly new quantity of testimony was provided by Jack Taylor, whom Maple seems to have missed, and it was wholly in harmony with the latter's other evidence. I print one story here, as it so dramatically illustrates the powers of a traditional cunning man:

When my sister and I were children, we wanted to ride our pony and trap to Rochford Fair; but that day the beast just wouldn't move, no matter what we did with it. Then we suddenly saw George Pickingill staring at us with those terrible eyes of his. He came over and told us to put down the reins and not to interfere with the pony at all. Then he whispered in its ear for a few minutes and stood back and hit it; and it started off, and found its own way down the lanes to Rochford, without our needing to touch it.[20]

This, at the least, indicates that something more was at stake in 'horse-whispering' than immobilization and attraction by use of scents, as George Ewart Evans suggested.[21] Jack was born in 1888 and became a labourer alongside the Pickingills; George took an especial liking to him. He likewise did not remember that the wise-man was consulted by clients from outside the region, or left the village more than very rarely, or had any relationship with groups or individuals outside it.

This seems to be all that can at present be said about *The Pickingill Papers*. Three different possibilities can be envisaged for their future. One is that their material will positively be demonstrated to be fraudulent. This could really only be achieved by a retraction on the part of Bill Liddell himself, and such a development is most unlikely. A second is that solid evidence will be uncovered or provided to vindicate some of it; but it is hard to avoid the feeling that if any had been forthcoming then it would have been found by now. The third, and perhaps the obvious one at the present, is that when eventually Bill Liddell himself passes on, the dossier of his testimony will be closed, to remain as an article of faith among the covens which were founded by people inspired by it.

I confess that I have myself become charmed by Liddell during the course of our correspondence. Repeatedly, he has responded to often forceful criticisms with patience, modesty, and good humour, never once taking refuge in vilification or angry self-justification. I want to believe that his Brethren and elders do or did exist; although if this were proven, it would still not remove any of the difficulties which I have with the actual assertions made by them concerning the history of pagan witchcraft.

*   *   *

It is time to consider some other, less complex, claims to separate traditions. The very first to come to the attention of Wiccans was advanced by Charles Cardell, who took the name of Rex Nemorensis, the title of the divine king in Frazer's *Golden Bough*. He lived in a house with large grounds at Charlwood in the Surrey North Downs, and in a London flat from which he practised (after a fashion) as a psychologist. His personal life was unusual; in the 1930s he had made a pact with a woman called Mary, twenty years his junior, to become brother and sister, changing their respective names to Cardell by deed poll. They had lived together as siblings ever since. In mid-1958 they thrust themselves to the attention of Wiccans with an article in a magazine for occultists and spiritualists, *Light*, proclaiming themselves 'Wiccens' and inviting all genuine witches to contact them; this move was probably precipitated by the publicity recently given to Wicca in *The People*. The moment was opportune for Doreen Valiente and the group that had seceded with her from Gardner's Hertfordshire coven and were looking for new allies. They talked to Charles Cardell, who claimed that his mother had been a 'Wiccen', and had left her *athame* to him and her bracelet to Mary. Valiente and her high priest were initially impressed by him and put him in touch with Dafo, who coolly rebuffed his questions about the New Forest coven and warned Gardner of his machinations. Soon after that, Valiente herself lost faith in him, as he tried to pass off a nineteenth-century tripod as one dug up at Pompeii, and a statue of Thor as Celtic, and tried to hypnotize her.[22]

Cardell's response, in September 1958, was to declare war upon the whole Gardnerian family, informing Gardner himself grandiloquently that he would only recognize him and his initiates as real witches if they produced the traditional passwords, of which they seemed to be ignorant. In 1959 fortune provided him with a willing tool in this feud, when Olive Greene, having turned against

Gardner, became starstruck by Cardell and made him her new mentor. As said before, it is possible that she had been his agent all along, but this seems more likely to have been a fiction contrived to flatter and soothe them both. During the next few years the Cardells republished Leland's *Aradia* on their own press, gave interviews as 'Wiccens' to magazines and newspapers, advertised magical tools and ointment for sale, and put out their own periodical, *The Witch Evening News and Star*. None of this won them any friends or followers, although they did run a coven at their Surrey home for a time, and by 1962 they were sliding from view.

As soon as Gardner died, the Cardells cut their losses by publishing a venomous attack upon him, his priestess, and Valiente, including personal details about the latter, and Greene's hostile reminiscences about her initiations. It also printed the whole of her copy of the Book of Shadows, to render it public and so devalue it, and informed readers that there were no genuine witches in Britain and never had been. In 1967, apparently in the hope of earning both reputation and money, they sued *The London Evening News* for running an unsolicited article upon them as witches back in 1961. Their defence was that they had been masquerading as practitioners of witchcraft in order to explore its world and expose its falsehoods. The jury took twenty-four minutes to decide against them, and costs were awarded to the newspaper. They were financially ruined, and Charles died almost forgotten in 1976.[23]

This sequence of events makes it impossible to take the initial claims of the Cardells seriously, or even to warm to them much as human beings, but they had some impressive qualities. Charles could be an attentive and sympathetic teacher,[24] and *The London Evening News* had portrayed a ritual of theirs conducted with some style. It was held in the wood on their property, and involved six men and six women wearing robes. Charles, in a black cloak with a silver pentagram, cast the circle with a sword and blew a hunting horn to the quarters. Mary, cloaked in red, then went into trance, seated in the fork of a tree, to communicate with the spirits of the dead. At the close, Charles shot an arrow into the air, from a long bow.[25]

This scene is connected to a different claim about traditional pagan witch-craft, made by one Raymond Howard, who had worked for the Cardells as a handyman. It was he who had led the journalist to spy upon the ceremony in the wood, in vengeance after a falling out with his employers; at the trial they repaid him by describing him as being pathologically dishonest. He also showed the reporter a possession of his own, a large carved and painted wooden head, bearing horns, which he claimed had been given to him by a gypsy woman and which represented a pagan god called Atho. In the mid-1960s Howard re-established himself as the owner of an antique shop at field Dalling near the Norfolk coast, edited a short-lived magazine called *Witchcraft* and continued to show people the head, now joined by a 'rune stick', as a relic of surviving pagan witch-craft bequeathed by the gypsy; he claimed that it was 2,200 years old. In 1967, however, it was reported stolen. Doreen Valiente later recorded the details that it had been given to him in 1930, that the donor had been an old witch called Alicia French, who had lived with the gypsies and trained the young Howard in witch-craft, and that the name 'Atho' derived from the Welsh *Arddhu*, 'the dark one'.[26] There are no means of investigating this story, and it is hard to take on trust the word of somebody who would betray his employers; all that can be said with confidence is that the head existed, and that 'Atho' duly took his place as a god in some subsequent Wiccan liturgies.

A more flamboyant character than any of these emerged in 1962, when Sybil Leek first came to public attention. She was a big, jolly, dark-haired woman who ran an antique shop at Burley in the New Forest and worked for the local televi-sion station. In that year, at the age of forty, she began to promote herself as a witch, leader of a local coven, and in late 1963 the national press started to inter-view her. What really enabled her to seize the limelight, however, was the lecture-tour of the academic Russell Hope Robbins, to attack the Murray thesis. Leek, who had set herself up as a hereditary priestess of the very Old Religion which he was calling into question, informed journalists that he was a 'fool'. She attended his address to the Folk-Lore Society, equipped with her pet jackdaw (or 'familiar') Hotfoot Jackson, who sat upon her shoulder and was encouraged to croak loudly whenever Robbins said something of which she disapproved. She also barracked him directly, and the event confirmed her national profile. Journalists found her engaging—she was, after all, herself a member of the world of the mass media and understood it well. By mid-1964 they had given her the title of 'Britain's Number One Witch', and she had acquired the legal status of a company, Sybil Leek Incorporated.[27]

Her subsequent adventures will be recounted later. Here, the concern is with her claims regarding the origin of her practices. In her autobiography she stated that she came from a long family of witches, descended from one who died in 1663, and that she had inherited her great-grandmother's *athame*. Her prickli-ness towards academics appears again in her remark that she could easily have won a scholarship to university had she wished it; the fact that she actually left school after only three years had been due to the fact that her grandmother had decided to train her as a witch instead. Through this relative, she was eventually initiated into Wicca in her late teens, in an international gathering of witches in France. She had also been trained by Aleister Crowley, who was a friend of her family and regularly visited it; she later paid calls upon him, until the last year of his life. She subsequently studied with gypsies, and began to lead a coven in the New Forest in about 1950. Her practical proof of her powers as a witch lay in her remarkable abilities to heal and to divine, by magic.[28]

Only one part of this story can be tested by independent evidence, and that is her relationship with Crowley. His diaries, much cited above, cover in detail what would have been the last dozen years of it, and reveal no trace of such an acquaintance, with a family and a young woman of the sort described in some detail in the autobiography. If her training by Crowley is a fiction, then there is a strong possibility that her initiation into an international Wiccan network in about 1940 is likewise; and indeed no trace of this network has ever been encountered by other Wiccans. It might be added that, given Leek's appetite for publicity, there is something odd about the account of her running a coven for about twelve years before surfacing. Her shaky grasp of history is indicated by such references as that to 'Lady Castlereagh, the unfortunate confidant of Charles I in the sixteenth century', a line which manages in twelve words to confuse a nineteenth-century personality with a seventeenth-century one, and locate both in the wrong period. Doreen Valiente, who was well disposed towards her, noted that her 'hereditary' ritual practices seemed Gardnerian,[29] and indeed her use of an *athame* would bear this out. That is all that can at present be said about them.

A different sort of retrospective claim was made in 1989, by a woman who, like Bill Liddell, had grown up in England but emigrated. In her case the destination was Australia, and she wrote under the name of Rhiannon Ryall. The result was a book published in America, by Phoenix, and entitled *West Country Wicca*. It purported to be a description of the Old Religion as still practised in Ryall's youth in the borderland of Devon and Somerset. There, the village children were taught by the old women, the Elders, who were no longer fertile and thus not eligible to Draw Down The Moon (embody the goddess, as described earlier). When ready, they were initiated into covens in two degrees, the second being by sexual intercourse. They worshipped the horned god and the Green Lady, worked robed except for the Drawing and for initiation, and had special ceremonies for naming children and wedding couples together. Their rites were on the whole those of Gardner, differing in many minor details, and in the lack of the festivals of February Eve, August Eve, and the Autumn Equinox, and of a Book of Shadows, the sword, scourge and cords, the Charge, the Legend of the Goddess, the Witches' Rune, and the third degree. It was a simpler and more rustic variety of Wicca.

The essential problem with this picture is that the region concerned has been studied by folklorists repeatedly since the twentieth century began, most of them people native to it and rooted in it.[30] None of them recorded even a rumour of a pagan witch religion in the locality. I know it very well myself, and my circles of acquaintances there include several people with a special interest in witchcraft and magic, yet again I hear of no trace of what Ryall describes, even though she claims that it was still thriving during her youth in the 1940s, which is well within living memory of many. Spells, stories and recipes printed in her book can indeed be found in the records or present practices of the area, but not anything of the religion to which she attaches them. Embedded in her account are also a few stunning pieces of historical misinformation, such as the declaration that 'Cornwall in particular remained Pagan long after the rest of England had embraced Christianity' (p. 33). The truth is the exact opposite; that early Christianity in Cornwall is well attested in both history and archaeology—not least in its famous quantity of Celtic saints—and that it remained Christian all through the period in which most of England reverted to paganism under

Anglo-Saxon conquerors. If Ryall's claims had concerned just a coven or two, then they might have been more plausible, but to portray a widespread and deeply-entrenched folk religion stretches credulity to breaking-point. The possibility must therefore be accepted that, while in Australia, she has developed her own variety of Wicca, which she has tried here to pass off as an old tradition.

In contrast with these well-publicized stories is that of the man who wrote regularly in pagan magazines, most commonly under the name of 'Bob', until his death in January 1998. Born in 1930, he first surfaced to the view of other witches in the mid-1960s, as the leader of three covens in Warwickshire, which he claimed to descend from a different tradition to that of Gardner. In 1993 he published some information about it, starting with the story of how he had come across a coven which met in the wooded hills of Alderley Edge, Cheshire, in the early years of World War Two. His parents had a weekend retreat there, and he discovered the witches by following his mother's maid, who was one of them, as she left the house to join a meeting. He was initiated in 1943, and found the group to be part of a network which extended across Cheshire, Shropshire, and North Wales. In describing its practices, he displayed a commendable honesty in warning readers that his statements were limited by two caveats. One was that he was still bound by his original oaths of secrecy, which severely curtailed what he could reveal. The other was that he had suffered permanent brain damage (in circumstances which compel especial sympathy and respect). This not only caused partial loss of memory, but carried the possibility that he would confuse the witches with a group of ritual magicians whom he had known in the same period.

He then provided the following information: that the Alderley Edge coven differed from Wiccans in having no Book of Shadows, sword, scourge, or high priestesses and high priests, and in working with a chalice, three ritual knives, a rod and a staff, using a ninefold ceremonial kiss instead of a fivefold one, and wearing robes. Despite these characteristics, the basic form of the rites is still recognizably a Wiccan one: the sacred circle and quarters, the moon goddess and horned god, the female and male leader of the group, the ritual kiss, and the consecration of cake for a sacred meal. 'Bob' himself declared that both he and his wife had known Gerald Gardner. With this his information ends, and there are no points at which it can be checked—which adds a further poignancy to the loss of him.[31]

A better-publicized record of 'traditional' pagan witchcraft had quiet beginnings in a survey of modern ritual magic by Kenneth Grant, published in 1972. In his section about the London occultist Austin Osman Spare, whom he had known before Spare's death in the 1950s, he included the information that this very original magician had first gained his interest in sorcery from friendship with an old lady called 'Mrs Paterson', who told fortunes, made thought-forms materialize, and claimed descent from the people charged with witchcraft in the celebrated trials at Salem in 1692. Three years later (by which time Bill Liddell had published the first of his claims about George Pickingill) Grant's information had grown to include the news that Mrs Paterson was herself a witch and had a 'sister' in the craft who ran a coven in Essex. In 1994 he revealed that he had now been contacted by a surviving member of a coven which Yelg Paterson herself had led, and which had worked in various places but mostly in South Wales.[32] It is impossible to tell, in the face of this testimony, whether the latter represents a useful piece of history now just coming to light, or else a tale which has grown in the telling since 1972, and recently been appropriated and augmented by Kenneth Grant's informant.

What is clear is that the 1990s have been a particularly fertile decade for the appearance of claims concerning what is called 'Traditional' or 'Old' Craft, to distinguish it from Wicca. There are particular reasons why this should be so, which will be considered later. Here there is space to examine only one of the recent batch of unsupported assertions, chosen partly because it is fairly typical, partly because it involved the present writer, and partly because it says something interesting about the complex relationship between academics, the mass media, and modern pagan witches. It appeared at the end of 1996, when one John P. Williams, born in 1927 and a native of the large North Welsh island of Môn (Anglesey) began to publicize the survival of 'the Old Religion' there until the present. His claims were treated with most sympathy and in most detail by the Welsh-language television show *Elidir*, which devoted a programme to them in early 1997. On this, he spoke of the long and secret persistence of 'circles' of this religion in the island, meeting at prehistoric megaliths, holy wells, and sacred lakes, and casting offerings of special leaves and other natural objects in woven baskets into the latter. Their greatest festival was on the Thursday after the January full moon. Their total numbers were about 500 in his youth and about 1,200 at the present, and they were led by women, one of them elected to supreme authority by the others. These were feared as witches in the neighbourhood, and indeed they killed individuals who offended them, by blowing a poisonous mixture made from local plants at them from a squill of paper; death resulted immediately from a heart attack. He had been initiated into his circle at the age of twelve (at the end of the 1930s), by being presented with a charm to hang about his neck. The cult objects of the religion were stone heads, one of which was now in the island museum at Llangefni, and its god was Gwydion, who had three divine sons who were also venerated. It has a tradition of sacred roads, which Williams suggested were equivalents to the English ley-lines, and of communication at certain places and times between the human world and the 'otherworld'.

Elidir asked three academic scholars for their views upon his claims, all based within easy reach of Môn or the studio—experts, respectively, in modern paganism, ancient Celtic culture, and medieval Celtic literature. The first was myself; I was sent a transcript of the interview and my reactions were subsequently filmed. They were mixed, for on the one hand there was much in the picture of this religion which seemed authentically old, while other parts (such as the ley-lines) appeared to be modern accretions. The centrality of Gwydion as the cult figure argued for a modern provenance, as he was not recorded as a pagan god, but was instead the greatest enchanter in *The Mabinogion*, the group of medieval Welsh stories translated and popularized by Lady Charlotte Guest in 1849. She had effectively turned that body of tales into the Welsh national epic, so that Gwydion was one of the most popular names to be taken at initiation by modern witches who turned to Celtic literatures as their main source of inspiration. Certain other details of the information, such as the account of murders carried out infallibly and without fear of detection by blowing a toxic mixture in the victim's face, seemed a little far-fetched.

The expert on pagan Celtic religion was Anne Ross, who had pioneered the field in the 1960s and early 1970s, and been its leading authority during that period. Subsequently, she has stated her own belief that pagan traditions may have survived steadily until the present. I was, accordingly, not surprised to find that, in the programme which emerged, she emphasized the similarities between Williams's practices and those of the ancient Celts. More unexpected were the televised views of Gwyn Thomas, the specialist in medieval literature. In a letter before the filming, the director had told me that Thomas considered the group in Môn to represent 'probably a nineteenth-century development'.[33] On screen, however, he stressed the similarities between its practices and those found in early texts, and took direct issue with my point that the modern prominence of Gwydion was due to the publication of *The Mabinogion*; he told viewers that the oral tradition of Welsh folk had always preserved tales of Taliesin, Myrddin, and Arthur. This missed the point that those three figures are not Gwydion, but much more prominent in medieval and early modern Welsh tradition. Either because of inclination or of editing, at no stage did either Anne Ross or Gwyn Thomas face the obvious question of whether the archaic elements in this 'Old Religion' might not have been incorporated into a modern one as a result of the reading of works on Welsh history and archaeology; in the transcript of the interview (but not on screen), Williams himself had revealed an acquaintance with Anne Ross's own books, and mentioned that one member of his own circle at the time of his initiation was a professor at the nearby University College at Bangor. My own views were represented without distortion in the programme, and the narrator returned an open verdict. For all this, the use of actresses and actors to represent episodes in Williams's recollections lent an enhanced sense of reality to them, some of his less probable claims in the transcript (such as the possession of near-perpetual youth by members of the religion, and the miraculous power of its healing magic) were struck out of the televised version, and (perhaps above all) it appeared that the academic experts had decided by a two-thirds majority in favour of Williams's assertions.

I have no complaint to make of this, which seems to be a far better result than its opposite; that a nice old man was submitted to trial by television and condemned. What interests me more is the mechanism at stake, whereby a television company, faced with such a claim, automatically submits it to arbitration by academic experts. This is undoubtedly the swiftest and easiest response for hard-pressed staff to take, but it also embodies a traditional, top-down, view of the function of television. At no point did the production team show any interest in the views of the local people of Môn, nor even of experts in the island's folk traditions or modern culture. Once Williams had separated himself from them, by professing himself the bearer of arcane knowledge, the discussion was simply elevated above their heads, leaving them to become the recipients of knowledge along with the rest of the viewing public. Having seen the programme, I reacted by talking to the one person with whom I am personally acquainted who had grown up in Môn (in the 1950s and 1960s) and asking her if she had heard of Williams's circle. The latter immediately passed the test which Rhiannon Ryall's religion had failed, because she replied that she had indeed known about it, apparently operating very much on the lines which he had described; she thought, however, that it had been founded in the early twentieth century, as a local aspect of Welsh cultural nationalism.[34]

John Williams, then, belongs to a genuine local spiritual tradition, which differs markedly from Wicca and may well pre-date it. It would be fascinating now, and seems important, to discover what can be known of its history, of how far its past—even its twentieth-century past—is at all mythologized in the version provided for *Elidir*, and whether at any point its identity as a system of paganism became more self-conscious. If this research is to be conducted from an academic base, then University College of Wales, Bangor, would seem to be the obvious one; but not exclusively so.

*   *   *

There may well be problems here of both definition and chronology. Quite frequently in the 1990s individuals who identify with the label of 'Hereditary' or 'Traditional' witchcraft have told me that their religion has descended to them from their family or from older people known in their youth. Almost as often, they have added upon further conversation that these forebears did not apply the words 'pagan' or 'witch' to themselves, 'but their beliefs were just the same'. If enquiry goes further, those beliefs and actions usually turn out to consist of one or more of the components from which pagan witchcraft developed, such as popular charms and magical remedies, fortune-telling, ritual magic, and a mystical identification with an inherent sanctity in the natural world, or with pre-Christian monuments or literatures; but not the whole construction, as represented by Wicca and its derivatives or rivals. During the 1990s, also, pagan witches have generally become aware of the lack of any documentary evidence for their history before the 1940s and of the desirability of finding some. From time to time rumours have swept the British Pagan world of the existence of some unequivocal record, but, on enquiry, such documents always seem to vanish like wills-o'-the-wisp.

A spectacular illustration of this pattern, in an apparently public, accessible, and secure context, is provided by the Ryedale Folk Museum in the North Yorks

Moors. In 1998 Patricia Crowther published her autobiography, *One Witch's World*, and on p. 201 told readers that one exhibit which she had seen in the museum was 'a copy of a "Witch's Garter Book". The pages shown were filled with the names of witches who had received a garter and the dates upon which they were bestowed (The copy had been made by a vicar of Kirkbymoorside, and the date of the book was given as 1824).' The existence of such a manuscript seemed to me remarkable, because it appeared to be unequivocal proof of an initiatory organization of witches in the early nineteenth century (and presumably earlier than that as well). I immediately followed up the reference, only to find that no such item was now on display in the museum. Upon enquiry I was told that some of the exhibits concerning witchcraft had been replaced a few years before, to make the display 'more factual'. Those withdrawn had been placed in store, and to locate these I was reliant upon the efficiency and goodwill of the curator, Martin Watts, who excelled in both; he not only found the manuscript but made a photocopy of the whole thing for my own collection. It turned out to have itself consisted of a photocopy, of selected portions of an original handwritten book which seems to have disappeared, and represented a collection of information upon popular beliefs and customs made by somebody in that district of Yorkshire around the year 1830. Many of the entries—at least among the material which had been selected for copying—had consisted of spells and divinatory techniques. The first one was a means of divining the future of clients by applying a garter to a table of figures, once used by a local wise-woman called Peggy Duel. It seems to have been a previous curator who labelled the whole work, misleadingly, a 'witch's garter book'; but Patricia Crowther's interpretation of it appears to have been her own. At any rate, that does not match the evidence.

At times I have indeed been shown actual books of rituals owned by witches, and alleged by them to be centuries old; but with two exceptions they have either been recognizably modelled on Wiccan work composed in the 1950s or else consisted of entirely unfamiliar and unprovenanced rites written on modern paper and so impossible to date. The two exceptions were both shown to me by Andrew Chumbley, author of an intelligent modern grimoire which combines his own experiences with traditions of different groups of witches and magicians with whom he has worked.[35] He obtained permission from two of the latter to present me with copies of texts which had been handed down to them from what they believed to be traditional witchcraft. These were treasured by them, and thought to be significantly older than Wicca. On face value, I think that this belief is probably correct. One document consisted of notes originally taken by a man who was initiated into a magical group of four elderly women in the Oxfordshire village in which he lived in the years around 1940. They were part of the teachings of this group, and consisted of the various magical uses to which twenty-six of the biblical psalms could be put, sometimes consisting of the whole psalm and sometimes of a single verse. They are obviously classic Christian folk magic, of a sort recorded copiously from the early Middle Ages to the twentieth century, although the special importance of the psalms to Protestants would suggest that this use of them post-dates the Reformation. The second document had been passed from a mother to a daughter, also in about 1950, and had an alleged point of origin in South Wales. It consisted of a series of magical incantations in Latin. One was clearly the work of somebody equipped with an English–Latin dictionary but no knowledge of Latin grammar, so that words were fitted together without any use of cases or tenses. The others had been composed by an accomplished Latinist with a real ear for the music of the language and of its classical metres; and a talent for plagiarism. This person had constructed four polished incantatory poems by fitting together verses concerned with magic and enchantment, and taken from two of the most famous ancient Latin authors, Virgil and Petronius, and from a medieval song or poem, 'The Cock's Crow is the Herald of Hope'. The lines and metres were flawlessly adapted to blend the quotations into each other. The mingling of different styles and ages of the language, and the prominence of Petronius, suggests a nineteenth- or early twentieth-century date of composition.[36] The use of these two very different bodies of magical literature, in groups of modern traditional witches, indicates again the sheer richness of the inheritance of pagan witchcraft.

* * *

The methodology of this chapter has consisted hitherto of a linear approach—of trying to work backwards from individual claims and to test them from independent evidence. It may be fruitful, and just, to conclude it by substituting a lateral one; that of trying to identify those areas of England in which pagan witch traditions apparently independent of Wicca appeared early and remained strong. Three of these appear to be particularly significant. One is Cheshire, which has featured in the recollections of 'Bob' and which produced a group, 'the Cheshire Traditionals', who were especially respected among Wiccans by the 1980s as an authentic and parallel strand of the pagan Craft.[37] Another is Lincolnshire, where Charles Bowness described a pair of covens in 1979 which had been in existence for a long time, and which worked robed under the direction of a male Magister, supported by a male lieutenant carrying a blackthorn rod and a Lady who acted as his medium. Traditional groups still flourish there, and I have met a member of one who impressed me as honest and who told me that it seemed to have taken shape in 'about the 1940s'.[38]

The third region consists of the Sussex Downs. The activities of a group of witches there in 1951 have already been mentioned, and by the 1960s it was generally recognized that the oldest coven in the county (perhaps the same one) worked at Chanctonbury Ring, the ancient monument and landmark eulogized by Jacquetta Hawkes. Doreen Valiente has described this group as being of unusual antiquity, and the Ring as having been a meeting-place for covens long before the archaeological discoveries there.[39] It must be admitted that the principal living expert on Sussex folklore, Jacqueline Simpson, disagrees. In her survey of the lore connected with the place, it was associated (light-heartedly) with the Devil by 1909, and with a Druid by the 1920s, but not with witches until the 1960s, when various different covens worked there.[40] Whatever the truth of the matter, by the late 1960s the longest-established of these claimed to have existed since time immemorial. It used no Book of Shadows, nor magical tools, and worked robed except for initiations and certain other rites. It did not so much worship deities as honour the forces of the earth (called 'Her' or 'the Mother') and the sky (called 'Him'). Its main purpose was to work magic, using chants and trance states. There was no high priestess or high priest, although one woman was the most influential member, and each person took a leading role in rotation, personifying an animal associated with the season of the rite. The admission ceremony consisted of a symbolic rebirth, the laying-on of hands and the giving of words, and a scourging.[41]

What is beyond doubt is that by the early 1960s, at the latest, covens were established in many parts of England which regarded themselves as having an independent origin to Gardner's groups; in 1962 Valiente wrote that she had heard of them in Sussex, several places in the West Country and the Cotswolds, Lancashire, Yorkshire, Essex, Surrey, and the New Forest. Between them, distinctive styles of pagan witchcraft were evolving.[42] Their antecedents all remain mysterious, as does their connection with the older popular magic and cunning craft. It is certainly plain that when the profile of the latter provided in Chapter 6 of the present book is compared with the coven witchcraft of the mid- and late-twentieth century, there are obvious discrepancies. On the other hand, that same chapter emphasized the dynamism, literacy, and adaptability of cunning folk, and it would not be surprising if some had not transformed themselves rapidly and easily into pagan witches of the modern sort. I am content to leave the last word on the matter to Andrew Chumbley:

We have inherited an oral tradition of magical practice, a tradition which relates a path of historical descent to the present day and which leads onward into a changing future. As part of this tradition we accept that each generation has its own version of practice and teaching; ours is a blend of practical spell-craft and pure mysticism, combining to form what I term 'transcendental sorcery'. I can make no claims that this is what my initiator practised or indeed her own teacher. What I do claim is that each generation in our tradition has maintained certain teachings and principles of magical practice, combining the cultural elements of their time and place according to need and disposition. It is not surprising therefore that if you go back more than three generations, pre-1940, you will find vast differences [of] practice and self-representation of practice by initiates of this and other magical traditions of Britain. . . . To my mind it is needful for Vision to embrace past, present and future. The Old Craft has changed drastically since the days of [the teacher of my initiator], how much more so since the days of her own predecessors. None the less, as a path of magical practice, it has continuity and will transform according to its own power.[43]

16

THE MAN IN BLACK

I⊤ has been stated that two of the pagan witch traditions allegedly independent of Gerald Gardner were to produce particularly important recent legacies. One of these, associated with a man who published as a witch under the name of Robert Cochrane, will be the main subject of this chapter. It is perhaps most interesting to approach it through the experience of Doreen Valiente, who had contributed so powerfully to the first variety of pagan witchcraft to reach the public eye, and was now to perform the same service for others. In the late 1950s she had moved to Brighton, arguably the most culturally sophisticated of the towns on the south coast, and there she continued to train and initiate people into Wicca, as her rank as a high priestess entitled her to do.[1]

In 1962 she followed in Gardner's footsteps in another sense, by publishing a book. Like her mentor in *Witchcraft Today*, she claimed to be a disinterested scholar, informing the public of the practices of pagan witches whom she had encountered and from whom she distanced herself in print. The result was *Where Witchcraft Lives*, produced by the Aquarian Press, and remains a remarkable work in several respects. It was essentially a county study, of past and present witchcraft in Sussex, and incorporated genuine primary research into local archival records of the witch trials; something never attempted by another pagan witch before or since. This she interwove with Sussex material from the published researches of the excellent scholar of the subject, L'Estrange Ewen, in the manner of a true historian. The whole body of material, however, was interpreted strictly and explicitly in terms of the Murray thesis, which underpinned Wicca, even though Ewen's work itself called this into question; Valiente had almost made a breakthrough in writing Wiccan history, only to draw back to the party line. Another aspect of her nature was shown in her embellishment of the book with her own poetry, which had already contributed so significantly to Wiccan liturgy. Its greatest single theme was the manner in which witches could escape from the everyday world into a secret, free, and nocturnal one of joyous rites and dances and communion with nature.

A third abiding aspect of her writings was aired in this work for the first time: her willingness to credit stories of evil witchcraft in the modern world. One sentence told the reader that anybody who denied the existence of 'black magic' was 'either simply ignorant of the facts or trying to conceal the truth for his own ends'.[2] Such a confident statement, made by somebody so experienced in modern witchcraft, commands belief. It is rather a shock to find that the evidence which she then provided for it consisted of the sensational press reports cited in earlier chapters, plus the finding of chalk marks and black candle stubs in a house in Brighton by a friend of hers, and a report which she had received from a young stranger that he had accidentally stumbled on a ritual of cat sacrifice at a country pub. He had claimed that the group had forced him to drink drugged wine and swear a fearful oath of silence; neither of which had prevented him from furnishing the details to Valiente. It is not asserted here that such evidence was necessarily wrong, only noted that Doreen Valiente was instinctually inclined to accept it on face value whereas others were not.

The greatest value of her first book to a historian, however, lies in its portrayal of witch ceremonies in the very early 1960s. One was a full moon ritual held on the South Downs, similar but not identical to Gardner's practices. The leader stood before a bonfire, *athame* in right hand and pentacle in the left, and invoked the Old Ones and the elements to bless the proceedings. The group stood in a semicircle before him, and one woman presented a horn of wine to him for blessing with the *athame*, after which all passed it and drank. A ring dance followed, performed to a recorder played by an old man who kept the fire. A second ceremony was also at full moon, but upon the seashore, and seems to have been by the same coven, as again a dance was made to a recorder played by an elderly man; but this time by a single young woman wearing a necklace of silver and moonstones. A circle had been drawn upon the sand with an *athame*, for the people, and a triangle outside it, in the manner of medieval ritual magic, to contain the elemental spirits of water. A seer described the appearance of these spirits, who were invoked together with the Old Ones and the moon goddess. Three people carried working tools—a censer, and pentacles respectively bearing a pentagram and sigils representing the moon. The pentagram was presented to the quarters at the end to license the spirits to depart.

The term 'Old Ones' was not found in Gardner's rites, although it is very prominent in the fictional stories of Lovecraft. It occurred again in Valiente's description of the third ritual, as part of a toast in which it was added to the parting cry alleged of seventeenth-century Somerset witches (recently given new prominence in Graves's *The White Goddess*), 'Merry Meet and Merry Part'. A seer featured prominently in this rite as in the seashore one, and may be the same man. He was identified as an inhabitant of an old East Sussex town, who had inherited a crystal ball and a hand-written book of sigils and invocations from his parents. His other working tools included an *athame*, censer, and pentacles, and he obtained visions from the ball while seated in a chalked-out magical circle with his back to the north, surrounded by the rest of the coven standing with linked hands. All this suggests a piece of old-fashioned cunning craft carried out in a setting influenced by Wicca or by a common tradition which lay behind both Wicca and this working.

It is hardly surprising, in view of such rich description, that following the publication of the book, one newspaper, *The Sunday Citizen*, could declare

Brighton to be the centre of British witchcraft.[3] What is less clear is whether Valiente was describing more than one coven, and if not, whether she had encountered it already working in Sussex or founded it herself—unless it was actually the group with which she had seceded from Gerald Gardner. What seems reasonably clear from subsequent events is that she was still searching for a tradition of pagan witchcraft which seemed to be older and more 'authentic' than that revealed to her by Gardner. In 1964 she thought that she had found one, when mutual acquaintances introduced her to a young man whom she thought very handsome, intelligent, and plausible. He was tall and dark-haired, married to an attractive woman, worked as a designer, and lived on a modern housing estate in the Thames Valley just west of London. He told her that he practised a type of pagan witchcraft very different from that of Gardner, which had been passed to him by a member of his family. He had established a coven to carry it on, and she was subsequently initiated into this and placed all her considerable talents as composer of poetry and ritual at its disposal.[4]

The time was an exciting one for British witches in general and Valiente in particular. Gardner had died at the opening of the year, leaving pagan witchcraft bereft of its traditional leading figure even as the mass media was—as shall be discussed in the next chapter—paying it more attention than ever. Valiente had been reconciled with the old man before he departed,[5] but never again did she identify herself wholly or even primarily as one of his priestesses. Instead, she had begun to explore the apparent heritage of pagan witchcraft in general, and during the first half of 1964 she began to represent it to the public in talks and articles, although keeping clear of the national press and confining herself to local societies and occult magazines.[6] She was thus in an excellent position to benefit, unexpectedly and unintentionally, from the disaster which overtook the person who had seemed at the opening of the year to be best equipped to replace Gardner as the most recognizable public face of British witchcraft, Sybil Leek.

In February 1964, riding the crest of the wave of press attention which she had stirred up during the previous year, Leek had announced the formation of a Witchcraft Research Association under her presidency. It was almost certainly inspired by two events—the death of Gardner and the lecture tour of Russell Hope Robbins, attacking the Murray thesis—and had the double purpose of providing a national organization to unite Britain's witches and a means by which they might reclaim their own history. At this point Leek's own zeal for self-promotion backfired upon her. It had already got her evicted from her cottage and shop at Burley in November when the landlords refused to renew her leases, forcing her to resettle at New Milton on the southern edge of the New Forest. Now witches turned against her. The winter of 1963–4 was the time of the most serious and highly organized acts of ritualized vandalism against churches, by a group or groups which attacked five in Sussex and attempted a raid on one at Christchurch, Hampshire, the old setting for the Rosicrucian Theatre and now only a few miles from Leek's house. Leek claimed that signs chalked over the door by the vandals at Bramber Church, Sussex, were dedicated to her and proved that the leader of the attack was a 'black' magician whom she had healed of an illness. She did not condone the desecrations—indeed she vehemently condemned them—but some witches felt uneasy about this apparent link between her and evil magic and associated it with her other claim, to have been trained by Aleister Crowley. The latter, it has been suggested earlier, was almost certainly false, and her reading of the chalked signs may similarly have been intended to enhance her own public importance. If so, the error was tragic, for in July she was forced to resign from her newly created association because of the damage done to her reputation. Following this blow Leek emigrated to the United States, where she had found sympathetic audiences on an earlier speaking tour, and flourished there for the rest of her life. Her career as Britain's leading witch had lasted less than twelve months.[7]

By August, Doreen Valiente had been installed as her successor to preside over the Witchcraft Research Association,[8] and the latter had acquired its own magazine, *Pentagram*, edited by a friend of Cochrane, to which she contributed an approving foreword. On 3 October the association held a dinner, where she made an address calling for the identification and reunion of all the different traditions of the Old Religion which had survived in secret across the British Isles; her vision was that each represented a fragment of a whole which could now be reconstituted. Fifty witches were present; it was probably the first and last gathering in modern Pagan history where most of the men wore black ties and dinner jackets. One of them was Cochrane, who contributed an article to the next edition of *Pentagram*, reinforcing Valiente's call for a proper study of the surviving groups of pagan witches, so that the ancient mystery religion which lay behind them could be set free again, and engage with the wider society.[9]

That engagement was represented at the dinner by a sympathetic journalist, who had a personal interest in psychic phenomena and wrote the 'women's page' for a national newspaper, *The Daily Sketch*. Her pen-name was Justine Glass. She was already working on a book about modern English witches, published by Spearman in 1965 under the title *Witchcraft: The Sixth Sense—and Us*. This made it the fourth major text to appear on the subject, and one which reflected the aims and spirit of the Witchcraft Research Association. It accepted without question the identity of modern pagan witchcraft as the fragmented survival of Murray's Old Religion, and credited its practitioners with the utilization of genuine powers of extra-sensory perception and hypnosis. In Glass's words, it enabled people to 'become complete, integrated human beings'.[10] She took Valiente's line on the existence of 'black magic', suggesting that its devotees celebrated the same festivals as most witches, with the addition of the sacrifice or mutilation of animals. Indeed, Glass was more specific, stating that four 'black' covens existed in the provinces—in Sherwood Forest, the New Forest, and Brighton—and several in London, charging high entrance fees and demanding the desecration of churches and churchyards. Whether this information consisted of more than gossip, and how far it can be taken as truth, is unknown, but Glass suggested that the Church was justified in using its own spiritual powers to curse, and so fight against, such evil. In most of the rest of the book, she outlined the Gardnerian system of working, and her frontispiece showed Doreen Valiente making a toast to the horned god with Pat Crowther, the leading Gardnerian high priestess in northern England. There was also, however, considerable input from Robert Cochrane, who was introduced as a hereditary witch near the opening, displayed his own working tools in two illustrations, featured as the leader of one ritual described in the text, and actually contributed one section, interpreting medieval symbols carved upon a prehistoric standing stone in Brittany as 'a complete capitulation of Craft theology'. Valiente donated a poem inspired by an aspect of Cochrane's tradition. The book launch was a merry affair, the guests including Valiente and Patricia Crowther, and was followed by a live television programme on which Glass appeared with six witches.[11]

*   *   *

What, then, was Robert Cochrane's tradition, which was thus starting to take its place alongside Gardner's as a prominent component of modern British witchcraft? Reconstruction of it is attended by various difficulties, of which the greatest are that Cochrane himself never published more than selective and limited comments upon it, and that his wife destroyed all his private papers after his death.[12] A systematic attempt is at last being made to collate and publish the available information, but is not complete at the time of writing.[13] As a result, this chapter is dependent largely upon what has been recorded or remembered of his workings by others. The first to publish any of these was Glass, but here we encounter the problem that Cochrane afterwards boasted to friends that he had deliberately misled her.[14] It therefore seems wise to set aside most of the material with which he provided her, except at such points where it is confirmed by other information, and cite only the single ritual of his which she attended in person. This was a May Day celebration, in which Glass describes only a series of dances in a candle-lit room, interrupted when one priestess went into trance and spoke a message from the Other World.[15]

The most reliable sources of information derive from two people who worked regularly with Cochrane—Doreen Valiente herself and a Welshman called Evan John Jones, both of whom published impressions more than twenty years later. From these, with details fleshed out by other witnesses, the following picture can be built up. Cochrane was indeed young: twenty-eight years old in 1964.[16] Valiente learned that he had formerly worked as a blacksmith, which is why he had named his coven 'The Clan of Tubal Cain', after the great smith of Hebrew legend.[17] It is said that his first published work dates to 1962, when he, a friend calling himself 'Taliesin' (of whom more below), and a third person put a joint advertisement in the *Guardian* newspaper, inviting anyone interested in the ideas of *The White Goddess* to contact them at a box number.[18] What is certain is that he came to public attention on 9 November 1963, with an article in the spiritualist newspaper, *Psychic News*. This defended witchcraft as the last survivor of the ancient mystery religions of Europe, a complex and a sophisticated body of philosophy. At the time that Valiente was initiated into it, in 1964, his coven consisted of himself, his wife, and three other men; two more women joined later.[19]

The basic pattern of his rites is recognizably that of Gardner: the sacred circle, the quarters with elemental associations, the veneration of a nature-goddess and horned god, the leadership by a man and woman, and the prominence of symbolic working tools. Valiente, however, was more impressed by the differences: that his people worked in black robes instead of nude, that they never used the scourge, that they preferred to hold rituals out of doors (around a fire) if at all possible, and that the elemental correspondences were fire to east, earth to south, water to west, and air to north. He dominated the coven, as Magister, whereas Gardner's had been led by high priestesses. The emphasis upon the god as lord of death was more pronounced, and the working tools were distinctive, consisting of one knife, a cord, a cup (preferably of horn), a stone, and a forked staff known as a 'stang'. Like Gardnerians, Cochrane's coven ceremonially consumed cakes and wine, but again it did so in its own way, with different words of blessing and prefacing the dipping of knife in wine by the Magister with a rite in which the moon was reflected into the cup by use of a mirror.[20]

Jones has endorsed Cochrane's preference for outdoor rituals, but whereas Valiente has tended to stress the simpler, wilder, and more earthy nature of them (in comparison with those of Gardner), he has explained more of the quite complex spiritual system which lay behind them. Thus, some of the outdoor workings were held on a hilltop, which enabled celebrants to focus on the four winds, and on the goddess from whose castle they proceeded. Some were held in a woodland clearing and dedicated to the horned god, and others took place in a cave, representing the cauldron of rebirth, kept by the goddess in her three forms as mistress of fate. The goddess was also the mother of a young horned god, deity of truth and beauty, and behind all these deities was 'the unknown God', the primal force of creation. The 'stang' was the supreme ritual implement, representing either the goddess or one of the gods, according to how it was placed and with which ornaments. The Magister functioned as high priest and representative of the divine sacrificial king of *The Golden Bough*, with a woman, the Maid, to support him, and sometimes to stand in for him, in the name of the goddess. He also had a male lieutenant, the Summoner.[21]

All this he claimed to have been passed to him through his family, after he was initiated at the age of five. Valiente at first believed this story, but came to have serious doubts about it. For one thing, his assertion of a hereditary status remained curiously insubstantial. At one moment he told people that he had been taught by his mother; at another, that he had been initiated by a male relative. He claimed that two of his ancestors had been hanged for witchcraft, but never named them. It also rankled with Valiente that she caught him out in specific tricks, above all that she had bought him a copper dish in a Brighton antiques shop to carry the cakes for rituals, only to see it feature in Justine Glass's book as one of the ritual tools passed down through his family for centuries. She began to sense that he was making up ceremonies as he went along, and concluded that he was even more devious than Gerald Gardner. He had, in fact, become the third magus (after Gardner and Cardell) first to attract Valiente and then to alienate her.[22]

Jones, who was probably his closest friend in the coven, endorses these criticisms. He has written of Cochrane's 'attitude of trying to baffle, bewilder, and mystify everyone he met, in order to prevent them from forming a clear opinion of him. He called this technique his "grey magic", and by using it on people, he claimed that it gave him power over them. Since they were never as sure about him as he was about them, they were therefore weaker than he.' Jones noted, however, that Cochrane had another belief which might account for an element of deception in his claims; that things became real if people believed in them fervently enough, and that therefore acts which began as trickery could be turned into genuine magic.[23]

The basic form of his rituals, as outlined above, is perfectly compatible with a situation in which he had obtained some rough idea of Wicca, and then developed it in accordance with his own ideas and interests before propagating it as an inherited tradition. On the other hand, it could also be explained by the derivation of both Wicca and his practices from a common original of which no historical trace apparently remains. The influence of Graves and Frazer upon it is obvious enough in places, as is that of the medieval Welsh mythology upon which Graves had drawn at times; but all were interpreted within a novel, and highly idiosyncratic framework. The American academic James Baker has suggested that the idea for the 'stang' was derived from the forked staff described as a symbol of the Berber Dhulqarneni cult in a book by Idries Shah published in 1962, which is possible.[24] Cochrane collaborated closely with one of Britain's most famous ritual magicians, William G. Gray, an expert on the cabbala and tarot; he moved in a sophisticated circle of occultists.[25] In default of any evidence to the contrary, there must therefore be a strong suspicion that he created his own tradition—but it is a suspicion that falls a long way short of proof.

Something common to the accounts of all those who worked with him is an appreciation of his excellence as a focalizer or leader of ritual. Jones and Valiente agree upon the way in which participants felt genuinely swept up and transformed by arcane powers, and the latter has declared that they were some of the finest such experiences which she had known in all her long and varied career as a witch. Jones has recalled that 'we all knew what it felt like to be one of "Diana's darling crew"', while Valiente has recalled the wildness of the dances around the hilltop bonfires and how at one she saw a green fairy-fire spread across the ground beneath her dancing feet. Another witness has told me of how much of the magic seemed to emanate from Cochrane himself, who seemed at times in ritual like a being transfigured by supernatural energy.[26] This at least testifies to a remarkable talent; if he actually did compose all the rituals and their under-pinning ideas himself, then the word for him is surely not 'charlatan', but 'genius'.

*   *   *

Tragically, that same wildfire energy which made him so potent in the circle was in the process of spinning him off the planet, and the year 1965 saw the collapse of most of the achievements in which he had collaborated during the previous one. In the first issue of *Pentagram*, Valiente had expressed the hope that the Witchcraft Research Association would become 'The United Nations of the Craft'. The first step in the programme which she had outlined there and at its dinner was that the different traditions surviving should declare themselves and accept each other. The Association fell at this initial hurdle. In 1965 Patricia Crowther, and her husband and high priest Arnold, published their own first book, entitled *The Witches Speak*. It emphasized that witchcraft was both the Old Religion and a practical application of magic, by which initiates could use the powers of their own wills and of their deities to influence other people, for the latter's good and at their request. There was no place in their definition of it, however, for the notion that it was expressed through different traditions. Instead, they represented the Gardnerian one as normative, declaring (for exam-ple) that nude working was both the ancient way and the best, and that the wear-ing of 'monk-like' robes was 'completely out of keeping with the ancient craft'. The Crowthers also articulated a dramatically contrasting view of evil magic to that declared three years before by Doreen Valiente: 'Black Magic doesn't exist. There is no such thing as Black Witches [*sic*] and never has been.'[27]

This was abrasive stuff, but at least the provocation was implicit. It was the magazine of the Association itself, *Pentagram*, which was to be the occasion for open war. As said earlier, it was edited by one of Cochrane's friends, and largely a mouthpiece for them. Another of them, 'Taliesin', now claimed to be a member of a hereditary tradition operating in the West Country, which was Celtic and goddess-focused, and used the hallucinogenic mushroom, *Amanita muscaria*, to obtain trances. In a series of articles in the magazine between May and December he both extolled it and poured scorn on others. The first described Valiente's speech to the Association as representing 'the Gardnerian atmosphere of sweetness and light coupled with good clean fun under the auspices of a Universal Auntie'. This was probably the first time that the term 'Gardnerian' had been used in print to characterize practitioners of the oldest publicly declared form of modern pagan witchcraft; and by December the 'sweetness and light' of some of them had evaporated, at least where 'Taliesin' was concerned. Two, Arnold Crowther and a man using the pseudonym of 'Monsieur', defended the Gardnerian tradition, only to elicit an even nastier reply, in which 'Taliesin' accused it of 'maudlin sentimentality'. This level of rancour destroyed *Pentagram*, for contributions to it fell off to the point at which it folded in 1966; and the Witchcraft Research Association perished with it. Deprived of a public platform, 'Taliesin' vanished from view.[28]

Cochrane himself had been implicated in this disaster, and it rebounded on him. He had certainly encouraged his friend in these polemics. Evan John Jones has remarked that 'he seemed to want to be at loggerheads with most other occultists', and the latter certainly included the Gardnerians, against whom he fulminated in private with increasing passion.[29] He contributed a piece to the August issue of *Pentagram* which extolled his mystical interpretation of witch-craft as if it were the best and most true. This partisan hostility broke his rela-tionship with Valiente. It was already frayed by her growing suspicions of the authenticity of his tradition, and she had no respect for 'Taliesin', whom she had discovered to her own satisfaction to be a former member of Gardner's own Hertfordshire coven, living in the Thames Valley near Cochrane and with no perceptible connection with any West Country tradition. Although she no longer identified herself primarily as a Gardnerian, she still respected some of those who did, and regarded them as practitioners of a valid form of pagan witchcraft. Cochrane's ever more determined refusal to do so, and his growing authoritarianism within the coven, precipitated her withdrawal from it. In large part, these developments were a reflection of a general destabilization of his personality, and by 1966 his coven and his domestic and professional lives were all in serious disarray. He apparently committed suicide, upon Midsummer's Eve.[30]

Despite the brevity and tragedy of his public life as a witch, his legacy has been both considerable and complex. One part of it was represented by the London-based group known as the Regency—according to some, because the external human personality is a regent for the divine one within; according to others, because the group was formed to carry on Cochrane's tradition until his son came of age and could lead it, which he was never willing to do. It was formed at Hallowe'en 1966 by two former members of Cochrane's coven, one of them his Summoner. After about a year, another powerful character became influential in it; the actress and voice coach who used the name Ruth Wynn Owen, and who had been known since the 1950s as an occultist with claims to a hereditary family tradition of psychic powers. During the 1960s she founded groups of her own in London and Yorkshire, to work a tradition which she also claimed had come through her family, from Wales, and which she called 'Plant Brân'. From her own pamphlet upon it, it bears basic similarities to Wicca—the label of the Old Religion, the veneration of a god and a threefold goddess, the intent of working operative magic, the eight seasonal festivals, and the belief in reincarnation—but also differences of detail as distinctive as those of Cochrane. The Regency subsequently combined ideas drawn from the latter, with those of Wynn Owen and a fresh infusion of inspiration from the work of Robert Graves, to produce a sophisticated and fast-evolving set of rites. It also instituted the novelty of outdoor ceremonies open to anybody who wished to celebrate the seasonal festivities in a pagan manner. It lasted until 1974, and former members and guests have subsequently given birth to a number of different groups.[31]

Another direct continuity of the Cochrane tradition was provided by his friend Evan John Jones, who began in the 1990s to publish concepts and rituals which were based upon the original work of the coven but explicitly developed and supplemented in new ways. Doreen Valiente collaborated with him in one such book, adorning it with more of her own poetry and talent for devising ceremony.[32] A third tradition rooted in Cochrane's work had its origins in a correspondence which he had carried on towards the end of his life with one Joseph Wilson, who had written to *Pentagram* requesting an exchange with anyone interested in the Old Religion. Wilson went on to develop a major branch of American pagan witchcraft, the '1734 Tradition'; the figures refer not to a date but to a special value which they possess in numerology based on *The White Goddess*. Although drawing on many sources, including Wilson's own ideas, it does possess an important component derived from Cochrane.[33] During the late 1980s and 1990s other varieties of witchcraft have emerged into public view which clearly likewise embody images and concepts first associated with him.

The brief and traumatic nature of his life as a leader and teacher, the fragmented state of his legacy, and his disinclination to gather his concepts and practices into a volume, either a published one or an equivalent to the Book of Shadows, have all tended to conceal the contribution of Robert Cochrane to the history of modern pagan witchcraft. Had his career as a witch been longer and more stable, it is extremely likely that 'Cochranian' witchcraft would have become a readily identifiable strain, to compare with Gardnerian or (to anticipate) Alexandrian. Instead, the different forms of working descended from his practices have all tended to employ for themselves the labels 'traditional', or 'hereditary', which merely perpetuate the polemics of 1965. It should be emphasized that, as none of the traditions in this group has a documented history earlier than 1962—to compare with the Gardnerian base-line of 1948—for their proponents to describe themselves as 'traditionalists', and Wiccans as 'revivalists', is to deploy an unhelpful language of partisan strife. What is beyond doubt is the remarkable nature of the man who stands at the identifiable root of them. Doreen Valiente has described Robert Cochrane as 'perhaps the most powerful and gifted personality to have appeared in modern witchcraft', and she is probably better placed than anybody else to make such a judgement.[34]

17

ROYALTY FROM THE NORTH

O NE of the easier conclusions to which to leap in the history of modern pagan witchcraft is that treatment of it by the mass media was at first mainly hostile, continued as such for a long time, and then after a few decades began to display a greater sympathy and understanding, which is manifest at the time of writing. This is at best a half-truth. It can certainly be plausibly suggested that journalists became much better informed about modern witchcraft during this passage of time, and that it eventually achieved a much more secure and respectable public image; these suggestions will indeed be argued below. The actual relationship between witchcraft and the British mass media has been, however, much more complex than a simple progression from hostility to sympathy. The very first treatment of it, by Allen Andrews in 1951 and 1952, had been supportive, and only in the mid- and late 1950s did condemnation predominate, catalysed by Peter Hawkins's campaign. Even then, friendly voices were still sometimes heard in journalism; on 3 November 1958, just after the siege of her coven by hostile reporters at Hallowe'en and shortly before her exposure by *The People*, the *Daily Mail* printed an interview with Dayonis which recorded her fairly and refrained from any negative comment. During the early and mid-1960s, this tone predominated in press coverage, and Wicca seemed to be winning the battle for accurate, and even supportive, representation. The only outstanding exception was a Sunday paper especially notorious for scandalmongering, the *News of the World*, which on 1 September 1963 launched a short series on 'black magic', which it equated with pagan witchcraft and declared to be a 'terrible new menace to youth' in the style of the denunciations of the 1950s. In keeping with those, also, it cited Robert Fabian as its key 'expert'. Generally strong in rhetoric but weak in actual material, the articles instituted a tradition, maintained with a few lapses until the present, of hostility to pagan witches on the part of this particular newspaper. This attitude, it must be stressed again, was relatively rare among journalists of the time.

Such success was largely due to the efforts of the three high priestesses who represented the public face of the Gardnerian tradition in the 1960s: Patricia Crowther, Ray Bone, and Monique Wilson. Jack Bracelin sometimes assisted them, but after the bruising experiences of 1959, the Hertfordshire coven had become media-shy. The first two, in particular, gave regular interviews to local and national newspapers and radio and television programmes, and addressed universities and other societies in large numbers. In this work, Pat Crowther possessed the three considerable advantages of a supportive and eloquent husband (Arnold, also her high priest), glamorous blonde looks, and a training for the stage. Ray Bone, however, lacked all of those assets and yet accomplished just as much, scoring a notable symbolic victory in 1966 when the Oxford University Liberal Club chose her to replace the reigning Prime Minister, Harold Wilson, as an honorary member.[1] By that year, with Gardner and Cochrane dead, Sybil Leek in America, and Doreen Valiente retired once more into the background, these Gardnerian high priestesses were in a good position to lead British witchcraft between them, and to speak for it most frequently to the wider society. As they were only too aware, however, that position was already being challenged by two newcomers, who were rapidly to achieve an undoubted position as Britain's most famous witches.

One of them had been known to Patricia Crowther for a number of years— allegedly since she had received a letter from him dated 9 November 1961. This document, which has remained in her personal possession, has now been cited twice in books,[2] and although it has never been published in full, and its authenticity has apparently never been established beyond doubt, it fits well enough into the context of other records from the time. As quoted, the writer identified himself as a resident of Manchester called Alex Sanders. He stated that he had seen the Crowthers on a television programme, and had always wanted to be a witch but had never till then encountered anybody who could help him in this. He had always been interested in the occult, had had several experiences of 'the second sight', had been told by his grandmother of a witch ancestress who had lived near Mount Snowdon in Wales, and understood instinctually what Patricia Crowther had meant about the 'power' which witches could raise. He sought further help and advice from her and Arnold.

She has subsequently recorded that she invited him to visit her, which he did on three occasions between January and June 1962, and that she took a steadily reinforced dislike to him. This feeling was strengthened further in September, when Sanders accomplished a project which he had suggested to her during one of their meetings: to put Wicca onto the front page of his local newspaper, the *Manchester Evening Chronicle and News*. The resulting article was long, detailed, and illustrated with photographs. It described a ritual held on a Cheshire hillside—apparently Alderley Edge—and included an interview with Sanders himself, who extolled witchcraft as a benevolent pagan religion and claimed that although his adherence to it had broken up his marriage, he counted this loss worthwhile if it allowed him to practise it. The ceremony itself, however, was not Wiccan, but one devised by Alex and based on the Egyptian Book of the Dead, with robes woven with symbols from the *Key of Solomon*. The group which acted it out was a bunch of friends gathered for the occasion.[3]

The result was a multiple disaster for Sanders himself. For one thing, the newspaper ran the story under a headline of 'black magic', the very phenomenon from which he had tried to distinguish pagan witchcraft; he wrote a letter of protest to a subsequent issue. For another, the publicity cost him his job, at the library from which he had borrowed the copy of the Mathers edition of the *Key of Solomon* which had supplied the symbols for the robes; it was a confined volume, which he had taken without permission.[4] A third ill consequence was that the event won him the enduring hostility of the Crowthers. Their own home was in Sheffield, but they assumed a general responsibility for witchcraft in the North of England and had founded a second coven in Manchester.[5] They regarded themselves as having a commitment to quality control in Wicca; which to others, of course, could look simply like control. Furthermore, Sanders had antagonized them further by using two of Arnold's own paintings as stage-props in the ritual, apparently borrowed from a man to whom they had been entrusted for sale.[6]

In the interview, Sanders claimed that he had been an initiated witch for a year, and that he worked in a coven led by a woman from Nottingham. Neither of these facts matches up to any other contemporary evidence, but if they indicated wish-fulfilment then they were uncannily accurate, for within a year he was indeed one of a coven run by a high priestess who lived on the outskirts of Nottingham. She was called Pat Kopanski, and a long letter written by her to Gerald Gardner on 5 September 1963 represents a rare, and crucially important, example of a contemporary document surviving to clarify this tangled story.[7] She began by saying that she had just had a letter from Sanders, telling her that Gardner had sent him best wishes in response to one which Sanders had written to him. She then referred to a period which she had spent in the Crowthers's coven at Sheffield, being initiated to the first degree. She had left it because of a general low-level dislike of its ways, catalysed when Patricia accused her of being involved in Sanders's publicity stunt on Alderley Edge; in fact she had not even known of the latter until Gardner himself had sent her the press cuttings. Her relationship with Sanders himself had until now been a distant one, kept up by post and consisting of letters written by him to her. On receiving the cuttings, and quarrelling with the Crowthers, she sent Sanders a furious reply, only for him to visit her and to prove to her that the Crowthers had lied to her about the circumstances of the press article. Charmed by him, she became his friend and ally.

During the winter of 1962–3, she also found a place in another coven, based in Derbyshire around a high priestess using the name of Medea, who was independent of the Crowthers and disliked them. She and her husband had come originally from Shropshire. Kopanski asked Medea if she would initiate Sanders to the first degree, and she did so on 9 March 1963. The following day Kopanski herself was raised to the second degree and a dear friend of hers, Sylvia, was initiated also (apparently to the first). Tragedy then struck Medea, in the death of her husband, and she retired from witchcraft and moved out of the area. The trio of initiations permitted Kopanski to establish her own coven, with Sylvia as Maiden and Sanders as a member, presumably acting as high priest. Two more people had been initiated by the time of writing, and Kopanski was especially impressed by Sylvia, who was a powerful magical healer and shared with her a rapturous love of the Goddess. Their main problem was that Kopanski's sudden break with the Crowthers and the equally sudden dissolution of the Derbyshire coven had left them without all of the rituals. They hoped that they could meet Gardner for further instruction.

The letter, of course, raises as many problems as it solves. One is that it may itself represent a subterfuge, describing events which never occurred—which charge will be considered below. If it is accepted on face value, it then begs the obvious question of the origin of Medea's coven. There seems to have been no sense on the part of Kopanski and her friends that it derived from a different tradition from that of Gardner, and they equally plainly regarded him as the fount of wisdom on the subject and their natural leader. What is entirely unclear is how, if at all, Medea's Derbyshire group fitted into the Gardnerian family tree. All that the letter demonstrates beyond doubt was that at the time of writing both Kopanski and Sanders were very anxious to do so themselves.

Patricia Crowther's memoirs do something to put the letter in perspective, while also confusing matters still further. They supply the detail of how Kopanski and Sanders first met: at her own home on 28 June 1962 when the former was a member of her coven and the latter a visitor to the house. They also reveal the contents of the letter from Sanders to Gardner to which Kopanski had referred in her own, the original of which has now vanished. Gardner sent Patricia Crowther a copy of it on 27 August 1963, presumably soon after receiving it. Her précis of it exactly matches the information provided in Kopanski's letter, a copy of which was also sent to her. Having cited one of these documents and mentioned the other, Crowther then sets out to destroy their credibility. She quotes another letter which Gardner had copied to her from a lost original, on 8 June. It was from a man in the Midlands, who mentioned having known a witch who had used the name of Medea and stated that this woman had died on 12 January. She suggests that this was the same person as the one mentioned by Sanders and Kopanski, and who could not, therefore, possibly have been able to initiate anybody in March. The suggestion is possible, but unproven; it is not unbelievable that there should have been two women using the name of the great witch from Greek mythology in the same region at the same time. Crowther's reading of the letters also causes her to declare that they claim that Medea initiated both women and men, which would have been totally irregular by Gardnerian canons.[8] So it would; but the original letter from Kopanski makes no such claim. It certainly does not mention Medea as acting with a high priest, but nor does it state that she worked without one, and her husband, whose death allegedly destroyed the coven, might well have fulfilled that role. As matters stand, it seems impossible to verify whether or not Kopanski and Sanders cooked up the whole story of their respective initiations into Medea's coven. It seems an elaborate sort of ruse to employ in order to ingratiate themselves with Gardner; but such it may have been.

Similar difficulties attend the question of whether they succeeded in winning his regard. Doreen Valiente has stated categorically that Sanders visited Gardner on the Isle of Man and obtained the whole Book of Shadows from him. Patricia Crowther has asserted as firmly that Gardner rebuffed him, wanting nothing to do with him after the newspaper article.[9] It is certainly true that Crowther was more in contact with Gardner at this period than Valiente, but equally so that the opening remarks in Kopanski's letter suggest strongly that Gardner had responded favourably to the one from Sanders. If he had been angered by the press report, therefore, he may (like Kopanski herself) have been won round afterwards. This all raises a thicker question-mark over the problem of how Sanders did obtain the Gardnerian Book of Shadows. Crowther's answer is that he did so from a friend or initiate of their own, whom they had taken to visit Gardner on the island, and who had borrowed a copy of the Book from another Gardnerian witch living in Man. The trouble with the story is that no evidence is provided to connect the borrowed copy with Sanders; there is merely an assumption that he was somehow involved. At another point Crowther states that the version of the Book of Shadows later used by Sanders was peculiar to her own coven, including a spell written by herself; which seems to conflict directly with the previous positive assertion that he obtained the Book from Man.[10] All that can be confidently concluded from all these details is that if Sanders and Kopanski were anxious to be part of the Gardnerian family, the Crowthers were even more determined that Alex Sanders should be kept out of it. This determination—justified or not—is plain enough in their surviving correspondence with Gardner, in which they did their utmost to turn him against Sanders;[11] the same sources indicate as strongly that they had only a hazy idea of the movements and activities of the latter at this time. Patricia Crowther has maintained her vendetta to the present, and it is difficult to tell whether her efforts do more to clarify or to distort the history of the events in question.

Equal mystery hangs over the collapse of Pat Kopanski's coven, which seems to have occurred at some point in the winter of 1963–4. In 1967 Kopanski told a newspaper that she had disbanded it because she had become tired of the theatrical nature of the rites and concluded that they were a waste of time. The irritation in her tone, however, must have been related to the fact that she was facing hostile journalists whom Sanders had put on her trail long after he and she had parted company. She told them also that the coven had only ever consisted of the two of them plus one more man who had subsequently emigrated to Australia.[12] In that, she was clearly protecting the members, for her letter to Gardner shows that there were at least five of them; and the 'man' who emigrated was in fact Sylvia, who moved to New Zealand and Australia in the mid-1960s. There she became something of a figure in the development of pagan witchcraft in those countries, and the partner of E. W. Liddell, the public source of The Pickingill Papers.[13] Sanders later expunged all reference to the coven, and to all his activities between 1962 and 1964, from the official story of his tradition.

One conclusion can be drawn at this stage; that in most respects Sanders's early career as a witch had been catastrophic. His first foray into media exposure had rebounded painfully on him in almost every possible respect. He had secured a place in a coven—perhaps two in succession—which had collapsed. He had made bitter enemies of the most powerful and prominent witches in his region. A different personality would have given up at that stage; it is a measure of Sanders's distinction that he did not.

*　　*　　*

Not a single contemporary record of Sanders's life as a witch is known to survive from between September 1963 and June 1965; but this period represented the launch-pad for his subsequent career. It was in 1964 that he was joined by two remarkable people, both fellow Mancunians. One was a handsome, muscular man called Paul King, who worked for a rubber company and was aged twenty-one in that year. The other, about to become world-famous, was then seventeen. She was called Maxine Morris and had just left a convent school. She was tall, had long red hair which she had just dyed blonde, and was in the first flowering of an almost eerie beauty. All accounts agree that Sanders met her through his friendship with her mother, who was interested in esoteric religions, but thereafter her representation of her adolescence diverges from that of Sanders. In his memoirs, she is a shy and spiritually inexperienced girl, whose latent powers as a witch are released by his influence; in hers, she is already an initiate of a lodge of Egyptian magic, into which she has been admitted at the age of fifteen in rites set in an enormous cave system hidden under Alderley Edge.[14] In the winter of 1964–5 there took place a succession of joint ceremonies in which Sanders initiated Morris, and she initiated King, into all three degrees of Wicca.[15]

By the summer of 1965 the three of them had a coven up and running, and it emerged into public view as Sanders had done before, through a local newspaper. This time the latter was the *Manchester Comet*, and the effort paid off. To say that the witches set out to attract press notice would be unjust; in 1965, as in 1962, a calculated decision was made to take an opportunity for publicity which had arisen naturally. In this case King met a reporter for the *Comet* in a pub, and having befriended him obtained the consent of the coven to admit him to its midsummer ceremony at Alderley Edge. Photographs were taken of it there, both in the outdoor rites and in an indoor setting either before or after. Most were very coy, making recognition of individuals difficult, but there was one close-up of Morris, her head and shoulders visible above the altar as she consecrated salt and water upon it before casting the circle. A black bar was added to blot out half of her face, but her grin of wild joy was plain. The article represented her 'coming out' as a witch, although she herself has later stated that she did not give permission for either the photographs or the personal details to be obtained.[16] Referring to her only by her first name, it recounted that she had left home a few weeks before, when her widowed mother had discovered that she was a witch and refused to accept the fact.

The piece also contained apparently the first public statement of what was to become the foundation legend of Alex Sanders's tradition; that he had been initiated into Wicca by his grandmother. It gave his age as thirty-nine, and described him as having become a full-time, professional witch. It also provided details of the rituals, which were standard for the Gardnerian Book of Shadows. The tone was respectful, objective, and sympathetic, with no more talk of 'black magic'. Publication was on 23 June, and the edition of the 30th carried a follow-up article by Sanders and King, describing witchcraft as the Old Religion of nature- and goddess-worship. It also printed a letter from a reader, expressing praise and admiration for the witches; the publicity barrier had been broken.

The rewards were rapid and obvious; further interviews followed, for increasingly important newspapers, and by the autumn all this publicity had attracted recruits to the point at which Sanders could claim to have founded two more covens, and a large post poured in to them from people seeking information or—increasingly—magical healing. Again, the initiative came from the journalists themselves, who would contact the witches asking for interviews and generally be granted them. The most spectacular story given to them was an announcement in early December, that Sanders was marrying Morris according to Wiccan rites. By now the two of them were certainly a couple, and so the team of Alex and Maxine Sanders (or vice versa) was formed. For Maxine, the second half of 1965 must have felt rather like riding a whirlwind. She had been reconciled to her mother, only for the latter to die soon after and leave her parentless and estranged from the rest of the family. Neighbours had then stoned her in the street and smashed the windows of the house which had been her mother's, while she had been evicted from the flat which she had rented for herself. Strand by strand, her ties with everyday society were being cut, and she was forced further and further into the roles of witch priestess and media figure.[17]

Her wedding to Alex was not the first Wiccan marriage ceremony to be reported in the press; this distinction probably goes to that of the Crowthers, who had been united in a ritual led by Gardner himself, while also going through a legal form in a registry office. The first known Wiccan marital ceremony of all seems to have occurred in the Gardnerian Hertfordshire coven in August 1960, being that of Frederic Lamond.[18] There is no marriage ceremony in the 1950s Book of Shadows, but Gardner's own last version of the Book, preserved with his papers in Toronto, does have one. Along with distinctive Gardnerian elements, it contains two which were to become common in later Pagan wedding rites; that the couple were bound together by one hand, and that they swore to be true to each other only as long as love for each other truly remained in their hearts. The Sanders union—whether it actually occurred or was merely a story devised for the press—was the first of which details were provided in the newspapers, and was also distinguished by the fact that it stood on its own; the legal, registry office, wedding did not follow for a couple of years.

The rite, conducted by King, had in common with Gardner's version the binding of hands, but the couple were robed (Maxine in white, Alex in gold), mixed
their blood together, and jumped a fire made in a cauldron.[19] Not until the 1980s
did Wiccan marriage ceremonies begin to be standardized in anything like a
common form, and this was largely due to the influence of published texts, to be
discussed below.

By mid-1966 the couple had established themselves as some of the best-
known public representatives of witchcraft, through the visual, aural, and
printed media and public speaking engagements. In April it became known that
Metro Goldwyn Meyer had hired Alex as a consultant for a film which the
company was making on the subject—and this was too much for the
Gardnerians, who had been observing his rise to prominence with growing irritation. At the opening of May their two leading spokespeople, Ray Bone and Pat
Crowther, joined forces, with Jack Bracelin's encouragement, to denounce him
to the press as an imposter without proper initiatory credentials. It was a tactical
move of almost breathtaking folly, for it virtually forced Alex into a simple and
obvious response—that he, having been initiated by his grandmother, represented the old and authentic tradition of the Craft, whereas the Gardnerians
were practitioners of a modern and less reputable imitation.[20] From that
moment may be dated the inception of his distinctive form of pagan witchcraft,
and the two Gardnerian high priestesses—and, in view of her earlier efforts to
exclude him, Crowther in particular—may be credited with a crucial role in its
development.

No necessity, however, lay behind an even more audacious course of action
which Alex took at about this time; his assumption of the title of king of
Britain's witches. Both he and Maxine have stated that it was taken during late
1965,[21] but the claim apparently does not appear in the press reports of this
period, so that it does not seem to have become public knowledge until later.
There is equally little contemporary data for the expansion of the network of
covens which owed him allegiance. Alex later claimed that at the time when this
network offered him the name of king, it consisted of 1,623 witches. Maxine likewise subsequently stated that before their wedding they had presided over 127
covens in the North.[22] This is a steep jump from the three that were claimed by
Alex in press interviews at that time. It seems, to put things at their mildest, that
some inflation of the actual numbers is made in these retrospective sources, and
in 1967 one newspaper printed a story which may possibly indicate one means
by which the process operated. Alex had told it that he counted among his initiates a vicar of the Church of England, whom he named. When the journalist
spoke to the clergyman concerned, the latter replied with amazement that he
had merely written to Alex for information on witchcraft.[23]

What is hardly in doubt is that the network of initiates was indeed growing
steadily in the years 1965–7, and that it included what was, for pagan witchcraft
at the time, an unusually large number of young people. Gardner had never
initiated anybody younger than twenty-one;[24] Sanders reduced his minimum

age to eighteen. This was perfectly in tune with the times, in which people between those two ages were playing an ever larger part in public life, and would soon be given the vote. It also provided him with an exceptionally good-looking pool of witches upon which to draw for press photographers. His covens were available for portrayal in ritual, both nude and robed, and by 1967 pictures of them were becoming the standard public images of modern witchcraft in action.[25] Again, this achievement was part of a broader trend, whereby northern cities at this time because powerhouses of national youth culture; what Liverpool was to popular music in the mid-1960s, Manchester was to Wicca.

Alex and Maxine also followed the trend in forsaking their northern base after they had made their names, to move to London in June 1967. The former had quarrelled with and separated from Paul King, in circumstances which seem to have been particularly traumatic. King vanished completely from witchcraft and from the public view; if he is still alive (which seems very likely) and were prepared to tell his part of the story of the birth of Alex's tradition, then an invaluable addition of source material for it might be made. There were other, and probably stronger, reasons for the move, not least the simple one of a wish to be part of the life of the capital, in the first great burgeoning of the counter-culture of the time, to which Wicca, as a rebel religion, might so easily assimilate. Assimilate it did. By 1970 there were two really famous basements in Alternative London: the one from which *Oz* magazine was edited, and that from which the Sanders operated. In my own experience, most members of that counter-culture who were interested in the occult could chant their telephone number without pausing to think. Alex kept open house each week for members of the public who wished for an introductory talk on witchcraft. Those wanting magical aid, and especially healing, sought and often received a welcome without appointment; Maxine later remembered that the door-bell and telephone would ring constantly each evening until 3 a.m., and that her home was 'virtually an out-patients' clinic for drug-addicts'. She handled correspondence and telephone calls while Alex concentrated on speaking engagements; when he could not attend an event himself, he would often send a tape-recording.[26]

A remarkable illustration of the public position which the couple had achieved by 1969 was provided by a series run by the *News of the World* in the spring of that year. The newspaper had treated witchcraft only in passing after its big attempt to scaremonger in 1963—until 1967, when it printed a pair of major articles which followed the prevailing trend of the time in speaking objectively and even supportively of Wicca. One featured the Sanders, the other Monique Wilson, who was credited with powers of mediumship and healing, and whose religion was carefully distinguished from devil-worship.[27] Then, two years later, the paper changed its policy. Its journalists went out again to collect information on leading Wiccans, but this time in order to denounce them anew, as having links with Satanism and, above all, for luring young people into exploitative sexual practices. The material was, as before, short on actual evidence for those claims and long on suggestion and innuendo, but the intent was relentlessly destructive. The names and addresses of the witches chosen as targets were printed along with their photographs, and the purpose (next to that of increasing sales of the newspaper) was clearly to ruin their public reputations and so their lives.

Gardnerians were the worst affected, and the greatest victim was Monique Wilson, whose guard was obviously down after the favourable coverage which she had received from a succession of papers, including the *News of the World*. Her weak point was that she had a young daughter, whom the reporters alleged had been involved in her rites. The girl was subsequently placed under the supervision of a probation officer for three years, to ensure that such involvement did not take place. The impact upon the Wilsons can be judged by the fact that after the probation period had expired they emigrated permanently to Spain, selling the whole of Gerald Gardner's museum collection, library, and archive to a North American firm. In this manner, the biggest single deposit of evidence for the history of Wicca passed out of the British Isles. The fortunes of Alex and Maxine in this series could not have presented a greater contrast; the journalists actually *avoided* naming them, apparently as they had courted public attention so boldly that to attack them would merely augment their profile still further. Instead, the articles concentrated on exposing individuals among their initiates, but this tactic itself did not produce any conclusive results as the people concerned proved to be loyal and grateful to the Sanders and failed to provide any evidence of the exploitation which the newspaper was trying to prove to be inherent in Wicca. Maxine and Alex had taken on the sensationalist press on its own ground and defeated it, providing too large and obvious a target to be worth hitting. It was a remarkable achievement.[28]

Alex meanwhile ensured, like the Gardnerians and Cochrane before him, that he could publish his views at greater length and in a form over which he exerted more direct control—through the medium of books. His precise use of this, however, was distinctively his own. Whereas the Gardnerians, from Gerald onwards, had written their own texts, and Cochrane had preferred to appear anonymously in part of one produced by a professional writer, Sanders preferred to find trustworthy journalists who would turn him into an icon. Two of them obliged. The first was June Johns, who had published a feature on him for a light popular magazine, *Tit-Bits*, on 15 January 1966, and then wrote a biography of him, relying wholly upon his own testimony, which incorporated an interview and selections from the Book of Shadows. Brazenly entitled *King of the Witches*, it appeared in 1969. Two years later a companion volume came out from a male reporter with a very similar background, Stewart Farrar, who had begun by interviewing Alex for an identical sort of periodical, *Reveille*, in late 1969. Its title was *What Witches Do*, and it accordingly provided a range of ritual and magical practices inherited or developed by the Sanders, including paraphrases or quotations of much of the rest of their Book of Shadows. Maxine featured in both as Alex's junior partner, but in the mid-1970s she found her own voice at last, first in a series of interviews to the *News of the World* in 1975, then in an autobiography published during the following year, and finally in a study of her by a freelance journalist which came out in 1977.[29]

Stewart Farrar, moreover, initially supplied a double bonus; he was so impressed by the religion that he was portraying that he became an enthusiastic and enduring member of it. In the Sanders coven he met an intelligent, forceful and pretty young woman called Janet Owen, with whom he formed a partnership which led to the establishment of their own group in 1970. They married in 1975 and moved to Ireland in the next year, where they became another of the most influential partnerships in the history of modern witchcraft, and produced one of its major bodies of literature.[30] It was Stewart, in 1971, who gave Alex's tradition its enduring and distinctive name.[31] To term it 'Sandersian' would have been clumsy, and he coined instead the word 'Alexandrian', which both honoured its leader and made reference to the greatest city of the Hellenistic ancient world, in which the magical teachings of Egypt, Babylon, and Greece had been combined. With that title affixed to it, the new strain of pagan witchcraft may finally be said to have come of age.

*   *   *

A closer look should now be taken at this tradition, and at the two people at the centre of it. Several published descriptions survive of Alex Sanders at the apogee of his fame around 1970. June Johns noted that he was five feet and seven inches in height, with a low voice and gentle eyes, both of which could alter in ritual. Stewart Farrar met 'a slim balding man in his early forties, wearing dark glasses, answering questions in a soft Northern voice and giving a quick genuinely humorous smile every now and then'. He had 'an unmistakeable air of authority and knowledge, and his eyes are compelling, some would say disturbing'. Writers of potboilers on modern witchcraft were of course more florid. Thus, Frank Smyth:

At first sight, the gaunt features with their convex, impenetrably dark glasses are sinister in the extreme. Above the tall narrow forehead, brown hair is brushed forward in a Nero-like fashion. . . . The hands are long-fingered and sensitive and the rings on them look far too heavy. At second glance, with the blank black spectacles removed, Alex Sanders looks anything but sinister. The rather sad brown eyes and finely modelled cheekbones give him a totally fragile, vulnerable appearance, and impression which is increased when he speaks in his soft Lancashire voice.

And Eric Maple: 'There are many who regard Sanders with an unfriendly eye, but those who know him personally find it difficult to dislike him. The more perceptive become conscious of the sadness in his eyes, and his voice betrays a note of weariness with the world.'[32]

All the media interviews with him listed in the source notes to this chapter bear out these portraits. The suggestion of melancholy in some of these descriptions may have been real—at times he gives the impression of a man riding a whirlwind of attention and demands and starting to wear out—but it is balanced by characteristics which obviously came to the fore in other moods, such as sociability, vivacity, and loquacity. The reports also bring out his flamboyance, his instinctual sense of theatre and his unscrupulous appetite for fun. Those who knew him well[33] discovered other consistent traits. Like most people who have risen by their own talents, and to an insecure prominence, he seems to have been very sensitive to his treatment by others, responding with tremendous affection and kindness to those who behaved well towards him and savagely to those who did not; his sharp and witty tongue could occasionally be exercised against the latter without mercy. He showed the same duality in the manner in which he ruthlessly exploited individuals for whom he lacked liking and respect and was outstandingly generous to those for whom he had both.

Significantly, during the time in which they were together, Maxine was described mainly in terms of her physical characteristics: her beauty, her height and the dignity of her bearing, her taste for diaphanous white dresses. Indeed, she seems to have been content, on the whole, to let Alex do the talking. In the mid-1970s, as described, she claimed a voice of her own, and was made the subject of a full-length character-study. The latter portrays her as iron-willed, imperious, and capricious—an absolute monarch among her witches—and yet also possessed of a ready sense of humour.[34] The present writer can amply testify to that, and also to her shrewd wit, practicality, and charm; among Wiccan grandees (in general a convivial bunch) she is one of the most ready and entertaining of conversationalists.

Her family background and early life are relatively well known and objectively portrayed in the books written about her. Alex's life before fame as a witch, so much longer than her own, is proportionately more shadowy. He deprived historians of an invaluable cache of evidence by making a bonfire of his own accumulated collection of family records, papers, and correspondence, at an emotional moment in his later years. From a few that remain in the hands of Maxine it can be stated now that he was born Orrell Alexander Carter, in Church Road, Birkenhead, on 6 June 1926. The name of Sanders was assumed later, and finally confirmed by deed poll. He was married once before Maxine, but this first wife has never told her story.[35] The account of his past life which he gave June Johns is reasonably detailed, but some of it has to be fictional; the tale of his initiation into Wicca by his grandmother, and inheritance of the Book of Shadows from her, is contradicted by the sequence of events outlined above, and by the fact that his version of the Book is recognizably a Gardnerian one from the late 1950s or early 1960s. His statement to another author, that he had known Aleister Crowley during his boyhood, is contradicted by Crowley's diaries; but then (as must be obvious from earlier chapters) this was now a fairly standard claim for occultists to make.

When all this is said, certain themes are stated so powerfully in his recollections given to Johns that it is virtually certain that truth lies behind them: the financial insecurity of his childhood, resulting from the uneven fortunes of his

musician father Orrell, the importance of his grandmother in kindling his interest in magic and in spiritualism, the impact upon his life of occupational
misfortune and family tragedy, and the constant sense that he possessed
uncanny abilities. Maxine has confirmed two of those points. One is the prominence of the figure of his grandmother, Mrs Bibby, who was born at Bethesda
where the Snowdon massif runs down to the North Welsh coast, and was skilled
in cunning craft. The other is the centrality of spiritualism for his formative
experiences of the occult; his mother Hannah introduced him to it, and he
himself became a medium and spiritual healer famed in the Manchester area.[36]
It should be emphasized again that the man who emerged into public notice was
very much a figure of his times: a working-class northern lad who found fame
and relocated himself in a metropolitan and classless setting, by contributing to
the contemporary counter-culture with an especial but not exclusive appeal to
youth. It is significant that during the period he was a celebrity nobody seems to
have found it natural to call him 'Alexander', just as it does not seem to have
occurred to anybody to refer to Gardner as 'Gerry'.

The tradition of witchcraft which he developed with Maxine and their
covens was also distinctive in important respects. Its basic ceremonial framework was indeed that of the Gardnerian Book of Shadows, with some differences of detail; but the latter are significant. The preferred god-name was not
Cernunnos but 'Karnayna', which Doreen Valiente and the Farrars later assumed
to have been the result of a straightforward mishearing. It seems instead to have
derived from Margaret Murray's *God of the Witches*, where the Arabic for 'the
Horned One' (best known from the Koran) is given as 'Dhu'l Karnain'. The
specific reference in the Koran is to Alexander the Great, in his divine, ram-
horned, aspect, which would have made a pleasing pun for Alex; and the alteration of the name to Karnayna would have fitted the cadence of the verses in
which it substituted for 'Cernunnos'.[37] More generally, the Alexandrians
invested ceremonies with much of the 'high' ritual magic which Gardner had
declined to put into his own; the full eight different pentagrams for calling and
banishing elemental spirits, and the Qabbalistic Cross. In his teaching sessions
Alex lifted whole passages from the works of Levi and from Franz Bardon's
Initiation into Hermetics. He placed more public emphasis than other leading
Wiccans of the time upon practical magical techniques such as clairvoyance,
astral projection, thought-transference, and the use of charms, talismans, and
complementary colours, objects, and patterns. It is characteristic of him that he
especially recommended a glass of Guinness as a medium in which to scry. He
was anxious that his initiates should regard their craft primarily as a means of
achieving genuine results for themselves and others.[38]

This strong practicality, and readiness to borrow from Judaeo-Christian
sources, was made easier by the manner in which he and Maxine blurred the
boundaries of their paganism. He told Johns that Christians were welcome in
his covens if they recognized this his god was also theirs and described witchcraft to Maple as 'another form of prayer', while she claimed that her astral body

had visited the Christian heaven and found it 'useful and beautiful'.[39] All this made a striking contrast with Gardner's depiction of Wicca as a wholly separate and autonomous system of religion, and his ghosted autobiography was utterly different from the biographical accounts provided for themselves by the Sanders. Whereas Gardner had depicted himself as a scholar discovering a surviving ancient religion, they told their life stories as medieval hagiographies, full of illustrations of their psychic powers (effectively, miracles) and portraying themselves as warriors in a constant battle of good magic against bad.

In that, too, they resonated with a powerful chord in the contemporary wider culture. The notion of a conspiracy of devil-worshipping witches, secretly at work in modern society and protected by the scepticism and incredulity of prevailing attitudes, reached its cinematic apotheosis in 1968, with Roman Polanski's *Rosemary's Baby*. The enormous commercial success of this encouraged further deployment of the theme by the film industry. Between 1968 and 1974 it became embedded in a genre in which Britain at that time led the world; the popular horror movie. The company which specialized in this, Hammer, had already adapted Nora Lofts's novel *The Devil's Own* (discussed earlier) for the screen in 1966, with the title *The Witches*. There followed two adaptations of books by Dennis Wheatley, *The Devil Rides Out* (1968) and *To The Devil A Daughter* (1976). Between those came a set of Dracula films which cast the vampire as the leader of a Satanic cult. *Dracula A.D. 1972* made him the centre of a group of debauched adolescents holding rites in a ruined church. Hollywood meanwhile employed the concept of the real existence of the Devil in the modern world, working through the vulnerable or the corrupt and to be fought only with the traditional power of Christianity, in a sequence of much-viewed works, beginning with *The Exorcist* (1973) and continuing in *The Omen* trilogy. During the late 1960s, moreover, a genuine Church of Satan had developed in California, amid widespread publicity. It did not, in fact, worship the conventional Devil, but the divine force which it believed to be within humans, but its adoption of the traditional trappings of Satanism generally impressed journalists more than the subtlety of its theology, and its adherents were commonly described as 'witches'.

In the early 1970s, also, the nocturnal desecration of graveyards reached a spectacular climax, in events which have been made the subject of a full scholarly study by Bill Ellis.[40] After the spate of attacks on churchyards and churches in 1963–4, there was something of a lull, punctuated by incidents at Tottenham Park Cemetery, London, at Hallowe'en 1968, and at a burial ground at Tunbridge Wells, Kent, in the following February, which press reports interpreted as evidence of 'black magic'. Thereafter, public attention began to focus upon a single site, the famous, sprawling, decaying, and overgrown Victorian cemetery of Highgate in North London. From 1966 onward this became a regular venue for groups of young people, holding parties and seeking entertainment. One of these grew into a British Occult Society, the most prominent member of which was a youth with fragile blonde good looks and a taste for foreign au pair girls called David Farrant. During the early 1970s he recklessly courted press publicity, playing up to his growing image as a witch, magician, and necromancer. He also made enemies of the local police, most obviously with a stunt in which he sent voodoo dolls to detectives who had questioned one of his associates, warning them that he would use his magic against them if they repeated the offence. In 1973 they charged him with arson after catching him holding a 'Wiccan' ceremony around a fire in a derelict house, only to see him acquitted by the jury.

The following year they tried again, this time charging him with most of the increasingly spectacular and grisly japes with tombs and corpses which had been occurring at Highgate. Farrant had always taken care in his statements to distinguish himself from Satanists, and now claimed that he was a Wiccan, concerned with doing good to living and dead and being accused of offences actually committed by devil-worshippers. He faced a hostile judge, was pilloried in the press coverage, and had to reckon with a prominent writer on ritual magic, Francis King, who informed the court that a photograph of graffiti left on one tomb in the cemetery proved that a ritual had taken place there to restore life to a dead body. Farrant was acquitted of the most serious charges but found guilty of a set of minor offences, and gaoled for four years. He has always maintained his innocence, and Bill Ellis's careful analysis of the case suggests that he be given the benefit of the doubt—although it also demonstrates that there is actually no evidence that real Satanists ever operated in Highgate, and that the damage there may all have been the result of adolescent misbehaviour. It makes clear also how much Farrant brought his fate on himself—however unjust it may have been—by playing up to the newspapers and provoking the police. His trial remains the most sensational one involving a self-professed Wiccan in the alleged practice of the religion, and gave a very bad public impression of it.

In this context, Alex and Maxine operated in a fashion which reinforced some negative public stereotypes even while it challenged others. In 1971 they let themselves be talked by a theatrical entrepreneur into staging a show to present witchcraft to a live audience. It did not portray it as a pagan mystery religion so much as emphasize the traditional image of the craft as sorcery, the preserve of a magus who calls up spirits, or (in one press statement, 'demons'). This was an understandable way out of the problem of how to avoid divulging the secrets of an initiatory mystery tradition, but ran the risk of giving a misleading impression of what Wicca was actually about. The venture was marked by mishaps, which were gleefully reported by newspapers and have been chronicled by Doreen Valiente.[41] From the perspective of the present book, it seems more revealing to look in detail at a single case-study of the complex way in which the Sanders's stage show interacted with the press, public opinion, local communities, and other witches. The setting is Ilford, an old south Essex town which by the early 1970s had become an extension of the eastern London suburbs, and was characterized by a mixture of physical dinginess and cultural vibrance.

One aspect of the latter was represented in late 1971 by a man of thirty-three called Lee Hansen, who moved to the borough in the summer. His adult life had hitherto been marked by periods in gaol and detention centres; now he set himself up as a witch. His practices mixed Wicca, ritual magic on a vaguely ancient Egyptian model, the Chinese divinatory system of the I Ching, and the use of Scandinavian runes. In November he began to form a coven, and advertised himself by the now traditional means of giving an interview to the local newspaper, in which he claimed to be one of the most powerful practitioners of witchcraft in Britain. The immediate result was that Hansen was evicted from his lodgings. For Sybil Leek and Maxine Sanders, this had been a rite of passage on the way to international fame; for Lee Hansen, it was a blow at the start of his descent into the obscurity from which he had briefly risen. For that fortnight in which the newspaper was portraying him, however, witchcraft was brought to the attention of the people of Ilford, and this fact was almost immediately relayed to Alex Sanders. He booked a discotheque in the town for a performance of his show in the following week, and that in turn further stimulated interest in witches, at least on the part of the same local paper which, unable to send a reporter to see the performance itself, obtained an interview with Alex at his home afterwards.

He began by informing the feature-writer that to be a good witch enabled a person to become an even better Christian. He then rounded on a small pet dog which was growling in a chair nearby and told it to shut up or be turned back into a grandmother. Upon being asked to describe the performance which had been given at the discotheque, he replied that 'it was about a magician who lived centuries ago and who invoked a goddess to his circle. He tries to seduce her several times after stepping out of the circle. The magician rips off her gown and she is naked. Then she attacks him with a whip. Later she is carried out after being sacrificed.' Casting around for an alternative informed view of witchcraft, the reporter found a Yorkshireman called Owen Appleton who lived in the East End of London and claimed to be the 'Magister' of three covens there and to lead an Order of the Knights of Taliesin. Upon being asked about the nature of his beliefs and practices, he replied vaguely that he regarded himself as more of a sorcerer than a witch; his main concern seemed to be to denigrate Sanders and to insist upon the superior nature of his own strain of magic. Appleton, like Hansen, was not to enjoy a more lasting reputation, nor to leave a greater impact upon witchcraft, than that accorded by a few inches of newspaper column; but then it was through newspapers that the vast majority of the British public learned anything about the subject. In this case the readers of the *Ilford Recorder* had been treated to three weeks' worth of information, from three different sources, of which the reporters were clearly struggling to make sense. None of it really conveyed anything of the essence of Wicca as a pagan religion. Between journalistic ignorance and the opportunism, rivalry, and flamboyance of three different sets of self-professed witches, the issue had been reduced to almost complete confusion.[42]

Perhaps because of a combination of local episodes such as this, national events such as the Farrant trial,[43] and the broader cultural developments discussed above, it does seem that press coverage of witchcraft in Britain was distinctly harsher in the 1970s than it had been in the previous decade.[44] There was little emphasis upon it as a system of worship, concerned with specific deities, the world of nature, and the passage of the seasons, and a heavy stress upon it as a means of personal empowerment through invocation of supernatural forces. Even when the *Daily Star* ran a series in 1979 which included interviews with Maxine Sanders and Patricia Crowther about their work as priestesses, of the sort common in the 1960s, it was still packaged under the title 'The Devil's People'.[45]

The response of the leading Alexandrians to this problem was entirely consistent; they accepted completely the Dennis Wheatley view of the universe as divided into warring good and evil forces, and declared that they were on the side of good. When talking to June Johns, Alex had emphasized that one of his duties was to fight the bad magic practised by other witches, and that some of the latter drugged, whipped, and sexually abused their initiates. He also claimed that for a time in his youth he had himself held drunken orgies stimulated by parodies of devil-worship, to which he referred as his 'black-magic period'. He suggested that during that period he had been in contact with genuinely bad supernatural entities, and portrayed himself as a man redeemed by rededication to the powers of healing and love.[46] In the course of the 1970s Stewart Farrar published three novels which had in common the theme of good witches locked in magical battle with evil opponents who are eventually destroyed; the wicked magus in the most lurid of them is called Gerald.[47]

It was Maxine who went the furthest of all in this respect. Her autobiography concluded with the declaration that the occult world is 'a perpetual battle of white against black, of good against evil. It's really what life is all about anyway.' In the preceding pages she portrayed witchcraft as an activity which had become corrupted by a host of dabblers and self-seekers bent upon the exploitation and abuse of initiates, and doing serious harm to the latter. She also claimed that a Druid group in Britain bred children for human sacrifice, and that she herself had been present as a horrified guest in groups which had enacted ritual rape and the ceremonial killing of animals. Her most sensational first-hand account was of her rescue of a young woman who had been laid bound on an altar at a mansion in the Midlands, and seemed likely to become a victim of human sacrifice; it concluded with the warning that the group concerned was still operating. This and the most gruesome of the other assertions in the book were rehearsed in the series of interviews which she gave to the *News of the World* in the preceding year, 1975, and seemed to bear out the worst of the suspicions which that newspaper had voiced about witches and magicians in its previous attacks on them, and indeed the whole hostile stereotype of them developed since the 1950s.

Upon further enquiry, however, many of them break down. The autobiography in which they appear was ghosted, written by a *News of the World* journalist after further interviews with Maxine; she herself has never even read it. Some of the assertions, such as that about Druids (for whom Maxine herself has nothing but good to say) and the eye-witness account of animal sacrifice, are complete inventions. She does, however, stand by the story of saving the girl from apparent imminent sacrifice, despite the dreamlike quality of the whole episode which makes it seem more like an adventure on the astral plane. I asked her whether the group concerned had been Wiccans, or other kinds of witch, or pagan, or representatives of a tradition of ritual magic. She replied that they were none of the above, but just a set of rich, bored people, entertaining themselves with the trappings of ritual. This distinction may well explain why no other Wiccan—including the many to whom I have myself spoken in private and at length—has claimed to have had such experiences. As they stand, therefore, they appear to be a curiously isolated body of testimony but one which, given the importance of Maxine Sanders in the Wiccan community, must be taken seriously. What can hardly be in doubt is that these accounts must have done something to reinforce the suspicion and fear of pagan witchcraft which had been articulated since its first appearance, and which had become more rather than less pronounced in public discourse in Britain during the 1970s.[48]

*   *   *

In 1971 the Sanders acquired a retreat at Selmeston, a village tucked on the inland side of the South Downs. Between 1972 and 1973 their marriage broke down, although they remained close friends. Alex chose to stay at the Sussex house, moving a few miles east in 1975 to the coastal town of Bexhill. Maxine lived on in their old stronghold of the Bayswater flat, and continued to run a coven there, with a steady flow of initiations and of interviews, until the end of the 1970s. As that decade wore on it became increasingly obvious that by retiring from London Alex had chosen also to walk out of the blaze of public attention which he had occupied for eight years.

During those years witchcraft in Britain had continued to follow the trajectory which it had apparently held since 1950, of becoming an ever larger and more complex phenomenon. The Sanders themselves, and their initiates, had added another distinctive tradition to it. Although now overshadowed, the Gardnerians had also continued to expand their network, the South London coven known as Whitecroft, of Rae Bone's line, being particularly productive of new groups. In addition, strains of coven-based witchcraft which had no clear relationship with either continued to proliferate. The increasingly sulphurous atmosphere with which the press invested modern witches clearly only increased their glamour for many, creating a circular process. The apparent increase in media hostility was probably itself due in part to the replacement of a situation in which a closely related group of high priestesses represented Wicca to the press with one in which mavericks like Farrant, Hansen, and Appleton had become the most commonly encountered public face of witchcraft. This was, of course, precisely the development which Crowther and Bone had tried to prevent, in seeking to obtain for themselves and their kind a monopoly of public attention and credit. It was also one to which Alex had greatly contributed, by showing how that attention and credit could be seized by an outsider; but it was probably inevitable. At any rate, having held the initiative in the process for almost a decade, Alex Sanders was now relinquishing it to others.

One of these was Marian Green, a clever, practical and courageous woman who had met members of various magical groups in the 1960s, including Robert Cochrane and Doreen Valiente. From the opening of the 1970s she edited a magazine called *Quest*, as the journal of an organization which she built up with the purpose of training people to express their own personalities through the practice of magic, either individually or in groups. Almost immediately *Quest* became the mouthpiece of a kindred spirit of Green calling herself Diana Demdike, who attacked Alex's title of king and with it the whole notion that pagan witchcraft depended upon group-training, initiation, and two clearly defined deities. Instead, she declared that the old divinities had been elemental forces, whom would-be witches should encounter directly and in their own manner. In subsequent contributions, she denounced the Book of Shadows as a fossilization of witchcraft, and encouraged people to do away with all prescribed forms. She declared that most Gardnerian practices were superfluous, and urged readers to question all rules and to seek direct personal revelation from contact with the natural world.[49]

At the other end of the 1970s a former leading Gardnerian was saying the same thing, although more gently and implicitly. This was Lois Bourne, who had served as high priestess of Gardner's Hertfordshire coven in the early 1960s, and published the first of two sets of memoirs in 1979.[50] Although these paid tribute to her time as a coven member and to the Book of Shadows, and to the notion of Wicca as the Old Religion, most of her emphasis was on her preceding and succeeding life as a solitary practitioner, and testified to the richness of experience open to somebody functioning in that manner. She also, in passing, provided one half of a piece of evidence which, reunited with the other, furnishes a good example of the manner in which the wider society could be instructed in the myth of the Old Religion. In the mid-1960s the archaeologist Philip Rahtz was excavating the summit of Glastonbury Tor. One day he was visited at the work by a witch, who informed him that her people had been accustomed to engage in rites of pagan worship in this dramatic and historic place for centuries. In her book Lois Bourne revealed that the witch was herself, whose acquaintance with pagan witchcraft had been made through Gerald Gardner, and whose notions of it had been received from him.[51]

The gap between Bourne's two sets of writings was filled by a spate of publication from the most enduring heavyweight whom modern British witchcraft has yet produced, Doreen Valiente. In 1971 she had met 'Diana Dendike' halfway, by praising the sort of Craft which she had encountered with Cochrane more than that which she had known through Gardner, and agreeing that initiation was not necessary to become a witch. Between 1973 and 1978 she produced a trio of books in which she finally presented herself as a practitioner of pagan witchcraft.[52] The first introduced the public to the known story and nature of the modern version, and set it in a historical background. This background was furnished by combining popular works on the subject with those of Murray, Graves, and Frazer, to reinforce the claims of modern witches to represent a survival of ancient paganism. Having thus edified her readership, she went on to provide it with a handbook of practical magic, relying heavily on the notion of correspondences within natural phenomena. This, she made clear, was intended to show that witchcraft could be employed for benevolent purposes by anybody, and to undermine the recent 'charlatanry' of those who had set themselves up as experts. The third went further, to include a complete Book of Shadows of her own composition for those who wished to set themselves up as witches, including a ritual for self-initiation.

The emphasis laid by these three writers upon the permissibility—or even virtue—of personal exploration and independent operation, free of initiatory traditions, prescribed practices, and magisterial figures, was no doubt in part a reaction against the appearance of self-proclaimed leaders, using the mass media to promote themselves, of the sort which had become relatively common by the early 1970s. It also, however, accorded well with a more general characteristic of the decade: a glorification of individual self-discovery and self-knowledge through personal spiritual pilgrimage. Alex Sanders should have been fairly well placed to take advantage of this mood; after all, he had always emphasized the practical and experimental aspects of witchcraft and, as Stewart Farrar pointed out in a reply to 'Demdike', he had taught his initiates that occultism represented a continuous spectrum of ideas and activities upon which each coven could draw to develop a particular combination for itself.[53] In retirement, however, he had effectively lost his voice, for he had never been confident enough to publish his own words and had depended largely upon journalists and followers to promote him. Once he had withdrawn into Sussex, he cut most of his links with the former. Maxine's ghosted autobiography paid tribute to his talents, but also told some stories against him. More serious than any of this, however, were the consequences of his quarrel with the most articulate of their initiates, the Farrars, producing a breach which was complete by the end of the 1970s.

This estrangement became particularly significant when the couple, anxious to investigate the origins of Wiccan traditions, made an alliance with Doreen Valiente. The result was a pair of major works in the early 1980s which represented the first sustained textual analysis of the various recensions of the Book of Shadows. In the process the principal versions of the Book were at last all published in their entirety, with a full commentary upon the known provenance of each part and various additions made by the Farrars of their own, clearly acknowledged, composition. The exercise reasserted the identity of Wicca as a distinctive pagan religion, bound up closely with the seasonal rhythms of the natural world and the human life-cycle, honouring a goddess and god and with a claim to immemorial transmission from the past. Following the partial disclosures of the 1950s, the pirated texts of the 1960s, and the alternative liturgy of the 1970s, it provided a full public version of the central documents of that religion, and so completed the materials available to those who wished to found their own covens from scratch. It gave public credit for the first time to the major contributions made by Valiente, and established beyond reasonable doubt that the tradition taught by Alex Sanders was based upon the Gardnerian one and not inherited from his grandmother.[54]

Alex's own reaction to all these developments was both subdued and dignified. In 1979 he sent a letter to one of the two magazines most widely read by British witches, calling for unity among them, asserting that they could rightly claim authenticity for their work whether they used his version of the Book of Shadows, or the Gardnerian, or none, and declaring that he now wished to make amends for his 'past hurts' and 'many public stupidities'.[55] It was an astonishingly brave and magnanimous statement. Thereafter he continued to train and initiate people at his new base in Sussex, and made two further notable contributions to the history of his Craft. One was to develop forms of it which were more accessible to gay or bisexual men, breaking down the hostility to homosexuals which Gardner had embedded in the Book of Shadows and which was deeply implicit in the Wiccan emphasis upon gender polarity. The other was to train initiates from Continental Europe, giving Alexandrian Wicca a presence in several of its countries before his death from cancer in 1988. With that touch of flamboyant showmanship which remained with him until the end, he made his exit on 30 April, the date of one of the greatest seasonal festivals of the Wiccan calendar.

18

UNCLE SAM AND THE GODDESS

✴︎ ✴︎

Fʀᴏᴍ the 1970s onward the United States, and not Britain, has been the world
centre of modern paganism, exerting the greatest influence over its development, as over most forms of Western culture, and probably containing the
largest number of its adherents. As was indicated in the introduction, this
present book will not attempt to include a proper treatment of pagan witchcraft
in America, as the task far outruns my capabilities and probably would that of
any British academic. This chapter and the next will be largely concerned with a
different, though related, phenomenon: the impact which American ideas have
had upon pagan witchcraft in Britain. This has, it will be argued, been great
enough to turn the recent history of that witchcraft into one aspect of the
'special relationship' between the two countries. As such, this book will concentrate wholly upon those figures and works in American Pagan culture that have
had obvious influence in Britain, and ignore others that are of major importance in the United States, but have scarcely registered over here.

There is no doubt that the USA had its own indigenous pagan revival;
indeed, it produced the very first self-conscious modern pagan religion, the
Church of Aphrodite, established in Long Island in 1938.[1] It seems possible, also,
that it contained groups of witches working initiatory traditions before Wicca
was imported from England—perhaps as far back as the 1930s. The history of
these is as vexed by unsupported personal testimony, dearth of contemporary
evidence, and suspicion of later Wiccan overlays as that of 'traditional' and
'hereditary' covens in England.[2] One study of such an apparent local witch religion far exceeds all the others in importance: Vance Randolph's survey of popular beliefs in the Ozark highlands, published in 1947. The Ozarks are the only
extensive uplands in the Mid-West, and by the 1940s contained a relatively
isolated rural population among which Randolph found many traditional ideas
and practices brought over from Europe. Among them was a division between
cunning folk and suspected witches of the sort found until recently in England,
and discussed earlier in this book. One belief was that witches were initiated
into the full use of their powers in a ceremony in a graveyard at midnight,
whereby they renounced Christianity in favour of the Devil and had sexual
intercourse with an existing initiate in the presence of two witnesses, all involving being nude. Randolph added that he himself had spoken to women who had
claimed to have undergone the experience. He does not seem to have believed

them; earlier in the same section of his book, he stated that they were 'quite mad, of course'.[3] As no other research has been carried out to corroborate or refute his, it is likely that the question of whether they were repeating a fantasy or had undergone initiation into a real satanic cult will remain unanswered. It can be said that the ritual described bears some obvious resemblance to the stereotype of giving oneself to Satan found in early modern witch trials—which is generally agreed to be an imaginative construct. It is equally significant and important that from Gerald Gardner in the 1950s to Aidan Kelly in the 1990s, commentators have accepted that Randolph had uncovered a genuine witch religion.[4]

What seems beyond doubt is that all the main English branches of pagan witchcraft arrived in the United States during the 1960s and early 1970s, and that the books of Murray, Graves, and Gardner found a wide readership there during the same period. Among the readers were people versed in a range of traditions of European popular magic, imported into the country from the whole span of peoples who had supplied immigrants to it. The result was a very rich variety of strains of modern witchcraft.[5] America's most distinctive single contribution to that witchcraft, however, arose from a different phenomenon: its assimilation to the women's spirituality movement. This was based upon the simple and fundamental fact that the witch is one of the very few images of independent female power which historic European cultures have bequeathed. As the United States became the main source of modern feminist thought in general and radical feminist thought in particular, the appropriation of this image became virtually inevitable.

It was apparently first effected in 1968, when an organization called WITCH (Women's International Conspiracy from Hell) was formed in New York, with a manifesto which stated that witchcraft had been the religion of all Europe before Christianity and of European peasants for centuries after. Its persecution in the early modern period had therefore been the suppression of an alternative culture by the ruling elite, but also a war against feminism, for the religion had been served by the most courageous, aggressive, independent, and sexually liberated women in the populace. Nine million of these had been put to death. To gain freedom, therefore, modern women needed to become witches again, and could do so simply 'by being female, untamed, angry, joyous and immortal'.[6]

WITCH, however, disbanded in 1969, and not until the mid-1970s did the view of witchcraft expressed by it become embedded firmly in American radical feminism. This occurred then largely as the result of the work of two of the movement's most celebrated writers, Mary Daly and Andrea Dworkin. What they did was to repeat at length the assumptions and assertions made in the WITCH manifesto: that the witch trials had represented both the suppression of the Old Religion and the control of women, who might now regain their old power by identifying with witches. The emphasis was far more upon witchcraft as an obstacle to patriarchy, however, than as a system of religion; to Dworkin the witch trials were simply 'gynocide', while to Daly witches were women who had remained true to themselves and to sisterhood.[7] Daly also came to incorporate into her image of witchcraft a notion suggested in a booklet by two other feminist writers, Barbara Ehrenreich and Deirdre English—that the women persecuted as witches had been the traditional healers and midwives of their communities, and that their destruction had not merely been a blow against female power but against (wise and effective) natural medicine and therapies. The witch trials were therefore a victory for both patriarchy and a flawed, male-dominated, modern science. During the same period another American, Merlin Stone, took up the now long-established theory that ancient Europeans had worshipped a single great goddess, and restated it with renewed populism and polemical force. Daly incorporated these ideas in turn, declaring that the patriarchal overthrow of the prehistoric woman-centred cultures with their worship of the Triple Goddess, Maiden, Mother, and Crone, had been the beginning of the world's ills. She called upon modern women to rediscover their true being in the image of the Goddess.[8]

By 1978, therefore, the full-blown American radical feminist concept of the witch trials had been formed. According to this concept, the first grand assault of the patriarchal revolution had been the destruction of primitive matriarchy and of the supremacy of the Goddess. Witchcraft had, however, preserved remnants of Goddess-centred religion and of the former sacred status of women, not merely through the period of the historic ancient world but long after the triumph of Christianity. The early modern trials represented, therefore, the second wave of male aggression, to wipe out these remnants. In the words of Cynthia Eller, historian of American feminist spirituality:

the European witch burnings work both as a persecution history for women and as a symbol of the resilience of women and their goddess-loving religion. As a persecution history, the witch burnings intensify spiritual feminists' sense that they are anathema to the patriarchal powers; it bolsters their conviction that feminism is a question of life and death, of the very survival of women.

The figure of nine million deaths could be used to show that women had suffered more, and less justifiably, than any other group on record.[9]

How was this concept put together? Mostly, it drew upon materials which had long existed in the Western radical tradition in general and in the American one in particular. Pretty well the whole of it had been formed almost a hundred years before by Matilda Joslyn Gage, and to some extent its reappearance in the 1970s represented a rediscovery of Gage's work by later feminist writers; above all, Daly. Daly, however, also relied heavily upon Margaret Murray and Robert Graves to fill out aspects of the construct, while for Dworkin the crucial authorities were Murray (imbibed mostly through a 'pop' history of witchcraft by Pennethorne Hughes), and Gage's mentor Michelet. Both of them, plus Ehrenreich and English, drew for quotation upon the modern translation of that eccentric and rabidly misogynist work, the *Malleus Maleficarum*. Merlin

Stone tended to stress the novel and pioneering nature of her own work, and the way in which it ran counter to the religious and gender bias of most academics, but at times she acknowledged her appropriation of ideas from Murray, Jane Ellen Harrison, Jacquetta Hawkes, and Sir James Frazer.

There were, however, further reasons why this construction of the early modern witch trials should have had particularly strong resonances in the United States at this period. American academe had, as discussed earlier, become the world stronghold of the extreme rationalist interpretation of the trials—that they were the result of a manipulation of a gullible populace by an unscrupulous, power-hungry, and obscurantist Church (which, according to the bias of the writer, tended to be identified either with that of Rome or with New England Puritanism), allied with secular elites propelled by the same motives. This top-down concept of the trials was given added impetus by the drive against American Communists during the late 1940s and 1950s. The victims and opponents of these turned the prosecution of witches into the classic model for the persecution of intellectual and social dissidents, a pattern set by Bert Andrews, in *Washington Witch Hunt* (1948) and fully developed by Carey McWilliams in *Witch Hunt: The Revival of Heresy* (1950). It was given celebrated literary expression in Arthur Miller's *The Crucible* and Aldous Huxley's *The Devils of Loudon*. What feminist writers were doing was adding an essential component of gender to this model. In the process, they added an additional component of associations from the peculiarly American historization of the Nazi murder of most of the Jewish population of Europe during the 1940s, which became popularly known as the Holocaust. That a crime of such magnitude should provoke feelings of horror is perfectly natural, but it is equally plain that remembrance of it has taken different forms in different parts of the Western world. In much of Continental Europe, there has been a tendency to celebrate the many positive achievements of Jewry over the past two thousand years, and their contribution to world civilization, and to play down the great slaughter of the 1940s as a nightmarish aberration. In Israel, the latter is given full prominence, but the experiences of survivors and escapees, and of Jews who joined movements of armed resistance, are also emphasized. For a set of complex reasons, it has only been in the United States, and only since the 1970s, that full emphasis has been placed upon the sufferings of the victims, and the totality of the tragedy. In that decade it was appropriated, with considerable mass media promotion, as part of American popular culture.[10] As America turned into the most Holocaust-conscious nation on earth, the images and emotions associated with the murder of six million Jews by an ideologically inspired state machine were applied to the execution of alleged witches in early modern Europe. The figure which Gage had provided for the death-toll of those executions—of nine million—provided a symmetrical counterpart to that of the Nazi death-camps.

In all, therefore, the feminist writers were drawing upon an existing body of information and interpretation, and responding to wider cultural patterns.

Occasionally, however, they would engage in some wanton invention upon their own part. The outstanding example of this is in the work of Mary Daly, and commenced with a passage in a nineteenth-century work on epidemic disease, which dealt with the outbreaks of hysteria in southern Italy between the fifteenth and seventeenth centuries, attributed to the bite of the tarantula spider. One aspect of this hysteria was an acute longing for water, and the text reported that sufferers would sometimes throw themselves into the sea to assuage it. It appended an Italian song which purported to express this longing. Two decades after the publication of this passage, the great Victorian historian Lecky incorporated it into his history of European morality, beneath the comment that in the same period accused witches were said often to have committed suicide in prison. Daly put Lecky's two pieces of material together, to produce a lurid fantasy of mass suicides of witches who, fearing arrest, torture, and execution, preferred to walk into the sea together and drown.[11] It became one of the most compelling images of an episode of history and pseudo-history for which American feminism was now starting to employ Gerald Gardner's emotive name, 'the Burning Times'.

The identification of feminist and witch was, as Cynthia Eller has emphasized, not a specifically religious one; witches were held up for admiration as women who had refused to submit to demeaning and limiting roles, even at the cost of their lives. By the late 1970s, therefore, witchcraft had become a symbol without a practice in most feminism.[12] There was, however, an exception to this rule which existed in California and was becoming increasingly significant; it centred upon the figure of a Hungarian refugee calling herself Zsuzsanna Budapest. She was the daughter of a psychic who had taught her how to work ritual magic, had arrived in the United States in 1956, and founded the Susan B. Anthony Coven No. 1 in Hollywood at Midwinter 1971; it was named after a leading American campaigner for votes for women. Budapest was later to credit Jane Ellen Harrison as her main source of inspiration, but her work also shows signs of the influence of Leland and Gardner. She later claimed that between the foundation of the coven and her own removal to the Bay Area of central California in 1980, a total of seven hundred women had been initiated into her tradition. During the mid-1970s she simply referred to it as Wicca, but it subsequently became distinguished by the appellation of 'Dianic', after the classical goddess who features as the deity of the witches in Leland, but also had another especially relevant ancient association: of shunning men. From 1980, when Budapest published *The Holy Book of Women's Mysteries*, it became an international phenomenon.[13]

Eller has made a revealing comparison of the manifesto of the Susan B. Anthony Coven No. 1 with that of WITCH, pointing out that the former was much more religious and apocalyptic in character, calling for a revolution to usher in a new age for women. It held a view of magic as something which could be learned from a tradition, rather than simply manifested by every woman. It expressed the goals of seeking the female principle of the universe, gaining women power over their own souls, fighting patriarchal oppression, and restoring the lost golden age of prehistoric matriarchy. With this, comments Eller, radical feminism had become feminist religion.[14] It is also characteristic of the place and time that the six women who founded the coven intended it to be part or source of a movement which would transform the entire world.[15] Their practices were based upon those of Wicca—down to such details as the fivefold kiss and the set of ritual tools of which the '*athalme*' was the most important—with a heavy emphasis upon the spontaneous creation of ritual and of spells and the crucial distinction that a goddess alone was revered and only women were admitted.[16] Heavy emphasis was laid upon the persecution of 'the Burning Times', as an attempt 'to rid the land of the last vestiges of nature religions'.[17] The essence of female spiritual liberation, according to Budapest, was 'to abide in an all-female energy environment, to read no male writers, to listen to no male voices, to pray to no male gods'.[18] Her tradition was a spiritual expression of radical feminist separatism.

There was an obvious considerable difference between the concepts of witchcraft represented by any of the writers discussed above and the Wicca imported from England. The use of the image of the witch made by WITCH, Daly, and Dworkin had, as said, no necessary religious dimension at all, and moreover depended upon the concept that witchcraft was something inherent in all women, or at least something to which all liberated women could relate. Budapest had crossed these ideas with the structure of Wicca, but the result defined a specifically female mystery religion which still made a stark contrast with the English one, in which the genders were balanced in creative polarity. The tension between the two was to be brilliantly resolved by another Californian, Miriam Simos, who took the pen-name of Starhawk. In the mid-1970s she was an unpublished writer struggling—without success—to have a novel accepted. Ten years later she was the most famous witch in the world.

*   *   *

Starhawk was a feminist who had been trained by Gardnerians and then initiated into one of the home-grown American strains of pagan witchcraft which had absorbed some material from Wicca, the Faery, taught by Victor Anderson. She had also made contact with Zsuzsanna Budapest.[19] At Hallowe'en 1979, in San Francisco, she published a book called *The Spiral Dance*,[20] which represented her own views of what witchcraft should be. It subsequently became the best-selling work on the subject yet written, and replaced *Witchcraft Today* as the model text for would-be witches. Two outstanding qualities of it ensured that it would do so. The first was simply that Starhawk is a writer of remarkable talent; it is difficult to take notes from her books without copying entire sentences, so perfectly are her thoughts expressed and so marked is her genius for aphorism. A clear and melodious prose is enhanced by an underlying passion of feeling, so that her sentences seem to heave with emotion. The second tremendous virtue of the book was that it reworked the whole image of witchcraft to give it a new significance, and respectability, to a modern liberal reader. She showed how the coven could be turned into a training group in which women could be liberated, men re-educated, and new forms of human relationships explored which were free of the old gender stereotypes and power structures. She reinterpreted magic in terms of human psychology, as a set of techniques for self-discovery, self-fulfilment, and the realization of true individual human potential. To her, it was a means of exploring and releasing the positive qualities within people, effacing the negative and dissonant, and placing humans in the best possible relationships with themselves, with each other, and with the planet. The Craft was made at once a form of therapy, art, and creative play. Starhawk suggested that a network of covens after this pattern could be a potent mechanism for the transformation of society into a healthier and more sustainable model.

One of the most remarkable aspects of this refashioning is that it employed materials which by then were wholly traditional to modern pagan witchcraft. It incorporated wholesale the concept of witchcraft as the Old Religion of Europe, re-emerging after centuries of persecution, and embodying features of prehistoric matriarchy; Starhawk declared that her own Faery tradition went back 'to the Little People of Stone Age Britain', and that the eightfold pattern of festivals had been established in the neolithic. Her writings drew heavily on those of Graves and Merlin Stone. She celebrated the Craft as a joyous, life-affirming, tolerant path, 'a religion of poetry, not theology', which yet demanded responsibility. She reinforced the primacy of the goddess in the duotheism of Wicca, and made her a truly transcendent deity: 'we connect with Her; through the moon, the stars, the ocean, the earth, through trees, animals, through other human beings, through ourselves. She is here. She is within us all.' So was she then merely a name for the life-giving forces within us? Starhawk both affirmed and denied this: 'I have spoken of the Goddess as psychological symbol and also as manifest reality. She is both. She exists, *and* we create her.' At the same time she restated the importance of the horned god, transforming his image into that of the ideal New Man, strong and virile but tender and loving, acknowledging the primacy of the female: 'She is Mother and Destroyer; He is all that is born and is destroyed'; 'He has no father. . . . His power is drawn directly from the Goddess.'[21]

If her approach to the literal existence of deity could be positively described as subtle and open-ended and, less generously, as evasive, then her attitude to magic was of a piece. She defined it at the opening of the book as 'the art of sensing and shaping the subtle, unseen forces that flow through the world'. So did operative magic literally work? Here Starhawk fulfilled once more her own dictum that her religion was one of poetry, by cocooning the issue in imagery which at once illuminated and obscured it. Magic 'opens the gates between the conscious and unconscious minds'. 'The primary purpose of magic is connection. The universe is a fluid, ever-changing energy pattern, not a collection of fixed and separate things. . . . Its warp and weft are energy, which is the essence of magic. Energy is ecstasy. . . . No drug can take us so high, no thrill pierce us so deep, because we have the essence of all delight, the heart of joy, the end of desire. Energy is love, and love is magic.' So how, then, do spells work? 'To cast a spell is to project energy through a symbol.' 'Spells also go one step further than most forms of psychotherapy. They allow us not only to listen to interpret the unconscious but to speak to it, in the language it understands.' Magic is 'part of the discipline of developing power-from-within'. 'Emotion is a strobe light; directed energy is a laser beam.' To Starhawk, morality should be inherent in magicians because the energy projected affects the projector even more than the target: 'If you send out healing energy you are healed in turn. If you hex or curse, you yourself are cursed.' Clearly there is some kind of system of physics at work here, but whereas Starhawk explores or celebrates the effects, she remains very vague about the structure; indeed, she glorifies the vagueness, for 'Magical systems are highly elaborated metaphors, not truths.' Is there, then, any actual truth in what she is saying? Apparently it doesn't matter: 'The value of magical metaphors is through them we identify ourselves and connect with larger forces; we partake of the elements, the cosmic process, the movements of the stars'.[22]

This was, indeed, not theology but poetry, and great poetry at that. Starhawk was holding out to her readers the prospect of knowing divinity themselves by becoming at one with the cosmos: 'Feminist religion does not make false promises . . . while we can't stop the earth from turning, we can choose to experience each revolution so deeply and completely that even the dark becomes luminous'.[23] The tendency of *The Spiral Dance* was not to explain or to instruct so much as to intoxicate; which doubtless explains much of its tremendous popularity. It also, however, provided a practical guide to ritual, including an initiation rite which combined elements from the Gardnerian first- and second-degree rituals, and so furnished materials for readers who wanted to found their own covens after reading the book; and it has indeed been popularly credited with having inspired the foundation of hundreds of groups of witches all over Europe and North America. During the course of the 1980s Starhawk followed it with two more works, which have also achieved a wide circulation in both continents, even though their sales and impact have not matched the tremendous achievement of *The Spiral Dance*. Both have always been recognized as responding to the changing climate of radical culture, as the emphasis upon self-exploration and deep cultural change prevalent under the liberal governments of the 1970s gave way to a much more embittered and confrontational activism in the face of the aggressively right-wing regimes which partnered each other in the United Kingdom and United States in the 1980s.

In 1982 came *Dreaming the Dark*, in which Starhawk applied her notion of witchcraft to direct political action, examining in detail the implications of one for the other.[24] Magic had now become 'the art of evoking power-from-within and using it to transform ourselves, our community, our culture, using it to resist the destruction that those who wield power are bringing upon the world'.[25] In applying it in this fashion, Starhawk drew more heavily and explicitly upon history, and especially upon the American radical feminist image of 'the Burning Times', which she characterized as a persecution which 'shattered the peasants' connection with the land, drove women out of the work of healing, and imposed the mechanist view of the world as a dead machine'.[26]

In a long appendix, she provided her own history of the witch trials, which attempted to give the feminist portrait of them an enhanced scholarly rigour. She still held Christian institutions fundamentally to blame—'Church history is a history of persecution'—but also provided a socio-economic basis for the trials. In her reading, they were the result of the disruptions caused by a shift from landed to mercantile wealth, the enclosure of the common land, and the rise of the medical profession, all involving an attack on nature-related religion and a shift to a mechanistic model of the earth. None of this was based upon any actual research; rather, it was inferred from a blending of selective secondary sources, in which feminist polemicists such as Daly, Ehrenreich, and English took their place alongside old-fashioned Marxist historians such as the Englishman Christopher Hill, whose work was discussed earlier. Had Starhawk carried out any actual archival work to prove her assertions, she would have needed to show that the trials were driven on by new-style merchant capitalists, enclosing landlords, and professional doctors, or else took place especially in areas affected by the processes which they represented.[27] An examination of the results of actual research into the witch trials will be made later in this book; for the time being it may be helpful to anticipate by stating that there is absolutely no evidence to support either possibility, and much against. Starhawk had suggested what *should* have happened in early modern Europe, while making no attempt to discover what really did happen.

The main thrust of *Dreaming the Dark*, however, lay not in its excursion into history but in its deployment of the same inspiring rhetoric which had characterized *The Spiral Dance*, to drive home the message that by using magic we can change ourselves for the better, and by changing ourselves we can change the world. This was also the message of the third book, *Truth or Dare* (1987), in which the hardening of tone and darkening of mood went further, a measure of the bitter experience which Starhawk had now undergone, of arrest and imprisonment for non-violent direct actions undertaken in protest against installations where nuclear weapons were made or stored.[28] The book reasserted all her old themes, of witchcraft as 'the old, pre-Christian tribal religion of Europe', of magic as 'liberation psychology', of the need to reclaim the ' "mother-times" when power-over did not exist'. It restated the essential unity of all life and the real existence of the 'Goddesses and Gods', sensed primarily as forces within human beings: 'they are the mysteries that cannot be known intellectually but only through ourselves becoming what we are.' Conversely, it much more explicitly identified women, witches, Jews, black people in predominantly white cultures, and tribal peoples in the modern world as having undergone a common experience of dispossession and disempowerment. It also concentrated more upon a mythology of ancient matriarchy and its brutal destruction than a history of the witch trials, and upon rituals which built group solidarity than those which led to individual transformation.[29]

The shift of tone between the books was only one of degree, but it was significant. In *The Spiral Dance* Starhawk had proclaimed that 'The Goddess liberates the energy of our anger' and that 'Anger becomes a connecting force that spurs honest confrontations and communications with others'; but it was not, on the whole, an angry book. During the writing of the early parts of *Dreaming the Dark*, she 'was haunted by visions of annihilation', and it was the 'despair' which attended these that pushed her into her 'obsession' with the witch trials. Later in that work she proclaimed that 'We come out of jail angry, on fire with rage that does not retreat.' This is the informing emotion of *Truth or Dare*. At one point in this book, she describes how she led a workshop in which participants 'cried and screamed and raged as we named the wrongs we felt our country was committing in our name'. At another she tells of a visit to Stonehenge upon which 'I found myself crying with deep, deep, sobs and saying to myself "It's been so long! It's been so long!" As if I could feel the earth was so hurt and damaged, and the spirit of the stones was there to help us and yet it felt weak and tired and overwhelmed by the magnitude of the destruction.'[30]

In this there was something of a paradox. Throughout her books, Starhawk emphasized the essential unity of all beings and the interrelation of all life, while celebrating the virtues of tolerance and diversity. In all these respects she drew sharp contrasts with established monotheistic religions. In *The Spiral Dance* she denounced opposed dualisms, and the 'Righteousness Syndrome', according to which 'there is One Right True and Only Way—Ours!—and everybody else is wrong'. *Dreaming the Dark* spoke of the need to 'fight' such dualisms, and with them notions of the 'Chosen Few' and of salvation and damnation. At the same time a central message of this book was a call to resist powers which were threatening to destroy the world, and would do so unless society was converted to a better way of thinking.[31]

This is also the central message of *Truth or Dare*, but with much more livid emotion, and the tensions and conflicts in her world-view are proportionately more obvious. She bids readers realize that we are 'made of the same materials as the stars, the eucalyptus, the jaguar and the rose'. Yes, but are we also made of the same materials as the louse, the tapeworm, and the typhoid bacillus, and if so are we still justified in destroying such life-forms for our own comfort and survival? In a universe of complete magical interconnection, should we still pluck weeds out of our gardens and vegetable patches, and if so, with what justification? This is exactly the sort of basic question that Starhawk's 'religion of poetry' never confronted. Her political stance raises questions of its own. There is no sense in *Truth or Dare* that Starhawk is living in a democracy, in which issues can be settled by public debate and the election of new governments. Instead, she articulates a view of the mass of society as brainwashed by malign power-holders into the perpetuation of their lethally destructive systems of rule.

She calls upon her readers to 'rage at the culture-created demon, the monster thought form of authority'. To her, hope lies only in the actions of small groups who spread the word and example of resistance and alternative ways of being, and so attempt to renew the older and better relationships with the world, following in the footsteps of the early modern witches, 'the dedicated few who preserved remnants of the Old Religion'.[32] The distinction between a 'Chosen Few' and a 'dedicated few', between a world-view based on salvation and damnation and one which regards all-out resistance to the established authorities as necessary to save the world from destruction, is at best a fine one.

The power of these three books lay in Starhawk's remarkable talent for rhetoric, an emotional and lyrical outpouring intended to sweep people away without making them think too hard about all the implications of the images which they were absorbing. In the process she had accomplished two projects. One was to present witchcraft as a system of personal and group development, self-discovery, and liberation, for women above all. The other was to link it to a particular brand of activist politics. The fusion was accomplished by inculcating a belief in a specific reading of history and prehistory. Just as she blurred answers to the questions of whether magic literally worked or deities really existed, so she seemed to tell readers that it did not ultimately matter whether her view of the past was objectively correct; the crucial issue was that belief in it would make the world a better place. Consistently she lauded emotion, sensation, myth, and imagination, over reason, intellect, science, and scholarship. If her readers absorbed the beliefs which she was trying to inculcate, and then encountered rational objection to them, then the response which her writings seemed to recommend was blind rage.[33]

This analysis has paid full tribute to Starhawk as a creative and original writer; but she was not an original thinker. Her genius lay in taking ideas from others and combining and applying them in powerful new ways. Some of the influences upon her thought have been cited above. Others whom she acknowledged included Gerald Gardner, the philosopher Ivan Illich, and the radical feminist writer Adrienne Rich. In addition she came increasingly to recognize the importance of her childhood of devout Judaism and of her identity as a Jew. By *Truth or Dare* she was explicitly equating the social experiences of Jews and witches, and whereas other Pagan writers had excoriated the whole Judaeo–Christian tradition as the source of the earth's problems, she was now inclined to regard criticism of Judaism as anti-Semitism while retaining the animosity towards Christian Churches. She held Jewry up for admiration as an example of the capacity of the dispossessed to survive because of spiritual bonds, and her view of politics as a struggle carried on by small groups of right-thinking people amid hostile and ignorant masses drew at least partly upon this example.[34]

It could be argued, however, that it is at least as significant that she is a Californian, and that her attitudes represent in some aspects an application to witchcraft of what Alston Chase has termed 'the California Cosmology'. This was a development of nineteenth-century American pantheism, that strain of thought associated with writers such as Ralph Waldo Emerson, Henry David Thoreau, and John Muir, which relied on the twin propositions that God is good and that God's spirit is inherent in the natural world. To these thinkers, therefore, humanity could be brought closer to God by a closer relationship with that world.[35] Chase has traced the evolution of their ideas through the early and mid-twentieth century, in the work of Ansel Adams, Joseph Wood Krutch, William O. Douglas, Charles Lindeburgh, Sigurd Olson, Aldo Leopold, Rachel Carson, and David Brower, who all agreed upon the immanence of the divine in nature, as part of a sacred interconnected wholeness in the cosmos. All agreed likewise with the other major proposition of the pantheists: that humans had somehow become disconnected from nature, which needed to be defended from them as well as venerated.

What Chase has characterized as the Californian contribution to these ideas was made in the 1970s by academics based at Berkeley, Stanford, and the various divisions of the University of California—above all by Fritjof Capra, Theodore Rozak, Bill Devall, George Sessions, Willis Harmon, Marilyn Ferguson, Jacob Needleman, Alan Watts, Gary Snyder, John Rodman, Paul Shepherd, Rod Nash, Ray Dasmann, J. Peter Vajk, and William Everson. In Chase's exuberant prose, these writers

buzzed around a flowerbed of exotic religions and an eclectic cornucopia of offbeat ideas—Tao, Hinduism, Zen Buddhism, Hua-Yen Buddhism, Mahayana Buddhism, Gnosticism, Manicheanism, Vedanta, Sufism, Cabbalism, Spinozistic Pantheism, Whiteheadian metaphysics, Heideggerian phenomenology, Jungian archetypal symbolism, Yoga, biofeedback, Transcendental Meditation, psychedelic drugs, self-awareness exercises, psychotherapy, pre-Socratic philosophy, the 'Inhumanism' of Robinson Jeffers, Gandhian pacifism, animism, panpsychism, alchemy, ritual magic.[36]

It was a mixture ideally suited to the social circumstances of California at the time; a remarkable mixture of races and cultures, situated geographically between East and West, North and South, equipped with tremendous wealth and opportunity in general, and with a superbly funded university system in particular. Out of this brew a number of beliefs were developed, which united all these writers: that everything in the cosmos is both sacred and interconnected; that humans in the developed world have become tragically—perhaps fatally—disconnected from the cosmos; and that reconnection is possible given only a change of attitudes. The relevance of all this to Starhawk's thought is obvious, but she was particularly and explicitly influenced by an application of it made by a feminist trained in Marxist polemic and based at Berkeley, Carolyn Merchant. She provided a history of attitudes to nature in the early modern period, which linked the triumph of the new, world-controlling and exploiting, science, to specifically male attitudes and languages.[37]

Also important to Starhawk's cosmology was a separate, and equally dramatic, development of pantheistic thought made during the same period, and which first surfaced within the American Pagan community itself. It was articulated by the Church of All Worlds, an organization of radical mystics who had originally been inspired by science fiction and utopian writings, and was formed in Missouri in 1967. The moving spirit was Tim (later Otter) Zell, who propagated his ideas through the late 1960s and early 1970s in the Church's newsletter, which grew into the periodical *Green Egg*. It established the identity of modern paganism as a response to a planet in crisis, and its spiritual core lay in the concept of the earth as a single, divine, living organism. The mission of Pagans, according to this concept, was to save 'her' by a transformation of the values of Western society. Zell's definition of magic was 'the science you don't understand, the science you take for granted.'[38]

It is very likely that this view of the earth, although rooted in some ancient ideas and images, and very obviously derived from the modern notion of female divinity as inherently related to the natural world, was given final impetus by the first photographs of the planet from space, in the 1960s. The scientific concept of the biosphere was greatly enhanced by these, and proved integral to a parallel development of the idea of earth as an entity, which took place in the world of professional science. It was associated with one particular scientist, James Lovelock, who, in 'a flash of enlightenment' at Pasadena, California, in 1965, came up with the idea that 'life defines and maintains the material conditions needed for its survival', and that the whole planetary ecosystem 'seemed to exhibit the behaviour of a single organism—even a living creature'. Lovelock was an Englishman with a home base in a Wiltshire chalkland village, who had set himself up in the previous year as a freelance biochemist, developing instruments and performing other services for private companies, later including giants such as Shell Oil and Hewlett Packard. He published a brief note on his idea in 1968, in *The Proceedings of the American Astronautical Society*, and another as a letter to *Atmospheric Environment* in 1971. It began to become widely known among scientists in the mid-1970s, as he teamed up with the biologist Lynn Margulis, gave a series of papers at conferences and published them in *Tellus* and *Icarus*, and found a charismatic name for the theory. It was suggested by a friend, the novelist William Golding, and echoed the ancient Greek myth of a female divinity who represented the earth: 'the Gaia hypothesis'.

By this time Lovelock had already begun to demonstrate what became his characteristic habit of veering by sudden turns between science and poetry. In an interview in 1975, he expounded his theory as a matter of biochemistry, and agreed that it was as yet unproven. At the same time he referred in emotional language to the threat posed to the planetary eco-system by modern Western civilization, urging his fellow humans to 'make peace with Gaia on her terms and return to peaceful co-existence with our fellow creatures'. At another moment he suggested that a defence of 'Gaia' might actually awaken her, 'giving her awareness of herself and the universe'.[39] In 1979, the year of *The Spiral Dance*, Oxford University Press published Lovelock's first book on the subject, *Gaia: A New Look at Life on Earth*. Designed to appeal to a wide audience, it embodied the double aim which Lovelock had already expressed: to convince readers that the planet functioned like a living entity, and to suggest that it would be good for the world if everybody believed this.

During the 1980s the 'Gaia hypothesis' became common knowledge, and was taken up with particular ease and enthusiasm by people whose attitude to religion and ecology was already predisposed to it—most of all, of course, modern pagans in both America and Europe. In 1988 Lovelock wrote a second book to restate his theory and to review reactions to it. He retained the ambiguity which had been present in the hypothesis from the beginning; he began by speaking of 'the largest living organism, Gaia', went on to suggest that this organism was the sum of processes operated 'automatically and unconsciously' by all living beings within it, and later defined it as 'alive in the sense that it was a self-organizing and self-regulating system'. There is a distinction between a single living organism, an entity which is the sum of millions of living organisms, and a self-regulating system, which could be a mechanism; but Lovelock never explores it. Instead, when looking at the moral implications of his theory he was concerned with two other issues.

One was the fact that his hypothesis had so far failed to win general acceptance from the community of professional scientists, and had indeed met with heavy criticism. Lovelock's reaction was not to point out to his readers precisely what these criticisms had been, and to meet them one after another, but to issue a blanket condemnation of all scientists who were not, like himself, freelance: 'they have traded freedom of thought for good working conditions, a steady income, tenure and a pension.' To Lovelock they were victims of 'a finicky gentility' or 'creatures of dogma'. By contrast, he saw himself as 'a radical scientist' or 'a scientist-hermit', able to perceive truths denied to his more blinkered colleagues.[40]

The other issue that he tackled consisted of the religious implications of his hypothesis. He declared that he had no personal faith in God but was touched by those who did have, and then moved suddenly and astonishingly to seeming to declare that a faith in Gaia had the same status: 'it is otiose to try to prove that Gaia is alive. Instead Gaia should be a way to view the Earth, ourselves, and our relationships with living things.' In a fascinating illustration of the crosscurrents, or circularity, in which ideas can move, he now drew explicitly on American feminist spirituality (specifically on the writer Charlene Spretnak), to announce that until the coming of patriarchal Indo-European invaders destroyed 'the peaceful, artful, Goddess-oriented culture in Old Europe', humanity in general had accepted his hypothesis, and been the better for it. He mourned the fact that city-dwellers 'seemed to have lost interest in the meaning of both God and Gaia', and then announced that 'God and Gaia . . . are not separate but a single way of thought'. He concluded that 'I am too deeply committed to science for undiluted faith; equally unacceptable to me spiritually is the materialist world of undiluted fact.' It was, indeed, the essence of Lovelock's hypothesis that he had always spoken at one moment with the authority of science, and at the next with the rhetoric of a priest; at one moment it was a matter of biochemistry and, at the next, of faith. Just as Starhawk had seemed to do in the fields of prehistory and history, so in his own, Lovelock appeared to be saying that whether or not his suggestions were true, it would be best for people to believe them.[41]

The confusions inherent in this position became still plainer in his third book on the subject, published three years later. He was now prepared to admit much more specifically that his theory 'may be wholly or partially in error', and his condemnation of established science was less wholesale. His critics were still 'pedantic and wrong', but now identified as 'a small but vociferous group'. He was no longer a 'radical' or a 'hermit', but 'an old-fashioned scientist'. His qualifications of his concept of Gaia were likewise more elaborate. He began by saying that he was 'well aware . . . that the Earth is not alive in the same way as you or me, or even a bacterium', and that his usage of the term 'is more like that of an engineer who calls a mechanical system alive to distinguish its behaviour when switched on'. He asserted that 'the goal of zero pollution' is 'pointless and unobtainable', and suggested that ozone spots, greenhouse gases, and acid rain might possibly be 'no more than harmless growing pains of the planet'. He next described Gaia as 'a control mechanism for the Earth—a self-regulating system like the familiar thermostat of a domestic iron or oven'. He denied that Margulis or he had 'ever proposed that planetary self-regulation is purposeful'.[42]

On the very next page, however, his language started to change again. He suggested that 'the Earth might in certain ways be alive—not as the ancients saw her, a sentient goddess with purpose and foresight—more like a tree'. Lovelock was, therefore, still very clearly distancing himself from pagans, ancient and modern, but does not seem to have realized that to most people a thermostat and a tree are two very different entities; one is alive in a basic sense that the other is not. Likewise, a mechanical system, switched on by an engineer, cannot be said to have 'growing pains'. Lovelock, on the other hand, was now shifting his ground over those also. Having said that some of the best-known signs of global pollution might be harmless, he now asserted that the planet was in emergency after all, and that we 'cannot wait for big science planetary medicine to find the cure; there is no time'. At this point his dislike of institutional scientists blazed forth again. His readers were told that his aim was 'to deflate the tumescence of macho big science' and that 'good science . . . too often waits upon the appearance of a key thought in the mind of a genius' (such as the Gaia hypothesis?). 'The mere employment of a hundred new brightly polished doctors of philosophy from great universities to tackle the problems of global change is most unlikely to achieve anything other than provide them with secure and comfortable employment.' finally, this self-proclaimed agnostic launched again into the language of full-blooded pantheist mysticism, proclaiming that 'I find myself looking upon the Earth itself as a place of worship, with all life as its congregation.' After this, he devoted the remainder of the book to the technicalities of biochemistry.[43]

This analysis has been concerned with Lovelock's use of language, not with his work as a scientist; it may well be both that his hypothesis is wholly or partly correct, and that it would be good for people to believe it whether it is objectively true or not. A historian cannot pronounce professionally upon such issues. The purpose here has been, instead, to show how complex can be the relationship between science and spirituality in general, and science and modern alternative spiritualities in particular, and how rich the context was for the dogmatic statement made by Starhawk, in *Truth or Dare*, that 'to witches, the cosmos is the living body of the Goddess, in whose being we all partake'.[44]

Starhawk's last published pronouncement upon witchcraft, before the time when this is written, seems to have been made in the 1989 edition of *The Spiral Dance*. The amendments that she now wished to make to the book related mostly to perceptions which she had since achieved through her subsequent acquaintance with shamanist practices and evolving feminist theory. She did not see any reason to alter any of the view of history or prehistory which she had provided in it, and restated her view of the early modern witch trials as a mass brainwashing of the public by those who controlled power, to stigmatize as dangerous any power which they did not control, and women's power in particular.[45] During the 1990s she turned at last to the role of a novelist, which she had sought at the beginning of her career, and has produced fictional works which illustrate still further her political and social ideals.

*   *   *

During the 1980s Starhawk and Zsuzsanna Budapest—and especially the former—had many admirers and followers in the field of feminist witchcraft, but few literary imitators. The most significant book on the subject published in the decade by a different author was not a treatise but a novel. It was *The Mists of Avalon*, brought out in 1982 by another Californian, Marion Zimmer Bradley. A remarkable and thorough reworking of the classic British epic, the Arthurian legends, it presented a huge reading public—on both sides of the Atlantic—with the concept of witchcraft as the Old Religion, integrally associated with female power and suppressed by a patriarchal and puritanical Christianity.

The component parts of the concept, on the other hand, continued to flourish independently and luxuriantly in American feminist culture. The notion of 'the Burning Times' as a key episode in the male disempowerment of women continued to be taken up within that culture.[46] Still more widespread, and potent, was that of the prehistoric Great Goddess, usually linked with that of ancient woman-centred cultures, which grew in strength through the decade and into the 1990s. It was linked, in some cases inseparably, with the larger phenomenon of the movement to develop or recover a specifically female spirituality. By the late 1980s this was commonly subsumed under the label of 'Goddess spirituality', or simply 'the Goddess'. The terminology was loose enough to be both convenient and confusing. To some it simply represented a general female right to a separate spirituality, irrespective of whether this involved actual belief in deities; it could, indeed, signify simply the spiritual power within women. To others, it meant the putative prehistoric Great Mother Goddess, or the triple lunar deity of Graves, Maiden Mother, and Crone, or the living and divine body of the planet. By yet others it was understood to mean a composite figure in whom were subsumed all the female deities revered in any part of the world and at any age, who retained something of their individual identity as her 'aspects'. All these definitions embodied ideas which were very different from the polytheism manifested by the vast majority of pagans in the historic ancient world. They were in most respects modern religious concepts—but all the more potent for that.[47] Feminist witchcraft formed only a part of this movement, most of which is therefore only partly or tangentially relevant to the themes of the present book. Any full-scale appraisal of it would need to take into account not only the theoretical writings at its core and the practical experience of encounter and discussion groups, but works of utopian speculation crossed with archaeology such as Riane Eisler's *The Chalice and the Blade* (1987), and fiction such as Jean M. Auel's enormously popular series of novels about the palaeolithic.

Among the many American writers who dealt with the wider issues of feminist spirituality in the 1980s, a few do need to be considered for their relationship with pagan witchcraft. One was Charlene Spretnak, mentioned above in connection with the Gaia hypothesis. Her own books dealt with archaeological and ecological aspects of that spirituality, rather than witchcraft, but she is notable for having encouraged the recognition and enhancement of spiritual feminism within a scholarly context. In 1982 she edited a large collection of essays from contributors inside and outside of academe, which explored the implications of the movement for political and social issues. One was from an associate professor at Ottawa, Naomi Goldenburg, who seems to have been the first academic to characterize witchcraft as the feminist religion *par excellence*, the only one in the modern West 'that recognizes woman as a divinity in her own right'.[48]

A third author whose impact on both sides of the Atlantic has been great enough to deserve special consideration is Marija Gimbutas, the only front-rank professional archaeologist in recent years to give full support to the idea that prehistoric European cultures were woman-centred in both society and religion, and that the destruction of such cultures by patriarchal invaders represented a tragedy for humanity. Her ideas have met with an increasing volume of criticism from fellow archaeologists,[49] and no attempt will be made here to judge the truth or falsehood of them; although, in view of the quantity of the censure which they have attracted, it may be worth pointing out that at the time of writing they are by no means disproven, and may well never be. The controversy has centred upon the issue that the evidence is susceptible of alternative interpretations.

Two aspects of Maija Gimbutas's work are of particular relevance here. The first is that it represented an attempt to provide an objective basis for the prehistory which the feminist spirituality movement, and especially its more radical representatives, had already provided. A refugee to the United States from Lithuania, her most considerable asset lay in her command of the languages and knowledge of the cultures of Eastern Europe, which combined with her other abilities to make her the foremost Western expert upon the archaeology of the region. Her earlier works, of the 1950s and 1960s, were not greatly concerned with prehistoric religion or gender issues.[50] In 1974 she published a celebrated analysis of the figurines which had long been recognized as one of the most remarkable features of neolithic and Copper Age sites in south-eastern Europe. Following the collapse of general scholarly belief in a Great Goddess, she treated these as representations of individual deities and interpreted their symbolism—elaborately and boldly—according to a system which had been developed in its essentials by the Jungian psychologist Erich Neumann, whom she acknowledged and praised.[51]

It was only in the late 1970s that feminist theory replaced Jungian psychology as her major conceptual tool, and this may not be unrelated to the fact that she taught in the University of California, Los Angeles. In 1977 and 1980 she published a pair of major articles which tried to provide archaeological evidence for the overthrow of peaceful goddess-centred cultures by patriarchal and patrilinear Indo-European warriors; the second was notably more vehement and judgemental in tone than the first.[52] In 1982 she reissued her earlier book on figurines, in a paperback edition with the title reversed to give priority to goddesses and—more significant—a preface in which she stated her new opinions regarding Indo-European invasions and referred to the different female deities which she had identified in the Balkan neolithic as 'the Goddess Creatrix in her many aspects'.[53] This deity became to some extent part of her personal cosmology; in 1989 she told a feminist magazine how, on commencing her famous excavations at Achilleion, she found a figurine 'of the Goddess' which had been washed to the ground's surface by rain, and thought this 'surely a blessing on her work and her destiny'.[54]

Her life's labours were crowned by two huge books in 1989 and 1991, *The Language of the Goddess* and *The Civilization of the Goddess*, both designed for a mass readership and dedicated to propagating the idea that before the coming of the Indo-Europeans and the patriarchal dark ages which had persisted ever since, all Europe had been occupied by peaceful, creative, woman-focused cultures which had venerated the Goddess in all her aspects. Although Gimbutas believed that these had been matristic, matrilinear, and run by queen-priestesses advised primarily by councils of women, this did not to her imply the subservience of one sex to the other, but 'a condition of mutual respect'. She incorporated into her story the whole American radical feminist interpretation of the early modern witch trials: that the latter represented the 'murder of over eight million women' who 'had learned the lore and secrets of the Goddess from their mothers or grandmothers', 'wise women, prophetesses and healers who were the best and bravest minds of their time'. *The Language of the Goddess* concluded with a declaration of religious faith:

The Goddess gradually retreated into the depths of the forests or onto mountain tops, where she remains to this day in beliefs and fairy stories. Human alienation from the vital roots of earthly life ensued, the results of which are clear in our contemporary society. But the cycles never stop turning, and now we find the Goddess reemerging from the forests and mountains, bringing us hope for the future, returning us to our most ancient roots.[55]

The later work of Marija Gimbutas was as much a product of the American feminist spirituality movement as it was a source of inspiration for it.

It must be obvious to readers of this present book that the basic structure of that work had been developed long before, by a succession of writers (mostly British) beginning with Jane Ellen Harrison and culminating in Jacquetta Hawkes. It is true that most of the detail was provided by Gimbutas herself, and that she added new emphases to it, most of all to condemn earlier associations of the Goddess primarily with motherhood, which were no longer acceptable to feminist thought. This said, it is remarkable how little she chose to put herself in a tradition of writers and how much she preferred to disassociate herself from all predecessors. The works of Hawkes and others appeared in her footnotes, but the only one to be cited in the texts was Neumann, and then to distance herself from his work in accordance with the feminist critique of it which had developed since the 1970s.[56] Instead she emphasized that she had been the first to present the 'the pictorial "script" for the religion of the Old European Goddess', and allowed the psychologist and author of popular books on the history of religion, Joseph Campbell, to claim in a foreword to her work that she had deciphered neolithic symbolism just as Champollion had the Egyptian hieroglyphics. She attacked previous authors (anonymously) for having been too simplistic in their approach and too imprecise in their collection of evidence, and claimed to be the first 'to bring into our awareness essential aspects of European prehistory that have been unknown or simply not treated on a pan-European scale'.[57]

At least one honourable reason may be suggested for her stance: that the whole concept of the prehistoric Great Goddess had been developed through the twentieth century by writers whose politics and purpose were often at a polar opposite from hers; they were equally disgusted by many aspects of modern culture, but this was part of a wider conservatism. Jacquetta Hawkes had specifically praised the woman-centred nature of the European neolithic as she imagined it, because, to her, women were forces of resistance to change.[58] To Marija Gimbutas, women needed to be agents of radical change. In 1982, the year in which Gimbutas declared her belief in a single prehistoric Goddess, Hawkes announced that the world had now perhaps become too much dominated by 'the female principle', and that 'all females who allow their instincts to prevail' have 'a willing deference to the naturally dominant male, the leader born and bred'.[59] It is easy to see why Gimbutas might not have wished to acknowledge any debt to forerunners such as her.

British and Irish scholars may have special reason for unease with the final work of this remarkable colleague—with the fact that in it Gimbutas violated one of her own tenets, namely, that analyses of neolithic culture should rest upon the close and detailed knowledge of a particular region, rather than a superficial overview of the whole continent. For most of her career she had held to it admirably, basing her arguments upon the archaeology of Greece and the Balkans in which she was herself an expert; even though her characterization of this corner of the land-mass as 'Old Europe' did indicate a tendency to see it as typical of the whole. This last tendency was enhanced in *The Language of the Goddess*, where she was still relying on the Greek and Balkan material but now declared that 'its systematic associations indicate the extension of the same Goddess religion to all Europe, the Near East, and the Mediterranean region as a cohesive and persistent ideological system'. In *The Civilization of the Goddess* she finally abandoned caution and incorporated material from all over this region. Having no expertise in that of the British Isles at all, she took it from whichever sources seemed most fitted to her purpose, including the books of Michael Dames, whose grasp of archaeology was so weak that he treated the Wessex long barrows and superhenges as belonging to the same phase of prehistory instead of being monuments from different millennia and cultural packages. To her, the Irish Linkardstown cists were clearly relics of patriarchal Indo-European society, whereas the Boyne Valley passage graves and the English superhenges were as obviously part of the Goddess's civilization, 'the products of collective work, dedication, and love'. In fact, the Linkardstown cists are slightly older than the Boyne Valley tombs and pre-date the superhenges by about a thousand years.[60] This time there is a clear and simple explanation for such elementary mistakes; by the time that Gimbutas wrote her last two, and biggest, books, she was in the grip of a protracted and debilitating illness, which she resisted with considerable courage and which eventually killed her in 1994. Her aim in these works was to publish her message to as large and wide an audience as possible, and to make the greatest possible claims for it, and in the circumstances in which she was writing she would have been quite unable to pay any close attention to material which she was taking from areas beyond her personal knowledge. This does mean, however, that her ideas are best evaluated in the area of Europe upon which she was a leading expert, and not one in which she never even grasped the basic chronology of cultures.

As well as equipping the world with books, American feminist witchcraft also provided it with a different, and equally potent, vehicle for conveying ideas and emotions: songs and chants. These were the product, in turn, of another development of the 1970s: the growth in numbers of American Pagans to the point at which large conventions of them became possible. Cost and convenience meant that these commonly took the form of summer camps, a phenomenon with which Americans of the time were often familiarized in youth but which have no real equivalent in British culture. A feature of such camps had always been fireside singing and chanting, and witches responded to the need for these. In particular, those of the West Coast did so. Zsuzsanna Budapest composed the classic chant 'We All Come From The Goddess', which first became widely known at the Pan–Pagan Festival held in Indiana in 1980. In that year, also, a young Seattle musician called Charlie Murphy wrote a song, 'The Burning Times', which summed up the American radical feminist view of the witch trials. It subsequently became not merely an international Pagan favourite but was recorded by at least one celebrated folk singer. Starhawk provided a chant of her own, 'She Changes Everything She Touches', and popularized one by Deena Mezger, 'Isis, Astarte, Diana'. These devices spread and internalized the American feminist witches' notions of deity, prehistory, history, and contemporary politics among people all over North America and Europe who hardly looked at books, and their constant repetition and recital gave those who used them an even stronger sense of belonging to a pan-global movement for the improvement—or salvation—of the world.[61]

It would be simple to conclude that pagan witchcraft left Britain for the United States as a quietist religion, seeking a private but secure place within a wider society, and returned transformed into an evangelical one, seeking to alter the world. Though possessed of some truth, it would indeed be too simple. For one thing, Wicca always posed an implicit powerful challenge to social and religious norms, as has been made clear earlier in the present book, and attracted people who were out of sympathy with some of those norms. For another, American feminist witchcraft usually recognized the need for pluralism in belief. When Starhawk came to project her blueprint image of an ideal society in the twenty-first century, in one of her novels,[62] it was a San Francisco in which all citizens had not been converted to Paganism, but followed many different spiritual paths in harmony with each other. The point was that all of them also embraced a common culture of tolerance, egalitarianism, decision-making by consensus, pacifism, and self-sustaining, non-pollutant economics with a reverence for nature. Embedded in this, and in all of Starhawk's work, however, was a different assumption: that it was impossible to be a pagan witch without believing in all these things.

This was an assumption very much at variance with the British historical experience, as represented both by the first public representatives of Wicca and the magicians from whom they had drawn ideas. Mathers had been fascinated by militarism and aristocracy. Yeats's right-wing tendencies developed into a flirtation with fascism. Crowley was a lifelong high Tory, and all Dion Fortune's expressed political and social attitudes point in the same direction. Gardner, as said, was almost certainly a Conservative, and while Alex Sanders disclaimed any associations with specific parties, he consistently expressed admiration for monarchy and hierarchy.[63] A writer who interviewed several Wiccan groups in England in the 1960s noted that most of their members were politically right-wing.[64]

There was no paradox in this; for most of these people their interest in paganism and magic was part of a wider rejection of modernity, a phenomenon

in which for many people in the early and mid-twentieth century, industrialization, urbanization, and high technology all formed parts of a package with
socialism. Their spiritual interests marched closely with three different
emotional aspects of right-wing ideology: nostalgia for a better past, elitism and
suspicion of the masses, and a desire for a free market, in magic and sex as in
economics. A dislike of the modern world was something which united personalities as different as Gerald Gardner and Robert Cochrane.[65] It was also an
emotion perfectly compatible with egalitarian and communitarian values, and
these could readily be made part of a package with ecological conservation and
patheism or paganism, as the history of woodcraft movements shows. What
matters here is simply that in the case of pagan witchcraft it was—as far as the
record shows—the conservatives who got there first, and produced ideas,
images, and practices which were then appropriated by others. The transition
from Gardner's witchcraft to that of Starhawk marks the process of appropriation, a parallel effect to the transformation of the Goddess of Jacquetta Hawkes
into the Goddess of Marija Gimbutas. Pagan witchcraft travelled from Britain to
the United States as a branch of radical conservatism; it returned as a branch of
radical socialism. What remains in this chapter is to explore the impact of this
new kind of witchcraft upon the parent country to which it was rebounding.

*　　*　　*

The fully formed American feminist review of the witch trials, crossing the
Atlantic towards the end of the 1970s, had to compete for the minds of the
British public with an alternative view of the past starting to emanate from
academics. The latter was not in self-conscious competition with the former,
because few university-based scholars—and very few prehistorians and historians—had read the feminist literature, even though the latter was itself partly
rooted in earlier academic scholarship; the concepts of historical witchcraft held
by mainstream academe and radical feminism were diverging out of a common
stock of ideas. The forces propelling the developments in academic research into
the subject were twofold. One was the widespread foundation of new universities and public funding of research in the mid-twentieth century Western world,
resulting in a much greater number of practising historians than ever before and
the increasing professionalization of their activities. The other was that spirit of
iconoclasm, that willingness to question traditionally held models and teachings, which was a feature of the West in the same period and from which the
feminism of the time had itself sprung.

One of the models to be questioned was, as shown earlier, that of the universal prehistoric Great Goddess. During the 1970s it collapsed further in European
academe as specialists challenged the evidence for her worship alleged in regions
which had been added to her domain during the previous generation, and
formed part of the staging-posts between which her cult had been said to have
been carried from the Near East: Italy and the Maltese Islands.[66] It must be

stressed once more that none of these developments had disproved the former worship of such a deity; they had simply shown that it could not be proven. Furthermore, the evidence from the historic ancient world was full of unmistakable proof of the widespread veneration of *goddesses*, often locally regarded as superior to gods and associated with functions—rulership, justice, city-building, industry, agricultural processing, learning—which could make excellent role models for modern feminists. The problem was that the American feminist spirituality movement generally wanted a Goddess, partly as a convenient abstraction for female spiritual power, and partly as a straightforward answer to dominant male monotheism.

Academic research into the early modern witch trials also underwent an important shift in the 1970s, with the definitive collapse of faith in the Murray thesis. It was directly and energetically attacked by two British historians, Keith Thomas and Norman Cohn, and the latter in particular exposed the tactics by which Margaret Murray had distorted evidence to support it.[67] Perhaps more potent still in bringing about its demise was the revival of intensive study of archival records of the trials, and the setting of them in their local context; notable studies of this sort were produced between 1970 and 1979 by the British scholar Alan Macfarlane, the Americans Erik Midelfort and William Monter, the Frenchman Robert Muchembled, the German Gerhard Schormann, the Norwegian Bente Alver, and the Swede Bengt Ankarloo.[68] They left no doubt that the people tried for witchcraft in early modern Europe were not practitioners of a surviving pagan religion. Writers of textbooks on the period, such as Christopher Hill, deleted passages which had supported that idea from new editions and omitted them from new publications.[69] Carlo Ginzburg, as has been shown earlier, denied his earlier apparent support for the Murray thesis. Until the late 1970s it was possible to have an up-to-date knowledge of early modern history and to believe in that thesis; after that time it was out of the question. In 1991, however, at an international conference on the trials, held at the University of Exeter, Sir Keith Thomas (as he had become) told participants that he despaired that the public would ever foresake the mythology which had grown out of the work of Murray and her predecessors and followers. His statement met with widespread sympathy and assent. How had this situation come about?

In part it was simply a matter of the time-lag which follows the publication of research. A quarter of a century had been required for Margaret Murray's own ideas to enter popular knowledge, and it was hardly surprising that at least the same would be needed for them to be widely rejected. Many of the earlier textbooks and popular works on witchcraft remained in schools and public libraries well into the 1980s, and people who had left education before the mid-1970s were likely to preserve the impressions of history which they had acquired before then. The feminist view of witchcraft arriving from America thus had the advantage of falling on ground already prepared to receive it. Even when new textbooks were revised or old texts revised to take account of the new scholarly research, their authors almost never attacked the obsolete ideas about witchcraft head-on, but ignored them or deleted them silently.

The feminist history, furthermore, had various component packages. If the concept of the Old Religion was removed, it still left that of the early modern 'witch hunt' as a mechanism for repressing women, and especially midwives and healers. The 1970s studies had not really addressed this, partly because they had been written by people not yet aware of the American feminist literature, and partly because of a general insensitivity to the gender issues in the witch trials which that literature would remove, thus making a genuinely valuable contribution to scholarship. The one expert who did respond fairly rapidly to the American feminist stereotype was the Scottish historian Christina Larner, who challenged it in an essay in 1984, which denied that persecution of witches was indeed persecution of women.[70] Her work does not, however, seem to have been widely read outside her circle of colleagues, a fact which must in part be attributed to her tragically early death. In general, there was a relative dearth of publication on the witch trials by British and American historians in the 1980s, as an earlier generation of researchers withdrew and a new one was only just settling to work.

This still remains, however, only part of the reason for the walkover which the American view was to have among most British feminists and Pagans. Some of the former, at least, were very much attuned to the realities of the evidence provided by the trials. Between 1982 and 1985 two women called Rachel Halsted and Lynette Mitchell contributed essays to an avowedly radical feminist magazine called *Trouble and Strife*.[71] They had read the most important of the recent academic monographs and in Halstead's case at least had carried out original research. In the light of these they submitted the American feminist view to a withering and accurate factual criticism and questioned in addition whether a view which focused upon women wholly as victims was indeed beneficial to female liberation. This was good history—more to the point it was good radical feminist history—but in talking to many British feminists and witches between 1985 and 1990, I did not come across a single one who had heard of them. It was not that their views had been read and rejected, but that they were not know to exist, so that the American assertions had gone completely uncontested. This no doubt has something to do with the fact that *Trouble and Strife* was a cheap and infrequent production edited in Leeds, while the main British women's presses were republishing the American feminist works for mass distribution as essential texts. It does not explain, however, why the work of Halsted and Mitchell never made the transition to the feminist mainstream. Only when the history of British feminism in the 1980s comes itself to be written may answers to a question like this become easier to find. What is very clear is how completely the American construct became internalized in that feminism, so that its origins were often forgotten. It was a frequent experience for me in the mid-1980s to hear female British radicals inveigh against America as the world powerhouse of exploitative capitalism, nuclear weaponry, polluting industry, and materialist consumerism, and in the next breath to propound a view of the history of witchcraft which had been manufactured in the United States, just as surely as cruise missiles.

It is a much simpler matter to discern why British witches and other Pagans should have absorbed the same view. For one thing, it was partly based upon their own teachings. For another, many British witches were not merely separated from university-based scholarship but instinctually antipathetic to it. The writer who noted the right-wing politics of Wiccans in the 1960s also recorded that most of them had been educated at grammar schools and technical colleges.[72] This makes a good fit with what is known of their leading figures in the 1950s and 1960s, all of whom were highly intelligent, intellectually curious, literate people, and none of whom had been to university. In later life Gerald Gardner came to resent the rejection of many of his ideas by mainstream scholarship—even by his own Folk-Lore Society—and to speak of its inherent narrow-mindedness. Doreen Valiente echoed these feelings, emphasizing to her readers the benefits of never having had 'the brainwashing of a formal and respectable education'.[73] Embittered remarks about institutional scholarship could be found in works which pagan witches drew upon during the 1960s, such as those of Tom Lethbridge and George Ewart Evans, and others which followed, such as those of James Lovelock—all of whom have been quoted earlier. Starhawk, with her elevation of imagination over intellect, could be relied upon to compound the prejudice against those who lived most by the latter. This is exactly what she did, declaring that those who proceed to the higher echelons of the educational system are the most habituated to authority and the most temperamentally suited to obey it.[74]

Pagan witchcraft was therefore fertile ground for the counter-cultural phenomenon of 'alternative archaeology' or 'earth mysteries' which blossomed in the late 1960s and all through the 1970s, and centred most obviously upon the entity of the ley, commonly called the 'ley-line'. Propagated by writers such as John Michell, Tom Graves, and Paul Screton, this consisted in its fully developed form of the belief that the surface of the planet was crossed by straight lines or corridors of energy, which had been recognized by ancient peoples and marked by them with a range of different monuments. This was never accepted by professional archaeologists, and its proponents often gloried in the fact, representing their views to be part of an assault upon orthodoxies of all kinds, leading to the creation of a better world. It ran out of steam during the late 1980s and 1990s, but not—it should be stressed—before it had anticipated, and perhaps contributed to, some very useful developments in archaeology itself: a heightened awareness of the importance of landscape and of the relationship of monuments to it, of the cognitive factors in ancient sites, and of the very different ways in which succeeding ages have related to and interpreted prehistoric structures. By the early 1990s professional and alternative archaeologies were on a converging course, in a way that would have seemed unthinkable ten years earlier.

In that earlier phase, however, pagan witches readily absorbed the concept of ley-lines in its most obdurately counter-cultural form; it had certain obvious resonances with their view of the inherent sanctity of nature, only reinforced by the Church of All Worlds, the California Cosmology, and the Gaia hypothesis. Doreen Valiente swallowed it whole, Alex Sanders worked with 'ley energy' at his Sussex retreat, Bill Liddell's Elders were soon reporting to him that the ancient Druids and witches had done the same, and Janet and Stewart Farrar approvingly cited the writings of earth mysteries researchers such as John Michell. Those writings leaped the Atlantic, to get built into the American feminist model; Starhawk told her readers that the ley-lines had been traced in the neolithic, by priestesses.[75]

It is hardly surprising, therefore, that developments in academic scholarship would not make any rapid impact upon British pagan witches, while American feminist witchcraft would have just such an impact. It was, necessarily, an uneven one, for most of the established covens carried on more or less as before. On the other hand, the main Wiccan authors responded rapidly. Doreen Valiente was converted to an indignant feminism by reading the work of the pioneering American radical feminist Robin Morgan. She learned 'the truth about the ancient past' from that of Merlin Stone, and praised Starhawk. In the succession of books published by Janet and Stewart Farrar between 1981 and 1989, the words 'matriarchy' and 'patriarchy' became recurrent. They declared that all goddesses were part of the one Goddess, who was also the planet, issued a list of 'acceptable' god-forms which were not too much like patriarchs, and declared that all environmental and anti-nuclear activists, Jungian psychologists, and fringe medics 'whether they realize it or not (and an increasing number of them do) are battling for an end to the patriarchal phase in human evolution'.[76]

As well as affecting British Wicca, American feminism also planted its own strains of witchcraft in Britain, through the followers or (much more commonly) the books of Starhawk and Zsuzsanna Budapest. These could be openly antagonistic towards Wicca itself. John Rowan, a therapist who had discovered 'the Great Goddess' through The Spiral Dance, warned people of the possibilities of patriarchal subversion within Wicca and declared that 'the Craft was not designed to overthrow patriarchy, it was designed to ignore patriarchy'. He reshaped the figure of the Horned God in Starhawkian fashion, to enable men to recognize and transcend the impact of feminism.[77] A critique of Wicca along the same lines was articulated by a more flamboyant figure who emerged in the mid-1980s: Shan Jayran, a warm-hearted, well-educated, energetic, confident, and determined woman with a zest for publicizing her work which equalled anything manifested by Sybil Leek or Alex Sanders. She had commenced as a Dianic witch, in the separatist tradition inspired by Budapest; other influences which she has celebrated included Robin Morgan, Merlin Stone, Starhawk, and Marija Gimbutas. Her London home, the House of the Goddess, became the centre of an eclectic form of feminist witchcraft which she developed for herself, and which embodied the whole American version of the history of witchcraft. In 1987 she and her group held a Hallowe'en Festival at Battersea Town Hall, which was attended by 1,350 people, making it the largest gathering of British Pagans in modern times, and a harbinger of the more organized and public paganism which was to appear in the 1990s.[78]

Feminist witchcraft of the American sort flourished, above all, in the many covens which developed out of consciousness-raising groups and sets of friends under the influence of texts such as *The Spiral Dance*. Its ideas deeply permeated the whole radical British counter-culture of the 1980s, and became part of its folklore. Here, again, rumour, gossip, and sing-alongs could carry messages further and even more effectively than the original printed texts, and internalize them more rapidly. It must be significant that whenever I encountered groups of British pagan witches between 1987 and 1997, and heard them perform a song or chant which virtually all in the company knew, it was one that had been composed in either California or Washington State in the years around 1980. It may be more so that I almost never met somebody in those groups who knew by whom any of these works had been written, and very few, indeed, even realized that they had originated in the United States; they had become part of a timeless and amorphous Pagan culture, already consigned by some simply to 'the oral tradition'.

It is time to sum up a balance sheet for the impact of American feminist witchcraft upon British witches, and that wider, more diffuse, modern paganism which was starting to form around them. Such balances are commonly composed by putting positive effects first and negative second, which can lean final impressions towards the latter. To avoid building in any tendency to this result, I am going to reverse the sequence, and suggest the liabilities of the impact first. The most important of these was that the American feminist view of the history of witchcraft was in large part wrong, in the straightforward factual sense that it is wrong to say that Manchester is the capital of the United Kingdom. Its view of prehistory, on the other hand, may well be correct, but was presented as a proven fact, rather than as one interpretation of a remote past of which the truth may never be retrieved. No talk of the need to read history as myth, of the crucial short-term empowering effects of having a mythology of one's own, of the way in which things that are not literally true can be poetically true, was going to get round that problem indefinitely. As a large part of the force of the message of American feminist witchcraft lay in its claim to be expressing neglected or concealed facts about the past, and in having those facts accepted as objectively correct, it was, in this sense, built around a time-bomb.

This was linked to another disadvantage, and one which (as shall be shown) was recognized by some British Wiccans: that by identifying pagan witchcraft so firmly with a particular radical counter-culture, the American feminist model would box it into a corner, in which it would wither once political and social preoccupations moved on. The combination of a radical creed with the myth of the Old Religion and of the Burning Times as its destruction, made the questioning of those myths by witches very difficult without attracting charges of defending patriarchy or betraying the great struggle to defend the planet. The glorification of myth, poetry, and imagination compounded this difficulty by calling rational disputation itself into question. Between the late 1970s and the late 1980s British pagan witchcraft was often an uncomfortable place for an intellectual; for one with a state-of-the-art knowledge of history and archaeology it had become virtually uninhabitable. It seemed possible during that period that Wicca and its relations would be marginalized in a new and more enduring fashion, as a spectrum of fundamentalist sects.

Against all this, it must be argued that the same process also produced considerable gains. As mentioned above, the American feminist history of witchcraft was even of benefit to academic scholarship, in that it eventually directed the attention of such scholars to gender issues in the trials which had previously been undervalued. Feminist witchcraft also rescued British witches from the fate to which media stereotyping—and some of their own more opportunist representatives—had threatened to consign them in the 1970s: of having their craft perceived as a means to personal empowerment of an individual, amorphous, and non-ethical kind. American feminist spirituality had reinvested witchcraft with a pagan spiritual identity and invested it with a passionate ethic of world improvement or salvation through female liberation and conservation of the natural environment. It had given it a much larger and better-defined constituency of support, brought it out of the occult fringe into the mainstream of international cultural politics, and greatly enhanced its obvious relevance to contemporary issues and needs. In the process, it had provided a sense of purpose, and an opportunity for self-realization and self-actualization, to thousands of British people, and especially to women.

Let's look at Lesley[79] in 1983, getting onto a bus with her life packed into two shopping bags. Her hair is in plaits, she is overweight (or so she insists), and she is walking out on a conventional existence which has made her feel trapped, disempowered, and unhappy to the point of desperation. One of the worst aspects of her misery is that it is so isolated and inarticulate; she knows that there must be a better world out there but has no real idea of how to find it, or even why it has been that normal living has failed so utterly to provide her with the contentment and fulfilment which it had traditionally promised. What is driving her into flight is an incoherent, but irresistible, instinct. The bus actually takes her to France, where she finds work harvesting crops, and meets and joins people with socially and politically radical ideas. Through them she enters activist politics, encounters the ideas of feminist witchcraft, and reads *The Mists of Avalon*. Now, Lesley doesn't know much about the history of witchcraft, but she has a very shrewd suspicion that witches weren't women who got kicked around by men, imprisoned in hopelessly dreary and self-denying domestic labour, and allowed no opinions, no adventures, no true existence of their own; and that is enough for her. She becomes one. In this process, and that of working with other witches, she develops a self-confidence, a self-knowledge, and a range of practical abilities which she has before only sensed and hoped to be latent within herself. Above all, she discovers words, words that 'fly like arrows' (Lesley is a Sagittarian), that truly express her thoughts and emotions and that have the power to sweep up others. She discovers a new sense of kinship with the world around her—natural and human—and a true sense of place in it. She has come home.

That, at any rate, is Lesley's story, as she told it to me sitting in a Somerset meadow in August 1994; a happy, freckled, red-haired woman with a vulpine smile of mischief, an irrepressible sense of humour, and (as the account suggests) a genuine power to infuse and use words. It is not an unusual story, and that is the point of it. I have heard the like from hundreds of other women in the late 1980s and 1990s. In this sense Lesley is quite ordinary; she is a reminder, like so much else in the history of modern pagan witchcraft, of how wildly, fantastically, marvellously extraordinary, ordinary people can be. If this is magic, then so be it.

19

COMING OF AGE

༞ ༞

 O NE of the most impressive qualities of modern American culture is that it is so self-critical; it is hard to find an ideological position taken up by one citizen of the United States that is not ably contested by another. This pattern holds good for its Pagan community. Only a few years after Wiccan beliefs had arrived in the USA, they were questioned and investigated by other members of that community; it was a process launched by two individuals above all. During the first half of the 1970s Isaac Bonewits ruthlessly and accurately exposed the shortcomings of the authors upon whom most Wiccans relied, notably Margaret Murray and Robert Graves. He argued against the notion of a Europe-wide pagan witch religion, and suggested that the reality had been a scattering of different survivals from a pre-Christian ancient world. During the second half of the decade he developed these ideas further to divide witchcraft into several different categories specific to time and place. The other person was Aidan Kelly, who between 1971 and 1975 conducted the first textual research into Wiccan writings and commenced the process—to be taken much further by the Farrars—of revealing the series of revisions which they had undergone even since 1950.[1]

It is significant that both men were intellectuals who had allegiances to alternative modern pagan traditions, a reflection of the much greater early diversity of modern paganism in the United States, which itself reflected a much more heterogenous society. Bonewits was a magician with an interest in Celtic literatures, who subsequently defined himself as a pagan Druid. Kelly was the author of the liturgy of a pagan witch religion founded in California in the late 1960s, with New Reformed Orthodox Order of the Golden Dawn, which openly and honestly took its material from literary sources and creative experimentation and did not claim to be a continuous tradition. Their impact, although in the case of Bonewits initially acrimonious, was profound; it has been claimed (by a well-informed author) that by the mid-1970s many American witches were already starting to accept the Old Religion more as metaphor than reality.[2] It must be commented that nobody would get this impression from the books of Zsuzsanna Budapest and Starhawk, precisely the American witches who were (put together) the most widely read. It may well, however, have been true of many Wiccans in the United States. One of them was a high priestess called Margot Adler.

At Hallowe'en 1979, the day when *The Spiral Dance* was published in San Francisco, a Boston press brought out Adler's first book, *Drawing Down The Moon*. The contrast between the two was in many ways the stereotypical one between the more poetic and visionary radicalism of the West Coast and the more rational and intellectual kind of the East. Like most stereotypes, it can be faulted. Plenty of feminist witches of the Dianic and Starhawkian kind appeared on the eastern seaboard, and Aidan Kelly (as said) was a Californian. Adler's own early career displays some striking similarities to that of Starhawk, including a Jewish family background, direct involvement in radical politics, and association with California, to which Adler came, as a student at Berkeley, like a refugee entering a promised land.[3] That said, the distinction to some extent stands up. Starhawk's love of San Francisco is one of the enduring themes of her career, while Adler was a New Yorker, and returned to the East Coast. *The Spiral Dance* was plainly produced by a creative writer, while *Drawing Down The Moon* was as obviously the work of a highbrow journalist. The former was a celebration and a prospectus, the latter a history and an analysis. Adler defined religion as 'any set of symbolic forms and acts that relate human beings to ultimate conditions of existence, cosmic questions and universal concerns',[4] and she set out to show that paganism in the modern United States represented a constellation of newly appeared religions. She portrayed their differing natures and explained their development, constantly displaying a sophisticated sense of the special character of times and places and of the considerable differences between individual spiritual experiences and needs. She celebrated the power and utility of myth but also drew a firm distinction between myth and reality. She recognized that Wicca had probably been built upon a pseudo-history, and then suggested that this was normal for the development of religious traditions and that Wiccans deserved credit for the fact that they were increasingly conscious of this without losing a sense of the viability of their actual experience of the divine. What emerged from *Drawing Down The Moon* was an argument for modern paganisms as ideal religions for a pluralist culture, and for witchcraft as one of these.

Nothing as intellectually rigorous and powerful as this had emerged from a modern pagan's pen before, but as it was more demanding, more expensive, and less intoxicating than *The Spiral Dance*, its impact was proportionately more muted, and especially so in Britain where its readership was long mostly confined to Wiccan intellectuals. There has never, in fact, been a British equivalent to the work. British witchcraft was eventually to achieve the degree of self-knowledge and self-analysis which Margot Adler gave to that in America, but the process took more than a decade longer. The roots of it were, to be sure, very long; they reached back to 1968 when a small group of Gardnerians started an informal newsletter to keep in touch with each other. It was entitled *The Wiccan*, and had an initial circulation of eight people. The editor, commonly known as 'M', has been described to me as 'a Saturnine figure dressed in a trenchcoat and trilby'. He lived at this time in a New Forest village, was a keen vegetarian and practitioner of natural medicine, and had a personal sense of mission for the revived Old Religion, as a means of restoring freedom and authority to women and a close and productive relationship between Western humanity and the natural world. The thirteenth issue, on 2 September 1970, announced the formation of a Pagan Front to promote these aims in the wider society. It was open to all who accepted the concepts of paired female and male divinity, of the Wiccan ethic 'do what you will as long as it harms none', of reincarnation with reward or punishment for behaviour in life (the Hindu concept of karma), and of kinship with Nature, seen as an interplay of complementary forces. A separate and parallel body with similar aims, the Pagan Movement, had been founded shortly before.[5]

The Front was supported by leaders of covens of at least three different kinds—Gardnerian and two varieties of traditional—and secured the approval of Doreen Valiente. In November 1970 she produced a full moon ritual with which people could inaugurate local divisions of the organization, and on May Day 1971 she chaired its first national meeting, at Chiswick in West London. Just as in the short-lived Witchcraft Research Association in the previous decade, she called for unity. The Front did not collapse in acrimony as the Association had done, but nor did it generate enough interest to justify more than one further national convention. Instead, it survived through the 1970s as a contact service and defence mechanism for pagan witches, with *The Wiccan* as its mouthpiece. The views of the latter remained very much those of 'M' himself, a passionately opinionated man with a talent for making both friends and enemies; he favoured feminism, care for the environment, and free contraception and abortion, and was hostile to the concept of prehistoric matriarchy, homosexuality, capital punishment, and Alex Sanders. In 1976 a second magazine was founded to cater for pagan witches, edited by Michael Howard who had been active among pagans and ritual magicians since the early 1960s. Entitled *The Cauldron*, it gave space in particular to non-Gardnerian traditions of witchcraft and so provided some balance to the opposite tendency of *The Wiccan*.[6]

Both journals, and the Pagan Front, continued into the 1980s, with only two significant changes. One was that 'M' died in November 1979 and was replaced as editor of *The Wiccan* and co-ordinator of the front by a friend of his, a Gardnerian high priestess called Leonora James. She was a Cambridge graduate, trained as a philosopher and grounded in the Greek and Roman classics. As such, she brought an intellectual rigour to Wicca which was generally lacking in British pagan witchcraft at the time. She was also a powerful, energetic, brazen-haired woman of boundless enterprise and courage, as leonine as her name would suggest. The other alteration was that in October 1981 the Pagan Front became the Pagan Federation, a result partly of the contamination of the former term by extremist politics such as those of the right-wing National Front, and partly of the need to reflect better the organization's nature as an affiliation of different groups. In May 1985 James and her circle of friends founded another body, the Pagan Anti-Defamation League, for the specific purpose of replying to public misinformation concerning modern paganisms and responding to attacks upon individual Pagans. All these remained, however, shoestring exercises. The two magazines were essentially products of cottage industry—in the case of *The Cauldron*, literally so—and consisted of roughly typed sheets of paper, clipped together. The Federation and League both depended upon the efforts of a small group of dedicated people personally linked to Leonora James.[7]

The ground was, however, being prepared for expansion, by a multiplication of varieties of modern paganism equivalent to that which has taken place much earlier in the USA. From the 1970s small groups were practising versions of the religions of the ancient Norse and Anglo-Saxons, and the Fellowship of Isis was founded to provide a common framework for celebrating goddess-focused traditions. The second half of the 1980s saw a dramatic expansion in pagan Druidry. In large part these movements were encouraged by the example of Wicca, and to a much smaller extent they sprang from it; the founders of two of the four new pagan Druid orders of the period had been Wiccan high priests, and the two most celebrated authors of popular books upon pagan Celtic spirituality had briefly been members of a Gardnerian and a traditional coven respectively. It is also true that many of these people were reacting against Wicca and striving for a different way of working, rather than inspired by it, but the common experience was important. By the last years of the decade the potential existed for a national alliance of Pagan traditions (the capital letter indicating a self-conscious modern application of the term).

Two events in 1988 provided the catalyst for one. The first was the death of Alex Sanders on 30 April. A gathering of his friends held after his death decided that it was inappropriate to choose a successor to his title of king, and that collective leadership and action would be preferred in future. This cleared the way for a true rapprochement between Alexandrians and the Gardnerians, whose rejection of the title and refusal to recognize a need for it had been one of the main points of division between the traditions. The other development was again an American initiative in origin, but this time of a very different kind to those before; a widespread public panic over alleged ritual abuse of children by Satanist networks (readily conflated with Pagans in the relevant literature), conceived and propagated by fundamentalist Christian organizations. It arrived in Britain in 1988 with the agitation of the Reachout Trust, and rapidly made some impression upon social workers and police. The result was a sequence of tragedies which was finally ended in the early 1990s by the work of an academic, Jean La Fontaine, former professor of anthropology in the London School of Economics. She was formally commissioned by the government to carry out a thorough, rigorous, and impartial investigation of the claims made by the Reachout Trust and its allies. The result was a lengthy report which concluded that although a few child-abusers had incorporated an element of ritual into their practices, there was absolutely no evidence of the existence of an organized network of Satanists who made child-abuse a part of their religion. Three comments upon this succession of events can be made here. The first is that whereas between the 1950s and 1970s the proponents of scare-stories had made young adult women the objects of their concern as likely victims of pagans, witches, and occultists, during the 1980s the focus had shifted to children. The second is that the panic over satanic ritual abuse in England had most of the features of a classic early modern witch-hunt, lacking only the use of torture or the death penalty and a belief in the literal involvement of the Devil on the part of (most) authorities involved. The third is that none of the prosecutions brought during the time in which it operated, between 1988 and 1993, affected pagan witches. This may be ascribed partly to the fact that the latter are better integrated into society than some other groups, but also to the speed and vigour with which Wiccans responded to the threat.

One of the first and most important steps in that response was taken on the day of Alex's death, May Eve, when the Pagan Federation was refounded with a larger and more formal structure; five executive officers, a treasury, and an extended framework for dealing with correspondence and for production of *The Wiccan*.[8] The president was Leonora James, the secretary another high priestess, Vivianne Crowley, who had been trained in both Alexandrian and Gardnerian Wicca in the 1970s and come to prominence in the 1980s. She was also an accomplished poetess, a natural speaker, with a gentle, musical voice, and a very proficient Jungian psychologist. She was the closest thing that Britain possessed to an informal successor to Alex in leading his tradition, and she and James were to operate as the moon and sun of the British Wiccan world (respectively) in the 1990s.

In 1989 Crowley published a first book, *Wicca: The Old Religion in the New Age*, which at last provided British witchcraft with a writer to match the spiritual power of Starhawk. In Crowley's pages her religion was portrayed as an elevated series of Neoplatonic mysteries, in which each stage of training and initiation corresponded to parts of the human psyche and led eventually to a personal wholeness. It extinguished the distinction between flesh and spirit, matter and energy, human and divine, in both an individual and a universal transcendence: 'We cannot have other than free will because each of us in our innermost centre is divine.' To Crowley, magic was a metaphor for profound transformations in the human psyche, induced by ritual and meditative practices and having a knock-on impact upon the surrounding world: 'The most important piece of magic we will ever do is the magic we do on ourselves.' If Crowley's elegant prose pleased the intellect, the senses were nourished by the power of her verse, and the whole exuded a profound spirituality. She was representing a mature religion, capable of taking its place alongside the more established varieties; symbolically, in the same year she led a Pagan ceremony as part of a Festival of Faith held at Canterbury Cathedral.[9]

Simultaneously, Crowley and her colleagues on the committee of the Federation were pushing forward their work under the forceful leadership of James, bombarding national and local politicians, the mass media, and educational institutions, with objective information about British Paganism. A structure of regional groups rapidly developed to underpin it, and made possible the adoption of an elective system for the ruling committee from 1991. The same process drew in representatives from the range of other Pagan traditions which had now developed, and the Wiccan dominance of the Federation gave way naturally and painlessly to an equality of representation. Membership swelled from hundreds to thousands, and annual conferences were held from 1989. Both *The Wiccan* and *The Cauldron* changed to a full magazine format at the end of the 1980s, and in 1994 the former went glossy, with the significant change of title to *Pagan Dawn*.[10] In 1990 Vivianne Crowley started an annual Pan-European Wiccan Convention, developed initially directly from the network of initiates established by Alex Sanders on the Continent. Held in a different country of northwest Europe each year, it has involved witches from all over this region and some from further east and south; since 1990 various recensions of the Book of Shadows have been translated into German, Norwegian, Portuguese, flemish, Dutch, and Polish.[11] In acquiring a federative European identity, Wicca was of course once again following the general drift of British culture in a particular decade.

The system of elections to the Pagan Federation leadership had brought with it a regular change of presidency, releasing James to foster the intellectual life of British Paganism. Her academic training had made her impatient of the increasingly emotional, anti-rational, and counter-cultural drift of British witchcraft in the 1980s, and determined to realize more of the potential of Paganism to become a stable and imposing complex of religions drawing upon a tremendous inheritance of ancient civilization.[12] At the end of the decade, therefore, she began to make her mark upon 'serious' television and radio. Witches had of course been appearing in the mass media since the 1950s, but almost invariably as a branch of the entertainment industry, in the format of the feature interview or chat show. James now weighed in as a participant in religious affairs programmes and the columns of the quality press, representing the merits of Wicca and a broader Paganism successfully against theological pugilists such as the Archdeacon of Durham. At the same time she fostered links between the Pagan Federation and academic scholars; the present book would not have been possible without her encouragement and practical support in providing information and introductions.

In the academic study of modern pagan witchcraft, as in so much else, Britain had trailed behind the United States, where scholarly notices of the phenomenon—however crude and rudimentary by later standards—had begun to appear from the opening of the 1970s. During that decade, indeed, Kenneth Rees began to incorporate an analysis of it, and of contemporary magical practices, into his classes at London's City University. For these he merits the honour due to a pioneer, but City was too marginal an institution, and Rees's own research profile too low, for him to make the impact on wider academic culture that his work deserved. Only with the opening of the 1980s did British scholarly institutions begin to take some notice of pagan witchcraft, and then as no more than a very minor and incidental part of the work of institutions set up to provide objective data on apparently novel or recently imported religions. There were two of these: the Centre for New Religious Movements founded at King's College London in 1982 and INFORM, established at the London School of Economics, with government funding, soon after. There was at first no direct contact between these bodies and Pagans, but information came to be mediated between them by a young postgraduate student who embarked in 1981 upon the first systematic academic study of contemporary British occultism.[13] She was an anthropologist called Tanya Luhrmann.

Luhrmann was also an American, and her work represented an application to British material of techniques of study and analysis developed in the United States during the previous ten years; although, in the nature of academic discourse, she was to challenge aspects of those. Her own interest was in the phenomenon of magic, as practised in a contemporary society, rather than in Paganism, and so much of her research was devoted to groups of ceremonial magicians who would not fall into the latter category at all. None the less, she also worked with a number of witches, from a feminist group in Kent which used rituals adapted from the books of Budapest and Starhawk to the oldest continuously existing Wiccan coven in the world, that which had been founded by Gerald Gardner in Hertfordshire. She furthermore became the first academic to receive the help of Leonora James. The eventual result was a book published in 1989, *Persuasions of the Witch's Craft*. It represented the most sophisticated study of modern magic and its relationship with religious experience produced up to that time, and also the most informed and perceptive academic commentary upon the nature of Wiccan belief and practice; some of its ideas will be taken up later. For now it is sufficient to note that a powerful tension ran through the whole work. On the one hand, it placed itself firmly in an investigative and sceptical academic tradition, so that while it invalidated conclusions drawn (or assumptions made) by earlier scholars, it did so using conceptual tools developed within mainstream scholarship. It suggested, systematically and carefully, that operative magic was a creative and potentially valuable self-delusion. On the other hand, it admitted that this approach was itself the result of a largely arbitrary choice, to place within this explanatory framework experiences which had impressed her at the time as uncanny. Luhrmann was quite explicit that at a point in her research she had to make a conscious decision to view phenomena as an academic and not as a witch, although as systems of interpretation each made sense in its own way.[14] Reactions to her book among British witches were proportionately divided, some emphasizing the fact that it had at last brought their religion to the attention of mainstream intellectual culture, while others were more concerned with her apparent dismissal of their practices as founded on delusion.[15] The feelings of the latter were to some extent enhanced by Luhrmann's own return to the United States as soon as her project was complete, her entry into the academic profession assured, and her subsequent lack of any obvious interest in Paganism or magic. It is beyond dispute that her book represented a prominent milestone in academic anthropology, and her work for it may have had the additional effect of encouraging Wiccans themselves to start writing more rigorous books which bid more obviously for the attention of professional scholars.

Whatever the truth of this last possibility, *Persuasions* certainly had the effect of hastening a convergence between Pagans and academics which became very marked during the 1990s, because of a number of different factors. One was the new size, sophistication, and public profile of Paganism in Britain, and its continued rapid growth, which inevitably drew scholarly interest to it. Another was the panic over alleged satanic ritual abuse, and the damage which it inflicted, revealing the persistent ignorance of newly arrived or appeared religions in general among public bodies of all kinds. A third was the appearance within academe of scholars who were themselves sympathetic to Pagan ideas, as part of the general diffusion of those ideas through society. By the mid-1990s Pagan chaplains were being appointed in British universities, and Paganism was recognized as a valid complex of religions, meriting its own official visitors, by the hospital and prison services. In September 1994 the first full-scale academic conference on Paganism in contemporary Britain was held at the University of Newcastle, and in April 1996 it was followed by another on Paganism in the contemporary Western world, a huge international event hosted by the University of Lancaster. Both produced published collections of papers,[16] and a third conference on the same themes was held at King Alfred's College, Winchester, in September 1997. From 1993 onwards a sprinkling of one-day schools on the same or similar subjects were held at a number of different institutions, the first being Bath Spa University College. Although no major set-piece study of Wicca has yet appeared, two works of research in the mid-1990s devoted some space to it. Another American postgraduate, Amy Simes, produced a study of Paganisms in the East Midland region, including witchcraft, and a chapter was accorded to it in Graham Harvey's survey of contemporary British Pagans.[17]

All this represented, admittedly, a small quantity of scholarly work in comparison with that carried out during the same period into 'new' religions of other kinds, and into the wider cultural phenomenon of 'New Age' spirituality. It was also a feeble movement of contact compared with the convergence between professional and 'alternative' archaeologies which occurred in the 1990s. Furthermore, it was essentially confined to the disciplines of anthropology, sociology, and (especially) religious studies. Modern pagan witchcraft had, after all, appeared as a movement with a very specific historical claim, and sooner or later it had to make a relationship with current academic historiography in order to put itself into a more secure, and durable, perspective. A first step in this direction had been taken by Margot Adler, as described, but although she suggested that the notion of the Old Religion should not be treated as literal fact, she still suggested that there might be some truth to it. A similar hedging was made by Vivianne Crowley in her book in 1989, which took note of the criticisms of the Murray thesis but told readers that they could themselves be flawed; in the same year, by contrast, Tanya Luhrmann accepted the thesis as defunct.[18] The decisive breakthrough was apparently made at a seminar convened at King's College London in December 1990 to discuss the comparisons and contrasts between Paganism and other varieties of religion. It was attended by several notable Wiccans, including Crowley, Leonora James, and Frederic Lamond, and a number of academics including myself, invited in my capacity as a historian of ancient paganisms. One of the most significant aspects of the occasion was the spectacle of one Wiccan after another speaking of the Murray thesis as a foundation myth, and of the Old Religion as metaphor, in the manner of Margot Adler—but with a yet greater sensitivity and erudition. As in America earlier, so now in Britain, Wiccans had broken out of the trap of fundamentalism which has often seemed to be the natural course of minority religions whose basic assumptions are questioned by the wider society. The greatest barrier between pagan witchcraft and academic scholarship (which was one major gateway for it to the national community) was dissolving.

It was hardly a moment too soon, for in the 1990s there broke a tidal wave of accumulating research which swept away not only any possibility of doubt regarding the lack of correlation between paganism and early modern witchcraft, but virtually the whole set of assumptions upon which both the original concept of the Old Religion and its later, evolved, American feminist version, had been based. In Witchcraft studies this corresponded (accidentally or not) to a major geographical shift in the centres of scholarly expertise in the field. For a hundred years the United States had consistently supplied historians at the forefront of it, and this pattern held until the 1970s. During the 1980s, despite the appearance of one or two leading figures,[19] it began to be overshadowed by work undertaken in other nations. Whether because of a generation gap, or even because of a destructive effect of the radical feminist model upon scholarship, the American market in books on the topic ceased to be dominated by works which treated the witch trials as manifestations of a complex web of beliefs in societies significantly different from our own. Instead it became in the 1990s largely the preserve of writers whose own expertise lay in other fields or periods and who regarded the trials as an awful warning for the present, an example of a viral infection of social bodies which could be used for polemical purpose to denounce the phenomenon targeted by the author's particular set of beliefs, whether patriarchy (Anne Llewellyn Barstow), Catholicism (Hans Sebald), or Puritanism (Frances Hill).[20]

The one world-class historian of the subject whom America bought in during the period was, significantly, its most brilliant maverick, Carlo Ginzburg. He accepted a chair at the University of California, Los Angeles, and justified it with a large-scale work on the concept of the witches' sabbat, which traced its roots to ancient beliefs in shamanism and spirit-flight. Like all his work, it was something which probably nobody else could have written, and which broke important new ground. It had the faults common to such bold and broad-brush enterprises, of covering too much ground too fast, and with too much dependence upon the author's original, narrower body of expertise; in this case, his impressions of tribal shamanism and ancient paganism were both somewhat sketchy, and arguably too much was extrapolated from the very unusual phenomenon of the *benandanti* of Friuli, his first study. Most significant for the present book was his representation of the historiographical context of his work. His ideas actually represented an extensive and fruitful development of a point central to Norman Cohn's major study, *Europe's Inner Demons*, published in 1975, that underlying the early modern stereotype of satanic witchcraft lay not merely intellectual constructs but a network of ancient popular beliefs regarding night-flying spirits and goddesses, with their retinues. Cohn had, however, presented his book as a refutation of the Murray thesis, and in the process taken a swipe at Ginzburg for his apparent endorsement of at least some aspects of it in *I Benandanti*, discussed earlier. Ginzburg now portrayed his latest work, once again, as a recognition that Margaret Murray had got certain things right—in particular, that ancient pagan concepts underlay those of early modern witchcraft. In a phrase that was to cause tremendous confusion among modern British witches, he declared that the Murray thesis 'contained a core of truth'. This approach rescued him from having to make any retractions of earlier views, but it skirted the fairly obvious issue that he was actually fulfilling Cohn's agenda, of showing how ancient dream-worlds, or operations on non-material planes of consciousness, helped to create a new set of fantasies at the end of the Middle Ages. The 'core' of the Murray thesis, by clear contrast, was that the witches' sabbats were real and material events in which people celebrated the rites of a secret religion; which is pretty well the opposite of what Ginzburg, as well as Cohn, was saying.[21]

These works had a considerable impact on the general public. Barstow's became a (perhaps the) standard radical feminist text on the subject, while Ginzburg's achieved the position of being the academic book that most British witches have read. This success may be attributed both to their lucid and exciting style and the promotion which they have been given by major presses. Much less well known to date has been the outpouring of research from scholars in Britain and Continental Europe since 1980, which has represented cumulatively the most intensive and sophisticated investigation of early modern witchcraft beliefs and prosecutions ever made and has by now involved more than a hundred academics, from virtually every European state. fifteen international conferences were held between 1980 and 1995—seven in Germany, while Sweden, Austria, Hungary, Britain, France, the Netherlands, and Switzerland hosted one each. As this pattern suggests, German scholars have made the running, although few of their individual monographs or conference proceedings have been translated into English.[22] The mid-1990s, however, saw a major contribution to the field by English historians, representing research that had in some cases been twenty years in the making. five books in particular turned Britain into one of the world centres of work on the subject.[23]

All this outpouring of information had the effect of dismantling many previous assumptions and models, including that provided by American feminism.[24] It has established beyond any reasonable doubt that there was no long-lasting or wide-ranging persecution of witches in early modern Europe, trials which involved the charge being neither routine nor common in any district. Only a tiny percentage of people suspected by their neighbours of witchcraft were executed as a result, and mass arrests only occurred in very exceptional circumstances. Virtually all were concentrated in a few specific places and times during the period 1560–1630, a short span in the whole extent of the medieval and early modern epochs. The number of people put to death for the alleged crime was miniscule compared with those executed on other criminal charges or killed in battle during the centuries involved. The distinction was that the overwhelming majority of the dead in those other two categories were male, whereas most of the victims of witch trials were women; the patriarchies which ran early modern Europe were much more effective in destroying their sons than their daughters.

The predominance of female defendants in the trials is an overall figure, ignoring northern and eastern lands where most were male and some such as Switzerland where men formed a large minority of the accused. None the less, the overall figure matters and makes gender stereotyping an important aspect of the phenomenon. The women accused were virtually never powerful, independent, popular figures who posed any threat to the dominant structures of their society. In most cases they were already poor, marginalized, and anti-social, and where accusations spread they mostly reflected tensions between neighbours in the lower reaches of society. Victims were rarely midwives, who were far more commonly found searching suspects for signs of witchcraft, and although some were healers or cunning folk, the proportion of these was always small; the two categories together supplied 26 of 400 people accused in a series of records from Lorraine, and this seems typical. Accusations of witchcraft were not merely made against women but very often—in some areas mostly—initially made by women, not in the name of male power but because the alleged spells cast by witches most commonly affected those spheres of activity—small children, domestic work and the physical home, the animals of the in-field—which were normally the responsibility of females.

The traditional paradigm of witch trials as a means by which people in power regulated and indoctrinated their inferiors, which flourished from the eighteenth century to the 1970s, has collapsed almost completely. It is now obvious that the main force in driving on persecution was pressure from common people, who genuinely feared and hated witches and wanted their rulers to act against them in times of social upheaval and economic crisis. The greatest single factor in keeping trials relatively infrequent was the disinclination of those rulers to oblige, so that hunts flourished not where states were larger and more powerful, but where they were smallest and most fragmented, and had a decentralized system of justice which put magistrates most directly in contact with the populace. Opinion concerning the efficacy of witch trials—or even the reality of witchcraft—remained divided in most places, at all levels of society. A belief in the need to try witches was found scattered through the whole range of social, political, and confessional structures across most of Europe; the most determined persecutors of all were German Catholics and Scottish Calvinists. Churchmen were rarely prominent in the trial processes except where—as in parts of Germany—they doubled as territorial rulers. Witchcraft could, at times, be a self-empowering fantasy for the dispossessed, but not a single person tried for witchcraft in Europe between 1400 and 1800 has been demonstrated to have adhered to a pagan religion.[25]

During the same years other research demolished any plausible context for the Wiccan creation myth. Historians of late medieval and early modern religion revealed that Christianity permeated the thought-world of the people at the time, and had the value of being developed into an enormous range of discourses to serve all needs, from those of bishops and rulers to those of working people who belonged to devotional guilds and revered favourite saints, popular rebels who talked of hanging or castrating all priests, or ritual magicians seeking to obtain practical ends by controlling demons.[26] Studies of heterodoxy in the period have revealed that it is possible to track even tiny and secretive sects through the centuries, both through their own private papers and literature and the observations of outsiders, whether neighbours or local or central authorities. This is true even of the sixteenth century, let alone the seventeenth, when the breakdown of central controls during the Civil War allowed sectarian groups to flourish, and to be systematically monitored and catalogued by their polemical opponents. It obtained equally for rural and urban districts.[27] This discovery harmonized with another, that the Victorian and Edwardian assumption that a distinctive and ancient 'oral tradition' had endured among country people until modern times, sealed off from literate culture in an essentially unchanging provincial world, had been badly wrong. Systematic research has now proved that England had ceased to be a pre-literate society before the end of the sixteenth century, that reading, writing, and published works were an integral part of even small agricultural communities by that time—even if only a few people in each settlement could deploy them, on behalf of the rest—and that oral and written traditions intermingled and constantly enriched and informed each other. Written culture and spoken culture were not two different worlds, but mirrors which reflected each other. To a lesser extent this last point had been true since the early Middle Ages.[28] In all these fields, the view of the past taken in the 1960s seemed by the late 1990s to belong to another age of the world.

These discoveries will take several more years to filter through to the general public and alter received opinions built up in some cases over a century or two. Already in the 1990s, however, enough of them were reaching parts of British Paganism to produce a knock-on effect of revisionism and adaptation. Since the

1970s, after all, pagan witchcraft had developed its own literature, to which practitioners could refer in the first instance without need for recourse to more general reading. Changes in that small and fairly self-contained body of writing could therefore produce a dramatic impact. There is no doubt that the most sensationally revisionist piece of writing of all was another American initiative: Aidan Kelly's long-delayed monograph on Gerald Gardner and the origins of Wicca which was published in 1991 under the title of *Crafting the Art of Magic*. It performed two principal tasks. One was to draw public attention to the vital importance of Gardner's papers in Toronto, as discussed earlier. The other was to launch a savage polemical attack upon the weakening idea of the Old Religion and to suggest that Gardner and his friends had essentially developed a new one. His treatment of this issue was ambivalent. On the one hand, he held that new religious movements were admirable in themselves and represented a regular and essential replenishment of human spirituality. On the other, he declared that certain aspects of Gardner's practices, of which he himself disapproved, had been related directly to the man's own idiosyncratic psychopathology—of which, by implication, Kelly himself also disapproved. The overall effect was to defend the notion of Wicca as a viable new religion while discrediting Gardner himself, by casting doubt both upon his historical claims and his personal tastes. In this, perhaps, he did another service to scholarship, by presenting Wiccan revisionism in such an intemperate and provocative guise that any subsequent scholar who tackled the matter was bound to appear moderate by comparison, and therefore to be the more welcome to Wiccans.

During the mid-1990s a clutch of publications by British Wiccans did a great deal to lead their religion towards the new millennium with a new maturity and security of self-identity. Leonora James, using the name of Prudence Jones, teamed up with a friend who was himself a long-established writer on ancient Northern European paganism, and earth mysteries, Nigel Pennick. Together they produced a *History of Pagan Europe* for a mainstream press, which circumvented and rendered largely redundant the debate about direct connections between ancient and modern paganism, by exploring the extraordinary richness of different pagan traditions in old Europe, and the ways in which their images and ideas had persisted in Western cultures ever since. Vivianne Crowley published a second title, *Phoenix from the flame*, which concentrated on the nature of Pagan spirituality and ethics, and built up an argument for a pluralist, tolerant, joyous religion which celebrated the world as a sacred place and depended upon mutual responsibility, co-operation, and respect. More explicitly than Starhawk, she treated deities as entities formed and activated by humans, 'human images of reality, rather than reality itself', which needed to be treated as real because once activated they became forces of genuine power. Magical techniques to her are 'not important in themselves, but are ways of focusing the mind on what is to be accomplished'; they provide a deep connection to the unconscious which enables humans to transform themselves and the world about them.

The crux of her argument was summed up in a compound sentence:

It is the task of Paganism today to give to those who seek its ways the inner knowledge, light, energy and peace with which to live our lives in harmony with one another and with all living creation and to answer the eternal questions of humankind: 'Who am I? What must I do to live well and honourably? What is the meaning of the mystery of life and of the divine?'

Those same questions were being tackled simultaneously by Frederic Lamond, in a work which was published under the title of *Religion Without Beliefs* and represented an attempt to put Wicca into a dialogue with other religions. A large part of the value of the book was that it showed how different it was from conventional theology, in its absence of dogma and its reliance upon direct experience and practical results. In the process, it took a double attitude towards the divine as delicate as that of Starhawk and Vivianne Crowley (the deities exist but we help to create them, they are real in one sense and not in another), but different in essence. On the one hand, Lamond related Wicca to broad cultural patterns in modern society—feminism, environmentalism, pluralism—and suggested that religions take particular forms to suit particular times. On the other, he accepted deities as real forces for response, intervention, and change in the universe, whatever their origin (and here he allowed for at least three different Pagan theories), and suggested that cultural processes might actually be driven by their manifestation. He also provided a series of case-studies to argue that operative magic actually works, as a form of energy manipulation comparable to electronics.[29]

*   *   *

Thus far, the story is a triumphalist one of successful development and adaptation in the face of social and intellectual challenges; but human affairs are rarely so neat and the reactions of pagan witches to the challenges of the period between 1988 and 1998 were proportionately more varied and complex than this account would suggest. This is already apparent when considering only the publications of those Wiccan elders who, like Lamond, had survived from the early years of the public history of the religion. The greatest of all, of course, was Doreen Valiente, whose formidable energy carried her into the new decade with undiminished impact. In 1989 she published her own history of modern pagan witchcraft, which was largely, and valuably, autobiography. It proved to be another work with a curious double aspect. One of these was obscurantism, a restatement of the tenets which she had embraced cumulatively during the previous four decades with no overt concessions to criticisms of them other than hostility. Thus, she noted that the Murray thesis had been questioned, but avoided tackling the specific doubts which had been raised, stating instead that it was 'hard to see' why she 'should have aroused the ire of other scholars to such an extent'. She then banged the feminist drum by quoting another (non-academic) opinion that 'Dr Murray's anthropological and sensitive approach to the subject, allied to some genuine "field-work" caused some jealousy among her male colleagues'. Later in the book she declared that the classic texts of ley-hunters from the 1960s and 1970s—already starting to be questioned by earth mysteries researchers themselves—'are practically required reading for the modern witch', and that Michael Dames had discovered the true purpose of the Avebury monuments. One constant feature of the book was her heavy reliance upon newspapers for information about witches with whom she was not herself acquainted. This had a particularly dramatic result when it combined with her other long-term tendency to credit tales of devil-worship and evil magic, to cause her to believe the early reports of satanic ritual abuse and even to give some support to Geoffrey Dickens, the fundamentalist Christian MP who campaigned to bring them to the attention of Parliament: 'I wish I could say, as some witches and occultists have said, that such allegations are all nonsense. Unfortunately, I have press cuttings which bear out Mr Dickens' statements to the letter.'[30]

The book had, however, another aspect which was to be equally important in its impact upon contemporary witches. It actually avoided giving any unequivocal endorsement to the idea of a continuously surviving pagan religion, and placed more emphasis upon the reasons why pagan witchcraft should have appeared at that particular time: its significant choice of term for its modern experience was 'rebirth'. Still more significant, Valiente candidly and ruthlessly drew attention to the points in which she had caught out Gardner and Robert Cochrane in apparent deceptions concocted to lend weight to their claims of perpetuating existing traditions. She printed the evidence which suggested that Alex Sanders had no experience of witchcraft before meeting the Crowthers, and emphasized that key texts of the Wiccan tradition had been written by herself. She ultimately left open the question of whether there had been any pagan witchcraft before Gardner, but had dealt some heavy incidental blows to belief that there had been.

Her next major publication, the following year, was still more curious, for it appeared to condemn that very Wicca which she herself had helped to develop, by declaring that the witchcraft promulgated by Gardner and Sanders was 'airy-fairy'. Instead, with Evan John Jones, she now provided a blueprint for a different variety based upon that of their common mentor Robert Cochrane, with material added from their own thoughts and workings, and the books of Robert Graves and a selection of modern feminist and earth mysteries writers. On two consecutive pages, Valiente declared both that Cochrane's claim to a surviving tradition could never be verified and that he represented an older witchcraft than Wicca; indeed, she termed the book which she and Evans had put together to be the only one entirely dedicated to 'traditional witchcraft'.[31] This pattern, at first sight confusing, was in longer perspective wholly typical of Valiente's career; her enduring greatness lay in the very fact that she was so completely and strong-mindedly dedicated to finding and declaring her own truth, in a world in which the signposts to it were themselves in a state of almost complete confusion.

Other notable survivors were more clear-cut in their attitudes, even if these in turn departed from those developing within the new generation of leading Wiccans. In an interview with a writer who published in 1993, Lois Bourne disassociated herself from Wicca, and represented herself as a solitary witch working (effective) spells after the pattern of old-time cunning folk. In her autobiography, five years later, she confirmed this stance and was agnostic on the subject of the origin of Gardner's practices. Her pen-portrait of Gardner himself was the best published until that time, showing him to have been at once fascinating, inspiring, lovable, and devious.[32] The only one of his followers to write in the 1990s who suggested that he had no faults and that his account of Wiccan origins should be taken at face value was Patricia Crowther. This was equally true in her own autobiography, which also appeared in 1998, and in her republication six years earlier of a book which she and Arnold had produced in the 1970s, without any further comment or amendment.[33]

That such a range of responses was possible among former leading Gardnerians provides a miniature of the now luxuriant complexity of pagan witchcraft in Britain. By the 1990s all of the varieties in place by the 1960s—Gardnerian, Cochranian, Alexandrian, and those which claimed an independent origin to any of those—were still flourishing and reproducing, as were aberrant offshoots of all. In addition there was the very large number of covens founded by people who had read books—above all Gardner's, Valiente's, Starhawk's, Budapest's, and those of the Farrars—and developed their own practices from them. Sometimes these founders would declare them to be in the tradition of the author(s) who had most inspired them, and sometimes they would subsume them under the general label of 'traditional'. Alongside coven-based pagan witchcraft there appeared at the end of 1980s a formally constituted strain which catered for the solitary practitioner. It was largely given identity by one book, by the West Country writer Rae Beth, who standardized for such people the delightful term of 'hedge witch'. The book concerned, published in 1990, was essentially a handbook of Wicca without a coven structure and formal initiation, embellished with Beth's own powerful poems, meditations, and invocations. It also embodied, wholesale and without question, the myth of the Old Religion as developed by American feminism. The following year the veteran Marian Green, who had always argued against the necessity for prescribed structures and liturgies, produced another manual for lone working, and thereafter those who would not or could not operate in groups were well supplied, and represented a major growth area in British witchcraft.[34]

To do justice to the various personalities who came to prominence in the latter during the 1980s, flourished through the 1990s, and yet remained outside the national literary or administrative leadership, would need a book in itself. Three regional portraits may suffice to indicate the range. In the West was Paddy Slade, who represented herself as a lifelong witch in the solitary tradition, worked with groups of ritual magicians, and devised rituals which gave comfort and inspiration to many, and particularly to women who had suffered physical abuse. The dominant figure in south-east Midland witchcraft was the magnificent Dot Griffiths, a warm-hearted dragon who mixed elements of native American, Egyptian, Romany, Greek, English folk and voodoo spiritualities into a Wiccan mould, and trained and campaigned tirelessly from her base in the House of Avalon. From Sussex came Kevin Carlyon, who was one of the last individuals to court public attention in the manner which had been so common in the 1970s—by regular and audacious appearances in the mass media. It was a device that was passing its time, and had the effect of isolating Carlyon from the bulk of British witches, but some of the rituals which he staged with a press presence had the useful effect of providing a mutually supportive interaction with local people as well as keeping images of a benevolent and public-spirited witchcraft before the national gaze.

During the 1990s an ill-defined but perceptible division began to occur in British pagan witchcraft, propelled by two different, but interactive forces. One was structural. Until the end of the 1980s the only regional or national hierarchy which existed among witches was an informal one, based on the respect and affection given naturally to especially prominent elders in particular traditions, or the handful of authors of well-read books or editors of the main magazines. With the growth and elaboration of the Pagan Federation, including elected leaders, honorary councillors, annual conferences, a glossy periodical, regional co-ordinators, official visitors, a press hotline, and local meetings for ritual or to hear speakers, a Pagan aristocracy began to emerge, producing a counterbalancing emotion of alienation among those unwilling or unable to participate in the processes which had produced it. This could combine at times with the effects of revisionist historiography. During the 1980s the Farrars, in combination with Doreen Valiente, had inflicted damage upon the reputation of Alex Sanders, which Valiente compounded in her own book at the end of the decade. This process still left Gardner's standing intact, as the great transmitter of the ancient ways, but it was dealt a devastating blow by Aidan Kelly, who seemed to reduce him to a deceiver of dubious personal tastes. Kelly's avowed purpose was to make people give Wicca its due as a new religion, but his impact upon many British witches or would-be witches was to make them reject Gardner himself while preserving a wish for an unbroken and ancient descent of practice. The result was to give new appeal to those groups who wore the tag of 'traditional' or 'hereditary' or in an increasing number of cases simply 'the Old' Craft. Gardner and Wicca could be elbowed aside by them, and they could assert their identity as the authentic transmitters of the Old Ways. I have personal knowledge of three covens which had been formed in the 1980s (largely using information from books) with the tag of 'Wiccan', and hastily converted their self-description to 'traditional' in the mid-1990s. As Gardner's remains the oldest variety of coven-based pagan witchcraft securely recorded in the Western world, there is some injustice in the process, just as the denigration of him which has frequently appeared in the wake of Aidan Kelly's book misses what was genuinely remarkable about the man and what explains his undoubted impact.

The result of all this was to create not two opposed blocs, but a spectrum. At one end were witches, mostly Wiccan, who were prominent in the Pagan Federation, wrote the books which represented pagan witchcraft to the wider intellectual culture of the nation, and had assimilated the changes in historiography to view their religion as one which, while drawing heavily upon ancient ideas and images, was essentially a modern development especially well suited to the resolution of modern needs by applying selected old concepts and practices in a new way. At the other were witches who self-consciously belonged to the conceptual if not literal backwoods, claiming to work in an unbroken hidden succession of practitioners stretching back to antiquity, using appellations such as 'traditional', and often articulating a generally counter-cultural stance. The delineation here is of extremes and, in the nature of things, the majority of British pagan witches conformed precisely to neither of these models.[35]

All were now operating within a profound shift in attitudes to that witchcraft which had taken place within society in general since 1980. In place of the 1970s notion of it as a means to an often unethical personal empowerment, most journalists had come to view witches as practitioners of a pagan religion based upon feminism and nature-worship and with a benevolent and life-affirming ethic; at worst, harmlessly idiotic. The change began in the early 1980s, was pronounced by the end of the decade, and had made the new stereotype general by the 1990s. It was taken up in particular by the quality press or by local newspapers, while the more sensational popular daily and Sunday papers either dropped the subject of witchcraft as no longer newsworthy or—in just one or two cases—continued to play upon the old, hostile image.[36] The alteration in journalistic opinion may actually have helped to save witches from becoming targets in the scare over alleged satanic ritual abuse, while the collapse of the panic and the disproof of the claims which had supported it further discredited the image of the witch as a devil-worshipper and menace to society.

The transition was vividly illustrated in that most popular and influential of all media, television; and here the fact that the United States was undergoing just the same shift of perspective assisted the process considerably, as so many programmes shown on British television were made there. On 27 November 1995 an episode of the cult science fiction series, *The X files*, neatly had its ideological cake and ate it. It portrayed the exposure of a genuine sect of Satanists, who had worshipped secretly in a small American town for seven generations and were eventually destroyed by the demon which they had called up; thus far the script was still living in the world of Lovecraft, Wheatley, Summers, and their followers. On the other hand, when the investigators debated the question of whether they might have been part of a wider network of groups, the heroine (Agent Scully) burst out that the allegations of a nationwide conspiracy of Satanists made on television chat shows were 'crap', and that Wiccans 'love all living things'—and that settled the matter. Suddenly the story was in the 1990s.

More subtle and significant still was the episode of the British Independent Television detective series *Wycliffe*, screened on 28 July 1996. It began by suggesting that a Cornish pagan group was guilty of child sacrifice, after the finding of the body of a baby. Viewers were initially encouraged to share the instinctive hostility and suspicion felt towards the pagans by the investigating police officers, and the most sinister possible interpretation was invited of such standard Pagan trappings as the pentagram symbol, robed workings in a circle, and the invocation of elemental powers. Then the plotline twisted, to reveal that the group concerned was completely harmless and innocent, and that the killer of the infant was actually its own mother, daughter of a friend of the leading detective. The policewoman who had led the investigation of the pagans, and who had at first been deeply prejudiced against them, came slowly to understand, respect, and defend them, and was last seen reading a textbook upon the nature of ancient paganism by the Oxford historian Robin Lane Fox.

A different form of acceptance and integration was manifested by the way in which Pagan (and often specifically Wiccan) imagery began to take its place in both popular and elite culture. Novels began to appear from authors who were not themselves celebrities among the pagan communities and yet which were steeped in a knowledge of, and sympathy towards, pagan witchcraft, whether comic (Jessica Berens) or dramatic (Freda Warrington).[37] A public exhibition of paintings on pagan themes was held at the Piers Feetham Gallery, London, in the autumn of 1996, with the title 'Drawing Down The Moon'. Rock bands with local followings, mostly in the Gothic style, identified their music wholly with Paganism, and so did one star performer, Julian Cope. Three examples, perhaps more than any other, illustrate the extent to which it had penetrated mainstream culture, by the mid-1990s. The internationally successful rock band, The Pretenders, released a song, 'Hymn to Her', which was a paean of praise to the goddess of modern witchcraft. The first episode of a very popular American soap opera about a dynamic woman in middle life, *Cybill*, shown in Britain on 5 January 1996, was entitled 'Virgin, Mother, and Crone'.

In 1996 also the twentieth book was published in a series by the most popular British comic novelist of the late twentieth century, Terry Pratchett. Pratchett never allowed his readers to forget that the world in which he set his stories was imaginary, intentionally reversing that suspension of disbelief which is traditionally integral to fiction. At the same time he used the slapstick humour of his fantasies to explore serious questions about time, belief, and religion. The result was a set of stories which any thirteen-year-old could find hugely entertaining and yet which required a very broad and sophisticated education for every joke to be fully appreciated. As part of this pattern he treated Wicca and ritual magic as a normal and acceptable part of human life, and showed a deep knowledge of both. In fact, some of his wisecracks about modern pagan witchcraft could only be understood by insiders—which, since Pratchett has been careful to disassociate himself from any direct knowledge of it, must be the result of very shrewd reading.[38] Even his works, however, probably did not represent the most widely known and influential public display of motifs taken ultimately from Wicca during the 1980s and 1990s. This distinction belongs to the television series 'Robin of Sherwood', made by Goldcrest Productions for HTV between 1984 and 1986 and written by Richard Carpenter. It portrayed Robin Hood as a pagan guided by the antlered god of the greenwood—here called Herne, one of the names attributed to the male deity of the witches by Margaret Murray—and proved to be one of the most successful programmes that this television company has ever released.

It is important not to make too much of these developments. As shall be made plainer later, attitudes among journalists and scriptwriters were by now often in advance of those held even among the more wealthy and educated sections of society in general. It must also be significant that when a multi-faith directory of religions in the United Kingdom was published in 1993, pagan witchcraft was included in the section on paganism in general, which was given just two pages; in the same work the Baha'i sect of Islam, which has about 6,000 adherents in Britain, was given twenty-four. This is an illustration partly of the lack of information on Wicca and its sisters then circulating among inter-faith networks, but perhaps also of the much greater importance attributed by such networks to religions associated with other cultures in an ethnically diverse society than those which had been home-grown within that society.[39]

On the other hand, it is also important not to underestimate the changes in the public position of pagan witchcraft between 1988 and 1998. One consequence of them was that the figure of the witch herself was starting to recede within that craft, to be replaced by those of the priestess and priest. Wiccans were ceasing to identify primarily with the victims of the early modern trials and starting to look over and around them, to reclaim the heritage of classical antiquity, and of the Celtic and northern literatures. They were less and less the representatives of an age-old peasant resistance movement and more and more a trained group of religious and magical practitioners, answering a growing call from mainstream society. They were no longer so much the inheritors of an archaic faith as members of the earliest, and foremost, of an important constellation of modern successors. These changes were symbolized neatly by the increasingly rare usage of the word 'witch' itself, at least in public discourse, and the substitution of 'Pagan'. For all this, however, the challenge which pagan witchcraft still poses to established notions of religion is not the less radical because it has become more familiar; and at the heart of its mysteries lies a particular notion, and experience, of the transformative power of something that is commonly called magic. In those senses, its practitioners will always be witches.

20

GRANDCHILDREN OF THE SHADOWS

In the course of carrying out the research for this book, it was essential for me to gain the trust and friendship of a relatively large number of pagan witches, or else I would have been bereft of a vital quantity of my source material and lacked an interpretative context for much of what remained. As well as having an indispensable practical value, the process was exciting in itself, propelled by an intense curiosity on my own part and ameliorated by the pleasure which I took in the company of many of the individuals concerned. It was never intended to be a sociological or anthropological exercise, for not only have I never been trained in those disciplines but had I conducted myself from the beginning with the formal rigour and regard for quantitative analysis associated with them, including systematic and standardized questioning, then it is most unlikely that I would ever have won the trust of the people concerned. It was the fact that I was identified as a historian, committed to a quest which had intrinsic interest for many of them, while not being bent upon studying them directly, which permitted the growth of that mutual familiarity which has made the writing of this book possible. None the less, this looser and more informal set of relationships has acquired a depth which has implications for scholarship. Between 1991 and 1998 I made the acquaintance of hundreds of British witches, and obtained a knowledge of the full membership, beliefs, and working practices of twenty-one covens; four were firmly identified as Gardnerians, five as Alexandrian, three as traditional, and nine displayed a mixture of the first two, or were derived from one of the successors to them such as the 'reformed Alexandrian' variety developed by the Farrars. To most of these I was an occasional, often a one-time, visitor, but I was continuously in touch with five of them over a period of at least three years each.

This length and depth of contact may well exceed that of any academic who has yet published upon British pagan witchcraft. The total number of covens of which I have first-hand experience represents, for example, almost three times that recorded by my main predecessor in the field, Tanya Luhrmann. It probably, in fact, exceeds that of most pagan witches, given the rule which binds most, that nobody should belong to more than one coven at once; my status as an academic scholar was very generously held to exempt me from the latter. My sample is clearly heavily weighted towards the Wiccan end of the spectrum of modern witches, but my acquaintance with many individuals who represent

Traditional, Hereditary, or Hedge Witchcraft suggests that their beliefs and rituals are essentially the same. Even given the impressionistic and casual manner in which I have gained my material, it may therefore be arguable that there is value in setting down my own observations of the nature of pagan witchcraft in Britain during the 1990s, half a century or one long adult lifetime after its first appearance.

The Pagan Federation has, since 1989, issued three statements of belief which, in its view, define a Pagan, and to which its members are expected to subscribe. As that Association was founded by Wiccans, and dominated by them until the mid-1990s, the definition may be presumed to apply to them with particular strength. The first component is an acceptance of the inherent divinity of the natural world, and a rejection of any notion of the creation of that world by a power outside itself. Such acceptance is immediately recognized to take a range of possible forms, from the animist belief that the cosmos is empowered by an apparently infinite number of spirit forms to that form of monotheism which suggests that the planet is the living body of a single divine entity. The second component is the rejection of any concept of a divinely prescribed law for human behaviour, and therefore of the concepts of sin and salvation. In place of those is an ethic of freedom to express and gratify individual needs and desires, and so pursue personal growth and happiness, with the single major limitation of an undertaking to avoid harming others in the process. This restriction is given a mystical quality for many by the concept of the inherent sanctity of all living things. The two aspects of this morality are summed up in 'the Wiccan Rede': 'Do as ye will an' ye harm none.' The third component is an acceptance that divinity can be both female and male. This formulation leaves room for a further range of conceptualizations, from a single bisexual Great Spirit to a genuine polytheism, although duotheism—by which a goddess and a god appear in various aspects—is the most commonly articulated. The essential practical expression of this principle is that women are held to represent religious power at least as effectively as men.

At a glance it should be obvious that these principles can also characterize not only every other variety of modern Paganism, but some varieties of Hindu and Shinto beliefs and many tribal religious systems. They could, indeed, be endorsed by liberal Christians, with some reformulation such as the recognition of a Supreme Being who is beyond gender, incorporating both female and male. As already indicated, they leave room for a very wide span of beliefs, let alone practices, of a sort quite large enough to characterize separate religious systems. An unspoken definition is therefore crucial, that Pagans today are people who hold those tenets and turn for symbolism, kinship, and inspiration to the pre-Christian religions of Europe and the Near East, and that pagan witches identify in addition with a refashioned, positive version, of the traditional figure of the witch.

*　　*　　*

390

I would now like to add five more features of modern pagan witchcraft, based upon my own observation of it, which are not usually identified by its practitioners but seem to me to be important. First, *it aims to draw out and enhance the divinity within human beings*. Second, *it abolishes the traditional Western distinction between religion and magic*. Third, *it is a mystery religion, or set of mystery religions*. Fourth, *its essence lies in the creative performance of ritual*. Fifth, *it is eclectic and protean*. They will now be examined in detail, as stated. The first depends upon the notion that modern pagan witches aim both to honour and work with superhuman forces and to recognize and develop the potential for divinity or semi-divinity within themselves. This notion strikes to the heart of the debate over the definition of religion which has been conducted in the West since ancient times. The first chapter of this book opened with the statement that no resolution of it has ever been made, and adopted as a working formulation that of Tylor: a belief in the existence of spiritual beings, and in the need of humans to form relationships with them. It may be added here that the very meaning of the word has never been generally agreed. The Romans produced it, but among them Cicero traced it to a root word signifying 'observation', and suggested that its essence was a reading of signs given by the divine, while Servius opined that its root lay in a different term, meaning 'to bind', and that its essence was therefore a relationship, and communion, between human and superhuman. In practice, of course, these definitions are perfectly compatible, and most Western writers have used the word to indicate a blend of both.[1] Pagan witches, however, tend in practice to place a much heavier emphasis upon Servius's definition, because they do not generally believe that divinities have set plans or commands for humans, and so correspondingly have less need to read their directions. By contrast, the notion of communion between human and superhuman is central to pagan witchcraft, with the vital additional dimension that the superhuman is also, at least implicitly, present within human beings as part of the immanent and integral existence of the sacred within the natural world. Thus the central act of pagan witchcraft is invocation, by which a deity-form is invited to enter into the living body of a witch, and so make manifest, or supercharge, the divine nature of the human concerned. It is a striking, and intense, fulfilment of that very common element of religiosity, a yearning for integration with the divine, with the rest of the cosmos, and with oneself.

It is this yearning, and its resolution, which distinguishes pagan witchcraft from a straightforward process of therapy, self-development, or human potential. It makes explicit reference to a supernatural and at least partially external source of empowerment; deities matter to it. On the other hand a literal belief in the existence of those deities is not necessary to practitioners. Among pagan witches I have found people who think of their goddess and god as archetypes of the natural world or of human experience, others who regard them as projections of human need and emotion which have taken on life of their own, others who see them merely as convenient symbols, and yet others who have a belief in them as independent beings with whom relationships can be made. Some of the latter see themselves as having been 'called' by those divinities, and having been guided by them subsequently. More remarkable, and significant, I have encountered all those viewpoints within a single coven, co-existing in perfect harmony because the members never usually felt the need to articulate or debate them; a set of radically different belief systems was existing in complete harmony because the people who held them were co-operating with great success to work with a common stock of images and actions. Tanya Luhrmann is correct that modern paganism, including witchcraft, can be the perfect religion for a romantic rationalist,[2] but it is worth emphasizing that many witches are full-blown theists of a wholly traditional kind, and that many more hold perspectives between these two extreme positions.

The essence of religious experience in modern pagan witchcraft lies in the awakening or enhancement of powers within the participant, by contact with deity forms which may or may not be regarded as objectively real but are treated as though they are. As long as the stimulant effect is produced, then the reality of the goddess or god form invoked is more or less irrelevant. A common theme to this witchcraft, found in the books of exemplars such as Starhawk and Vivianne Crowley, and key ritual texts such as the Charge, is that the vital first step in attaining a better life and perhaps a better world is to know and fully express one's own self. This means at the least a gain in positive and productive action, and to more ambitious practitioners the development of actual 'occult' abilities such as clairvoyance, prophecy, psychokinesis, and magical healing. Associated with this process is the belief that it is both possible and desirable to gain a better understanding of how the world functions as a whole, by discerning its inner workings and symbolic patterns. A related important feature of these projects is that pagan witchcraft can have no congregations or audiences; everybody present at its workings must be an active participant.

This pattern is reinforced by the concentration of this witchcraft upon the present world and life. The latter is one consequence of its lack of a concept of salvation, and of eternal reward or punishment, and its emphasis upon self-realization. The doctrine of afterlife articulated by most pagan witches to whom I have spoken, and which is built into the Wiccan liturgy, is that expounded by Gardner—of reincarnation, after an interval of rest and pleasure in an Otherworld known variously as 'the Summerland' or as 'the ecstasy of the Goddess'. This doctrine was taken by him, in every detail except the second name for the resting-place between lives, directly from a particular branch of spiritualism, which was itself already well developed by the 1870s and 1880s.[3] Some of the witches to whom I have spoken incorporated into it a detail that was (as has been illustrated) precious to Gardner himself, that devout Wiccans would be able to live again alongside those whom they had loved most in a present incarnation. Some had absorbed the Eastern doctrine of karma, and believed that the form of future lives would be to some extent determined by good or bad deeds in an existing one. Most, however, accepted the prospect of reincarnating as a simple, secure, and pleasant future, and gave it no further thought. Some had vivid memories of what they took to have been previous lives, and considered these to be significant to their present identity, but none seemed to attach the same degree of importance to lives to come. Rituals at Hallowe'en (in Irish, Samhain), the seasonal festival commonly associated with death and the dead, usually only served to confuse the issue. A very common component of these was the expectation that the spirits of the beloved dead— including the very long dead—would return to join the living celebrants. If these spirits were in new incarnations, such a process ought to be difficult to achieve. A reconciliation of the two concepts is, of course, perfectly possible to propose, and according to a number of different schemes, but not only is there no standard one prescribed in pagan witchcraft, but even within the same coven it is generally left up to individual members to resolve the apparent problem according to their choice; and most do not seem to pay attention to it at all. It can be no coincidence that of all the rites of passage used among modern witches, those concerned with funerals are the least discussed, encountered, or standardized.

The instinctual position of most pagan witches, therefore, seems to be that if one makes the most of the present life, in all respects, then the next life is more or less certainly going to benefit from the process and so one may as well concentrate on the present. If this is the case, then it certainly has empirical strength, and if it is simpler than (say) a belief in a cycle of constant dreary rein-carnation from which the wise and the blessed break free, or in a single process of judgement, salvation or damnation, then it is not necessarily more naïve. It is related to the attitude of pagan witches to suffering. The sociologist Bryan Wilson has declared that 'all religions provide a vocabulary of sufferings, whether these are personal, communal, societal, or even universal in kind, and they provide, no less, a repertoire of methods for their relief.' The anthropologist Clifford Geertz has suggested that as 'a religious problem, the problem of suffering is, paradoxically, not how to avoid suffering but how to suffer'.[4]

Both comments have relevance to pagan witchcraft, but within a distinctive idiom. Pagan witches do not regard pain and distress as experiences inflicted by deities, or as aspects of a material world which is itself inherently flawed, corrupt, and filled with grief. On the contrary, they tend to emphasize the beauty, sanctity, and potential for pleasure of the apparent world, and draw no sharp distinctions within it between matter and spirit. This does not mean that their religion does not recognize suffering, which is vividly symbolized by the presence of the scourge among the working tools and highlighted by a crucial question upon initiation as to whether the postulant is willing to endure discomfort in order to learn. Rather, they regard it as a series of experiences from which humans may learn, and in learning equip themselves better to encounter and to overcome it in the future. Pains and ordeals are to witches a part of the process of training themselves to become wiser and more effective beings, individually and collectively; not phenomena to be passively endured but to be treated as object lessons, and—if possible—to be tackled and defeated.

In this attitude, as in its attitude to death, pagan witchcraft reflects its central concept of humans as miniature divinities, or parts of the divine, who may enhance or further discover their divine selves by their own efforts, assisted by co-operation with greater divinities, or parts of the divine, which are represented by pagan deities.

My second personal observation was that this witchcraft *abolishes the traditional Western distinction between religion and magic*. This was defined earlier as recognizing that both religion and magic are means by which humans negotiate with supernatural beings, but that in the former they are dealing with forces outside their control, while in the latter they are seeking to compel and manipulate them. Pagan witches both honour the deities and spirits with whom they work and expect these entities to assist with tasks once invited, enticed, or summoned, to the consecrated space. They have little sense of a continuous need to propitiate and satisfy divine beings. One consequence of this attitude is that pagan deities, Hebrew daimons and archangels, and elemental spirits, are commonly called by witches to their circles for the same ritual, although only a (or the) goddess and god are actually invoked into humans. The eclectic nature of the entities involved reflects the roots of this witchcraft in both ancient pagan religion and ceremonial magic. Another consequence is the total absence of the concept of sacrifice, as the ritual is expected to be satisfaction enough for the supernatural beings involved. The deliberate union of religious and magical traditions is signalled very obviously by the title commonly given to initiates, of 'priest (or priestess) and witch'. It gives emphasis to the fact that pagan witches are expected not to be passive servants of the divine but to take the initiative in working with it. Priestesses and priests can have passive roles; a witch must not. The traditional concept of the magician as a person who dominates and directs spiritual forces has largely been replaced among modern witches by a different one, also with ancient precedents—that the greater harmony with the cosmos and greater understanding of it produced by training as a witch, together with concomitant changes produced within oneself, allow the solution of formerly intractable problems and the attainment of formerly unreachable goals.

Since ancient times Western intellectual culture has accorded respect to religion and treated magic with a much greater degree of suspicion, and the only effect of a relative shift to rationalism and secularism has been to compound the latter with derision. The effects of this tradition are visible even in fairly recent and deeply respected scholarly works such as that upon religious practices in modern America published by Rodney Stark and William Bainbridge in 1985:

Many current cults, such as the various witchcraft and pagan groups, have reacted to secularization by a headlong plunge back into magic. They reject the whole scientific culture as well as Christian-Judaic religious traditions. . . . In our judgement, these cults are reactionary and have little future. They are utterly vulnerable to the same forces of secularization that have corroded much better organized and accommodated faiths. They will not thrive unless the modern world itself collapses.[5]

The tremendous condescension of this passage is matched by the total lack of any research to underpin it; it is a clear example of how even by the 1980s leading academics could make confident declarations based upon blatant prejudice when confronted with the phenomenon of modern witchcraft.

It was exactly this combination of ignorance and dismissiveness which Tanya Luhrmann worked to stop, and which her book in 1989 has indeed largely brought to an end, at least among specialists in religious studies. She demonstrated that witches and ritual magicians in modern Britain were not reactionaries who dismissed the whole scientific culture; on the contrary, a large number were in jobs at the cutting edge of it, such as computer technology. She went on to explain how ritual magic operated in its own way upon scientific and technological principles, and how its practices could 'directly confront powerful psychological issues' while exhibiting an intellectual strategy of ambivalence to religious truth of the sort found among modern Christian theologians. As said earlier, however, she also suggested that there was an element of self-deceit involved in the manner in which modern ritual magicians, including witches, persuaded themselves of the literal efficacy of their spells and invocations.[6] This last aspect of her work has been criticized by Amy Simes, in her thesis on Paganism in the North-East Midlands, with the observation that the standard of verification employed among pagan witches is personal and subjective, lacking the external objectivity which Luhrmann had apparently assumed to apply. Simes added the suggestions that Pagan magicians were seeking a persuasive metaphorical meaning for action, and that the results of that action were generally less important to them than the action itself, which could be as symbolically valuable and therapeutically effective as Luhrmann herself had pointed out.[7]

The following points can be made here to extend the observations of these two writers. The first is that, as shown earlier, modern ritual magic is itself the product of a period imbued with the notions of evolution, progress, and sequential scientific discovery. It has evolved to take account of developments in scientific thinking, and in particular chaos and quantum theory, which both portray a universe which functions in some respects more like that of ceremonial magicians than the mechanistic one assumed by scientists between the eighteenth and mid-twentieth centuries. I have met many pagan witches who are considerably better educated in such recent scientific speculation than the average highly literate person, and employ it to defend their practices. The second point is that my own conversations with witches suggest that their attitude to operational magic is indeed very complex. All of those to whom I have spoken have articulated the issue raised by Tanya Luhrmann and reinforced by Amy Simes, that the therapy involved in the action of carrying out the ritual is generally perceived as valuable in itself. If the beneficiary is intended to be the person or people enacting the rite or casting the spell, then it provides an opportunity to confront and work through problems and choices. If the action is requested by somebody outside the group, or other than the witch, performing it, then the knowledge that magic is apparently being performed to help them can be immensely reassuring and supportive. All, therefore, would acknowledge the importance of magical work as therapy, placebo, and moral assistance.

All, however, have also insisted to me that operative magic is sometimes literally effective, and here it is necessary to take into account Luhrmann's portrait of a process by which magicians remember apparent successes and dismiss apparent failures, and so build up faith in the efficacy of their actions. I have observed this myself, and would place it in the following context. To most witches to whom I have spoken, magical working is an imperfect, hit-and-miss craft, and therefore they expect a failure rate. It is entirely consistent with this that they remember and prize those occasions when they seem to have achieved spectacular success. All agree that magic should be resorted to either as a supportive action for practical responses to problems or when all apparent practical measures have failed. It appears to me in addition that their operations often divide into two categories. One consists of requests for magical working undertaken on appeal from others which are treated as formalities or points of honour. No great emotional investment is made in them and the result of the operation is not a matter of great interest or memory. The other consists of those workings in which the operators have a deep personal interest and invest powerful emotions. They are rarely undertaken if they appear to run against the natural course of events or to be based upon unreasonable expectations. They are employed most commonly, and avidly, if a natural process ought to have occurred but seems to be mysteriously blocked, or if the odds for a desirable and an undesirable outcome to a process seem to be evenly balanced. This pattern has been very clear in the five covens which I have observed steadily over lengthy periods, and the apparent success rate of that class of operation is very high indeed. A sceptic might plausibly argue that this reflects the reasonable conditions for expectation of a happy outcome in which it is undertaken; but this is as impossible to demonstrate as the literal efficacy of the magic.

Two further observations may be of value. One is that all of the pagan witches to whom I have spoken regard cursing as an activity which is not merely ethically abhorrent but genuinely dangerous. This is formally expressed as the much-quoted 'law of threefold return': that any magical working rebounds upon the operator with three times the force—benevolent or malevolent—with which it was sent forth. In practice, few of the witches who have been my partners in conversation accepted this in its full, literal sense, but all had a less precise but still powerful feeling that a piece of magic directed with evil intent carried some kind of psychic penalty for the person directing it, sufficient to make such operations unacceptable in all but the direst extremity of self-defence. The other observation is that for every witch whom I have encountered who has rationalized the operation of magic in terms of quantum physics, chaos mathematics, or electronic particle theory, I have met many more who have not the least idea of why their spells and ritual workings appear to be effective and are happy to leave the matter open. One of them summed up the matter for me thus: 'The first stage is when you totally believe in witchcraft. The second is when you realize that it's a complete lot of rubbish. The third is when you realize that it's a complete lot of rubbish; but that somehow it also seems to work.'[8]

The third major characteristic which I would myself attribute to modern pagan witchcraft is that *it is a mystery religion, or set of mystery religions*. This has already been emphasized by Margot Adler, who has defined the characteristics of such religions as their concern with the processes of growth and regeneration, and the manner in which their devotees undergo experiences of death and rebirth and confront the questions of the source of all life and the place of humans in the cosmos. This concern is also central to the view of Wicca taken by Vivianne Crowley.[9] I would endorse it, and also draw attention to structural aspects of this identity. Modern pagan witchcraft has no public places or acts of worship. It is almost wholly the preserve of closed groups or solitary individuals, operating a process of training and initiation which usually takes some considerable time. Much of its joy and effectiveness lies in its self-image as a religion of secrets, associated with the night and wild or hidden places. It is usually recognized as requiring considerable dedication and hard work, and as being unsuitable for the faint-hearted, lazy, or flippant. It is, accordingly, highly selective and exclusive, and is mandated to care only for those who seek its aid. While many of its members believe that it has a wider benevolent implication for their society, or even their planet, they still do not envisage that a majority of people should or could practise it. They instinctually assume the existence of other religions alongside it, which cater for other needs and other sorts of personality.

The fourth major characteristic of pagan witchcraft consists of its essential reliance upon *the creative performance of ritual*. Its only holy writings are books of ceremonies, which most practitioners regard as starting-points for the development of their own practices. Its only sacred words are those used to evoke or invoke divinity, and considerable time and trouble is usually devoted to preparing the space for each working. Although witches often have favourite places in which to work—special rooms set aside in their homes and commonly described as 'temples', or attractive and secluded rural settings— these are virtually never used until the invisible shrine of the consecrating circle has been erected. This is, in turn, carefully removed at the end of the rite. Unlike some other varieties of modern pagan, witches have no special and fixed attachment to the ceremonial monuments of previous ages, such as prehistoric stone circles, although they generally regard these sites as having sanctity and will work there if occasion permits. To them, sacred action is crucially necessary to produce a sacred place, and functions as the channel or vehicle by which humans can achieve a direct and personal experience of the divine. If the Judaeo-Christian tradition has depended on the proposition 'this is how you should feel about the divine', modern pagan witchcraft says 'this is how you *feel* the divine; now work out what it means for yourself, if you wish.' Not for nothing is the most ambitious attempt to examine its structures of thought made hitherto, the book by Frederic Lamond, entitled *Religion Without Beliefs*. If the informative action of ancient paganism was *propitiation*, the process of appeasing and pleasing superhuman forces, then the equivalent action of modern paganism is *consecration*, the treatment of people, places, and objects in such a way as to make them seem more spiritually powerful, effective, and significant.

In its attitude to ritual, pagan witchcraft embodies something at once very ancient and very modern. Some of the leading pioneers of the sociology of religion gave primacy to ceremony in all human religious behaviour. Robertson Smith declared that practice and not theory was fundamental to religion, that most people are concerned with observance and not doctrine, and that modes of worship are more revealing to a scholar than stated beliefs. R. R. Marett agreed that ritual is essential and belief secondary, and that emotion rather than reason is the key to religious ceremony: 'savage religion is not something so much thought out as danced out'. Max Weber suggested that traditional religions consist of a multitude of loosely ordered deities and a collection of acts and images which involve themselves in an independent, segmental, and immediate manner with almost any sort of event. They lack abstraction, logical coherence, and inclusive formulations, but meet problems creatively, specifically, and opportunistically.[10] These views are certainly borne out by studies of ancient European paganisms, which suggest a strong primacy of ritual and direct experience of divinity, and a much lesser importance of conceptual and doctrinal structures.[11] In this sense, pagan witches are just going back to basics, but with a distinctively modern application, to personal accomplishment and development. Their emphasis upon individuality, self-discovery, and pluralism is characteristic of aspects of late twentieth-century Western thought. In particular, it has been noted of the counter-culture of the period that it gives priority to 'experience, creativity, symbolic communication, and openness to the transcendent that brings about a transformation of consciousness'.[12] All this is true of modern pagan witchcraft.

The fifth and last feature of that witchcraft stated above is that *it is eclectic and protean*; it takes ideas from many sources and applies them in many—and often constantly altering—ways. This also is typical of aspects of the period, already noted in an extreme form in the case of the 'California Cosmology'. Images, texts, and concepts are taken from the cultures of ancient Greece, Egypt, Rome, Mesopotamia, Ireland, and Wales, from the Anglo-Saxons and the Vikings, and from the folklores of the British Isles, the structure of prehistoric monuments, Hinduism, Buddhism, Taoism, eighteenth- and nineteenth-century Celtic romanticism, native America, the modern earth mysteries movement, and American radical feminism. Techniques for raising energy can include dancing, drumming, chanting, scourging, and singing, while operative magic can take the form of meditation, visualization, spiral dancing, sacred drama, astral projection, and a very large number of different spell-casting operations. Ritual is often used as a means of communication—between members of the coven or between human and divine—and equally often as a means of resolving and altering situations, and both usages regularly take place within the same ceremony. It is used both to transform and to confirm, to challenge and to reinforce, to bond a group together and to achieve practical and external effects—for all the ends, in fact, which sociologists of religion have deemed ritual to be worked.[13]

The basic format of modern pagan witchcraft can therefore contain a rich kaleidoscope of cultural borrowings from all over the globe, fashioned according to the tastes of the person or group working within it. None the less, that basic format is still a strong one, and common structures of activity still pronounced. In large part this is due to the existence of the Books of Shadows, but also to the inherent power and utility of the basic forms: the duotheism of the divine couple (sometimes reduced to the goddess alone), the sacred circle with its cardinal points, the blessing and sharing of food and drink, the personification of divine beings by celebrants, ritual work of healing and consecration, a system of training and initiation (usually through three degrees), and the observation of ceremonies at the full moon and the eight major seasonal festivals.

There are other aspects of modern pagan witchcraft which, although much less important than these five, and not found ubiquitously among its practitioners, are none the less both pronounced enough, and unusual enough among religions of any period, to require some comment. One is the tradition, firmly observed by most covens, of alternating reverence and mirth in the circle, in such a way as to balance the solemnity of some rites with others which are designed to provoke joy and merriment: a consecration of play. Tanya Luhrmann described witches as 'perhaps the only magicians who incorporate humour into their practice' and quoted one high priest as saying that all of his co-religionists had a little of 'the goat and the gazelle'.[14] The second aspect is the celebrated tradition of ritual nudity, which is still very common amongst Wiccans. Their authors have provided a number of mystical justifications for it, the most common being that it helps to release magical power from the body.[15] Without necessarily discounting any of these, I would suggest from my personal acquaintance with witches that there are two practical reasons for its persistence. One is that it demands a high degree of trust and confidence between members of a coven, and so is a powerful test for the existence of harmony and unity, without which the rituals cannot be effectively worked. The second is that, in combination with other components normally present, such as candlelight, incense, and music, it conveys a very powerful sense that something abnormal is going on; that the participants in the circle have cast off their everyday selves and limitations and have entered into a space in which the extraordinary can be achieved. If the experience generates a degree of nervousness—as is initially at least the case for most people—then the latter increases their sensitivity, and receptivity, to what is occurring. Ideologically, it forms part of the pattern whereby modern witchcraft challenges most of the fears, and reverses the polarities, of traditional Western culture. This is why, of course, although nudity is a great rarity in the history of religion, it is an important theme, worldwide, in that of magic.

*　　*　　*

It is time to turn now to more straightforward sociological aspects of the subject, the first one being the number of adherents to modern pagan witch-craft. In this respect its stronghold is certainly the United States; Aidan Kelly suggested in 1991 that America contained about 200,000 Pagans, and the major-ity of these would be witches.[16] In Canada and Australia they can probably be counted in thousands, while most European countries have populations rang-ing from a few hundred to a few thousand; these estimates are suggested by the representatives at recent Pan-European Wiccan Conventions. My own calcula-tion for Britain is based upon the pagan Druid orders, who keep track of their membership in a way that other varieties of pagan do not. Their combined totals yielded a figure of about 6,000 Pagan Druids in the nation in 1996. In the local Pagan festivals, gatherings, moots, and networks, Druids are generally outnumbered by witches, with a ratio which causes me to believe that about 6,000 Pagan Druids indicates the present existence of about 10,000 pagan witches in initiatory traditions.[17]

This figure, however, represents a much stricter and more parsimonious computation than that normally accorded to religions in modern Britain. Others, from the Established Church to those closely associated with immigrant communities, generally count among their adherents the children automatically brought to worship by their parents. Pagan witches, in my observation absolutely, adhere to a rule whereby eighteen is the minimum age for initiation. On the other hand, some allow their children to help prepare the space in which rites will later be held without them, others hold specific summer celebrations for youngsters, in which the songs and the decorations have a distinctively pagan character, and most imbue their offspring with an outlook upon life which—deliberately or not—to some extent reflects their religion. None of these children, however, is counted in the total.

The latter also conceals the existence of an important and growing phenome-non of non-initiated Pagans who are starting to treat initiates as clergy. This is illustrated by the case of a Wiccan coven in a Midland city, which I have been observing consistently for six years. In early 1995 it had five members, and took to holding rituals at the eight seasonal festivals for members of the local Pagan community who wished to celebrate them but did not themselves belong to working groups. It immediately attracted from twenty to thirty-five of these on each occasion, joined after the ceremony by ten to twenty-five more, who partic-ipated in the feasting and merry-making. These were still wary of being involved in ritual, but wished none the less to be present in a sacred space on a sacred night, and have fellowship with those who had just enacted one there; people who simply wanted a party were not encouraged to attend. A year later, the coven had swelled to fourteen members, and the number of guests at its cere-monies varied between fifty and a hundred, and would have grown further had a ceiling not been imposed. I could count people in the circle precisely, but have a hazier idea of those who came when the rites had concluded; it was apparently between twenty and thirty on most occasions. According to the criteria used to quantify adherents of most religions in modern Britain, I should have included up to 100 people—if not 130—from this one sequence of gatherings as followers of modern pagan witchcraft. My total given above would only include the fourteen formally inducted into the coven.

This is part of a general development in present-day Paganism, so that at local assemblies of the sort described above initiates are always now considerably outnumbered by non-initiates who look upon the former as the foci of traditions. If I add to about 10,000 initiated pagan witches and about 6,000 Pagan Druids the approximate number of members of other kinds of initiatory Paganism (those in groups inspired by ancient Germany, Scandinavia, or Egypt, or working explicitly pagan ceremonial magic, such as the Ordo Templi Orientis, or in trained and initiatory shamanist traditions), the resulting figure is an approximation of 17,000–20,000 initiated Pagans in Britain in the late 1990s. The ratios which I have tabulated from 261 local Pagan gatherings—moots, meetings, talks, picnics, open rituals, and conferences—held in that decade suggest that the total of initiates represented by those figures indicates the existence of between 90,000 and 120,000 non-initiated Pagans in Britain by that time. These are people who have an active Pagan identity, honour Pagan deities and make an effort to attend Pagan ceremonies, but are not inducted into a particular Pagan tradition. It is interesting that the same approximate total has been reckoned independently—according to means unknown to me—by two other scholars, David Burnett, an evangelical Christian who has made an objective if unsympathetic study of modern British Paganism, and Joanne Pearson, a member of a university department of religious studies who has considered the same subject.[18]

British pagan witches are, as Tanya Luhrmann found in the 1980s, drawn from a wide range of backgrounds and occupations.[19] There are, however, some patterns to that range. My close acquaintance with twenty-one covens has yielded biographical information for a total of 213 individuals (membership of the covens varied between six and fifteen, but most had a turnover of members in the time in which I have known them). The pattern shown by these is borne out by the many more casual encounters which I have had with pagan witches in local gatherings, from Cornwall to Lothian and from Ceredigion to Norfolk, although it may well be challenged or amended by further research. It suggests that modern pagan witches in Britain are drawn overwhelmingly from the upper levels of the working class and the lower levels of the middle one. None in my sample had above-average wealth or political importance, or held inherited titles of honour. None directed large companies, and they included only two doctors (both in general practice) and three lawyers (both solicitors). Only two held tenured university posts, in contrast to thirty-four who were students in higher education for some at least of the time in which I knew them; significantly, fully thirty of these were not undergraduates of the conventional age-group but older people who had returned to college or university as mature students. On the other hand, only thirteen were seeking employment during the time in which I knew them, and only ten were unskilled labourers. None was a factory worker, miner, or farmhand. Instead they were, overwhelmingly, artisans (carpenters, blacksmiths, painters and decorators, skilled gardeners, builders, and plumbers), shopkeepers, artists, service engineers (most often specializing in computers or sound systems), financial advisers or insurance salespeople, or owners of small businesses. Public employees were virtually all represented by the three schoolteachers, the five librarians, the two archivists, and the six who worked in provincial offices of civil service departments. The professional element was provided most obviously by the eight psychologists. The common theme to this occupational profile is a higher than usual amount of independence and self-organization. This combined with another almost universal trait among them, a greater than usual love of reading and a commitment to constant self-education. All the covens concerned held firmly to the rule of initiating nobody under the age of eighteen, and only 46 of the 213 were over the age of fifty, the rest being distributed fairly evenly across the span of ages between. The gender balance was also relatively even, but with a significant majority (136 of 213) being female.

When I have mentioned the subject of my research for this book to friends, acquaintances, and colleagues who themselves have no direct knowledge of pagan witches, the most common prejudicial opinion which I have encountered about the latter is that they must be sad individuals who lead exceptionally dull working and domestic lives, and so need an unusually lurid spiritual existence to make up for the general inadequacy of the rest. My fieldwork indicates that on the contrary (to employ similarly crude and simple terms) they are unusually lively, independent, and adventurous people who demand a proportionately exciting and unusual religion, which affords them the maximum scope for self-development. This suggestion does have some reflection upon much more sophisticated and respected opinions expressed by academic leaders in religious studies. A long tradition among these, commencing with Max Weber, Ernst Troeltsch, and Richard Niebuhr, holds that religious movements appear in response to feelings of disinheritance and disadvantage. It was given its most elegant expression in 1964 by Charles Glock, who suggested that all new religions arose as a result of deprivation, but that this could take a number of different forms, which he classified as economic, social, organismic, ethical, and psychic. The same basic idea was given different form by Rodney Stark and William Bainbridge, in their dictum that 'when rewards are very scarce, or not available at all, humans create and exchange compensators—sets of beliefs and prescriptions for action that substitute for the immediate achievement of the desired reward'. According to this scheme, new religions 'are social enterprises primarily engaged in the production and exchange of novel or exotic compensators.'[20]

There are some aspects of Glock's model which can be made to fit my observations of pagan witchcraft. Its practitioners could be said to have taken it up because they were ethically or psychically deprived, in the sense that other religions available in their society did not furnish them with the experience which they found in witchcraft. At the same time a nagging doubt remains about the terminology—that to deprive somebody of something means to take it away from them. Modern witches are not people who have lost anything, or been left in a situation of relative disadvantage. Rather, they have impressed me as people who have an unusual degree of enterprise and of control over their own lives, and demand even more from them, extending this pattern by asking more of religious life than most people do. They perceive themselves as having the opportunity and the will to gain more than most people, by a more adventurous and demanding spiritual practice. My difficulty with the Stark–Bainbridge formulation is broader: that the witches whom I have observed do not strike me as people who are creating religious compensators for the lack of more straightforward and obvious rewards. One does not have to possess a particularly religious temperament, or to be speaking of pagan witchcraft, to suggest that the rewards furnished by religious experience are not necessarily compensations for other sorts of experience, as they have a peculiar quality of their own. A taste for vintage wine or a love of painting landscape is not automatically regarded as a compensator for other, scarce or unobtainable, rewards, and the pleasures taken by witches in their religion seem to me to fall into the same category.

Overwhelmingly, the witches to whom I have spoken entered their covens through personal contact with existing members, although most had already been predisposed towards witchcraft by books or reports in the mass media. Many, therefore, regarded their acceptance by a coven as the completion of a quest. There is no doubt that by the 1990s at latest the demand for places in covens far exceeded space in them. In the middle of the decade a national Wiccan organization was set up to receive applications from individuals wishing to join a group, and to refer them to witches working in their district. Although it has achieved some notable successes, a large log-jam has accumulated, of people waiting for a coven to take them in; which is in itself one reason for the boom in solitary practice and self-initiation using books. The coven structure is itself somewhat ponderous and inelastic, a concomitant effect of its strength. The supply of high priestesses and high priests—especially of the latter—is restricted by the special qualities needed for those roles, which combine those of clerics, teachers, parents, poets, actors and actresses, orators, mediums, and colleagues, and most covens like to keep their numbers small in order to maintain the intensity of group working. Above a strength of a dozen, indeed, a group rapidly ceases to be viable.

Entry is further restricted by the screening process which all or virtually all covens apply to prospective members. Some religions, including several which have recently appeared in the West, place an emphasis upon recruiting people who have suffered disabling misfortune, or drug or alcohol abuse, or depression, and giving them a new purpose in life. To judge by the representatives whom I have known, pagan witchcraft looks for people who have already found their purpose in life and wish to enhance and fulfil it. It seeks individuals who combine vivid imagination and high creative power with stability and stamina, and on the whole it finds them. If they do not already possess unusual powers of eloquence, group management and dramatic improvization, then they develop these in the course of the training. Such personalities tend often also to be hypercritical, impatient, demanding, competitive, volatile, and opinionated, traits which can all become social vices. The pagan witchcraft which I have observed, however, seems to be remarkably free of the demented, the malleable, the humourless, the unscrupulous, or the unworldly. Eileen Barker has stated that new religious movements tend to contain 'a slightly above average peppering of both rogues and saints'.[21] Pagan witchcraft, in my experience, does not.

The demanding nature of the training and activity, and the intensity of personal relationships inherent in the coven structure, result in quite a high wastage rate. The five covens which I consistently knew well contained a total of sixty-four people over the time in which I closely followed their fortunes—which makes them generally larger than the average. Of these, twenty-five dropped out of the group without (as far as I know) joining any other witches. When these are added to the twelve who departed in the traditional and laudatory manner of going on to found their own covens, the extent of mobility inside pagan witchcraft can be perceived. Nothing was done to put pressure upon any of those who had expressed a wish to depart from following it up, and in most cases it was recognized that they had not, after all, been suited to the work or to the group. Covens tend to resemble lobster pots in reverse, being very difficult to enter and very easy to leave.

In general, political issues in the conventional sense were not of great interest to the witches to whom I talked, and even at general elections were not discussed much among them. This being so, I can only surmise from stray remarks that most were either Labour or Liberal Democrat in their party allegiances; I only met two (out of the 213) who were certainly Conservative. None made an expressed point of not voting at all, and this pattern fits well with the fact that pagan witchcraft is not a religion which demands any withdrawal of its adherents from mainstream society or any distinguishing marks within it; indeed, it encourages the exact reverse. Some of the witches whom I met adopted clearly counter-cultural lifestyles and appearances, and regarded these as entirely compatible with their witchcraft and an expression of it; but they did not assume that all witches would or should express it in the same way and worked in covens alongside some who did not. The point has been made repeatedly that pagan witchcraft challenges social and religious norms by its very nature, but its identity as a mystery religion automatically insulates it from any direct impact upon the outside world. Upon only two subjects which could more loosely be called political were the attitudes of witches both fairly homogenous and clearly related to their Craft. One was that all believed in a tolerant and pluralist society with maximum potential for individual choice and self-expression. The other was a concern for environmental issues, and especially those which directly affected their own home districts. Even here, however, the degree of engagement was limited, for although some of the members of the covens which I knew well or visited actively supported campaigns to stop construction or extractive projects in their localities, none actually joined protest camps formed to halt the latter—in sharp contrast with Pagan Druids and non-initiatory Pagans with whom I was also acquainted.

Of the sixty-four individuals whom I knew well in the five covens, a total of seventeen had professed a personal religious belief of a different kind before becoming a witch, or else had come from a family background of devout piety. Most of these professions had been either of Roman Catholicism or of sectarian strains of radical Protestantism. In addition, two had come from a Jewish family background, although it was not clear that this had been a devout one. All the remainder had been agnostics or atheists—overwhelmingly the former—and had been brought up with the same tepid level of religious commitment; witchcraft represented their first engagement with active religiosity, although (as said above) its lack of doctrine and of need for literal and dogmatic belief in deity means that it demands less from agnostics than most religious traditions. Only one member of these five covens was the child of Wiccan parents. The ethnicity of British pagan witches is overwhelmingly white and European; of the 213 in covens which I knew well or visited, only one was from an Asian family background, and only one from an African or Afro-Caribbean one. On the other hand, the remainder showed a fairly diverse European heritage, with about a fifth of them having at least one parent of non-British origin. At moments the impression of ethnic diversity could be quite strong, if misleading; of three women ceremonially accepted as trainees of one coven upon a particular night, one was of Spanish parentage, one Jewish, and one Nigerian.

A striking sociological fact of pagan witchcraft in Britain which became apparent to me in the course of my research was its very marked similarity to the fastest-growing sector of British Christianity, the house church movement.[22] The basic unit of both is a small gathered group of enthusiasts, meeting in private homes. Both show a remarkable diversity of practice within a common framework, and relatively high mobility or instability of membership. Both draw inspiration from ancient literature, in the house church case, the Bible. Both place heavy emphasis on irrational qualities in religion, which can be called magical, the house churches describing these as faith-healing, speaking in tongues or possession by demons or the Holy Spirit. Both are suspicious of public or formal authority but have recently begun to form into national and regional associations. Both instinctually feel that the future is likely to be especially favourable to them. Both draw upon similar social groups; both, overall, are aspects of the important contemporary phenomenon of the privatization of religion. In terms of ideology, of course, they could hardly be more different, members of most house churches being dogmatic, evangelist, salvationist, and intolerant in their attitudes. Another distinction is that house church members benefit from the generally positive public value still accorded to the word

'Christian', while witches still suffer from the traditionally negative connotations of their name.

It is time to look at some of the negative stereotyping of pagan witches—whether in works of modern fiction, written or visual, or in the public gossip which feeds upon them—and check them against the actuality suggested by my research. First, it is very clear that the only drug used in their rituals is alcohol, in the form of the wine which is blessed and served as a communion with the divinity within the natural world. Furthermore, although some coven members drink to calm nerves before a ceremony, and many more do so to relax afterwards, it is generally considered very undesirable to be intoxicated in the course of ritual working, when minds are required to be clearest and willpower and attention most sharp. A drunken coven member can easily wreck the whole proceeding. Furthermore, it is perfectly clear to me that the ritual experience itself can produce effects upon sober people which can, depending upon one's viewpoint, be described as altered states of consciousness, apparitions, or hallucinations, quite as vivid as those induced by mind-altering drugs, and rendering the latter superfluous.[23] These can affect individuals or entire groups, and manifest with equal strength for people who do not normally hear or see things which have no obvious and mundane source. Unlike (say) spiritualism, pagan witchcraft does not depend upon such phenomena as a source of self-justification or expect them to occur. They are the more powerful in being an incidental, occasional, and unexpected effect of the rites.

Sexuality has a similar relationship with this witchcraft to that of wine; it occupies a central symbolic place in the ceremonies (most notably when blessing the wine itself), but remains confined to this. Pagan witches hold that sexual acts are sacred, and this tenet can have entirely opposite effects, according to individual personalities. To some, it justifies a promiscuous lifestyle, while to many more, it suggests that sex should be treated with the reverence of a religious act and reserved for occasions when it can be invested with profound significance—most obviously, with deep love. The result is a spectrum of behaviour which seems to me no different from that found in society as a whole; and Amy Simes's research suggested the same conclusion.[24] It is rare for members of a coven to become sexually involved with each other, because the consequences of falling out are likely to be so destructive for the group.

Even more to the point, I have never encountered, or heard of, a single example of actual sexual intercourse being employed in a coven working. Ethical considerations aside, there is a practical reason for this: that group ritual magic depends largely upon the raising of willpower and energy by joint co-operation and concentration, and its direction and release towards a particular aim. Whereas sexual excitement can certainly build energy effectively, orgasm just as effectively scatters it, as a person loses control and willpower. It is certainly possible to use the moment of sexual release to direct the accumulated energy to a target—this is, indeed, a long-established form of operative magic—but for fairly obvious reasons this is most easily performed alone or in a couple of devoted lovers. A group simply cannot co-ordinate the process. One partial exception to the absence of ritual sex in coven witchcraft is the fact—built into Books of Shadows—that the high priestess and high priest are encouraged to make love privately after the group ceremony is over and the others gone, to complete and honour the whole proceeding; but this only occurs if they are already a couple. Another, more important and more controversial, is that the highest initiation ceremony, the third degree, is built around a rite of actual or symbolic sexual intercourse between the person initiating and the one being initiated. All the covens which I have visited or observed continuously agreed that no initiate should be required to go through an actual act unless she or he clearly wished to do so. A few of them had leaders who made clear that they would refuse to oblige even in such a case. The others all had the rule that at the crucial stage of the ceremony the couple concerned were left alone and that nobody outside knew what truly passed between them; and that naturally concludes what I can say about the matter.

In general, the rites of pagan witchcraft are dedicated to purposes which require discipline, concentration, and control, and the balance to the solemnity of many of these is provided by the mirth and games referred to above, which function most often as means of relaxing and returning to normality after an intense period of ritual activity. Witch ceremonies usually, therefore, lack the ecstatic, euphoric, and abandoned quality of many tribal and shamanist ritual practices; the object is usually not to lose consciousness but to enhance and deploy it. If the practices of pagan witches therefore easily give the lie to the fictional libel that they must be orgiastic, then their structures are more vulnerable to a different charge made in those fictions; that they encourage domineering and manipulative ways on the part of the leaders. It is true that in theory the typical coven is a despotism run by the high priestess, to whom the high priest acts as a mixture of consort and chief vizier. My own observations, however, indicate that in reality coven working has to be consensual in order to operate effectively; a situation which is greatly enhanced by the sort of independent and self-assertive personality most commonly attracted to pagan witchcraft. A high priestess who succumbs to the temptations of absolute power is likely to find herself abandoned by her group. Rather than ruling fiefs, those whom I have watched generally chair boards; they listen, recommend, adjudicate, guide, and lead by example.

The most colourful charge ever levied against pagan witches is that they worship devils, and this can only be sustained by those who firmly believe that any deity or deities except their own must automatically be demonic. Like Tanya Luhrmann before me,[25] I have never encountered anything remotely resembling Satanism in my entire experience of pagan witches. To do so would, indeed, be something of a conceptual impossibility, as belief in the Devil itself requires a Christian cosmology, and modern Pagans of all kinds do not perceive any inherently evil forces to exist in the non-human world. Graham Harvey has carried out a systematic study of Satanism in modern Britain, and found fewer than a hundred people who belonged to organized groups which used that label; and even these did not worship the Devil in the Christian sense but took the myth of Lucifer as an empowering symbol of the divine forces latent within human beings. He found rather more people who used the term of themselves without belonging to groups, almost all being young people who had adopted it as a posture of rebellion, with which to shock and provoke the (in most cases literally) parent society. As a posture it almost wholly lacked genuine religious commitment.[26] The only overlap which I have found between these individuals and pagan witches is represented by a total of three among the latter (none members of the twenty-one covens which I have known as groups) who told me that they had adopted Satanist trappings in their youth as part of such a gesture politics. All made the point that they had turned to pagan witchcraft as a process of manifesting greater spiritual maturity. It would be amusing to forge a polemical point from this; that instead of acting as an antechamber to Satanism, as some uninformed critics have asserted, pagan witchcraft serves to rescue people from it. The sample of people represented by this process, however, is far too small to sustain such a suggestion.

Even friendly critics may be tempted to wonder whether, in making this survey, I have naturally only managed to observe the 'nice' witches, and whether there are pagan covens in England which have kept out of the way of national and local associations, and avoided any contact with me, and which are every bit as unpleasant in their practices as hostile fiction has made out the type to be. My answer to this proposal is that British Pagan networks are both remarkably dense and overlapping at local level, and riddled with rivalry and gossip, and that the latter phenomena affect witches at least as much as any. I have listened assiduously to the views which they have expressed about each other, in public and private, and have fairly frequently found them to include sentiments of hostility and disapproval. It is also a recognized function of the local networking to provide warnings of individuals or groups who are said to violate the generally accepted ethics of the Craft, by sexual or financial exploitation of initiates, so that newcomers can be headed off from joining them and they can be made to feel the weight of peer-group disapproval. In the ten-year period, from 1988 to 1998, in which I was constantly in contact with witches, I only heard such allegations made about three covens in the entire country. In two of those cases, I followed up the stories by contacting the group concerned, and found that if the charges had ever been true, then they no longer held good by the time that I made my investigation. The third really concerns a single individual, who certainly has a dubious legal record and considerable notoriety and unpopularity in the Pagan community. Even here, however, the allegations amounted to no more than claims of exploitation of trainees for pecuniary profit or sexual pleasure—squalid, rather than lurid, varieties of human misconduct.

If there are pagan covens in Britain which engage in sexual orgies, or blood sacrifice, or worship of demons, then they have not merely escaped my notice but that of the vast majority of witches, and other Pagans, who operate in this country. If they exist at all, indeed, they must be so atypical as scarcely to belong to the same category of religion. To broaden the picture, it must be noted that British pagan witchcraft has been strikingly free of the scandals which have attended other religious groupings during the past thirty years, such as the homicidal or suicidal frenzies which have marked the implosion of Christian sects, or the accusations of gross exploitation of followers and personal enrichment which have been levelled against leaders of some new religious movements, or the systematic abuse of children which has been proved against clergy of some of the older and more institutionalized religions—and, for that matter against people holding responsible positions in the caring and penal services and woodcraft movements. Nor has there been any recognized admission of people to mental homes or prisons who have been driven to breakdown or crime by the practice of pagan witchcraft. Leaving aside any benefits which it might bestow upon its members or upon the wider society, it certainly seems to do remarkably little harm to either.

*   *   *

It is time now to try to locate pagan witchcraft within the pattern of modern religion in general, and of newly appeared Western religions in particular, and in doing so to test some of the categories defined by academic specialists within the field. Is it, for example, a sect? This was the term most commonly used for new religious movements in the first half of the twentieth century, and in the second half was still employed in that sense by a leading British sociologist of religion, Bryan Wilson. He defined it as applicable to any 'religiously separated group' or any 'self-consciously and deliberately separated religious minority who espouse a faith divergent from that of other religious bodies'. According to this definition, pagan witchcraft would certainly represent a sect. Wilson himself, however, noted uneasily that new religious movements may not always be 'adequately designated' as such, but can be called so in the context of Western cultures because they are 'readily distinguished from what appears normal religion'.[27]

It is indeed not an 'adequate designation', upon straightforward linguistic grounds, and this point has been effectively made by American scholars. They have drawn attention to the fact that the word 'sect', properly speaking, applies only to religions which are formed by separation from an existing religious body and tradition, such as a Church.[28] This is indeed how most new movements emerged in the West in the nineteenth and early twentieth centuries, which is why the term was generally and properly applied then; but it does not fit a large number of those which have appeared in the second half of the century, including pagan witchcraft, because they are not schismatic. Wicca and its sisters would only be sects if they had split off from a larger and more inclusive body of modern Paganism, but the historical process was the reverse; Paganism has been formed largely out of the example set by the earlier appearance of pagan witchcraft. The term is therefore a precise and valuable one to describe a particular sort of religious group, but its value is negated if it is applied to pagan witches.

Do the latter, then, represent a 'cult'? This term has commonly been used to characterize new religious movements in the late twentieth century, especially in the United States. Its utility was already questioned in 1977, by Colin Campbell, who emphasized that the only consensus over the word was a negative one; that cults were religious groups which were not Churches, denominations, or sects. According to this process of relegation, pagan witchcraft would certainly be a cult, but Campbell himself was very unhappy about the notion of creating a residual category for human groups which did not fit neat stereotypes based upon Christian religious experience. He also made the important point that the term also represented a dumping-ground for movements which scholars held to represent forms of religious deviancy, and questioned whether such a category is still appropriate at all in a modern, pluralistic, religious culture. He went on to provide his own definition of cultic religion, as a mysticism which recognizes that all religious forms are essentially the same, and cannot be identified with any one tradition. Cults are therefore forms of religious phenomena which are not social groups, and groups which form out of them will soon dissolve again.[29] By this definition, pagan witchcraft is very obviously not a cult.

In the 1980s the American usage of the term in exactly the fashion which had disturbed Campbell was determinedly restated by Rodney Stark and William Bainbridge, who divided it into 'audience cults', 'client cults', and 'cult movements'. Only the last of those comprised actual religions, which could be distinguished from other religious movements by being both deviant from the parent society and non-schismatic. Paganism, including witchcraft, was explicitly consigned by them to this category.[30] For some reason, this indisputably fine and inspiring pair of sociologists have not fared well in this chapter, and they shall not do so again here, for their process of definition is vulnerable to the same technical criticism which they have themselves, cogently, applied to a sweeping employment of the term 'sect'. It is interesting to note that neither Amy Simes[31] nor I have ever met a single British Pagan (including witches) who did not regard the application of the word 'cult' to her or his religion as offensive. Academics are perfectly entitled to impose definitions upon social groups which the latter resent, if some clear scholarly purpose is served by doing so, but in this case the resentment is based upon a sound sense of traditional terminology which undermines the scholarly usage.

In British discourse at least, both literary and colloquial, the term 'cult' has often been deemed to signify a reverence paid to a single deity, fictional work, person, object, or practice. Thus, one can have a cult of Krishna, or *Star Trek*, or Elvis Presley, or brown rice, or transcendental meditation. This definition would actually fit most of the social phenomena which Stark and Bainbridge group under the word, including all their 'audience cults' and 'client cults', and indeed many non-schismatic, recently appeared, religious movements. It might also cover Dianic witchcraft, which could be classified as a cult of a goddess, although a reasonable objection to this could be that the purpose of that tradition is not merely or perhaps even primarily to pay reverence to a deity, but to develop spiritual powers in its practitioners. At the limits of this definition, other pagan witchcraft could perhaps be termed a cult of a goddess and god, but apart from incurring the same objection, the usage has to break down in the face of those witches who are polytheists, and genuinely work with different deity-forms at different times. It may also be asked whether working with a deity is the same thing as making a cult of that divinity. For these reasons, pagan witchcraft seems to be too complex a system of belief to be represented by the label of 'cult' and the latter, like that of 'sect' should be reserved for its proper and precise connotation. This form of witchcraft is neither a sect nor a cult, but a fully developed, independent, religion.

Can it, then, be regarded as an integral part of the New Age Movement? Here there is a very clear division of viewpoint. Scholars who have specialized in studying the New Age have generally accepted Paganism, including witchcraft, to be an aspect of that movement.[32] Those who have studied Paganism are insistent that it is not. In large part, this pattern merely reflects the views of the groups under study. I have myself met many New Agers who have considered pagan witchcraft to be a part of their movement; I have never yet encountered a pagan witch who did. There is a simple historical reason for according more credit to the latter view—that pagan witchcraft is a movement which originated in the United Kingdom and attained its enduring form in the 1950s, and the New Age is one which attained its enduring form in the United States during the 1970s. The former therefore cannot possibly be an aspect or outgrowth of the latter, and what has happened instead is that the latter has to some extent attempted to appropriate the former. The big question which remains, therefore, is whether they are essentially similar phenomena, making a convergence and conjunction of them an easy matter.

Here the judgement of the scholars of British Paganism is clearly negative. Amy Simes has pointed out that Paganism in general is much more overtly religious and precisely defined than the New Age; that it emphasizes natural cycles, whereas New Agers emphasize karmic law and judgement; that it integrates plans of being within a concept of polarity, whereas they imply a hierarchy of planes with the spiritual one being superior; that it sees the feminine as a divine force, while they see it as an inner self; and that it looks for links with the past, from which they cut themselves off. She agreed that British witches sometimes used the term 'New Age', but demonstrated that they did so in a different sense; to signify a coming era, and not a current movement. Joanne Pearson's critique has focused on the following characteristics of the New Age: that it is based on the premises that the modern world is not working and that rejection of that world is needed to create a better future; that it conceives of the physical world as inherently imperfect and representing a trapping of spirit in matter; that it perceives present existence to be marred by fragmentation, and humans as needing to seek wholeness as a part of their quest for perfection; that it locates authority wholly in the individual; that it suggests that specific courses of study or self-preparation need to be pursued for specific ends; and that therefore it regards people as free to draw upon any historical traditions which can assist them in the quest for transition to a better way of living. By contrast, the Wiccans whom she has studied cultivated a pragmatic middle way between acceptance and rejection of modernity. They treated perfection as an individual perception, aimed not to escape contemporary life but to enhance its positive aspects, and regarded matter and spirit as aspects of the same essential sanctity of the natural world. They accorded respect to deities and elders as well as to their own experience and opinions, required sustained commitment to a single process of training and initiation, and very much regarded themselves as following a specific tradition.[33]

From my own research, it is clear that the two movements have some points of similarity and overlap. Both have drawn members from modern counter-cultures, and both regard themselves as providing an enhancement of lifestyle, leading to better personal development and self-expression. I would also, however, endorse all the points of difference to which Simes and Pearson have drawn attention, and add to them. The New Age Movement is based largely upon the quest for a common basis for world spirituality, while pagan witches tend to be instinctually pluralist and to stress the distinctive nature of their own religion and to accept that it is likely only to suit a minority in a world made up of many different faiths. As part of that eclecticism, the New Age draws far more wholeheartedly and explicitly upon both Eastern and Western concepts, pagan witchcraft being a Western tradition to which ideas from Hinduism and Buddhism are added only incidentally and marginally, and only in some groups. Despite its emphasis upon the authority of the individual, the New Age is far more obviously built around guru figures and study courses. Pagan witches are much less likely to refer to 'teachers' or 'guides', and far more likely to value group dynamics. All told, the atmosphere of pagan witchcraft is much more practical and earthy than that of the New Age, with a stronger sense of history and a weaker sense of the global context and of utopian ideals. One of the most celebrated claims of the New Age is that humans make their own reality; I have yet to meet a pagan witch who would agree. In essence, witchcraft is one of the religions upon which New Agers attempt to draw in their effort to create an ideal spirituality, but British witches do not generally collaborate in this process.

Is pagan witchcraft a New Religious Movement? At first sight the answer is obviously affirmative. It is new in the sense that it has appeared or surfaced only in the relatively recent past, and it is certainly both religious and a movement of sorts. The capital letters should, however, give an informed observer pause, for they define a particular category of religion delineated by academics, of whom the outstanding figure in Britain is Eileen Barker.[34] It is true that she herself has indicated that it is a rag-bag category like that of 'cult' in some scholarly usage, admitting that all that New Religious Movements have securely in common is that the label is attached to them. She does, however, also emphasize that many of them have several other similarities, and her research abundantly confirms that proposition. It is highly significant in this context, therefore, to note three things. The first is that she includes pagan witchcraft as a New Religious Movement. The second is that it is not a religion to which she and her colleagues have devoted any research, preferring to concentrate instead upon Christian sects and religious groups of Eastern provenance. The third is that in several respects it is remarkably unlike most of the other movements in this category. It does not depend heavily upon one or a few charismatic leaders. It does not appeal overwhelmingly to a particular age group or cultural group. It does not offer a radical break with existing family and social relationships, and does not openly challenge the wider culture. Nor is the essence of its message an assured means of personal salvation.

In part these contrasts may simply be because, after half a century of public existence, it is no longer new; dominant figures were certainly more obvious in the first two decades of its recorded development. On the other hand, those who knew Gerald Gardner have commonly made the point that he lacked both the disposition and the behaviour of a charismatic religious leader, and there is no sign that pagan witchcraft ever possessed the other characteristics outlined above. It may be relevant to this pattern that all the other movements under the label, except for the other varieties of Paganism, are genuinely 'new', in Western terms. Either they have been founded, or divided from traditional Churches, in the recent past because of fresh revelations claimed by founders, or else they have arrived in Britain from a different continent. Pagan witchcraft does not claim to be new at all; on the contrary, its self-image was first that of a survival of ancient native religion and later that of a selective revival of one, with some elements of continuity. This does raise doubts as to whether it should be consigned to even a residual category with the others.

It seems at least arguable, therefore, that pagan witchcraft qualifies as a full-blown, independent religion. It is more than a shared set of stories, language, or images, and more than a common store of deities and texts. It has a common identity and a common institutional structure, of the coven supplemented by solitary practice of the same tradition. It is more than the veneration of a single deity or object, and has not separated off from a larger religious body or movement. This discussion has not got us, however, any closer to an answer to the question of what sort of religion it is, or how it should be categorized, if it does indeed need to be separated from the categories discussed above. The problem is not much assisted by the fact that the only obvious relatives and parallels which it possesses in the West are the other traditions of Paganism, with which it forms a very clear family group of which it is the eldest known member. To make that statement is only to enlarge the question of whether this family is itself *sui generis*. It is necessary to look at some different sorts of classification.

One of these was proposed in 1984 by Roy Wallis, who divided New Religious Movements into three varieties. The first was 'world-denying', hostile to the dominant values of the society around it and bent upon their transformation.

This kind of religious movement usually enjoined upon its members some degree of withdrawal from participation in normal social activities. The second was 'world-affirming', and described those movements which lauded and sought to reinforce prevailing social norms, and whose members engaged easily with the society around. The third was 'world-accommodating', and denoted those which aimed to withdraw their members into a private, interior, life of religious experience from which society in general could be excluded as irrelevant.[35] It should be obvious at once that this scheme, though helpful and meaningful in itself, cannot readily be applied to pagan witchcraft, which overlaps all three varieties. It comes closest to being 'world-accommodating', but Wallis's usage of this term is not wholly applicable to a religion which regularly works to help people who are not members of the sealed group, which increasingly sponsors 'open' rituals for non-initiates at festivals, and which regards the surrounding world as essentially sacred.

Pagans themselves sometimes try to locate their traditions within a wider group of 'native' religions. Thus, Paganism is 'native European religion', in a family with 'native American religion', 'native African religion', and so forth. This does have the merit of coming close to the original meaning of the word paganism itself, in Chuvin's sense of the *pagus*, the local unit, and conveys the qualities of rootedness and immemorial ancestry associated with the ancient European religions. It is more doubtful, however, whether these associations can be so easily applied to a religious movement which (as this book has attempted to argue) has no straightforward continuity with the ancient past and owes much of its success to the manner in which it has embodied modern forms and modern needs. For these characteristics, also, it may not be so easily identified with those tribal religious systems which have been preserved in unbroken descent to the present day. It has more kinship with tribal practices which represent modern developments and recastings of old ways, such as the Handsome Lake tradition or peyote-based rituals among native North American groups—which themselves beg the question of the term 'native religion'. Nor is it obvious that a label such as 'native Indian' can at once embrace the tribal ways of that sub-continent, the developed Hinduism of temples, priesthoods, and pilgrimage, and the more austere philosophical systems of some teachers. If it does, then it becomes little more than an expression of geography.

More useful is the recent development by North American academics of the concept of 'nature religion'. This was popularized by Catherine Albanese and given further expression by Peter Beyer.[36] In his formulation such religion is characterized by a comparative resistance to institutionalization and legitimation in terms of identifiable socio-religious authorities and organizations. Instead it regards nature as the embodiment of divinity or sacredness. It has a concomitant distrust of politically orientated power, and a corresponding faith in individual authority; a valorization of physical space as a vital element of spirituality; a this-worldly emphasis with a corresponding one upon personal experience as the final arbiter of truth or validity; a value of non-hierarchical community; a stress on holistic conceptions of reality; and a conditional optimism with regard to human capacity and the future. To Beyer, this all added up to a critique of contemporary global society, stressing local place and individual and group difference.

Most of this description makes a perfect fit with pagan witchcraft, but three difficulties remain. This first is simply that not all the clauses apply; as Joanne Pearson has demonstrated, witches are not particularly given either to holistic conceptions of reality or to purely individual authority. The second is that it is a very Western concept of 'nature religion', excluding all those tribal systems which likewise regard nature as the embodiment of the sacred but lack virtually all the other parts of the description. The third is, as Vivianne Crowley has pointed out[37] that pagan witchcraft has only identified itself closely with the natural world since the 1970s; before that it was not a nature religion but (in part) a fertility religion, which is not the same thing. Its seizure of the moral high ground of environmentalism represented a response to changing global circumstances, even if this seizure was facilitated by the fact that it already elements compatible with such a change of emphasis.

A different sort of descriptive category was suggested by James Beckford in 1992, when he spoke of 'post-modern' religion.[38] He associated post-modernity with 'a refusal to regard positivistic, rationalistic, instrumental criteria as the sole or exclusive standard of worthwhile knowledge', 'a willingness to combine symbols from disparate codes or frameworks of meaning, even at the cost of disjunctions and eclecticism'; 'a celebration of spontaneity, superficiality, fragmentation, irony, and playfulness', and 'a willingness to abandon the search for over-arching or triumphalist myths, narratives, and frameworks of knowledge'. Aside from some doubt about the single word 'superficiality', Beckford had got pagan witchcraft bang to rights, especially after its abandonment of the 'overarching and triumphalist' myth of the Old Religion and the Burning Times. He proceeded, however, to dismiss it almost immediately, declaring that it was hard to find actual illustrations of post-modern sensibility in the modern world once 'we disregard the glittering baubles on the exotic fringe of religion'. As such a 'bauble', witchcraft was tossed out of the realm of worthwhile discussion.

A new classification might be proposed here, of 'revived religion'. This is the only one which truly does justice to what is arguably the central and enduring characteristic of pagan witchcraft; that it is a modern development which deliberately draws upon ancient images and ideas for contemporary needs, as part of a wholesale rejection of the faiths which have been dominant since the ancient ways of worship were suppressed. The category has the limited utility that at present it is effectively confined to Western Paganism, but it is likely to grow; there are already signs that native Hawaiian religion, for example, is going to provide an exact parallel. The difficulty then, of course, would be whether such religions would have anything in common except the fact of revival.

The true conceptual significance of Paganism, including pagan witchcraft, is that it occupies the ground at which nature religion, post-modern religion, and revived religion intersect. None of these is a religious model which scholars trained in traditional history, theology, sociology, and anthropology find easy to understand; which is probably why, although pagan witchcraft has had a prominent public profile in Britain for half a century, it has been much less studied than other religious movements which have appeared or arrived more recently. Perhaps the present book will do something to alter that pattern.

❧ NOTES ❧

Full details are given of place and publisher for all works dating from after 1920 (a date arbitrarily chosen simply because it fits the cataloguing system of the Bodleian Library, the nearest copyright institution to my own university of Bristol). For books dating from before then, only place of publication is supplied, unless it happens to be London, when the date alone is given.

CHAPTER 1

1. Summed up recently by Malcolm B. Hamilton, *The Sociology of Religion: Theoretical and Comparative Perspectives* (London: Routledge, 1995).
2. Robin Lane Fox, *Pagans and Christians in the Mediterranean World from the Second Century to the Conversion of Constantine* (London: Viking, 1986), 30–1.
3. Pierre Chuvin, *A Chronicle of the Last Pagans* (Cambridge, MA: Harvard University Press, 1990), 7–9.
4. The biography is by Eric Quayle: *Ballantyne the Brave* (London: Rupert Hart-Davis, 1967).
5. John Lubbock, *Prehistoric Times* (1865), 115–16, 336–447.
6. *Ibid.*, 485.
7. Edward B. Tylor, *Primitive Culture* (1871), vol. I, 424–5.
8. *Ibid.*, 108.
9. Charles Grant B. Allen, *Falling in Love: With Other Essays* (1889), 296–7.
10. Sam Smiles, *The Image of Antiquity: Ancient Britain and the Romantic Imagination* (New Haven, CT: Yale University Press, 1994), 86–109.
11. Paul Newman, *The Meads of Love: The Life and Poetry of John Harris* (Redruth: Dyllansow Trurian, 1995), 25.
12. Smiles, *Image of Antiquity*, 96–7.
13. T. R. S. Boase, 'The Decoration of the New Palace of Westminster, 1841–1863', *Journal of the Warburg and Courtauld Institutes* xvii (1954), 341.
14. Quoted in Smiles, *Image of Antiquity*, 210.
15. Ernest Marston Rudland, *Ballads of Old Birmingham* (Birmingham, n.d.), 95–6. I am grateful to Elizabeth Taylor for this reference.
16. Sir Mark Sykes, *The Caliph's Last Heritage* (1915), 88.
17. William Force Stead, *The House on the Wold* (London: Cobden-Sanderson, 1930), 41.
18. Boswell's *Life*, quoted in Peter Gay, *The Enlightenment: An Interpretation* (London: Weidenfeld, 1966), 39.
19. The quotation is taken from the edition of 1839, p. ix.
20. Quoted in James Sutherland, *A Preface to Eighteenth-Century Poetry* (Oxford: Oxford University Press, 1948), 142.
21. Gay, *Enlightenment*, 42.
22. Theodore Zeldin, *France 1848–1945: Taste and Corruption* (Oxford: Oxford University Press, 1980), 59.
23. *The Victorians and Ancient Greece* (Oxford: Blackwell, 1980), *Dignity and Decadence*

(London, HarperCollins, 1991), and 'Late Antiquity in English Novels of the Nineteenth Century', *Arion* 3 (1995–6), 141–66. See also Norman Vance, *The Victorians and Ancient Rome* (Oxford: Blackwell, 1997).

24. Jenkyns, *Victorians*, 16, 68–91, and *Dignity and Decadence*, 105, 111–13.

25. Jenkyns, *Victorians*, 71, 91–3, 200–31.

26. There is a good recent overview of the scholarship in Burton L. Mack, *The Lost Gospel: the Book of Q and Christian Origins* (Shaftesbury: Element, 1993), 15–39.

27. Sir Walter Scott, *Letters on Demonology and Witchcraft* (1831), 63.

28. Kenneth Robinson, *Wilkie Collins: A Biography* (London: Bodley Head, 1957), *passim*.

29. Charles Merrivale, *History of the Romans Under the Empire* (1875), vol. III, 23–6.

30. The most recent biography is Syliva Cranston, *HPB* (New York: G. P. Putnam, 1993). Compare Richard A. Hutch, 'Helene Blavatsky Unveiled', *Journal of Religious History* 2 (1980), 320–41.

31. Cranston, *HPB*, makes the bravest possible case for the defence.

32. *Personal Memoirs of H. P. Blavatsky*, ed. Mary K. Neff (London: Rider, 1947), 289.

33. Summarized in Cranston, *HPB*, 183–242.

34. Howard Eilberg-Schwartz, 'Neopaganism and Goddess Worship as Enlightenment Religions', *Journal of Feminist Studies in Religion* 5.1 (Spring, 1989), 77–95.

35. The above paragraph can all be illustrated from Gay, *Enlightenment*. The final quotation is on p. 44.

36. E. M. Butler, *The Tyranny of Greece over Germany* (Cambridge: Cambridge University Press, 1935), 94–148; Suzanne L. Marchand, *Down from Olympus: Archaeology and Philhellenism in Germany, 1750–1950* (Princeton, Princeton University Press, 1996), 1–30.

37. Butler's translation in *Tyranny of Greece*, 166.

38. *Ibid.*, 209.

39. The passage is on pp. 731–2 of the journal.

40. *The Diary of Benjamin Robert Haydon*, ed. Willard B. Pope (Cambridge, MA: Harvard University Press, 1960), vol. II, 68.

41. *The Athenians*, ed. Walter Sidney Scott (London: Golden Cockerel Press, 1943), 43–4.

42. *Shelley at Oxford*, ed. Walter Sidney Scott (London: Golden Cockerel Press, 1944), 61.

43. Walter Jackson Bate, *John Keats* (Cambridge, MA: Harvard University Press, 1964), 133–6.

44. *Ibid.*, 217, 474, 482, 589–91, 689; Robert M. Ryan, *Keats: The Religious Sense* (Princeton: Princeton University Press, 1976), *passim*; and *The Romantic Reformation: Religious Politics in English Literature, 1789–1824* (Cambridge: Cambridge University Press, 1997), 152–78.

45. Quoted in Patricia Merivale, *Pan the Goat-God: His Myth in Modern Times* (Cambridge, MA: Harvard University Press, 1969), 64.

46. Ellsworth Barnard, *Shelley's Religion* (Minneapolis: Minnesota University Press, 1937), *passim*; Ryan, *The Romantic Reformation*, 193–223.

47. Jenkyns, *Victorians*, 178.

48. Havelock Ellis, *The Dance of Life* (London: Constable, 1923), 196.

48. *Inter alia*: Aleister Crowley, *Moonchild* (1929: 1970 repr., York Beach, Maine: Weiser), 227–9; Dion Fortune, *The Winged Bull* (London: Aquarian, 1935), 134–42, 151; G. B. Gardner, *The Meaning of Witchcraft* (London: Aquarian, 1959), 139–41.

50. For this and most above, see Jean Overton Fuller, *Swinbourne: A Critical Biography* (London: Chatto and Windus, 1968), 35, 147–8; and Donald Thomas, *Swinburne: The Poet in his World* (London: Weidenfeld, 1979), 111–13, 137, 155, 181–2, 206–7, 224.

51. Douglas Bush, *Mythology and the Romantic Tradition in English Poetry* (New York: Pageant, 1957), 423–8.

52. John Addington Symonds, *Studies of the Greek Poets* (3rd edn, 1893), 329–404.

53. *Ibid.*, 367–83.
54. The quotations are from the 1990 Oxford University Press edition, pp. 62, 262, 390.
55. Edward Carpenter, *Civilization: Its Cause and Cure* (1889), 44–7.
56. Peter Green, *Kenneth Grahame* (London: Murray, 1959), 138.
57. W. F. Barry, 'Neo-Paganism', *The Quarterly Review* 172 (1891), 272–304.
58. Matthew Sturgis, *Passionate Attitudes: The English Decadence of the 1890s* (London: Macmillan, 1995), 218.
59. Gilbert K. Chesterton, *Heretics* (1905), 153–70.
60. John Sherwood, *No Golden Journey: A Biography of James Elroy Flecker* (London: Heinemann, 1973), *passim*.
61. Published in *The Occult Review* 25 (1917), 84.
62. Algernon Blackwood, *Strange Stories* (London: Heinemann, 1929), 106.
63. D. H. Lawrence, *Lady Chatterley's Lover* (Penguin edition, 1961), 312.
64. H. J. Massingham, *Wold Without End* (London: Cobden-Sanderson, 1932), 171.
65. This is the theme of the latter half of Butler, *Tyranny of Greece*; see also the latter two-thirds of Marchand, *Down From Olympus*.
66. Jean Laroque, *L'Angleterre et le peuple Anglais* (Paris, 1882), 326; my translation.
67. Armand Silvestre, *Le Nu au Salon des Champs Elysées* (Paris, 1896), n.p.; my translation.

· CHAPTER 2 ·

1. Eric Smith, *A Dictionary of Classical Reference in English Poetry* (Cambridge: Brewer, 1984), and sources cited there under goddess names.
2. For example, by writers as different as Pierre Abelard in the twelfth century, Christine de Pisan in the fifteenth, and Giordano Bruno in the sixteenth.
3. This was based on a personal survey of public architecture in the following sample of cities: Venice, Paris, and London.
4. Notable pictorial examples of it are in Robert Fludd, *Utriusque Cosmi Historia* (Oppenheim, 1617), and Athanasius Kircher, *Oedipus Aegyptiacus* (Rome, 1652).
5. Carolyn Merchant, *The Death of Nature* (San Francisco: Harper Row, 1980).
6. Geoffrey Chaucer, *The Parlement of Briddes*, or *The Assembly of Foules*, ll. 295 ff. For the development of the concept, see George D. Economou, *The Goddess Natura in Medieval Literature* (Cambridge, MA: Harvard University Press, 1972).
7. Most relevant for this study have been Keith Thomas, *Man and the Natural World: Changing Attitudes in England 1500–1800* (London: Allen Lane, 1983), 243–68; Sam Smiles, *The Image of Antiquity: Ancient Britain and the Romantic Imagination* (New Haven, CT: Yale University Press, 1994), 21–2; Marjorie Hope Nicholson, *Mountain Gloom and Mountain Glory* (Ithaca, NY: Cornell University Press, 1959), *passim*; C. A. Moore, 'The Return of Nature in English Poetry of the Eighteenth Century', *Studies in Philology* xiv (1917), 243–92.
8. Smith, *Dictionary of Classical Reference*.
9. 'I Stood Tip-toe Upon A Little Hill', ll. 116–22.
10. *Endymion*, Book III, ll. 141–88.
11. 'Song of Proserpine' (1820), ll. 1–5.
12. 'Artemis Prologizes', ll. 1–6.
13. *Jane Eyre* (1847), chs. 27–8. I owe this reference to Lisa Raduolvic Hutton.
14. 'Hertha', ll. 1–15, in *Songs Before Sunrise* (1867).
15. Especially in the *Werke* of Johann Herder, August and Friedrich von Schlegel, and Ludwig Tieck.

16. Eduard Gerhard, *Über Metroen und Götter-Mutter* (Berlin, 1849), 103.

17. Peter J. Ucko, *Anthropomorphic figurines of Predynastic Egypt and Neolithic Crete with Comparative Material from the Prehistoric Near East and Mainland Greece* (Royal Anthropological Institute Occasional Paper, 1968), pp. 409–10, and sources listed there.

18. Theodore Dent, 'Researches among the Cyclades', *Journal of Hellenic Studies* 5 (1884), 42–59.

19. Eduard Piette, 'La Station de Brassempouy et les statuettes humaines de la periode glyptique', *L'Anthropologie* 6 (1895), 129–51.

20. R. Bosanquet, 'Archaeology in Greece 1900–1901', *Journal of Hellenic Studies* 21 (1901), 334–54. See also M. Salomon Reinach, 'La Sculpture en Europe avant les influences Greco-Romaines', *L'Anthropologie* 5 (1894), 15–34, 173–86, 288–305.

21. Arthur J. Evans, *Cretan Pictographs and Prae-Phoenician Script* (1895), 124–31.

22. A. J. Evans, 'The Palace of Knossos', *Annual of the British School at Athens* viii (1901–2), 1–124, and ix (1902–3). 74–94.

23. Sir Arthur Evans, *The Palace of Minos* (London: Macmillan, 1921), vol. I, 45–52.

24. Charles Henry Hawes and Harriet Boyd Hawes, *Crete: The Forerunner of Greece* (1909), 135–9; J. D. S. Pendlebury, *The Archaeology of Crete: An Introduction* (London: Methuen, 1939), 273; Charles Picard, *Les Religions prehelleniques* (Paris: Presses Universitaires de France, 1948), 74–80.

25. Especially Martin P. Nilsson, *A History of Greek Religion* (Oxford University Press, 1925), 18–33, and *The Minoan–Mycenaean Religion and its Survival in Greek Religion* (Lund: Gleerup, 1950), 290–394.

26. E. K. Chambers, *The Medieval Stage* (Oxford, 1903), vol. I, 264.

27. Jane Ellen Harrison, *Prolegomena to the Study of Greek Religion* (Cambridge, 1903), 257–322.

28. J. G. Frazer, *Adonis, Attis, Osiris: Studies in the History of Oriental Religion* (1907), 34–6, 105–10, 219–35.

29. J. G. Frazer, *Spirits of the Corn and of the Wild* (1914), vol. I, 35–91, 129–70.

30. Joseph Dechelette, *Manual d'archeologie prehistorique Celtique et Gallo-Romaine*, vol. 1 (Paris, 1908), 594–6.

31. E.g. Hawes and Hawes, *Crete*, 135–9; Arthur Bernard Cook, *Zeus: A Study in Ancient Religion* (Cambridge, 1914), vol. I, 776–80; Gilbert Murray, *Four Stages of Greek Religion* (New York, 1912), 45–6; Lewis Richard Farnell, *An Outline History of Greek Religion* (London: Duckworth, 1920), 24–36.

32. G. D. Hornblower, 'Predynastic figures of Women and their Successors', *Journal of Egyptian Archaeology* xv (1929), 29–47.

33. E. B. Renaud, 'Prehistoric Female figurines from America and the Old World', *Scientific Monthly* 28 (1929), 507–13.

34. Gordon Childe, *The Dawn of European Civilization* (London: Routledge, 1925), 208–24, *The Prehistory of Scotland* (London: Kegan Paul, 1935), 22–105, and *Prehistoric Communities of the British Isles* (London: Chambers, 1940), 46–118; Grahame Clark, *Prehistoric England* (London: Batsford, 1940), 103; O. G. S. Crawford, *Long Barrows of the Cotswolds* (Gloucester: John Bellows, 1925), 23–4.

35. H. J. Massingham, *Wold Without End* (London: Cobden-Sanderson, 1932), *passim*.

36. Stuart Piggott, 'Ancient British Craftsmen', *Antiquity* 60 (1986), 190.

37. Gillian Varndell, 'The Ritual Objects', in Ian Longworth *et al.*, *Excavations at Grimes Graves, Norfolk 1972–1976: Fascicule 3* (London: British Museum, 1991), 103–6.

38. John Punnett Peters, *Nippur* (New York, 1898), 141–71.

39. Arthur J. Evans, 'The Neolithic Settlement at Knossos and its Place in the History of Early Aegean Culture', *Man* 1 (1901), 185.

40. Patrick Benham, *The Avalonians* (Glastonbury: Gothic Image, 1993), 15–20.
41. *Ibid.*, 21–43.
42. Robert Briffault, *The Mothers* (London: Allen and Unwin, 1927), ch. 23.
43. Massingham, *Wold Without End*, 171.
44. In chapters 13 and 34.
45. Eleanor Farjeon, *Pan-Worship and Other Poems* (1908), 61, 71.
46. *Selected Poems by A. E.* (London: Macmillan, 1935), 17, 85.
47. The brief quotation is on p. 345, the long one on p. 263.
48. Quotations are from the Penguin edition, pp. 365 and 516.
49. Quotations from the Penguin edition, pp. 244, 276–80, 348.

CHAPTER 3

1. Eric Smith, *A Dictionary of Classical Reference in English Poetry* (Cambridge: Brewer, 1984).
2. Patricia Merivale, *Pan the Goat-God: His Myth in Modern Times* (Cambridge, MA: Harvard University Press, 1969).
3. *Ibid.*, 227.
4. Ken Dowden, *The Uses of Greek Mythology* (London: Routledge, 1990), 126.
5. Merivale, *Pan*, 1–53.
6. 'Lines Written in Kensington Gardens.'
7. Merivale, *Pan*, chs 2–4, to which I would add the works of J. B. L. Warren, Lord de Tabley, Roden Noel's 'Pan' (1868), Geoffrey Sephton, *In Pandean Vale* (Amalthea: Zurich, n.d.).
8. Merivale, *Pan*, 118.
9. 'Pan's Pipes', in *Virginibus Puerisque and Other Papers* (1881), 264–70.
10. 'The Rural Pan', in *Pagan Papers* (1893), 34–8.
11. *The Longest Journey* (1907), ch. xiv.
12. *The Letters of Maurice Hewlett*, ed. Laurence Binyon (London: Methuen, 1926), 84.
13. London: Grant Richards.
14. *The Complete Works of William Hazlitt*, ed. P. P. Howe (London: Dent, 1931), vol. VI, 192.
15. Richard Le Gallienne, *Attitudes and Avowals* (1910), 19.
16. Chs xiii, xxii.
17. *The Story of a Panic* (1902).
18. Max Beerbohm, 'Hilary Maltby and Stephen Braxton', in *Seven Men* (London: Heinemann, 1920), 53.
19. Algernon Blackwood, 'A Touch of Pan', in *Tales of the Uncanny and Supernatural* (London: Spring Books, 1962), 304.
20. Lord Dunsany, *Fifty-One Tales* (1915), 5, 25, 109.
21. London: Putnam, 1927.
22. p. 133.
23. Somerset Maugham, *Cakes and Ale* (London: Heinemann, 1930), ch. 11.
24. Teresa Hooley, *Selected Poems* (London: Jonathan Cape, 1947), esp. 19, 116–17.
25. Saki, 'The Music on the Hill', first published in *The Chronicles of Clovis* (1911).
26. Especially as republished in Aleister Crowley, *Magick*, eds John Symonds and Kenneth Grant (London: Routledge, 1973), 125–7.
27. Included in *Vale and Other Poems* (1931).
28. Merivale, *Pan*, 220.
29. p. 235 in the 1971 Edward Arnold edition.
30. *Ibid.*, 196.

Note Since this chapter was written, Patricia Merivale's work has been supplemented by a short survey of the use of the image of Pan since antiquity by John Boardman: *The Great God Pan: The Survival of an Image* (London: Thames and Hudson, 1998).

CHAPTER 4

1. *The first Freemasons* (Aberdeen: Aberdeen University Press, 1988), and *The Origins of Freemasonry* (Cambridge: Cambridge University Press, 1988).
2. Margaret C. Jacob, *Living the Enlightenment: Freemasonry and Politics in Eighteenth-Century Europe* (Oxford: Oxford University Press, 1991).
3. Bernard E. Jones, *Freemasons' Guide and Compendium* (London: Harrap, 1956), 80–3, 283–4.
4. Francis Consitt, *The London Weavers' Company* (Oxford: Oxford University Press, 1933), 194–5, 307.
5. Frank Taverner Phillips, *A Second History of the Worshipful Company of Cooks, London* (London: Cooks' Company, 1966), 38–9.
6. Eric Bennett, *The Worshipful Company of Wheelwrights of the City of London 1670–1970* (Newton Abbot: David and Charles, 1970), 154.
7. *Gould's History of Freemasonry*, ed. Herbert Poole (London: Axton, 3rd edn, 1951), vol. I, 155–6.
8. Henry Carr, *The Freemason at Work* (London: privately printed, 1977), 28; *The Early Masonic Catechisms*, ed. Douglas Knoop, G. P. Jones, and Douglas Hamer (Manchester: Manchester University Press, 1943), 31–62.
9. Alexander Slade, *The Free Mason Examin'd* (1754), 9–11.
10. Reprinted in Knoop, Jones, and Hamer, *Early Masonic Catechisms*, 104.
11. Jones, *Freemasons' Guide*, 353–4; J. M. Roberts, *The Mythology of the Secret Societies* (London: Secker and Warburg, 1972), 52.
12. William Preston, *Illustrations of Masonry* (1775), 75–109.
13. Jones, *Freemasons' Guide*, 267–80.
14. *Ibid.*, 290; E. H. Cartwright, *Masonic Ritual* (London: Lewis Masonic, 1947), 1–49.
15. Albert G. Mackey, *A Lexicon of Freemasonry*, ed. M. C. Peck (1919), 232, 242–9, 358–9, 374; Cartwright, *Masonic Ritual*, 121; James Dewar, *The Unlocked Secret: Freemasonry Examined* (London: William Kimber, 1966), 133–75; H. L. Haywood, *Symbolic Masonry* (London: Allen and Unwin, 1924), 70–93; A. E. Mason, *The Accepted Ceremonies of Craft Freemasonry* (1874), *passim*; Chalmers A. Paton, *Freemasonry. Its Symbolism, Religious Nature, and Law of Perfection* (1873), 290–322.
16. (James Anderson), *The Constitutions of the Freemasons* (1723), and *The New Book of Constitutions of the Free and Accepted Masons* (1738).
17. Eric Grant, 'The Sphinx in the North', in *The Iconography of Landscape*, eds Denis Cosgrove and Stephen Daniels (Cambridge: Cambridge University Press, 1988), 241–2.
18. W. L. Wilmhurst, *The Masonic Initiation* (London: Rider, n.d.), and *The Meaning of Masonry* (London: Rider, 1922); A. E. Waite, *A New Encyclopaedia of Freemasonry* (London: Rider, 1921); Mark C. Carnes, *Secret Ritual and Manhood in Victorian America* (New Haven, CT: Yale University Press, 1989), 28–62; plus sources at n. 15.
19. J. S. M. Ward, *Freemasonry and the Ancient Gods* (London: Simpkin, Marshall, Hamilton, Kent and Co., 1921).
20. Jacob, *Living the Enlightenment, passim*; Roberts, *Mythology of the Secret Societies, passim*; Peter Partner, *The Murdered Magicians* (Oxford: Oxford University Press, 1981), *passim*.

21. Carnes, *Secret Ritual, passim.*
22. *Ibid.*
23. T. F. Thiselton Dyer, *British Popular Customs* (1876), 320–1.
24. Henry Pelling, *A History of British Trade Unionism* (3rd edn, Harmondsworth: Penguin, 1976), 40.
25. John Rule, 'Against Innovation? Custom and Resistance in the Workplace, 1700–1800', in *Popular Culture in England, c. 1500–1800*, ed. Tim Harris (Basingstoke: Macmillan, 1996), 172.
26. Leslie F. Newman, 'Notes on some Rural and Trade Initiation Ceremonies in the Eastern Counties', *Folk-Lore* 51 (1940), 34–7.
27. David Neave, *Mutual Aid in the Victorian Countryside 1830–1914* (Hull: Hull University Press, 1991), 1.
28. Sherri J. Brown, 'Friendly Societies and their Symbols and Rituals', *Group for Regional Studies in Museums* 10 (October 1982), 8–9. I owe this reference to Martin Gorsky.
29. Carnes, *Secret Ritual*, 22.
30. *Ancient Order of Shepherds, Ashton Unity. Centenary Souvenir 1826–1926* (Manchester: Ancient Order of Shepherds, 1926), 5.
31. Brown, 'Friendly Societies', 10.
32. Walter G. Cooper, *The Ancient Order of Foresters Friendly Society* (Ipswich: Ancient House, 1984), 4–16.
33. *Ancient Order of Druids: Introductory Book* (1889), *passim*; Brown, 'Friendly Societies', 8.
34. James Spry, *The History of Odd-Fellowship* (1867), 3–4; P. H. J. H. Gosden, *The Friendly Societies in England 1815–1875* (Manchester: Manchester University Press, 1961), 132; Carnes, *Secret Ritual*, 17–21, 51.
35. G. J. Holyoake, *Sixty Years of an Agitator's Life* (1906), 205–7.
36. Brown, 'Friendly Societies', 8.
37. J. M. McPherson, *Primitive Beliefs in the North-East of Scotland* (London: Longman, 1929), 290–2.
38. Thomas Davidson, 'The Horseman's Word', *Gwerin* 2 (1956), 70–2.
39. George Ewart Evans, *The Pattern under the Plough* (London: Faber, 1966), 228–35; *The Leaping Hare* (London: Faber, 1972), 225; *The Days That we Have Seen* (London: Faber, 1975), 42–3; and *Horse Power and Magic* (London: Faber, 1979), 137–41.
40. William Singer, *An Exposition of the Miller and Horseman's Word* (6th end, Aberdeen, 1865), *passim*; Anon, *Eleven Years at Farm Work* (Aberdeen, 1869), *passim*; J. F. S. Gordon, *The Book of the Chronicles of Keith* (Glasgow, 1880), 149; Neil Roy, *The Horseman's Word* (1895), *passim*.
41. Hamish Henderson, 'A Slight Case of Devil Worship', *New Statesman and Nation* (14 June 1962), 696–8.
42. Ian Carter, *Farmlife in Northeast Scotland 1840–1914* (Edinburgh: John Donald, 1979), 154–6.
43. *Ibid.*, 154–5. See also McPherson, *Primitive Beliefs*, 292–3.
44. Carter, *Farmlife*, 154–5, and 217, n. 85.
45. Published examples include 'Sic Iubeo', i.e. 'Thus I Command' (George Ewart Evans, *The Horse in the Furrow*, London: Faber, 1960, 271), 'Collar and the Hames' (Davidson, 'Horseman's Word', 68), 'Both as One' ('An Old Buchan Ploughman', 'The Horseman's Word', *Scottish Notes and Queries* 2nd series, 3, March 1902, 143), and 'a common monosyllable spoken backwards' (Ernest Marwick, *The Folklore of Orkney and Shetland*, London: Batsford, 1975, 192; cf. Henderson, 'Devil Worship', 697).
46. Different versions have been printed in Henderson, 'Devil Worship', 696; Evans, *Pattern under the Plough*, 230–1; Anon, *The Horseman's Oath, as Written Down by a Buchan*

Horseman in 1908 (Edinburgh: Scottish Country Life Museums Trust, 1972); Andrew Fenton, *Scottish Country Life* (Edinburgh: John Donald, 1976), 223–4.

47. Marwick, *Orkney and Shetland*, 66–8, 192; Evans, *Days That We Have Seen*, 36–40; Carter, *Farmlife*, 154–6; 'Buchan Ploughman', 'The Horseman's Word', 143; McPherson, *Primitive Beliefs*, 290–2; Henderson, 'Devil Worship', 696–8; J. T. Smith Leask, 'How Willo o' Iver Tuack Became a Horseman', *Old Lore Miscellany of Orkney, Shetland, Caithness and Sutherland* 9 (1933), 75–81.

48. Davidson, 'Horseman's Word', 67, 73.

49. *Ibid.*, 67–70; Ralph Whitlock, 'Horse Sense and Nonsense', *Guardian Weekly* 8 (March 1992), 9.

50. Evans, *Horse in the Furrow*, 271.

51. Sources at ns. 45–7, but esp. Henderson, 'Devil Worship', 696–8.

52. Davidson, 'Horseman's Word', 69.

53. Evans, *Horse Power*, 152–69.

54. William Youatt, *The Horse*, ed. E. N. Gabriel (1859), 456–8.

55. Evans, *Horse in the Furrow*, 245–8, *Pattern under the Plough*, 204–18, *Days That We Have Seen*, 29–35, and *Horse Power*, 97–138; Whitlock, 'Horse Sense', 9; G. W. Pattison, 'Adult Education and Folklore', *Folk-Lore* 64 (1953), 425–6; Christina Hole, 'Popular Modern Ideas on Folklore', *Folk-Lore* 65 (1955), 328–9; Ronold Blythe, *Akenfield* (London: Allen Lane, 1969), 54.

56. Carnes, *Secret Ritual*, 1.

CHAPTER 5

1. For example *Arcana Mundi*, ed. Georg Luck (Baltimore, MD: Johns Hopkins University Press, 1985), 3; *Magic, Witchcraft and Curing*, ed. John Middleton (Austin, TX: University of Texas Press, 1987), ix–x.

2. The debates have recently been summarized in Malcolm B. Hamilton, *The Sociology of Religion: Theoretical and Comparative Perspectives* (London, Routledge, 1995), 28–44.

3. J. E. Cirlot, *A Dictionary of Symbols* (London: Routledge, 1962), 196–7.

4. William of Auvergne, *De Legibus*, cap. 27.

5. Sloane MSS 313, 3854, and 3883.

6. The outstanding exception at the time of writing seems to be Bradford J. M. Verter's Princeton University PhD thesis, 'Dark Star Rising: The Emergence of Modern Occultism, 1800–1950' (1997).

7. Gerald Suster, *The Legacy of the Beast* (London: Allen, 1988), 9.

8. Some of my own work for this present book would hardly have got off the ground were it not for Caduceus Books, of York, and its golden-hearted proprietor.

9. I am grateful to Julian Vayne and Rufus Harrington for conveying some of the essence of these to me.

10. The biography is Francis X. King, *The Flying Sorcerer* (Oxford: Mandrake, 1992).

11. Francis King, *Ritual Magic in England: 1887 to the Present Day* (London: Spearman, 1970), 25–7.

12. King, *Flying Sorcerer*, 19–20.

13. Mircea Eliade, *Occultism, Witchcraft and Cultural Fashions* (Chicago, IL: Chicago University Press, 1976), 49–54; King, *Ritual Magic*, 22–4; Christopher Macintosh, *Eliphas Levi and the French Occult Revival* (London: Rider, 1972), *passim*.

14. The basic works are Eliphas Levi, *Historie de la magie* (Paris, 1860), and *Dogma et ritual*

de la haute magie (Paris, 1861). His views on the pentagram can be found translated into English in the last pages of Eliphas Levi, *The Key to the Mysteries* (1896) and *Transcendental Magic* (1896), 60–5.

15. Peter Partner, *The Murdered Magicians: The Templars and their Myth* (Oxford: Oxford University Press, 1981), 115–69.

16. King, *Ritual Magic*, 27–38; Israel Regardie, *The Golden Dawn* (4th edn, St Paul, MN: Llewellyn, 1971), vol. I, 19–20); Ellic Howe, *The Magicians of the Golden Dawn* (London: Routledge, 1972), 26; R. A. Gilbert, *The Golden Dawn: Twilight of the Magicians* (Wellingborough: Aquarian, 1983), 16–20; *Gould's History of Freemasonry*, ed. Herbert Poole (3rd edn, London: Caxton, 1951), vol. IV, 270.

17. Francis King, *Astral Projection, Ritual Magic and Alchemy* (London: Spearman, 1971), 17–18; Gilbert, *Golden Dawn*, 16–20; John Hamill, *The Rosicrucian Seer: Magical Writings of Frederick Hockley* (Wellingborough: Aquarian, 1986), *passim*; Patrick Curry, *A Confusion of Prophets: Victorian and Edwardian Astrology* (London: Collins and Brown, 1992), 83. I am very grateful to Dr Curry for the gift of this book.

18. King, *Ritual Magic*, 28.

19. Gould's *History of Freemasonry*, vol. IV, 270.

20. Gilbert, *Golden Dawn*, 20.

21. Gould's *History of Freemasonry*, vol. VI, 270.

22. Hargrave Jennings, *The Rosicrucians: Their Rites and Mysteries* (1887).

23. King, *Ritual Magic*, 40.

24. Curry, *Confusion of Prophets*, 117–18.

25. Howe, *Magicians of the Golden Dawn*, 40–1; Gilbert, *Golden Dawn*, 22–3; Sylvia Cranston, *HPB* (New York: Putnam, 1993), 367.

26. Differing views are found in John Symonds, *The Great Beast* (London: Macdonald, 1971), 16–17; Francis King, *The Magical World of Aleister Crowley* (London: Weidenfeld, 1977), 16–17; King, *Astral Projection*, 17–18, and *Ritual Magic*, 42–5; George Mills Harper, *Yeats's Golden Dawn* (London: Macmillan, 1974), 9–10; Howe, *Magicians of the Golden Dawn*, 5–26; Gilbert, *Golden Dawn*, 27–32; Gerald Suster, 'Answer to Howe', in Israel Regardie, *What You Should Know About the Golden Dawn* (Phoenix, AZ: Phoenix, 1983), 111–20. The best work on Westcott is R. A. Gilbert, *The Magical Mason* (Wellingborough: Aquarian, 1983), while the biography of Mathers is by Ithell Colquhoun, *Sword of Wisdom: MacGregor Mathers and the Golden Dawn* (London: Spearman, 1975). Photostats of the cipher manuscripts are available to scholars in the Warburg Institute, Gerald Yorke Collection.

27. Gilbert, *Magical Mason*, *passim*.

28. Warburg Institute, Gerald Yorke Collection, copy of 'The Historic Lecture to Neophytes. 1888'.

29. Mary K. Greer, *Women of the Golden Dawn* (London: Park Street, 1995).

30. Between 1887 and 1898 he published an exposition of the cabbala and editions of *The Key of Solomon the King*, *The Grimoire of Armadel*, and *The Book of the Sacred Magic of Abramelin the Mage*, and circulated an edition of the *Goetia* in manuscript.

31. Howe, *Magicians of the Golden Dawn*, ix–xxv; Charles Wycliffe Goodwin, *Fragment of a Graeco-Egyptian Work upon Magic* (Cambridge Antiquarian Society, 1852).

32. Regardie, *Golden Dawn*, *passim*; King, *Ritual Magic*, 57–74, and *Astral Projection*, *passim*; R. G. Torrens, *The Secret Rituals of the Golden Dawn* (Wellingborough: Aquarian, 1973), *passim*.

33. Regardie, *Golden Dawn*, vol. I, 68–76, vol. II, 264–8. Compare the data in Richard Kieckhefer, *Magic in the Middle Ages* (Cambridge: Cambridge University Press, 1990), 159–61; *The Book of the Goetia of Solomon the King*, ed. S. Liddell MacGregor Mathers

(1892); the *Art Armadel* in BL Sloane MS 2731, f. 16; and Dee's papers in the BL Sloane MSS 3188–9 and 3191.

34. King, *Ritual Magic*, 57–8; Howe, *Magicians of the Golden Dawn*, ix–xxv.
35. Regardie, *Golden Dawn*, vol. I, 94–5, vol. II, 12; King, *Astral Projection*, 24–5; Gilbert, *Golden Dawn*, 36.
36. Regardie, *Golden Dawn*, vol. I, 68, vol. II, 264–8.
37. *Ibid.*, ii. 79.
38. *Ibid.*, ii. 290.
39. Cf. Kieckhefer, *Magic in the Middle Ages*, 9–15, 163–61.
40. Regardie, *Golden Dawn*, vol. II, 183–4.
41. King, *Ritual Magic*, 81.
42. Howe, *Magicians of the Golden Dawn*, ix–xxv.
43. Mathers' text was eventually published by his pupil Crowley, and is cited at n. 33. The *Goetia* first appears in the famous polemic of Johann Wier (Weyer), *De Praestigiis Daemonum* (Basle, 1563), and this version was translated into English by 'T.R.' in 1570. Mathers used a different recension from the seventeenth century, in BL Sloane MS 3648.
44. King, *Ritual Magic*, 94–5.
45. *The Confessions of Aleister Crowley: An Autohagiography*, eds. John Symonds and Kenneth Grant (London: Routledge, 1979), 174–93.
46. King, *Astral Projection*, 58–9.
47. Crowley, *Confessions*, 193–7.
48. Colquhoun, *Sword of Wisdom*, 85–9; Harper, *Yeats's Golden Dawn*, 19, 71, 210.
49. King, *Ritual Magic*, 94–151; Crowley, *Confessions*, 196–7, 559–640; Gilbert, *Golden Dawn*, 71–2; Howe, *Magicians of the Golden Dawn*, 233–71.
50. Traditionally taken to stand for Astrum Argentum, though this is sometimes denied.
51. The manuscript is in the Bibliothèque de l'Arsenal, Paris, which was the other archive to which Mathers had access, apart from the British Museum. His edition is *The Book of the Sacred Magic of Abramelin the Mage* (1898).

CHAPTER 6

1. Willem de Blecourt, 'Witch doctors, Soothsayers and Priests. On Cunning Folk in European Historiography and Tradition', *Social History* 19 (1994), 299.
2. Owen Davies, 'The Decline in the Popular Belief in Witchcraft and Magic' (Lancaster University PhD thesis, 1995), 1.
3. Brian C. Luxton, 'William Jenkin, the Wizard of Caxton-juxta-Barry', *Morgannwg* 24 (1980), 31–60; Glyn Penrhyn Jones, 'Folk Medicine in Eighteenth-Century Wales', *Folk Life* 7 (1969), 60–75; Kathryn C. Smith, 'The Wise Man and his Community', *Folk Life* 15 (1977), 24–37.
4. Owen Davies, 'Decline in the Popular Belief'; 'Cunning Folk in England and Wales during the Eighteenth and Nineteenth Centuries', *Rural History* 8 (1997), 91–107; 'Urbanization and the Decline of Witchcraft: An Examination of London', *Journal of Social History* 30.2 (1997), 597–615; 'Newspapers and the Popular Belief in Witchcraft and Magic in the Modern Period', *Journal of British Studies* 37 (1998), 139–65; 'Charmers and Charming in England and Wales from the Eighteenth to the Twentieth Century', *Folklore* 109 (1998), 41–52; 'Cunning Folk in the Medical Marketplace during the Nineteenth Century', forthcoming in *Medical History*. Manchester University Press have commissioned Dr Davies to write a book, *Witchcraft, Magic and Culture,*

1736–1951, which is well under way at the time of writing these words. I am very grateful to him for reading through this chapter of my own for me and tendering his comments, for showing me much work of his in manuscript, and for a long correspondence in the course of which he has exchanged many ideas and pieces of source material.

5. In my essay 'The Rise of Modern Paganism', in *Paganism Today*, eds. Graham Harvey and Charlotte Hardman (London: Thorsons, 1996), 6.

6. Davies, 'Cunning Folk', 91.

7. Theo Brown, *The Fate of the Dead* (Ipswich: Folklore Society, 1979), 46–7; Tony Deane and Tony Shaw, *The Folklore of Cornwall* (London: Batsford, 1975), 117–18.

8. Davies, 'Cunning Folk', 91.

9. *Ibid.*, 92–4.

10. Davies, 'Charmers and Charming', *passim*.

11. Davies, 'Cunning Folk', 93–4.

12. Eric Maple, 'Cunning Murrell', *Folklore* 71 (1960), 36–43. The quotation concerning Murrell's appearance is found on p. 42.

13. Gordon Ridgewell, 'Swimming a Witch, 1863', *Folklore Society News* 25 (1997), 15–16.

14. William Henderson, *Notes on the Folk-Lore of the Northern Counties of England* (1879), 215–19.

15. J. C. Atkinson, *Forty Years in a Moorland Parish* (1891), 113–17.

16. Richard Blakeborough, *Wit, Character, Folklore and Customs of the North Riding of Yorkshire* (Saltburn, 1911), 180–2; *County Folk-Lore II: North Riding of Yorkshire, York and the Ainstey*, ed. Mrs Gutch (1901), 185–7.

17. Henderson, *Northern Counties*, 213.

18. *County Folk-Lore II*, 187.

19. *Ibid.*, 208.

20. William Chaloner, *Palatinate Studies* (Chetham Society, 1992), 21–35.

21. William Bottrell, *Traditions and Heatherside Stories of West Cornwall* (Penzance, 1870), 79–89.

22. Paul Karleek, 'A Budget of Witches', *Report and Transactions of the Devonshire Association* 14 (1882), 387–90.

23. R. B. Span, 'West Country Superstitions', *Occult Review* 22 (1915), 284–7.

24. Davies, 'Cunning Folk', 94.

25. *Ibid.*, 97.

26. Beatrix Albinia Wherry, 'Wizardry on the Welsh Border', *Folk-Lore* 15 (1904), 76–7.

27. Jacqueline Simpson, *The Folklore of Sussex* (London: Batsford, 1973), 72–3.

28. M. R. T. Taylor, 'Witches and Witchcraft', *Folk-Lore* 46 (1935), 171–2.

29. *The Ashton-under-Lyne Reporter* (17 January 1857), reprinted in *FLS News* 16 (1992), 12–13.

30. Olive Knott, *Witches of Dorset* (Milborne Port: Dorset Publishing Co., 1974), 33–9.

31. Thomas Hancock, 'Llanrhaiadr-yn-Mochnant', *Montgomeryshire Collections* 6 (1873), 329–30.

32. Davies, 'Cunning Folk', 93.

33. On this see, particularly, Barry Reay, 'The Context and Meaning of Popular Literacy: Some Evidence from Nineteenth-Century Rural England', *Past and Present* 131 (1991), 89–121.

34. Bottrell, *Traditions and Hearthside Stories*, 90–1.

35. Span, 'West Country Superstitions', 285.

36. Elias Owen, *Welsh Folk-Lore* (Oswestry: Woodall, 1887), 252.

37. Edward Hamer, 'A Parochial Account of Llangurig', *Montgomeryshire Collections* 3 (1870), 267.

38. Simpson, *Folklore of Sussex*, 77–8.
39. Jacqueline Simpson, *The Folklore of the Welsh Border* (London: Batsford, 1976), 62–3.
40. E.g., *ibid.*, 62–3; James Obelkevich, *Religion and Rural Society: South Lindsey 1825–1875* (Oxford: Oxford University Press, 1976), 289; Wherry, 'Wizardry', 76–7; Jonathan Ceredig Davies, *Folk-Lore of West and Mid-Wales* (Aberystwyth, 1911), 246–9.
41. Davies, 'Decline in the Popular Belief', 189–91, and 'Cunning Folk', 97–8.
42. Eric Maple, *The Dark World of Witches* (London: Hale, 1962), 174–82, and 'Cunning Murrell', 40.
43. Brown, *Fate of the Dead*, 47.
44. Mary L. Lewes, 'The Wizards of Cwrt-y-Cadno', *Occult Review* 40 (1934), 17–24; Davies, *Folk-Lore*, 252.
45. Maple, 'Cunning Murrell', 40.
46. W. Habutt Dawson, *History of Skipton* (1882), 391–3.
47. Wellcome Institute, London, MS 3770.
48. Cwrtmawr MSS 97 and 672.
49. University College of North Wales, Bangor, MS 3212.
50. Davies, 'Decline in the Popular Belief', 191–2.
51. In the University of London, Harry Price Collection, Wonderful Magical Scrapbook.
52. Francis X. King, *The Flying Sorcerer* (Oxford: Mandrake, 1992), 26–51.
53. Maple, *Dark World*, 174–82.
54. University of London, Harry Rice Collection, Wonderful Magical Scrapbook, f. 367.
55. Patrick Curry, *A Confusion of Prophets: Victorian and Edwardian Astrology* (London: Collins and Brown, 1992), 46–60, suggests that the somewhat obscure Edwin Medhurst held the post. I am very grateful to Dr Curry for the gift of this work, the classic one upon the subject. Owen Davies, 'The Decline in the Popular Belief in Witchcraft and Magic', 326–7, states that Medhurst did not take over until *c.* 1846, and proposes for his predecessor the famous occultist Frederick Hockley. There is good circumstantial evidence for this, but none is conclusive, and the matter may well remain undecided.
56. Lewes, 'Wizards of Cwrt y Cadno', 17–24.
57. These issues are explored in Owen Davies's paper, 'Charmers and Charming'.
58. Best surveyed in Owen Davies, 'Healing Charms in Use in England and Wales 1700–1950', *Folklore* 107 (1996), 19–32.
59. W. H. Howse, *Radnorshire* (Hereford: Thurston, 1949), 199.
60. Bottrell, *Traditions and Hearthside Stories*, 116.
61. *County Folk-Lore II*, 187–9.
62. Atkinson, *Forty Years*, 94–6.
63. Davies, 'Charmers and Charming', *passim*; Theo Brown, 'Charming in Devon', *Folklore* 81 (1970), 37–47; Chaloner, *Palatinate Studies*, 21–35; Margaret Courtney, *Folklore and Legends of Cornwall* (1890), 147; Deane and Shaw, *Folklore of Cornwall*, 121–2; Maple, *Dark World*, 163–6; Charlotte C. Mason, 'Witchcraft and Magic in Essex', *Essex Review* (April 1928), 63–4; Spar, 'West Country Superstitions', 285–7; C. W. Whistler, 'Local Traditions of the Quantocks', *Folklore* 19 (1908), 89; John Symonds Udal, *Dorsetshire Folk-Lore* (Hertford: Stephen Austin, 1922), 216; Charles Thomas, 'Present-Day Charmers in Cornwall', *Folk-Lore* 64 (1953), 304–5; Enid M. Porter, 'Some Folk Beliefs of the Fens', *Folk-Lore* 69 (1958), 118–19; Margaret Eyre, 'Folk-lore of the Wye Valley', *Folk-Lore* 16 (1905), 167–8; Knott, *Witches of Dorset*, 39–41; Hamer, 'Account of Llangurig', 269; J. Moreton Pearson, 'Montgomeryshire Folk-Lore', *Montgomeryshire Collections* 37 (1915), 191.
64. Brown, 'Charming in Devon', 46–7.

65. *Ibid.*, 42–3; Thomas, 'Present-Day Charmers', 304–5; Deane and Shaw, *Folklore of Cornwall*, 121.

66. George Ewart Evans, *The Horse in the Furrow* (London: Faber, 1960), 239–61.

67. Simpson, *Folklore of the Welsh Border*, 61; Henderson, *Folk-Lore of the Northern Counties*, 215–19; Simpson, *Folklore of Sussex*, 72–3; F. W. Mathews, *Tales of the Blackdown Borderland* (Somerset Folk Series 13: 1923), 103–4; Edward Hamer, 'Parochial Account of Llandiloes', *Montgomeryshire Collections* 10 (1877), 250–1.

68. Simpson, *Folklore of the Welsh Border*, 64, and *Folklore of Sussex*, 73–4; Jon Raven, *Staffordshire Folklore* (London: Batsford, 1978), 140; L. J. Dickinson, 'Charms and Witchcraft of Today', *Occult Review* 29 (1919), 334; Ella Mary Leather, *The Folk-Lore of Herefordshire* (Hereford, 1912), 59; Blakeborough, *Wit, Character, Folklore*, 184; Enid Porter, *Cambridgeshire Customs and Folklore* (London: Routledge, 1969), 177; Maple, 'Cunning Murrell', 39; Edmund Vale, *Shropshire* (London: Hale, 1949), 12–14; Dawson, *History of Skipton*, 390.

69. Taylor, 'Witches and Witchcraft', 171.

70. L. F. Newman, 'Some Notes on the History and Practice of Witchcraft in the Eastern Counties', *Folk-Lore* 47 (1946), 30.

71. Henderson, *Folk-Lore of the Northern Counties*, 215–19, 244–5; Blakeborough, *Wit, Character, Folklore*, 182; Christopher Marlowe, *Legends of the Fenland People* (London: Cecil Palmer, 1926), 213–16.

72. Simpson, *Folklore of the Welsh Border*, 64; Bottrell, *Traditions and Hearthside Stories*, 79–89, 118; Courtney, *Folklore of Cornwall*, 140; Mason, 'Witchcraft and Magic', 63–4; Henderson, *Folk-Lore of the Northern Counties*, 219–31; Mathews, *Blackdown Borderland*, 107–10; 'Consulting a Witch', *Folk-Lore Record* 2 (1879), 207; 'Witchcraft in the Midlands', *Folk-Lore Record* 4 (1881), 181; Ralph Whitlock, *The Folklore of Devon* (London: Batsford, 1977), 43–7; Davies, *West and Mid-Wales*, 239–41; Mark R. Taylor, 'Norfolk Folklore', *Folk-Lore* 40 (1929), 131; T. A. Davies, 'Folklore of Gwent', *Folk-Lore* 48 (1937), 52–3; Porter, 'Folk Beliefs', 121–2; Atkinson, *Forty Years*, 124–4; John Nicholson, *Folk Lore of East Yorkshire* (1890), 91–2; Charles Henry Poole, *The Customs, Superstitions and Legends of the County of Somerset* (1877), 55; Maple, 'Cunning Murrell', 38–9; Dawson, *History of Skipton*, 394.

73. Mathews, *Blackdown Borderland*, 107; Taylor, 'Norfolk Folklore', 130; 'Scraps of English Folklore', *Folk-Lore* 40 (1929), 78–9; Taylor, 'Witches and Witchcraft', 171–2; Blakeborough, *Wit, Character, Folklore*, 191–2; Simpson, *Folklore of the Welsh Border*, 64; Courtney, *Folklore of Cornwall*, 140, 145.

74. Taylor, 'Norfolk Folklore', 100.

75. Mason, 'Witchcraft and Magic', 63–4.

76. Davies, 'Cunning Folk', 98–100.

77. Blakeborough, *Wit, Character, Folklore*, 168–71.

78. Ruth Tongue, *Somerset Folklore*, ed. K. M. Briggs (Folk-Lore Society, 1965), 65–89; Sarah Hewett, *Nummits and Crummits* (1900), 63–5.

79. A theme constant among experts from Alan Macfarlane, *Witchcraft in Tudor and Stuart England* (Cambridge: Cambridge University Press, 1970) to James Sharp, *Instruments of Darkness: Witchcraft in England 1550–1750* (London: Hamish Hamilton, 1996).

80. Robert Hunt, *Popular Romances of the West of England* (Truro, 1881), 328.

81. Courtney, *Folklore of Somerset*, 145.

82. Bottrell, *Hearthside Stories*, 245–7.

83. Marie Trevelyan, *Folk-Lore and Folk–Stories of Wales* (1909), 208–9.

84. Wherry, 'Wizardry', 80.

85. See Ronald Hutton, *The Stations of the Sun: A History of the Ritual Year in Britain* (Oxford: Oxford University Press, 1996), 420–1, and notes appended. My attitude has hardened since then.

86. Christopher Marlowe, *Stories of the Fenland People* (London: Palmer, 1926), 200–11.

87. Ethel H. Rudkin, 'Lincolnshire Folklore', *Folk-Lore* 45 (1934), 250.

88. John Symonds Udal, *Dorsetshire Folk-Lore* (Hertford: Austin, 1922), 212.

89. H. P. Whitcombe, *Bygone Days in Devonshire and Cornwall* (1874), 83.

90. Raven, *Staffordshire Folklore*, 36.

91. Simpson, *Folklore of Sussex*, 75–6.

92. 'Witches over the Crouch', *The Times* (27 January 1959), 5.

93. Eric Maple, 'The Witches of Canewdon', *Folklore* 71 (1960), 241–3.

94. Porter, *Cambridgeshire Customs*, 167.

95. James Obelkevich, *Religion and Rural Society: South Lindsey 1825–1875* (Oxford: Oxford University Press, 1976), 280.

96. De Blecourt, 'Witch Doctors', 299–301.

97. Obelkevich, *Religion and Rural Society*, 290–1.

98. *County Folk-Lore V: Lincolnshire*, ed. Mrs Gutch and Mabel Peacock (Folk-Lore Society, 1908), 73–4.

99. Simpson, *Folklore of the Welsh Border*, 64; Hamer, 'Account of Llangurig', 268; Deane and Shaw, *Folklore of Cornwall*, 121–2; Davies, 'Folklore of Gwent', 45–6; Thomas, 'Present Day Charmers', 304–5; Blakeborough, *Wit, Character, Folklore*, 182; Atkinson, *Forty Years*, 124–5; Margaret Eyre, 'Folklore of the Wye Valley', *Folk-Lore* 16 (1905), 168–9; Brown, 'Charming in Devon', 41–5; Knott, *Witches of Dorset*, 41.

100. Courtney, *Folklore of Cornwall*, 147; Span, 'West Country Superstitions', 284–5; C. W. Whistler, 'Sundry Notes from West Somerset and Devon', *Folk-Lore* 19 (1908), 88; Dawson, *History of Skipton*, 392–4; Hamer, 'Account of Llangurig', 269–70.

101. Simpson, *Folklore of Sussex*, 82–3; Raven, *Staffordshire Folklore*, 120; Hardwick, *Traditions, Superstitions, Folklore*, 120–1; D. Edmondes Owen, 'Pre-Reformation Survivals in Radnorshire', *Transactions of the Honourable Society of Cymmrodorion* (1910–11), 111; Charlotte S. Burne, *Shropshire Folk-Lore* (1888), 181–2.

102. Simpson, *Folklore of Sussex*, 82–3; Raven, *Staffordshire Folklore*, 23–4; Dawson, *History of Skipton*, 393–4.

103. Raven, *Staffordshire Folklore*, 41.

104. Nicholson, *East Yorkshire*, 91–2.

105. L. Salmon, 'Folklore in the Kennet Valley', *Folk-Lore* 13 (1902), 426.

106. Simpson, *Folklore of the Welsh Border*, 67; Davies, *West and Mid-Wales*, 234; Davies, 'Folklore of Gwent', 47; Owen, *Welsh Folk-Lore*, 242.

107. Burne, *Shropshire Folk-Lore*, 151–3.

108. C. W. Whistler, 'Local Traditions of the Quantocks', *Folk-Lore* 19 (1908), 45; 'Scraps of English Folklore', *Folk-Lore* 39 (1928), 383; Rudkin, 'Lincolnshire Folklore', 259; Davies, *West and Mid-Wales*, 231.

109. Hermione L. F. Jennings, 'A Cambridgeshire Witch', *Folk-Lore* 16 (1905), 188–9; 'Superstition in Essex', *Folk-Lore* 27 (1916), 299–300.

110. 'Scraps of English Folklore', *Folk-Lore* 37 (1926), 78; *County Folk-Lore V*, 104; Porter, *Cambridgeshire Customs*, 161–75; Maple, *Dark World*, 170–87.

111. Lewes, 'Wizards of Cwrt y Cadno', 17–24; Davies, 'Cunning Folk', 95–6.

112. *Ibid.*, 96–7.

113. Maple, *Dark World*, 174–82; Henderson, *Folklore of the Northern Counties*, 215–20; Atkinson, *Forty Years*, 124.

114. Obelkevich, *Religion and Rural Society*, 289.

115. Davies, 'Cunning Folk', 97; Blakeborough, *Wit, Character, Folklore*, 180–1; Maple, 'Cunning Murrell', 36–7.

116. Davies, 'Charms and Charming', *passim*; Brown, 'Charming in Devon', 37–9; J. Moreton Pearson, 'Montgomeryshire Folk-Lore', *Montgomeryshire Collections* 37 (1915), 191; Leather, *Herefordshire*, 70; Thomas, 'Present Day Charmers', 304–5; John Rhys, *Celtic Folk-Lore* (Oxford, 1900), vol. I, 300.

117. E. O. Begg, 'Scraps of Folk-Lore from Somerset', *Folk-Lore* 56 (1945), 293–4; Eric Maple, 'The Witches of Dengie', *Folklore* 73 (1962), 178–9; Owen, *Welsh Folk-Lore*, 222–3; Davies, *West and Mid-Wales*, 221.

118. Hardwick, *Traditions, Superstitions and Folklore*, 112–23; Simpson, *Folklore of Sussex*, 76; Porter, *Cambridgeshire Customs*, 161; Eyre, 'Wye Valley', 120–1; Maple, 'Witches of Canewdon', 246–7; Maple, 'Witches of Dengie', 181.

119. Rudkin, 'Lincolnshire Folklore', 262.

120. Davies, 'Charmers and Charming', *passim*; Chaloner, *Palatinate Studies*, 21–35; Eyre, 'Wye Valley', 167–8; Brown, 'Charming in Devon', 41.

121. Knott, *Witches of Dorset*, 38–9.

122. Maple, 'Cunning Murrell', 38–9.

123. Davies, *West and Mid-Wales*, 237–8.

124. Hamer, 'Account of Llangurig', 270–1; Roy Palmer, *The Folklore of Warwickshire* (London: Batsford, 1976), 82–3.

125. Nicholson, *Folklore of East Yorkshire*, 93–4; Hardwick, *Traditions, Superstitions, and Folklore*, 120–1.

126. Henderson, *Folklore of the Northern Counties*, 221–2; Maple, *Dark World*, 144; Obelkevitch, *Religion and Rural Society*, 287–8.

127. Raven, *Staffordshire Folklore*, 50.

128. E. A. Rawlence, 'Folk-Lore and Superstitions still obtaining in Dorset', *Dorset Natural History and Antiquarian field Club* 35 (1914), 85–7.

129. Davies, 'Urbanization and the Decline of Witchcraft', 600–1.

130. Courtney, *Folklore of Cornwall*, 142.

131. M. A. Hardy, 'The Evil Eye in Somerset', *Folk-Lore* 24 (1913), 382–3.

132. 'Witchcraft in the Midlands', *Folk-Lore Record* 2 (1879), 181.

133. Taylor, 'Norfolk Folklore', 128, and 'Witches and Witchcraft', 171–2.

134. Whitlock, *Folklore of Devon*, 387–90.

135. Taylor, 'Norfolk Folklore', 132; Enid. M. Porter, 'Some Folk Beliefs of the Fens', *Folk-Lore* 69 (1958), 120.

136. Taylor, 'Witches and Witchcraft', 171–2.

137. Raven, *Staffordshire Folklore*, 40, 50; Palmer, *Folklore of Warwickshire*, 82–3.

138. Davies, 'Cunning Folk', 94–5.

139. *Ibid.*, 95; Edward Hamer, 'Parochial Account of Llandiloes', *Montgomeryshire Collections* 10 (1877), 249.

140. Marlowe, *Fenland People*, 213–20.

141. Nor can I, in any contemporary source. There is, however, the testimony by Cecil Williamson, that as a boy, during World War One, he saw four or five drunken farm-workers stripping an old woman at North Bovey, on the edge of Dartmoor in Devon, to search her for a witch's teat on the assumption that she had bewitched their cattle. They were halted by the vicar, and their victim later revealed herself to Williamson as a wise-woman and commenced his instruction in cunning craft. There is something odd about this account, for belief in a witch's teat, along with the associated one in a familiar, is not a West Country one, but East Anglian. If true, it is by far the most recent occasion of a witch-mobbing ever recorded, more than half a century after the

last properly documented one: 'A Conversation with Cecil Williamson', *Talking Stick* 7 (1992), 26–7.

142. Davies, 'Decline in the Popular Belief', 42–219, and 'Cunning Folk', 104–5.
143. Davies, 'Decline in the Popular Belief', 195.
144. Maple, *Dark World*, 142–3.
145. *Ibid.*, 143–9.
146. Newman, 'Witchcraft in the Eastern Counties', 32.
147. *County Folk-Lore II*, 187–9.
148. *The Croydon Chronicle* (8 November 1856), 3c.
149. Davies, 'Urbanization and the Decline of Witchcraft', 600–1, and 'Cunning Folk', 101.
150. Palmer, *Folklore of Warwickshire*, 82–3; *Folklore Society News* 16 (1992), 12–13.
151. Hardwick, *Traditions, Superstitions and Folklore*, 120–1.
152. Davies, 'Decline of the Popular Belief', 217–19, 326–52, and 'Cunning Folk', 104.
153. Davies, 'Decline of the Popular Belief', 351–75.
154. Brown, 'Charming in Devon', 47.

CHAPTER 7

1. *The Stations of the Sun: A History of the Ritual Year in Britain* (Oxford: Oxford University Press, 1996).
2. Gillian Bennett, 'Geologists and Folklorists: Cultural Evolution and the Science of Folklore', *Folklore* 105 (1994), 25–37.
3. Wilhelm Mannhardt, *Roggenwolf und Rogenhund* (Danzig, 1866), *Die Korn damonen* (Berlin, 1868), *Antike Wald- und Feldkulte* (Berlin, 1877), and *Mythologische Forschungen* (Strasburg, 1884).
4. Mary Beard, 'Frazer, Leach and Virgil: The Popularity (and Unpopularity) of *The Golden Bough*', *Comparative Studies in Society and History* 34 (1992), 203–24.
5. Robert Ackerman, *J. G. Frazer: His Life and Work* (Cambridge: Cambridge University Press, 1987), 1–32; John Burrow, *Evolution and Society* (Cambridge: Cambridge University Press, 1966), 241–4.
6. Burrow, *Evolution and Society*, 245–59.
7. Henrika Kuklick, *The Savage Within: The Social History of British Anthropology 1885–1914* (Cambridge: Cambridge University Press, 1991), 78–9.
8. Ronald Hutton, *The Rise and Fall of Merry England* (Oxford: Oxford University Press, 1994), 144–5.
9. Ackerman, *J. G. Frazer*, 1–32, 164–7.
10. In the introduction: vol. I, pp. xxi–xxii.
11. pp. 300–1.
12. R. Angus Downie, *Frazer and "The Golden Bough"* (London: Victor Gollancz, 1970), 20–1.
13. Ackerman, *J. G. Frazer*, 236–48.
14. *Ibid.*, 212.
15. See especially Edward B. Tylor, *Primitive Culture* (1871), vol. II, 443–53.
16. Ackerman, *J. G. Frazer*, 97.
17. Haskell M. Block, 'Cultural Anthropology and Contemporary Literary Criticism', *Journal of Aesthetics and Art Criticism* 11 (1952), 46–54; John P. Vickers, *The Literary Impact of "The Golden Bough"* (Princeton: Princeton University Press, 1973), *passim*; Sir

James Frazer and the Literary Imagination, ed. Robert Fraser (Basingstoke: Macmillan, 1990), *passim*.

18. Many of which are collected in Trinity College, Cambridge, Frazer MS 22.
19. Raymond Williams, *The Country and the City* (London: Chatto and Windus, 1973), ch. 21; W. J. Keith, *The Rural Tradition* (Toronto: Toronto University Press, 1975); Martin Wiener, *English Culture and the Decline of the Industrial Spirit* (Cambridge: Cambridge University Press, 1981); Jan Marsh, *Back to the Land: The Pastoral Impulse in England from 1880 to 1914* (London: Quartet, 1982); Alun Howkins, 'The Discovery of Rural England', in *Englishness: Politics and Culture 1880–1920* (London: Croom Helm, 1986), 62–88; Gillian Bennett, 'Folklore Studies and the English Rural Myth', *Rural History* 4 (1993), 77–91.

   Peter Mandler, 'Against "Englishness": English Culture and the Limits to Rural Nostalgia, 1850–1940', *Transactions of the Royal Historical Society* 6th series 7 (1997), 155–76, has argued forcefully against an overstatement of this position, suggesting that the 'rural myth' was the preoccupation of only a section of society, and not dominant in England in general. His words are well taken, and do not diminish my own case, which depends only on the belief that this 'myth' was prevalent in a significant part of the literary culture, and came under no direct attack or opposition at this time. Likewise, John Ashton, 'Beyond Survivalism: Regional Folkloristics in Late-Victorian England', *Folklore* 108 (1997), 19–24, has reminded us that provincial England contained a number of important folklore collectors who did not share the contemporary pre-occupation with folk customs as pagan survivals. This does not alter the fact that they did not articulate any alternative theory to challenge the latter, and that 'survivalism' was dominant among the metropolitan scholars who presided over the movement.

20. Marsh, *Back to the Land*, 35.
21. Morton Cohen, *Rudyard Kipling to Rider Haggard: The Record of a Friendship* (London: Hutchinson, 1965), 51.
22. *Our Old Home* (repr. 1890), 92.
23. Alice Chandler, *A Dream of Order: The Medieval Ideal in English Literature* (London: Routledge, 1971); fiona MacCarthy, *The Simple Life: C. R. Ashbee in the Cotswolds* (London: Lund Humphries, 1981); John Burrow, *A Liberal Descent: Victorian Historians and the English Past* (Cambridge: Cambridge University Press, 1981); Roy Edmund Judge, 'Changing Attitudes to May Day 1844–1914' (Leeds University PhD thesis, 1987). And see also Hutton, *Stations of the Sun*, ch. 28.
24. *Scenes from Clerical Life* (1858), 1.
25. 'Inaugural Address', *Journal of the Folk Song Society* 1 (1899), 1.
26. Vic Gammon, 'Folk Song Collecting in Sussex and Surrey 1843–1914', *History Workshop* 10 (1980), 80–5.
27. Bennett, 'Folklore Studies and the English Rural Myth', 88–9.
28. Joseph Jacobs, 'The Folk', *Folk-Lore* 4 (1893), 234–6.
29. Ivor Clissold, 'Alfred Williams, Song Collector', *Folk Music Journal* 1.5 (1969), 293–300.
30. E. Sidney Hartland, 'Peeping Tom and Lady Godiva', *Folk-Lore* 1 (1890), 225.
31. G. L. Gomme, 'Opening Address', *Folk-Lore* 2 (1891), 5–11, 'Opening Address', *Folk-Lore* 3 (1892), 4–12, *The Village Community* (1890), 2–4.
32. E. Clodd, 'Presidential Address', *Folk-Lore* 7 (1896), 47–8, 56.
33. Walter Johnson, *Folk-Memory or The Continuity of British Archaeology* (Oxford: Oxford University Press, 1908), and *By-Ways in British Archaeology* (Cambridge: Cambridge University Press, 1912).
34. H. J. Massingham, *Downland Man* (London: Cape, 1926), 327, *The English Countryman* (London: Batsford, 1942), 11–14, and *Remembrance: An Autobiography* (London: Batsford, 1944), 49–68.

35. H. J. Massingham, *The Tree of Life* (London: Chapman and Hall, 1942), 210.

36. H. J. Massingham, *Wold Without End* (London: Cobden-Sanderson, 1932), 40, 47, 86–90, 156, 205. See also his *The English Countryside* (London: Batsford, 1939), 1.

37. R. R. Marett, 'Survival and Revival', *Journal of the English Folk Dance and Song Society* 1.2 (1933), 74.

38. For the latest survey of the evidence see *Church Archaeology: Research Directions for the Future*, eds. John Blair and Carol Pyrah (Council for British Archaeology Research Report 104, 1996), 6–12, 53.

39. Hutton, *Stations of the Sun*, passim.

40. G. L. Gomme, 'Opening Address', *Folk-Lore* 5 (1894), 69.

41. Edmund R. Leach, 'Golden Bough or Gilded Twig?', *Daedalus* (Spring 1961), 383.

42. Jane Ellen Harrison, *Reminiscences of a Student's Life* (London: Hogarth, 1925), 81–4.

43. Sandra J. Peacock, *Jane Ellen Harrison: The Mask and the Self* (New Haven, CT: Yale University Press, 1988), 206.

44. Harrison, *Reminiscences*, 84.

45. Peacock, *Jane Ellen Harrison*, 49, 68–90. See also Thomas W. Africa, 'Aunt Glegg Amongst The Dons', and Sandra J. Peacock, 'An Awful Warmth About Her Heart: The Personal in Jane Harrison's Ideas on Religion', in *The Cambridge Rituals Reconsidered*, ed. William M. Calder III (Atalanta: Illinois Classical Studies, Supplement II, 1991), 21–35 and 168–83.

46. Harrison, *Reminiscences*, 83.

47. Peacock, *Jane Ellen Harrison*, 99.

48. *Ibid.*, 186–200; Renate Schleiser, 'Prolegomena to Jane Harrison's Interpretation of Ancient Greek Religion', in *The Cambridge Rituals Reconsidered*, ed. Calder, 187–219; Jane Ellen Harrison, *Prolegomena to the Study of Greek Religion* (Cambridge, 1903), and *Themis: A Study of the Social Origins of Greek Religion* (Cambridge, 1912).

49. Gilbert Murray, *Four Stages of Greek Religion* (New York: Columbia University Press, 1912), 16–18, 45–6; Arthur Bernard Cook, *Zeus: A Study in Ancient Religion* (Cambridge: Cambridge University Press, 1914), vol. I, 776–80. See Robert Ackerman, 'The Cambridge Group: Origins and Composition', and Robert L. Fowler, 'Gilbert Murray: Four (five) Stages of Greek Religion', in *The Cambridge Ritualists Reconsidered*, ed. Calder, 1–19 and 79–95.

50. Louis Richard Farnell, *Outline History of Greek Religion* (London: Duckworth, 1920), 16–36.

51. John Cuthbert Lawson, *Modern Greek Folklore and Ancient Greek Religion A Study in Survivals* (Cambridge, 1910).

52. The best study is Janet Grayson, 'In Quest of Jessie Weston', *Arthurian Literature* 11 (1992), 1–80.

53. *Primitive Culture*, ii. 452.

54. Ackerman, *J. G. Frazer*, 213.

55. *Ibid.*, 211.

56. Johnson, *Folk Memory*, 17.

57. Massingham, *Wold Without End*, 85.

58. Marett, 'Survival and Revival', 75–6.

59. Gammon, 'Folk-Song Collecting', 84–5.

60. Theresa Buckland, 'English Folk Dance Scholarship: An Overview', in *Traditional Dance*, ed. Theresa Buckland (Crewe: Traditional Dance Conference Series, 1982), vol. I, 3–18.

61. Violet Alford, 'Folklore Gone Wrong', *Folklore* 71 (1961), 599–611.

62. M. M. Banks, 'The Padstow May Festival', *Folk-Lore* 49 (1938), 392–4.

63. Simon Lichman, 'The Gardener's Story and What Came Next: A Contextual Analysis of the Marshfield Paper Boys' Mumming Play' (Pennsylvania University PhD thesis, 1981), 1–2, 213–15.

64. Hutton, *Stations of the Sun*, 117.

65. Alice B. Gomme, 'The Character of Beelzebub in the Mummers' Play', *Folk-Lore* 40 (1929), 292–3.

66. E. C. Cawte, *Ritual Animal Diguise* (Ipswich: Folklore Society, 1978), 157–68; Judge, 'Changing Attitudes to May Day', 410–11.

67. Banks, 'The Padstow May Festival', 393–4.

68. Roy Judge, *The Jack-in-the-Green* (Ipswich: Folk-Lore Society, 1979), *passim*.

69. Lady Raglan, 'The Green Man in Church Architecture', *Folk-Lore* 50 (1939), 45–77. Brandon Centerwall has recently argued persuasively that Lady Raglan had indeed chosen the correct, and traditional, name for the carved figures in churches. The identification is not completely proven, however, while her extension of it to the May Day figure was certainly wrong, and the connection of the church figures with paganism remains dubious: Brandon S. Centerwall, 'The Name of the Green Man', *Folklore* 108 (1997), 25–34.

70. Hutton, *Stations of the Sun*, 70–80; Stephen D. Corrsin, 'The Historiography of European Linked Sword Dancing', *Dance Research Journal* 25 (1993), 1–13.

71. Violet Alford, *Sword Dance and Drama* (London: Merlin, 1962), 13–28, 201–16.

72. S. H. Hooke, 'Time and Custom', *Folk-Lore* 48 (1937), 17–24.

73. Sir Flinders Petrie, *The Hill figures of England* (Royal Anthropological Institute, 1926), 10; Stuart Piggott, 'The Character of Beelzebub in the Mummers' Play', *Folk-Lore* 40 (1929), 193–95, and 'The Name of the Giant of Cerne', *Antiquity* 6 (1932), 214–16; O. G. S. Crawford, 'The Giant of Cerne and other Hill figures', *Antiquity* 3 (1929), 277–83, and *The Eye Goddess* (London: Phoenix House, 1957), ch. 13.

74. E. K. Chambers, *The Medieval Stage* (Oxford: Oxford University Press, 1903), *passim*.

75. G. C. Coulton, *five Centuries of Religion, Volume 1* (Cambridge: Cambridge University Press, 1925), 179–83.

76. Analysed and criticized in detail by Joseph Fontenrose, *The Ritual Theory of Myth* (Berkeley: University of California Press, 1964), ch. 2.

77. Cecil Sharp and Herbert Macilwaine, *The Morris Book. Parts 1–3* (2nd edns, 1912–24); Cecil Sharp, *The Morris Book. Parts 4–5* (2nd edns, 1911–13). For Sharp's evolving thought, see John Forrest, *Morris and Matachin* (English Folk Dance and Song Society, 1984), 2–8.

78. Sir Lawrence and Lady Gomme, *British Folk-Lore, Folk–Songs and Singing Games* (National Home-Reading Union Pamphlets, Literature Series 4, n.d.), 10.

79. Gammon, 'Folk Song Collecting', 82; A. H. Fox Strangways, *Cecil Sharp* (Oxford: Oxford University Press, 1933), 23, 60–6.

80. David Harker, 'Cecil Sharp in Somerset—Some Conclusions', *Folk Music Journal* 2.3 (1972), 220–40.

CHAPTER 8

1. This figure was calculated independently by myself, in *The Pagan Religions of the Ancient British Isles; Their Nature and Legacy* (Oxford: Blackwell, 1991), 306, 370, and Robin Briggs, 'Women as Victims?', *French History* 5 (1991), 438–50. My detailed account of the reasoning and data behind my own calculation is contained in a paper which will be published in a forthcoming collection of essays. In 1996 the figure was accepted

by the four experts who made up the participants in the episode on 'The Great Witch Hunt' in my BBC Radio Four parlour game, 'Battling With The Past': Robin Briggs, James Sharpe, Diane Purkiss, and Anne Lawrence. It has also been endorsed in public speech by Wolfgang Behringer, probably the leading contemporary authority on the German trials, and so appears to be becoming an orthodoxy; cf. Robin Briggs, *Witches and Neighbours: The Social and Cultural Context of European Witchcraft* (London: HarperCollins, 1996), 8, 260. The sole dissenting voice within academe seems to be Anne Llewellyn Barstow, in her feminist polemic *Witchcraze: A New History of the European Witch Hunts* (San Francisco: HarperCollins, 1994), 179–81, where the figure is estimated at about 100,000. Professor Barstow very helpfully lists her sources, and having worked over them independently I believe that she has misunderstood them; but that dispute is for a different publication.

2. For this and much of what follows below, see E. William Monter, 'The Historiography of European Witchcraft; Progress and Prospects', *Journal of Interdisciplinary History* 2 (1971–2), 435–51, and Leland L. Estes, 'Incarnations of Evil: Changing Perspectives on the European Witch Craze', *Clio* 13.2 (1984), 133–47.

3. Nikolaus Paulus, *Hexenwahn und Hexenprozesse vornehmilch im 16.Jahrundert* (Freiburg, 1910).

4. George Bancroft, *History of the United States. Volume 3* (Boston, 1845), 74–99.

5. James Russell Lowell, *Literary Essays. Volume 2* (London, 1911), 313–98.

6. See Estes, 'Incarnations of Evil', 136–7, and sources cited there.

7. *Ibid.*, plus Wallace Notestein, *A History of Witchcraft in England from 1558 to 1718* (Washington: American Historical Association, 1911), and George Lyman Kittredge, *Witchcraft in Old and New England* (Cambridge, MA: Harvard University Press, 1929).

8. C. L'Estrange Ewen, *Witch Hunting and Witch Trials* (London: Kegan Paul, Trench and Trubner, 1929).

9. Charles Mackay, *Memoirs of Extraordinary Popular Delusions* (1841), vol. II, 167–323.

10. Thomas Wright, *Narratives of Sorcery and Magic* (1851), 2 vols.

11. E. Lynn Linton, *Witch Stories* (1861); quotation on p. 428.

12. W. E. H. Lecky, *History of the Rise and Influence of the Spirit of Rationalism in Europe* (1865), vol. I, 1–150; quotation on p. 149.

13. Edward B. Tylor, *Primitive Culture* (1871), vol. I, 141.

14. Gordon Ridgewell, 'Swimming a Witch, 1863', *Folklore Society News* 26 (1997), 5.

15. St John D. Seymour, *Irish Witchcraft and Demonology* (Dublin, 1913), 248–53.

16. Karl Ernst Jarcke, 'Ein Hexenprozess', *Annalen der Deutschen und Auslandischen Criminal-Rechts-Pflege* 1 (1828), 450. The vital importance of Jarcke, and Mone (below), was first noticed by Norman Cohn, *Europe's Inner Demons* (Falmer: Sussex University Press, 1975), 103–5.

17. Franz Josef Mone, 'Uber das Hexenwesen', *Anzeiger fur Kunde der Teutschen Vorzeit* (1839), 271–5 and 444–5; cf. Cohen, *Europe's Inner Demons*, 104–5.

18. In *Del Congresso Notturno delle Lamie*. For a typical misinterpretation of his text, see Lewis Spence, 'Modern Theories about Witchcraft', *Occult Review* 69 (1942), 89–91.

19. Jacob Grimm, *Teutonic Mythology*, trans. J. S. Stallybrass (1883), vol. III, 1044–93.

20. first noticed in this context by Prudence Jones and Nigel Pennick, *A History of Pagan Europe* (London: Routledge, 1995), 206.

21. For this and the biographical details below, see Oscar A. Haac, *Jules Michelet* (Boston: Twayne, 1982), 84–144.

22. *Ibid.*, 85, 93.

23. Lucien Febvre, 'How Jules Michelet invented the Renaissance', in *A New Kind of History, from the Writings of Febvre*, ed. Peter Burke (London: Routledge 1973), 265.

24. *Ibid.*, 267.
25. Haac, *Jules Michelet*, 85–93.
26. *Ibid.*, 117.
27. Cohn, *Europe's Inner Demons*, 107.
28. Haac, *Jules Michelet*, 137.
29. *Ibid.*, 138.
30. Quotations taken from the English translation by A. R. Allinson (Paris, 1904); in this case pp. 1–2.
31. *Ibid.*, 39, 93, 111, 120–3.
32. *Ibid.*, 11, 87, 92, 122.
33. *Ibid.*, 48–50, 141–2, 180–3, 300.
34. *Ibid.*, 3, 150, 245.
35. *Ibid.*, 221.
36. *Ibid.*, 329.
37. Haac, *Jules Michelet*, 138.
38. Sigmund Freud, *The Origins of Psychoanalysis: Letters to Wilhelm Fliess*, ed. Ernst Kris (London, 1954), 188–9.
39. James Webb, *The Occult Establishment* (La Salle, IL: Open Court, 1976), 381.
40. My interpretation of Gage and her role is based on the study made by Rachel Halsted, in 'The New Myth of the Witch', *Trouble and Strife* 2 (Spring 1982), 10–17, and 'Mothers of Invention', *Trouble and Strife* 7 (Winter 1985), 17–25.
41. Grimm, *Teutonic Mythology*, vol. III, 1067.
42. Lecky, *History of the Rise and Influence of the Spirit of Rationalism*, vol. I, 149.
43. Mackay, *Memoirs of Extraordinary Popular Delusions*, vol. II, 168.
44. Matilda Joslyn Gage, *Women, Church and State* (Chicago, 1893), 106–7.
45. Apart from *Aradia*, below, see Charles Godfrey Leland, *Etruscan Roman Remains in Popular Tradition* (1892), 209–10.
46. *Ibid.*, 221.
47. Charles Godfrey Leland, *Gypsy Sorcery and Fortune Telling* (Privately printed, 1889), 3–12, 177–83.
48. *Ibid.*, 55–6.
49. Leland, *Etruscan Roman Remains*, 210.
50. Charles Godfrey Leland, *Legends of Florence* (1895), vii, and *Aradia, Gospel of the Witches* (1990 reprint; Phoenix: Custer, WA), vi.
51. Leland, *Gypsy Sorcery*, 242–3.
52. Elizabeth Robins Pennell, *Charles Godfrey Leland* (1906), vol. II, 311, 356.
53. Such as J. B. Andrews, 'Neapolitan Witchcraft', *Folk-Lore* 8 (1897), 1–9.
54. Leland, *Etruscan Roman Remains*, 203–4, and *Legends of Florence*, 268–9.
55. For example, 'The Goblin of the Tower della Trinita', in *Legends of Florence*.
56. Cf. Cohen, *Europe's Inner Demons*, ch. 11; Jeffrey Burton Russell, *Witchcraft in the Middle Ages* (Ithaca, NY: Cornell University Press, 1972), chs 3–4; Carlo Ginzburg, *Ecstasies: Deciphering the Witches; Sabbath* (London: Penguin edn, 1992), 6–299, *passim*.
57. Leland, *Etruscan Roman Remains*, 4, 193, 198, 203–10.
58. *Ibid.*, 2.
59. *Ibid.*
60. Leland, *Aradia*, vii–viii, 101–2.
61. *Ibid.*, v–viii, 102–3, 116–17.
62. *Ibid.*, 116–17.
63. Carolly Erickson, *The Medieval Vision* (Oxford: Oxford University Press, 1976), 96.
64. For books based upon these records and published in English, see Carlo Ginzburg, *The*

Cheese and the Worms (London: Routledge, 1980), and *The Night Battles* (London: Routledge, 1983); Ruth Martin, *Witchcraft and the Inquisition in Venice 1550–1650* (Oxford: Blackwell, 1989); David Gentilcore, *From Bishop to Witch* (Manchester: Manchester University Press, 1992); Guido Ruggiero, *Binding Passions* (Oxford: Oxford University Press, 1993).

65. Pennell, *Leland*, vol. II, 310, 341, 404.

66. I put this case very crudely in *Pagan Religions of the Ancient British Isles*, 301, where I was reacting against the view, which I had often heard in conversation in Britain, that Leland was duped by Maddelena. This passage in my book was an extreme case of the overall problem of the work, of the compression of a vast amount of subject-matter into a small span. Hence the criticisms in Chas. S. Clifton, 'Leland's Aradia and the Revival of Modern Witchcraft', *The Pomegranate* 1 (1997), 2–27.

67. Leland, *Etruscan Roman Remains*, 13–14.

68. The obituary is printed in *Folk-Lore* 14 (1903), 162–3.

69. The controversy and its conclusion are well summarized in John MacInnes's preface to the Floris edition of *Carmina Cadelica* (Edinburgh, 1992).

70. Leland, *Aradia*, 103–6.

71. *Ibid.*, 102.

72. *Ibid.*, 102, 104.

73. *Ibid.*, 111–14.

74. Here my eye is particualrly upon Professors Robert Matthiesen of Brown University and Chas Clifton of the University of Southern Colorado, who have both worked on these papers and are contributing to a new edition of *Aradia*. See Clifton, 'Leland's *Aradia*', above.

75. George Lawrence Gomme, *Ethnology in Europe* (1892), 48–57.

76. Karl Pearson, 'Woman as Witch', in *The Chances of Death and other Studies in Evolution* (1897), vol. II, 1–50.

CHAPTER 9

1. D. S. Higgins, *Rider Haggard: the Great Storyteller* (London: Cassell, 1981), 137; Tom Pocock, *Rider Haggard and the Lost Empire* (London: Weidenfeld and Nicolson, 1993), 91–2.

2. Higgins, *Rider Haggard*, 137.

3. Pocock, *Rider Haggard*, 80, 91–2.

4. Charles Carrington, *Rudyard Kipling: His Life and Work* (London: Macmillan, 1955), 182–3.

5. *Ibid.*, 240, 487.

6. In Ch. 7; source at n. 21.

7. Peter Keating, *Kipling the Poet* (London: Secker and Warburg, 1994), 154–5; Carrington, *Rudyard Kipling*, 444.

8. Carrington, *Rudyard Kipling*, 487–8.

9. Peter Green, *Kenneth Grahame* (London: Murray, 1959), 137.

10. Alison Prince, *Kenneth Grahame: An Innocent in the Wildwood* (London: Alison and Busby, 1994), *passim*; Green, *Kenneth Grahame*, *passim*.

11. Green, *Kenneth Grahame*, 300.

12. Prince, *Kenneth Grahame*, 169–72.

13. A. Norman Jeffares, *W. B. Yeats: Man and Poet* (London: Routledge, 1962), 53.

14. *The Collected Works of William Butler Yeats* (Stratford-upon-Avon, 1908), vol. VIII, 191.

15. Jeffares, *W. B. Yeats*, 52.

16. George Mills Harper, *Yeats's Golden Dawn* (London: Macmillan, 1974), 71, 259–68.

17. Quoted in Richard Ellmann, *The Identity of Yeats* (London: Faber, 1954), 51.

18. *Ibid.*, 55–60.

19. Maud Gonne, 'Yeats and Ireland', in *Scattering Branches: Tributes to the Memory of W. B. Yeats* (London: Macmillan, 1940), 22–33.

20. W. B. Yeats, *Fairy and Folk Tales of the Irish Peasantry* (1888), ix–xvi.

21. W. B. Yeats, 'Rose Alchemica' in *The Secret Rose* (1897), 244–5.

22. Elizabeth A. Sharp, *William Sharp* (1910), 277, 282.

23. W. B. Yeats, 'The Tribes of Danu', *New Review* 17 (November 1897), 550.

24. W. B. Yeats, *The Celtic Twilight* (1902), 192.

25. W. B. Yeats, *Autobiographies* (London: Macmillan, 1926), 253–4.

26. Richard Ellmann, *Yeats: The Man and the Masks* (London: Faber, 1949), 125–8.

27. Ellmann, *Identity of Yeats*, 29.

28. W. B. Yeats, *The Speckled Bird*, ed. William O'Donnell (Toronto: McClelland and Stewart, 1976).

29. W. B. Yeats, *The Wind Among The Reeds* (1899), 75.

30. Ellmann, *Yeats: The Man and the Masks*, 130–7.

31. Ellmann, *Identity of Yeats*, 171–3.

32. Yeats, *Autobiographies*, 142.

33. John Eglinton, *A Memoir of A.E.* (London: Macmillan, 1937), *passim*.

34. Ellmann, *Yeats: The Man and the Masks*, 123–4.

35. Æ, *The Candle of Vision* (Wheaton, IL: Theosophical Publishing House, 1965).

36. Emile Delavenay, *D. H. Lawrence and Edward Carpenter: A Study in Edwardian Transition* (London: Heinemann, 1971).

37. pp. 141 and 389 in the Penguin edition.

38. 'The Proper Study', reprinted in *Phoenix: The Posthumous Papers of D. H. Lawrence*, ed. Edward D. Macdonald (New York: Viking, 1936). Quotation on p. 723.

39. *Phoenix*, 31.

40. *Ibid.*, 22–31; quotations on p. 31.

41. Quotations from the Penguin edition (of 1961), pp. 144, 312.

42. D. H. Lawrence, *Apocalypse* (London: Heinemann, 1931).

43. D. H. Lawrence, *Etruscan Places* (New York: Viking, 1932), 39, 83.

44. *Ibid.*, 86.

45. *Ibid.*, 87.

46. *Ibid.*, 123.

47. Timothy Mowl, 'In the Realm of the Great God Pan', *Country Life* (17 October 1996), 54–9.

48. All of the above is based upon Brian Morris, 'Ernest Thompson Seton and the Origins of the Woodcraft Movement', *Journal of Contemporary History* 5 (1970), 183–94.

49. I. O. Evans, *Woodcraft and World Service* (London: Douglas, 1930); Derek Edgell, *The Order of Woodcraft Chivalry 1916–1949* (Lewiston: Mellen, 1992); J. L. finlay, 'John Hargrave, the Greenshirts, and Social Credit', *Journal of Contemporary History* 5 (1970), 53–71.

50. Evans, *Woodcraft and World Service*, 160–8.

51. *Ibid.*, 172–3.

52. James Webb, *The Occult Establishment* (Glasgow: Drew, 1981), 88–91.

53. John Hargrave, *The Great War Brings It Home* (1919), 224–39.

54. John Hargrave, *Young Winkle* (London: Duckworth, 1925), 171–7.

55. John Hargrave, *The Confession of the Kibbo Kift* (London: Duckworth, 1927), 136–47.

56. 'A Soldier of Pan', *Aisling* 8 (1996), 9.

57. Edgell, *Order of Woodcraft Chivalry*, as at n. 49; and thereby hangs a tale. This book was

based upon a full use of the Order's archive at Luton. Its publication caused disquiet among some members, resulting in a decision to close the archive for a period sufficient to allow more distance to be put between the Order's earlier history and the present. This was the point at which I sought access to it. I obtained this on condition that I cited only the published items within it, and four specific letters in which I was specially interested. I was duly admitted, with the greatest degree of kindness and trust, and shall honour that by adhering to the terms; although I included within them a brief to check the accuracy of Derek Edgell's use of manuscript documents (which is perfect) and to state if necessary what is not in the collection; which may be important later, as readers will see. I would like to thank Charlotte Jones and Julian and Sue Brown for their support in this delicate process. Blue Sky!

58. Edgell, *Order of Woodcraft Chivalry*, 1.

59. Pitt Rivers Museum, *Westlake Collection*, Box 2, five letters, 11 May–19 September 1909.

60. Edgell, *Order of Woodcraft Chivalry*, 65, to which more can be added from the list appended to Ernest Westlake, *The Place of Dionysos* (Woodcraft Way Series 9, 1927).

61. Ernest to Aubrey Westlake, 17 September 1917 and 29 July 1921, in Archive of Order of Woodcraft Chivalry, file A.121.

62. Westlake, *The Place of Dionysos*, 9–22.

63. Aubrey T. Westlake *et. al.*, *An Outline History of the Order of Woodcraft Chivalry* (Woodcraft Way Series 25, 1979), 6–9; cf. Edgell, *Order of Woodcraft Chivalry*, 152. On 14 October 1995 I attended a recreation of the original fire-lighting ceremony by the Order in the original folkmoot circle at Sandy Balls, and was impressed by its beauty and touched by the welcome which I received from all involved. I am especially grateful to Martin Westlake for the invitation.

64. Edgell, *Order of Woodcraft Chivalry*, 72, 136.

65. Margaret A. Westlake, *The Theory of Woodcraft Chivalry* (Woodcraft Way Series 2, 1918), 25.

66. Edgell, *Order of Woodcraft Chivalry*, 172.

67. Ernest Westlake to Miss A. Milner Barry, 20 December 1918, and to Aubrey Westlake, 18 September 1922.

68. Edgell, *Order of Woodcraft Chivalry*, 184–8.

69. *Ibid.*, 131, 139–40; Westlake *et al.*, *Outline History*, 6–7.

70. Edgell, *Order of Woodcraft Chivalry*, 191–203, 279; *Pine Cone*, issues 1–5 (July 1923–September 1924).

71. Edgell, *Order of Woodcraft Chivalry*, 206–51.

72. Westlake, *The Place of Dionysos*, 1–9.

73. Edgell, *Order of Woodcraft Chivalry*, 177, 239.

74. *Ibid.*, 292, 300–1, 367, 376.

75. *Ibid.*, 250, 302, 368–70, 432–8; Westlake *et al.*, *Outline History*, 17–20. I have myself viewed the graves at Sandy Balls, with Martin Westlake's kind permission.

76. Edgell, *Order of Woodcraft Chivalry*, 612–13; Vera G. Pragnell, *The Story of The Sanctuary* (London: Vine Press, 1928); Jean Overton Fuller, *The Magical Dilemma of Victor Neuburg* (London: W. H. Allen, 1965), 78–9, 229–36.

77. Edgell, *Order of Woodcraft Chivalry*, 503–84; quotation on p. 584.

CHAPTER 10

1. Gerald Suster, *The Legacy of the Beast* (London: Allen, 1988).

2. Colin Wilson, *Aleister Crowley: The Nature of the Beast* (London: Aquarian, 1987).

3. Alex Owen, 'The Sorcerer and his Apprentice: Aleister Crowley and the Magical Exploration of Edwardian Subjectivity', *Journal of British Studies* 36 (1997), 99–133.

4. See the reading list in Jean Overton Fuller, *The Magical Dilemma of Victor Neuburg* (London: Allen, 1965), 129–31, and the pantheon in Aleister Crowley, *Moonchild* (1929: repr. Samuel Weiser, York Beach, Maine, 1970), 227–9.

5. Aleister Crowley, *777* (1909: repr. Neptune, London, 1955), x, and *Magick*, eds John Symonds and Kenneth Grant (London: Routledge, 1973), 217, 309.

6. Aleister Crowley, *The Book of Lies* (1913: repr. Samuel Weiser, York Beach, Maine, 1980), 32.

7. Suster, *Legacy of the Beast*, 8.

8. *The Magical Record of the Beast 666*, ed. John Symonds and Kenneth Grant (London: Duckworth, 1972); quotation from pp. 235–6; *The Confessions of Aleister Crowley: An Autohagiography*, eds John Symonds and Kenneth Grant (London: Routledge, 1979), 148–9.

9. These diaries will be discussed in detail in the next two chapters.

10. Aleister Crowley, *The Magical Record of the Beast 666*, eds John Symonds and Kenneth Grant (London: Duckworth, 1972), *passim*, esp. 'Rex de Arte Regia'.

11. That with Neuburg, which ended in 1914, seems to have been his last.

12. Crowley, *Book of Lies*, 80.

13. Aleister Crowley, *The Commentaries of AL*, ed. James Wasserman (London: Routledge, 1976), 44–5.

14. Suster, *Legacy of the Beast*, 86.

15. Crowley, *Magick*, 4, 133, and *Moonchild*, 213.

16. Lon Milo Duquette, *The Magic of Thelema: A Handbook of the Rituals of Aleister Crowley* (York Beach, Maine: Samuel Weiser, 1993), 108. I am very grateful to Melissa Montgomery for the gift of this volume.

17. Crowley, *Magick*, 131, 133, 137, and *Confessions*, 176–7.

18. Aleister Crowley, *Magick Without Tears*, ed. Israel Regardie (Phoenix, AZ: Falcon, 1982), 38, 64, 219.

19. Kenneth Grant, *The Magical Revival* (London: Muller, 1972), 135.

20. Crowley, *Magick*, xvii.

21. *Ibid.*, 219–20.

22. *Ibid.*, 296.

23. Suster, *Legacy of the Beast*, 87.

24. Crowley, *Magic*, 239, and *Moonchild*, 273–4.

25. In 'The Vision and the Voice', first published as *The Equinox* I.v (1911), Special Supplement, and reprinted several times since.

26. *The Equinox* I.iv (1910), 239.

27. Wilson, *Aleister Crowley*, 88: John Symonds, *The Great Beast* (London: Macdonald, 1971), 239.

28. pp. 154 and 209 in the Weiser edition.

29. *Ibid.*, 309.

30. Crowley, *Magick Without Tears*, 75.

31. Symonds, *Great Beast*, 197, 235.

32. *The Secret Rituals of the O.T.O.*, ed. Francis King (London: Daniel, 1973), 172, 180, 223.

33. Suster, *Legacy of the Beast*, 57–8.

34. Crowley, *Magick*, 151, 287.

35. p. 285 in the Weiser edition.

36. Crowley, *Book of Lies*, 6.

37. Symonds, *Great Beast*, 235.

38. Crowley, *Magick Without Tears*, 23.

39. p. 204 in the Weiser edition.

40. Symonds, *Great Beast*, 157–79.
41. Crowley, *Magick Without Tears*, 23.
42. Crowley, *Magick*, 143–4.
43. Duquette, *Magick of Thelema*, 229.
44. King, *Secret Rituals of the O.T.O.*, 173.
45. p. 32 in the Weiser edition.
46. Crowley, *Confessions*, 839.
47. p. 147 in the Weiser edition.
48. Symonds, *Great Beast*, 194–5.
49. pp. 187–8 in the Weiser edition.
50. Crowley, *Magick*, 48–117.
51. Duquette, *Magick of Thelema*, 95–101.
52. Crowley, *Magick Without Tears*, 23, 217, 464–5.
53. Alan Richardson, *Priestess: The Life and Magic of Dion Fortune* (Wellingborough: Aquarian, 1987); Janine Chapman, *Quest for Dion Fortune* (York Beach, Maine: Weiser, 1993).
54. Richardson, *Priestess*, 66–143; Chapman, *Quest for Dion Fortune*, 6–22, 122.
55. Dion Fortune, *The Training and Work of an Initiate* (London: Rider, 1930), 99; and *The Secrets of Doctor Taverner* (1926; repr. Aquarian, Wellingborough, 1989), 61.
56. Richardson, *Priestess*, 68–9.
57. Quotations from pp. 57–8 in the Aquarian reprint of 1989 and p. 218 in the original Noel Douglas edition of 1927.
58. p. 40 in the original Rider edition of 1928.
59. p. 100 in the original Rider edition of 1930.
60. Violet M. firth, *The Problem of Purity* (London: Rider, 1928), *passim*; Fortune, *Training and Work of an Initiate*, 130–2; Dion Fortune, *Sane Occultism* (London: Rider, 1929), 127–30; and *The Esoteric Philosophy of Love and Marriage* (London: Rider, 1924), *passim*.
61. Fortune, *Sane Occultism*, 115, and 'How Ritual Works', *London Forum* 62 (1935), 32.
62. See also Fortune, *Training and Work of an Initiate*, 100–3.
63. pp. 127–8 in the Rider edition of 1929.
64. Richardson, *Priestess*, 147–64.
65. Dolores Ashcroft-Nowicki, *The Forgotten Mage: The Magical Lectures of Colonel C. R. F. Seymour* (Wellingborough: Aquarian, 1986).
66. Alan Richardson, *Dancers to the Gods* (Wellingborough: Aquarian, 1985), 173–5.
67. Richardson, *Priestess*, 169–70; Grant, *Magical Revival*, 178.
68. Dion Fortune, 'The Broken Tryst', *Occult Review* 56 (1932), 23.
69. Richardson, *Dancers to the Gods*, 52–3; Dion Fortune, *The Mystical Qabalah* (1935: repr. Benn, London, 1957).
70. Dion Fortune, *Avalon of the Heart* (London: Aquarian, 1934), esp. 10, 27, 37, 47–8, 110.
71. Dion Fortune, 'How Ritual Works', *London Forum* 62 (1935), 32–4.
72. Quotations from pp. 10, 56, 96, and 140–1 of the 1989 Aquarian reprint. I am very grateful to Caitlin Matthews for lending me copies of this and of *Moon Magic*.
73. Quotations from pp. 37, 87–8, 108–9, 165, 294, 307, and 381 of the original Aquarian edition of 1936.
74. Richardson, *Priestess*, 208–9, 225, and *Dancers to the Gods*, 79.
75. pp. 156–7, 216, 285–6 in the Aquarian edition of 1989.
76. See pp. 76 and 210–11 in the original Aquarian edition of 1956.
77. Richardson, *Priestess*, 213–29, and *Dancers to the Gods*, 79; Chapman, *Quest for Dion Fortune*, 44–5, 84, 158.

78. For example, Alan Richardson thinks that the breakdown of her marriage was crucial, while Janine Chapman argues that she was largely indifferent to it; and the evidence is proportionately equivocal.

79. Here I follow Richardson's reasoning, that given Fortune's love of contemporary detail it could hardly have been written after 1939 as she would never have described its London setting so carefully without mentioning the Blitz.

80. Richardson, *Priestess*, 229–31, and *Dancers to the Gods*, 55; Chapman, *Quest for Dion Fortune*, 95, 128.

81. Francis King and Isabel Sutherland, *The Rebirth of Magic* (London: Corgi, 1982), 149–50.

82. Dion Fortune, *Applied Magic* (London: Aquarian, 1962), 61–2.

83. Chapman, *Quest for Dion Fortune*, 145.

84. Warburg Institute, Gerald Yorke Collection, MS 23.

85. Chapman, *Quest for Dion Fortune*, 154–5.

86. These points were made to me, eloquently and persuasively, by Gareth Knight, who has undertaken the work of editing a succession of the manuscripts for publication. I am very grateful indeed to him for this correspondence, and to John Matthews for making the introduction which opened it.

87. Martin Seymour-Smith, *Robert Graves: His Life and Work* (London: Hutchinson, 1982), 383–430; Richard Perceval Graves, *Robert Graves and the White Goddess* (London: Weidenfeld, 1995), 58–104.

88. p. 10 in the original, Cassell, edition of 1944.

89. pp. 353–4 in the original, Cassell, edition of 1946.

90. p. 25 in the (Faber) edition of 1966.

91. p. 9 in the 1946 edition.

92. pp. 10 and 338–9 in the 1946 edition.

93. p. 371 in the 1994 edition.

94. *Passim* in Seymour-Smith, *Robert Graves*, and Richard Perceval Graves, *Robert Graves: The Assault Heroic 1895–1926* (London: Weidenfeld, 1986), and *Robert Graves: The Years With Laura 1926–40* (London: Weidenfeld, 1990), and *Robert Graves and the White Goddess*.

95. p. 67 in the 1966 edition. For the evolving legend of Ceridwen, see Ronald Hutton, *The Pagan Religions of the Ancient British Isles* (Oxford: Blackwell, 1991), 320–3, and *The Stations of the Sun* (Oxford: Oxford University Press, 1996), 368, and the comment on the latter in the review by Malcolm Jones in *Folklore* 108 (1997), 140.

96. I owe this suggestion to Mike Howard.

97. Hutton, *Stations of the Sun*, 259.

98. On which, see Seymour-Smith, *Robert Graves*, 404.

99. pp. 10 and 21 in the Faber edition of 1966. Cf. Seymour-Smith, *Robert Graves*, 85–7, 370–1, 398, 517.

100. R. P. Graves, *Robert Graves: The Assault Heroic*, 313, and *Robert Graves: The Years With Laura*, 103.

101. Seymour-Smith, *Robert Graves*, 370–1, 393, 509.

102. R. P. Graves, *Robert Graves and the White Goddess*, 103–4.

103. Max Mallowan, 'Margaret Murray', *Dictionary of National Biography* (1961–70), 777; Sandra J. Peacock, *Jane Ellen Harrison: the Mask and the Self* (New Haven: Yale University Press, 1988), 68–90; Janet Grayson, 'In Quest of Jessie Weston', *Arthurian Literature* 11 (1992), 1–6.

104. Margaret Murray, *My first Hundred Years* (London: William Kimber, 1963), esp. chs 5 and 7 and pp. 116, 96–8, 160–2.

105. M. A. Murray, 'Organisations of Witches in Great Britain', *Folk-Lore* 28 (1917), 228–58, and 'Witches and the Number Thirteen', *Folk-Lore* 31 (1920), 204–9; Charlotte S. Burne, 'Witchcraft in Great Britain', *Folk-Lore* 28 (1917), 453.

106. M. A. Murray, 'Witches' Fertility Rites', and 'The Devil's Officers and the Witches' Covens', both in *Man* 19 (1919), 55–8 and 137–40; and 'The "Devil" of North Berwick', *Scottish Historical Review* 15 (1918), 310–21.

107. Oxford University Press Archive, file 881053.

108. For a historian's view, see Norman Cohn, *Europe's Inner Demons* (Falmer: Sussex University Press, 1975), 102–25. For that of a folklorist, Jacqueline Simpson, 'Margaret Murray: Who Believed Her, and Why?', *Folklore* 105 (1994), 89–96.

109. Margaret A. Murray, *The God of the Witches* (1931: repr. Oxford University Press, 1970), 29.

110. *Ibid.*, 65, 75, 110, and Plate 10.

111. Martin Almagro Basch, *El Covacho con Pinturas Rupestres de Cogul* (Lerida) (Instituto de Estudias Ilerdenses, 1952).

112. Hutton, *Pagan Religions*, 308–16.

113. See Mallowan, 'Margaret Murray', 776–8.

114. *Folk-Lore* 33 (1922), 224–30.

115. *Ibid.*, 43 (1932), 114, and 45 (1934), 95–6.

116. Murray, *My first Hundred Years*, 103–5.

117. Oxford University Press Archive, file 881053.

118. G. C. Coulton, *five Centuries of Religion. Volume One* (Cambridge: Cambridge University Press, 1923), 179–83.

119. Lewis Spence, 'The Witch Cult in Scotland', *Scots Magazine* (January 1930), 17–20, and 'Modern Theories about Witchcraft', *Occult Review* 69 (1942), 89–93; Fortune, 'The Brocken Tryst', 102–7; Ashcroft-Nowicki, *The Forgotten Mage*, 187–9; Ralph Shirley, 'Notes of the Month', *Occult Review* 38 (1923), 193–205; J. W. Brodie-Innes, 'Witchcraft Rituals', *Occult Review* 25 (1917), 329–34, and 'The Cult of the Witch', *Occult Review* 35 (1972), 150–63.

120. J. W. Wickwer, *Witchcraft and the Black Art* (London: Herbert Jenkins, 1925); Theda Kenyon, *Witches Still Live* (London: Rider, 1929).

121. Oxford University Press Archive, file 881053; Murray, *My first Hundred Years*, 104–5.

122. C. N. Deedes, 'The Double-Headed God', and Violet Alford and Rodney Gallop, 'Traces of a Dianic Cult from Catalonia to Portugal', both in *Folk-Lore* 46 (1935), 194–243 and 350–61.

123. *Ibid.*, 57 (1946), 12–33; 58 (1947), 285–7; 60 (1952), 244–5; 61 (1955), 307–8.

124. Christina Hole, *Witchcraft in England* (London: Batsford, 1945), 22–7.

125. G. N. Clark, *The Seventeenth Century* (Oxford: Oxford University Press, 1929 and 1945), 245–8.

126. Hugh Ross Williamson, *The Arrow and the Sword* (London: Faber, 1947); Arne Runeberg, *Witches, Demons and Fertility Magic* (Helsingfors: Societas Scientarum Fennica, 1947); R. Trevor Davies, *Four Centuries of Witch Beliefs* (London: Methuen, 1947).

127. Murray, *My first Hundred Years*, chs 1–4.

128. Simpson, 'Margaret Murray', 89.

129. Murray, *My first Hundred Years*, 196–204.

130. *The Sunday Dispatch* (4 November 1951), 4; Murray, *My first Hundred Years*, ch. 11.

131. Max Mallowan, 'Margaret Murray', 777.

132. It is preserved in Oxford University Press Archive, file 881053, under the year 1962. As the writer is still alive, I shall provide no further details here.

133. McCormick gives the date of the interview as 2 September 1950. I have been unable to find it in that issue; the date may have been misprinted in his book, or the copy which I obtained may have been incomplete.
134. Donald McCormick, *Murder By Witchcraft* (London: Long, 1968), 64–80.
135. See n. 130.
136. Gerald B. Gardner, *Witchcraft Today* (London: Rider, 1954), 15–16.

Note Since completion of this manuscript, I managed to obtain copies of three further works of relevance to this chapter. The first was Israel Regardie, *The Eye in the Triangle: An Interpretation of Aleister Crowley* (Las Vegas, NV: Falcon, 1970), lent to me by Robert Hardy, whom I thank for this. It is, in my opinion, the finest detailed analysis of most of Crowley's earlier work and thought which has yet been made, and draws the comparison between Crowley and Mathers which I have made in this chapter. On pp. 8–10 he bravely prints Crowley's libel against him to which I refer in my own Chapter 11, and cite there from a manuscript copy in n. 58.

The second book, bought at the suggestion of Gareth Knight, was the 1998 reprint of the scarce first biography of Fortune, *The Story of Dion Fortune As Told to Charles fielding and Carr Collins* (Loughborough: Thoth, 1985). Although invaluable for the early history of the (now) Society of the Inner Light, and worthy of respect for supplying the first basic biographic details of Fortune herself, its material has little bearing on the issues discussed in this third.

The third was *A Coven of Scholars: Margaret Murray and her Working Methods*, by Caroline Oates and Juliette Wood (Folk-Lore Society, Archive Series 1, 1998). It illustrates even more vividly than before how ruthless and unscrupulous Murray was in her selection and presentation of evidence, and her promotion of her own reputation, but also how much the latter process was assisted by her gift for making friends, which ensured that she usually had an ally in an influential position when she needed to get something accepted for publication.

CHAPTER 11

1. J. L. Bracelin, *Gerald Gardner: Witch* (London: Octagon Press, 1960). The circumstances of its authorship were confirmed to me by F. Lamond (*pers. comm.*, 15 August 1996).
2. The review, by Wilfrid Bonser, is in Folk-Lore 66 (1955), 312–14. See Katherine Briggs's recollections in James W. Baker, 'White Witches: Historic Fact and Romantic Fantasy', in *Magical Religion and Modern Witchcraft*, ed. James R. Lewis (Albany: State University of New York Press, 1996), 184–5.
3. Doreen Valiente, *The Rebirth of Witchcraft* (Custer, WA: Phoenix, 1989), 41–2.
4. John Hammill, *The Rosicrucian Seer* (Wellingborough: Aquarian, 1986), 90; Alan Richardson, *Priestess: The Life and Magic of Dion Fortune* (Wellingborough: Aquarian, 1987), 80.
5. Janet and Stewart Farrar, *The Witches' Way* (London: Hale, 1984), 282–93.
6. Bracelin, *Gerald Gardner*, 166–7.
7. Valiente, *Rebirth of Witchcraft*, 45–6.
8. Amado Crowley, *The Secrets of Aleister Crowley* (Leatherhead: Diamond, 1991), 105–32, and *The Riddles of Aleister Crowley* (Leatherhead: Diamond, 1992), 6.
9. 'Aleister Crowley: An Interview with Cecil Williamson', *Talking Stick* 9 (Winter 1992), 25–6.
10. Warburg Institute, Gerald Yorke Collection, MSS 21–3.

11. I am very grateful to Melissa Montgomery for putting me in touch with people who could furnish copies of the documents concerned.

12. Warburg Institute, Gerald Yorke Collection, Scrapbook EE2, ff. 223–8. I owe thanks to Bradford Verter for drawing my attention to this manuscript.

13. Warburg Institute, Gerald Yorke Collection, MS 23, entry 25 January 1937.

14. Bournemouth Reference Library, *Christchurch Times*, *passim*, but esp. 23 July 1938, 3 and 6 June 1939, 19 January 1951.

15. I owe this information to Ian Stevenson.

16. The documents are all in the probate division of Somerset House, under his name.

17. *Christchurch Times*, 27 August 1938, 10 June 1939, 19 January 1951. The will is in Somerset House.

18. Bournemouth Reference Library, *Bournemouth Evening Echo*, 25 February 1986 and 13 May 1988.

19. The invaluable Ian Stevenson made the introduction; and I was introduced to Mr Stevenson, in turn, by Caroline Wise.

20. Ian Stevenson, *pers. comm.*, 16 April 1997. Mr Stevenson has a collection of paintings by, and photographs of, Dorothy Clutterbuck and her friends.

21. Valiente, *Rebirth of Witchcraft*, 37–8.

22. *Christchurch Times*, 18 June 1938.

23. *Ibid.*, *passim*, but esp. 11 and 18 June 1938, 18 November and 2 December 1939, 25 May 1940, 12 August 1944; Bournemouth Reference Library, DR.942.33 CHR (pamphlet on theatre); Bracelin, *Gerald Gardner*, ch. 13; Doreen Valiente, *An ABC of Witchcraft Past and Present* (London: Hale, 1973), 153–4; Aidan Kelly, *Crafting the Art of Magic* (St Paul, MN: Llewellyn, 1991), 32.

24. Bracelin, *Gerald Gardner*, ch. 13.

25. *Christchurch Times*, 8 and 29 July, and 12 August 1944. I am very grateful to Ian Stevenson for drawing my attention to these reports.

26. Valiente, *Rebirth of Witchcraft*, 43.

27. Doreen Valiente, 'Witchcraft and Fertility', *The Cauldron* (Samhain, 1981), n.p. A later full list of directors (from 1960) is among the Gardner papers in Toronto, to be discussed below.

28. Jennie Cobban, 'The Witch's Cottage', *Talking Stick* 10 (Spring 1992), 8–9; Bracelin, *Gerald Gardner*, ch. 12; Martin Short, *Inside The Brotherhood* (London: Grafton, 1989), 138–9.

29. Valiente, *Rebirth of Witchcraft*, 38, 66.

30. Frederic Lamond, *pers. comm.*, 19 July 1996.

31. *Ibid.*; Ameth to Dafo, 17 July 1958, printed in Kelly, *Crafting The Art of Magic*, 137–9 (I have seen the original in Toronto); Toronto Collection (for which see below), Dafo to Charles Cardell, 20 July 1958.

32. Francis King, *Ritual Magic in England: 1887 to the Present Day* (London: Spearman, 1970), 176–81.

33. He had, at least in some quarters, a reputation for such embroideries: John Matthews, *pers. comm.*, 4 February 1998; Bradford Verter, *pers. comm.* 20 September 1988.

34. Brian Vesey-fitzgerald, *Portrait of the New Forest* (London: Hale, 1966); Mary Boase, *The Folklore of Hampshire and the Isle of Wight* (London: Batsford, 1976); Winifred G. Beddington and Elsa B. Christy, *It Happened in Hampshire* (Winchester: privately printed, 1937); J. R. Wise, *The New Forest* (1863).

35. Steve Wilson, 'Woodcrafting the Art of Magic', *Aisling* 8 (1996), 12–14.

36. 'Bran', *pers. comm.*, 26 June 1993.

37. Derek Edgell, *The Order of Woodcraft Chivalry 1916–1949* (Lewiston: Mellon, 1992), 503–84, 649–58.

38. Valiente, *Rebirth of Witchcraft*, 58.

39. Allan H. Greenfield, 'Wicca and the Ordo Templi Orientis', *LASHTAL* 1 (1988), 47. I am very grateful to Melissa Montgomery for providing the introduction which enabled me to obtain this article.

40. Amado Crowley, *Secrets of Aleister Crowley*, 142–6; E. W. Liddell and Michael Howard, *The Pickingill Papers* (Chieveley: Capall Bann, 1994), 152–3.

41. Warburg Institute, Gerald Yorke Collection, MS 23, under dates given.

42. King, *Ritual Magic in England*, 176–9; Baker, 'White Witches', 188.

43. Warburg Institute, Gerald Yorke Collection, Scrapbook EE2, note on letter from Ameth, n.d., and personal copy of *High Magic's Aid*. I thank Bradford Verter for this reference.

44. Gerald Suster, *The Legacy of the Beast* (London: Allen, 1988), 201, 218; Amado Crowley, *Secrets of Aleister Crowley*, 142–6; Liddell and Howard, *Pickingill Papers*, 91–4.

45. Kelly, *Crafting the Art of Magic*, 171–7.

46. I am very grateful to Rufus Harrington for sending me a copy of the relevant email posting.

47. Barbara Smith-LaBorde, *pers. comm.*, 14 March 1977.

48. Bracelin, *Gerald Gardner*, ch. 14.

49. Patricia Crowther, 'The Day I Met Aleister Crowley', *Prediction* (November 1970), 14; King, *Ritual Magic in England*, 176–81.

50. Liddell and Howard, *Pickingill Papers*, 19–30; Mike Howard, 'Gerald Gardner: the Man, the Myth and the Magick', *The Cauldron* 84 (1997), 17.

51. Warburg Institute, Gerald Yorke Collection, Scrapbook EE2, fo. 340.

52. Patricia Crowther, *Lid Off The Cauldron* (London: Muller, 1981), 26–27.

53. Liddell and Howard, *Pickingill Papers*, 32.

54. Howard, 'Gerald Gardner', 16–17; Warburg Institute, Gerald Yorke Collection, Scrapbook EE2, n.p., Ameth to Yorke and attached note by Yorke. I owe this reference to Bradford Verter.

55. Liddell and Howard, *Pickingill Papers*, 162–3.

56. James Webb, *The Harmonious Circle* (London: Thames and Hudson, 1980), 214–15; Suster, *Legacy of the Beast*, 92.

57. E.g. Warburg Institute, Gerald Yorke Collection, MS 22, under 10 April 19451; 'the spirit of the Jew, which has rotted the soul of Mankind'.

58. In Warburg Institute, Gerald Yorke collection, Scrapbook EE2.

59. *Ibid.*, MSS 10 and 104.

60. Aleister Crowley, *The Confessions of Aleister Crowley* (London: Cape, 1969), 109.

61. Warburg Institute, Gerald Yorke Collection, MS D5, Crowley to Yorke, 9 May 1947, and E21, Gardner to Crowley, 14 June 1947.

62. Crowley, *Confessions*, 700–10; Francis King, *The Secret Rituals of the O.T.O.* (London: Daniel, 1973), *passim*.

63. Clive Harper, 'Gerald Gardner and the O.T.O.', *Nuit-Isis* 10 (1991), 8–10.

64. Warburg Institute, Gerald Yorke Collection, Scrapbook EE2, fo. 340.

65. These letters are in the OTO archive in the USA and were published in an edition of Thelema Lodge Newsletter. I am very grateful to Melissa Montgomery for making the introduction which enabled me to obtain the latter.

66. 'Notes on Two Uncommon Varieties of the Malay Kris', and 'Notes on Some Ancient Gold Coinns from the Johore River', *Journal of the Malayan Branch of the Royal Asiatic Society* 11 (1933), 173–82 and 182–6; *Keris and other Malay Weapons* (Singapore: Progressive Publishing, 1936); 'Le Problème de la Garde de l'Epée Cypriote de l'Age du Bronze', *Bulletin de la Societé Préhistorique Française* 12 (1937), 1–8; 'Ancient Beads from

the Johore River as Evidence of an Early Link by Sea between Malaya and the Roman Empire', *Journal of the Royal Asiatic Society* (1937), 467–70; 'More Coins from the Johore River', *Numismatic Chronicle* 5th ser. 19 (1939), 98–103.

67. G. B. Gardner, 'Witchcraft', *Folk-Lore* 50 (1939), 188–90.

68. Instrument of Appointment of Chief, Winter Solstice 1946, in order's archive. I am very grateful to Philip and Stephanie Carr-Gomm for a copy of this document.

69. Doreen Valiente, *Rebirth of Witchcraft*, 39, 49, and *Witchcraft for Tomorrow* (London: Hale, 1978), 14; Liddell and Howard, *Pickingill Papers*, 155.

70. Quotations and images taken from chs 3, 5, 9, 14, 15.

71. Gardner to Gordon B., n.d., quoted in the preface to the 1993 Pentacle Enterprises reprint of *High Magic's Aid*, 1; Warburg Institute, Gerald Yorke Collection, Scrapbook EE2, fo. 340.

72. Janet and Stewart Farrar, *Eight Sabbats for Witches* (London: Hale, 1981), and *The Witches' Way* (London: Hale, 1984).

73. Aidan Kelly, *Crafting the Art of Magic* (St Paul, MN: Llewellyn, 1991). I am very grateful to Dr Kelly for presenting me with a manuscript of this work which contained the full set of source references and transcriptions missing from the published version, and much additional information. This tremendously facilitated both my evaluation of his conclusions and my use of the original material. I thank Dr Shelley Rabinovich for an introduction to the Wiccan Church of Canada through which I was able to obtain a full transcription of 'Ye Bok of ye Art Magical'. My access to the Toronto Collection itself was made possible by introductions given initially by John Yohalem and Judy Harrow and ultimately by Tamarra and Richard James. Any further enquiries regarding it should be made through the Wiccan Church of Canada. I would also like to thank Allyn Wolfe, another scholar who has worked upon 'Ye Bok of ye Art Magical', for debating its significance with me and so providing additional perspectives to those of Aidan Kelly and myself. During my stay in Toronto I was provided with wonderful hospitality by Professor Ian Gentles and his wife Caroline, and Richard and Tamarra James showed me many kindnesses in addition to the vital service mentioned above.

74. British Library, Additional MS 10862, fos. 12v and 13v.

75. British Library, Sloane MS 3847, fos. 48–50; Bibliothèque de l'Arsenal, MS 2350, fo. 60.

76. Valiente, *Witchcraft for Tomorrow*, 78; Baker, 'White Witches', 176–7; C. J. S. Thompson, *The Mysteries and Secrets of Magic* (London: Lane, 1927), 235; Emile Grillot de Givry, *Witchcraft, Magic and Alchemy* (Paris: Librairie de France, 1931), fig. 74. Patricia Crowther, in her autobiography *One Witch's World* (London: Hale, 1998), 49–57, tells of how in 1962 she was sent material from a Scottish family witch tradition, which to her confirmed the existence of pagan witchcraft as an unbroken tradition from the remote past. The rituals were both similar to Gardners and yet had differences; the difficulty in dealing with such material will be explored in Ch. 15 of the present book. For Patricia Crowther the most important evidence was the gift of an *athame* (by that name) which had allegedly belonged to her correspondent's grandmother and had the same shape and signs as those upon the Gardnerian *athame*. It was clearly worn by use. If this evidence is taken on face value, it seems to me to suggest three different explanations. first that the knife indeed derives from an old witch tradition. Second, that it was made by somebody who had obtained Mathers's printed text of the *Key of Solomon*, which represents such a tool. Third, that its maker had used a manuscript recension of the *Key*, which is one of the most famous and common of grimoires; the British Library alone has eight copies. There is no confirmed dating for the knife to which Pat Crowther refers, and tools show wear from frequent use as much as great age. The most

telling piece of evidence supplied by her is that witches' *athames* differ in the shape of
the blade and a few symbols from that illustrated in the Mathers *Key*; and this is
certainly true of that drawn by Gardner in 'Ye Bok' (p. 23). The blade in the Key,
however, has a particularly awkward shape to make or obtain, and the variation in
symbols may reflect the haste or taste of copyists. To be solid evidence, Patricia
Crowther's Scottish *athame* needs a firm provenance and dating, which at present it
clearly lacks.

77. Kevin Danaher, *The Year in Ireland* (Cork, 1972), 226; Mical Ross, 'The Knife Against
    The Wave', *Folklore* 105 (1994), 83–8. I am grateful to Christine Oakley and Vanessa for
    obtaining for me some of the references upon which this latter work was based.

78. These, and the initiations, are printed with commentary in Kelly, *Crafting the Art of
    Magic*, 47–9, 54–67.

79. Valiente, *Rebirth of Witchcraft*, 60.

80. Valiente, *Witchcraft for Tomorrow*, 134–5.

81. I intend to publish an essay documenting these observations in a forthcoming collec-
    tion.

82. The quotation is from *Moon Magic* (London: Aquarian, 1956), 151. This novel and *The
    Sea Priestess* contain passages which perfectly illustrate my point.

83. p. 63 in the Pentacle reprint.

84. J. F. C. Fuller, 'The Black Arts', *Occult Review* 43 (1926), 231.

85. De Givry, *Witchcraft, Magic and Alchemy*, 102–17; Kurt Seligmann, *The History of Magic*
    (New York: Pantheon, 1948), 153.

86. Valiente, *Rebirth of Witchcraft*, 51–2; Baker, 'White Witches', 177; Toronto Collection, 'Ye
    Bok of ye Art Magical', pp. 94–5.

87. *Ibid.*, pp. 267–88. These entries are printed in Kelly, *Crafting the Art of Magic*, 52–4,
    67–72. They are, however, reproduced there with some surprising inaccuracies, which
    do not cumulatively seem to serve any obvious polemical purpose so that they seem to
    be bizarre editing errors. Dr Kelly's privately circulated manuscript of the book not
    only provides the transcripts very accurately but contains a much more sensitive and
    reflective commentary. It would be a real service to scholarship if this could be
    published to replace the existing Llewellyn edition, although the realities of the
    publisher's trade make such a development unlikely.

88. Kelly, *Crafting the Art of Magic*, 80–2, 91–3.

89. *Ibid.*, 88–90.

90. Valiente, *Witchcraft for Tomorrow*, 147–8, and *Rebirth of Witchcraft*, 59–60.

91. Farrars, *Witches' Way*, 31, 50–1.

92. These passages are in 'Ye Bok of ye Art Magical', pp. 8r, 151–4, 203, 277. Most are printed
    in Kelly, *Crafting the Art of Magic*, 76–86.

93. As in his letter to Symonds, in Warburg Institute, Gerald Yorke Collection, Scrapbook
    EE2, fo. 340.

94. Valiente, *ABC of Witchcraft*, 157, and *Rebirth of Witchcraft*, 57.

95. For published examples, see Valiente, *Rebirth of Witchcraft*, 41–2, 47; Frank Smyth,
    Modern Witchcraft (London: Macdonald, 1970), 30–2. Fred Lamond has provided me
    with others from his own experience (pers. comm., 15 August 1996).

Note Since this chapter was written, one of Gardner's later high priestesses, Lois Bourne,
has published her memoirs, *Dancing with Witches* (London: Hale, 1998). To my surprise,
she has become the first person to put into print my research and reservations regarding
Dorothy Clutterbuck (pp. 59–60). She has clearly heard of them through gossip circulating
in the Gardnerian community after I had discussed my ideas with two members of it, and

simply incorporated them into her own work. She makes plain that the information given is not her own, while seeming to have no idea of its true source; and therefore was not in a position to seek the permission of the author before putting these ideas before the public. An academic, in this position, would never publish another's material, but I do not apply such standards to private writers, and take no offence here.

The book has other points of relevance to the themes of this chapter. It confirms the horror of Dafo at Gardner's decision to publicize their religion, and her doubts about the quality of the people whom he initiated (pp. 58–9). In the process it 'outs' her identity in a way which I have avoided here. It adds to the body of testimony as to Gardner's capacity for duplicity and 'inventiveness' (p. 38), while repeatedly augmenting that regarding his charm and ability to inspire affection. It also provides a very valuable insight into his 'longing to escape back into some long-vanished age' and 'a more leisurely and gentle way of life than that of the harsh and demanding nineteenth and twentieth centuries of which he had been a part'. Gerald Gardner was thus another representative of that romantic conservatism and dislike of modernity which has already been emphasized in this book as an important feature of the development of modern paganism.

A further important aspect of the work is that (on pp. 28–9) it finally declares to the public—from impeccable inside knowledge—the identity of Idries Shah as the true author of *Gerald Gardner: Witch*, which had long been known within the community of Gardner's witches.

CHAPTER 12

1. I owe this reference to Allyn Wolffe: *pers. comm.*, 8 December 1997.
2. These possibilities were all thrashed out in a correspondence carried on since 1992 with Ceisiwr Serith and Prudence Jones, and joined since 1997 by Allyn Wolffe. Gardner's definition is in *Witchcraft Today* (London: Rider, 1954), 121.
3. Doreen Valiente, *The Rebirth of Witchcraft* (Custer, WA; Phoenix, 1989), 37, 47.
4. Rex Nemorensis, *Witch* (Charlwood: Dumblecott Productions, 1964), 44.
5. Jack Bracelin, *Gerald Gardner: Witch* (London: Octagon, 1960), 6, 8.
6. Patricia Crowther, *Lid Off the Cauldron* (London: Muller, 1981), 27–8.
7. *Pers. comm.*, 11 September 1996.
8. The subsequent reminiscence of neither man do full justice to the other or to the facts: 'An interview with Cecil Williamson', *Talking Stick* 14 (1994), 33; Bracelin, *Gerald Gardner*, ch. 15; Cecil Williamson, 'The Witchcraft Museums', *Pentagram* NS 6 (1967), 28–9. See the newspaper reports cited in Valiente, *Rebirth of Witchcraft*, 10–14, especially Allen Andrews, 'Calling All Covens', *Sunday Pictorial* 29 June 1951, 6.
9. Allen Andrews, 'Witchcraft in Britain', *Illustrated* 27 September 1952, 19–20.
10. Warburg Institute, Gerald Yorke Collection, Scrapbook EE2, ff. 348–50. This letter casts interesting light upon Williamson's later claims to have known Crowley personally, cited in Ch. 11 of this book.
11. Andrews, 'Witchcraft in Britain', 41–2.
12. See the comments on these articles in Valiente, *Rebirth of Witchcraft*, 49, and Gerald Gardner, *The Meaning of Witchcraft* (London: Aquarian, 1959), 213.
13. Valiente, *Rebirth of Witchcraft*, 35–7. Biographical information upon Doreen Valiente was published (maliciously) in Rex Nemorensis, *Witch*, 6r.
14. See the sources at n. 8, as well as the drift of all Williamson's reminiscences, cited in this chapter and the last.

15. This fact, long rumoured in the Pagan community, was confirmed by Doreen Valiente in her speech to the Pagan Federation on 22 November 1997.

16. *The Witch Cult in Western Europe* (Oxford: Oxford University Press, 1921), 13.

17. Gardner, *Witchcraft Today*, esp. 26–7, 44–6, 166–72, 186.

18. Warburg Institute, Gerald Yorke Collection, Scrapbook EE2, n.p., Ameth to Yorke, n.d., and Yorke's notes on it, December 1953, and Gardner to Yorke, 24 October 1952.

19. Janet and Stewart Farrar, *Eight Sabbats for Witches* (London: Hale, 1981), 45, 72–9, 93–101, 116–20, 148; Aidan Kelly, *Crafting the Art of Magic* (St Paul, MN: Llewellyn, 1991), 116–20.

20. Farrars, *Eight Sabbats*, 35–47; Valiente, *Rebirth of Witchcraft*, 60–3; Kelly, *Crafting the Art of Magic*, 114–15.

21. Rex Nemorensis, *Witch*, 46.

22. Analysed by Ceisiwr Serith in *Enchante* 21 (1996), 22–5.

23. Frederic Lamond, *pers. comm.*, 28 March 1992.

24. *Ibid.*

25. Kelly, *Crafting the Art of Magic*, 109–67.

26. The string of reports is itemized and analysed in Gardner, *Meaning of Witchcraft*, 216–49, and Valiente, *Rebirth of Witchcraft*, 65–8, and preserved in Doreen Valiente's collection of press cuttings, which I was able to read with the assistance and hospitality of Rufus Harrington and Melissa Montgomery.

27. Valiente, *Rebirth of Witchcraft*, 68; Bracelin, *Gerald Gardner*, ch. 15.

28. Valiente, *Rebirth of Witchcraft*, 68–72. The proposed rules and Gardner's 'Craft Laws' are printed in Kelly, *Crafting the Art of Magic*, 103–5, 145–61.

29. The reports are in *The People*, 27 October 1957, 1; 3 November 1957, 9; and 13 January 1959, 1. An account of the projected raid is in the Toronto Collection, while Valiente's comments on these events are in *Rebirth of Witchcraft*, 72–5. Further information was provided by Frederic Lamond, *pers. comms.* 3 September 1996 and 8 May 1998.

30. Valiente, *Rebirth of Witchcraft*, 59–60; Toronto Collection, D. to Gardner, 28 June 1959.

31. *Pers. comm.*, 11 September 1996. For published examples of my experiences, see Frederic Lamond, *Religion Without Beliefs* (London: Janus, 1997), 3–8.

32. Frederic Lamond, *pers. comm.*, 11 September 1996. Correspondence of all these women with Gardner, detailing their activities, is in the Toronto Collection. The quotation is from L. H. to Gardner, 15 October 1962.

33. Dayonis, *pers. comm.*, 4 June 1998; Lois Bourne, *Dancing with Witches* (London: Hale, 1998), 27–8.

34. Rex Nemorensis, *Witch*, 44–46; I am very grateful to 'Bran' for presenting me with this scarce text. A file of documents in the Toronto Collection chronicles the whole sad story, and suggests strongly that Greene only met and turned to her mentor, Charles Cardell, after disillusion with Gardner, and so therefore that the spy tale is a fiction. A parallel story of rescuing a maiden from Gardner, put about by a rival magician, is that in Francis King, *The Magical world of Aleister Crowley* (London: Weidenfeld, 1977), 179–80. It was told by Kenneth Grant, but as neither Doreen Valiente nor Fred Lamond can recall any of the characters or incidents concerned in this drama, its truth remains unconfirmed. Other doubts hang over the details of Grant's story of a ritual in 1949 attended by Gardner, in Kenneth Grant, *Nightside of Eden*, and discussed in Valiente, *Rebirth of Witchcraft*, 50, and Mike Howard, 'Gerald Gardner: the Man, the Myth and the Magick', *The Cauldron* 84 (1997), 19.

35. Richard Perceval Graves, *Robert Graves and the White Goddess* (London: Weidenfeld, 1995), 326–7.

36. 'Witches', *Daily Mail*, 1 October 1964, 15.

CHAPTER 13

1. See especially *The Dream-Quest of Unknown Kadath* (n.d.), *The Rats in the Walls* (n.d.), *The Dreams in the Witch House* (n.d.), *The Silver Key* (1926), *The Case of Charles Dexter Ward* (1929), *At the Mountains of Madness* (1931), and *The Dunwich Horror* (1935).

2. L. Sprague de Camp, *Lovecraft: A Biography* (New York: Putnam, 1975), *passim*.

3. p. 65 in *The H. P. Lovecraft Omnibus* (London: Grafton, 1985).

4. Joseph Jerome, *Montague Summers: A Memoir* (London: Woolf, 1964); Timothy d'Arch Smith, *A Bibliography of the Works of Montague Summers* (London: Vaner, 1964); Roger Dobson, 'Hell-fire, fiends and Black Magic', and 'Montague Summers—Oxford's Demonologist', in *Strange Oxford,* ed. Chris Morgan (Oxford: Golden Dawn, 1987), 39–43, 44–6. The opinion quoted is that of Mr Dobson.

5. Montague Summers, *The History of Witchcraft and Demonology* (London: Kegan Paul, 1926) (quotations from pp. xii and xiv); *The Geography of Witchcraft* (London: Kegan Paul, 1927); edition of *Malleus Maleficarum* (London: Rodker, 1928).

6. Montague Summers, *Witchcraft and Black Magic* (London: Rider, 1946) (quotation from p. 10).

7. Sylvia Cranston, *HPB* (New York: Putnam, 1993), 367.

8. Arthur Machen, *The Great God Pan* (1894) and 'The Novel of the Black Seal' in *The Three Imposters* (1895).

9. J. W. Brodie-Innes, 'Witchcraft' and 'Witchcraft Rituals', *Occult Review* 25 (1917), 264–71, 328–36; 'An Egyptian Ritual Against Apophi and its Relation to Modern Witchcraft', *Ibid.* 26 (1917), 75–84; *For The Soul of a Witch* (1910); *The Devil's Mistress* (1916).

10. See Alice Mary Hadfield, *Charles Williams: An Exploration of his Life and Work* (Oxford: Oxford University Press, 1983), for his background (and Underhill's) in magic.

11. See especially 'The Return of the Ritual', 'The Scented Poppies', and 'The Death Hound' in *The Secrets of Doctor Taverner* (London: Douglas, 1926).

12. Kenneth Grant, *The Magical Revival* (London: Muller, 1972), 190–2, and *Images and Oracles of Austin Osman Spare* (London: Muller, 1975), 23–6.

13. Aleister Crowley, *Magick*, eds. John Symonds and Kenneth Grant (London: Routledge, 1973), 295, and *Magick Without Tears*, ed. Israel Regardie (Phoenix, AZ: Falcon, 1982), 9, 72, 109–21.

14. Aleister Crowley, *777* (repr. Samuel Weiser, York Beach, Maine, 1973), 164–5, and *Magick*, 164–5.

15. A. Lillie, *The Worship of Satan in Modern France* (1896); H. T. F. Rhodes, *The Satanic Mass* (London: Rider, 1954); Christopher Macintosh, *Eliphas Levi and the French Occult Revival* (Rider: London, 1972), chs. 16, 18.

16. Theda Kenyon, *Witches Still Live* (New York: Washburn, 1929) (quotation from p. ix); Elliott O'Donnell, *Strange Cults and Secret Societies of Modern London* (London: Allan, 1934) (quotations from pp. 213, 203–5, 233–9).

17. Published in London by Harrap.

18. Published in London by Long. Quotations from pp. 257–9.

19. Warburg Institute, Gerald Yorke Collection, MS 83.

20. Robert Fabian, *Fabian of the Yard* (London: Naldrett, 1950), esp. 105–11.

21. Best known in the edition by S. L. Mathers, 1898.

22. Robert Fabian, *London After Dark* (London: Naldrett, 1954), esp. 4, 70–7.

23. 'Ancient Sorceries', repr. in Algernon Blackwood, *Strange Stories* (London: Heinemann, 1929), and *John Silence* (1908), *passim.*

24. A. E. W. Mason, *The Prisoner in the Opal* (London: Hodder and Stoughton, 1929).

25. Warburg Institute, Gerald Yorke Collection, MS E.21, Wheatley to Crowley, 123 May 1934.

26. For Wheatley's view of Crowley and Summers, see Dennis Wheatley, *The Time Has Come. Volume III: Drink and Ink 1919–1977* (London: Hutchinson, 1979), 131–3, 261. The debunking of the Crowley anecdote is in Gerald Suster, *The Legacy of the Beast* (London: Allen, 1988), 88–9.

27. Wheatley, *The Time Has Come. Volume III*, 266.

28. *The Devil Rides Out* (1935); *Strange Conflict* (1941); *The Haunting of Toby Jugg* (1948); *To the Devil—A Daughter* (1943); *The Satanist* (1960); *Gateway to Hell* (1970); *The Irish Witch* (1973). All published in London by Hutchinson.

29. Foreword to the 1988 reprint of *The Devil Rides Out*, vii–x.

30. Wheatley, *The Time Has Come. Volume III*, 216.

31. *Ibid.*, 131–41; Rollo Ahmed, *The Black Art* (London: Long, 1936), dedication and 7–9.

32. Dennis Wheatley, *The Devil and All His Works* (London: Hutchinson, 1971), author's note and 238–57.

33. Printed by Arrow Books, 1971.

34. Wheatley, *Devil and All His Works*, 10–88.

35. This is a major theme of all three volumes of his memoirs, *The Time Has Come*, published by Hutchinson between 1977 and 1979.

36. E.g. Wheatley, *Haunting of Toby Jugg*, 73, 121, 127, and *The Time Has Come. Volume III*, 166–7, 254–5.

37. *Ibid.*, 88–114.

38. Wheatley, *Haunting of Toby Jugg*, 126.

39. *Ibid.*, 103.

40. *Dangerous Inheritance* (London: Hutchinson, 1965) is devoted to this argument.

41. Ch. 12 of the original, Hutchinson, edition.

42. In *The Sultan's Daughter* (1968) and the eponymous *The Ravishing of Lady Mary Ware* (1971).

43. Wheatley, *The Time Has Come*, 196.

44. Wheatley, *Devil and All His Works*, 13–41, 87–8.

45. The key articles are listed in Gerald Gardner, *The Meaning of Witchcraft* (London: Aquarian, 1959), 213–84. A full coverage of press attention to these issues from the 1950s to the 1990s is provided by Doreen Valiente's collection of cuttings, now deposited with the Pagan Federation. I am very grateful to Ms Valiente for making the deposit and to Melissa Montgomery and Rufus Harrington for obtaining access to it for me.

46. Peter Curtis, *The Devil's Own* (London: Macdonald, 1960), republished as *The Witches*, by Pan, 1966.

47. The fullest reports were in *The Daily Herald*, 3 and 5 December 1956.

48. These phenomena are considered in *Gardner, Meaning of Witchcraft*, 213–88; Eric Maple, *Witchcraft* (London: Octopus, 1973), 97–9; Doreen Valiente, *The Rebirth of Witchcraft* (Custer, WA: Phoenix, 1989), 75–8, 146–51. Ms Valiente's cutting collection contains the full range of press coverage of them.

49. See, for example, his words to *Psychic News*, 23 July 1955; the *Observer* 16 December 1956; *Two Worlds* 11 May 1957; *Weekend* 26–30 June 1957; and the *Daily Mail* 3 September 1960.

50. Colin Wilson, *Aleister Crowley: The Nature of the Beast* (London: Aquarian, 1987), ch. 1.

CHAPTER 14

1. Robert Graves, 'An Appointment for Candlemas', repr. in *Collected Short Stories* (London: Cassell, 1965), 85–9; and 'Witches Today', repr. in *The Crane Bag and Other*

Disputed Subjects (London: Cassell, 1968), 216–24. I am grateful to John Yohalem for the first reference and Mike Howard for the second.

2. For reactions of two very different sorts of journal, see the *Daily Mail* 4 September 1963, and *Psychic News*, 14 September 1963.

3. *Inter alia*, see Arkon Daraul, *Witches and Sorcerers* (London: Muller, 1962); Gillian Tindall, *A Handbook on Witches* (London: Baker, 1965); Ronald Seth, *Witches and their Craft* (London: Odhams, 1967); Peter Haining, *Witchcraft and Black Magic* (London: Hamlyn, 1971); Raymond Lamont Brown, *A Book of Witchcraft* (Newton Abbot: David and Charles, 1971); Clifford Lindsay Alderman, *A Cauldron of Witches: The Story of Witchcraft* (Folkestone: Bailey, 1973); Frank Donovan, *Never On A Broomstick* (London: Allen and Unwin, 1973).

4. Arkon Daraul, *Secret Societies* (London: Octagon, 1961), 163–78. For Shah's reputation as a Sufi scholar, and his relationship with Graves, see Martin Seymour-Smith, *Robert Graves: His Life and Work* (London: Hutchinson, 1982), 505–27, and Richard Perceval Graves, *Robert Graves and the White Goddess* (London: Weidenfeld, 1995), 431–72.

5. Michael Harrison, *The Roots of Witchcraft* (London: Muller, 1973), esp. 19–32, 85, 147–74, 262.

6. For a full chronology and documentation, see Ronald Hutton, 'The Local Impact of the Tudor Reformations', in *The English Reformation Revised*, ed. Christopher Haigh (Cambridge: Cambridge University Press, 1987), 114–28.

7. A brief sympathetic biography, a bibliography, and selections from works, are provided in Tom Graves and Janet Hoult, *The Essential T. C. Lethbridge* (London: Routledge, 1980). For a general statement of his views, see T. C. Lethbridge, *Ghost and Ghoul* (London: Routledge, 1961), and for a balanced account of the Wandlebury controversy, Paul Newman, *Lost Gods of Albion: The Chalk Hill-figures of Britain* (2nd edn, Stroud: Sutton, 1997), 114–25.

8. T. C. Lethbridge, *Gogmagog: The Buried Gods* (London: Routledge, 1957), and *Witches: Investigating An Ancient Religion* (London: Routledge, 1962).

9. The references are collected and printed in *County Folk-Lore III: Leicestershire and Rutland*, ed. C. J. Billson (Folk-Lore Society, 1895), 4–9.

10. Elliott Rose, *A Razor For A Goat* (Toronto: Toronto University Press, 1962), quotation on pp. 14–15.

11. Carlo Ginzburg, *The Night Battles: Witchcraft and Agrarian Cults in the Sixteenth and Seventeenth Centuries* (London: Routledge, 1983), xix in preface to 1966 edition; Emmanuel Le Roy Ladurie, *Paysans de Languedoc* (Paris: Ecole Pratique des Hautes Etudes, 1966; translated into English 1974), 407–14.

12. See particularly Christopher Hill, *Society and Puritanism in Pre-Revolutionary England* (London: Secker and Warburg, 1964), 187 and 486, n. 4, and *Reformation to Industrial Revolution* (London: Weidenfeld, 1967), 115–18, and his use of the Murray thesis to berate Peter Laslett in his review of the latter's *The World We Have Lost*, in *History and Theory* 6 (1967), 121.

13. These notices are reviewed in Ginzburg, *Night Battles*, xiii–xiv. To them may be added the influential intervention of the very distinguished American-based scholar of comparative religion, Mircea Eliade. He published a collection of essays in 1976 which rejected Murray's portrait of the witch religion in its fully developed form, but drew explicitly upon Ginzburg to underpin a theory that medieval witchcraft could have represented a religion of rebellion against Christian institutions, drawing upon pagan fertility practices: *Occultism, Witchcraft, and Cultural Fashions: Essays in Comparative Religions* (Chicago: Chicago University Press, 1976), 57–8, 69–92.

14. Ginzburg, *Night Battles*, 133–4 and n. 254.

15. *Ibid.*, p. xiii.

16. Carlo Ginzburg, *Ecstasies: Deciphering the Witches' Sabbat* (1989: published in English by Hutchinson, London, 1991).

17. See Joseph Fontenrose, *The Ritual Theory of Myth* (Berkeley, CA: University of California Press, 1964).

18. Ginzburg, *Night Battles*, 22–30.

19. C. F. C. Hawkes, *The Prehistoric Foundations of Europe* (London: Methuen, 1940), 84–9, 153, 180, 198; Jacquetta Hawkes, *Early Britain* (London: Collins, 1945), 16–18.

20. Jacquetta Hawkes, *A Land* (London: Cresset, 1951), 158–61; *A Guide to the Prehistoric and Roman Monuments of England and Wales* (London: Chatto and Windus, 1954), 20–1, 198, 243–4; *Man on Earth* (London: Cresset, 1954), *passim*; *Man and the Sun* (London: Cresset, 1962), 57–87; *UNESCO History of Mankind. Vol. 1* (New York: Unesco, 1963), 204–344; *Dawn of the Gods* (London: Chatto and Windus, 1968), *passim*. See also her fictional works *Fables* (London: Cresset, 1953), and *Providence Island* (London: Chatto and Windus, 1959).

21. Hawkes, *A Land*, 143, 198, 200–1.

22. Jacquetta Hawkes, 'The Proper Study of Mankind', *Antiquity* 42 (1968), 260; Hawkes, *Man and the Sun*, 240–1.

23. J. B. Priestley and Jacquetta Hawkes, *Journey Down A Rainbow* (London: Heinemann-Cresset, 1955), 227; Hawkes, *A Land*, 159; Dustjacket notes to Jacquetta Hawkes, *King of the Two Lands* (London: Chatto and Windus, 1966).

24. Hawkes, *Man On Earth*, ch. 8; Priestley and Hawkes, *Journey Down A Rainbow*, 111–16.

25. Hawkes, *A Land*, ch. 10.

26. Hawkes, *Guide to the Prehistoric and Roman Monuments*, 56–7. The dismissal of urban sites is on p. 36.

27. V. G. Childe, *What Happened in History* (Harmondsworth: Penguin, 1954), 64–5, 268, and *The Prehistory of European Society* (Harmondsworth: Penguin, 1958), 21, 46, 58, 124–39; O. G. S. Crawford, *The Eye Goddess* (London: Phoenix House, 1957); Glyn Daniel, *The Megalith Builders of Western Europe* (London: Hutchinson, 1958), 74.

28. O. G. S. Crawford, *Said and Done* (London: Weidenfeld, 1955), 301–2; *The Eye Goddess*, *passim*.

29. G. R. Levy, *The Gate of Horn* (London: Faber, 1948), 54–164; E. O. James, *The Cult of the Mother Goddess* (London: Thames and Hudson, 1959); Johannes Maringer, *The Gods of Prehistoric Man* (London: Weidenfeld, 1960), chs. 4–5.

30. T. Zammit and Charles Singer, 'Neolithic Representations of the Human Form from the Islands of Malta and Gozo', *Journal of the Royal Anthropological Institute* 54 (1924), 67–100; J. D. Evans, *Malta* (London: Thames and Hudson, 1959), 136–67; Levy, *Gate of Horn*, 131–8.

31. James Mellaart, 'Excavations at Catal Huyuk. first Preliminary Report', *Anatolian Studies* 12 (1962), 41–65; 'Excavations at Catal Huyuk, 1962', *ibid.* 13 (1963), 43–103; 'Excavations at Catal Huyuk, 1963', *ibid.* 14 (1964), 39–120; 'Excavations at Catal Huyuk, 1965', *ibid.* 16 (1966), 165–91; *Earliest Civilizations of the Near East* (London: Thames and Hudson, 1965), 42–107; *Catal Huyuk A Neolithic Town in Anatolia* (London: Thames and Hudson, 1966), *passim*. His journalism is found in successive issues of the *Illustrated London News*, in February and May 1964. Note the difference in tone in his earlier work, 'Beycesultan Excavation. Fourth Preliminary Report', *Anatolian Studies* 8 (1958), 93–126, and 'Excavations at Hacilar. first Preliminary Report', *ibid.*, 8 (1958), 127–56; and in his later, *The Neolithic of the Near East* (London: Thames and Hudson, 1975), 66, 101–8.

32. Carl Jung, *Collected Works. Volume IX, Part 1: The Archetypes and the Collective Unconscious* (London: Routledge, 1959), 75–102.

33. Erich Neumann, *The Great Mother: An Analysis of the Archetype* (Princeton, NJ: Princeton University Press, 1963), esp. 1–2, 336.

34. Hawkes, 'Proper Study of Mankind', 260.

35. P. J. Ucko, 'The Interpretation of Prehistoric Anthropomorphic figurines', *Journal of the Royal Anthropological Institute* 92 (1962), 38–54.

36. Stuart Piggott, *British Prehistory* (Oxford: Oxford University Press, 1949), 82–95; *The Neolithic Cultures of the British Isles* (Cambridge: Cambridge University Press, 1954), 46; *Ancient Europe* (Edinburgh: Edinburgh University Press, 1965), 114–15.

37. P. J. Ucko, *Anthropomorphic figurines of Predynastic Egypt and Neolithic Crete with Comparative Material from the Prehistoric Near East and Mainland Greece* (London: Royal Anthropological Institute, 1968); Andrew Fleming, 'The Myth of the Mother Goddess', *World Archaeology* 1 (1969), 247–61.

38. Peter Ucko, *pers. comm.*, 13 March 1996.

39. Hawkes, 'Proper Study of Mankind', 255–62, and *A Land* (2nd edition, David and Charles, Newton Abbot, 1978), ix.

40. Michael Dames, *The Silbury Treasure: The Great Goddess Rediscovered* (1976) and *The Avebury Cycle* (1977), both published in London by Thames and Hudson.

41. This process is the major theme of Ronald Hutton, *The Stations of the Sun: A History of the Ritual Year in England* (Oxford: Oxford University Press, 1996).

42. Cf. Ralph Whitlock, *Wiltshire Folklore and Legends* (London; Hale, 1992), esp. p. 90.

43. The autobiography of George Ewart Evans is in two parts: *The Strength of the Hills* (1983) and *Spoken History* (1987). All his books were published in London by Faber.

44. George Ewart Evans, *Horse Power and Magic* (1979), 3.

45. Evans, *Strength of the Hills*, 255.

46. For example, *The Farm and the Village* (1969); *When Beards Wag All* (1970); *From Mouths of Men* (1976).

47. See *Ask the Fellow Who Cut The Hay* (1956), 108–13; *The Pattern Under The Plough* (1966), 94–5, 144–8, 160–1, 259; *The Days That We Have Seen* (1975), 31–41.

48. This is one theme of *The Strength of the Hills*. See also *The Crooked Scythe* (1993), xv.

49. Evans, *Pattern Under The Plough*, 141–2.

50. George Ewart Evans and David Thomson, *The Leaping Hare* (1972), 143.

51. Evans, *Days That We Have Seen*, 19, 27: quotation on p. 22. See also *Pattern Under The Plough*, passim.

52. Evans, *Pattern Under The Plough*, 62–3, 101, 123–42, 184, 192–4, 220–30; *Days That We Have Seen*, 42–3; *Spoken History*, 62–5, 139; *Crooked Scythe*, xvii; Evans and Thomson, *Leaping Hare*, 15–16, 105–7, 142–5, 221–5.

53. Evans, *Pattern Under The Plough*, 220; *From Mouths of Men*, ii; *Spoken History*, 215.

54. For biographical details, see David Sweetman, *Mary Renault* (London: Chatto and Windus, 1973).

55. See especially *The Golden Strangers* (London: Bodley Head, 1956) and *The Green Man* (London: Bodley Head, 1966).

56. Especially *The Eagle of the Ninth* (1954); *Warrior Scarlet* (1958); *The Lantern Bearers* (1959); *Knight's Fee* (1960) (all published in Oxford by Oxford University Press); *Sword at Sunset* (London: Hodder and Stoughton, 1963); *The Mark of the Horse Lord* (Oxford: Oxford Universty Press, 1965); *The Witch's Brat* (Oxford: Oxford University Press, 1970); *The Capricorn Bracelet* (Oxford: Oxford University Press, 1973); *Sun Horse, Moon Horse* (London: Bodley Head, 1977); *Song for a Dark Queen* (London: Pelham, 1978). Her autobiography is *Blue Remembered Hills* (London: Bodley Head, 1983), while her

literary interest in paganism is studied in Barbara L. Talcroft, *Death of the Corn King; King and Goddess in Rosemary Sutcliff's Historical fiction for Young Adults* (Metuchen, NY: Scarecrow, 1995).

57. Sean French, *Bardot* (London: Pavilion, 1994), 77.

CHAPTER 15

1. Allen Andrews, 'Witchcraft in Britain', *Illustrated*, 27 September 1952, 20, 42.
2. Lois Bourne, *Dancing With Witches* (London: Hale, 1998), 48–55, 97–103. The presence of this lady in the Hertfordshire coven at this time is confirmed by two other surviving members of it, Frederic Lamond and the man who features prominently as 'Enoch' in Tanya Luhrmann, *Persuasions of the Witch's Craft* (Oxford: Blackwell, 1989): Lamond, *pers. comms.*, 17 August 1996 and 19 June 1998, and 'Enoch', *pers. comm.*, 9 July 1998. There are, however, some discrepancies between their memories of her and those of Lois Bourne; they do not recall that she was a member of the coven for as long a term as Bourne implies, nor that her hereditary coven seemed, from her accounts, to be as grand or elaborate. This emphatically does not refute anything that Bourne says upon the matter, but it does deprive her account of that independent endorsement in all its details which would turn it into reliable historical evidence.
3. E. W. Liddell and Michael Howard, *The Pickingill Papers* (Chieveley: Capall Bann, 1994), 1–2, 11–14; Leonora James, *pers. comm.*, 25 May 1990; Lugh, *Old George Pickingill and the Roots of Modern Witchcraft* (Wiccan Publications, 1982); Doreen Valiente, *Witchcraft for Tomorrow* (London: Hale, 1978), 17–20, and *The Rebirth of Witchcraft* (Custer, WA: Phoenix, 1989), 198–206; James W. Baker, 'White Witches: Historic Fact and Romantic Fantasy', in *Magical Religion and Modern Witchcraft*, ed. James R. Lewis (Albany: State University of New York Press, 1996), 185–7.
4. Liddell and Howard, *Pickingill Papers*, 24–5, 56–8, 63–6, 78–80, 89, 111.
5. Bill Liddell, *pers. comm.* 18 May 1998.
6. Liddell and Howard, *Pickingill Papers*, 24.
7. *Ibid.*, 23, 57, 60–3, 119–22.
8. *Ibid.*, 19–26, 72, 102–17, 124–8.
9. *Ibid.*, 27, 89, 154, 157.
10. *Ibid.*, 19–30, 82–6, 96–9, 115–17, 146–8, 150–4.
11. *Ibid.*, 37–41, 163.
12. *Ibid.*, 16–17.
13. *Ibid.*, 24, 45–54, 63–9; Pennethorne Hughes, *Witchcraft* (London: Longman, 1952), plate 3a; Bodleian Library, Rawlinson MS D410, fo. 1; compare the parallel scene reproduced in Russell Hope Robbins, *An Encyclopaedia of Witchcraft and Demonology* (London: Hamlyn, 1959), 31.
14. Liddell and Howard, *Pickingill Papers*, 85, 89.
15. Twelve of these survive in the archives of the Wellcome Institute, London, and of the United Grand Lodge of England at Freemasons' Hall, London.
16. Francis X. King, *The Flying Sorcerer* (Oxford: Mandrake, 1992), 25–6.
17. Eric Maple, 'Cunning Murrell' and 'The Witches of Canewdon', *Folklore* 71 (1960), 37–43, 241–9; 'The Witches of Dengie', *Folklore* 73 (1962), 178–83; 'Witchcraft and Magic in the Rochford Hundred', *Folklore* 76 (1965), 213–24.
18. See his obituary by Alan Smith in *Folklore* 106 (1995), 87–88, and the review of *The Dark World of Witches* by H. A. Beecham in *ibid.*, 77 (1966), 230–1.
19. Charles Lefebvre, *Witness to Witchcraft* (New York: Ace, 1970), 51–6, 156.

20. Jack Taylor, *pers. comm.*, 4 April 1967. Mike Howard, talking to Lillian Garner in October 1977, heard a slightly different account of Pickingill from her, notably the detail that he had visitors 'from all over, including abroad', which accords better with Bill Liddell's portrait: Michael Howard, *pers. comm.*, 24 June 1998. It is not clear, however, what this expression exactly signified.

21. See Ch. 4 of this book.

22. Personal details are given in *The Times* Law Reports, 10–13 October 1967. Valiente's account is printed in Aidan Kelly, *Crafting the Art of Magic* (St Paul, MN: Llewellyn, 1991), 137–40, supported by letters in the Toronto Collection from Valiente to Dafo, 17 July 1958, and Dafo to Cardell, 20 July 1958.

23. Toronto Collection, Cardell to Gardner, 9 September 1958, Bruce to Gardner, 19 November 1959 and 12 May 1961, and Valiente to Kelly, 5 October 1983; *The County Post*, 24 March 1961; *The Times* Law Reports, 10–13 October 1967; Rex Nemorensis, *Witch* (Charlwood: Dumblecott, 1964).

24. 'Bran', *pers. comm.*, 27 September 1995.

25. *London Evening News*, 7 March 1961, 5.

26. *Ibid.*; *The Times* Law Reports, 10–13 October 1967; *Eastern Daily Press*, 6 March 1967; Doreen Valiente, *An ABC of Witchcraft Past and Present* (London: Hale, 1973), 24–6; Bourne, *Dancing With Witches*, plate 24.

27. Especially significant interviews and profiles are in the *Daily Herald*, 16 September 1963; *London Evening News*, 31 October 1963; and *Daily Mail*, 1 October 1964. Other portraits are provided by Valiente, *Rebirth of Witchcraft*, 144–6; Alan W. Smith, 'Which Witch Was Which?', *Folklore Society News* 16 (November 1992), 7–8; and Clifford Lindsey Alderman, *A Cauldron of Witches* (Folkestone: Bailey and Swinfen, 1973), 169–70.

28. *Diary of a Witch* (Englewood Cliffs, NJ: Prentice, 1968), 1–131.

29. Valiente, *Rebirth of Witchcraft*, 145–6.

30. F. W. Mathews, *Tales of the Blackdown Borderland* (Somerset Folk Series 13, 1923); R. L. Tongue, *Somerset Folklore* (Folklore Society, 1965); Kingsley Palmer, *The Folklore of Somerset* (London: Batsford, 1976); Ralph Whitlock, *The Folklore of Devon* (London: Batsford, 1977).

31. Alastier Clay-Egerton, 'Crafty Ones', *The Cauldron* 70 (1993), 8–9, and 'Craft Teachings', *The Cauldron* 81 (1996), 3–4.

32. Kenneth Grant, *The Magical Revival* (London: Muller, 1972), 182; Liddell and Howard, *Pickingill Papers*, 32–2; Kenneth Grant, *Outer Gateways* (London: Skoob, 1994), 17–31.

33. Emlyn Davies, *pers. comm.*, 29 January 1997.

34. Levannah Morgan, *pers. comm.*, 5 June 1998.

35. The Azoetia (Chelmsford: privately published, 1992).

36. Andrew Chumbley, *pers. comms.*, 239 March, 20 April, and 12 May 1996. I am very grateful to my colleague at Bristol, Duncan Kennedy, for confirming the attributions of the Latin texts and showing precisely how they had been adapted.

37. Cf. their prominence in Janet and Stewart Farrar, *The Life and Times of a Modern Witch* (London: Piatkus, 1987).

38. Charles Bowness, *The Witch's Gospel* (London: Hale, 1979), *passim*. My meeting with the Lincolnshire man took place at Nottingham on 8 March 1995.

39. Doreen Valiente, *Where Witchcraft Lives* (London: Aquarian, 1962), 54; *ABC of Witchcraft Past and Present*, 63; *Rebirth of Witchcraft*, 139.

40. Jacqueline Simpson, 'Legends of Chanctonbury Ring', *Folklore* 80 (1969), 112–31.

41. John Matthews, 'Breaking the Circle', in *Voices from the Circle*, eds Prudence Jones and Caitlin Matthews (Wellingborough: Aquarian, 1990), 127–36. 'Delenath' 'and all at Chanctonbury' are thanked in the preface to Caitlin and John Matthews, *The Western*

Way (London: Arkana, 1985). I am very grateful to John Matthews for clarifying some points for me at a meeting on 26 December 1995.

42. Valiente, *Where Witchcraft Lives*, 81–2.
43. *Pers. comm.*, 13 October 1997.

CHAPTER 16

1. Toronto Collection, Richard G. to Gardner, 27 May 1960.
2. On p. 95.
3. On 7 October 1962.
4. Doreen Valiente, *The Rebirth of Witchcraft* (Custer, WA: Phoenix, 1989), 117, 122.
5. *Ibid.*, p. 80.
6. See the report on her speech to the Brighton Forum Society in *The Evening Argus*, 16 April 1964, and *Prediction*, May 1964.
7. *Daily Herald*, 19 February and 2 July 1964; *Daily Express*, 29 November 1963; *Daily Mirror*, 2 July 1964; *Daily Sketch*, 2 July 1964; Valiente, *Rebirth of Witchcraft*, 146, 150; Sybil Leek, *Diary of a Witch* (Englewood Cliffs, NJ: Prentice, 1968), 161.
8. *Evening Argus*, 29 September 1964.
9. *Pentagram* 1 (August 1964) and 2 (November 1964); *Prediction* (December 1964); Valiente, *Rebirth of Witchcraft*, 130; Marian Green, *pers. comm.* 12 February 1997.
10. Quotation from p. 21.
11. Reported most fully in *Prediction* (April 1966).
12. Evan John Jones, *pers. comm.*, 3 April 1997.
13. By Evan John Jones and Chas S. Clifton.
14. Valiente, *Rebirth of Witchcraft*, 121.
15. Justine Glass, *Witchcraft: The Sixth Sense—And Us* (London: Spearman, 1965), 135–7.
16. *Ibid.*, 135–6.
17. Valiente, *Rebirth of Witchcraft*, 118–19.
18. Michael Howard, *pers. comm.*, 19 June 1998.
19. Valiente, *Rebirth of Witchcraft*, 120, 122.
20. *Ibid.*, 117–25.
21. Evan John Jones and Chas S. Clifton, *Sacred Mask, Sacred Dance* (St Paul, MN: Llewellyn, 1997), 155–63. Several of Cochrane's concepts have been expounded further by Jones in successive issues of *The Cauldron* during the 1990s.
22. Glass, *Witchcraft*, 64–5, 135–6; Valiente, *Rebirth of Witchcraft*, 120–2.
23. Jones and Clifton, *Sacred Mask, Sacred Dance*, 164–5.
24. James W. Baker, 'White Witches: Historic Fact and Romantic Fantasy', in *Magical Religion and Modern Witchcraft*, ed. James R. Lewis (Albany, NY: State University of New York Press, 1996), 187.
25. Jones and Clifton, *Sacred Mask, Sacred Dance*, 156; Marian Green, *pers. comms.*, 12 February 1997.
26. Jones and Clifton, *Sacred Mask, Sacred Dance*, 164–5; Valiente, *Rebirth of Witchcraft*, 125–7; Marian Green, *pers. comms.* 12 February 1997 and 21 May 1998.
27. Patricia and Arnold Crowther, *The Witches Speak* (Douglas: Athol, 1965); quotations from pp. 15–16, 102–3, 148.
28. *Pentagram* 3 (May 1965), 4 (August 1965), 5 (December 1965); M.H., 'Out of the Shadows', *The Cauldron* 76 (1995), 2–3.
29. Jones and Clifton, *Sacred Mask, Sacred Dance*, 164; Valiente, *Rebirth of Witchcraft*, 128–9.
30. Valiente, *Rebirth of Witchcraft*, 128–35.

31. M.H., 'Out of the Shadows', 3–4; Michael Howard, *pers. comms.*, 28 November 1997, 25 June 1998; Marian Green, *pers. comm.*, 21 May 1998; Gwenfran Gwernan, *Introduction to Witchcraft* (London: Quest, 1970: 2nd edn, 1980); Patricia Crowther, *One Witch's World* (London: Hale, 1998), 94–5; *Pentagram* 6 (NS)(February 1967). I am very grateful to Marian Green for presenting me with a copy of the Gwenfran Gwernan pamphlet.

32. Evan John Jones and Doreen Valiente, *Witchcraft: A Tradition Renewed* (London: Hale, 1990); Jones and Clifton, *Sacred Mask, Sacred Dance*; Evan John Jones, *pers. comms.*, 3 and 15 April 1997.

33. M.H., 'Out of the Shadows', 3; Ann Finnin, 'The Riddle of Four Figures', *The Wiccan* 96 (1990), 3–4.

34. Valiente, *Rebirth of Witchcraft*, 135–56.

CHAPTER 17

1. See, *inter alia, Sunday Mail*, 17 September 1961; *Sunday Citizen*, 7 October 1962; *Sunday Times*, 27 October 1963; *Evening News*, 31 October 1963; *Everywoman*, November 1963; *Daily Express*, 7 March 1964; *Sunday Telegraph*, 3 May 1964; *Life International*, 18 May 1964; *Parade*, 17 October 1964; *Sun*, 31 October 1964; *Reading Standard*, 15 April 1965; *Weekend Telegraph*, 21 May 1965 and 17 June 1966; *The Star*, 30 October 1965; *Daily Telegraph*, 4 June 1966; *Daily Mirror*, 4 June 1966; and *Woman's Mirror*, 20 August 1966. Patricia Crowther's own view of the process is represented in her autobiography, *One Witch's World* (London: Hale, 1998), 32–9.

2. Crowther, *One Witch's World*. 63–64; Doreen Valiente, *The Rebirth of Witchcraft* (London: Hale, 1989), 165–6.

3. For Crowther's side of the story, see *One Witch's World*, 63–7; for Sanders's, see June Johns, *King of the Witches: The World of Alex Sanders* (London: Davies, 1969), 64–9. Both Crowther and Valiente, *Rebirth of Witchcraft*, 166–8, give the date of the article as 15 September 1962, but it is not in that edition of the newspaper: I have, however, seen the cutting of it in Valiente's own collection, for use of which I again thank her, Melissa Montgomery, and Rufus Harrington. In the same collection is the letter of protest mentioned below.

4. Johns, *King of the Witches*, 61–7.

5. Toronto Collection, Monique Wilson to Gardner, 5 December 1963.

6. Crowther, *One Witch's World*, 66.

7. It is in the Toronto Collection. The signature could read 'Kopanski' or 'Kopinski'. Aidan Kelly took it as the former (*Crafting the Art of Magic*, St Paul, MN: Llewellyn, xiii), which is also the version given in the interview with her in the *News of the World*, 9 April 1967, 4. I have therefore adopted it here, as the 'public' version. However, Maxine Sanders, who knew her well, tells me that her name was actually 'Kospinski': *pers. comm.*, 12 September 1998.

8. Crowther, *One Witch's World*, 67–8.

9. *Ibid.*, 68–9; Valiente, *Rebirth of Witchcraft*, 166.

10. Crowther, *One Witch's World*, 68–70.

11. This is especially true of one long letter from Arnold to Gardner in the Toronto collection, undated but clearly from 1963.

12. Alan Whittaker, 'The Witches', *News of the World*, 9 April 1967, 4.

13. E. W. Liddell, *pers. comm.*, 6 July 1998.

14. Johns, *King of the Witches*, 72–81; Maxine Sanders, *Maxine: The Witch Queen* (London: Star, 1976), 14–35.

15. A newspaper report in June 1965 states that the initiations had occurred in November: Chris Robbins, 'Witches Dance Pagan Rituals Under Moon', *Manchester Comet*, 23 June 1965, 32. Johns, *King of the Witches* 80–4, gives the date as after Christmas. Maxine, however, now says that Alex and Paul King met as members of an existing coven based at Poynton, south-east of Manchester, which worked outside the Gardnerian network, and in which Alex spent his time between the collapse of the group run by Kopanski (or Kospinski) and his re-emergence into the public eye in mid-1965; *pers. comm.* 12 September 1998.

16. Sanders, *Maxine: The Witch Queen*, 59–67; Jim Bennett, 'In Conversation with Maxine Sanders', *Pagan Dawn* 121 (Samhain, 1996), 14–15; Maxine Sanders, *pers. comm.*, 12 September 1998.

17. Sanders, *Maxine: The Witch Queen*, 56–80; Richard Deutch, *The Ecstatic Mother: Portrait of Maxine Sanders* (London: Bachman and Turner, 1977), 79–86; *Manchester Evening News*, 21 September 1965; *News of the World*, 17 October 1965; *The People*, 5 December 1965; *Sun*, 8 December 1965; *Tit Bits*, 15 January 1966; *Manchester Comet*, 4 May 1966; Maxine Sanders, *pers. comm.* 12 September 1998.

18. The Crowther wedding is recorded in an unattributed press cutting dated September 1962, in Doreen Valiente's collection, where they also give the date of their initiation as the previous Yule. However, Crowther, *One Witch's World*, 30, 40, gives the date of the latter as April 1960, and that of the wedding as 9 November 1960, with the second and third degrees in October 1961. In the history of Wicca little is simple. The information about Fred Lamond's marriage comes from the man himself: *pers. comm.*, 24 August 1998.

19. *The People*, 5 December 1965; *Sun*, 8 December 1965. Maxine now says that there was in fact no such ritual, and that the account of it was devised to keep journalists happy.

20. The press report with these exchanges is in the *Sun*, 3 May 1966. For the background to her part, see Crowther, *One Witch's World*, 72.

21. Johns, *King of the Witches*, 96–104; Sanders, *Maxine: The Witch Queen*, 68–80. Maxine confirms that the title was indeed offered to him by a gathering of witches, and not simply assumed by him upon his own initiative.

22. Johns, *King of the Witches*, 96; Sanders, *Maxine: The Witch Queen*, 68.

23. Alan Whittaker, 'The Witches', *News of the World*, 9 April 1967, 4.

24. Valiente, *Rebirth of Witchcraft*, 170.

25. Cf. Whittaker, 'The Witches'; *Tit-Bits* 18 February, 25 February, 4 March 1967; *Swank*, March 1966.

26. Sanders, *Maxine: The Witch Queen*, 81, 122–3; Deutch, *The Ecstatic Mother*, 102.

27. Alan Whittaker, 'The Witches', *News of the World*, 2 April 1967, 1, 4; 9 April 1967.

28. 'The Priest and the Black Mass', *News of the World*, 2 February 1969, 2–3; 'Witchcraft Puts Their Little Girl in Peril', *ibid*, 9 February 1969, 2–3; 'Witch Child: Police Act', and 'My Initiation', *ibid.*, 16 February 1969, 1, 3; 'How Young Girls Are Lured By The Witches', *ibid.*, 23 February 1969, 2–3; 'We Name The Satanist All The Witches Fear', *ibid.*, 2 March 1969, 9; cf *The Times*, 16 April 1969.

29. *News of the World*, 13 and 20 April 1975; Sanders, *Maxine: The Witch Queen*; Deutch, *The Ecstatic Mother*.

30. Stewart Farrar, *What Witches Do: A Modern Coven Revealed* (London: Hale, 3rd edn, 1991), preface and p. 4; Janet and Stewart Farrar, *Eight Sabbats for Witches* (London: Hale, 1981), 17; and *The Witches' Way* (London: Hale, 1984), 3–4, 22, 188.

31. Jim Bennett, 'In Conversation with Maxine Sanders', *Pagan Dawn* 121 (Samhain, 1996), 16.

32. Johns, *King of the Witches*, 120–1; Farrar, *What Witches Do*, 3–4; Frank Smyth, *Modern*

Witchcraft (London: Macdonald, 1970), 115–16; Eric Maple, *Witchcraft* (London: Octopus, 1973), 136.

33. For my purposes, Maxine Sanders and Vivianne Crowley, from whom I have learned much in conversation.

34. Deutch, *The Ecstatic Mother, passim.* For a parallel portrait of Maxine in action at this time, see Margot Adler, *Drawing Down The Moon* (Boston: Beacon, 2nd edn, 1986).

35. I am very grateful to Maxine Sanders for showing me these papers, and to her and her family for agreeing to my use of them. For some of the misapprehensions which have circulated, see Deutch, *The Ecstatic Mother*, 104; Valiente, *Rebirth of Witchcraft*, 174; David Alford, 'Witch King Wanted Men Not Me', *The People*, 14 September 1986, 4; Smyth, *Modern Witchcraft*, 119.

36. Johns, *King of the Witches*, 15–28; Smyth, *Modern Witchcraft*, 115–18; Maxine Sanders, *pers. comm.*, 12 September 1998.

37. Farrar and Farrar, *The Witches' Way*, 14–15; Margaret A. Murray, *The God of the Witches* (London: Sampson Low, 1931), 25. I am grateful to David James for drawing my attention to this point.

38. Farrar, *What Witches Do* (1993 edn), preface and 93–106. This should emphatically not be taken as suggesting that other Wiccans, and especially Gardnerian Wiccans, were less practical and results-related in their magic. It only suggests that in interviews and lectures they tended to talk somewhat more about the Old Religion, and Alex and Maxine somewhat more about practical magic.

39. Johns, *King of the Witches*, 121; Maple, Witchcraft, 137; Sanders, *Maxine: The Witch Queen*, 144–5.

40. Bill Ellis, 'The Highgate Cemetery Vampire Hunt: the Anglo-American Connection in Satanic Cult Lore', *Folklore* 104 (1993), 13–35.

41. Valiente, *Rebirth of Witchcraft*, 173; Maxine Sanders, *pers. comm.*, 12 September 1998.

42. *The Ilford Recorder*, 18 and 15 November, and 2 December 1971. I am grateful to Christine Hooper for locating these references for me in the Ilford Local History Library.

43. For another example of adverse publicity which featured in the national press, see the misadventures of Marie Unsworth, chronicled in the *Daily Express*, 21 October 1972, 1 September 1973, and 15 May 1977.

44. This is certainly the impression given by Doreen Valiente's huge collection of cuttings.

45. *Daily Star*, 3 April 1979.

46. Johns, *King of the Witches*, 36–44, 113.

47. *The Twelve Maidens* (London: Joseph, 1974); *The Serpent of Lilith* (London: Arrow, 1976); *The Sword of Orley* (London: Joseph, 1977), 'Gerald' features in the second of these.

48. Sanders, *Maxine: The Witch Queen*, 94–121, 134–43; *News of the World*, 6, 13, and 20 April 1975; Maxine Sanders, *pers. comm.*, 12 September 1998.

49. Diana Demdike, 'Witches: Cult or Craft?', *Quest* 3 (September 1970), n.p.; 'The Gardnerian "Heresy"', *ibid.* 6 (June 1971), n.p.; column in *ibid.* 9 (March 1972), n.p.; 'Don't Let Witchcraft Die', *ibid.* 15 (September 1973), n.p.

50. Lois Bourne, *Witch Among Us* (London: Satellite, 1979).

51. *Ibid.*, 52. I have heard Philip Rahtz speak of this encounter on several occasions.

52. Doreen Valiente, *An ABC of Witchcraft Past and Present; Natural Magic* (1975); *Witchcraft for Tomorrow* (1978). All published in London by Hale.

53. Stewart Farrar, 'The Demdike "Heresy"', *Quest* 7 (September 1971), n.p.

54. Farrar and Farrar, *Eight Sabbats, and The Witches's Way*.

55. Published in *The Cauldron* (Lammas 1979).

CHAPTER 18

1. Margot Adler, *Drawing Down The Moon* (Boston, MA: Beacon, 2nd edn, 1986), 233–6.
2. *Ibid.*, 67–9; Aidan Kelly, *Crafting the Art of Magic* (St Paul, MN: Llewellyn, 1991), 23–6.
3. Vance Randolph, *Ozark Superstition* (New York: Columbia University Press, 1947), 265–6.
4. Gardner expressed his opinion to the *Observer*, 16 December 1956; Kelly, *Crafting the Art of Magic*, 25–6.
5. On this see Adler in particular: *Drawing Down The Moon*, 70–8.
6. Adler, *Drawing Down The Moon*, 179; Alice Nichols, *Daring To Be Bad: Radical Feminism in America 1967–1975* (Minneapolis, MN: University of Minnesota Press, 1989), 79–119.
7. Mary Daly, *Beyond God The Father* (Boston, MA: Beacon, 1973), 63–8, 146–59, and *Gyn/Ecology: The Metaethics of Radical Feminism* (Boston, MA: Beacon, 1978), 178–222; Andrea Dworkin, *Woman Hating* (New York: Dutton, 1974), 118–50.
8. Barbara Ehrenreich and Deirdre English, *Witches, Midwives and Healers* (London: Writers and Readers Publishing Cooperative, 1973); Merlin Stone, *When God Was A Woman* (New York: Harcourt, Brace and Jovanovich, 1976); Daly, *Gyn/Ecology*, 13–14, 75–7.
9. Cynthia Eller, *Living in the Lap of the Goddess: The Feminist Spirituality Movement in America* (Boston, MA: Beacon, 1993), 174, 260–1.
10. Peter Novick, 'Holocaust Memory in America', in *The Mart of Memory: Holocaust Memorials in History*, ed. James E. Young, *The Texture of Memory: Holocaust Memorials and Meaning* (New Haven, CT: Yale University Press, 1993), ch. 4. I am grateful to Tim Cole, my colleague at Bristol University, who is himself working upon the subject, for providing me with these references.
11. J. F. C. Hecker, *The Epidemics of the Middle Ages*, trans. B. G. Babington (1844), 120–1; William E. H. Lecky, *History of European Morals* (1869), vol. II, 57–8.
12. Eller, *Living in the Lap of the Goddess*, 55.
13. *Ibid.*, 56; Adler, *Drawing Down The Moon*, 76–7; Zsuzsanna E. Budapest, *The Grandmother of Time* (San Francisco, CA: Harper and Row, 1989), *passim*.
14. Eller, *Living in the Lap of the Goddess*, 56–7.
15. Budapest, *Grandmother of Time*, 16.
16. Zsuzsanna Budapest, *The Holy Book of Women's Mysteries* (Oakland, CA: Susan B. Anthony Coven No. 1, 1980), *passim*.
17. *Ibid.*, 239.
18. Budapest, *Grandmother of Time*, 168.
19. A brief autobiography is given in the 1989 reprint of *The Spiral Dance*, ix, 2–6.
20. Starhawk, *The Spiral Dance: A Rebirth of the Religion of the Great Goddess* (San Francisco, CA: Harper and Row, 1979).
21. Quotations from pp. 22, 25, 91, 95, 109, 111.
22. Quotations from pp. 27, 123–6, 128–9, 142, 204.
23. p. 206.
24. Starhawk, *Dreaming the Dark: Magic, Sex and Politics* (Boston, MA: Beacon, 1982).
25. Quotation on p. xi.
26. Quotation on p. xii.
27. pp. 183–219. Quotation on p. 184.
28. Starhawk, *Truth or Dare* (San Francisco, CA: Harper and Row, 1987).
29. Quotations from pp. 6–7, 32–3, 106.
30. Starhawk, *The Spiral Dance*, 95; *Dreaming the Dark*, xiv-xv, 95; *Truth or Dare*, 215, 252.
31. Starhawk, *The Spiral Dance*, 201; *Dreaming the Dark*, xi, 15–32.

32. Starhawk, *Truth or Dare*, 6, 7, 93.

33. This analysis of Starhawk's writings is heavily influenced by the interpretation made, and the effect registered, by the many readers whom I have encountered in Britain. My own readers may, quite legitimately, wonder whether my responses are conditioned by my attitude to her politics. That is true, in the sense that during the 1980s I was a supporter of exactly the same causes, extending to non-violent direct action, as she, and my beliefs have not significantly altered since then; she and I have very similar ends, and I am concerned here purely with her means.

34. Starhawk, *Truth or Dare*, 18, 159. See also her introduction to the 1989 edition of *The Spiral Dance*, 2.

35. *The Portable Emerson*, ed. Carl Bode (New York: Penguin, 1981), *passim*; Henry David Thoreau, *Walden* (1854), *The Natural History Essays* (Salt Lake City, UT: Peregrine Smith, 1980), and *A Week on the Concord and Merrimack Rivers* (Boston, MA: Houghton Mifflin, 1961); John Muir, *Our National Parks* (Madison, WI: University of Wisconsin Press, 1981); *The American Transcendentalists*, ed. Perry Miller (Baltimore, MD: Johns Hopkins University Press, 1957).

36. Alston Chase, *Playing God in Yellowstone: The Destruction of America's first National Park* (New York: Harvest, 1987), 303–59; quotation on p. 347.

37. Carolyn Merchant, *The Death of Nature* (San Francisco, CA: Harper and Row, 1980). Starhawk repeatedly cited her in *Dreaming The Dark*, 183–219.

38. Adler, *Drawing Down The Moon*, 293–309; quotation on p. 309.

39. James Lovelock and Sidney Epton, 'The Quest for Gaia', *New Scientist* 65 (1975), 304–6.

40. James Lovelock, *The Ages of Gaia: A Biography of Our Living Earth* (Oxford: Oxford University Press, 1988), xiii–xvi, 19, 21, 225.

41. Ibid., 203–23.

42. James Lovelock, *Gaia: The Practical Science of Planetary Medicine* (London: Gaia Books, 1991), 6–11.

43. Ibid., 12–17.

44. On p. 7.

45. Starhawk, *The Spiral Dance*, 1–11, 213–30.

46. For a well-informed and scholarly analysis of this process, see Diane Purkiss, *The Witch in History* (London: Routledge, 1996), 7–29.

47. They may be found expressed by the wide range of writers cited in Eller, *Living in the Lap of the Goddess*.

48. Neomi Goldenburg, 'Feminist Witchcraft: Controlling our own Inner Space', in *The Politics of Women's Spirituality*, ed. Charlene Spretnak (New York: Anchor Press, 1982), 213–18.

49. The literature of which is now vast: key names among the authors of it are Ruth Tringham, Margaret Conkey, Lynn Meskell, Juliette Wood, Lucy Goodison, Brian Hayden, Caroline Malone, Simon Stoddart, Andrew Townsend, B. M. Fagan, and Lauren Talalay.

50. Marija Gimbutas, 'Battle Axe or Cult Axe?', *Man* 53 (1953), 51–4; *The Prehistory of Eastern Europe* (Peabody Museum Bulletin, 1956); *The Balts* (London: Thames and Hudson, 1963); *The Slavs* (London: Thames and Hudson, 1971).

51. Marija Gimbutas, *The Gods and Goddesses of Old Europe* (London: Thames and Hudson, 1974).

52. Marija Gimbutas, 'The first Wave of Eurasian Steppe Pastoralists into Copper Age Europe', *Journal of Indo-European Studies* 5 (1977), 271–338; 'The Kurgan Wave No. 2 (*c.* 3400–3200 BC) into Europe and the Following Transformation of Culture', *ibid.* 8 (1980), 272–315.

53. Marija Gimbutas, *The Goddesses and Gods of Old Europe* (London: Thames and Hudson, 1982); quotation on p. 9.

54. Vicky Noble, 'Marija Gimbutas: Reclaiming the Great Goddess', *Snake Power* 1 (1989), 6.

55. Marija Gimbutas, *The Language of the Goddess* (London: Thames and Hudson, 1989); quotations from pp. 319, 321; *The Civilization of the Goddess* (San Francisco, CA: Harper Row, 1991) quotation from p. xi.

56. See, for example, Rosemary Radford Ruether, *New Woman, New Earth* (New York: Seabury, 1975), 154–7.

57. Gimbutas, *Language of the Goddess*, xiii–xxi, 316; *Civilization of the Goddess*, vii.

58. Jacquetta Hawkes, *A Land* (Newton Abbot: David and Charles, 1978 reprint), 159.

59. Jacquetta Hawkes, *Mortimer Wheeler: Adventurer in Archaeology* (London: Weidenfeld, 1982), 2–3.

60. Gimbutas, *Language of the Goddess*, xv–xvi; *Civilization of the Goddess*, 206–19, 341. Cf. Peter Harbison, *Pre-Christian Ireland* (London: Thames and Hudson, 1988). 42–104.

61. Adler, *Drawing Down The Moon*, 346–7, 424; Frederic Lamond, *Religion Without Beliefs* (London: Janus, 1997), 86; Z. Budapest, *pers. comm.*, relayed by John Yohalem, 25 November 1996.

62. *The fifth Sacred Thing* (New York: Bantam, 1993).

63. June Johns, *King of the Witches* (London: Davies, 1969), 127.

64. Frank Smyth, *Modern Witchcraft* (London: Macdonald, 1970), 19.

65. Lois Bourne, *Dancing With Witches* (London: Hale, 1998), 17–93; Doreen Valiente, *The Rebirth of Witchcraft* (Custer, WA: Phoenix, 1989), 120; Michael Howard, *pers. comm.*, 21 August 1998.

66. Ruth Whitehouse, 'Megaliths of the Central Mediterranean', and David Trump, 'Megalithic Architecture in Malta', in *The Megalithic Monuments of Western Europe*, ed. Colin Renfrew (London: Thames and Hudson, 1981) chs 4, 5.

67. Keith Thomas, *Religion and the Decline of Magic* (London: Weidenfeld, 1971), 514–19; Norman Cohn, *Europe's Inner Demons* (Brighton: Sussex University Press, 1975), 102–35.

68. Alan Macfarlane, *Witchcraft in Tudor and Stuart England* (Cambridge, 1970); Bengt Ankarloo, *Trolldomsprocesserna i Sverige* (Stockholm, 1971); Bente G. Alver, *Heksetroog Troldom* (Oslo, 1971); H. C. Erik Midelfort, *Witch-hunting in South-Western Germany* (London, 1972); E. William Monter, *Witchcraft in France and Switzerland* (London, 1976); Robert Muchembled, *Sorcieres du Cambresis* (Paris, 1977); Gerhard Schormann, *Hexenprozesse in Nordwestdeutchland* (Hildensheim, 1977); M. S. Dupont-Bouchet, W. Frijhoff and R. Muchembled, *Prophetes et Sorcieres dans le Pays-Bas* (Paris, 1978).

69. Compare, for example, the first and second editions of Hill's *Reformation to Industrial Revolution*.

70. Christina Larner, *Witchcraft and Religion* (Oxford: Blackwell, 1984).

71. Rachel Halsted, 'The New Myth of the Witch', *Trouble and Strife* 2 (Spring, 1982), 10–17, and 'Mothers of Invention', *ibid.* 7 (Winter, 1985), 17–25; Lynette Mitchell, 'Enemies of God or Victims of Patriarchy?', *ibid.* 2 (Spring, 1982), 18–20.

72. Smyth, *Modern Witchcraft*, 21.

73. J. L. Bracelin, *Gerald Gardner: Witch* (London: Octagon, 1960), chs 6, 7; Valiente, *Rebirth of Witchcraft*, 43.

74. Starhawk, *Truth or Dare*, 83.

75. Doreen Valiente, *Rebirth of Witchcraft*, 214–15, and *Witchcraft for Tomorrow* (London: Hale, 1978); 'The Sussex workings', *The Cauldron* (Hallowe'en, 1979), n.p.; E. W. Liddell and Michael Howard, *The Pickingill Papers* (Chieveley: Capall Bann, 1994), 60–86; Janet and Stewart Farrar, *Eight Sabbats for Witches* (London: Hale, 1981), 18–20; Starhawk, *Spiral Dance*, 18.

76. Valiente, *Rebirth of Witchcraft*, 180–7; Janet and Stewart Farrar, *Eight Sabbats for Witches*, 18–20; *The Witches' Way* (London: Hale, 1984), 157; *The Witches' Goddess* (London: Hale, 1987), *passim*, but especially 1–17, with quotation on p. 78; *The Witches' God* (London: Hale, 1989), *passim*, but especially 75–113.

77. John Rowan, *The Horned God: Feminism and Men as Wounding and Healing* (London: Routledge, 1987); quotation from pp. 127–8.

78. Valiente, *Rebirth of Witchcraft*, 193–4; Shan, Circlework: *A DIY Handbook for Working Ritual, Psychology and Magic* (London: House of the Goddess, 1988); and *Which Craft?* (London: House of the Goddess, 3rd edn, 1988). I am very grateful for her characteristically generous gift of the last two works.

79. It's her real name; she likes it.

CHAPTER 19

1. Margot Adler, *Drawing Down The Moon: Witches, Druids, Goddess-Worshippers, and Other Pagans in America Today* (Boston, MA: Beacon, 2nd edn, 1986), 67–78; Isaac Bonewits, *Real Magic* (Berkeley, CA: Real Books Co., 1971), *passim*, and 'Witchcult: Fact or Fancy', *Gnostica* 3.4 (1973), n.p.; Aidan Kelly, *Crafting the Art of Magic* (St Paul, MN: Llewellyn, 1991), xiv–xvii.

2. Adler, *Drawing Down The Moon*, 86–7.

3. Margot Adler, *Heretic's Heart: Journey Through Spirit and Revolution* (Boston, MA: Beacon, 1997), passim.

4. Adler, *Drawing Down The Moon*, 11.

5. Leonora James, *pers. comm.*, 29 September 1996.

6. *Ibid.*

7. *Ibid*; issues of *The Wiccan*, 1983–9, and *The Cauldron*, 1979–89, deposited in the Bodleian Library, Oxford.

8. Leonora James, *pers. comm.*, 29 September 1996; *Guardian*, 14 May 1988; *Daily Telegraph*, 14 May 1988.

9. Vivianne Crowley, *Wicca: The Old Religion in the New Age* (London: Aquarian, 1989); quotations on pp. 112, 142.

10. Leonora James, *pers. comm.*, 29 September 1996; issues of *The Wiccan*, 1989–94, and *The Cauldron*, 1989–94.

11. Vivianne Crowley, *pers. comm.*, 29 November 1996.

12. Leonora James, *pers. comm.*, 29 September 1996.

13. *Ibid.*

14. T. M. Luhrmann, *Persuasions of the Witch's Craft* (Oxford: Blackwell, 1989).

15. This is a personal impression, based on conversations with scores of witches.

16. *Paganism Today*, eds Graham Harvey and Charlotte Hardman (London: Thorsons, 1996); *Nature Religion Today: Paganism in the Modern World*, eds Joanne Pearson, Richard H. Roberts and Geoffrey Samuel (Edinburgh: Edinburgh University Press, 1998).

17. Amy Caroline Simes, 'Contemporary Paganism in the East Midlands' (Nottingham University PhD thesis, 1995); Graham Harvey, *Listening People, Speaking Earth: Contemporary Paganism* (London: Hurst, 1997).

18. Adler, *Drawing Down The Moon*, 49–52; Crowley, *Wicca*, 47; Luhrmann, *Persuasions*, 42–5.

19. One at least: Brian Levack, who produced the best textbook of the decade, *The Witch Hunt in Early Modern Europe* (London: Longman, 1987).

20. Anne Llewellyn Barstow, *Witchcraze: A New History of the European Witch Hunts* (San

Francisco: Pandora, 1994); Hans Sebalt, *Witch-Children: From Salem Witch-Hunts to Modern Courtrooms* (New York: Prometheus, 1995); Frances Hill, *A Delusion of Satan: The Full Story of the Salem Witch Trials* (London: Hamilton, 1996).

21. Carlo Ginzburg, *Ecstasies: Deciphering the Witches' Sabbath* (New York: Pantheon, 1991); quotation on p. 9.

22. An exception is Wolfgang Behringer's major study of south-eastern Germany, republished by Cambridge University Press in 1997 as *Witchcraft Persecutions in Bavaria*; but this translation appeared ten years after the original. For a recent overview of publication in German, see Behringer again, 'Witchcraft Studies in Austria, Germany, and Switzerland', in *Witchcraft in Early Modern Europe*, eds Jonathan Barry, Marianne Hester and Gareth Roberts (Cambridge: Cambridge University Press, 1996), 64–95.

23. Lyndal Roper, *Oedipus and the Devil* (London; Routledge, 1994); Robin Briggs, *Witches and Neighbours: The Social and Cultural Context of European Witchcraft* (London: HarperCollins, 1996); James Sharpe, *Instruments of Darkness: Witchcraft in England 1550–1750* (London: Hamilton, 1996); Diane Purkiss, *The Witch in History: Early Modern and Twentieth-Century Representations* (London: Routledge, 1996); Stuart Clark, *Thinking with Demons: The Idea of Witchcraft in Early Modern Europe* (Oxford: Oxford University Press, 1997).

24. For publications expressly aimed at this, see, *inter alia*, David Harley, 'Historians as Demonologists: The Myth of the Midwife Witch', *The Social History of Medicine* 3 (1990), 1–26; Stuart Clark, 'The "Gendering" of Witchcraft in French Demonology: Misogyny or Polarity?', *French History* 5 (1991), 426–37; Robin Briggs, 'Women as Victims?', *ibid.*, 438–50; James Sharpe, 'Witchcraft and Women in Seventeenth-Century England: Some Northern Evidence', *Continuity and Change* 6 (1991), 179–99, and 'Women, Witchcraft and the Legal Process', in *Women, Crime and the Courts in Early Modern England*, eds Jenny Kermode and Garthine Walker (London: University College Press, 1984), 106–24; Roper, *Oedipus and the Devil*, esp. 1–52; Briggs, *Witches and Neighbours*, 257–87; Sharpe, *Instruments of Darkness*, 169–89; Purkiss, *Witch in History*, esp. 7–29; Clark, *Thinking with Demons*, 108–33. In justice, readers may like to compare a lone English academic voice on the other side, the explicitly revolutionary feminist Marianne Hester, *Lewd Women and Wicked Witches* (London: Routledge, 1992).

25. Evidence to support this summary can be found in the list of titles given above, representing a fraction of the hundreds published in Europe since 1980. For two editions of conference papers in English, see *Witchcraft in Early Modern Europe*, eds Barry, Hester and Roberts, and *Early Modern Witchcraft*, eds Bengt Ankarloo and Gustav Henningsen (Oxford: Oxford University Press, 1990).

26. See, among many titles, Eamon Duffy, *The Stripping of the Altars: Traditional Religion in England c.1400–c.1580* (New Haven, CT: Yale University Press, 1992); Christopher Haigh, *English Reformations* (Oxford: Oxford University Press, 1992); Richard Britnell, *The Closing of the Middle Ages* (Oxford: Blackwell, 1997); *Conjuring Spirits: Texts and Traditions of Medieval Ritual Magic*, ed. Claire Fanger (Stroud: Sutton, 1998); Andrew P. Brown, *Popular Piety in Late Medieval England* (Cambridge: Cambridge University Press, 1995); R. N. Swanson, *Religion and Devotion in Europe c.1215–c.1515* (Cambridge: Cambridge Medieval Press, 1995).

27. Christopher W. Marsh, *The Family of Love* (Cambridge: Cambridge University Press, 1994); *The World of Rural Dissenters, 1520–1725*, ed. Margaret Spufford (Cambridge: Cambridge University Press, 1995).

28. R. A. Houston, *Literacy in Early Modern Europe* (London: Longman, 1988); Tessa Watt, *Cheap Print and Popular Piety* (Cambridge: Cambridge University Press, 1991); Margaret Spufford, 'The Pedlar, the Historian and the Folklorist: Seventeenth-Century

Communications', *Folklore* 105 (1994), 13–24; Adam Fox, 'Ballads, Libels and Popular Ridicule in Jacobean England', *Past and Present* 145 (1994), 47–83; Pauline Croft, 'Libels, Popular Literacy and Public Opinion in Early Modern England', *Historical Research* 68 (1995), 266–85; *Popular Culture in England c.1500–1850*, ed. Tim Harris (Basingstoke: Macmillan, 1995); Adam Fox, 'Custom, Memory and the Authority of Writing', in *The Experience of Authority in Early Modern England*, eds Paul Griffiths, Adam Fox and Steve Hindle (Basingstoke: Macmillan, 1996), 89–116; Adam Fox, 'Rumour, News and Popular Opinion in Elizabethan and Early Stuart England', *Historical Journal* 40 (1997), 597–620; Matthew Innes, 'Memory, Orality and Literacy in an Early Medieval Society', *Past and Present* 158 (1998), 3–36.

29. Prudence Jones and Nigel Pennick, *A History of Pagan Europe* (London: Routledge, 1995); Vivianne Crowley, *Phoenix from the Flame: Pagan Spirituality · in the Western World* (London: Aquarian, 1994); quotations from pp. 40, 213, 255; Frederic Lamond, *Religion Without Beliefs: Essays in Pantheist Theology, Comparative Religion and Ethics* (London: Janus, 1997).

30. Doreen Valiente, *The Rebirth of Witchcraft* (Custer, WA: Phoenix, 1989); quotations from pp. 27, 210, 214.

31. Evan John Jones and Doreen Valiente, *Witchcraft: A Tradition Renewed* (London: Hale, 1990); quotations from pp. 7–8.

32. John Parker, *At the Heart of Darkness: Witchcraft, Black Magic and Satanism Today* (London: Pan, 1993), 97–9; Lois Bourne, *Dancing with Witches* (London: Hale, 1998).

33. Patricia Crowther, *One Witch's World* (London: Hale, 1998); Arnold and Patricia Crowther, *The Secrets of Ancient Witchcraft* (1974: repr. Citadel Press, New York, 1992).

34. Rae Beth, *Hedge Witch: A Guide to Solitary Witchcraft* (London: Hale, 1990); Marian Green, *A Witch Alone* (London: Aquarian, 1991).

35. These generalizations are based upon many personal conversations and views and exchanges published in *Pagan Dawn, The Cauldron, Talking Stick, Aisling, The New Wiccan, White Dragon, Dragon's Brew, The Singing Head, Comhairle, Dark Mirror, Pagan Dusk, Pagan Voice, Twisted Tree,* and *Manchester Pagan Wheel*.

36. Early examples of the change were published in the *Sunday Times*, 21 August 1983, and *Living*, June 1984. For a sample from the year 1989 along, when the scare over satanic ritual abuse was rising to its peak, see the *Independent*, 20 March, 5 April, 17 June, 6 July, and 4 September; the *Guardian*, 14 and 22 May; *St Albans Herald*, 8 June; and *The Bucks Advertiser*, 28 October. The lone example of sustained hostility in the mid-1990s was *News of the World*, a newspaper which had come to rely for sales almost wholly upon the tactic of the 'shock exposé'.

37. Jessica Berens, *Queen of the Witches* (London: Arrow, 1993); Freda Warrington, *Dark Cathedral* (London: Penguin, 1995), and *Pagan Moon* (London: Penguin, 1997).

38. For especially clear examples of his exploration of religious issues, see *Small Gods* (1992) and *Hogfather* (1996). His trilogy which affectionately satirizes Wicca is *Wyrd Sisters* (1988), *Witches Abroad* (1991), and *Lords and Ladies* (1992). All these titles were published in London by Gollancz and later brought out in Corgi editions.

39. *Religions in the UK: A Multi-Faith Directory*, ed. Paul Weller (Derby: University of Derby, 1993), 47–72, 589–90.

CHAPTER 20

1. This pattern is reviewed in A. C. Bouquet, *Comparative Religion* (London: Cassell, 1961), 11–12.

2. Tanya Luhrmann, *Persuasions of the Witch's Craft* (Oxford: Blackwell, 1989), 336.

3. Alex Owen, *The Darkened Room: Women, Power and Spiritualism* (London: Virago, 1989), 93–4.

4. Bryan Wilson, *Religion in Sociological Perspective* (Oxford: Oxford University Press, 1982), 27; Clifford Geertz, *The Interpretation of Cultures: Selected Essays* (1973: HarperCollins, repr. 1993), 104.

5. Rodney Stark and William Sims Bainbridge, *The Future of Religion* (Berkeley, CA: University of California Press, 1985), 455–56.

6. Luhrmann, *Persuasions of the Witch's Craft*, esp. 321–41; quotation on p. 340.

7. Amy Caroline Simes, 'Contemporary Paganism in the East Midlands' (Nottingham University PhD thesis, 1995), 511–22.

8. Rob Hardy, *pers. comm.*, 31 October 1992.

9. Margot Adler, *Drawing Down The Moon* (Boston, MA: Beacon, 2nd edn, 1986), 441; Vivianne Crowley, *Wicca: The Old Religion in the New Age* (London: Aquarian, 1989), *passim*.

10. W. Robertson Smith, *Lectures on the Religion of the Semites* (Edinburgh, 1889), *passim*; R. R. Marrett, *The Threshold of Religion* (1914), *passim*; quotation on p. xxxi; Max Weber, *The Religion of China* (trans. Glencoe, Il, 1958), 226–49.

11. Herbert Jennings Rose, *Ancient Roman Religion* (London: Hutchinson, 1948); Martin Henig, *Religion in Roman Britain* (London: Batsford, 1984); Robin Lane Fox, *Pagans and Christians* (London: Viking, 1986); Ken Dowden, *The Uses of Greek Mythology* (London: Routledge, 1992).

12. Robert A. Evans, *Belief and the Counter-Culture* (Philadelphia: Westminster Press, 1971), 23.

13. Cf. Simes, 'Contemporary Paganism', 186–201; Gilbert Lewis, *Day of Shining Red* (Cambridge: Cambridge University Press, 1980); Victor Turner, *The Forest of Symbols* (Ithaca, NY: Cornell University Press, 1967), and *The Ritual Process* (Chicago: Aldine, 1969); Bruce Lincoln, *Discourse and the Construction of Society* (Oxford: Oxford University Press, 1989), 51–5; Emile Durkheim, *The Elementary Forms of the Religious Life* (1915: 1874 trans., Allen and Smith), 387–419.

14. Luhrmann, *Persuasions of the Witch's Craft*, 54.

15. Gerald Gardner, *Witchcraft Today* (London: Rider, 1954), 19–24; Justine Glass, *Witchcraft: The Sixth Sense—And Us* (London: Spearman, 1965), 101; Patricia and Arnold Crowther, *The Witches Speak* (Douglas: Athol, 1965), 148; Doreen Valiente, *Witchcraft for Tomorrow* (London: Hale, 1978), 98–9; Starhawk, *The Spiral Dance* (San Francisco, CA: Harper and Row, 1979), 60; Janet and Stewart Farrar, *The Life and Times of a Modern Witch* (London: Piatkus, 1987), 85–92; Vivianne Crowley, *Wicca: The Old Religion in the New Age* (London: Aquarius, 1989), 59–60.

16. Aidan Kelly, *Crafting the Art of Magic* (St Paul, MN: Llewellyn, 1991), ix.

17. Amy Simes's regional research suggests the same ratio: Simes, 'Contemporary Paganism', 434.

18. David Burnett announced his computation in a discussion with me broadcast on BBC Radio Four on 18 December 1994, and Joanne Pearson presented hers in the international Nature Religion electronic forum on 7 August 1998.

19. Luhrmann, *Persuasions of the Witch's Craft*, 99–111.

20. Charles Y. Glock, 'The Role of Deprivation in the Origin and Evolution of Religious Groups', in *Religion and Social Context*, eds Robet Lee and Martin E. Marty (Oxford: Oxford University Press, 1964), 24–36; Stark and Bainbridge, *The Future of Religion*, 172.

21. Eileen Barker, *New Religious Movements: A Practical Introduction* (London: HMSO, 2nd edn, 1995), 5.

22. Paul Badham, 'Religious Pluralism in Modern Britain', in *A History of Religion in Britain*, eds Sheridan Gilley and W. J. Shiels (Oxford: Blackwell, 1994), 488–502; Grace Davies, *Religion in Britain Since 1945* (Oxford: Blackwell, 1994), esp. 163.

23. A classic example is given in Doreen Valiente, *The Rebirth of Witchcraft* (Custer, WA: Phoenix, 1989), 127–8.

24. Simes, 'Contemporary Paganism', 389–91, 424.

25. Luhrmann, *Persuasions of the Witch's Craft*, 81.

26. Graham Harvey, 'Satanism in Britain Today', *Journal of Contemporary Religion* 10.3 (1995), 283–96.

27. Bryan R. Wilson, *Religion in Sociological Perspective* (Oxford: Oxford University Press, 1982), 88–114; quotations on pp. 88, 104; and 'Sects and Society in Tension', in *Religion, State and Society in Modern Britain*, ed. Paul Badham (Lewiston, NY: Mellen, 1989), 159–84; quotation on p. 160.

28. Glock, 'The Role of Deprivation', 24–6; Stark and Bainbridge, *The Future of Religion*, 25.

29. Colin Campbell, 'Clarifying the Cult', *British Journal of Sociology* 28.3 (1977), 375–88.

30. Stark and Bainbridge, *The Future of Religion*, 26–7. In this respect these authors were just asserting forcefully and dogmatically what had already become a tradition. In 1980 Gini Graham Scott had entitled her study of newly appeared religious groups in California (which included the first extensive survey of a modern pagan witch tradition) *Cult and Countercult* (Westport, CT: Greenwood). Stark and Bainbridge may well, however, have hardened an orthodoxy: in 1985 J. Gordon Melton lumped 'Witchcraft, Neopaganism and Magick' together as 'newer cults' in his *Encyclopedic Handbook of Cults in America* (New York: Garland). He defended this terminology on the grounds that 'social scientists' defined a cult as any religious group 'foreign and alien to the prevalent religious communities' (pp. 3–4).

31. Simes, 'Contemporary Paganism', 369.

32. Pre-eminently contributors to *Perspectives on the New Age*, eds J. R. Lewis and J. G. Melton (Albany, NY: State University of New York Press, 1992); and Paul Heelas, *The New Age Movement* (Oxford: Blackwell, 1996). Michael York, *The Emerging Network* (Lanham, MD: Rowman and Littlefield, 1995), associates the two without integrating them. Melton himself clearly distinguishes them in his *Encyclopedic Handbook*, as does Scott, *Cult and Countercult*. On the other hand, the British government publication, *Aspects of Britain: Religion* (London: HMSO, 1992), lists Wicca only as a contribution to the New Age Movement.

33. Simes 'Contemporary Paganism', 490–8; Joanne Pearson, 'Assumed Affinities: Wicca and the New Age', in *Nature Religion Today*, eds Joanne Pearson, Richard H. Roberts and Geoffrey Samuel (Edinburgh: Edinburgh University Press, 1998), 45–56.

34. Eileen Barker, *New Religious Movements*; 'Authority and Dependence in New Religious Movements', in *Religion: Contemporary Issues*, ed. Bryan Wilson (London: Bellew, 1992), 237–55; and 'New Religious Movements in Europe', in *Religion in Europe: Contemporary Perspectives*, eds Sean Gill, Gavin D'Costa and Ursula King (Kampen: Kok Pharos, 1994), 120–40.

35. Roy Wallis, *The Elementary Forms of the New Religious Life* (London: Routledge, 1984).

36. Catherine L. Albanese, *Nature Religion in America* (Chicago: Chicago University Press, 1990); Peter Beyer, 'Globalization and the Religion of Nature', in *Nature Religion Today*, eds Pearson, Roberts and Samuel, 11–21.

37. Vivianne Crowley, 'Wicca as Nature Religion', in *ibid.*, 170–9.

38. James A. Beckford, 'Religion, Modernity and Post-Modernity', in *Religion: Contemporary Issues*, ed. Wilson, 11–23.

❋ INDEX ❋

Casaubon, Isaac 63
Castlerigg, Cumbria 289
Çatal Höyök, Turkey 281
Catholicism:
    and Leland 142–7, 148
    and Michelet 137–40
    and Soldan 132
Cauldron, The (journal) 289, 371–2, 374
Cecil, Robert 209
Centre for New Religious Movements (King's
    College London) 375
ceremonial magic 93, 255–6
ceremonies *see* rituals
Ceres (or Demeter) 33
Cernunnos (Gallic deity) 196, 234, 331
Chaffer, Clayton 89, 91, 109
Chalice and the Blade, The (Eisler) 356
Chambers, Sir Edmund 36, 129
Chanctonbury Ring, Sussex 279–80, 307–8
Chandler, Alice 118
Chapman, Janine 181
'Charge' (incantation) 247, 392
charmers (healers) 85, 94–5
    and Christianity 101–2
    and inherited powers 103–4
    payment as 104–5
Chase, Alston 350–1
Chaucer, Geoffrey 33
'Cheshire Traditionals' 302, 307
Chesterton, G. K. 11, 29
child abuse allegations 372–3, 376
Childe, Gordon 38, 280
Christchurch Times 209, 211, 213
Christian Mystical Lodge 181
Christianity:
    and Alexandrian Wicca 331–2
    and charming 101–2
    Crowley's attitude to 175–6
    Fortune's opinion of 181, 184–5
    and *Golden Bough* 114–17, 119, 122, 123–4,
        127, 172, 277
    house church movement 405–6
    and pagan survivals 114–17, 120–3
    and persecution of witches 132–40, 348
    secret societies and 61, 236
Chumbley, Andrew 306, 308
Church of Aphrodite, Long Island 340
churches:
    desecration of 268, 311–12
    female fertility figures in 198
    over pre-Christian sites 122, 185, 284
    phallic symbols inside altars 274
Chuvin, Pierre 4, 414
Cicero 21, 391
Circle of the Universal Bond *see* Ancient Druid
    Order
Civilization of the Goddess, The (Gimbutas) 357,
    359

Clark, Sir George 200, 275–6
Clark, Graham 38
classical paganism 11–17, 177–8
classicism 21–31, 115, 124–5, 165
Clodd, Edward 121
Clutterbuck, Dorothy ('Old Dorothy') 205–6,
    207–8, 209–12, 238
Cochrane, Robert 311, 312, 313–18, 361, 383
Cogul, north-eastern Spain (rock paintings) 197
Cohen, Norman 362, 378
Coleridge, Samuel Taylor 22, 119
Collins, Wilkie 14
Column of Dust, A (Underhill) 256
Co-Masonry 58, 213, 236
Communism 262, 264
Conrad, Joseph 126, 205
consecration of play 399
Conservative Association, Highcliffe 210, 251
Constant, Alphonse Louis *see* Levi, Eliphas Zahed
Cook, Arthur Bernard 124–5
Cope, Julian 387
Coral Island, The (Ballantyne) 6–7
Cornwall:
    charmers 103
    cunning folk 108
    pellars 105
    Ryall on 301–2
Corpus Hermeticum 82
cosmology:
    Californian 350–1, 398
    Haggard on 152
    Yeats on 156
Cotton, Elijah 106
Coulton, G. C. 129, 199
counter-culture 364–5
countryside, idealization of 33–4, 44, 117–20, 127
craft guilds 54–5
'Craft of the Wise, the' 233, 241
Crafting the Art of Magic (Kelly) 381
Crawford, O. G. S. 38, 129, 280
Creasy, W. K. 186
Crosby, Humberside 104
Crow, W. B. 222
Crowley, Aleister 171–81
    caricatured by Somerset Maugham 261
    and ceremonial magic 257
    and Fortune 187
    and Gardner 206, 216–23, 226, 247
    and Golden Dawn 81
    High Toryism of 360
    and Neuberg 49
    and Operation Mistletoe 208–9
    and Pan 50
    and references to witch religion 220
    and Sanders 330
    Swinburne's influence on 26
    and Sybil Leek 300–1
    and Wheatley 261–2